The Army of the Potomac

Birth of Command

VOLUME I

The Army of the Potomac

Birth of Command

November 1860 - September 1861

VOLUME I

Russel H. Beatie

Da Capo Press

Maps by Blake Magner
Text design by Theodore P. Savas

Cataloging-in-Publication data for this book is available from the Library of Congress.

First Da Capo Press edition 2002
ISBN 0-306-81141-3

Published by Da Capo Press
A Member of the Perseus Books Group
http://www.dacapopress.com

Da Capo Press books are available at special discounts for bulk purchases in the U.S. by corporations, institutions, and other organizations. For more information, please contact the Special Markets Department at the Perseus Books Group, 11 Cambridge Center, Cambridge, MA 02142, or call (800) 255-1514, or (617) 252-5298, or email j.mccrary@perseusbooks.com

1 2 3 4 5 6 7 8 9—05 04 03 02 01

Printed and bound in the United States of America

TO

THE AMERICAN FIGHTING MAN

than whom no better ever stood for his flag, especially to the men of Viet Nam, who have not received the recognition their countrymen owe them

and

MY BELOVED NOISY FRIEND

at last a sturdy, upbeat, supportive wife who does not require reassurance for the obvious;

and, in order of altitude

THE PRINCE
IMPUS MAXIMUS
GORGEOUS (OF LESSER STATURE)
THE MERMAID
THE TOAD
THE OGM

All taken together a real family

Contents

Contents (continued)

Contents (continued)

Contents (continued)

List of Illustrations

Illustrations appear in the Dramatis Personae

List of Maps

List of Maps (continued)

Acknowledgments

Over the years of research and thought, scattered in patches among the labors of a hard-working trial lawyer, many have laid hand on this thing in constructive, even vital, ways, too many to name. But some contributions were also too great to pass without mention, specifically:

My two liberal arts schools, the Hackley School and Princeton University, which created, nurtured, and reared a thriving love of history, the historical process, and the work ethic necessary to do it thoroughly. In the course of the studies, which sometimes included savage instruction in written communication, I fell across a number of marvelous works with messages worth carrying into the project: Sir Edward Creasy, *The Fifteen Decisive Battles of the World*; Herbert Butterfield, *The Whig Interpretation of History*; Jacques Barzun, *Darwin, Marx, and Wagner*; R. G. Collingwood, *The Idea of History*; D. S. Freeman, *Lee's Lieutenants*; and John Keegan, *The Face of Battle*.

Saint Barbara, the patron saint of artillery, under whose protective cloak I was honored to serve my country as a company grade officer and learn something about an army in real life.

Saint Ives, the patron saint of lawyers, who grudgingly gave free time for research in out-of-the-way places on business trips and for writing from 11 p.m. to 2 a.m. but who made everything possible.

Tom Broadfoot, who connected me with El Supremo and arranged for scrutiny of part of an early draft by a learned scholar whose mission was to say, "Finish it," or "Switch to plumbing." No man has contributed as much to the Civil War researcher as Tom, who always sounds like a "Tuckahoe" or a "Cohee" (whichever cannot read) but who is an intelligent, creative, imaginative, human willing to go more than the extra mile to help his fellow man.

Theodore P. "Ted" Savas, El Supremo of the former Savas Publishing Company, who was willing to read the entire manuscript after almost every living person at every press, trade or scholarly (except for Oxford) had refused to read even two chapters. I am forever in his debt.

Blake Magner, superb cartographer who thankfully replaced me and whose excellent work can be found in many recent publications on the war.

Francis Minot Weld, M.D., ("Timmo") excellent friend, fellow cigar smoker, hunting companion (together we exhausted our supplies of Cubanos Puros in Africa after the first week), and consultant on all manner of human ailments from McClellan's typhoid to Lander's probable infection and Holmes' lung wound.

Jennifer Pariser, Esq., ("Raspberry") cranky, demanding princess who, between legal problems, found time to unravel the mysteries of the French language for me.

Monica Mehta, who edited in the face of heavy fire from the front ("Why should it be read by an editor. It doesn't need one," said the egomaniac, thinking to himself, "And I won't accept the changes anyway.")

Jim Murray and Ben Coleman, who can find anything, whether it be the unfindable old book or the elusive typographical error that has escaped countless proofreadings.

Hans Bielenstein ("Rittmeister"), former officer in the Guards Regiment (Sweden), and scholar extraordinaire in his own right, who read several chapters and made a diagnostic suggestion that can be found in these pages.

Nothing contributes to learning on a subject unless it finds its way to publisher and print. In the current state of technology, word processing, discs, electronic transfer, etc., dominate the writing of Civil War History. Because I am a man of the nineteenth century in more ways than one (I hunt dangerous game on foot with bolt action rifles), I have relied on the continuous hard work of Esther Rosa (my secretary, the "other" woman in my life after my Beloved Noisy Friend) to create the modern manuscript from my hieroglyphics, and Fran Vecere (whom, working at some distant place, I have not seen in almost twenty years) to transcribe the research.

L (or "the L"), who unfortunately had not the emotional peace to last the course but whose affectionate generosity built the foundation for one of the finest Civil War libraries in private captivity and whose "No peeking in Dornbush!" preserved most of the surprises for many Christmas, Easter, and birthday events.

CB (or "Little Connie" as my children affectionately referred to her), who provided steady, warm encouragement to stay the course when the research mountain seemed too tall and who, for all her youth, gave sage and intelligent (Princeton, four year 4.0) advice.

The many men—and they are all men for this has always been a man's war and the work of men—who lit the lanterns on the paths to the primary sources and even went out of their way to give specific help: Lieutenant-colonel Robert N. Scott (supervisor of the *Official Records*), Stephen Sears (researcher, writer, and finder par excellence), Gary Gallagher (who said, "Finish it"), Edward Longacre, James McPherson, Bell Wiley, Michael Burlingame, John Keegan (creator of many original ideas), David Chandler (model of clarity, form, and detachment), Ernest Fergurson, Thomas Hennessy, T. Harry Williams, and John C. Ropes (superb researcher and writer, whose crippled spine kept him from serving in the war that killed his brother and whose fairness drew compliments from all sides of every issue he touched).

The largest, indeed numberless, group is the legion of thoughtful, helpful, patient archivists at the many great libraries and historical societies that house the life-giving collections of private papers beyond the *Official Records*:

Tom Camden, once at the New Hampshire Historical Society; Michael Musik at the National Archives—than whom no man knows more about the subject and whose willing assistance is truly encyclopedic and always available; Library of Congress (Staff of the Madison Annex); Alice Dowd and Frederick W. Bauman, Jr., of the New York Public Library—now one block from my office, with everything published on the subject including an endless collection of nineteenth century periodicals and pamphlets and their willing, helpful staff colleagues too many to name; Abigail Salerno at the Pennsylvania Historical Society; Peter Drummey of the Massachusetts Historical Society; Boston University Library (the Mugar Library, whose secrets are always ready to be made known by the indefatigable "Charlie"); John C. Harriman at the William L. Clements Library at the University of Michigan; John Rodehamel, scholar in residence at the Huntington Library and facilitator of research that would have ended on the conduct of die alte frauen waffen SS who masquerade as curators and librarians; and Chuck Hill at the Missouri Historical Society.

Preface

This is the story of a group of men during a short but extraordinary period in their lives. At the same time the story is meant to give, by the biographical sketches of the men, a snapshot of the momentous political, social, and economic issues of mid-nineteenth-century America.

When this undertaking found life forty years ago, I was concerned that, unlike my role model D. S. Freeman, I would not have access to the marvelous letters and diaries that gave his men so much life. He seemed to be tightly bound with members of the Southern aristocracy who held many important personal papers in their possession. I had no similar connection with the holders of private papers in the north. In fact, I could not even identify any similar northern aristocracy. My men, I feared, would be two dimensional and lifeless. If they are, the fault is mine because I soon learned that the available primary sources, even when I limited myself to the papers of officers, were mountainous. The task of consuming them was Herculean. And I could always find new things.

This great problem grew greater still with the addition of a work ethic instilled by the law firm that gave me "shelter" after law school. When the immense transaction or litigation hung on an unresolved legal issue, the senior partner would command the junior associate to "exhaust the field," to read every relevant decision, then answer the question with clear reasoning and sound judgment. My mission in writing the book, as it is in the practice of law, stood clear . . . and impossible. But I would adjust it after an intelligent suggestion of moderation.

More than five years ago, I was visiting Indianapolis on business and sneaking a peek at the contents of the Indiana Historical Society. Sure enough, I found two items I had never seen in any bibliography or catalogue. That night I was to have dinner with Alan Nolan, author of the superb unit history *The Iron Brigade* and many other well-regarded works on the Civil War. I could hardly order my meal before I blurted a description of my discoveries.

"That's great," he said, disappointingly non-plussed.

A moment passed.

"Let me suggest something," he continued. "You are a lawyer. I know your training. You were taught to 'exhaust the field.' And you probably approach research on the Civil War that way. But I guarantee that with your thoroughness you will always be able to find new material. At the end you will have far more unused material than anyone else and you will still be finding new things."

I thought to myself, I *can* find it all. I *can* read it all. My field, after all, is narrow.

Alan concluded with the same devastating point made by all my good friends who confront my stubbornness with their marvelous intellects.

"While you are still finding new, even important, material, you will die. And you will never have picked up your pen. You will not leave one word behind! You must say to yourself, 'I have found enough to make an original contribution.' You must leave what's left to the next guy, and you must write. The undiscovered material belongs to your successors."

As always, I was unconvinced. My guiding light had been the word "definitive." I could not achieve that without finding and reading everything. In the two or three years that passed I suffered the nightmares of producing nothing, of telling no story. I concluded that I would not find the important collections I knew had survived the war, the letters and diaries of Irvin McDowell, Daniel Butterfield, H. E. Tremain, Charles Griffin, A. E. Burnside, William L. Candler, and John Pope.

But if the correct conclusion is sound and compelled by logic, it usually takes hold in time. I would follow Alan's advice. If I have missed an important work or not found important manuscripts and, therefore, facts important to the story, I can only say I tried and ask forgiveness. For balance, James McPherson kindly took the time to read and comment with the wise advice that I be careful not to tell the reader more than he wants to know.

I rescued two pieces written as an undergraduate, updated their research, improved their presentation, and was appalled at the amount of improvement they could absorb. And I refined my theory for the work. Although the first hundred pages of my copy of Hegel are dog-eared and dirty, the remainder, in spite of my many tries, are pristine and unread. Nor have I ever been certain they would have been understood if I had read them. My many forays into the philosophy of history have provoked thought . . . but understanding? Who knows. Walsh, Croce, Becker, Popper, Butterfield, Collingwood, Evans. I have struggled with them all.

I reject the idea that history is a science governed by rigid rules, unmodified and untempered. Even the law—"an ass"—is not so wooden. But the rigorous standards of the great Leopold von Ranke serve anyone well, and I try to follow them. I also reject J. B. Bury's annihilation (Evans's word) of art in the telling of history and espouse the standard typified by Macaulay and Trevelyan. My specific methodology (assuming I understand it) is Collingwood's approach: treat historical facts as if they were ideas and put myself "inside the idea" where I can think it as if I were the historical actor.

From this flows my adoption of the "fog of war" theory. My copy of Collingwood from my undergraduate days, reread many times, pages yellow from age and exposure, coverless, is filthy and battered from traveling in my pack with foul-smelling cosmoline and the usual extra ammunition. Hopefully, I have applied rigorous scholarship like von Ranke and produced beautiful art like Macauley and Trevelyan without compromising either; and in the likelihood that I have failed, at least that was my goal. I do not aspire to be Bell Wiley, Douglas S. Freeman, or James McPherson, but I would be honored if people were willing to say I was one of the "historians" of a small part of this era and I could justifiably have on my stone, after ashes to the winds and the woods:

My old friends of the
American Civil War—
I have camped with you,
marched with you,
stood in line of battle with you
charged with you,
tended you bleeding and dying
on fields of great courage,
and now at long last join you.

Dramatis Personae

Winfield Scott

Seventy-four years old and suffering all the infirmities of his years, Winfield Scott, towering in more ways than one, dominated the military scene on both sides in 1861. To the Lincoln government he provided experience and judgment that would be important assets in the early days of the Republican administration. He alone could stand and look Lincoln square in the eye. In his prime Scott dwarfed most men, weighed two hundred thirty pounds, and had the strength of an ox. In his old age, though he remained huge, gout plagued him, he could not sit a horse, he walked with difficulty, and his eyesight was bad. Nevertheless, in 1861 he was the only high-ranking American officer with broad experience and an international reputation.

By the end of the War of 1812, Scott had compiled an admirable record, was a brigadier general in the Regular Army, had a brevet for major general, and was a national hero. At the outbreak of the war with Mexico, President Polk kept him from the field to avoid development of his potential as a political opponent. Finally and with great reluctance, Polk gave him command of a military force that would land at

Princeton University

Winfield Scott

Vera Cruz on the Mexican coast, march inland, and capture Mexico City. With an army of less than 15,000 men in a country of several million, Scott executed a campaign that was a miraculous demonstration of virtuosity. By 1861, he was a brevet lieutenant-general and the general in chief of the United States Army.

Throughout his life Scott had been a man of marked eccentricities and sensitivities. In his old age they became sharper and more dominant. Anecdotes about his career he told . . . and retold . . . and retold. Busts and portraits of himself filled his quarters. He was not, he was always quick to say, six feet four inches tall; he was six feet four and one quarter inches. He would comment frequently about the youthfulness, attractiveness, and sturdiness of his figure, and the freedom of his skin from the marks of old age. He would compare his own exploits with those of the great military commanders. Nevertheless, he remained a man of broad learning, a true military expert, widely read and current in his reading, with an international reputation. In 1859 when sectional problems were already dominant, he offered the position of military secretary to his favorite officer, a Southerner. If the officer had accepted, the general in chief's staff would have been Southern to a man.

"What will they say, General," asked one of his junior aides, "if all the staff are Southerners?"

"If the Southern rascals will have so much merit, how can we fail to advance them?" he responded.

When questioned about his loyalty, he stood firmly for his country. "If necessary, I shall plant cannon at both ends of Pennsylvania Avenue; and if any of the Maryland or Virginia gentlemen who have become so threatening and troublesome of late show their heads or even venture to raise a finger, I shall blow them to hell!"

Nevertheless, his deep love for his home state of Virginia interfered with his strategic judgment and reduced his usefulness. By advocating promotion for George B. McClellan, he created a mortal competitor who would end his career.

Charles P. Stone

Born in Greenfield, Massachusetts, on September 30, 1824, from the stock of New England Puritans who had resided in the Commonwealth for many years, Stone's ancestors had served in every American war; one of them, Benjamin Lincoln, served as a general under Washington. Unlike Scott, who was from a state of slave holders and uncertain loyalty, Stone came from the most determined abolitionist state in the Union. He entered the United States Military Academy as a cadet on July 1, 1841, graduating seventh in a class that had numbered one hundred thirty-nine at the outset.

"By his courteous bearing, springing from the pure teachings of his youth, strengthened by his Christian principles," one of his friends wrote years later, "he secured the lasting respect of his instructors, and the esteem and affection of his comrades. The utmost confidence in his honor and integrity was felt by all." He was impulsive, "ever ready for duty, firm in decision and prompt to action. His impulsiveness often caused him trouble in after life; not so much from his methods of action as from his want of tact."

Library of Congress

Charles P. Stone

When Scott selected Stone's commanding officer to be chief of ordinance for the Mexico City column, Stone went as his assistant at army headquarters and to serve with the only siege battery used during the Mexican War. "By efficient service with the battery and also on General Scott's staff, both in the siege of Vera Cruz and on the march to and capture of the City of Mexico, he secured the ever abiding confidence of General Scott."

Visiting Washington on business on New Year's eve, 1860, he paid a social call on Scott and was rewarded with an appointment as inspector general for the District of Columbia, with responsibility for peace in the national capital, the weak loyal militia units, the disloyal units, and development of plans and supplies. A lifelong Democrat but, like most Regular Army officers, indifferent to the burning political issues of the time, he would be promoted to brigadier general for his prewar services and after Bull Run be given command of a division stretched along the Potomac River north of the capital. Here he would find himself in command of an inadvertent battle initiated by his commanding officer and expanded by a popular political general. His political affiliations and his soldierly treatment of fugitive slaves and enemy property would become the focal point of a congressional investigation that would introduce many non-military issues to the officer corps of the Army of the Potomac.

Robert Patterson

Born in Ireland in 1798, Patterson was six years old when his father was banished for rebellion. The family sailed to the United States and settled in Pennsylvania. At fifteen he entered a counting house in Philadelphia, but his incipient business career was interrupted by the War of 1812 in which he served as the lieutenant-colonel, then colonel of the Second Regiment, Pennsylvania militia. As a captain in the Regular Army, he was mustered out in June of 1815.

When the Mexican War began, he was commissioned a major-general of volunteers to serve with Scott's Mexico City column. As a well-known Democrat, he had even been considered by President Polk for command of the column before it was finally given to Scott. At Cerro Gordo he was lifted from sickbed to horse in order to lead his division into battle, then led the pursuit to Jalapa. While serving as Scott's second in command, he and Scott developed a strong friendship which continued after the war. In 1861, he received a three-month commission as a major-general in the United States service and took command of the forces at the foot of the Shenandoah Valley, where he was to prevent the Confederate force in the Valley from joining Beauregard at Bull Run Creek. The burden of independent command and confusion with his friend the general in chief would confound him and would be the earliest, best proof that a skillful, courageous subordinate did not necessarily have the ability to operate on his own.

Robert Patterson

Fitz-John Porter

Porter was born in Portsmouth, New Hampshire, on August 31, 1822, the son of Captain John Porter, nephew of Commodore David Porter, both of the United States Navy, and cousin of Lieutenant David Dixon Porter, who would take the *Powhatan* to the rescue of Fort Pickens. His early education was at Phillips Exeter Academy, perhaps the best of the many extraordinary New England private schools. When he arrived, he was straight-limbed and slender, with bright dark eyes, a winning smile, and a frank, open-hearted manner. Just and generous in the settlement of questions or squabbles, his contemporaries regarded his decisions as fair and righteous. He was popular with his schoolmates, an amiable companion, and a lover of innocent fun with an unfailing flow of good spirits. Many years later, his roommate at Exeter described him as "rather retiring and quiet in disposition, rather strong with his prejudices, and warm in his attachments. [He] did not seek the company of everyone, and [was] somewhat diffident on first acquaintance. He was not a boy of many words—but, in what little he said, you would know what he meant. He was somewhat sensitive, perhaps might be called quick tempered. But he was not vindictive. He was not eminently sociable, but he enjoyed the society of his friends."

His personality would continue essentially unchanged to the end of his days. He would always have a narrow selection of close friends, would stand by them, and

Library of Congress

Fitz-John Porter

would enjoy their company. More importantly, his powers of persuasion would give him great influence even with his superiors, who would often seek and follow his advice on the most important matters.

In 1841 he entered the United States Military Academy at West Point, from which he graduated eighth in his class in 1845. Like so many others to achieve prominence he was reassigned from Taylor's army on the Rio Grande to Scott's Mexico City column. During the campaign he was promoted to first lieutenant and awarded brevets of captain and major for gallantry at Molino del Rey and Chapultepec. In the assault on the Belen Gate, one of the main gates into Mexico City, Porter's battery commander and the other officer in the battery were killed. Though wounded, Porter continued to command the guns.

As a grown man he was remarkably handsome and, in form, had a physique of perfect proportions. He moved with unaffected dignity, ease, and grace, whether walking or riding. His courtesy and gentleness were recognized by all who knew him. The cadets at West Point, keen observers of the character and ability of their instructors, regarded Major Porter as an ideal soldier and gentleman and valued commendation from him.

During his peacetime service he established a number of close friendships with fellow officers, among them George B. McClellan, who graduated one year behind him in the class of 1846, and Irvin McDowell, who had graduated from the Military Academy before Porter arrived. Fatalistically, he believed, as he would say or write, "All that is, is right and for the best."

Early in the war he, like Keyes, Averell, and other junior officers, was sent on a highly responsible mission where he attracted the attention of an important officer, who sought his services as adjutant and fell under his sway. Some would attribute Patterson's failure to Porter's influence; but when his good friend McClellan took command of the Army of the Potomac, Porter became a division commander, again exercised great influence, and was favored for command of a corps. Early he would attract the attention of the inquisitional forces that pursued Stone, but protected by his friend in command he would be safe . . . as long as his friend remained in power.

Benjamin F. Butler

In a long, active, and controversial career, Benjamin Franklin Butler was one of the true, life-long champions of the "little people" in American history. Unlike his contemporaries, he openly sought public office but was always

Princeton University

Benjamin F. Butler

governed by his principals, which he pursued though any party that promised support for them.

Born November 5, 1818, in Deerfield, New Hampshire, he was a mixture of unsuccessful Irish patriots and English who had settled in America. His father died of yellow fever when he was but six months old. Having a strong intellect and superb powers of retention, he was granted a scholarship to attend Phillips Exeter Academy some years before Fitz-John Porter but stayed only a short time, finally graduating from Lowell High School in 1834. He wished to attend West Point, but his mother had other ideas: the ministry. She enrolled him in Colby College, at the time Waterville College, in Waterville, Maine, where she believed he would receive a good Protestant education with strong Baptist overtones. His trip to the ministry ended when he petitioned the faculty to be excused from compulsory church attendance. After graduation he read law and over the years developed a lucrative law practice in which he always had time to represent the little man. He worked for laborers against their employers, supported the secret ballot to protect freedom of the vote, organized support for the ten-hour day, and made speeches on behalf of labor. Active in the machinery of the Democratic Party, he attended the presidential convention as a delegate in 1852, was elected to the state legislature, ran for governor, and served as a delegate to the tumultuous Democratic Convention in Charleston, South Carolina, in 1860.

In personality, he was intelligent, quick-witted, humorous, self-confident, confrontational, courageous, and insatiably curious. His meteoric temper had a microscopic fuse. For Regular Army officers, West Point graduates, and Boston blue-bloods, he enjoyed a thorough distaste. In appearance, his slender frame of youth disappeared in a fat, uncoordinated but not clumsy, and fair complected body with slightly flushed smooth skin. His clear and bright eyes, one of which was wall-eyed, were surrounded by heavy features and no hair on top but long white hair hanging from the sides.

He never let traditional factions or party lines direct his course. As he saw it, this was not a Republican war. It was a national war. And with his "military background," he believed he was as well-trained and qualified as any man, West Point graduate or not.

When the Confederates captured Fort Sumter on April 14, Butler was more ready than most men. Traveling by rail and water to Annapolis with an early contingent of Massachusetts militia, Butler saw the effect of the "Baltimore Bottleneck" on the salvation of the capital. He disobeyed orders from Scott, took a trainload of his men into Baltimore in a driving rainstorm in the dark of the night, and captured the city of Baltimore. Success in violation of the general in chief's orders never produced a promotion or a medal. He was banished. But he was more than a political general. He would rise again—soon—and much later would return to fight alongside the Army of the Potomac.

Colonel Elmer E. Ellsworth

In command of the Ninth New York, a regiment of Fire Zouaves, was Colonel Elmer E. Ellsworth, impetuous, headstrong, uneasy under restraint, but modest and deferential in social settings, temperate, and a man who never swore. Young Ellsworth, only twenty-four, had been plagued throughout his

Princeton University

Elmer E. Ellsworth

life by bad luck and failure. But he came into his own as war approached. He formed companies of Zouaves which he drilled and trained to high proficiency. The nearer the war, the better he became, exhibiting his men at public functions and to paying audiences, all the while preaching preparedness and stirring martial fervor. At the outbreak, he recruited a regiment of New York City firemen with the aid of the fire chief and set out for the capital. He had, at last, succeeded.

In late May, but only after all the official niceties of Virginia's secession had been completed, Scott agreed to an aggressive movement across the Potomac to establish control of the west bank of the river. The town of Alexandria would be approached from the north by an infantry regiment, and Ellsworth would take his men in three ships to the Alexandria waterfront. Once in the town, he saw a Rebel flag on top of a hotel and went to remove it. On his way down the staircase from the roof he encountered an armed secessionist civilian and was killed.

J. K. F. Mansfield

Born in New Haven, Connecticut, in 1803, Mansfield entered West Point two months before his fourteenth birthday, took the five-year course, graduated second in the class of 1822, and was commissioned in the Corps of Engineers. In the years that followed he toiled on the country's coastal defenses in New York, Virginia, North Carolina, South Carolina, Florida, and Georgia. Chief engineer under General Zachary Taylor along the Rio Grande River during the war with Mexico, he constructed and participated in the defense of Fort Brown, Texas, was awarded a brevet of major for gallant and distinguished service in the defense of the fort, and received a brevet of lieutenant-colonel for gallant and meritorious conduct in several conflicts at Monterey, where he suffered a painful wound while leading an assault on a redoubt. He was breveted colonel for gallant and meritorious conduct at Buena Vista.

From 1848 to 1853 he served on the board of engineers planning coastal defenses on the Atlantic and Pacific oceans. On May 28, 1853, Secretary of War Jefferson Davis, who had observed him during the war with Mexico, appointed him inspector-general. In the Department of Texas in 1860 and 1861, he became aware of activities that would lead to war and hurried to Washington to communicate his observations to the War Department. Once in Washington, he received recognition for his good work by a succession of responsible assignments including command of the Department of Washington. Appointed brigadier-general and considered indispensable in Washington by Scott, he would have preferred, and he continuously tried to obtain, a field command even though in his long service he had never commanded troops.

Although vigorous, his flowing white hair and white beard made him appear all of his years in a war that did not lend itself to older officers. A man of kind disposition, he showed his deeply religious and patriotic nature in a letter he wrote his daughter on June 17, 1861, "I feel that I am right, and I shall do my duty to the full extent of my ability and power. May God help me, & strengthen me with his strong arm, and uphold me with his mighty power. If God be with us, who can be against

Princeton University

J. K. F. Mansfield

us." After inactive commands he would achieve his desire for a command in battle in the fall of 1862 when he would lead his corps to a fence just north of a bloody corn field near a little town in Maryland.

Irvin McDowell

Born in October of 1818, Irvin McDowell was raised to be aristocratic in spirit and thought. Young Irvin was warm-hearted, affectionate, and outspoken. A year of school in Paris, followed by four years at West Point where he was a social standout despite his mediocre academic status, produced a repressive effect. His classmates nicknamed him "Squash McDowell." He became more reserved and formal although his polish remained unchanged.

Upon graduation in 1838, twenty-third of forty-five graduating cadets, he began with a tour of duty in the First Artillery Regiment and during the following years held a series of staff positions, which rewarded him with the derisive new nickname "Guts" McDowell. In the Mexican War he served as General John E. Wool's adjutant, won a brevet for captain for services at the Battle of Buena Vista, but somehow became the victim of rumors of cowardice. After the close of the war he continued his staff positions; and at the outbreak of the Civil War, he was a major on duty in Washington. Scott had known him since graduation and thought highly of him. Working as an assistant-adjutant-general in the defenses of the capital during April, the major, by his energy and intelligence, attracted the attention of important people in the inner circles of the government. During this time, he met his first important real backer, Salmon P. Chase, secretary of the treasury. Chase had great influence over early military decisions, earning himself the unofficial title of "General." Chase remembered McDowell as an Ohioan in the Regular Army and sought McDowell's advice on questions of military organization. Impressed with his intelligence and poise, the secretary determined that McDowell should be promoted to a higher rank, which resulted in a promotion to brigadier-general.

McDowell's first opposition came in the massive form of the general in chief, who shared the hostile opinion of many in the army toward the rapid promotion of junior officers. Despite the fact that he liked McDowell, Scott was annoyed because his advice had not been sought on McDowell's promotion.

Although tall and strong, McDowell had a torso too long for his short legs, a configuration that magnified the substantial girth in his middle. His legs were well-proportioned in themselves, but "were attached to his body by brawny rolling hips that worked up and down when he walked." Making expert horsemanship an impossibility, the short legs and large body, often caused him to lose his seat and tumble from his horse. Nevertheless, in spite of his clumsy and ungainly appearance he enjoyed a good dance, at which he had "elf-like grace." His head, attached to his fat body by a short thick neck, seemed "bullet-shaped;" and his florid face, fleshy and chubby, was made to appear even more fat by his jaws, which protruded on

Irvin McDowell

either side. He wore a brawly, bristling imperial and a bushy, drooping German mustache which emphasized his Teutonic appearance.

Hard liquor, wine, and spirits of any other kind he never used, a characteristic for which he was known throughout the army. In fact, he never even drank tea, coffee, or other lesser stimulants. Nor did he use tobacco in any form, a practice he found abhorrent. And he never swore.

A cold, distant superior, he lacked the kind of magnetic personality that would make him a natural leader of men; and he did not evoke great devotion in his subordinates, particularly the enlisted men who would be called to do his fighting.

McDowell had seen battle but had never in his military career held any line command. Now, he was to command an entire army. On May 27, General Orders No. 26 created an unnamed department to include all Virginia east of the Alleghenies and north of the James River "under the command of Brigadier General Irvin McDowell, U.S.A." McDowell would lead his country's most significant army to its first major battle, would feel the elation of victory as it progressed, and would personify the ignominy of defeat. When a young major general came east to assume command of the defeated army, McDowell would serve gladly as his best advisor and loyal friend. But a cruel confluence of circumstances would change all this when his general fell desperately ill in December.

Samuel P. Heintzelman

One of the older officers in the early war Samuel Peter Heintzelman was born in 1805, was appointed to West Point from Pennsylvania, and graduated in the class of 1826. His stern, hardy visage, pinched features which made his nose almost touch his chin, full beard, long thin hair, and sharp, scowling eyes made his nickname of youth, "grim old Heintzelman," an apt description. Over the years, he had acquired much battle experience. After the war another general described him as "a man of the keenest sense of honor, but captious and querulous oftentimes to such an extent, that, if the junior officers did not seek to avoid him, they rarely sought his society. And yet he was a man of vast and varied acquirements; a great reader, he had the best library in the garrison, and there was no one of the officers who could draw upon so wide a range of reading and study for information upon any point of history, ancient or modern. He was kind hearted in acts, far more so than in words. He was the only officer in the garrison whose pecuniary means had grown beyond his wants, and to those few subalterns who appreciated his real worth, in spite of a repellant manner, he was a true friend, and his purse was always open to aid his less prosperous brother officers."

Blunt and caustic, Heintzelman spoke his feelings on the many points that rankled him. Although he appeared to be pro-this and anti-that in a way that favored advancement, he had no strong views about the explosive issues of the war except his loyalty to his country, his profession, and his comrades in arms. High command would test his abilities, and he would not be found wanting, but would he shine?

Library of Congress

Samuel P. Heintzelman

David Hunter

Commander of one of McDowell's divisions at Bull Run, David Hunter, a native of the capital, had been born at the turn of the century and graduated in 1822 from West Point, where he stood below the middle of his class, twenty-fifth of forty. After several years service on the frontier against the Indians, he resigned his commission, but in 1842 he reentered the army.

David Hunter

As crisis followed crisis in 1861, Hunter concluded that conflict was inevitable. From his post at Fort Leavenworth, Kansas, he communicated this opinion to the newly elected president and was rewarded with an invitation to accompany the presidential train on the inaugural trip from Illinois to Washington. In the capital he organized a force of one hundred gentleman volunteers to guard the White House and its occupants day and night, living himself in the East Wing. Because he was constantly in the eye of the president, Hunter was a natural choice for promotion to full colonel on May 14 when the Regular Army was expanded. He brought to his new rank an entirely different attitude than Heintzelman. Handsome and unprepossessing, with dyed black hair and mustache, he was easy and friendly, almost like an adoptive father to his young staff officers as if they were the children he had never had. Service at Bull Run ended early with a bloody neck wound, which he followed by villification of the hapless McDowell, then a major appointment in the west. But he would return . . . this time to the graveyard of reputations, the Shenandoah Valley, where his skill at independent command and his politically correct views would create a bright light for the Union.

George B. McClellan

Among the passengers stepping from a train that had arrived in the capital in late July 1861 was a broad shouldered, muscularly built, short young man, perhaps five-feet-eight-inches tall. Although he appeared quiet and modest, his movements, active and graceful, showed no lack of confidence. He had a shapely head, dark hair and mustache, blue eyes, and a fine face, all resting on a short, thick neck. Leaving the platform, he headed at once to present himself to General Scott.

Consistent with his upbringing as a patrician and his affinity for aristocratic Southerners, George B. McClellan, West Point class of 1846, was dignified, reserved, friendly, quiet, and magnetic. His personal intercourse with the men about him was marked by kindness, modesty, and courtesy, even toward his enemies, military and civilian. In fact, one of his close friends thought he treated his enemies better than his friends. His manners were simple and unaffected. Nor was his personal conduct subject to criticism. No drinker, no gambler, no womanizer, he was known for the highest truthfulness and integrity. He had splendid talents as an organizer, administrator, and drillmaster. His distaste for, even disgust at, the volunteer soldiers and officers of the Mexican War he had, to some extent, put aside; but he had doubts about the willingness and ability of his men to fight.

A connoisseur of the arts, he read Latin and Greek, spoke French and Spanish fluently in a good voice without being very musical, and rode his huge horse Dan Webster like a professional horseman. His work, especially the mountains of organizational and administrative work necessary to create an army where none had existed, he did with tireless patience, energy, and good humor, which earned him the loyalty and support of the men who labored with him at headquarters.

In camp, he was genial, charming, and friendly to the men around him, a sociable, modest man "with a taste for jokes and good cigars." Always in uniform, he could nevertheless be approached by a junior officer or an enlisted man at any time. The hard-nosed confrontation born of a disagreement on an important subject was beyond him. Cursing, the emotional outburst, damning of those who were

Princeton University

George B. McClellan

wrong, vilification of his enemies, relief of a defaulting subordinate from command were not part of his personality.

In disagreement he showed a stubbornness exceeded by no man; but with his natural reserve, he always avoided antagonism. His resistance, according to a subordinate who saw him during the early days of the war and intermittently until the end of his military career, was unshakeable but was of "the feminine sort." He would discuss, rediscuss, raise, and reraise a question. Because many of the disagreements he had with his superiors involved time and McClellan usually wanted more, further talking gave him his way.

Nathaniel Prentiss Banks

The first of seven children born to the superintendent of a Massachusetts cotton mill, Nathaniel Prentiss Banks spent only a few years in school before, and while still a boy, he abandoned his education and began work in the cotton mill.

He taught himself Latin and Spanish, read voraciously, and took every opportunity to practice public speaking. After aligning himself with the Democratic party, he became an effective spokesman for the working man in a state then dominated by the Whigs, the party of wealth and class. Dabbling in acting, reading law sufficiently to be admitted to practice, marrying, and becoming an exceptional ballroom dancer, but always verging on poverty, he entered public service as an inspector in the Boston customs house, published a local newspaper supporting the working man, and at last in his thirties began a career in politics. In his seventh campaign he was finally elected to the Massachusetts Assembly. Two years later he showed the characteristics that would dominate his political and military life, an ability to avoid doctrinaire positions and a desire to harmonize conflicting forces or as others would see it, "a complete lack of principle." He formed a coalition between his Democratic Party and Henry Wilson's Free-Soil Party, a coalition that gave Wilson the presidency of the state senate and made Banks speaker of the assembly.

In 1853, he was elected to the United States Congress, where he served sporadically for ten terms representing over time no less than five political parties. His willingness to identify and pursue issues that attracted voter support and his need for the income of political employment, his sole means of support after the age of thirty-five, made him the perfect politician, a man who would support any issue that would provide gainful employment as an officeholder. Slavery and abolition were among these issues. He did not much care about the plight of the black man; but a successful politician in Massachusetts, the national caldron of abolition, required a strong position on the issue.

When Fort Sumter surrendered, Banks tendered his services to Lincoln. Although he had served briefly in the Lowell militia, had been a member of the House Committee on Military Affairs, and had been governor during the farsighted, effective reorganization of the Massachusetts militia, he knew nothing about military affairs, a fact he conceded freely.

His military and leadership characteristics reflected his humble origins and his natural reluctance to affect the superiority, power, and aristocracy of high military rank. Unlike Winfield Scott he would not insist on the personal perquisites of a major-general or demand precise military etiquette. Having come from "the

Nathaniel Prentiss Banks

people," he would remain one of them; and his leadership would be that of a "first among equals." Nor would he enforce strict military discipline. In fact, he would have difficulty enforcing discipline at all. And his willingness to associate with his enlisted men would put him in the category of "democratic leaders."

Although he dressed well, wore expensive military clothing, and ran an officers' mess that cost his military family dearly, he would wear the uniform of a common soldier and work at menial tasks with his men. Difficult to label at any time in his political career, Banks represented the kind of unifying appointment Lincoln wanted to make. A former Democrat, a spokesman for labor, an opponent of slavery, and a successful Republican candidate for political office, his advancement appealed to many groups beyond the Republican, Radical, antislavery men of Lincoln's party.

Early in command as a major general of the Potomac area around Harpers Ferry, he would find his way into the Shenandoah Valley where he would confront a Confederate stone wall.

Chapter 1

"I felt as confident that war would soon come as
that the sun would rise on the morrow."

— Lieutenant-Colonel Erasmus D. Keyes, General Scott's Military Secretary

Scott Proves His Loyalty

Following orders from President James Buchanan, Brevet Lieutenant General Winfield Scott, general in chief of all United States military forces, had moved his headquarters from New York City to Washington, D.C., in December of 1860. But when General Thomas S. Mather, the adjutant-general of Illinois, presented himself at the new temporary headquarters on January 29, 1861, Scott was not there. Lieutenant-Colonel Erasmus D. Keyes, Scott's military secretary, received Mather.[1]

By January of 1861, more and more letters threatening personal violence were being received by President-elect Abraham Lincoln. No man's loyalty could be taken for granted.[2] Even the loyalty of those in high places was uncertain. The last

1 Weik, Jesse, "Side Lights on Lincoln, How Lincoln Was Convinced of Scott's Loyalty," 89 *Century Magazine* 594 (1911) ("Weik, *Sides Lights*); Elliott, Charles Winslow, *Winfield Scott, the Soldier and the Man* 678-80, 687-89 (New York, 1937) ("Elliott, *Scott*"); Keyes, Erasmus D., *Fifty Years Observation of Men and Events Civil and Military* 360 (New York, 1884) ("Keyes, *Fifty Years*").

2 Weik, *Side Lights*, p. 593.

two secretaries of war, Jefferson C. Davis and John B. Floyd, staunch Southern Democrats, had dispersed the tiny regular army over the frontier where it could be of no use in the event of hostilities and had relocated many weapons depositories to the Southern states.[3]

From his post at Fort Leavenworth, Lieutenant-Colonel David Hunter, one of the rare abolitionists in the officer corps of the regular army joined the group of unsolicited correspondents sending warnings. In October, Hunter wrote that "a number of young men in Virginia had bound themselves, by oaths most solemn, to cause your assassination, should you be elected . . . 'on the institution' [of slavery] these good people are most certainly demented and being crazy, they should be taken care of, to prevent their doing harm to themselves or to others."[4] Through November and into December, Hunter reported more plots and Lincoln requested more information.[5]

Still in Illinois, Lincoln decided that someone must travel to Washington to learn "the real military conditions." Mather agreed to go. Lincoln instructed him to call on Scott, tell him about the threats, and learn if any efforts were being made to assure the president-elect's safety. But Mather's principle mission was to verify Scott's loyalty. Was he unreservedly for the Union?[6]

Lincoln had reason to be uncertain about, if not doubt, Scott's loyalty. The president-elect could probably put aside the fact that Scott was a Virginian, had many Southern friends, had a strong preference for Southern officers, was a long-standing personal friend of Lincoln's presidential opponent John J. Crittenden,

3 Nicolay, John G., and Hay, John, *Abraham Lincoln, a History* 10 vols. (New York, 1914), vol. 4, p. 207 ("N&H"); Rhodes, James Ford, *History of the United States from the Compromise of 1850 to the McKinley-Bryan Campaign of 1896* 8 vols. (New York 1920), vol. III, pp. 236-41; Nevins, Allan, *The Emergence of Lincoln, Prologue to Civil War 1859-1861* 2 vols., (New York, 1950), vol. 2, pp. 372-376. Moore, John Bassett, *The Works of James Buchanan, Comprising His Speeches, State Papers, and Private Correspondence* 11 vols. (New York, 1960) ("Moore, *Buchanan Works*"), vol. 11, pp. 279-82, letter dated October 28, 1862, Buchanan to the Editors of the *National Intelligencer*. Nevins stops short of charging Floyd with malfeasance but clearly finds him guilty of misfeasance; but contemporaries had no trouble finding guilt. Henry Jackson Hunt MSS (Library of Congress) draft letter December 16, 1861, from Hunt to McClellan; George B. McClellan MSS (Library of Congress) final version of letter dated December 16, 1861, from Hunt to McClellan.

4 Robert Todd Lincoln MSS (Library of Congress), letter dated October 20, 1860, from Hunter to Lincoln; Miller, Edward A., Jr., *Lincoln's Abolitionist General: The Biography of David Hunter* (Columbia, 1997) 49-50 ("Miller, *Hunter*").

5 Lincoln MSS (L.C.), letters dated November 1, 1860; December 18, 1860, from Hunter to Lincoln; Basler, Roy P., ed., *The Collected Works of Abraham Lincoln* 9 vols. and 2 supps. (New Brunswick, 1953) ("Basler, *Lincoln's Works*") vol. 4, pp. 132, 159 letters dated October 26, and December 22, 1860, from Lincoln to Hunter.

6 Weik, *Side Lights*, 593-94.

and had supported him in the election. Far more important, Scott had sent Lincoln a puzzling document in December. Entitled "Views Suggested by the Imminent Danger of a Disruption of the Union by the Secession of One or More of the Southern States," the "Views" had been laboriously written over eight or ten days. "Every morning," according to Keyes, Scott's military secretary, "he discussed them or rather he harangued me about them, as I disagreed with him in all his statements and conclusions. I was in favor of Lincoln for President and I felt as confident that war would soon come as that the sun would rise on the morrow."[7]

The "Views" did not leap off the page as the testament of a man firmly loyal to the federal government and opposed to secession. The original had been sent to Buchanan a short time before the election but had produced no response. In fact, they had produced no effect at all. An almost indecipherable mixture of conflicting military and political suggestions, they supported the Union, suggested that secession be condoned, advocated confrontation with the Southern states, and expressed an abhorrence for internecine war. They began, "To save time the right of secession may be conceded, and instantly balanced by the correlative right, on the part of the Federal Government, against an interior State or States, to reestablish by force, if necessary, its former continuity of territory." He followed this with a weak, affectionate plea that the states threatening secession not go, "particularly dear Virginia — being 'native here and to the manor born' . . ." He urged that the forts in Southern territory, including Fort Pickens on Santa Rosa Island in Pensacola Harbor and Forts Sumter and Moultrie in Charleston Harbor, be reinforced and held at all hazards. Any conflict, he believed, would be enormous and bloody.[8]

Most of all, the "Views" reflected his strong desire to avoid sectional fighting. He wrote from the heart, not the head, when he said, ". . . there is good reason to hope that the danger of secession may be made to pass away without one conflict of arms, one execution, or one arrest for treason. . . . the foregoing views eschew the idea of invading a seceded state." In an explanatory letter sent the following day to the secretary of war, he added unrealistically, "General Scott is . . . not without hope that all dangers and difficulties will pass away without leaving a scar or painful recollection behind."[9]

7 Keyes, *Fifty Years* 334; Elliott, *Scott* 683, 687-88.

8 Buchanan, James, *Mr. Buchanan's Administration on the Eve of the Rebellion* (New York, 1866) 288 ("Buchanan, *Administration*") The "Views" are not printed as an appendix in Elliott's *Scott*, but they do appear as appendices in Buchanan; *Administration* and in Townsend, Brevet Major-General Edward D., *Anecdotes of the Civil War in the United States* (New York, 1881) ("Townsend, *Anecdotes*").

9 Buchanan, *Administration,* 289-90.

In early January, Scott had written Lincoln to assert his loyalty, but the obvious facts and the incomprehensible "Views" must have caused a sense of uncertainty about the old general.[10] Perhaps the "Views" were a product of his early training as a lawyer: an attempt to give objective consideration to all aspects of the problem, even the unspeakable concept of secession. As unclear and perplexing as they were, the recipient could be forgiven for questioning the author's loyalty to the Union.

Lincoln decided he needed a direct personal assessment of the general in chief he would inherit from Buchanan and a long line of former presidents, almost all of them Democrats.

"Mr. Seward, Mr. Washburne and other good friends have certified to General Scott's loyalty, high character, and personal integrity," he said to Mather,

> and he himself has written to me offering his services without reserve; but he is a Virginian, you know, and while I have no reason or evidence to warrant me in questioning him or his motives, I shall feel better satisfied if you will visit him on my behalf. When you call, insist on a personal interview and do not leave till you have seen and sounded him. Listen to the old man and look him in the face, note carefully what he says and how he says it, and then, when you return with your report, I shall probably be well enough informed to determine with some degree of accuracy where he stands and what to expect of him."[11]

Only a few days before Mather arrived in the capital, Scott had arranged for the "Views" to be published in the *National Intelligencer*, an influential Washington newspaper with national circulation.[12] Buchanan, of course, was furious. In his mind, the document involved government affairs that should have been kept secret. He had been compromised by the old general in chief and not inadvertently. Later, replaced by Abraham Lincoln and his country at full war, Buchanan wrote about the "Views." After reading them, he explained, "you will admit that they constitute an extraordinary Document. Indeed, they tend to prove what has often been said about the gallant General, that when he abandons the sword for the pen, he makes sad work of it."[13]

Now that Mather had arrived at army headquarters only to find Scott absent, he and Keyes discussed current political and military affairs. Keyes believed that the North was strong and prosperous, that power was about to pass at long last from

10 Elliott, *Scott,* 679-80.

11 Weik, *Side Lights,* 594.

12 Keyes, *Fifty Years,* 353.

13 Moore, *Buchanan's Works,* 11, 206-09, Buchanan to Halleck, letter dated June 29, 1861.

Southern to Northern hands, that war was inevitable, and that this was as good a time as any to fight it out.[14] But strong steps were necessary. Keyes talked, as he always did, about the "miserable condition of the Northern States" and their inability to resist rebellion.

Mather agreed. Illinois, he said, had almost no arms and did not even have any record of the weapons given to it by the Federal government before 1856. Worse yet, in nearby St. Louis, the governor of Missouri was issuing the state's weapons to violent secessionists.

Both men were mindful of the conduct of Jefferson Davis and John Floyd, the two prior secretaries of war. Joseph Holt, another Democrat, had replaced John B. Floyd as secretary of war during Buchanan's lame-duck period before Lincoln's inauguration. Assuming that Holt's tenure would end when Lincoln was inaugurated in March, Mather and Keyes turned to the qualifications needed for a secretary of war in the new Lincoln administration.

According to Mather, President Lincoln wanted to know the opinions of the officers in the Regular Army about the person who should be appointed. As it was in the civil departments, all authority over the military was now in the hands of Southerners.

A man capable of reversing that was required, Keyes said. In Keyes's opinion only a solid Northerner willing to act with perseverance and firmness would satisfy such a need. The North had to be given power and patronage fully proportionate with its numbers. Anything short of that, Keyes warned the president, would lead to failure.[15]

Although Mather was probably pleased to find a kindred spirit so close to the general in chief, the real purpose of his visit was to meet Scott; but for some time the general in chief had been suffering from recurrences of amoebic dysentery, a disease he had contracted during his remarkable campaign in Mexico in 1847.[16] When Mather learned that Scott was recuperating at home, he went there. Scott's servant refused to deliver Mather's card, saying the general was too ill to receive anyone. The following morning, January 30,[17] Mather presented himself a second time, only to receive the same rebuff. He reached in his pocket and drew out a letter Lincoln had given him.

14 Keyes, *Fifty Years,* 351, 334.

15 Keyes, *Fifty Years*, 360-61.

16 Elliott, *Scott*, p. 688, n. 29.

17 The dates of these visits and conversations are unclear. The text reconciles the accounts of Weik and Keyes and produces a chronological narrative based on Keyes's reference to his meeting with Mather on January 29.

"It is very important," he said, "and should be delivered at once."

In a few moments he heard a commotion in the general's quarters, and a short time later he was invited upstairs to Scott's chambers. The old general, all six feet four and one-quarter inches of him, sat in his bed propped up by a bank of pillows. He was "grizzly, wrinkled, and pale," and his flesh lay in rolls across his warty face and neck. He breathed laboriously and with difficulty.

In his trembling hand lay Lincoln's letter.[18] He, too, had begun to receive letters threatening his life.[19] Had he been intimidated by the fire-eating Southerners? Had all the fight left his gout-ridden body?

"You may present my compliments to Mr. Lincoln when you reach Springfield," he said in a wheezy voice, "and tell him I shall expect him to come to Washington as soon as he is ready. Say to him also that, when once here, I shall consider myself responsible for his safety. If necessary, I shall plant cannon at both ends of Pennsylvania Avenue; and if any of the Maryland or Virginia gentlemen who have become so threatening and troublesome of late show their heads or even venture to raise a finger, I shall blow them to hell!"

His frame trembled. His eyes flashed. His demeanor and statement spoke an "unequivocal and righteous indignation at the perfidy of those of his countrymen who were so willing to destroy the Union which he had fought long and ardently to maintain."[20]

Beginning his adult life as a lawyer, young Scott had found the practice of law to be slow, difficult, and unrewarding. He flirted with military service. The outrage of the *Chesapeake-Leopard* affair drove him into the Virginia militia as a lance corporal in command of a squad of volunteer Virginia cavalry. With the increase of martial fervor in the period preceding the War of 1812, the United States regular army increased in size and with it the rank of young Scott, who succeeded in transferring from state militia to regular army. By the end of the War of 1812, a war notorious for incompetent military commanders, Scott had compiled an admirable record, was a brigadier general in the Regular Army, had a brevet for major general, and had become a national hero.

In the reduction of the regular army after the war five of every six officers were released, but Scott kept his commission and received command of a military department. In 1832 he had first-hand contact with secessionism when President Andrew Jackson sent him to command the military forces in South Carolina during

18 Weik, *Side Lights*, 593-94.

19 Keyes, *Fifty Years,* 361.

20 Weik, *Side Lights*, 594.

the Nullification Crisis. While there, he handled the Nullifiers with diplomacy, finesse, and aplomb, doing "much to preserve peace in a time of crises." He then saw service against the Seminoles, Creeks, and Cherokees and by 1841, had succeeded the deceased Alexander Macomb as general in chief of the army with headquarters in Washington. His administration was marked by excellence and innovation.

At the outbreak of the war with Mexico, Scott, now almost sixty, was victimized by politics. Throughout his life he had been a Whig. President James K. Polk, a Democrat and a ferocious political partisan, feared Scott's popularity and, to avoid his political potential, kept him from the field. When Polk at last decided that Zachary Taylor's campaign along the Rio Grande might continue forever without decisive result, that the public would not tolerate it, and that none of the other military candidates waiting in the wings were suited for the bold plan he had in mind, he turned to Scott.

Polk wanted a military force to land at Vera Cruz on the Mexican coast, march inland, and capture Mexico City, a plan he had considered from the declaration of war. With great reluctance, he gave Scott the command. The campaign that followed, with an army of less than fifteen thousand men in a country of several million, was a miraculous demonstration of Scott's virtuosity. Cooperating superbly with the navy, he managed a virtually bloodless landing and capture of Vera Cruz, a fortified coastal city. An unbroken string of victories followed, ending with the capture of Mexico City. All this he did in spite of severe obstructions from Democratic politicians at home. Worried as much by Scott's political popularity as they were by military issues, the Democrats attempted to court-martial him on silly charges that failed in the face of the returning hero's tremendous popularity. After the Mexican War, he continued to serve as general in chief except for a brief and woefully unsuccessful sojourn in politics as a badly defeated Whig candidate for president in 1852.

In his prime Scott towered over most men, weighed 230 pounds, and had the strength of an ox. In his old age, he remained huge and plagued by gout. He could no longer sit a horse, walked with difficulty, and had bad eyesight. Nevertheless, in 1861 he was the only high-ranking American officer of any real substance and the only one who could look Lincoln square in the eye.[21]

21 Johnston, R. M., *Bull Run, its Strategy and Tactics* (New York, 1913) p. 17 ("Johnston, *Bull Run*"); Malone, Dumas, ed., *Dictionary of American Biography,* 10 vols. (New York, 1964) vol. 9, pp. 505-11 ("*D.A.B.*"). The first edition of the Dictionary of *American Biography* was in twenty volumes. The current edition, used here, is in ten, each with two parts in one volume. For an objective and sound view of mobilization, officer appointment, and intemperate dealings between Scott and Polk, *see* Sellers, Charles, *James K. Polk: Continentalist 1843-1846* 2 vols. (Princeton, 1966) vol. 2, pp. 434-444. *Seriatim*, Polk offered Scott a command, Scott demanded

Throughout his life Scott had been a man of marked eccentricities and sensitivities. In his old age they became sharper and more dominant. His anecdotes diminished in number and increased in repetition. Busts and portraits of himself filled his quarters. He was not, he was always quick to say, six feet four inches tall; he was six feet four and one quarter inches. He would comment frequently about the youthfulness, attractiveness, and sturdiness of his figure, and the freedom of his skin from the marks of old age.

On his military career, Scott would often narrate the exploits of the world's great military commanders, then compare his own achievements with theirs. He would tell people about the threats he received in the mail and comment to others that he was puzzled when the listener showed such a lack of concern for him. This vanity he often recognized by saying, "At my time of life, a man needs compliments."

With retirement a real prospect at any moment, he had become concerned about his financial circumstances. Nevertheless, the daily requests he received for money from one person or another, many without merit, always touched his "kindness of nature" and often resulted in compensation to an undeserving imposter.

He remained, as always, a man of broad learning, widely read, current in his reading, and a true military expert with an international reputation. In 1861, "he was living in the past, and for the present he was absorbed in his fears of civil war and attention to his bodily weakness and pains." In 1861, a European officer visiting America was struck by his education and learning about military history, finding, however, that he had "too often the weakness of looking for points of comparison with his own career."

In 1859 when sectional problems were already dominant, he offered the position of military secretary to his favorite officer, a Southerner. If the officer had accepted, the general in chief's staff would have been Southern to a man.

"What will they say, General," asked one of his junior aides, "if all the staff are Southerners?"

"If the Southern rascals will have so much merit, how can we fail to advance them?" he responded.

According to Erasmus D. Keyes, a devoted Northerner who did accept the appointment as military secretary, "he would narrate the good qualities of his earlier

conditions, and Polk withdrew the offer. At one point, Scott wrote to Secretary of War Marcy, "I do not desire to place myself in the most perilous of all positions:— *a fire upon my rear from Washington, and the fire, in front, from the Mexicans*." Quoted in ibid., p. 441. Elliott, *Scott* in general. Elliott's work is by far the best of the many biographies of Scott, including the two very recent ones, and has been the object of reliance here above all others.

associates, and assign almost unimaginable virtues to many Southern men, making them much better than the men I have known in any part of my life."[22]

Now seventy-four years old and showing all the ravages of his years, he, his experience, and his judgment would, nevertheless, be important assets for the early days of Lincoln's administration.[23] His position was assured when Mather delivered a categorically favorable report which removed from Lincoln's mind all concern about the old general's loyalty.[24]

As the inauguration on March 4 drew near, men from the South visited their old friends in Washington to say last, heart-rending good-byes. Receiving numerous visits of this sort, the general in chief was among the sufferers but never showed a flicker of disloyalty.

Just before relations and communications between the sections ceased, Governor Morehead of North Carolina, an old friend, came to Scott's office. He was on his way south from Philadelphia where he had withdrawn his daughter from school to take her home while travel was still uninterrupted between the sections. The two old men had a touching interview. The cotton states had seceded, and many of the slave states were on the brink. Both men deprecated secession, but neither suggested that they might soon be together in any new country, and both viewed their parting as final. At last, Morehead arose and mournfully said farewell. He added that his daughter, who was in a carriage below, wished very much to see Scott once more and had asked if she might visit him. He consented, and she appeared immediately. After a few parting words of regret, she bent over the old general as he sat in his chair and kissed him on the forehead. Streaming tears, she and her father departed.

Judge Robertson, a small, thin, but venerable looking Virginian, also an old friend, came to Washington with two other Virginians to meet with Scott. The old general listened in silence as Robertson recalled the days when they were school boys together, the warm attachment Virginians had for their state, and their allegiance to it above all other ties. Turning to more concrete matters, he began to offer Scott command of Virginia's military forces.

22 Pisani, Lieutenant-Colonel Camille Ferri, *Prince Napoleon in America 1861, Letters from his Aide-de-Camp* (Bloomington, 1959) 103 ("Pisani, *Letters*"); Keyes, *Fifty Years*, 315-21, 325-326.

23 Seward, Frederick W., *Reminiscences of a WarTime Statesman and Diplomat, 1830-1915* (New York, 1916) 167 ("Seward, *Reminiscences*").

24 Weik, *Side Lights*, 594.

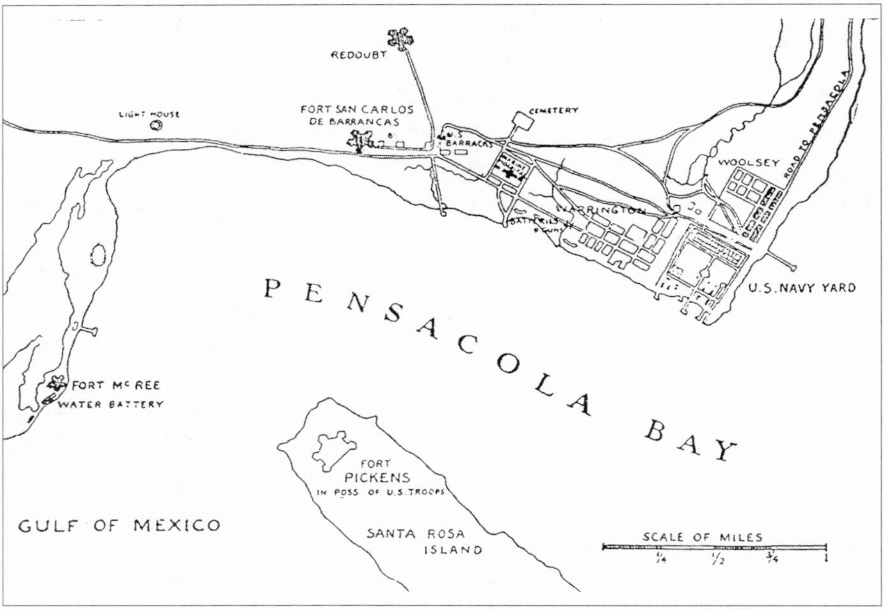

"I have served my country under the flag of the Union for more than fifty years," Scott responded to the offer, "and as long as God permits me to live I will defend that flag with my sword, even if my own native State assails it."

Robertson persisted, offering a large estate if Scott would take service with the South.

Scott stopped him.

"Friend Robertson, go no further. It is best that we part here before you compel me to resent a mortal insult."

When Scott's old and trusted friend Senator John J. Crittenden asked him about his reported intention to resign, Scott replied, "I have not changed. Always a Union man."[25]

Other matters were not so certain. As Scott had recognized in his "views," the forts in the South were destabilizing assets. They could not remain as they were. Some were deserted. Some had tiny, peacetime garrisons. Few could withstand an assault. None could withstand a siege. Worse yet, they were not all single powerful

25 *N&H*, 4, 103-104; Townsend, *Anecdotes*, 4-7. The first quote is from *N&H*, the second from Townsend. On April 22, 1861, the Charleston, South Carolina, *Mercury* stated that General Scott had resigned his position in the United States Army and offered to serve his native state of Virginia. In Mobile, Alabama, a one hundred gun salute was fired in honor of his resignation. Townsend, *Anecdotes*, 13.

structures. In both Charleston and Pensacola harbors, garrisons too small for one fortress had responsibility for three or more.

What should be done? This was not only a question of loyalty. It was a severe test of policy, analysis, judgment, decisiveness, and capacity for action.

Pensacola Harbor was shielded from the ocean by Santa Rosa Island, a forty mile strip of sand. To enter the harbor a ship had to cross a bar between the tip of the island and the mainland to the west, a space covered by Fort McRae on the mainland and Fort Pickens at the end of the Island. A triangle away, one and one half miles from Pickens and two miles from McRae, were Fort Barrancas and the village of Warrington, with a navy yard one mile and a half east of Barrancas. All were garrisoned by one under-strength, coast artillery company of less than one hundred men under the command of Adam J. Slemmer, a mere first lieutenant. He had forty-six enlisted men from his artillery company and thirty-one ordinary seamen from the navy yard. No orders gave Slemmer guidance; but, like Major Robert Anderson in Charleston Harbor, he decided to consolidate all his men in the fort easiest to defend and most difficult to assault.

After many false starts caused, among other things, by disloyal naval officers, Slemmer managed to have his men and some supplies towed on barges from Fort Barrancas to Santa Rosa Island. The families of Slemmer and his subordinate officer were put aboard a supply ship bound for New York.[26]

The ordnance and ordnance stores in Fort Pickens included more than two hundred large sea coast and garrison artillery pieces divided among 10-inch Colombiads, 10-inch mortars, 8-inch howitzers, and 42-, 32-, 24-, 18-, and 12-pounders with various quantities of powder and ammunition.[27] The fort had been

26 Lt. Col. J. H. Gilman, "With Slemmer in Pensacola Harbor," in Robert Underwood Johnson and Clarence Clough Buell, eds., *Battles and Leaders of the Civil War, being for the most part contributions by Union and Confederate Officers. Based upon "Century War Series,"* 4 vols. (New York, 1956, Yoseloff), vol. 1, pp. 26-28 ("*B&L*"). No enlisted men deserted even though their families remained on the mainland. From more than fifteen thousand enlisted men in the Regular Army in 1861, a mere twenty-six are known to have joined in the rebellion. Of the graduates of the Military Academy between 1802 and 1861, 1,249 were living in 1861. Of that total one hundred eighty-four on active duty and ninety-nine who had resigned their commissions or otherwise returned to civilian life joined the rebellion, a total of 283 or approximately twenty-three percent. Upton, Brevet Major-General Emory, *The Military Policy of the United States* (Washington, 1904), 238, 239 ("Upton, *Military Policy*").

27 *The War Of The Rebellion: A Compilation of The Official Records of The Union And Confederate Armies* 128 vols. (Washington 1899) (*OR)*, Series 1, vol. 1, 349. Published in four series each devoted to a different subject matter and each with a different number of volumes, the official records "volumes" are often in several "parts," each "part" being a separate book. Each part has its own volume number and part number. The related "parts" have the same volume number. All references are to Series I unless specifically stated. The separate "parts" are designated when necessary to identify the specific book.

designed for a garrison of twelve hundred.[28] When Slemmer took possession of it on January 10, only forty guns were actually mounted, the embrasures had no covers,[29] and the surrounding secessionist forces were numerous. Although both sides wanted the forts, neither was willing to precipitate a nationwide shooting war. Both sides maintained an undeclared truce.

On January 13, just after retreat, four men, three in uniform, presented themselves at the gate and demanded, as citizens of Florida and Alabama, admittance. Slemmer and Lieutenant J. H. Gilman went to the gate.

After a pause, one of the visitors said, "We have been sent to demand a peaceable surrender of this fort by the Governor of Florida and Alabama."

"I am here under the orders of the President of the United States and by direction of the general in chief of the Army," replied Slemmer. "I recognize no right of any governor to demand surrender of United States property. My orders are distinct and explicit."

A short time later, Colonel W. H. Chase and another rebel officer crossed the harbor in a small boat to the Fort's pier. Lieutenants Slemmer and Gilman, the entire officer corps for the Fort, met them on the pier.

"I have come on business which may occupy some time; and if you have no objection, we had better go inside to your quarters," said Chase.

"I have objections," responded Slemmer, "and it could hardly be expected that I would take you into the fort."

"As I built the fort and know all its weak and strong points, I would learn nothing new by going in it and had no such object in proposing it."

"I understand that perfectly," countered Slemmer, "but it would be improper for me to take you in. And however well you may have known the fort before, you do not know what it now contains nor what I have done inside."

"That is true, and I will state my business here. It is a most distressing duty to me. I have come to ask of you young officers, officers of the same army in which I have spent the best and happiest years of my life, the surrender of this fort. I would not ask it if I did not believe it right and necessary to save bloodshed, and fearing that I might not be able to say it as I ought, and in order, also, that you may have it in proper form, I have put it in writing and will read it."

He pulled a paper from his pocket and began to read. After a few lines, his voice began to shake and his eyes filled with tears. He stamped his foot as if ashamed, saying, "I can't read it. Here, Farrand, you read it."

28 *OR* 1, 334.

29 *OR* 1, 357.

He handed it to the officer accompanying him, who took it but refused to read saying his eyes were poor and he did not have his glasses with him. "Here, Gilman," he said to Slemmer's subordinate, "you have good eyes. You read it."

Gilman read it aloud and handed it to Slemmer. They stepped away to talk, then agreed they should bargain for an overnight rest for their small garrison. They walked back.

"Colonel," asked Slemmer, "how many men have you?"

"Tonight, I shall have eight hundred or nine hundred," replied Chase.

"Do you imagine you could take this fort with that number?"

"I certainly do. I could carry it by storm. I know every inch of this fort and its condition."

This was true, and Slemmer knew it. But now he made his real point. "With your knowledge of the fort and of your troops, what proportion of them, do you imagine, would be killed in such an attack?"

"If you have made the best possible preparations, as I suppose you have," said Chase, shrugging his shoulders, "and should defend it as I presume you would, I might lose one-half of my men."

"At least!" responded Slemmer. "And I do not believe you are prepared to sacrifice that many men for such a purpose."

"You must know very well that, with your small force," countered Chase, recovering his ability to posture, "you are not expected to and cannot hold this fort. Florida cannot permit it and our troops here are determined to have it. And if not surrendered peaceably, an attack and the inauguration of civil war cannot be prevented. If it is a question of numbers and if eight hundred is not enough, I can easily bring thousands more."

Slemmer, abandoning the mutual chest thumping, returned sharply to reality and maneuvered for a little rest for his men. "I will give this letter due consideration; and as I wish to consult with the Captains of the *Supply* and the *Wyandotte* before replying, I will give you my answer tomorrow morning."

Next day, Slemmer sent his refusal; and the two ships left with Slemmer still in his equivocal position. Two more demands for surrender were rejected, and a weak attempt to relieve the fort failed.[30] In a fort built for a garrison of twelve hundred, Slemmer with less than one hundred men awaited developments. Ahead of him was every form of the unknown and unpredictable, including his government.

General Scott, at least, had already gone on record to the public about the correct way to deal with Fort Pickens. It should be reinforced and defended to the

30 Gilman in *B&L*, 1, 30-32; *OR* 1, 337, 357.

utmost. In Florida, Lieutenant Slemmer's fort would not be shrouded by Scott's uncertainty about bloodshed on the soil of "dear Virginia."

Chapter 2

"Do you think that the government of the United States is stupid enough to allow a man to march armed men about the federal District under its authority, when that man hesitates to take the simple oath of office?"

— *General Charles P. Stone to a disloyal militia officer*

Colonel Stone Keeps Peace in the Capital

Throughout the time that his loyalty was being tested and verified, Scott was taking affirmative steps to deal with the important practical problem presented by the precarious geographic position of the national capital. Its social circles and most of its citizens were Southern in their sympathies.[1] In the heart of secession-prone territory, it was surrounded on all sides by potential military enemies. Virginia, just across the Potomac River and within easy shelling distance, leaned toward rebellion even though it had not yet seceded. Despite her loyal

1 Seward, *Reminiscences*, 156.

governor, Maryland looked as if she would secede shortly. The nerve center of the Union was potentially inside the outer lines of the Confederacy.[2]

On New Year's Eve, December 31, 1860, Scott was at Wormley's Hotel, his temporary quarters in Washington.[3] Charles Pomeroy Stone, a West Point graduate, a former Regular Army officer, a member of Scott's staff in Mexico, and now a civilian in Washington on business, visited his old commander to pay his respects. Scott received him warmly. For a few minutes, they chatted pleasantly, recalling their service in the Mexican War. When he deemed it appropriate, Stone remarked that he was glad to see Scott in good spirits because it showed that the general in chief took a more cheerful view of public affairs than the residents of Washington.

"Yes, my young friend, I feel more cheerful about the affairs of the country than I did this morning; for I believe that a safer policy than has hitherto been followed will now be adopted." Aiming directly at President Buchanan, he said, "The policy of entire conciliation, which has so far been pursued, would soon have led to ruin."

His attitude toward a sectional war remained unchanged. He could not tolerate the thought. "We are now in such a state that a policy of pure force would precipitate a crisis for which we are not prepared. A mixed policy of force and conciliation is now necessary, and I believe it will be adopted and carried out."

Scott looked at his watch. He rose and said, "I must be with the president in a quarter of an hour." He ordered his carriage. Then he paced up and down his dining room. Suddenly, he stopped and faced around.

"How is the feeling in the District of Columbia? What proportion of the population would sustain the government by force if necessary?"

"It is my belief, general, that two thirds of the fighting stock of this population would sustain the government in defending itself if called upon. But they are uncertain as to what can be done or what the government desires to have done, and they have no rallying point."

Once again, the general walked the room. Once again, he paced in silence. The carriage arrived at the door. Stone accompanied the old general to it. As he was leaving, Scott turned suddenly, looked Stone in the face, and placed his hand on Stone's shoulder. "Those people have no rallying point. Make yourself that rallying point!"

The next day, President Buchanan commissioned Stone a staff colonel and assigned him to the post of inspector general of the District of Columbia. On the

2 Butler, Benjamin Franklin, *Butler's Book A Review of his Legal, Political, and Military Career* (Boston, 1892), 218 (*Butler's Book*); Seward, *Reminiscences*, 156.

3 Scott's official headquarters were still located in New York City.

following day, January 2, 1861, he was mustered into the service of the United States at the special request of the general in chief and began his duties immediately. An office conveniently near the secretary of war was assigned to him in the War Department.[4]

Born in Greenfield, Massachusetts, on September 30, 1824, Stone was descended from New England Puritans who had resided in the Commonwealth for many decades. Unlike Scott, who was from a state of slave holders and uncertain loyalty, Stone came from the most determined, abolitionist state in the Union.

In every American war at least one of his ancestors had taken part, one of them, Benjamin Lincoln, having served as a general under Washington. After education in various schools in Massachusetts, he entered the United States Military Academy as a cadet on July 1, 1841, and graduated seventh in a class that had numbered one hundred thirty-nine at the outset.

While a cadet he became a member of the Episcopal church, then converted to Catholicism. "By his courteous bearing, springing from the pure teachings of his youth, strengthened by his Christian principles, he secured the lasting respect of his instructors, and the esteem and affection of his comrades. The utmost confidence in his honor and integrity was felt by all." He was impulsive, "ever ready for duty, firm in decision and prompt to action. His impulsiveness often caused him trouble in after life; not so much from his methods of action as from his want of tact. No act of his was ever tainted or tarnished by even the thought of injuring another or gaining any advantage by trick or deception. Whatever the occasion, he showed no fear, he fulfilled his promises and was ever true to his friends, his country, and his profession."

Upon graduation he was assigned to the ordnance corps and to duty at the military academy as assistant professor of history, geography, and ethics. Before the end of the first year after graduation he decided that war with Mexico was inevitable and wanted to escape duty at the military academy where he might miss all opportunity for distinction in the field. In January of 1846 he obtained an assignment to the Watervliet Arsenal, then to the arsenal at Fortress Monroe on the Virginia Peninsula, the only stations providing practical instruction in the manufacture of ammunition and the equipment and handling of siege artillery. At Fort Monroe "by his intelligence, activity, and energy in the line of his profession" he won the confidence of his commanding officer Captain Benjamin Huger.

Success in the army is often made possible by fortuitous assignments. So it was for Stone. Huger, selected by Scott to be his chief of ordnance for Mexico, chose

4 Schoff Collection (Stone MS) (Clement Library, Univ. Mich.) letter dated November 5, 1866, from Stone to Lossing; Stone, Charles P., "Washington in 1861," in *B&L*, 1, 8-11.

Stone to be his assistant at army headquarters and to serve with the only siege battery used during the Mexican War. "By efficient service with the battery and also on General Scott's staff, both in the siege of Vera Cruz and on the march to and capture of the City of Mexico, he secured the ever abiding confidence of General Scott, and won a brevet for first lieutenant for gallant and meritorious conduct in the battle of Molino Del Ray and a brevet of captain for similar conduct in the capture of Chapultepec."

In July of 1848 after the end of the war with Mexico, he was given a leave of absence and permission to visit Europe to study the great armies of the continent. During an absence of almost two years, he learned by watching the active armies of Europe, Syria, and Egypt in peace and war.

When he returned, he was assigned to duty in California at his brevet rank of captain.[5] Upon arrival in San Francisco he was assigned to duty as chief of ordnance on the Pacific Coast. Because lumber and wood products were vulnerable to the California weather, he used stone to construct the fortifications and storage depots for the arsenal whose location he had selected. Although he did this by order of the department commander, he incurred the wrath of the local lumber producers, who lost business opportunities with the army. They instigated a review of his financial activities, and his pay was stopped by the Treasury Department while the review was in process. To live, he was forced to borrow money at heavy interest rates. Under an old order, which he discovered some time later, a subordinate was relieved from liability for expenses incurred by direction of his superior officer; but it was too late. He already had great debts. Though his pay was restored, he was never compensated for his interest obligations and "was for a long time crippled financially." He continued on duty in the Department of the Pacific until 1856 when, in November, he resigned from the army and entered business as a banker in San Francisco. Again, financial disaster struck; and once again not of his own making: the treasurer absconded, and he was obliged to suspend business.

5 A brevet was often characterized by the expression, "A mule is a brevet horse." In an army with long, often seemingly infinite, periods between promotions, a brevet was an award of rank higher than the recipient's commissioned rank. Originally intended to give temporary rank, then to recognize gallantry or merit, then to reward ten years faithful service, a brevet simulated a promotion even though it was not a promotion. It came to be awarded for outstanding service. If the brevet officer were serving in a capacity or position that called for an officer of his brevet rank, he could wear his brevet rank on his shoulder straps and draw the higher pay of his brevet rank. Hunt, Roger D., and Jack R. Brown, *Brevet Brigadier Generals in Blue* (1990, Gaithersburg), introduction, p. v (Hunt and Brown, *Brevet Brigadier Generals in Blue*); Fry, James B., *The History and Legal Effect of Brevets in the Armies of Great Britain and the United States from their Origin in 1692 to the Present Time* 2 (New York, 1877); Coffman, Edward M., *The Old Army: A Portrait of the American Army in Peacetime, 1784-1898* (New York, 1986), 67 (Coffman, *The Old Army*).

In March, 1857, he was selected by a private association to be chief of a scientific commission for the survey and exploration of the State of Sonora, Mexico. During the summer and autumn of 1860, he was preparing his report of the operations of the scientific commission and supervising the preparation of maps of the reconnaissances made under his orders from 1857 to 1859. He was visiting Washington on this business on New Year's eve when he met Scott and was appointed inspector general.[6] In his new duties, he had to assure peace in the national capital by keeping its population stable, a duty complicated by the weakness of loyal militia units, the strength of disloyal units, and the lack of plans and supplies.

To learn the extent and condition of his command, he inspected the existing volunteer organizations. The Potomac Light Infantry, a company of infantry from Georgetown, he found well drilled, well armed, and dependable for the majority of its members but not all. The Washington Light Infantry and the National Guard he found to be old volunteer units composed of Washingtonians almost to a man loyal to the government. The officers, Major General Weightman and Major General Force were active and "true as steel."[7]

The National Rifles of Washington and the National Volunteers, two volunteer infantry companies, were another matter. These and other suspicious companies were carefully infiltrated and observed by detectives in Stone's employ. His secret service gave regular reports of the proceedings of these units.

On January 2, the day of his appointment as inspector general, he met Captain Schaeffer, the commanding officer of the National Rifles, at the entrance to the Metropolitan Hotel. Schaeffer had been a lieutenant and an excellent drill master in the Third United States Artillery, a Regular Army unit. He had not yet heard about Stone's appointment.

6 Cullum, George Washington, *Biographical Register of the Officers and Graduates of the U.S. Military Academy*, 2 vols. (New York, 1891) (*Cullum*) vol. II, no. 1237. In *Cullum*, the graduates are listed by class, in order of class standing, and are given consecutive numbers in order from first in the first class to last in the last class. In the notes here the citations are to volume number and to the officer's number, not to the page on which he appears; vol. 9 *D.A.B.*, pt. 2, 72; Caspar Crowninshield MS Diary (Boston Public Library) entry of November 21, 1861; John C. Tidball MS Reminiscences (L.C.) 101-05. Tidball wrote his reminiscences in spiral notebooks beginning with the period before the war. Several decades ago they were sold at auction, apparently one at a time. Regrettably, no master copy was made. The first Civil War volume is in the Library of Congress, the second in the library of the United States Military Academy. The remainder? Unfortunately, no one knows (another of the historian's nightmares—the valuable manuscript, like the earliest biographies of Alexander the Great, known to have existed but destroyed? secreted? lost?)

7 Porter, *Stone*, 12 (pam.).

When Stone congratulated him about the state of his company, which was remarkable for its drill, Schaeffer replied, "Yes, it is a good company; and I suppose I shall soon have to lead it to the banks of the Susquehanna!"

"Why so?" asked Stone.

"Why, to guard the frontier of Maryland and to help keep the Yankees from coming down to coerce the South!"

Stone said quietly that he considered it very improper for an employee of the Department of the Interior and the captain of a company of volunteers to say things like that.

Most of his men were Marylanders and would defend Maryland, Schaeffer responded.

He would soon learn, Stone told him, that he had been imprudent and suggested that he think more seriously about his position. He did not tell Schaeffer about the new appointment.

The ordinary infantry company had one hundred enlisted men and three officers; but when Stone inspected the National Rifles, he found that it had more than one hundred men on its rolls and was adding to its ranks daily. In addition to a full supply of rifles, the company had a large quantity of ammunition, two mountain howitzers with harness and carriages, and a supply of sabers, pistols, and other ammunition, all of which had been drawn from United States arsenals. Only the rifles were authorized equipment for an infantry company.

Stone went to the chief of ordnance to learn how a company of infantry happened to be issued pistols, sabers, artillery, and other unauthorized equipment. He was told that Secretary of War John B. Floyd, who had resigned only a few days earlier, had ordered the chief of ordnance to issue Captain Schaeffer any ordnance and ordnance stores "he might require for his company." He also learned that Floyd had recommended to the president that Schaeffer be promoted to major in the District of Columbia militia and that the commission had already been sent to the president for signature.

Stone immediately presented the entire issue to Joseph Holt, the new secretary of war. From Holt, loyal to the core, he obtained two orders: one to the chief of ordnance prohibiting the issuance of arms to any militia or volunteers in the District of Columbia without Stone's countersignature as inspector general; the second requiring that all commissions issued to officers of the District of Columbia be sent to the inspector general for delivery.

According to information from Stone's infiltrators, Schaeffer was part of a plot to take possession of the capital. With his battalion he was to seize the Treasury Department for a new provisional government. Schaeffer's men were far more heavily armed than any ordinary rifle company. Seizure of Schaeffer's armory would not disarm his growing force because he had begun to order his men to take their weapons and ammunition to their homes after drill. Meantime, Schaeffer's commission as a major was signed by President Buchanan and sent to Stone for delivery.

Stone reported all this to Scott, who ordered him to watch developments carefully and be ready to suppress any attempt at violence but not to cause any shock to the public. Still adhering to his belief that bloodshed should be avoided, Scott warned against outright conflict.

"We are now in such a state," he said, "that a dog fight might cause the gutters of the capital to run with blood."

Schaeffer was not Stone's only problem. Through his informants, Stone learned that a physician, well known for his ardent secessionism, was the driving force for the National Volunteers. He was assisted by other prominent citizens including members of congress and a connection to Governor Lechter of Virginia. The National Volunteers had grown in size to considerably more than three hundred men but had no weapons. At one of the company meetings the doctor suggested that they apply to "Old Stone" for arms, adding that Governor Lechter of Virginia would furnish them if Stone refused. Next morning, a full report was given to Stone, then by him to Scott.

To qualify for arms, the National Volunteers had to establish a proper organization: enroll the men, elect officers, certify the elections, and present the roster to the inspector general. A pretense company was organized, officers elected, and a requisition for arms prepared. Stone's infiltrator reported all this before the doctor, who had been elected captain, arrived to call for weapons.

When the doctor reported that he had raised a company of volunteers and that it was now ready for arms, he presented a certificate of election in the proper form. Stone said he could not give an order for weapons without a muster of all the men to prove that a full complement had signed the rolls. The doctor left and returned the following day with a muster roll containing the names and signatures of one hundred men in the proper form.

Stone took the muster roll, looked the doctor squarely in the face, smiled, put the muster roll in his desk, and locked it.

"Doctor, I am very happy to have obtained this list. And I wish you good morning."

The doctor understood that Stone had gotten the best of him. He smiled, bowed, and departed. He abandoned his extensive and valuable property in Washington and gave his service to secession. The National Volunteers dispersed without further effort.

The colonel now turned to Captain Schaeffer, who presented himself to the inspector general with an air of frustration and injury. He held in his hand a requisition for arms and ammunition. On presenting it at the Ordnance Office, he reported he had been told that no arms could be issued without the inspector general's approval.

Stone confirmed the accuracy of Schaeffer's statement, adding that the order of the secretary of war covered all weapons. Stone said Schaeffer already had more rifles than were necessary for a company and could have no more.

Schaeffer sulked. He said his company could easily take any arms he wanted.

"Where?" asked Stone.

"You have only four soldiers guarding the Columbian armory, where there are plenty of arms, and these four men could not prevent my taking them."

"Ah! In which part of the armory are those arms kept?"

Schaeffer replied that they were on the upper floor.

Stone knew this to be true. "Well," he replied, "you seem to be well informed. If you think it best, just try taking the arms by force. I assure you that, if you do, you shall be fired on by one hundred fifty soldiers as you come out of the armory."

In fact, part of Schaeffer's information was wrong. Only two enlisted men, not four, were on duty at the armory; but an artillery battery commanded by Captain William F. Barry had just arrived at the Washington arsenal, and a company of Regular Army sappers and miners stationed at West Point was on the way at Stone's request. Stone decided he could not wait. Ready or not, he had to disarm Captain Schaeffer and his men at once.

By the time Schaeffer returned to his own office, he found an order to deposit in the Columbian armory before sunset the two howitzers, their carriages, the sabers, the revolvers, and the other equipment that was not proper armament for a company of riflemen. Taken by surprise, Schaeffer did not have enough time to organize resistance. He knew that, if he did not comply with the order, Stone would take the guns with his loyal troops.

After complying, Schaeffer appeared again in Stone's office. Before he could speak, Stone said he had a commission as a major for him.

Schaeffer was pleased. He said, "Yes, I heard that I had been appointed."

The colonel handed the captain a slip of paper. "Here is a form of oath you are to take," he said. "You will find a Justice of the Peace on the next floor. Please qualify, sign the form in duplicate, and bring both to me. One would be filed with your letter of acceptance, the other would be filed in the clerk's office of the Circuit Court of the District."

Schaeffer took the paper, but not lightly. He was confronting a direct conflict with his integrity as a gentleman. His expression turned sober. He stood near Stone's table for several minutes while he looked quietly at the paper, turning it over and over in his hands. Stone, meanwhile, made himself appear to be busy with papers on his desk but watched Schaeffer closely.

Finally, he said, "Ah, Schaeffer, have you already taken the oath?"

"No."

"Well, please be quick about it as I have no time to spare."

Schaeffer hesitated. Then slowly he said, "In ordinary times I would not mind taking it, but in these times . . ."

Stone did not let him finish. "Ah! You decline to accept your commission of Major. Very well!" He opened his drawer, put the commission inside, and turned the lock.

"Oh, no. I want the commission," replied Schaeffer.

"But, sir, you cannot have it. Do you suppose that in these times, which are not, as you say, 'ordinary times,' I would think of delivering a commission of field officer to a man who hesitates about taking the oath of office? Do you think that the government of the United States is stupid enough to allow a man to march armed men about the federal District under its authority, when that man hesitates to take the simple oath of office? No, sir, you cannot have the commission; and more than that, I now inform you that you hold no office in the District of Columbia volunteers."

This was too much for Schaeffer. He would not be deprived of everything. "Yes, I do. I am captain. And have my commission as such signed by the president and delivered to me by the Major-General."

Stone had been a Regular Army officer for many years and had learned well the Byzantine administrative rules that have bedeviled young company grade officers for generations.

"I am aware," said Stone, "that such a paper was delivered to you, but you failed legally to accept it."

"I wrote a letter of acceptance to the Adjutant-General, and forwarded it through the Major-General," responded Schaeffer to Stone's suggestion of administrative failure.

"Yes, I am aware that you did." Stone replied, delivering the administrative coup de grace. "But I know also that you failed to enclose in that letter, according to law, the form of oath required to accompany all letters of acceptance; and on the register of the War Department, while the issuance of your commission is recorded, the acceptance is not recorded. You have never legally accepted your commission, and it is now too late. The oath of a man who hesitates to take it will not now be accepted."

Stone had defrocked the now-former captain. With no rank Schaeffer was forced to leave the National Rifles. He took with him the secessionist members of the company, true men took their places, a new election was held, and a loyal officer elected captain.

Having mastered the existing militia organizations, Stone wrote to forty well-known and highly regarded gentlemen of the District. He told each man that the government would like him to organize a company of volunteers to preserve order in the District. To some letters, he received no reply. To some, he received replies courteously declining the service. To some, he received letters sarcastically declining. But to many, he received enthusiastic acceptances.[8]

The Northern Liberties fire companies provided a quota of men, as did the Lafayette Hose Company. Masons, carpenters, stonecutters, painters, and groups from other employments formed companies and began industrious drill. Petty hostilities like those between the fire companies disappeared.[9] Each company tried to be better than the others.[10]

Soon, the companies he was organizing from loyal residents of the capital were ready to be armed. Stone approved requisitions by the captains of these units, but they reported that the Ordnance Department refused to issue any weapons. The inspector general was astonished. When he investigated, he was told by the chief of ordnance that an order had been received from President Buchanan not to issue any arms to District of Columbia troops. Stone went at once to secretary of war Holt.

He reported the facts, then said, "I do not feel disposed to be employed in child's play, organizing troops which could not be armed. Unless the order in question is immediately revoked, there is no use for me in my place, and I must at once resign."[11]

Stone was perfectly right, Holt responded. Unless the orders were revoked, it would be no use for him to hold his place. He added with a smile, "And I will also say, Colonel, there will be no use in holding my place any longer. Go to the President, Colonel, and talk to him as you have talked to me."

Stone went to the White House and was received by President Buchanan at his writing table. The president was wearing his dressing gown and had a harried, weary look on his face. Describing the restrictions on the issuance of arms, the colonel stated that immediate issue was necessary. A refusal to issue arms would stop the

8 Stone in *B&L*, 1, 11, 13-17.

9 At this time few cities had municipally funded and organized fire companies. They were usually privately owned, organized, and run; or they were volunteer organizations. They did not respond to fire calls from those who did not "support" them. Firefighting often began with a street brawl among companies to establish the right to put out the fire, to have the best fire plug, or to put the first stream of water on the fire. The brawls by "firemen" seeking patronage and support were sometimes more exciting and dangerous than the fires themselves. Banes, Charles H., *History of the Philadelphia Brigade Sixty-ninth, Seventy-first, Seventy-second, and One Hundred and Sixth Pennsylvania Volunteers* (Philadelphia, 1876), 11 (Banes, *Philadelphia Brigade);* Allen Oliver E., *New York, New York: A History of the World's most exhilarating and challenging City*, 133 (New York, 1990).

10 Stone in *B&L*, 1, 13.

11 This discourse has been converted from indirect to direct. No disservice to the facts would be done by the use of either form.

instruction, which the volunteers needed badly; would cause them to lose all confidence in the government; and would break the organizations. He finished his presentation.

"I beg your pardon for saying it. In case you decline to revoke your order, I must ask you to accept my resignation at once."[12]

Buchanan was distressed. He responded, "Colonel, I have given that order acting on the advice of the District Attorney Mr. Robert Ould."[13]

"Then, Mr. President, the District Attorney has advised your excellency very badly."

"But, Colonel, the District Attorney is an old resident of Washington, and he knows all the little jealousies which exist here. He tells me you have organized a company from the Northern Liberty Fire Company."

"Not only one, but two excellent companies in the Northern Liberty, your excellency."

"And then, the District Attorney tells me you have organized another company from among the members of the Lafayette Hose Company."

"Yes, your Excellency, another excellent company."

"And the District Attorney tells me, Colonel, that there is a strong feeling of enmity between those fire companies, and, if arms are put in their hands, there will be danger of bloodshed in the city."

"Will your Excellency excuse me if I say that the District Attorney talks nonsense or worse to you? If the Northern Liberties and the Lafayette Hose Men wish to fight, can they not procure hundreds of arms in the shops along the avenue? Be assured, Mr. President, that the people of this District are thinking now of other things than old war feuds. They are thinking whether or not the government of the United States is to allow itself to crumble out of existence by its own weakness. And I believe that the District Attorney knows that as well as I do. If the companies of volunteers are not armed, they will disband, and the government will have nothing to protect it in case of even a little disturbance. Is it not better for the public peace, your Excellency, even if the bloody feud exists — which I believe is forgotten in a greater question—is it not better to have these men organized and under the discipline of the government?"

Buchanan hesitated. Finally, he said, "I don't know that you are not right, Colonel; but you must take the responsibility on you that no bloodshed results from arming these men."

12 Indirect discourse converted to direct.

13 Ould, a secessionist, supported the South.

Stone accepted in a flash. The order was revoked, the companies received their arms, and the men began to drill with weapons.[14]

With thoughtful, shrewd maneuvering Colonel Stone had disabled the most powerful secessionist military units in the capital. The loyal units continued to acquire strength and skill. Units of the Regular Army joined the new companies of infantry organized from the citizens of the capital and Georgetown.[15]

Having eliminated disloyal and lukewarm elements, Stone soon had a small but reliable body of men. Added to this were Magruder's battery of the First U.S. Artillery, Barry's light battery of the Second Artillery, and from West Point, a battery composed of men, horses, and guns that had been used to instruct the cadets. Foot companies of artillery and infantry near the capital were brought to Washington, making a total of about three thousand men to guard the public buildings and the approaches to the city.

To cure the capital's vulnerability, Stone worked indefatigably to post his troops and collect provisions. He took large quantities of flour from the mills in Georgetown and stored them in the capital buildings. Troops were quartered in public buildings with stores of ammunition and provisions. Picket guards were assigned to the bridges and highways leading into the district and a signal for calling the troops to their positions was arranged. Colonel Townsend suggested to General Scott that a regular officer with proper rank be placed in charge of each public building and each important section of the city. Scott approved, and Stone and Townsend made the assignments.

Junior officers in the capital during this critical time began to assume prominence. Adjutant General Lorenzo Thomas was given command of Georgetown and the duty to guard the bridges. Major Irvin McDowell, an assistant adjutant general then employed to muster volunteers into the United States service, was assigned to Capitol Hill and especially to the Capitol building. This became an important and large command when regiments from the north began to arrive because many of them were quartered on Capitol Hill.[16] In the performance of his duties McDowell came to know and be known by prominent members of the government. Captain William B. Franklin of the Corps of Topographical Engineers was in charge of the extension to the Treasury Building, which was then being constructed and in which he collected a large magazine of supplies. Captain Andrew Atkinson Humphreys of the Corps of Engineers was assigned to guard the

14 Stone in *B&L*, 1, 14-18.

15 Keyes, *Fifty Years*, 356.

16 Townsend, *Anecdotes*, 11-14.

Smithsonian. The officers with these assignments tended to their regular duties during the day but were at their special posts every night to be ready for any emergency. For the defense of the president and the executive mansion, Townsend suggested several high officers but Stone objected to all of them. When Townsend at last asked him to name his choice, Stone replied, "I claim that post for myself as the most responsible and dangerous."

On January 20, the company of sappers and miners, commanded by Lieutenant J. C. Duane of the Corps of Engineers,[17] arrived from West Point and a short time later came the battery of regular artillery from West Point under the sharp-tongued, hot-tempered Captain Charles C. Griffin. The next evening Lieutenant Duane and Captain William F. Barry joined General Scott and Lieutenant-Colonel Keyes for dinner. While they were at the dining table, Colonel Stone arrived to deliver information about rumors of a contemplated attack on Harpers Ferry and the battery of artillery being drilled in Maryland by Captain John B. Magruder. Stone believed Magruder was disaffected. From his own information, Keyes agreed, advanced the view that Magruder was disloyal,[18] and said, "General, you must, or you ought to, take that young man in hand."

Magruder had graduated in the West Point Class of 1830, had served with Scott in Mexico, wore uniforms made in Europe of the finest cloth, had long been known to his fellow officers as "Prince John," and gave parties envied by wealthy civilians while he was stationed at Newport, Rhode Island. More important to the moment, he was a Southerner.[19]

With his long-standing preference for Southern officers, Scott would not tolerate criticism of them. He thought Keyes's manner and words showed a willingness to dictate to the general in chief. Although his sensitive feelings had been subjected to insults from presidents, he had found enough self-control to tolerate them, if not in silence, at least with respect. But a dictatorial speech from a lieutenant-colonel, a military secretary? Unthinkable! Always easily offended, especially on personal matters, and even more easily offended in his later years,

17 Keyes, *Fifty Years*, 356.

18 Describing this conversation in his journal for January 21, which he quotes in the book, Keyes says, "I derided the conclusion that Magruder was working with the enemies of the Union"; Keyes, *Fifty Years*, 357; but this must be an error because the context shows that Keyes believed Magruder was disloyal, and on January 29 he wrote in his journal, "To intrust Prince John Magruder with the safety of the capital would have been like placing a wolf to guard the sheepfold." *Id.*, 361. His assessment was correct. Casdorph, Paul D., *Prince John Magruder: His Life and Campaigns*, 108-109 (New York, 1996).

19 Vol. 6, *D.A.B.*, pt. 2, pp. 204-05; 1 *Heitman*, 684; 1 Cullum, no. 601; Freeman, Douglas Southall, *Lee's Lieutenants: A Study in Command*, 3 vols. (New York, 1942), vol. 1, pp. 15, 19.

Scott was enraged. He said he had long had an affection for Keyes but reminded the colonel of his recent habit of speaking in a dictatorial manner.

Keyes, too, was aroused. He was not to be repressed on this subject. He was a patriot, he said; and when so many people were treacherous, he would not measure his words against traitors. He disclaimed any intention of dictating to his superior officer but insisted that he must speak his mind as he thought best on matters of patriotism.

Scott was an egotistical, grudge-bearing chief; Keyes an outspoken, unrestrained subordinate. Both men were loyal to the Union to their very core. Scott could not bear the thought of insult to his beloved South, especially Virginia. Keyes thought war was necessary, even desirable, to repair his country. Both men rose to their feet. They argued vehemently.

At last the passions subsided, the argument ended, and the tempers of both men cooled. Concluding that this argument had ended his career as a member of Scott's staff, Keyes retired to his quarters, where he wrote in his diary: ". . . I intend to do my duty to all men and to the country, but it is not part of my duty to feel or to know in this contingency fear for any man."[20]

Meanwhile, the loyal Colonel Stone kept hard at his duties, doing his administrative work late into the evenings. Near midnight on a February evening, the colonel was working over his papers, the kind of work that has driven second lieutenants mad for generations but the kind that had permitted Stone to disable Schaeffer and purify his infantry company without firing a shot. A caller presented his card for delivery to the hard-working inspector-general.

Stone read "Mr. Leonard Swett", and in the unmistakable handwriting of General Scott, "Colonel Stone, inspector general, may converse freely with Mr. Swett." A tall man with features like Lincoln entered the room. Stone thought he was being visited by the president-elect. The visitor persuaded the Colonel that he was not Lincoln, that the card gave his true name, but that he had been sent by Lincoln "to see for him the state of affairs in Washington and report to him in person."

Swett remained in the capital several days; visited the armories of several volunteer companies, now peaceful and devoted to the federal government; and had frequent, long conversations with Scott and Stone. At the end of his visit as he and the colonel drove to the railway station, he said, "Mr. Lincoln, and, in fact, almost everybody is ignorant of the vast amount of careful work which has been done here this winter by General Scott and yourself to insure the existence of the government

20 Keyes, *Fifty Years*, 357.

and to render certain and safe the inauguration of Mr. Lincoln. He will be very grateful to both."

Known always as a man of straightforward bluntness that overwhelmed any weak instincts for tact, Stone replied, "Mr. Lincoln has no cause to be grateful to me. I was opposed to his election and believed in advance that it would bring on what is evidently coming, a fearful war. The work which I have done has not been done for him, and he need feel under no obligations to me. I have done my best toward saving the government of the country and to insure the regular inauguration of the constitutionally elected president on the fourth of next month."[21]

The congress was not oblivious to all this. A congressional committee of five was appointed to see if a conspiracy to seize the capital existed. Scott was asked to testify before it.[22] President Buchanan, with only weeks to serve and wanting to avoid war more than anything,[23] was asked by a House of Representatives resolution to explain the large number of troops in Washington. He was also to give any information he had about a conspiracy to "seize the capital and prevent the inauguration of the president elect." Buchanan, a deft politician if nothing else, evaded the heart of the question, did not mention the thirty-three companies of militia, and limited his answer to the Regular Army troops. There were not many, he said, a mere six hundred sixty-three, excluding marines; and the marines were not in the capital but at the Navy Yard. He closed, "At the present moment, when all is quiet, it is difficult to realize the state of alarm which prevailed when the troops were first ordered to this city. This almost instantly subsided after the arrival of the first company, and a feeling of comparative peace and security has since existed both in Washington and throughout the country. Had I refused to adopt this precautionary

21 Stone in *B&L*, 1, 22-23.

22 Keyes, *Fifty Years*, 361.

23 Buchanan had been willing to do anything, or nothing, to avoid provoking the South, an attitude that became stronger as he drew nearer the end of his term and the Southern states became more truculent. Lincoln was unwilling to allow the Southern states to push him around but wanted the South to "fire the first shot." As a result the army and its officer corps was no more prepared for the war than it had been ten years earlier. In major wars that followed the Civil War, military preparedness became a provocation and to some a validation of Buchanan's conduct if preservation of peace, no matter how great the loss, were the only goal. In the ten years before World War I the European powers, the combatants of the future, made military preparations and sometimes passed military legislation aimed directly at their adversaries. At least one historian believes these programs contributed to the commencement of active hostilities. Herrmann, David G., *The Arming of Europe and the Making of the First World War*, 225-226, 229 (Princeton, 1996). And in the tense period following World War II, the threat of war, of "massive retaliation," or at least of massive retaliatory power became formal foreign policy programs announced to the adversaries. Challener, Richard D., "The Moralist as Pragmatist: John Foster Dulles as Cold War Strategist," in Craig, Gordon, and Loewenheim, Francis L., eds., *The Diplomats 1939-1979* (Princeton, 1994), 146-150.

measure, and evil consequences, which many good men at the time apprehended, had followed, I would never have forgiven myself."[24]

By March 3, Colonel Stone had Washington well in hand and safe from internal disruption. On the following day, Inauguration Day, a battalion of his troops stood on the steps of the Capitol building; his riflemen were in the windows of its wings; and his plainclothes police were circulating through the crowd. Stone and his mounted marshals escorted the carriage taking Buchanan and Lincoln from Willard's Hotel to the inaugural platform on the Capitol steps. By intentionally inept use of his spurs, the colonel managed to keep the marshals' horses sufficiently uneasy and unsteady in their gait to make any shot at the occupants of the carriage extremely difficult, even for a marksman.[25]

The light artillery battery of Captain William F. Barry was stationed at the corner of South Capitol and B Streets during the inauguration. The guns, fully supplied with canister, stood ready to deploy in any direction at a moment's notice. A company of infantry was present as a support. The day was exceptionally fine for that season of the year. Although mild, it was still cool enough to make the warmth of a fire enjoyable. A citizen had generously allowed the artillerymen to use one of the rooms of his nearby house, where he had an open grate fire.

General Scott took his position with the battery for the moment. As the inaugural procession made its way down Pennsylvania Avenue, he received a quick succession of reports about its progress from aides and messengers stationed along the route. "He was evidently very anxious—everyone was anxious," wrote Captain John C. Tidball later.

As Lincoln gave his inaugural address, Scott, "showing the infirmities of age" but still magnificent, walked out to the corner of the street, from which he could see the inaugural ceremonies. Lieutenant Tidball, second in command of the battery, and some of the other officers were also there. Soon they saw an elderly gentleman, "tall and gaunt, running with all the vigor that his age permitted, down the hill towards us. His tall silk cap was pushed well back on his head disclosing a massive brow over which scant gray locks fluttered in the agitation caused by his running. At first everyone thought him a messenger of ill news; but as he approached the general, he cried out."

"It is finished! He is the President! He is safe!"

To which the general in chief replied, "Thank God. Thank God."

24 Moore, *Buchanan's Works*, 2, 152-54, Buchanan to House of Representatives, Mar. 1, 1861.

25 Stone in *B&L*, 1, 25.

Then the two old men fell into each others arms and hugged each other with the joy of schoolboys. The elderly gentleman who brought such cheering news was none other than Thurlow Weed, the veteran editor who had done so much to define the course which led Lincoln to the presidency.[26] Abraham Lincoln had been peacefully inaugurated as the sixteenth president of the United States.

Stone had fulfilled his duties. He had disarmed or disabled the forces of secession in the capital. He had instilled reliability and stability in its loyal volunteer forces, the three thousand men of the District of Columbia militia. He had seized steamboats for movement on the Potomac when the railroad tracks had been destroyed.[27] The electoral votes had been peacefully counted in February. He had seen the new president's arrival in the capital and installation without incident. The colonel had satisfied the desire of the general in chief to avoid fighting, bloodshed, and military confrontation. He had become favorably known by the most prominent families in Washington. Throughout, the inspector general had dealt firmly, deftly, and effectively with two presidents, the secretary of war, the general in chief, cabinet officers, and an array of junior officers. Although not the most tactful officer in the capital, he had, as always, behaved like a gentleman.[28]

In the last days of the Buchanan administration, Scott began to meet regularly with officials of the incoming government. One of these men was the cigar-smoking future Secretary of State William H. Seward, who favored abandoning the forts in the South and not provoking the Confederates to war.[29] Scott was still dominated by his fundamental beliefs that a war with the South would be long, bloody, and costly; that no effective peace would be possible at the end of it even if, as he was certain they would, the federal forces prevailed; and that civil war was a horror to be avoided at almost any cost. He believed and hoped that a firm show of great force would intimidate the Southern states and avoid war.[30] As the threat of war had grown more real, his truculence about the defense of the forts in the South had grown weaker.

26 Tidball MS Rem (L.C.), 123-127.

27 Schoff Collection (Stone MS) (Clement Library, Univ. Mich.) letter dated November 5, 1866, from Stone to Lossing; Nevins, Allan, and Thomas, Milton Halsey, eds., *The Diary of George Templeton Strong*, 4 vols. (New York, 1952), vol. 3, *The Civil War*, 206, entry dated February 12, 1862 (Nevins, *Strong Diary*).

28 Crowninshield MS Diary (M.H.S.) entry dated Nov. 21, 1861; Tidball MS Rem. (L.C.), 101-05.

29 *N&H*, 4, 434.

30 Although this sounds foolish under the circumstances of 1860-1861, the North never seemed to observers to be ready to fight for its principles even in the face of constant sabre rattling and threats by the South.

After conversations with Seward he once again unsheathed his pen, and once again he made "sad work of it" as he had with his "Views." He had delivered the "Views" to President Buchanan a few days before the election of 1860. He chose to deliver his new statement the day before another watershed event, the inauguration of the first Republican president on March 4. Although he addressed it to Seward, the new secretary of state probably had a strong hand in its preparation.[31] Scott unmistakably intended it for Lincoln, but Seward surprisingly kept it to himself.[32]

Scott regarded his new statement, which was unencumbered by the usual lengthy title, as a "Supplement" to his "Views." Once again probably harkening to his early career as a lawyer, he tried to discuss all reasonable courses of conduct. Four, he had determined, were available.

First, the Republican party should "throw off" its name and rename itself the Union Party. The secessionists, who hated them with a passion, called them "Black Republicans," which had much to do with the Southern perception of their hearts and nothing to do with the color of their skin. Unless the Republican party were replaced, the band of slave states (Maryland, Virginia, Kentucky, Tennessee, and Missouri) would join the cotton states (South Carolina, Georgia, Alabama, Mississippi, Florida, Louisiana, and Texas) in secession; a garrison of thirty-five thousand men would be needed in the capital; and a garrison of one hundred and fifty thousand would be needed in Maryland even if it did not secede. The party should adopt a program of conciliation like that proposed by his friend John Crittenden.

Second, the Southern ports lost to the Union could be blockaded, and the government should collect import duties at the blockade or close the ports. He did not define the economic or naval results a blockade would produce; but he probably believed it would, much later, induce the seceding states to rejoin the Union quietly.

Third, the government could invade and conquer the seceding states. This would require an army of three hundred thousand disciplined men, one third for garrisons and more than that for casualties of all kinds. The cost would be an unimaginable $250,000,000. The South, he thought, would suffer "destruction of life and property . . . [that] would be frightful, however perfect the moral discipline

31 Elliott, *Scott*, 697-98; the text also appears as part of Appendix A in Townsend, *Anecdotes*, 255-56. The letter came to be known as the "Wayward Sisters" letter.

32 Niven, John, ed., *The Salmon P. Chase Papers*, 4 vols. (to date), vol. 3 *Correspondence, 1858-1863*, 298, letter dated October 15, 1862, from Chase to Scott (Niven, *Chase Papers*). The letter was first publicized at a meeting of administration opponents at the Cooper Institute in New York City and was then printed in the *New York Times*, October 14, 1862, the day after the Cooper Institute meeting. 3 Niven, *Chase Papers* 299, n. 1. According to Chase's letter to Scott, "I had no knowledge of the existence of the [Wayward Sister's] letter; & I learn from the president today that he had none."

of the invaders." With acute prescience, he predicted the disharmony of Reconstruction: the "devastated provinces" would "not . . . be brought into harmony with their conquerors, but . . . be held for generations, by heavy garrisons" at great additional cost.

Last, "Say to the seceded states, Wayward Sisters, depart in peace?"

This "Supplement" was not a supplement at all but a new statement of the alternatives and their consequences,[33] and it differed in two important respects from the "Views": conciliation was prominent; and re-enforcement of the forts, a categorical position in the "Views" and reasserted after they were sent to Buchanan and Lincoln,[34] had vanished. Whether or not changes had taken place in his thinking, the "Supplement" rested on the bedrock of the "Views": do not force war by confrontation, and do nothing to compel the beloved State of Virginia and her "Wayward Sisters" to secede.

When they were delivered, the "Views" had no effect on Buchanan.[35] If Scott had meant to force the unwilling president's hand when he arranged for their publication in the *National Intelligencer*, he had failed. Like the "Views" the "Supplement" did nothing to direct national policy. The incoming Republican president had his own ideas, and they were firmly in place. In his inaugural address, Lincoln said the country simply could not tolerate secession. As he said clearly a short time later, "For my own part, I consider the central idea pervading this struggle is the necessity that is upon us of proving that popular government is not an absurdity. We must settle this question now, whether, in a free government, the minority have the right to break up the government whenever they choose. If we fail, it will go far to prove the incapability of the people to govern themselves." He deferred any statement on the volatile question of slavery. "There may be one consideration used in any stay of such final judgment but that is not for us to use in advance. That is, that there exists in our case an instance of a vast and far reaching disturbing element, which the history of no other free nation will probably ever present. That, however, is not for us to say at present. Taking the government as we found it, we will see if the majority can preserve it."[36]

He intended to reenforce the forts, he said in his inaugural address, especially Fort Pickens in Pensacola Harbor and Fort Sumter in Charleston Harbor. "The

33 Elliott, *Scott*, 698, agrees and considers them a statement of different "Views."

34 Townsend, *Anecdotes*, 254-55.

35 Seward, *Reminiscences*, 341.

36 Burlingame, Michael, and Ettinger, John R. Turner, eds., *Inside Lincoln's White House: The Complete Civil War Diary of John Hay* (Carbondale and Edwardsville, 1997) 20, entry dated May 7, 1861 (Burlingame, *Hay Diary*).

power confided in me will be used to hold, occupy, and possess the property and places belonging to the government."[37]

After a presidential inauguration, the officers in Washington customarily called in a body on the president by pre-arrangement a few days later. In 1861, an unusually large number of officers were in the capital.[38] In two long lines headed by General Scott and Simon Cameron, the secretary of war, they approached the White House. The secretary opened the door and entered. The general, less familiar with the place and its occupant, waited outside. The two columns of officers came to rest smartly behind him. Shortly, the secretary emerged to see why they had not followed him. Scott, having drawn himself to his full height, stepped forward, took the bell majestically in his hand, and rang it. When the proper attendant appeared, they entered. Compared to the diplomats, who had been introduced to the president a few days earlier, the officers were tall, well made, grave, handsome, and striking in their uniforms, altogether unlike the members of the previous group in their "brocaded and embroidered coats, bowing and dancing about."[39]

After they entered, the officers formed a crowd in the East Room of the Executive Mansion. All were in full dress, a spectacular exhibition, and "most gorgeous." Among those present were General Scott, the only veteran of the War of 1812; many veterans of the Mexican War including Robert E. Lee, Joseph E. Johnston, Samuel Cooper, and John Magruder, all shortly to become generals in the Confederate Army. At the reception, "Prince John" honored his nickname by appearing "in all the gorgeousness of dress brought by him from Europe." All these men were from Virginia except for Cooper whose wife was from Virginia and "proved the stronger of the two when the tug of war came." Officers from seceded states were conspicuous by their absence.

At the proper time, General Scott's aide formed the officers in a curved line in a single rank extending around three sides of a large room opposite the door through which the president would enter. They arranged themselves according to rank, Scott at the head and the most junior lieutenant at the rear.

The door opened, and the president, accompanied by the secretary of war and several other members of the cabinet, entered to take their stand near the head of the line. Scott gave the initial greetings to Lincoln, then the line slowly filed past, each man being introduced by General Scott or one of his aides.

37 Basler, *Lincoln's Works*, 266, inaugural speech, March 4, 1861.

38 Tidball MS Rem (L.C.), 128-129.

39 Riddle, Albert Gallatin, *Recollections of War Times: Reminiscences of Men and Events in Washington 1860-1865* (New York, 1895).

Lincoln "was thoughtful and almost silent. Occasionally, a faint smile lighted up his homely countenance, but immediately he would relapse into the appearance of sadness. The occasion was impressive for its solemnity, and . . . little calculated to inspire hope and confidence."

Some had expected to see a storytelling buffoon and to be kept in constant laughter. "But," wrote First Lieutenant John C. Tidball later, "I saw nothing of the kind. On the contrary I saw in him a dignified, though extremely awkward looking person; tall and gaunt to ungainliness, with a face of extreme homeliness relieved only by his surpassing expression of kindliness."[40]

The military and the president, about to begin a long and arduous partnership, had been introduced.

40 Tidball MS Rem (L.C.), 128-33.

Chapter 3

"From a knowledge of our Southern population it is my solemn conviction that there is some danger of an early act of rashness preliminary to secession, viz., the seizure of some or all of the following posts . . . Forts Pickens and McRee, Pensacola Harbor, with an insufficient garrison for one; Fort Pulaski, below Savannah, without a garrison; Forts Moultrie and Sumter, Charleston Harbor, the former with an insufficient garrison, and the latter without any."

— *General Winfield Scott's Statement in his "Views"*

Confusion at the Brink

A strange period of military quiet, thoughtful uncertainty, and feverish activity surrounded the inauguration. The North, especially the area around the capital, was anything but ready for war. The critical places on the eastern spurs of the Baltimore & Ohio Railroad, Baltimore, Relay House, Annapolis Junction, Annapolis, Harpers Ferry, and Frederick, were in disloyal hands. The cotton states had seceded. Virginia, Maryland, and the other slave states were on the brink of secession. The forts in the South continued to be undermanned, unreinforced, or even vacant. Confederate troops held Harpers Ferry, its weapons manufacturing equipment, and its storehouse of rifles. The telegraph was cut everywhere, and the management of the Baltimore & Ohio Railroad refused to carry federal troops. The capital could not communicate with the Northern states.[1]

Large questions were presented, many of them new and novel. In its brief history of less than one hundred years, the United States had never truly confronted its own dissolution. On the questions presented by secession, from the well of experience, that most vital contributor to judgment, no American had ever drunk. Without precedent for guidance, every decision was new, and every solution had to be developed for a population so badly divided that four parties with different candidates and policies had made strong showings in the recent election. No single philosophy dominated. Uncertainty, confusion, and disagreement were everywhere, even among those with the same intentions and goals. These problems existed as much for the military as they did for everyone else in 1861.

The tiny Regular Army, scattered on distant frontiers, had no relevant prior experience, could give no clearly reliable advice, and could offer little practical help in solving the many military problems presented to Lincoln and his government. Civilians and officers with no relevant political experience or military training would answer these unique and vital questions. Would the development of military preparedness provoke the South? Would full-scale occupation of the undermanned or vacant forts in Southern territory be viewed as an aggressive act? Would the Northern states be able to create an army large enough and soon enough to protect the national capital? What plan should the federal government devise to restore the departed states to the fold? Would the weather allow the new armies to fight when it was necessary? Where would the fighting take place. Where would the ordinary military lines be drawn? Would the entire controversy be resolved in one monstrous battle, one great Armageddon? Would a slow-acting policy satisfy the practical needs of the government and the reasonable demands of the people? Was war, if it came, to be an extension of political policy and subservient to it; or must it dominate decisions on delicate political and legislative questions? Were the military questions to be considered and answered exclusively by the few men with military experience and training? If so, who were they? How could they be identified? How chosen?

Few of these questions were even anticipated in March. Through no fault of their own, the members of Lincoln's government confronted a real risk of failure—but not because they violated the old maxim "those who are ignorant of history are doomed to repeat its mistakes." They had no history.

1 Nevins, *Emergence of Lincoln*, 2, 454-471; Margaret Leech, *Reveille in Washington, 1860-1865* (New York, 1941), 46-62 (Leech, *Washington*); Keyes, *Fifty Years*, 370-74; *Butler's Book*, 165-70; Festus P. Summers, *The Baltimore and Ohio in the Civil War* (Gettysburg, 1939), 45-50 (Summers, *B&O*).

The lack of precedent to guide the president and his principle advisers came with another problem, the greatest uncertainty of all: loyalty. Every man was subject to doubt. If an officer had been born in, raised in, or appointed to the military academy from the South, was he presumptively disloyal? If he were a Democrat, especially a Douglas Democrat or a Crittenden Democrat, was he unworthy of a risk on his loyalty? If a military leader tried and failed, was his failure necessarily a result of treachery? Was a general who failed in the field to be deemed disloyal? If he lost a battle, was it evidence of treason? If he disagreed with a strongly held civilian policy like abolition, was his disagreement proof of disloyalty? What policy should govern the treatment of Southerners, their families, and their property? What should be done, if anything, about the slave and his master? What limitations defined the boundaries of military discipline?

In the early months of the war the question of loyalty confused many men. The adjutant general of the army Samuel Cooper had resigned and gone South.[2] About his replacement, Lorenzo Thomas, one correspondent wrote Secretary of War Cameron, "In the present treacherous aspect of part of our Country, I feel however constrained to inform you as the head of the War department of opinions expressed by one of your subordinates in high position and who is necessarily in a situation to do mischief if he should act upon the principles so expressed. Col. Thomas who is or has been acting Quartermaster General some short time since in conversation with our mutual friend Mr. W. who you know took a warm interest in his promotion a year or two since expressed the recent decided sympathy with the rebels now in arms against the government, and justifies their proceedings."[3]

The issue also confounded the careers of many officers. While assigned on the West Coast, William H. Emory, a major in the First United States Cavalry, and another of the unusually numerous officers on duty in Washington, served in the office of the Inspector General of the Army. Emory had received orders to investigate "financial difficulties" plaguing the army in California and Oregon. He discovered the cause of the problems, recommended a solution to Secretary of War Floyd, and saw his suggested remedy effect a cure.[4] In April 1861, Lieutenant General Scott summoned Emory, now serving in Washington, to a meeting with Inspector General Samuel Cooper, and Arkansas Senator Mitchell. Robert E. Lee had resigned his commission as colonel of the First Cavalry; and Scott was, he told

2 *Heitman*, 1, 326.

3 Simon Cameron MSS (Library of Congress) letter dated April 12, 1861, from Price to Cameron.

4 Jed J. W. Nesmith MSS (Oregon Historical Society) letter dated June 25, 1861, from Emory to "General Nesmith."

Emory, not satisfied with the lieutenant colonel of the regiment. Scott told Emory he must leave his position in the Inspector General's Office and return to his regiment, which was on the frontier in Indian territory.[5] Scott recommended that Emory take with him his servants, whom he knew to be slaves; and he also stated that he, General Cooper, and Senator Mitchell being strong Union men had agreed that Cooper and Mitchell would meet him at Fort Smith, Arkansas, where they would give him all possible assistance. His assignment included command of Forts Arbuckle, Cobb, Smith, and Washita in the territory allocated to the Cherokee nation and the units stationed at them.

Although he had served eleven and a half of the preceding fourteen years on the frontier separated from his family,[6] Emory dutifully began his trip west on March 20 to meet Cooper and Mitchell at Fort Smith, then proceed to Fort Washita to assume command of the regiment. But when he reached Fort Smith, neither Cooper nor Mitchell kept the appointment. Although he stayed at Fort Smith nearly two weeks, he heard nothing from them. He learned that his position in Washington had been filled by an appointment. Mitchell and Cooper having not appeared, Emory decided that he had been sent to duty with his unit in order to remove him and make his position available to the person who had been appointed to it, a little personnel sleight of hand. He also believed that Mitchell's part in the instructions was merely another act by a pro-Southerner to trap the active forces of the United States Army in Indian territory where they could not help the government.

The condition and performance of the government during the months prior to the end of the Buchanan administration had deprived Emory of all confidence in the federal government. Having reached a remote frontier region, he learned that the government in Washington had been broken up, that Scott had resigned, and that Washington had been abandoned. He feared for the safety of his home and family in Maryland. Without any clear facts or conclusions, he wrote his resignation, gave it to persons he knew to be loyal to the country, and told them to deliver it to the government if Maryland seceded.

While on the road to Fort Arbuckle, Emory passed a gentleman driving very rapidly. The man said that all northern Texas was in arms and preparing to capture the federal garrisons in the Indian territories. He said that Emory would not be permitted to reach Fort Washita and that probably no United States soldiers would be allowed to leave the territory. But they would be allowed to join the Confederacy.

5 NA Off's MS Rpts (Emory), letter dated January 28, 1864, from Emory to the Adjutant General.

6 NA Off's MS Rpts (Emory), letter dated January 28, 1864, from Emory to the Adjutant General.

He said he was authorized to offer Emory command of those forces with a rank of major general. He refused decisively.[7] He did not know if his resignation had been sent, but he did know his command was threatened. He decided to cancel his resignation if it had not been sent and sent two messengers.[8]

Traveling mainly at night, he reached Fort Washita, where he ordered it reinforced by all the cavalry under his command, a total of five companies. All infantry was to concentrate at Fort Arbuckle. The commanders of all the forts except Fort Smith insisted that he was exceeding his orders and throwing the frontier open to the Indians by concentrating the troops. By this active, somewhat provocative measure he was also giving an excuse for an uprising against the United States government.

He concluded that he could not hold his position, broke up Fort Washita, destroyed the property he could not take with him, prepared the troops for a forced march, and withdrew in the direction of Fort Arbuckle. He would concentrate at a road junction five miles from the fort. Emory knew he could defeat any force of Texans he found in the open. All his units except those at Fort Cobb met on time at the designated rendezvous and marched to the open prairie.

There he was joined by Lieutenant William Woods Averell, West Point class of 1855.[9] Emory must have been glad to see Averell, who had served with him earlier on the plains and been a good friend. On February 25, 1860, Emory had written to Averell from the Kansas River, "I wish you were with me. I have no one to converse with," explained the lonely army major. "If I were only in love now with some fair damsel as I was when I crossed the Plains on a previous occasion I should have plenty of time to think about the loved one. But thank heaven I am cured of any such disease. I never think of our once admired Carlisle beauty but with disgust for the entire sex. Yet reason tells me that there must still be a fair sensible American woman left."[10]

Having taken all recent steps on his own initiative, he must also have been glad to receive the dispatches Averell brought with him from Washington. They validated his initiative by ordering him to act exactly as he already had. He realized

7 NA Off's MS Rpts (Emory) letter dated January 28, 1864, from Emory to the Adjutant General.

8 Nesmith MSS (Or. H.S.) letter dated June 11, 1861, from Emory to n.a.

9 Averell, *Ten Years*, 272; NA Off's MS Rpts (Emory) letter dated January 28, 1864, from Emory to the Adjutant General; Nesmith MSS (Or. H.S.) letter dated June 11, 1861, from Emory to n.a.

10 Averell MSS (N.Y.S.L.) letter dated February 25, 1860, from Emory to Averell.

that, if he had not done this, his troops would already have been taken by the Confederates.[11]

Having delivered his messages, Averell departed to return to Washington while Emory marched his column toward safety at Fort Leavenworth, Kansas.

In the middle of the first day's march, the rear guard reported an enemy force in pursuit. Emory prepared to go into camp as if nothing unusual had happened. Quietly, he detached Captain Sturgis and a squadron of cavalry with orders to interpose between the advance guard of the Confederates and its main body, capture the guard, and bring it into camp. This was done, and he took the entire guard, several officers and twenty-one men. The prisoners told Emory they were a day or more in advance of the main column, which consisted of four thousand troops. They also said that two thousand troops from Arkansas were marching on Fort Gibson. The Arkansas column would presumably intercept Emory because it had the shortest road to Kansas and would delay Emory's column long enough for the Texans to overtake it.

Early next morning, Emory's column, led by an Indian guide, struck for the open prairie where he met the missing command from Fort Cobb. The entire command now consisted of five companies of cavalry and seven of infantry. Seeing no reason to remain in the prairie under the circumstances, Emory marched rapidly toward Fort Leavenworth and safety.[12]

By the time Averell returned to Washington, Emory's resignation had been submitted and accepted. He was no longer Major Emory and no longer an officer in the army.

Averell did not know what to do. The next day Colonel Schuyler Hamilton, military secretary to General Scott, invited him to dinner at General Scott's. Only the general's military family were present. Averell was placed next to Scott. The old general asked about the journey and asked where Averell had found Emory's troops. Averell reported as briefly as possible, asked about Emory's resignation, and spoke of Emory's faithful conduct. Scott was interested. At the conclusion he put his massive arm about Averell's shoulders and gave Averell one of his rare compliments, which sent Averell "reeling."

11 Averell, *Ten Years*, 272; NA Off's MS Rpts (Emory) letter n.d. approximately 1872, from Emory to n.a.; Nesmith MSS (Or. H.S.) letter dated June 11, 1861, from Emory to N.A.

12 NA Off's MS Rpts (Emory) letter dated January 28, 1864, from Emory to the Adjutant General.

"My young friend, it is fortunate that Major Emory, whom I highly esteem, has one here to place his status in its proper light. I cannot restore him to his position, for that is filled, but I can help make him a lieutenant colonel of a new regiment."[13]

When Emory reached Fort Leavenworth, he learned that the withdrawal of his resignation had failed to reach the capital in time and that his resignation had been accepted. He hastened to Washington where he presented his case to the president and the secretary of war. Scott wrote a letter to Cameron recounting Emory's faithful execution of his orders and expressing satisfaction with his loyalty to the government.[14]

In a time of grave uncertainty, this was not enough. Rumors began to circulate that he had left three resignations when he departed for the Cherokee Territory; that he had been a confidential advisor to John B. Floyd, who was now serving in the Confederate army; and that, while serving on the United States and Mexican Boundary Commission, he had made a number of disloyal statements and had spoken abusively about the North. An article in the *New York Times* described Emory's disloyal acts and received widespread credence.[15] The mere fact that he had submitted his resignation during this time of turmoil, even though he might have tried to recall it, was enough to turn many against him, the secretary of war among them.

Professor Alexander Dallas Bache tried to persuade Montgomery C. Meigs, fresh from a successful adventure at Fort Pickens, that Emory should be reinstated but with little success. Bache said Emory "ought to be returned to the army and Scott thought so also." Emory's friends, he said, stated that he "acted so well in saving the command which he lead out of Texas, that he ought to have a brevet; that now they are willing to give up the Brevet and take only his restoration. That the officers of his own regiment are willing to sign a round robin asking this . . ."

Meigs thought "it would take much printing to make the Army generally think that an officer who when his country was in danger, resigned, should be restored. That there was the naked fact [of the resignation], and that other officers had also been told that Gen. Scott had resigned, had been cut off, been told that the country was broken up; that there no longer was a government, or U.S., etc., etc." Meigs

13 Averell, *Ten Years*, 278-279. Though Averell refers to Emory as a colonel, he had not yet reached that rank. *Heitman*, 1, 405. The references to Emory have been changed to reflect his real rank.

14 Nesmith MSS (Or. H.S.) letter dated July 6, 1861, from Matilda Emory to Nesmith with enclosed unsigned statement.

15 Nesmith MSS (Or. H.S.) letter dated June 25, 1861, from Emory to "General Nesmith"; Averell, *Ten Years*, 272; Basler, *First Supplement 1832-1865, Lincoln's Works*, 78, letter dated June 13, 1861, from Lincoln to Cameron.

agreed that differences existed "but only in degree; he was soldier enough to bring out his troops before deserting them, but he wrote a resignation and sent it to Washington . . ."[16]

Emory began his own campaign to recapture his commission. Having become acquainted with J. W. Nesmith, the senator from Oregon, he wrote Nesmith denying the various charges and rumors. His wife Matilde wrote Nesmith. He obtained a written statement from the three members of the boundary commission, who said, among other things, that Emory's critic had been a mere draftsman, had been fired for cause, had left the commission months before Emory had arrived to serve on it, and had been denied claims by Emory on the ground that they were fraudulent. He forwarded copies of supporting letters from friends in the army.[17]

Writing from Fort Leavenworth, Kansas, Lieutenant A. V. Colburn said, "Did I suppose that anything could induce you to join the army of the (so called) Southern Confederacy, or that you could under any combination of circumstances be induced to take up arms against the flag you have served under so long and so faithfully, God knows I would be glad that you are out of the Army, but during my long and intimate acquaintance with you, I have never known you to breathe a disloyal sentiment; and I am fully convinced not only by your words but by your actions, that next to your own honor, you value that of your country more than anything else."[18]

In June, the campaign succeeded. The president offered Emory the lieutenant-colonelcy of the Sixth United States Cavalry, a new regiment; and he accepted. On June 13, Lincoln wrote to the secretary of war, "Owing to the peculiar circumstances of Col. W. H. Emory's case, and especially because of the Commanding General's statement that he is perfectly satisfied of Col. Emory's loyalty to the Government . . . Col. Emory should be restored to the service

16 John G. Nicolay MSS, tr. Montgomery C. Meigs MS diary (L.C.) entry dated June 8, 1861. Meigs kept his diary in shorthand; and of the two systems (Gregg and Pitman) he used the more uncommon and had many of his own shorthand peculiarities, making a translation almost indispensable. Weigley, Russell F., *Quartermaster General of the Union Army: a Biography of M. C. Meigs* (New York, 1956). (Weigley, *Quartermaster General Meigs*) Nicolay and Hay obtained a partial transcript for their biography of Lincoln, and the copy is in the Nicolay MSS.

17 Nesmith MSS (Or. H.S.) letters dated June 25, 1861, from Emory to Nesmith; June 2, 1861, from A.V. Colburn to Emory; July 5, 1861, from Matilda Emory to Nesmith; June 11, 1861, from Emory to n.a.; statement with no signature; statement dated June, 1861, from John H. Clarke, Hugh Campbell, and John E. Weiss of the boundary commission. The sources for this series of events in Emory's career are unusually plentiful but extraordinarily unclear and conflicting. Even Emory's letters are inconsistent. These conflicts have been resolved in the most consistent and plausible way but generally in Emory's favor. Even if he had a flicker of uncertainty about his allegiance in the earliest period, he served throughout the war with undivided devotion to the flag and performed creditably if not outstandingly as commanding officer of the Nineteenth Corps under Banks in Louisiana and Sheridan in the Valley in 1864.

18 Nesmith MSS (Or. H.S.) letter dated June 19, 1861, from Colburn to Nesmith.

especially if it can be done, to his position of Colonel 1st Cavalry. I direct that said Col. W. H. Emory be allowed to withdraw what purports to be his resignation, and that he join his Regiment of 1st Cavalry." He was then sent to Pittsburgh to recruit and organize the regiment.[19] Emory's problem was at least temporarily solved, but the hostility to his resignation and the doubt about his loyalty continued even while he was campaigning actively against the Rebels.[20]

Like Emory, others were headed from the frontier posts to the capital with their Regular Army units; and they, too, faced charges about their loyalty. John Gibbon, appointed to the military academy from North Carolina; Philip St. George Cooke, an older officer from an aristocratic Virginia family; Wesley Merritt, a graduate of 1860 from Copperhead territory in southern Illinois and a member of an outspoken family of Douglas Democrats; and William P. Sanders, born in Kentucky, appointed from Mississippi and a member of the class of 1856, suffered charges of disloyalty. Their participation in the heated pre-war debates in the army and at West Point about abolition and secession reached Washington in the form of warnings about their loyalty.

The Second United States Cavalry, the "Old Second Dragoons," and other units, including several batteries of artillery, were stationed at Camp Floyd, Utah, where they had been waiting to participate in any fighting that might erupt with the Mormons. In spite of his Virginia background, Cooke spent much time attempting to persuade the officers at Camp Floyd to remain loyal. Buford, a troop commander in the Second and a West Point graduate; Gibbon, commanding one of the artillery batteries; Merritt, Buford's second lieutenant in the cavalry regiment; and Sanders, loyal throughout, were equally opposed to abolition and to secession. Other officers tending toward Radical Republicanism secretly reported them to the adjutant general as having disloyal sentiments and being potentially harmful to the government. When Cooke learned about this, he wrote the adjutant general to exterminate any effect the report might have and ordered the men who sent it arrested.

Buford and Gibbon had become close friends but, like most others, they found the subject of loyalty so sensitive they never declared themselves to each other during any of their long discussions about conditions in the country. One night after

19 NA Off's MS Rpts (Emory), letter dated January 28, 1864, from Emory to the Adjutant General; and letter n.d. approximately 1872, from Emory to n.a.; Basler, *First Supplement 1832-1865, Lincoln's Works*, 78, letter dated June 13, 1861, from Lincoln to Cameron. A few days later Lincoln ordered that Emory be made Colonel of the Fifteenth United States Infantry, an appointment that later went to Major Fitz-John Porter instead. *Lincoln's Works*, 4, 409, letter dated June 17, 1861, from Lincoln to Cameron; *ibid.*, 409, n.2.

20 Chandler MSS (L.C.) letter dated 1861, from Doubleday to Chandler.

the mail had arrived they found themselves in Buford's room locked in one of their conversations and speculations. In his characteristic slow, deliberate manner, Buford spoke.

"I got a letter by the last mail from home with a message in it from the governor of Kentucky. He sends me word to come to Kentucky at once, and I shall have anything I want."

Gibbon suffered a burst of anxiety. How would Buford declare? "What did you answer, John?"

"I sent him word I was a Captain in the United States Army," Buford replied while Gibbon enjoyed a rush of relief, "and I *intend to remain one*."

Of the four young officers whose careers might have been ended in 1861 by this report, Sanders would make the supreme sacrifice in battle as a Union brigadier general, Buford would die of exhaustion and disease the most respected cavalry officer in the Army of the Potomac, Gibbon would rise to corps command in the Army of the Potomac, and Merritt would end the war at the head of all three superb divisions of cavalry in the Army of the Potomac.

In the early days of the war they and their men, like Emory, headed for Fort Leavenworth, Kansas, a march of one thousand miles over arid plains. By August, Gibbon, Buford, and Merritt had reached Washington and been assigned to the main army in the east.[21]

The one officer with truly broad experience, an enviable international reputation, and a long string of successes was Winfield Scott. In his "Views" Scott had shrewdly predicted in 1860 that "From a knowledge of our Southern population it is my solemn conviction that there is some danger of an early act of rashness preliminary to secession, viz., the seizure of some or all of the following posts: Forts Jackson and St. Philip, in the Mississippi, below New Orleans, both without garrisons; Fort Morgan, below Mobile, without a garrison; Forts Pickens and McRee, Pensacola Harbor, with an insufficient garrison for one; Fort Pulaski, below Savannah, without a garrison; Forts Moultrie and Sumter, Charleston Harbor, the

21 John Gibbon MSS (Pennsylvania Historical Society) MS biography of John Buford by John Gibbon, 9-10; NA RG 80 M619, Letters Received, letter dated June 15, 1861, from F. E. Hunt, R. E. Clary, and J. B. Potter to Cameron; NA AGO recs. file 21 U 61 letters dated June 17, 1861, from Cooke to Lorenzo Thomas and Gibbon to Thomas; June 18, 1861, and June 19, 1861, from Clary to Gibbon; and MS Court of Inquiry; Gibbon, John, *Personal Recollections of the Civil War* (New York and London, 1928), 1-5 (Gibbon, *Recollections*); Lavery, Dennis S., and Jordan, Mark H., *Iron Brigade General: John Gibbon, A Rebel in Blue* (Westport and London 1993), 30-33 (Lavery and Jordan, *Gibbon*); Alberts, Done E., *Brandy Station to Manilla Bay: A Biography of General Wesley Merritt* (Austin, 1980), 16-19 (Alberts, *Merritt*); Longacre, Edward G., *General John Buford* (Conshohocken, 1995), 69-70 (Longacre, *Buford*); Warner, *Generals in Blue*, 52-53, 58-90, 321-322, 419-420.

former with an insufficient garrison, and the latter without any; and Fort Monroe, Hampton Roads, without a sufficient garrison. In my opinion all these works should be immediately so garrisoned as to make any attempt to take any one of them, by surprise or coup de main, ridiculous."[22]

President Buchanan spent many sleepless nights on the Southern forts but always found a reason not to reinforce them. Most of all he feared that reinforcement would provoke the cotton states to hostilities.[23] Three days after Scott moved his headquarters to Washington in December of 1860, the general and secretary of war Floyd met with Buchanan. Scott urged the president to send three hundred regulars to reinforce Major Anderson at Fort Moultrie in Charleston Harbor. Buchanan refused. He thought reinforcement by a contingent that small would be a confession of weakness, not the intimidating act Scott was postulating.[24]

During the last months of Buchanan's administration, no effective step was taken to reinforce any of the forts. A half-hearted attempt to reinforce Fort Pickens in Pensacola Harbor at the end of January had been a dismal failure.[25] On March 5, the day after the inauguration, Lincoln ordered Scott to reinforce the forts and repeated the order in writing a few days later. However, face to face with the increasing prospect that the prediction in his "Views" would come true and that reinforcement would provoke an "early act of rashness" and war, the old general's unequivocal, ardent insistence that the forts be made invulnerable dissolved. Favoring almost any course that would avoid war, his zealous wish to reinforce them dissolved.[26] He did nothing in response to the president's order.

After the paralysis of the Buchanan administration despair gripped Lieutenant-Colonel Keyes at the apparent unwillingness of the new Republican government to do anything. The forts would never be reinforced in sufficient strength to withstand attack, he concluded. By the middle of March, he was certain they would soon be surrendered or captured.[27] In this despondent state and knowing that Lieutenant Adam Slemmer held Fort Pickens with less than one hundred men, Keyes sent Scott a negative message from Scott's old headquarters in New York

22 Buchanan, *Administration*, 299; Townsend, *Anecdotes*, 249-55.

23 Tidball MS Rem (L.C.), 105; Moore, *Buchanan's Works*, 11, 185, letter of April 25, 1861, from Buchanan to Dix; 285, letter dated October 28, 1862, to the Editors of the *National Intelligencer*, "Answer to General Scott" from Buchanan.

24 Moore, *Buchanan's Works*, 11, 283.

25 *Ibid.*, 284-285.

26 Nicolay MSS (L.C.), tr. Meigs MS Diary (L.C.) entry dated March 31, 1861; *N.O.R.*, 4, 90; *OR*, 1, 200, 201; *N&H*, 3, 394; Elliott, *Scott*, 703; Keyes, *Fifty Years*, 379; Basler, *Lincoln's Works*, 4, 316, letter dated April 1, 1861, from Lincoln to Seward; Seward, *Reminiscences*, 166.

27 Keyes, *Fifty Years*, 379; *N&H*, 3, 393-394.

City about the difficulties of landing ordnance stores on the sandy beach near Fort Pickens on Santa Rosa Island.[28] He added that, if the fort needed all the supplies and equipment requested by the officer in command, it must be "in a bad way." The matter was serious, he felt; and General Scott should give it his personal, special attention. Upon his return from New York, Keyes suggested that the fort be abandoned, along with Fort Sumter, "as an act of grace." To justify this decision they could argue that the forts had been surrendered, in practical effect, much earlier by Buchanan's inaction.

By the end of March, Seward had become alarmed at Scott's advice to make concessions to the states in rebellion and seeing that the cabinet was unanimously against him, had changed his mind about the forts. He believed, as he always had, that Fort Sumter in Charleston Harbor should be abandoned because an attempt to supply or reinforce a fort so close to the capital might precipitate an attack on the capital itself. But Fort Pickens in Florida offered the geographic conditions he wanted: confrontation far from the capital, fighting on Southern not Northern ground, and selection of the ground by the federal government not the Rebels. Applying these criteria, he suggested to Lincoln that the country show force at Fort Pickens in Pensacola Harbor and in Texas "at every cost." He wanted to impose the burden of war on the people who had provoked it and do it on their soil.[29] At the same time Lincoln did not want to precipitate war, did not want to "fire the first shot."[30] Fort Pickens satisfied all these needs and would be, as well, a statement that the president meant to make good on his inaugural assertion that federal property, particularly the forts, would be preserved and protected. In the latter part of March, Seward and Captain Montgomery C. Meigs discussed the state of the forts, particularly Fort Pickens. Meigs believed it could be reinforced and, with proper support from the navy, held.[31]

28 Keyes, *Fifty Years*, 377.

29 Seward, Frederick H., *Seward at Washington*, 2 vols. (New York, NY, 1891), 2, 530-533 (Seward, *Seward at Washington*); Van Dusen, *William Henry Seward*, 279-284 (Van Dusen, *Seward*). Although Seward opposed sending reinforcements to Sumter and the other Cabinet officers had as many views as there were Cabinet seats, Lincoln wished, without hostilities, to reinforce Sumter. He assigned the task to Gideon Welles and the Navy Department, the specifics to be arranged by Gustavus V. Fox, a former naval officer who had recently resigned from the service. Two programs proceeded independently with neither coordination nor overall supervision. Each was in blissful ignorance of, and ultimately in conflict with, the other. *N&H*, 4, 1-2, 4-5; Morse, John T., ed., *Diary of Gideon Welles: Secretary of the Navy Under Lincoln and Johnson*, 3 vols. (Boston and New York, 1911) vol. 1, 7-25 (Morse, *Welles Diary*).

30 Donald, *Lincoln*, 292-294; see Lincoln's note to South Carolina, in Seward, *Seward at Washington*, 2, 536-37.

31 Porter, *Incidents and Anecdotes*, 13-14. Porter suggests, without personal knowledge, that Meigs first suggested this to Seward, but Seward had wanted to preserve the fort and press in

From his associations in the capital with important and high-ranking people, Captain Meigs, like Colonel Charles P. Stone, Major Irvin McDowell, and Captain William B. Franklin, was known to "Prime Minister" Seward. A graduate of West Point, class of 1836, Meigs, "young, vigorous, handsome, clever, and when he chose to be, seductive," was the engineer officer supervising the construction of the dome on the Capitol building, the Capitol's extension, and the Potomac aqueduct.[32]

Meigs discussed Fort Pickens with Lieutenant David D. Porter of the navy. The new secretary of the navy, Gideon Welles, believed Porter to be implausible, careless in his speech, and given to intrigues. Nor was his loyalty above suspicion. During the winter of 1861, he had paid too much attention to secessionists and had requested coast survey service in California when all men knew they would be needed in a war in the east. In Secretary Welles's view this was the act of a man who preferred to stand on the sidelines rather than yield his commission or choose a side and fight.

To Meigs, Porter was a naval officer with a mild and affable manner but a character laced with dash, energy, and audacity.[33] Together Meigs and Porter developed a plan for joint army and navy reinforcement of Fort Pickens. They would collect a good steamer, six or seven companies of infantry, and a number of large guns with the necessary ammunition.[34] The men, guns, and ammunition would land on the shore outside the fort under cover of a ship of war to protect against an enemy ground assault. The men, at their most vulnerable, would then drag the guns and equipment across the beach to the fort. Once inside, the reinforcements would make Fort Pickens impregnable. With proper naval support it could never be taken.[35]

On March 28, Lincoln penned a short note asking Scott to come to the White House for the president's first state dinner. All members of the cabinet would attend and be joined after dinner by other Washington dignitaries. The general in chief believed he would have to discuss Fort Sumter and Fort Pickens, and he expected the president to be willing to surrender both. Suffering from a severe attack of amoebic dysentery, Scott arrived early and met privately with the chief executive.

Texas for some time, and this must be an incorrect surmise by Porter, whose view that the fort could be held was just what Seward wanted to hear.

32 Porter, Adm. David D., *Incidents and Anecdotes of the Civil War*, 13-14 (New York, 1885) (Porter, *Incidents and Anecdotes*); Keyes, *Fifty Years*, 389-390; see generally Weigley, Russell *Quartermaster General Meigs*, 60-77; Warner, *Generals in Blue*, 318-319; *D.A.B.*, 7, pt. 2, 507-508.

33 Nicolay MSS (L.C.), tr. Meigs MS diary (L.C.) entry dated March 29, 1861.

34 Porter, *Incidents and Anecdotes*, 14.

35 Porter, *Incidents and Anecdotes*, 13-14.

Scott had been correct about the topic for discussion, but on the conclusion dead wrong. The president talked about Fort Sumter and also, very sharply, about the order given the day after his inauguration to reinforce the forts. Scott persisted in his objection to relieving Fort Sumter and Fort Pickens. In his opinion they should be yielded, an act which would halt all the cries of coercion. A "cold shock" this was to the president. He rightly implied a "want of consistency" in Scott's advice on the forts and said his administration would be broken unless "a more decided policy" were adopted. If the general could not execute his orders, the president would find some other person who could.

Any criticism irritated Scott. This criticism disturbed him greatly. In all probability Scott chose not to face the cabinet of this new Republican government which would talk about the necessity for reinforcing the forts, and remind him about his failure to perform the president's order. Undoubtedly announcing his old disorder as an excuse, he absented himself from the dinner and avoided a highly undesirable opportunity to "face the music," listen to the military prattling of a group of men with no military experience, and lose his temper on a subject charged with emotion. During the informal discussion between Lincoln and the cabinet after dinner, Postmaster General Blair denounced the old general.[36]

36 Nicolay MSS tr. Meigs MS Diary (L.C.), entries dated Mar. 29, 30, and 31, 1861; Keyes, *Fifty Years*, 378; *N&H*, 3, 394; Elliott, *Scott*, 702-03; Russell, *My Diary*, 27-29, entry dated March 28, 1861. Just before everyone departed, Lincoln took the cabinet aside and told them Scott had "that day" advocated abandonment of Fort Pickens and Fort Sumter, but the way the General made this recommendation is not stated in any source. The conversation between Lincoln and Scott is described in Keyes, *Fifty Years*, 378, on the basis of Scott's account the next day. Lincoln's reaction is in Meigs' Diary, entry for March 31, 1861, and *N&H*, 3, 394. The fact that Scott was present and could have attended the dinner is mentioned only in Russell, *Diary*, entry dated March 28, 1861. The excuse of his old disease for his departure is in Elliott, *Scott*, 702. According to Elliott, expressly, and *N&H*, by inference, the advice by Scott was given on March 28 in a written memorandum; but all other sources cite and quote a document printed in *OR*, 1, 200-201, as attachment D to Secretary Cameron's answer to a request, dated March 15, 1861, from Lincoln on the advisability of attempting to reinforce Fort Sumter. *OR*, 1, 196. According to the editors of *OR*, the answer by Cameron and attachments "A" through "H" were probably submitted to the President and then to the Cabinet the same day, March 15. If the written response to the president's March 15 request was given on March 15, the more complete statement of Scott's advice on both Sumter and Pickens, recited in *Keyes* and *N&H*, was probably given verbally before dinner; and the president's strong, hostile reaction, not the old "malady," was probably the reason for the general in chief's early departure.

Chapter 4

"The great Frederick used to say that, 'When the king commands, nothing is impossible.' Sir, the president's order shall be obeyed."

— *General Winfield Scott's Response to Lincoln's Orders to Reinforce Fort Pickens*

Keyes and Porter Emerge

Angry that he had been accused of tardiness, Scott spent the next two days preparing a short chronology of events relating to Forts Sumter and Pickens, no doubt to vindicate his conduct. As he was finishing, he and Keyes discussed the subject at length. They agreed that both forts should be surrendered or, at least, that the garrisons should be withdrawn. Keyes suggested that a paper be prepared by "an able writer" to give "an air of grace to the concession."[1]

When the cabinet convened at noon on March 29 to discuss the Southern forts, especially an expedition to reinforce Fort Sumter, Lincoln asked the members to write their views on the forts. Continuing his tirade about the general in chief from the night before, Postmaster General Blair wrote a strong, hostile characterization of Scott's unwillingness to deal firmly with the South, especially Virginia.

"As regards General Scott, I have no confidence in his judgment on the questions of the day. His political views control his judgment, and his course as remarked on by the president shows that, whilst no one will question his patriotism,

1 Keyes, *Fifty Years*, 379.

the results are the same as if he was in fact traitorous."[2] Fort Sumter drew a wide variety of responses. To a man, however, the members of the cabinet agreed that Fort Pickens should be held. Seward had already done his own investigation on this subject and, going beyond a mere suggestion, identified Captain Montgomery C. Meigs as the man for the job. In addition to his special training and merit, Captain Meigs had personally accompanied earlier reinforcements to Key West and Tortugas. In his detailed memorandum for Lincoln, Seward wrote "I would call in Captain M. C. Meigs forthwith. Aided by his counsel, I would at once, and at every cost, prepare for a war at Pensacola and Texas, to be taken, however, only as a consequence of maintaining the possessions and authority of the United States."[3]

After the cabinet meeting, Secretary Seward wrote a short note to his son Frederick saying, "Send a note by a messenger who will be sure to find Captain M. C. Meigs and bring him to the Department that I may introduce him to the president."[4]

Seward collected Meigs and took him to the president's quarters. On the way he explained that he wished the president to discuss the issue with a military man whose views would not be confounded by politics. Although Scott and Totten were available, he said, "no one would think of putting either of these old men on horseback."

Lincoln spoke freely with Meigs. After some inquiries about Sumter, he asked if Fort Pickens could be held.

"Certainly, if the navy had done its duty and not lost it already."

Lincoln then asked Meigs whether he could go there again and take command of the three great fortresses, Forts Taylor, Jefferson, and Pickens, and keep them safe. Meigs said he was only a captain and could not command the majors who were there.

Seward broke in saying, "I can understand how it is. Captain Meigs, you have to be promoted."

"That cannot be done. I am a captain, and there is no vacancy."[5]

Seward made light of this and told Lincoln that, if he wanted the Pensacola forts saved, he should follow the course of Lord Pitt when he wanted to take Quebec. He reminded the president that Lord Pitt did not send for any old general. Instead, he called for a young man he had noticed in the society of London, told him he had

2 *N&H*, 3, 395, 432.

3 Seward, *Seward at Washington*, 2, 534-35; *N&H*, 3, 429-433; Elliott, *Scott*, 704.

4 Seward, *Seward at Washington*, 2, 534.

5 The number of officers at each rank was fixed by Congress. If no vacancy existed at a rank, no promotion to that rank could be made unless Congress increased the number.

selected him to take Quebec, directed him to ask for the means, and ordered him to do it.[6] Seward asked the president to do this now. Lincoln replied that he would "consider on it" and let Meigs know in a day or two.

Seward and Meigs walked home together. The secretary was "much gratified at the result of this interview." The cabinet "had been in a strait" because of Scott's disheartening position. Then he explained his own view on Sumter and Pickens. All men of sense must see that war was coming, he felt, and that the burden of it should be imposed on those who had provoked it.[7]

Seward had solved half his problem. He had a favorable response from the army on the reinforcement of the forts and an army officer to do the job. But the navy would be necessary as well. Lieutenant David Porter, who had attracted the attention of many in the capital, was available and, probably through Meigs if not independently, was known to Seward. The next day Seward sent for Porter to visit him at once. This was the last day before Porter's departure for California. The carriage and the note found Porter having dinner with his family before he set sail for his new post. Porter left the dinner and his family to jump into the carriage for the ride to the secretary's office.

He found Seward lying on his back on a sofa with his knees up and reading a long document. Without moving, Seward greeted his new naval consultant.

"Can you tell me how we can save Fort Pickens from falling into the hands of the rebels?"

Porter answered promptly, "I can, sir."

"Then," said the secretary, "you are the man I want if you can do it."

"I can do it."

Seward rose to his feet. "Now, come, tell me how you will save that place."

A few days earlier Porter and Meigs had fortuitously devised a plan. He explained it. He then turned to naval means. Seward listened attentively. Meigs entered while Porter was talking.

"Give me command of the *Powhatan*, now lying at New York ready for sea, and I will guarantee that everything shall be done without a mistake."[8]

At breakfast on Easter morning, March 31, Scott was probably still smarting from the verbal whipping administered by Lincoln. His influence with the new Republican government had surely sunk to its lowest. His ideas were not unique, nor were they confidential. Many men, including Secretary of State Seward, agreed that

6 Keyes, *Fifty Years*, 380.

7 Nicolay MSS (L.C.), tr. Meigs MS diary, entries dated March 29 and 31, 1861.

8 Porter, *Incidents and Anecdotes*, 13-14.

much loyal sentiment existed in the South and that provocation should be avoided until that sentiment had a chance to prevail over the hotheads. Others, many others, had long since passed beyond this view and had developed strong feelings against treating the seceded states gently.

The old general encouraged Keyes to discuss the Fort Pickens situation. Turning to his own specialty, Keyes began a detailed recitation of the methods for landing heavy guns, gun carriages, and ammunition on a sandy beach like the one on Santa Rosa Island and the difficulty of moving them into the fort over that kind of terrain. The fort could never be reinforced, Keyes believed, with a weak effort. Although he spoke for almost half an hour, Scott never interrupted.

With amazement Keyes watched the expression on the general in chief's face. At least some of the time, the lieutenant general's thoughts appeared to wander. As soon as Keyes finished, the old man wheeled in his chair, took a long roll from a pile of maps and plans, and handed it to Keyes. It was a map of Pensacola Harbor and its surroundings.

"Take this map to Mr. Seward, and repeat to him exactly what you have just said to me about the difficulty of reinforcing Fort Pickens." Undoubtedly, Scott thought this would put the ugly, provocative subject of the forts, particularly "Prime Minister" Seward's notions about Fort Pickens, to rest.

Keyes stuck the roll under his arm and walked slowly down the avenue toward the Treasury Building. He knew the government would make no serious effort to reinforce or relieve Fort Pickens. He assumed Scott had sent him on an errand of form without substance, an unnecessary mission to dissuade the secretary from pressing for reinforcement, unnecessary because the secretary simply would not press for reinforcement. He would speak to Seward for ten minutes, then arrive early at St. Matthew's Church for services. On the way, he was stopped by an acquaintance who asked about the long roll under his arm. He said it related to "unfinished business" and he was taking it to the secretary of state.

When he arrived at Seward's house, he found the secretary standing by himself in the middle of his parlor. He gave a respectful salutation and said, "Mr. Seward, I am here by direction of General Scott to explain to you the difficulties of reinforcing Fort Pickens."

"I don't care about the difficulties. Where's Captain Meigs?"

"I suppose he's at his house, Sir."

"Please find him, and bring him here."

"I'll call and bring him on my return from church."

But Seward was in a much bigger hurry. "Never mind church today. I wish to see him and you here together without delay."

Keyes was not Seward's subordinate and was far removed from any chain of command headed by the secretary. For an instant, he considered a rebellious response, then decided that the secretary spoke from "the ambush of original power." He would obey at once.

Meigs was starting for church when Keyes found him. Within ten minutes of the order he and Meigs stood together before the secretary of state. Once again, Seward did not delay the conversation with preliminary pleasantries.

"I wish you two gentlemen to make a plan to reinforce Fort Pickens, see General Scott, and bring your plan to the Executive Mansion at 3 o'clock this afternoon."

Keyes and Meigs hurried to the Office of Engineers. The custodian allowed them entrance. Familiar with the record keeping system in the Engineer's Office, Meigs went directly to the cubicle containing maps and plans of Pensacola Harbor and Fort Pickens and spread them over a large table. Hardly speaking at all, they worked separately on plans to reinforce. For almost four hours they worked in silence, making lists of everything a vacant fort would need, calculating the weight of equipment and baggage, determining the necessary shipping tonnage, and determining the number of troops of different arms necessary for the fort to withstand a siege. Thinking far ahead, Meigs prepared sailing instructions and a requisition for machines that would purify sea water. The two men finished almost simultaneously, compared notes, and agreed; but by now they had insufficient time to report to Scott and present themselves at the White House by 3:00 p.m. Keyes decided to take his chances with Scott's sensitivity about the chain of command, his insistence on protocol, and his mercurial temper. They would skip the meeting with him and go immediately to the president. Directly to the White House they went, arriving at the door with five minutes to spare.

Lincoln and Seward were waiting for them, Lincoln sitting behind a table at the end of the room, his right leg resting on the table and his left leg on a chair. His hands were clasped on the top of his head.

"Gentlemen, are we ready to report?" asked Seward.

"I am ready," said Keyes, "but I have not had time to see General Scott, who is entirely ignorant of what I have been doing. As I am his military secretary, he will be angry if I don't let him know."

"I'm not General Scott's military secretary," responded Meigs, "and I am ready to report."

"There's no time to lose," said Lincoln. "Let us hear your reports, gentlemen."

Meigs went first while Keyes, who had not read Meigs's plan, listened carefully. Keyes then read his plan. Although different, the two did not conflict.[9]

9 According to Keyes, *Fifty Years*, 383, he knew nothing about the content of Meigs' plan; but Meigs wrote in his MS diary, entry dated March 31, 1861, that they "wrote out . . . our views, compared notes, agreed." Meigs' record, contemporaneous, is accepted.

Meigs had the engineering details and Keyes the details for artillery, their respective specialties. As they discussed scarps, counter scarps, terre plains, barbettes, trench cavaliers, and other forms of field and siege fortifications, Seward became impatient and interrupted.

"Your excellency and I don't understand all those technical military terms."

"That's so," said the president, putting both feet on the floor and clasping his hands between his knees. "But we understand that the *rare* rank goes right behind the front!"

During the conversation, Lincoln changed his physical position frequently. Keyes marveled silently. He had never seen "a man who could scatter his limbs more than he." He and Meigs at last took seats.[10]

Neither Lincoln nor Seward suggested an amendment or addition. Lincoln said, "Gentlemen, see General Scott; and carry your plans into execution without delay." They were to say that the president wanted this thing done and that Scott was not to let it fail "unless he can show the refusing [of] something he asked [as] necessary." In the end, he said, "I depend on you gentlemen to push this thing through."

By now, it was almost 6:00, the dinner hour. Keyes and Meigs hastened to the general's home. They found Scott seated alone at the table. In the old general's face, Keyes could see a mixture of anger and anxiety more intense than he had ever seen before. The two junior officers showed him their papers; and he approved them. Saying there was nothing in them not necessary and little to be added as necessary, he added a few details.

A short time later, Seward arrived, at least temporarily saving both junior officers from a tirade about superior officers, orders from others, and chain of command.[11]

"General Scott, you have officially advised the president of the United States," he said, "that, in your judgment, it will not be practicable to relieve Fort Sumter and Fort Pickens. I have come to you from the president to tell you that he directs that Fort Pickens shall be relieved."

The old general looked up. He saw both the humor and the gravity of the moment; but he must have been, as usual, irritated because matters in his domain had been decided by others. Nevertheless, he was "a soldier and a disciplinarian." He put

10 Keyes, *Fifty Years*, 382.

11 Nicolay MSS (L.C.), tr. Meigs MS diary (L.C.) entry dated March 31, 1861; Keyes, *Fifty Years*, 380-84, 436. These accounts do not duplicate or confirm each other on all matters, but they are not inconsistent. For example, the Keyes account does not say that Seward visited Scott's quarters while Meigs and Keyes do not report or recite the "Great King" colloquy. The two have been combined in a consistent manner although the order of events is governed generally by Meigs' account.

both hands on the table, rising slowly and with difficulty until he stood at his considerable full height.

"The great Frederick used to say that, 'When the king commands, nothing is impossible.' Sir, the president's order shall be obeyed."[12]

After a discussion about the assignment and the way it should be performed, Seward and Meigs departed. Alone with Keyes, Scott turned on him sharply. "Where have you been all day?"

In the fewest possible words, Keyes explained that Seward had refused to hear about chain of command or protocol. He explained that Seward had ordered them to make plans to reinforce Fort Pickens, told them to see General Scott, and ordered them to return to the White House at 3:00 p.m. The work, he said, had detained him until it was too late to report and return to the White House on time. Last, Lincoln had ordered him to read his plan without first reporting.

"Did he tell you that?" demanded the general.

"He did, Sir!"

A pause of at least five minutes followed. Like a dictator who had been overruled, Scott was struggling to control "a tremendous emotion." Instead of the threatening demeanor he so often manifested toward junior officers when his prerogatives had been infringed, his face showed, as if he were receiving honors while simultaneously being deprived of power, a gloomy sadness.

Keyes knew from long experience that these circumstances required a deferential silence; but his excitable temperament made that impossible. His eyes sparkled with happiness. His voice was joyous. Military efforts were to be undertaken, and he was to be a part of them. At the same time he had been hard at work for ten hours without food or drink. To the dinner table he took "the appetite of a Siberian wolf in winter, and the thirst of a Bedouin returned from a foray in the scorched sand of Arabia." He ate voraciously and charged himself with several bumpers of wine, throwing his head back to inhale the last drop of each glass.

The next morning, April 1, Meigs and Keyes began work in the various military bureaus to carry out the reinforcement. They had to select officers, troops, and equipment; learn where they all were; and accumulate them for shipment to Florida. Together, they drew up a letter of instructions to Colonel Harvey Browne, the officer they had selected to command the infantry and artillery for the expedition. The letter was given to Seward for review, then for signature to Scott, who signed it without comment.

12 Seward, *Seward at Washington*, 2, 534; Keyes, *Fifty Years*, 383, 436. There are several versions of this conversation, but the account in Seward is closest to one of the actual participants and is adopted.

Keyes and Meigs intended to accumulate the equipment in the harbor of New York City. Before leaving Washington, Keyes wanted a letter of authority that would produce instantaneous obedience in the New York City area. He prepared another order for Scott's signature.[13] For Colonel Browne, the president had already signed instructions to all officers of the army and navy to cooperate with the effort to collect men and material.[14]

Keyes took his order to Scott and handed it to him for his signature. The general in chief held the order in his hand, reading its few lines for two or three minutes. He handed it back. "You had better get the president to sign that order."

Keyes changed the heading and took it to the White House where he received Lincoln's signature at once.

Later that day Meigs collected Lieutenant Porter and went to the White House, where they arranged the naval aspects of the mission with Seward and Lincoln.[15] Porter was to go to New York, take any ready vessel, and sail with all steam for Pensacola Harbor. Once there, he was, as he and Meigs had planned earlier, to provide naval protection for the fort and the expedition by preventing any Rebel boat from taking troops across the harbor to Santa Rosa Island.

"Tell me," asked Lincoln, "how we can prevent Fort Pickens from falling into the hands of the rebels, for if Slemmer is not at once relieved there will be no holding it. Pensacola would be a very important place for the Southerners, and if they once get possession of Pickens, and fortify it, we have no navy to take it from them."

"Mr. President," responded Porter, "There is a queer state of things existing in the Navy Department at this time. Mr. Welles is surrounded by officers and clerks, some of whom are disloyal at heart. And if the orders for the expedition should emanate from the secretary of the Navy and pass through all the department red tape, the news would be at once flashed over the wires, and Fort Pickens would be lost forever. But if you will issue all the orders from the Executive Mansion, and let me proceed to New York with them, I will guarantee their prompt execution to the letter."

"But, is not this a most irregular mode of proceeding?"

"Certainly," replied Porter, "but the necessity of the case justifies it."

"You are commander in chief of the army and navy," added Seward, "and this is a case where it is necessary to issue direct orders without passing them through intermediaries."

13 Keyes, *Fifty Years*, 383-385, 387.

14 Basler, *Lincoln's Works*, 4, 315, letters dated April 1, 1861 from Lincoln to Porter; *OR*, 1, 367.

15 Nicolay MSS (L.C.) tr. Meigs MS diary, entry dated April 1, 1861.

"But what will Uncle Gideon say?"

"Oh, I will make it all right with Mr. Welles," said the secretary of state. "This is the only way, sir, the thing can be done."

As the conversation progressed, Porter took his measure of the secretary of state. An arbitrary man, he thought, and one accustomed to having his own way. The best feeling, he could see, did not exist between the Departments of State and the navy. Seward seemed to feel that he had not been "as much consulted as he ought to have been in the fitting out of the expedition for the relief of Sumter. He looked upon himself as Prime Minister and considered that the secretary of the navy should defer to him in all matters concerning movements against those in rebellion."

Porter wrote the necessary orders; Meigs recopied them; and Lincoln signed them, saying, "Seward, see that I don't burn my fingers."

With his three orders in hand Porter bid good-bye to the president and left with Meigs to see Scott. Keyes received them and showed them into the anteroom. Meigs asked to see the cranky old general in chief as soon as possible.

Keyes delivered the message.

Gruffly, Scott asked what they wanted.

Keyes explained that they were calling about Fort Pickens and Pensacola Harbor. The expedition, having, among other things, incited a tongue-lashing by the president for dereliction of duty, could not have been the most pleasant subject for Scott. This was a fair time for the most strict application of all rules, and he could give an intentional rebuff by doing it.

"Tell Captain Meigs to walk in. I won't see any naval officer. *He* can't come in."[16]

In a short while Meigs and Keyes rejoined Porter in the anteroom with the necessary approvals. The three men left. Porter headed for the train for New York.[17]

Next morning, Porter arrived at the New York Navy Yard with the three orders in his possession.[18] The first ordered Porter to proceed to New York, take command of the steam frigate *Powhatan*, and sail to Fort Pickens. Once there, he was to cross the bar, anchor in the harbor, and cover the fort. There, he should protect Meigs and his men and equipment while they landed.[19]

16 Porter attributes this intentional rudeness to a severe attack of gout, *Incidents and Anecdotes*, 16; but even if the condition were present, it would not have been the sole basis for Scott's capricious reaction to Porter's visit.

17 Porter, *Incidents and Anecdotes*, 14-17; Nicolay MSS (L.C.), Meigs MS diary, entry dated April 1, 1861.

18 Porter, *Incidents and Anecdotes*, 16.

19 Basler, *Lincoln's Works*, 4, 313-315, Series 1, *N.O.R.*, 4, 108-109. According to Basler, the originals have not been found. The copies reprinted in various works, many authoritative, vary

The second directed the commandant of the Navy Yard to fit out the *Powhatan* with all dispatch for "secret service." It concluded with the unmistakable but baffling injunction, "You will under no circumstances communicate to the Navy Department the fact that she is fitting out."[20] The last order, addressed to the commanding officer of the *Powhatan*, delivered command of the ship to Porter; but to confirm his continued confidence in the displaced officer, Lincoln had written that he would give him a better command to replace the *Powhatan*.[21]

At the Navy Yard, Porter found Commodore Breese, the commandant, absent on leave, the *Powhatan* disassembled, her officers on leave, and her crew dispersed. Porter considered at least part of this beneficial because Breese, an old, unimaginative, by-the-book officer, would not have moved without an order from the Navy Department in spite of the president's letter. In his place Porter found his old friend Captain Alexander H. Foote, more intelligent, but not necessarily so easy to persuade either. He showed Foote the orders, but they were not enough. Foote read them again and again, turned them upside down, examined the watermark and the Executive Mansion stamp, and surveyed Porter from head to foot.

"You see, Porter," he said, "there are so many fellows whom I would have trusted to the death who have deserted the flag that I don't know whom to believe. How do I know you are not a traitor? Who ever heard of such orders as these emanating direct from the president? I must telegraph to Mr. Welles before I do anything and ask further instructions."

"Look at these orders again, and then telegraph at your peril. Under no circumstances must you inform the Navy Department of this expedition. Now give me a cigar, let me sit here in quiet, and you may take an hour or two to look over those letters if you like; but if you telegraph to Mr. Welles, the president will consider it high treason, and you will lose the best chance you ever had in your life. If you must telegraph, send a message to the president or Mr. Seward."

significantly in language but not in substance. The issuance of the written orders by Lincoln cannot be doubted, and the variations can be explained in a variety of plausible but immaterial ways. This problem apparently applies to all five orders for the relief of Fort Pickens signed by Lincoln on April 1. Basler, *Lincoln's Works*, 4, 313-315. According to Porter, *Incidents and Anecdotes*, he was given one order; but Basler, *Lincoln's Works*, 315, and Series 1, *N.O.R.*, vol. 4, 108-109, show two orders issued by Lincoln to Porter on April 1. One could have been created later in the day for Meigs to deliver to Porter when Meigs joined Keyes at the Navy Yard in New York City. By its text the first and shorter of the two orders looks as if it might have been prepared after Porter departed.

20 Basler, *Lincoln's Works*, 4, 314, from Series 1, *N.O.R.*, vol. 4, 314.

21 Basler, *Lincoln's Works*, 4, 314, from Series 1, *N.O.R.*, 4, 314. In the parallel projects to reinforce Fort Sumter, a Navy Department effort, and Fort Pickens, a State Department project, both teams intended to use the *Powhatan* for firepower and close protection for the ships carrying men and equipment.

Foote, like many other loyal servants of the federal government at this time, could not tell who was reliable and who was not, who was a patriot and who a traitor.

"Yes, and what would prevent you from having a confederate at the other end of the line to receive the message and answer it? There is so much treason going on!"

Porter laughed. "What would you say, if I were to tell you that Frank Buchanan, Sam Barron, and Magruder were going to desert to the rebels?"

This substantiated Foote's worst fears and enhanced his greatest uncertainties. No one could be trusted. Porter nonchalantly lit a cigar and began to smoke. Foote jumped from his chair.

"God in heaven! What next? You don't expect me to trust you after that? How do I know you are not in league with the others? But, man, that can't be, for I saw by the morning papers that President Lincoln was at a wedding last night at Buchanan's, and Buchanan had the house festooned with American flags, and all the loyal men of Washington were there."

"So they were, but nevertheless, they will all desert in a few days, for their hearts are on the other side. Ingraham is going also — his chief clerk has already preceded him, and carried off the signal-book of the navy."

"Good Lord, deliver us! I must telegraph to Mr. Welles. I can't stand this strain any longer. It will kill me. You sit smoking and smiling as if this was not a very serious matter." He turned to his chief clerk. "Here, bring me a telegraph blank."

"Before you send that message, let me call your attention to a paragraph of the president's order: 'Under no circumstances will you make known to the Navy Department or any one else the object of this expedition, or the fact that the *Powhatan* is fitting out.' Just think of the president taking you into his confidence so early in these troubles. Think what a high position you may reach before the trouble with the South is over if we succeed in carrying out this expedition successfully. Then, again, think what a tumble you will get if you disobey a positive order of the president. He will believe rebellion rampant everywhere and won't know whom to trust. Think of Captain Foote being tried and shot like Admiral Byng[22] for failing to carry out his orders."

22 In the 1750s while England reigned supreme on the high seas and her old challengers, the Spanish and Dutch navies, had receded, Admiral John A. Byng, commanding ten ships of the line, had an inconclusive engagement with a French fleet. When the wind shifted to give Byng the advantage while the French were disorganized, Byng failed to renew the engagement. This he followed by abandoning his blockading position and withdrawing to Gibraltar. The sea lanes, to the amazement of the ineffective French maritime, were open. After horrific reactions at home, Byng was charged with, tried for, convicted of neglect of duty, sentenced to death under the new Twelfth Article of War, and executed on the quarterdeck of the *Monarch* in Portsmouth Harbor. G. J. Marcus, *A Naval History of England: The Formative Centuries*, 2 vols. (Boston and Toronto, 1961), vol. 1, 282-284.

"Hush, Porter! Hush at once! I believe you are a rebel in disguise, for after Frank Buchanan, Barron, and Magruder preparing to desert, and Ingraham, too, with his Kosta record, I won't trust any one. Where are your trunks?"

"At the Irving House."

Foote took the only compromise course that seemed to allow him to cover himself against deception by Porter while, at least temporarily, obeying the order not to communicate with the Department of the Navy.

"Send the postman here," he ordered.

When he arrived, Foote ordered him, "Go to the Irving House, pay Lieutenant Porter's bill, and take his trunks to my house, and tell Mrs. Foote to prepare the best room.—There, my boy, I have you now. You shall stay with me, and I will be ready to arrest you the moment I find there is any treason about you. After all, you have come on a wild-goose chase."

Porter had come to New York knowing that the *Powhatan* was in the New York Navy Yard and expecting it to be seaworthy and ready to sail. This was not the case.

"The *Powhatan* is stripped to a girt-line," Foote continued. "Her engines are all to pieces, her boilers under an order to survey, her boats are worn out, and the ship wants new planking all over. Her magazines are too damp to keep powder in, and we are pulling them all to pieces. She wants a new fore-yard and painting throughout. In fact, the ship is worn out, and I gave orders to haul her into dock this morning preparatory to thorough repairs."

"So much the better," said Porter undaunted. "She is just the ship I am looking for. Never mind paint, never mind repairing the boilers, never mind new spars, or repairs to magazines. I will take her as she is. Only set your people to work and put everything in place, and we can get off in four days. I want a ship that can be sunk without any great loss."

"But all the *Powhatan*'s officers have been granted leave, and her crew transferred to the receiving-ship."

"Telegraph the officers to return at once, and send the crew on board to rig and equip her."

"I can't do that, unless I telegraph to Mr. Welles."

Once again Porter called Foote's attention to the president's order. Foote was puzzled. He thought carefully.

"I will trust you, though I am utterly nonplused. It's such a doubtful business. I will set to work immediately, and by night we will have the spars up and by noon tomorrow I will have all the officers back. Come home with me now and take lunch, and I will give the sentry at my house orders to keep an eye on you when I return to the office."

Porter had not lost his sense of humor.

"And I will return to the office, and watch you to see that you don't telegraph to Mr. Welles. I want to save you, if possible, from the fate of Admiral Byng."

Foote laughed heartily. He had decided to obey the written instructions. A double set of men were ordered aboard the *Powhatan* with orders to work day and night to make the ship ready for sea in three days.

Resting later at Foote's home, Porter and his host talked nearly all night about the adventure on which they were embarking. Foote's concerns seemed to be, at least temporarily, allayed; and he was now driven by as much enthusiasm as Porter. He had become devoted to the success of the expedition and had begun to feel a sense of anticipation for it.

Although Foote hardly drank at all, he was a good host, kept a well-stocked larder, and had every kind of liquor handy for his friends. The weather was cold. A fire was burning in Porter's room. Porter offered an additional solution to the late winter chill.

"Suppose you send for a kettle of water, some lemons, and sugar; and let us have some hot punch."

"If you ever tell anybody, you bad fellow, that I sat up with you after midnight brewing punch, I'll never forgive you."

Porter took ten minutes to brew whisky-punch, then tasted it and declared it to be admirable.

"Let me make you one."

"Well, if you will take some hot water, lemon, and sugar, and mix them together, and put in a very little whisky 'unbeknownst' to me, I will keep you company."

At this time in the history of their country, no man in the American military could predict the course of events with any certainty. Through the long hours of the night, Porter and Foote discussed the prospects for their navy. By daylight Foote had decided he could trust Porter and had abandoned all notions of telegraphing Secretary Welles.[23]

Meanwhile, after Porter left Washington for New York, Meigs and Keyes had further discussions with Seward and Scott about the army officer who should command the expedition. Knowing the obvious problem of seniority but thinking Meigs was the man for this assignment, Seward wanted Meigs promoted.

Opposed to meteoric promotions of junior officers, Scott explained why, under existing legislation, this could not be done.

Undaunted, Seward asked Meigs if he would go anyway.

23 Porter, *Incidents and Anecdotes*, 16-20.

"I am ready for any duty in any place in any capacity at any pay, so long as it is in my country's service," replied Meigs stoutly.

Aware that Meigs was responsible, as engineer officer, for the capitol dome and other very important ongoing construction projects and no doubt swayed by the fact that a state of war did not exist, Scott opposed again.

"It is cruel to ask him to go away from the great works and in a rank so low as that which a captain's commission must give him."

The Pickens expedition was Seward's creation. Whatever happened to the relief of Fort Sumter, an adventure in the hands of the Department of the Navy, the State Department's mission to reinforce Fort Pickens in Pensacola Harbor must succeed.

"Any arrangement you can make for carrying on the work in your responsibility will be carried out," he said to Meigs. "To this, I pledge myself. You get your pay anyhow."

He discounted the fame, perhaps even the recognition, the capitol projects offered. He would go to the aid of Lieutenant Slemmer, his tiny force, and Fort Pickens. "Fame will come from Pickens as well as from the capitol. The capitol might stop. There is no use in a capitol unless we have a country."[24]

On the evening train, April 3, Keyes and Meigs set out for New York City. After midnight, they embarked on the ferry to cross the Delaware River to Philadelphia. As the boat was about to leave its mooring, Keyes overheard a group of men talking, one of whom said, "There's General Scott's secretary. What's up?"

Spies were everywhere, Keyes assumed. Surprise, therefore secrecy, was vital to the success of the reinforcement. Even the Navy Department and the secretary of the navy were unaware of the plan. If the Rebels learned about it, they could attack the ships while the men and equipment were landing on Santa Rosa Island or prepare an assault on land while the equipment was being moved tediously across the sandy beaches to the fort. To show that their trip was unimportant, Keyes assumed an air of indifference and casualness. "Meigs, I'm not going to travel all night. Please look out for my trunk, and I'll come on in the morning train if I don't oversleep myself."

Next morning, Meigs, fresh from his long train ride, arrived in Foote's office. Porter and Foote, having ended their long philosophizing about the future, had already sent for Captain Mercer, commanding officer of the *Powhatan*, read him the president's letter, and enjoined him to secrecy. Meigs explained his own part in the

24 Nicolay MSS (L.C.), tr. Meigs MS diary, entry dated April 1, 1861; indirect discourse has been converted to direct discourse. They also prepared, and arranged for the signature of, other orders. An order written by Meigs with a postscript written by Porter, and signed without reading by the president, rearranged one of the most important functions in the Navy Department. When Welles received it, he went straight to the president and had it revoked. Morse *Welles' Diary*, 1, 16-21.

expedition and told Foote he had transcribed all the orders in the president's presence. This settled any remaining qualms Foote had.

The work on the *Powhatan* proceeded rapidly. The boilers and machinery were repaired, and the officers returned in response to telegrams. Mercer took nominal command. Porter's presence in the navy yard caused no comment because he never went near the ship. That evening he unobtrusively sent his luggage on board.

On the fourth day the *Powhatan* was ready for sea with its steam up and the pilot on board. Meigs told Porter he would sail on the *Atlantic* at 3:00 p.m. with the troops under command of Colonel Harvey Browne. While Porter and Foote were making last minute preparations, a telegram arrived from the secretary of the navy ordering the *Powhatan* to be prepared for sea at once. Ignorant of the Fort Pickens program, he was ordering the ship into the Fort Sumter relief flotilla.

Dazed, Foote gave Porter the telegram. "There, you are dished!"

"Not by any means," answered Porter. "This telegram is all right, only the president has got uneasy about the ship not sailing, since he was under the impression that she was ready for sea at a moment's notice, and has made a confidant of Mr. Welles. Let me get on board and off, and you can telegraph that the *Powhatan* has sailed."

"No," said Foote. This was a development not anticipated by anyone, even the persuasive Porter. Foote called for pen and ink, "I must telegraph to Mr. Welles."

"Don't make any mistake," said Porter, still too quick for Foote. "You must obey the commander in chief of the army and navy in preference to all others." Again, he quoted the president's order against telling the Navy Department the object of the expedition.

Foote threw down his pen. "Porter, you will be the death of me; but I will send for Mercer and Captain Meigs to join our conference."

Both men arrived shortly. Both urged Foote to obey the president's order, and he decided to follow their advice.

"Now go right on board, my boy, and get off, and as soon as you are under way I will telegraph the secretary that you have sailed." Porter bid Foote good-bye and unnoticed in the crowd, slipped on board the *Powhatan*, where he locked himself in the captain's stateroom.

To complete the deception, Captain Mercer was to remain in command until the ship reached Staten Island, then go ashore while the ship proceeded down the bay under its first lieutenant. After it had passed the bar and the pilot[25] had left, Porter

25 Under long practice in the Port of New York, a practice that continues today, ships entering and leaving are handled by local pilots familiar with the peculiarities of the port, not by their regular pilot and captain.

would emerge. Meeting many obstacles in its progress down the East River, the *Powhatan* did not have full steam for an hour after leaving the navy yard and was an hour and a half reaching Staten Island. Another long hour was consumed landing Captain Mercer.

Just as the order was given to go ahead, the quartermaster reported to Porter, "A fast steamer a-chasin' and signalin' of us, sir, and an officer wavin' his cap!"

The first lieutenant did not know that Porter was below in the captain's cabin. He stopped until the steamer arrived. Foote had chartered the fastest little steamer in New York harbor and kept her steam up for any moment a telegram should arrive.

The steamboat was soon alongside the *Powhatan* and a lieutenant delivered a telegram. Perry walked into the cabin and, to his astonishment, found Porter there. He handed him the dispatch.

"Deliver up the *Powhatan* at once to Captain Mercer. Seward."

Porter prepared a telegram in response: "Have received confidential orders from the president, and shall obey them. D. D. Porter."

He then returned to the bridge and gave orders to go fast. In an hour and a half they were steering south, then east to confuse any pursuers.[26] In New York harbor Meigs and Keyes worked feverishly to load their large steamer with supplies, equipment, and men. To the secretary of state, whom both men rightly deemed "the originator and patron of the effort to reinforce Fort Pickens," Meigs wrote a prophetic letter. It read in part:

> This is the beginning of a war which every statesman and soldier has foreseen since the passage of the South Carolina ordinance of secession. You will find the Army and Navy clogged at the head with men, excellent men —patriots, who were soldiers and sailors forty years ago, but who now keep active men out of their places, in which they could serve the country.
>
> If you call out volunteers you have no general to command. The genius, born, not made, is yet to be found, who is to govern this great army which is to save the country, if saved it can be. Colonel Keyes has shown intelligence, zeal, activity, and I look for a high future for him.

> England took six months to get a soldier to the Crimea. We were from May to September in getting General Taylor to Monterey. Let us be supported. We go to serve our country, and our country should not neglect us or leave us to be strangled in tape, however red.[27]

26 Porter, *Incidents and Anecdotes*, 21-22.

27 Keyes, *Fifty Years*, 389-90; the letter also appears in *OR*, 1, 368.

The troops of the relief force and about one-fourth of the necessary supplies were on board with Meigs when his ship set sail.[28] Keyes remained behind to assure that the remaining supplies were loaded and shipped promptly.[29]

28 Keyes, *Fifty Years*, 391.

29 *Ibid.*, 396-97.

Chapter 5

"No, sir, the capital is not in danger. The capital is not in danger."

— Scott to Lincoln, Curtin, and McClure

The Beginning of Command

While Keyes, Meigs, and Porter worked feverishly to reinforce Fort Pickens, the Southerners transformed themselves from secessionists to Rebels on April 12. With Keyes diligently completing his tasks in New York and Meigs at sea, Rebel forces in Charleston Harbor opened fire on Fort Sumter. Two days later, its supplies dwindling, it surrendered. Three days after that, the Virginia Convention passed an ordinance of secession which was to be submitted in May to the people of the state for a vote. Civil and political turmoil had ceased to be Scott's worst nightmare. Now he confronted the reality of full-fledged war.[1] The forces prepared by Stone under Scott's watchful eye had been intended to keep order in the capital. They were not sufficient to defend it from attack. Infantry, artillery, and cavalry were needed at once and could come only from the states.

The most exposed of the border states and second in population, wealth, and military power was Pennsylvania; whose role as a leader among the loyal states was

1 John G. Nicolay, *Outbreak Of The Rebellion* (New York, 1882), 137-143 (Nicolay, *Outbreak*).

important. Lincoln wired Andrew Curtin, the governor of the state, to request a meeting. At 10:00 a.m. on the day after Fort Sumter surrendered, they met in the White House to discuss the posture of the state in the new war. Curtin and Colonel A. K. McClure, the chairman of the Military Committee of the Pennsylvania Senate, arrived a few moments early. Because the cabinet was in session in the room they were to use, they sat in the anteroom in two chairs by the window looking over the Potomac. A number of visitors arrived, filling all the other chairs. Scott, taller than all the others and obviously infirm, arrived. Curtin greeted him cordially and introduced McClure. They could see that Scott stood "with great agony." Both Curtin and McClure offered him their chairs. Always a model of form, Scott declined. He would not sit while one of the other men stood. All three men stood for thirty minutes until Lincoln was ready to talk with them.

As they finished their discussion about Pennsylvania's role in the war, Scott openly described Washington's exposure. McClure assumed that Scott did not have a large force at hand, and he knew that General P. G. T. Beauregard, commanding the Rebel forces in Charleston Harbor, had a "formidable force." That his army could move from South Carolina to Washington in a few days was clear. McClure became aware of "the utterly hopeless condition of the government" and felt free to ask Scott if the capital were in danger.

"No, sir, the capital is not in danger. The capital is not in danger."

"If it is a proper question for you to answer, I would like to know how many men you have in Washington for its defense."

Stone had created an internal security force, not a garrison for defense or an army for offense. Scott replied promptly.

"Fifteen hundred, sir. Fifteen hundred men and two batteries."

"Is Washington a defensible city?" asked McClure.

A shadow crossed the old general in chief's face.

"No, sir. Washington is not a defensible city." To emphasize the security of the capital, he pointed out the window to the Potomac. "You see that vessel? A sloop of war, sir. A sloop of war."

McClure looked out the window. He could see a sloop in the river; but beyond it, he could see Arlington Heights, from which one or two batteries, even decrepit, outmoded artillery, could "knock the sloop of war to pieces in half an hour." Upon reflection McClure must have known that direct fire from the heights could hit the capital buildings.

"How many men does Beauregard have at Charleston?"

Scott's head drooped toward his breast. A look of despair flickered across his face. He spoke in a tremulous voice.

"General Beauregard commands more men at Charleston than I command on the continent east of the frontier."

"How long would Beauregard require to transport his army to Washington?"

"It might be done in three or four days."

McClure assumed the risk of pressing his point to a state of rudeness with the sensitive old general.

"General, is not Washington in great danger?"

Aroused, Scott straightened himself in his chair and with crushing dignity responded a second time.

"No, sir. The capital can't be taken! The capital can't be taken, sir."

Throughout Lincoln listened intently. He twirled his spectacles in his fingers. Scott and McClure seemed to have come to the end of the dialogue.

"It does seem to me, general," said the president, "that if I were Beauregard I would take Washington."

"Mr. President," said Scott, affirming his conviction in the way that made Lincoln reluctant to do without his counsel, "the capital can't be taken, sir. It can't be taken."

About Scott, the president kept his own counsel as he did on all personnel matters unless the circumstances required activity. Curtin and McClure, however, concluded that "the great Chieftain of two wars and the worshiped Captain of the Age was in his dotage and utterly unequal to the great duty of meeting the impending conflict."[2]

In spite of his categorical statements to McClure and the president, Scott and many others feared greatly for the safety of the national capital. Specifically, Scott anticipated an attack across the Potomac River north of Washington, an advance to capture Baltimore, and a turn south for an easy capture of Washington. To oppose this he would collect a force in the capital for direct defense and two forces to threaten the flank of any movement on Baltimore. The one at Harpers Ferry, which had the most important and most difficult task, would assail the north flank of any force crossing the Potomac toward Baltimore, thus compelling the enemy to halt, face north, deploy, and fight. The two forces from Baltimore and the capital could then concentrate on the invaders.[3]

2 A. K. McClure, *Abraham Lincoln and Men of War Times: Some Personal Recollections of War and Politics during the Lincoln Administration* (Lincoln and London, 1996, 4th ed.), 65-69 (McClure, *Lincoln and Men*). In his superb work *Lincoln and his Generals* (New York, 1952), Professor T. Harry Williams implies that this conversation took place immediately after the loss of the Battle of Bull Run. The dialogue would fit, but McClure's narrative gives a precise date for the meeting, *op cit.*, 65. Miers, *Lincoln Day by Day*, 1862, p. 35, April 15.

3 Fitz-John Porter MSS (L.C.), letters dated November 24, 1890 (draft) and November 28, 1892, from Porter to Livermore.

The Regular Army, the only organized, disciplined, and equipped force, had a minuscule size that precluded it from being used alone to fight the war. Widely scattered, its positions made it useless for the immediate defense of the capital. On April 14, 1861, when Major Robert Anderson surrendered Fort Sumter, the regular army had less than seventeen thousand men of whom only six hundred were officers. Nearly half the officers holding active commissions resigned to take service with their states, including most of the higher ranking and more promising men.

Many of the Northern graduates of West Point in the years prior to 1861 had served their obligatory terms, then resigned their commissions to seek better opportunities in civilian life. Most of the older and more experienced of them had been civilians for some time. The shortage of active officers was complicated by imbalance. Artillery officers surpassed both infantry and cavalry officers in number. Even those in the infantry and cavalry had received instruction in artillery.[4] More officers would be needed.

To fill this void, the Regular Army could be used in two ways. It could be held together, compact, disciplined, and reliable in battle—a form of imperial guard. Or, the government could disperse it among the volunteers, the cadre or 100,000-man army theory. Napoleon's imperial guard had been created by taking the best men of all ranks from all units to form an elite organization saved for deployment at the critical moment, to brace any part of the line that sagged, to be the *schwerpunkt* or the *masse de decision* in the attack. The most difficult tasks would be given to these experienced, hardened campaigners while the remainder of the army filled the lines about them. Washington had used the Continentals as a small but solid and reliable nucleus while he used his militia units as fillers.[5] Scott had fought the Mexican War in this manner, volunteers and regulars being kept separate.[6]

The imperial guard theory, however, had several drawbacks. Because it was an elite organization and was composed of the best men of all ranks, both officers and enlisted men, it stripped the ordinary line units of their best men, the natural leaders, the most skilled, those who set the best examples.[7] When to use an elite force was

4 *N&H*, 4, 65; Comte De Paris, *History Of The Civil War In America*, 3 vols. (Philadelphia, 1875), vol. 1, 19 (Paris, *History of the Civil War*); Upton, *Military Policy*, 236-238.

5 See generally, Christopher Ward, *The War of the Revolution*, 2 vols. (New York, 1952).

6 See generally, Jack K. Bauer, *The Mexican War* (1974, Norwalk, Easton Press ed.).

7 John W. Gordon on Major General Orde Wingate, in John Keegan, ed., *Churchill's Generals,* 294 (New York, 1991). Gordon quotes Field Marshall Sir William Slim, who wrote after World War II, that special or elite units "lower the quality of the rest of the army—both by skimming the cream of it, but by encouraging the idea that only specially equipped corps d'elite could be expected to undertake . . . those most obviously demanding and hazardous missions."

always a question. In ordinary circumstances? In battle? Only when the most difficult task was presented?

Waiting for the right moment and jealously guarding his special troops, Napoleon saved his imperial guard too long. By the time he committed it at Waterloo, it simply could no longer perform the superhuman task expected of it.[8]

Nevertheless, the government could create and use an elite force without damage to the remainder of the army. Alexander the Great's Companion Cavalry, his personal bodyguard and an elite force, was not withheld from battle. Instead, he used it frequently, often giving it the place and the task of honor, the most difficult and critical assignment. Not losing its edge from lack of use, it always rewarded him in battle.[9]

In the alternative, the Regulars could have been used as a cadre for the volunteers by being interspersed among them to spread their knowledge and experience. The German Army of 1920 to 1935, under the brilliant General Hans von Seeckt, was the paradigm of this concept. Limited by the Treaty of Versailles to 100,000 men of all ranks, it became the living embodiment of the cadre theory: in mobilization, privates would become corporals; corporals, sergeants; lieutenants, captains; and so on to the top. Every man was expected to know and be able to perform the duties of the two ranks senior to him. By 1940 the 100,000-man army had given Hitler a military force which equaled the General Staff's most optimistic estimates for 1945, and the system proved itself by the German successes in the early years of the war.[10]

The United States Regular Army was used both ways in the Civil War but not by design. Certainly, it had no prewar plan. Ultimately, the officers were used as a cadre even though they had not intentionally been given training for higher ranks.

8 David Chandler, *The Campaigns of Napoleon*, 2 vols. (Norwalk, 1991) (Collector's Edition, Easton Press), vol. 2, 1088-1091 (Chandler, *Napoleon*); John R. Elting, *Swords around a Throne, Napoleon's Grande Armee* (New York, 1988), 183-205.

9 Peter Green, *Alexander of Macedon: 356-323 B.C. A Historical Biography* (London, 1991), 17-18 (Green, *Alexander*); Lesile J. Worby, *Hippies: The Cavalry of Ancient Greece*, 153-167 (San Francisco, 1994).

10 Walter Goerlitz, trans. Brian Battershaw, *History of the German General Staff 1657-1945*, chap IX, esp pts X and XI, 222-228 (New York, 1953); Gordon A. Craig, *The Politics of the Prussian Army 1640-1945*, chap. X, esp pts II and III, 389-408 (Oxford, 1955); Harold J. Gordon, Jr., *The Reichswehr and the German Republic 1919-1926*, chap. 8, esp pt VIII, 297-308 (Princeton, 1957). Restricted by the Treaty of Versailles to an army of 100,000 men, the Germans designed an army which could be increased to at least three times that size in the blink of an eye. With a bit more time the 100,000-man army would be the core of an army many times that size. The plan was intended for a Germany governed by a conservative form of democracy, but it worked superbly for an altogether different form of government.

The enlisted men, the "ground pounders," the "crunchies," the "mud crushers," were kept intact in units that would, by example, steady the green volunteer units.

The national military forces would mimic the armies of the past: a combination of Regulars, militiamen, and volunteers. The Regulars were creatures of the federal government. The state governments created the militia forces, top to bottom. The volunteers, although predominantly creatures of the states, would take birth from both. The resulting army would never be a truly federal force. Until the militia regiments were complete and mustered into the national forces, the governors controlled them. What authority the governors would have after the regiments were mustered into federal service was one of many uncertainties yet to be resolved.[11]

The Regular Army could never have purposely implemented an imperial guard concept. That would have conflicted with every American social and political concept. The democratic civil-soldier was the ideal even before the minute man of the Revolutionary War; and Andrew Jackson had proven that the training of an elitist school like West Point was unnecessary. Although all West Point graduates loyal to the Union were potential leaders, especially those still on active duty, the problems of tapping this source were great.[12] The Regular officers on active service instinctively cleaved to the imperial guard theory. They resisted the breakup of stable, proven units; and older Regular officers, including Scott, resisted the promotion of company grade Regular officers to higher ranks in the volunteers in the fear that it would cause a dearth of men capable of instructing and indoctrinating new Regular companies.[13] Initially these factors and the grass roots militia system united to prevent any plan that would intentionally disperse the officers of the Regular establishment.

Many officers did not want to command volunteers at the outset because of bad experiences with them in the Mexican War.[14] To the Regular Army officers, the

11 Fred Albert Shannon, *The Organization and Administration of the Union Army 1861-1865*, 2 vols. (Cleveland, 1928), vol. 1, 26-35.

12 *Annual Report of the Adjutant General of New York 1861* (Albany, 1862), 23 (*A.G. Report N.Y.*).

13 Oliver O. Howard, *The Autobiography of Oliver Otis Howard*, 2 vols., (New York, 1907), vol. 1, 106 (Howard, *Autobiography*).

14 George B. McClellan MSS (L.C.) letters dated May 10, 1861, from Porter to McClellan and June 29, 1861, from Burnside to McClellan (this letter was misdated and, therefore, misfiled by the curator. It describes events that took place in 1862 during Burnside's campaign on the coast); Porter MSS (L.C.) draft letter dated May 24, 1890, from Porter to Livermore (Scott's view); Robert P. Patterson, *A Narrative of the Campaign in the Valley of the Shenandoah of 1861* (Philadelphia 1865), 106, letter dated Aug. 8, 1964, from Thomas to Patterson (Patterson, *Narrative*); Henry D. Sedgwick, ed., *Correspondence of John Sedgwick, Major General*, 2 vols. (privately printed, 1902), 1, 35-36, letter dated November 11, 1846, from Sedgwick to his father; 39, letter dated November 26, 1846, from Sedgwick to his sister; 58, letter dated February 9,

essential ingredient of organization for war was discipline, generally deficient in militia units and nonexistent in volunteer units;[15] but if the war eventually became longer than the brief "walk in the park" anticipated by many, the mainstay of any army, both enlisted man and officer, would be the volunteer.

On April 15, the day after Major Anderson surrendered Fort Sumter, Lincoln called for 75,000 militia for three months and assigned quotas to the various states. In response, the governors summoned their militia organizations.

The militia units were led by non-commissioned, company grade, and field grade officers usually elected by the men of the regiment and approved by the governor, who had the final appointive power over every rank from corporal to major general. Once confirmed by the governor they could be deprived of "office" only if found unfit. The governors could also appoint officers who had no troops.[16] Before the war attitudes toward militia service ranged from democratic revulsion against standing military organizations, through popular ridicule for inefficiency, to hearty enjoyment of fine social events at "drill meetings." In 1861 the condition of the state militias reflected this widely varied spectrum.

In 1860 Nathaniel P. Banks, the governor of Massachusetts, and his adjutant general foresaw war and prepared for it. During the first two months of 1860, a series of legislative acts reorganized, enlarged, and made efficient the state military system. All those in the service were required to register at their headquarters, and all organizations were ordered to recruit to full strength. Banks wanted only those men who could respond at the moment of danger. Those who could not were discharged and their places filled by those who could. Clothing, arms, and equipment were gathered. Extensive, thorough drilling began. When newly elected Governor John A. Andrew received on April 5 Lincoln's telegram requesting troops, he was able to parade four full regiments in Boston the next day.[17]

1846, from Sedgwick to his father (Sedgwick, *Correspondence*); George Gordon Meade, ed., *The Life and Letters of George Gordon Meade Major-General United States Army*, 2 vols. (New York, 1913), 1, 162-165, letters dated December 2, 1846, from Meade to his wife; 231, letter dated November 24, 1861, from Meade to his wife; 237, letter dated December 21, 1861, from Meade to his wife.

15 W. T. Sherman MSS (L.C.) letter dated May 21, 1861, from W. T. Sherman to his brother; Heintzelman MS Diary (L.C.) (large diary) May, 1861; Mark de Wolfe Howe, ed., *Home Letters of General Sherman* (New York, 1909), 211, letter dated August 3, 1861, from Sherman (Howe, *Home Letters of General Sherman*); Elliott, *Scott*, 719.

16 *Annual Report of the Adjutant General to the Legislature of Minnesota, 1861* (Boston 1861), 4 ff (*Adj't Gen'l Rpt Minn*).

17 *Annual Report of the Adjutant General of the Commonwealth of Massachusetts, 1861* (Boston, 1861), 4 ff (*Adj't Gen'l Rpt Mass.*); George H. Gordon, *Brook Farm to Cedar Mountain* (Boston, 1883), 2 (Gordon, *Brook Farm*).

In the state of Minnesota, General Order No. 2, October 1, 1858, gave the citizens the right to organize, drill, and equip themselves at their own expense. Its militia had the worst organization of any state. When the guns ceased firing in Charleston Harbor, the muster rolls showed two hundred privates and one hundred forty-seven officers. A hasty legislative act enabled the state to accept the many new men who sprang forward at the call for troops.

These two states represented the extremes of preparedness.[18] Each other state lay somewhere in between. In the early months of 1861, a few far-sighted members of Pennsylvania's militia had created well-disciplined and well-equipped units like the Ringgold Light Artillery, which was ready to march on April 16. The majority of its forces, however, were under-strength and not well-organized when Lincoln called for seventy-five thousand men.[19] These militias, ready, inactive, or defunct, provided a framework of officers and men, particularly officers, for immediate mobilization.

In the militia the company, not the regiment, was the basic organizational unit. In 1861 it continued that role as the basic unit for recruiting. The fever which pervaded the North after Sumter prompted huge numbers to enlist. In a few days the seventy-five thousand man quota had been oversubscribed. Many sought military service in vain. Some went to other states or bought places in the "better" companies. Service as a private sold for as much as fifty dollars.[20]

In states lacking the militia officers to fill their quotas, the governors authorized capable, trustworthy, influential citizens to raise infantry companies. The man who recruited the company was generally elected or appointed as its commanding officer. The company officers then elected the field grade officers and the regimental

18 Rivaling Minnesota was the State of Maine, where only 1,200 men of 60,000 on the muster rolls answered the call for troops. Whitman, William E. S., and True, Charles H., *Maine in the War for the Union* (Lewiston, 1865), 3 (Whitman, *Maine in the War*).

19 The act that rejuvenated the Pennsylvania system was entitled "An Act for the Better Organization of the Militia of this Commonwealth" and was passed on April 12, the first day of the war. *Pennsylvania Archives: Papers of the Governors*, 9 Series (Harrisburg, 1902), 8, 420; Samuel P. Bates, *History of the Pennsylvania Volunteers 1861-1865* originally published as 5 vols. (Harrisburg, 1869, 1871), 1, 4 and fn. 4 (Bates, *Penn. Vols.*), the Broadfoot reprint, which is used here is in ten volumes with a four volume index published in 1994; Edward G. Everett, "Pennsylvania Raises an Army, 1861," *Western Pennsylvania Historical Magazine* (Summer, 1956) (Everett, "Pennsylvania Raises an Army").

20 John A. Dahlgren MSS (L.C.) letter dated Apr. 23, 1861, from "Charlie" to John A. Dahlgren; Walter F. Clowes, *The Detroit Light Guard* (Detroit, 1900), 34 (Clowes, *Detroit Light Guard*); John Robertson, *Michigan in the War* (Lansing, 1882), 23 (Robertson, *Michigan in the War*); Adj't Gn'l Rpt Mass 6; *Annual Report of the Adjutant General of the State of New Jersey for the Year 1861* (Trenton, 1861), 3ff (*Adj't Gen'l Rpt NJ*); *Annual Report for the Adjutant General of the State of Connecticut for the Year 1861* (Hartford 1861), 5ff (*Adj't Gen'l Rpt Conn*).

commander.[21] In almost all cases, an effort was made to select qualified men to be officers, both by the governors in granting authorizations and by the company commanders in selecting their colonels.[22] Many men of prominence and influence refused to accept high commissions because they did not feel qualified, while others started in lower positions to rise if they could.[23] Bypassing the states, the federal government briefly offered yet another way to enter the service. The new method began as Daniel E. Sickles's imaginative solution to his own problem.

College graduate, printer, lawyer, member of the New York State legislature, diplomat in the London mission, corporation counsel to the City of New York, state senator, and a member of the United States House of Representatives. Daniel Edgar Sickles had been all these things before 1861 and had done them well.[24] With many talents he had been blessed in abundance. Tall, blond, pleasant, and ingratiating in the manner befitting a skilled politician, his sharp, quick eyes capped a military mustache and goatee. Though his face bore a slightly distraught look, he had a martial appearance. His quick perception, energetic will, prompt and supple intelligence, and active temperament made the jump to rank in a wartime military plausible. He was often able to make a good impression on men predisposed against him. A vigorous enemy and a good friend, he would become at once indifferent to a friend who deserted him or an enemy who ceased to oppose him.[25]

21 Then, as now, company grade ranks were second lieutenant, first lieutenant, and captain; field grade ranks were major, lieutenant-colonel, and colonel. Ordinarily, a company was commanded by a captain and a regiment by a colonel.

22 Howard, *Autobiography*, 1, 110ff; Martin H. Haynes, *A History of the Second New Hampshire Volunteer Infantry in the War of the Rebellion* (Lakeport, 1896), 8 (Haynes, *Second New Hampshire*); Robertson, *Michigan in the War*, 23-24; *Adj't Gen'l Rpt Mass*, 24, 25; *Adj't Gen'l Rpt Minn*, 352; *Adj't Gen'l Rpt NY*, 6, 7. According to Johnston, *Bull Run*, 103, recruiting was like ward politics (*loc. cit.*, 5); the colonels were bad; and their field officers worse. This was primarily because they were elected. The facts are to the contrary. In most states "elected" officers had been previously selected by the governor. Were the officers, especially the company grade officers, inexperienced? Absolutely, they were. In general, were they the best choices under the circumstances? Yes, they were. And the officers and men who served in the "Three Months Campaign" under McDowell and Patterson would be the cradle of command for the Army of the Potomac in later years.

23 Ernest A McKay., *The Civil War and New York City* (Syracuse 1990), generally chap. 2, esp. 33-37 (McKay, *Civil War and NYC*).

24 *D.A.B.*, 9, pt. 1, 150; generally, Swanberg, W. A., *Sickles the Incredible* (New York, 1956) (Swanberg, *Sickles*); Edgcumb Pinchon, *Dan Sickles, Yankee King of Spain* (New York, 1946), 15-73 (Pinchon, *Sickles*); de Trobriand, *Four Years*, 426.

25 Comte de Paris MS diary (large diary) (A.N. de la M. de F.) entry dated December 7, 1861; Frank L. Bryne and Andrew T. Weaver, eds., *Haskell of Gettysburg: His Life and Civil War Papers* (Madison, 1970), 117 (Bryne, *Haskell Letters*); Rusling, *Men and Things*, 281, letter dated October 16, 1862, from Rusling to his father; Jesse Bowman Young, *What a Boy Saw* (New York, 1894), 215 (Young, *A Boy Saw*).

Like many other Democrats and residents of New York City in early 1861 he felt conciliatory[26] toward the South, but the overt act of rebellion drove him to choose country over party. "I sincerely hope the administration will press on in the uniform measures adopted to punish the insults to our flag and to destroy the power of those who have declared themselves our enemies," he wrote to Secretary of War Cameron. "Be assured of the loyal and hearty support of the masses in this City. You know very well that I have from boyhood mingled with the multitude here and if anybody knows them, I do. You can have thousands of the best troops raised in this city—intelligent, hearty brave men—who have always voted with the South, as I have done, but who now consider the Confederate States, a *foreign power*."[27] In favor of military action against the South and disgusted with his party, he believed himself dutybound to carry the war to a complete military victory for the federal government.[28]

Shortly before the outbreak of war, Sickles's young and beautiful wife had a torrid affair with United States attorney Barton Key, the son of Francis Scott Key, who had written the "Star Spangled Banner." When Sickles learned about it, he confronted his distraught young wife and extracted a written confession from her, then took a loaded pistol, found Key on the street, and killed him in cold blood. Relying on the defense of temporary insanity, he became the first man to use it and be acquitted. In a peculiar social twist, killing an unarmed man did not compromise his standing as much as his prompt willingness to take his unfaithful wife back to his bed.[29]

Stuck in the practice of law and outside the mainstream, Sickles was disconsolate. After the smoke over Fort Sumter had cleared, he went to the famous Delmonico's at Broadway and Chambers Street with his friend William Wiley. Several of their acquaintances were at the bar, the war their topic of conversation. Someone suggested that Wiley raise a regiment to assist in the defense of Washington.

"If he will," said Sickles with jocular disbelief, "I'll go as a private."

Wiley, who had embraced Sickles when he was acquitted, knew Sickles's abilities as an organizer, administrator, and thinker. Sickles would, he decided, be a good leader.

26 McKay, *Civil War and NYC*, generally chap. 2, esp. 33-37 (McKay, *Civil War and NYC*).

27 Cameron MSS (L.C.) letter dated April 17, 1861, from Sickles to Cameron.

28 de Trobriand, *Four Years*, 426-427.

29 Swanberg, *Sickles*, 40-76, especially 71-76; Pinchon, *Sickles*, 97-137.

"If you will command a regiment," he responded to Sickles, "I will raise, arm, and equip it."[30]

Sickles did not ignore this offer. In a short while he was busily recruiting not one but several regiments. Because New York had already filled its quota of regiments, Governor Morgan told him he must disband most of his companies. He was infuriated.

He headed for Washington. He had an idea for the president, an idea that could solve his problem. Lincoln received him with more than the usual kindness because Sickles's constituency, the staunchly Democratic, Irish-Catholic Tammany Hall of New York City, had abandoned its sympathies for the South when sectionalism turned to war. It announced its support for the federal government, recruited the Forty-Second New York from its members, and engineered the unanimous passage of resolutions of loyal support by the New York Common Council of the Board of Aldermen on April 19, 1861. Sickles had drafted the resolutions. Lincoln received this good news on the day the plug-uglies fired on the Sixth Massachusetts in Baltimore.

"We invoke in this crisis the unselfish patriotism and the unfaltering loyalty which have been uniformly manifested in all periods of national peril by the population of the City of New York," the resolutions said; "and while we reiterate our undiminished affection for the friends of Union in the Southern States for the preservation of peace, . . . we only give expression to the convictions of our constituents when we declare it to be our unalterable purpose, as it is their solemn duty . . . to crush the power of those who are enemies in war, as in peace they were friends."

Surrounded by factional bickering even among his supporters, Lincoln was grateful.[31]

"Sickles, I have here on my table the resolutions passed by your Common Council appropriating a million of dollars toward raising men for this war and promising to do all in the power of your authorities to support the Government. When these resolutions were brought to me by Alderman Frank Boole and his associates of the Committee, I felt my burden lighter. I felt that, when men break through party lines and take this patriotic stand for the Government and the Union,

30 Swanberg, *Sickles*, 115, quoting from the *New York World*, June 30, 1869.

31 Sickles, Daniel E., "Speech to Lincoln Fellowship," February 12, 1910; McKay, *The Civil War and NYC*, 38-40, 76-77; New York Monuments Commission for the Battlefields of Gettysburg and Chattanooga, *Final Report on the Battlefield of Gettysburg*, 3 vols. (Albany 1900) speech by Sickles, 1, 314 (Commission, *Report on Gettysburg*).

all must come out well in the end. When you see them, tell them for me they made my heart glad, and I can only say, 'God bless them.'"

Certainly Sickles was a man whose loyalty was not in doubt.[32] He turned indirectly to his problem with the governor of New York and the quota. He did not suggest that the time honored militia-volunteer system be dismantled, just that it be supplemented by a federal system of volunteers. His proposal was, in part, a common sense suggestion and, in part, a lawyer's appellate argument.

The government should establish one or more large camps as reserve depots for the entire federal army. In them the men would be trained for their branch, infantry, artillery, or cavalry, and sent to a unit in the field when they were ready. He also suggested that surplus recruits be made into regiments of United States Volunteers, in effect bypassing the state recruiting systems altogether. The War Department would have exclusive direction and command of these regiments from the beginning.

"The power to raise armies granted to Congress by the Constitution," he said, "conferred upon the federal government ample discretion to choose whatever manner and form of organizing the land and naval forces might be deemed most serviceable."

The president listened carefully, then rose to pace up and down the room.

"Sickles," he said, "I want your men, and I want you to command them. But we have no arms or equipments, and but little money to buy them if they could be found." He paused. "How long can you keep your men together?"

"I have my men quartered in private homes in the City and suburbs," Sickles answered promptly, "but if I am formally authorized by the government to organize my brigade as United States Volunteers, I personally and from my own resources will undertake their subsistence and equipment and hold the force subject to Your Excellency's orders."

The president's face brightened. Yet he seemed hesitant. "I like the idea of United States Volunteers, but do you see where it leads to? What will the governors say if I raise regiments without their having a hand in it? Let's hear what the secretary of war has to say about it."

He reached for the page bell and asked for the secretary of war. Promptly, Cameron appeared. When he heard the plan, Cameron not only approved it but also suggested that one of the reserve camps be placed at Harrisburg in his home state. He went to a large map on the wall and began to identify locations for other reserve camps.

32 de Trobriand, *Four Years*, 426-427.

"We shall need all the men we can get," continued Cameron, "and now is the time to enlist them. By all means let us have three or four of these camps for our own recruits. From Staten Island, to begin with, they can be sent anywhere by sea, or from Harrisburg by rail, and there are several other points equally advantageous."

"The subject of the various camps we will consider at a cabinet meeting," said Lincoln giving instant substance to the idea. "But meanwhile, Cameron, I'm going to ask you to give Sickles authority to raise five regiments as United States Volunteers, and we will see how this beginning ends."[33]

Sickles left to set gladly about his new work. Having trouble with quarters for his troops while he was collecting them,[34] he wrote to the Union Defense Committee of the Citizens of New York to request funds for the last tasks necessary to complete his brigade. "My Brigade (five thousand strong) has been accepted by the President of the United States to serve for the War. I am enjoined by the secretary of war to lose no time in preparing this force to take the field."[35]

Cameron issued a number of other authorizations for the direct recruitment of volunteer regiments. The men who raised these regiments could recruit in any state, then report directly to the federal government to be armed, equipped, and mustered into service. They followed in Sickles's footsteps.

From Massachusetts, Wilder Dwight, a Harvard graduate about to become the major of George H. Gordon's Second Massachusetts, traveled to Washington, visited the secretary of war, and obtained a letter authorizing the creation of a regiment under federal authority.[36] Several other regiments followed, including the Seventy-first Pennsylvania, to be known as the California Battalion for its commander Senator Edward D. Baker.[37]

Sickles was commissioned a colonel. After his regiments and a few others were mustered into the federal service, the program died. The governors, no doubt for a

33 Sickles, "Speech to Lincoln Fellowship," February 12, 1910 (pam).

34 Swanberg, *Sickles*, 118-119.

35 Union Defense Committee MSS (N.Y.H.S.) letter dated May 15, 1861, from Sickles to Richards.

36 Dwight, *Dwight Letters*, 62-63, letter of April 28, 1861, from Cameron to Wilder Dwight and George L. Andrews; Gordon, *Brook Farm to Cedar Mountain*, 7-9, letters dated April 25, 1861, and April, 1861 from Dwight to Gordon; Cameron received many inquiries from correspondents supporting candidates for appointment in the military, e.g., letter dated April 16, 1861, from George Erety to Cameron; letter dated April 16, 1861, from J. W. Goff to Cameron; letter from W. J. Howard to Cameron [dated April 16, 1861]; letter dated April 16, 1861, from George Lear to Cameron; letter dated April 20, 1861, from R. H. Austin to Cameron; letter dated April 21, 1861, from Reverend R. A. Kellen to Lincoln; letter dated April 22, 1861, from H. Diebitsch to Cameron.

37 Wistar, *Autobiography*, 355-357; Bates, *History of Pennsylvania Volunteers*, 4, 788.

multiplicity of reasons ranging from selfishness to zeal, opposed this program when they learned of it. So vociferous was their opposition that centralized Federal control of selection, training, and replacement of company and field grade officers fell as it left the starting blocks.[38]

38 Pinchon, *Sickles*, 157.

Chapter 6

"I have the honor to tender the resignation of my commission as Colonel of the 1st Regt. of Cavalry."

— Robert E. Lee to Scott

Persevering and Quitting

In the confusion of the early months of the war, with Washington's communications with the North severed, regiments ready to go to the aid of the capital could not always find ready acceptance. As always, knowing the right person helped. Daniel Butterfield, colonel of the Twelfth New York Militia, stood ready and so did his regiment. But they could not just appear unannounced in the capital. He went to Washington where he found himself wandering aimlessly in the outer rooms of Assistant Secretary of State Frederick Seward, his classmate at Union College in upstate New York. They had not seen each other for more than ten years, Butterfield having worked in the family stagecoach business that was to become the American Express Company.[1]

Seward's room was filled with visitors of all kinds, officials on business, members of Congress with protégés seeking office, reporters, loungers, and rumor

1 Seward, *Reminiscences*, 161-162; vol. 2, *D.A.B.* pt. 1 372-374; Warner, *Generals in Blue*, 62; Julia L. Butterfield, *A Biographical Memorial of General Daniel Butterfield Including Many Addresses and Military Writings* (New York, 1904), 10-11 (Butterfield, *Butterfield*).

mongers. In the crowd of faces, Seward noticed his old college friend. He took him by the hand.

"Why, Dan, where did you come from? And what are you doing here?"

"I am going back home, tired and disappointed," replied Butterfield despondently. "I thought I might be of some service, but I find I am not wanted. I have been all day at the War Department and can't get a hearing. The halls and rooms are crowded. The door keepers say they are not allowed to take any more names or cards to the secretary of war. The officials are all too busy to listen or if they listen, have no power to act."

"What was it you wanted at the War Department?" asked Seward.

"Only permission to bring my regiment on here to defend the capitol. I supposed troops were wanted."

"So they are, and urgently and immediately. There must be some misapprehension. Come with me, and I will go back with you and get you an audience with Secretary Cameron."

They hastened to the War Department where they found a state of chaos, just as Butterfield had described it. Known to the messengers and door keepers, Seward gained immediate access to the secretary. Cameron was sitting at his desk surrounded by an eager crowd, the foremost of whom seemed to be haranguing him about something they wanted to sell to the government.

"Mr. Secretary," said Seward, "here is my friend Colonel Butterfield, who has something to say to you that I think you will be glad to hear."

"What is it, Mr. Seward?"

"He has a regiment to offer to the government."

"Why, Colonel, that is just what we want. What is your regiment?"

"The Twelfth New York State Militia, sir, of which I am commander."

"But are they armed or equipped or clothed?"

"Yes, sir, and tolerably well drilled. We foresaw some time ago that there might be trouble, and so we got in readiness to respond to any call."

"And how soon could you get them here?"

"Within twenty-four hours after receiving orders to start."

"But how can you get through? You know communications with New York are cut off."

"We will march through Baltimore, sir. Or we can come round by sea and up Chesapeake Bay and the Potomac. I have made a provisional arrangement with the steamer *Coatzacoalco*, which is all ready to bring us on."

"Are you sure, Colonel, that the government can rely on these statements of yours?"

"I believe the secretary of state will vouch for me, sir."

Cameron looked much relieved. "Well, Colonel, your regiment will be very welcome. You shall have orders at once."

Butterfield departed hurriedly. Soon after, the Twelfth New York marched up Pennsylvania Avenue to ovations and cheers, the waving of flags, hats, and handkerchief, that all early arrivers received. Assigned Franklin Square for a campground, its companies were well-drilled in parade and tactical exercises and drew throngs of visitors. Butterfield's prompt performance and soldierly bearing made him a favorite at the War Department.[2]

The regiment had been in Washington only a few days when Butterfield became very well-known and well-received at the White House, particularly by Mrs. Lincoln. At some point, she told Butterfield that the White House cook was in trouble because the waterback of the range was out of order. She asked if he did not have in his regiment some "soldier plumbers" who could fix it.

Without really knowing the answer, Butterfield said he certainly had plumbers in his unit. When he returned to his camp, he promptly requisitioned plumbers to go to the White House.

The adjutant, who knew little and cared less about the problem, announced it to the engineer company: "Wanted: Plumbers for the White House, by order of Col. Butterfield."

None of the company were plumbers. One of them volunteered the opinion that plumbers might be found in other companies. He was detailed to find them and located four. He went along to supervise their work. With his four fully armed infantrymen, he marched into the White House kitchen, surrounded by an admiring group of black servants. The men stacked arms. In a few minutes they had yanked out the range, set it in the middle of the kitchen, then begun wrestling with its waterback.

While they were working, Lincoln entered the kitchen. Half sitting, half leaning on the kitchen table and holding one knee in his hands as he had in his meeting with Keyes and Meigs, Lincoln said, "Well, boys, I am certainly glad to see you. I hope you can fix that thing right off, for if you can't, the cook can't use the range, and I don't suppose I'll get any grub today!"[3]

When the seventy-five thousand man quota was filled, the federal government refused to accept more regiments. The states with surplus regiments had to do something with them. New York, for example, was given a quota of seventeen regiments totaling some thirteen thousand men; but a few days of recruiting

2 Seward, *Reminiscences*, 161-162.

3 James A. Scrymser, *Personal Reminiscences of James A. Scrymser in Times of Peace and War* (n.p. 1915), 17-18 (Scrymser, *Reminiscences*).

produced thirty-eight fully subscribed and eager regiments. The state could keep the excess regiments at its own expense while their fate was uncertain, disband them, or remand them to private support. In most circumstances a regiment could find some person or town willing to house and feed it until it was finally called to active service. Always showing an attitude of superiority, New York sent a special representative to Washington to discuss the problem. "With some difficulty" he induced the federal government to accept all extra regiments.

Andrew G. Curtin, governor of Pennsylvania, gradually accepted all the units recruited within his state's borders because he was certain all of them would be needed in the future. A loan was subscribed throughout the state to support them; and with the encouragement Curtin extended personally, recruiting quickly created a large force.[4]

Very quickly, everyone knew the war would last more than the three months for which the militia regiments had been called. As April gave way to May, Scott persuaded Lincoln to summon troops for three years and to expand the Regular Army. The presidential proclamation issued on May 3 called for 42,034 volunteers to serve for three years or the duration of the war should it be shorter and 22,714 more troops for the Regular Army.

The president called a special session of Congress, which met the fourth of July. Congress responded by authorizing five hundred thousand troops to serve three years.[5] This longer term of service did not diminish the enthusiasm for enlisting, and it created a federal home for the excess regiments. Some of the three-month regiments polled their men to identify and replace those who could not or would not serve for three years.[6]

As American manpower filled the numerous regiments, a few of Lincoln's advisers expressed the view that the Southern forces would not fight well or hard and disparaged the infant Southern military. They and the many others who shared their view would have done well to heed the advice of their president when he was preparing the call for seventy-five thousand men.

4 Everett, "Pennsylvania Raises an Army," 97; Samuel Bates, *Martial Deeds of Pennsylvania* (Philadelphia, 1875), 953-954 (Bates, *Martial Deeds*); *Pennsylvania Archives: Papers of the Governors*, ser. 4, vol. VIII, 337. Everett, in *Pennsylvania Raises an Army* says Curtin was reluctant to do this, 97. Curtin's speech in *Pennsylvania Archives: Papers of the Governors*, series 4, vol. VIII, 375 ff, and his correspondence with Patterson belie this.

5 Swinton, *Campaigns of the Army of the Potomac*, 28; Shannon, *Organization and Administration*, 46; *N&H*, 4, 254-255, 370-371.

6 Haynes, *Second New Hampshire*, 3; *Adj't Gen'l Rpt. Minn*, 83; Whitman, *Maine in the War*, 4.

"We must not forget that the people of the seceded states, like those of the loyal ones," said Lincoln, "are American citizens with essentially the same characteristics and powers. Exceptional advantages on one side are counterbalanced by exceptional advantages on the other. We must make up our minds that man for man the soldier from the South will be a match for the soldier from the North and *vice versa*."[7]

Meanwhile, the organization of commands larger than regiments ran haywire. For their militia regiments in state service, the governors had the power to appoint general officers to command brigades and divisions.[8] If each governor could appoint generals to command brigades and divisions of his troops bound for the federal service, the federal government would be left to appoint officers for the regular units, for volunteer units with regiments from more than one state, and for corps, and armies.[9]

This system would be intolerable. It would promote the kind of interstate rivalry that would impair morale, discipline, and recruiting. And it would not necessarily provide the most qualified generals, who should be selected for their competence without reference to their state of origin. A unified war effort was impossible without centralized control of the creation of higher command. In fact, the war effort would have been better served by federal selection of all officers, uniform training, and uniform standards for promotion; but this idea, a germ in Sickles' proposal, was in no man's mind and was far away in time.

If brigade and division commanders were responsible to their states, the army would have, in theoretical, if not practical, effect, many secretaries of war. Officers would be responsible to the general in command of their army, a federal officer, and so to Lincoln's government; but they would also be answerable to their state governments. One of the first and most important principles of command was

7 *N&H*, 4, 79.

8 Under ordinary circumstances, brigades were led by brigadier-generals, and divisions by major-generals. All larger units, corps, armies, departments, etc., were commanded by the senior officer present absent special intervention by the president. Most often these commands were assigned to major-generals. The only lieutenant-general in American history had been George Washington, Scott being only a brevet lieutenant-general. Like so many other things, this would change during the Civil War.

9 This problem was not a new one. As early as the American Revolution the governors of the states had insisted on the right to appoint general officers in proportion to the troops they raised. Richard K. Showman, ed., *The Papers of General Nathaniel Greene*, 3 vols. (Chapel Hill, 1980), vol. 3, 40, letter dated March 9, 1777, from John Adams to Greene (Showman, *Greene Papers*); Edmund C. Burnett, ed., *Letters of Members of the Continental Congress*, 7 vols. (Washington, 1923), vol. 2, 288, letter dated March 4, 1777, from Roger Sherman to Jonathan Trumbull, Governor of Connecticut; Thomas Burke, *Obstruct of Debates of the New York Provisional Congress*, February 12 to 19, 1777.

centralization, which had to exist at least at the higher headquarters. In the existing system, such a principle was impossible to implement.

To clarify the roles in this situation, General Orders No. 12 were issued on May 22 by the Office of the Adjutant General in Washington. The organization of a regiment was standardized from the number of officers and men to the pay per man. The governors of the states were authorized, indeed, ordered, to appoint all regimental officers from lieutenant to colonel; and the non-commissioned officers of each company were to be appointed by the colonel on the recommendation of the captain commanding the company. All brigade and division officers, whether staff or line,[10] would be "appointed by the president, by and with the consent of the Senate."

Governor Edwin D. Morgan of New York was incensed at this order. The secretary of war had promised him he could create New York divisions intended to be led by John A. Dix and James S. Wadsworth. The new orders took away the power to create brigades and divisions and to appoint their commanding officers. He decided to resist. The federal government held the reins tightly. Cameron coolly notified Morgan that, if he refused to honor the decree, no more New York troops would be accepted. Morgan could do nothing but capitulate.[11]

State interference, perhaps variation would be more fair, was further reduced by requiring that "the volunteers will be subject to the laws and regulations governing the army of the United States."[12] A unified, standardized, and centralized higher command system had been created, thus removing the major kinks after little more than a month. From this point, regimental officers would be appointed by the organizing authority, the governor of the state for a volunteer regiment and the federal government for a Regular Army regiment. Superior officers, in both rank and assignment, would be appointed by the federal government, specifically by the president "with the consent of the Senate." But problems had been created before the May standardization, and they lingered.

Meanwhile regiments poured into the important cities in droves, and the armies which would enforce union against secession began to take form. The basic unit of the state militias had been the company, many of which had their own names, uniforms, weapons, and social status. Before the war they had seldom held regimental camps or drills. As a result, regimental evolutions and duties were almost unknown. The basic recruiting organization for a unit that was not a militia

10 The exceptions were the personal aides of the general, who were appointed by him.

11 Pearson, *Wadsworth*, 63-64.

12 The complete text of General Orders No. 12, appears in *Adj't Gen'l Rpt Mass*, 25 ff.

organization was also the company. As a carryover from the militias and because almost any town or region could produce a company of one hundred men when it could not always recruit the eight hundred to one thousand men necessary for a regiment, the company continued to be the basic unit for recruiting. Governors rarely gave permission to recruit a regiment in the early months of the war. After the necessary companies had been banded together, the company officers would choose a regimental commander, usually a man with military experience. At first the companies varied in size from fifty to two hundred; but the General Order of May 22, which standardized all incoming organizations, denied mustering to any company that had less than ten or more than one hundred men.

Because all units had raw recruits, some being completely composed of them, basic fundamentals had to be taught. The most cohesive and easily manageable number of men, but most of all, the most traditional unit, the company, fell heir to this task when it was independent and from inertia, if nothing else, continued to have it after it had been regimented.

The governors of most states tacitly recognized the company's semi-independence by allowing them to choose their fellow companies for a regiment. Companies would refuse to accept membership in a regiment because its other companies did not come from their part of the state, because the attitude of the other units was deemed to be offensive, or because they had some other petty grievance.[13] Ethnic enlisting by Irish, Scotts, Germans, French, and Italians took place; and these companies sought regimentation with companies of their own nationality.[14]

The importance of the company foundation became more evident as the time for battle drew near. The officers were still trying to establish regimental cohesion, leaving little or no time for brigade or division exercises. Accustomed to direction at the company level, if at all, the men had to refocus. While their command and maneuver relationships were being reoriented, they were trying to learn the art of soldiering from boiling coffee and eating hardtack to marching with packs and firing

13 John D. Hicks, "The Organization of the Volunteer Army in 1861, With Special Reference to Minnesota," *Minnesota Historical Bulletin*, no. 5, Feb. 1918, 324-368 (Hicks, *Org. Vol. Army Minn.*); Howard, *Autobiography*, 1, 106-107; *Adj't Gen'l Rpt Mass*, 24-25; Curtis, *Bull Run to Chancellorsville*, 18 ff; Abner Small, *Road to Richmond* (California, 1939), 8-9 (Small, *Road to Richmond*); R. I. Holcombe, *History of the First Regiment Minnesota Volunteer Infantry* (Stillwater, 1916), 6 (Holcombe, *First Minnesota*); Bates, *Penn. Vols*, vol. 1, 3, 4, 5, 13-200.

14 Paris, *History of the Civil War*, 1, 177-79; T. Harry Williams, *Lincoln and his Generals* (New York, 1952), 11; Ella Lonn, *Foreigners in the Union Army and Navy* (Baton Rouge, 1951), chaps 5 and 6 (Lonn, *Foreigners*).

their rifles. Their progress left much to be desired when they set out for the enemy for the first time.

Many company officers had originally been in the militia, and some had served in Mexico. Men who recruited independent new companies and who subsequently became their commanders were not primarily political appointees, grafters, and unworthy friends of the governors. In the early months of the war they were the most qualified men who could be identified under the circumstances. They were chosen because they were responsible leading citizens, because they had prior military experience, or because they were social, economic, business, or political leaders who could be expected to lead a democratic "ploughshares into swords" military force. The governors generally tried to be as rational in their choices as they could.[15] The quality of leadership at the company level was, as a result, the best that could be attained without a pre-existing, centralized, standardized, uniform system. Before the acid test of battle no one could tell who would provide good leadership and who would fail; but using criteria which appeared to be reasonable, the people who chose the company and regimental officers, from selecting governor to electing militia, must be credited with a considerable amount of success. Many men who entered the stage as lieutenants and captains when the war began exited at the head of regiments, brigades, divisions, and even corps in 1865.

While all this happened at the small unit level in the states, the federal government attempted to identify officers who could command larger units in the new armies and devise a plan for the war. As Scott saw it, his problem was selection of an officer to lead an army so large and well-equipped that it would, he hoped, intimidate the seceders into a peaceful reunion with the federal states. Even now, he would do almost anything to avoid destructive military contact.

Scott particularly favored one officer, who had served with distinction on his staff in Mexico and who had in 1860 declined the position as his military secretary.[16] After Sumter surrendered, Scott asked Townsend if he had seen or heard of this

15 According to family members of an officer who served with Dwight D. Eisenhower while he was assembling his staff and commanders for the invasion of North Africa, Eisenhower acknowledged that many worthy officers were available but concluded that, with little time, he had no choice but to select men he knew personally and believed to be reliable and competent. For the importance of personal and professional relationships in the selection of officers for higher command, especially independent command, in World War II, see Arthur Bryant's two volumes of diaries and autobiographical notes by Field Marshall Alan Brooke, especially volume one *Triumph in the West: A History of the War Years Based on the Diaries of Field Marshall Lord Alanbrooke, Chief of the Imperial General Staff* (New York, 1959) (Bryant, *Triumph in the West*).

16 Keyes, *Fifty Years*, 205-207; Douglas Southall Freeman, *R.E. Lee. A Biography*, 4 vols. (New York, 1934), 1, 431-433 (Freeman, *Lee*).

officer. Townsend had not but knew that the officer was on leave and across the Potomac at the family home of his wife.

Scott said, "It is time he should show his hand and, if he remains loyal, should take an important command."

Townsend suggested that Scott write and ask him to come to the general's headquarters.

Scott replied, "I wish he would."

They wrote a note on April 18, four days after Sumter surrendered, and sent it across the river.[17] The problem of command had been recognized by others, particularly men in the cabinet. Scott had already worked at considerable length with Seward and had given him several written policy suggestions. Frequently, Seward would drive his carriage through the new troops and end his day with a call on the general in chief.

During a visit a short time after Scott's note had been sent across the river,[18] Seward remarked, "We are gathering a large army. What I do not yet foresee is how it is to be led? What are we to do for generals?"

"That is a subject, Mr. Secretary, that I have thought much about. If I could only mount a horse, I . . ."

The old general checked himself. He shook his head. Then he added mournfully, ". . . but I am past that. I can only serve my country as I am doing here now in my chair."

Seward was a shrewd observer of human affairs. He understood the indispensable role Scott could play for his country from the chair.

"Even if you had your youth and strength again, General, it might not be worth as much to us as your experience. In any case, you would need commanders with military training to carry out your orders."

"There are few who have had command in the field even of a brigade," said Scott. "But there is excellent material in the army to make generals of. There are good officers. Unfortunately for us, the South has taken most of those holding the higher grades. We have captains and lieutenants that, with time and experience, will develop and will do good service."

He began to name superior, promising West Point graduates, including George B. McClellan, William B. Franklin, Winfield S. Hancock, Joseph Hooker, Joseph K. F. Mansfield, W. Tecumseh Sherman, Edwin V. Sumner, and Henry W. Halleck.

17 Townsend, *Anecdotes*, 29-30.

18 This chronology does not appear in the original sources. It is reconstructed in Freeman, *Lee*, 1, 431-43, with the usual careful caveat, e.g., 432, fn. 2.

"There is one officer who would make an excellent general, but I do not know whether we can rely on him. He lives not far away, and I have sent over to see. I had expected to hear from him today. If he comes in tomorrow, I shall know."

"I will not ask his name until you hear from him, then, general," responded Seward, "for I think I guess whom you mean."[19]

In response to Scott's letter, the officer arrived the next day at Scott's new headquarters in the capital. Prior to reaching Scott's offices, he had visited Francis P. Blair, Sr., the father of Postmaster General Montgomery Blair, who was an old Missouri friend. The elder Blair offered him command of the entire Union army.

He responded, "If the union is dissolved and the government disrupted, I shall return to my native state and share the miseries of my people and, save in defense, draw my sword on no one."

Although he was opposed to succession and deprecated war, he added, he could take no part in an invasion of the Southern states, a statement he had made, in substance, repeatedly in the preceding months.[20]

Scott and his old subordinate usually agreed on important issues. Here, they must have disagreed about the state of affairs. Scott did not believe his choice to lead the Union army would be forced to fight against Virginia; but with him at the head of a force sufficiently powerful, perhaps no battles would ever occur. Both had been born in Virginia,[21] both loved the Union, both found the prospect of war abhorrent, and neither could bear the thought of drawing his sword against his home state. The old general hoped against hope that war could be avoided. His subordinate considered it inevitable.

When the officer entered Scott's office, Adjutant-General Townsend was at his desk in the corner; and the aides were in an adjoining room with the door closed. Townsend rose to see if Scott signaled that he wished to be alone. Scott quietly motioned him to keep his seat, and he sat down. The officer did not seem to notice that Townsend had risen or that Scott had signaled him to remain.

Scott invited the officer to be seated and began the conversation, saying, "You are at present on leave of absence?"

"Yes, general, I am staying with my family at Arlington." The subordinate described his conversation with Frank Blair.

19 Seward, *Reminiscences*, 167-168.

20 Freeman, *Lee*, 1, 405 ff, App. 1-1, 633-636, 436-437.

21 Keyes, *Fifty Years*, 206.

"These are times when every officer in the United States service," said Scott, "should fully determine what course he will pursue and frankly declare it. No-one should continue in government employ without being actively engaged."

Scott paused. He received no response.

"Some of the Southern officers," he continued, "are resigning, possibly with the intention of taking part with their states. They make a fatal mistake. The contest may be long and severe, but eventually the issue will be in favor of the Union."

He paused again. Still his old friend said nothing. Seeing that his visitor had no apparent disposition to respond one way or the other, Scott continued.

"I suppose you will go with the rest. If you propose to resign, it is proper you should do so at once. Your present attitude is an equivocal one."

Finally, the officer spoke. "The property belonging to my children, all they possess, lies in Virginia. They will be ruined if they do not go with their state. I cannot raise my hand against my children."[22]

Addressing his old companion in arms by name, Scott said, "You have made the greatest mistake of your life; but I feared it would be so."[23] Scott was grievously pained.[24] He had an almost idolatrous fancy for his friend and believed his military abilities to be far above those of any other officer in the army.

The following day Scott received by special messenger two letters, one official and one personal.[25] The official letter, addressed to the secretary of war, read as follows:

22 At this point, according to Townsend, the interview ended. *Anecdotes*, 31-32. Freeman in *Lee*, 1, 437, n. 28, rejects Townsend's account for a number of reasons, all of which are carefully delineated on 437-38, fn. 28. The reasons are inferential and were not taken from a direct, primary source. The author does not readily disagree with or contradict Freeman, who is the idol as a Civil War historian of every thinking man including the author. But Freeman's objectivity and his analysis were, no doubt, strained by this incident, the most problematic in Lee's career. Freeman's problem was much like the difficulty Winston Churchill faced when he dealt with the defection by his kinsman, John Churchill, and the Camaret Bay letter in which the young John Churchill supposedly betrayed the expedition against Brest. The similarities are striking. Both men were accused of betraying their country. Both writers finished their defense with a long paragraph composed of numbered points. Winston S. Churchill, *Marlborough: His Life and Times*, 4 vols. in 2 (London, 1966), 18-19 and chaps. 25 and 26, 368-394, especially 393-394. Freeman's arguments are outweighed by the fact that almost the very words quoted by Townsend were written by Lee in a letter to his sister two days later: "I have not been able to make up my mind to raise my hand against my relatives, my children, my home," Clifford Dowdy, *The Wartime Papers of R. E. Lee* (Boston, 1961), 9-10, letter dated Apr. 20, 1861, from Lee to his sister.

23 *Mason*, 73; Freeman, *Lee*, 1, 436-437.

24 Elliott, *Scott*, 713-714.

25 Freeman, *Lee*, 1, 442.

Arlington, Virginia (Washington City P.O.)
20 April 1861
Hon. Simon Cameron
Secy. of War

Sir:

I have the honor to tender the resignation of my commission as Colonel of the 1st Regt. of Cavalry.

Very resp'y Your Obedient Servant.

R. E. Lee
Col 1st Cav'y.

The personal letter, addressed to Scott, had been written after great anguish and, no doubt, was read by the recipient with equal anguish. It said:

Arlington, Va.
April 20, 1861

General:

Since my interview with you on the 18th inst. I have felt that I ought no longer to retain my commission in the Army. I therefore tender my resignation, which I request you will recommend for acceptance. I would have presented it at once, but for the struggle it has cost me to separate myself from a service to which I have devoted all the best years of my life and all the ability I have possessed.

During the whole of that time—more than a quarter of a century—I have experienced nothing but kindness from my superiors and a most cordial friendship from my comrades. To no one, General, have I been as much indebted as to yourself for uniform kindness and consideration, and it has always been my ardent desire to meet your approbation. I shall carry to the grave the most grateful recollections of your kind consideration, and your name and fame will always be dear to me.

Save in defense of my native State, I never desire again to draw my sword.

Be pleased to accept my most earnest wishes for the continuance of your happiness and prosperity, and believe me, most truly yours,

R. E. Lee.[26]

26 The full text of both letters appears in both Freeman, *Lee*, 1, 440-442; and Dowdy, *Wartime Papers*, 8-9.

A day later, Scott and Seward met again. Seward reminded him of their conversation about command of the Union forces.

"You were expecting to hear from some officer you thought well of. Did you?"

"Yes," said Scott, more angry than he showed, "It was too late. He had decided to go with his State, as the phrase is now. I am sorry, both on our account and his own."[27]

A short time later Lee was in the office of Adjutant General Lorenzo Thomas. While deciding what to do, he had been tortured by his dilemma. Worse yet, after he decided, he had heard recriminations about his decision.

"General Thomas," he said, "I am told you have said I was a traitor!"

Thomas rose and looked him in the eye.

"I have said so. Do you wish to know on what authority?"

Lee responded, "Yes."

"Well, on the authority of General Scott!"

This must have been an emotional blow. Lee muttered, "There must be some mistake."[28]

Mistake or not, Lee's decision had left the highest command position in the Union Army completely open. No candidate of clear-cut qualifications was apparent.

27 Seward, *Reminiscences*, 168.

28 Townsend, *Anecdotes*, 32; Ben Poore Perley, *Perley's Reminiscences of Sixty Years in the National Metropolis*, 2 vols. (Boston, 1986), vol. 2, 73. Townsend was a member of the adjutant general's office, and Poore was not. Nevertheless, their accounts, although they appear to have been written independently, are consistent almost word for word. Poore, by his precise and unnecessary reference to Captain Alexander Shiras, *Heitman*, 1, 884, a third officer who was present, appears to have received his account from Shiras.

Chapter 7

"I would march the troops through Baltimore," he said earnestly, "or over its ashes to the defense of the capital of the nation."

— Fitz-John Porter to Pennsylvania Governor Andrew Curtin

Early Stars Rise

On April 13, while Sumter was still under attack and shortly before Scott was rebuffed by Lee, Lieutenant-Colonel Keyes addressed his first report to the general in chief about the progress of his mission in New York City.[1]

Keyes had sent his earlier reports to Seward; but Simon Cameron, the secretary of war, complained about the secretary of state meddling in military affairs. Seward, the shrewd politician turned thoughtful diplomat, asked Keyes to address future communications to the War Department. On April 18, Keyes sent a report to Colonel Townsend in which he said defensively, "General Scott will understand the immense labor I have had to perform, and I trust you will let him know how uneasy I feel at being here, while he has such burdens on his shoulders. If you think the General would prefer I should join him before completing the business here, let me

1 Keyes, *Fifty Years*, 396-97.

know by telegraph, and I will set out Saturday morning. If not, I shall start Monday morning."[2]

While Keyes finished his work in New York, he found his absence from Washington to be a pleasant respite from the mercurial, typhoon-like temper of his old chief.[3] Independent, detached duty without his irascible commanding officer was enjoyable. Freedom from Scott's fragile sensitivity and snappish disposition had been, whether consciously or not, a huge emotional relaxation for the colonel.[4] Increasing the tension and the friction between the two was Keyes's ardent support for the North. Unswervingly loyal to his country, Scott was, nevertheless, a partisan of the South and Southern men. On frequent occasions, Keyes had offended his superior by not concealing his strong Northern sentiments. Although Scott had treated him "with uniform kindness" and they had had only one argument, Keyes had already concluded that the warmth of their relationship was dying.

While in New York, he had been offered service with Governor Morgan and planned to accept. But he thought duty required him first to report in person to Lincoln and particularly to Seward. He must also have thought that one last face-to-face meeting with the president and the secretary of state could not be harmful to his career. Of course, military etiquette, then and today, required him to report to General Scott, his superior, as well. For the trip to Washington, General Charles Sanford, commander of the New York State militia, gave Keyes authority over the New York troops being sent to the capital, the Sixth, Twelfth, and Seventy-first[5] Regiments of New York Infantry, and asked him to supervise them on the trip. Governor Sprague of Rhode Island gave him similar authority over the First Rhode Island Regiment under Colonel Ambrose E. Burnside.[6] Of course, this meant further delay in his return to Washington and predictable irritation on the part of the general in chief.

At the news of Fort Sumter's surrender, Keyes was overwhelmed with rage and despair; but it affected him less than the cowardice and imbecility he had seen in Washington before the attack. On April 21, one week after the surrender, he sailed from New York on ships carrying the four regiments under his supervision. Aboard

2 Keyes, *Fifty Years*, 399.

3 *Ibid.*, 401.

4 *Ibid.*, 404-05.

5 For winning a battle in a different kind of war, the author was made, and is proud to be today, an honorary member of the Seventy-first Infantry, the successor to the Seventy-first New York Infantry, a unit that has served with great honor in virtually every war involving the United States since the 1850s.

6 Keyes, *Fifty Years*, 401.

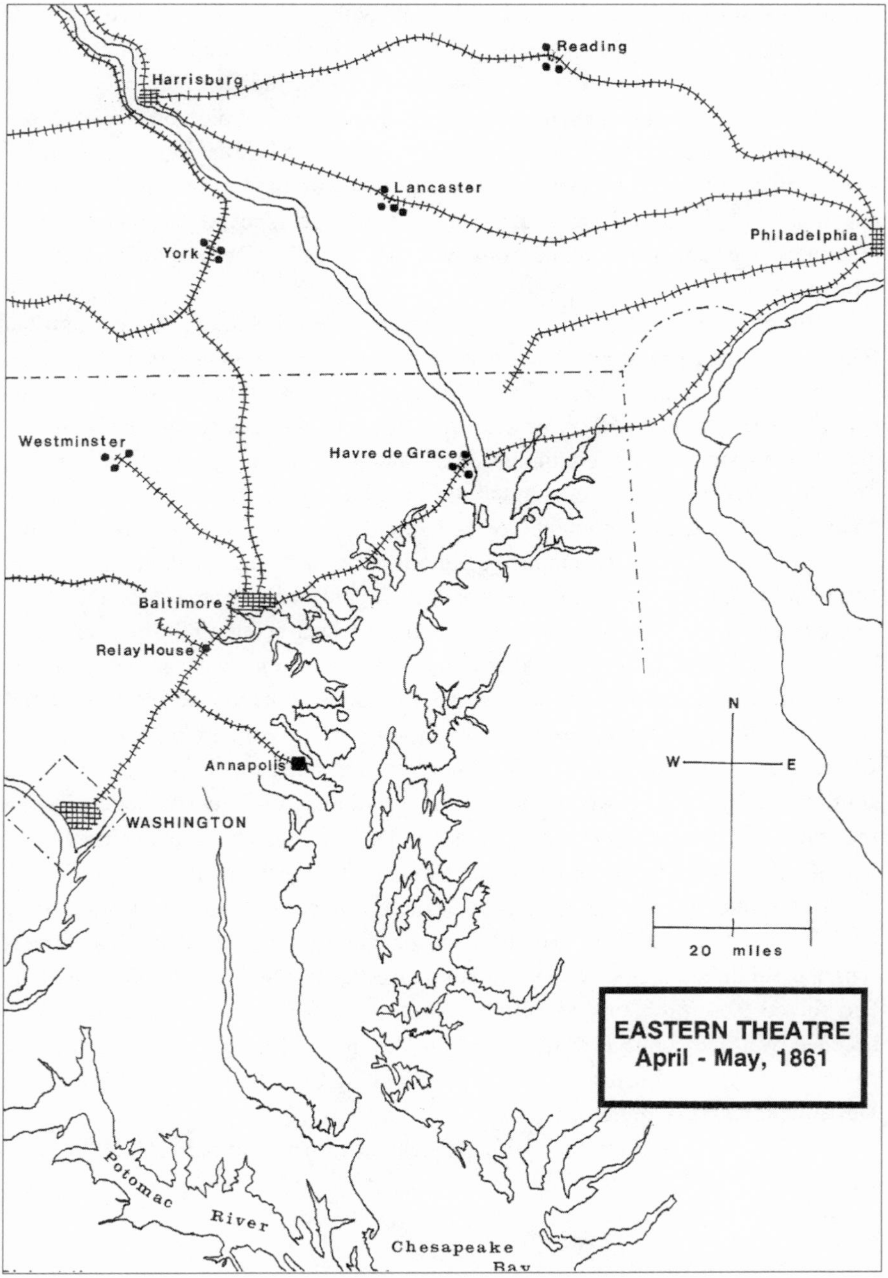
Reading
Harrisburg
Lancaster
Philadelphia
York
Westminster
Havre de Grace
Baltimore
Relay House
Annapolis
WASHINGTON
N
W
E
20 miles
EASTERN THEATRE
April - May, 1861
Potomac River
Chesapeake
Bay

one of the ships was Colonel Daniel Butterfield with his recently accepted regiment, the Twelfth New York. Keyes chose to sail on the ship with Colonel Butterfield and the Twelfth New York aboard. Intending to proceed up the Potomac River to Washington, the ships rendezvoused at Fort Monroe at 4:00 p.m. on April 22. The ships' captains decided the channel was too close to the Virginia shore and would be vulnerable to artillery; and they could not, at least with the larger vessels, leave the channel without risk of running aground. Keyes decided they should take the alternate route and ordered the convoy to sail up the Chesapeake Bay toward Annapolis.[7]

Within a matter of days after the surrender of Fort Sumter, Washington had fallen into a critical position. The Rebels had occupied Harpers Ferry and appeared to be prepared to send a strong column down the east bank of the Potomac toward the capital. Through the treachery of a naval officer, the Norfolk Navy Yard had been abandoned with all its equipment and tonnage including the steam frigate *Merrimack*. The relief force, arriving too late, ineptly destroyed the shipyard and abandoned its damaged contents to the Confederates. The city of Baltimore was dominated by secession sympathizers, who were armed. The states of Virginia and Maryland would secede within weeks or even days. The track, bridges, and facilities of the Baltimore and Ohio Railroad had been destroyed, severing the best land route between Washington and the Northern states. The management of the Baltimore and Ohio Railroad still refused to transport Union troops on its trains. The condition of Annapolis and the tracks between Annapolis and Washington was unknown. Confederate batteries on the Virginia shore fired at shipping on the Potomac River south of the capital. The Rebels had cut all communication between the capital and the states to the North, everyone in Washington "felt genuine fear for its safety,"[8] and those who could were moving their families from the capital.

Before the attack on Fort Sumter, Scott's problem had been protection of the capital against internal dissension because the majority of its residents sympathized with the South. Scott's personnel decisions and the masterful performance by Stone had solved these problems peacefully. As long as Virginia and Maryland had not seceded, war had not erupted outright, and Virginia had not prepared to attack, the safety of Washington from capture by an attacking force had not become an issue. But now, it was a genuine concern.

As the Confederate military forces began to form, Scott increasingly feared a Confederate attack across the Potomac north of the capital, a march to Baltimore,

7 Keyes, *Fifty Years*, 401-402.

8 Nicolay, *Outbreak*, 82-84; Chittenden, *Invisible Siege*, 5-8; N&H, 4, 148; Beatie, *Road to Manassas*, 45-50.

and an easy capture of Washington from the rear.[9] The District of Columbia militia was not sufficient to defend against it. A command organization and troops were needed immediately.

On April 16, two days after Fort Sumter surrendered and a month before the federal government reserved the power to appoint general officers to itself, the governor of Pennsylvania commissioned Robert Patterson a major general of militia. When Scott heard this, he was pleased. Patterson was a reliable friend and comrade in arms from the Mexican War. It was only natural, therefore, that Scott should want Patterson, a tried and proven subordinate with battle experience, commissioned a major general of volunteers in the service of the United States Government.[10] On April 19, Patterson's commission was transferred from the Pennsylvania militia to the United States Army to serve three months.[11] General Orders No. 3, published over Scott's signature, placed him in command of the Military Department of Washington, which included the District of Columbia and the states of Delaware, Pennsylvania, and Maryland. Patterson left his large business interests, established his headquarters in Philadelphia, and took command of the many regiments and companies beginning to report.[12]

A force under Patterson in the Hagerstown-Williamsport-Frederick area would deter any thrust across the Potomac toward Baltimore because it could fall on the open left flank or rear of a Baltimore column before the Rebels could achieve their

9 Fitz-John Porter MSS (L.C.) letters dated Nov. 24, 1890 (draft); and Nov. 28, 1892, from Porter to Livermore.

10 *D.A.B.*, 7, pt. 2, 306-307; *Martial Deeds*, 953-954; Elliott, *Scott*, 453; National Archives, Pennsylvania Military Files for the War of 1812 for Robert P. Patterson.

11 National Archives, General Staff File for Robert P. Patterson. In his encyclopedic work, *Generals in Blue* (Baton Rouge, 1964), Ezra Warner does not list Patterson, 601-602, or sketch him, 362-363, presumably because Warner believed him to have been a militia general who never had a federal commission. In an anomaly, however, Patterson was given a three-month commission in the federal service.

12 General Orders No. 3 in *OR*, 2, 579; Elliott, *Scott*, 453; Patterson, *Narrative*, 26. The notes here will not discuss the *Narrative's* many minor errors, particularly the order of letters, telegrams, dispatches, and orders and the inferences suggested by the order. Although he says the *Narrative* is generally accurate on the facts, which seems to be true, Fitz-John Porter, who had much reason to defend Patterson and the three month campaign in the Valley because of his dominant role in it, conceded later that the order of the documents was "inaccurate." Porter MSS (L.C.) letter dated November 28, 1892, from Porter to Livermore. The task of microscopic analysis has been ably and encyclopedically performed by Thomas L. Livermore in "Patterson's Shenandoah Campaign," in Theodore F. Dwight, ed. *Papers of the Military Historical Society of Massachusetts*, 13 vols., (Boston, 1881). The article by Livermore covers the missteps in Patterson's *Narrative* as well as it can be done. The society assigned a committee, usually of three men, to report on each major campaign of the war. The results, much like Herodotus, the grandfather of all historians, were usually based on the official records and personal knowledge. They are thoughtful and reliable even though somewhat dry by today's standards.

objective.[13] This was a perfect example of advantage from exterior lines, a condition not prized in American military thinking of the day.

Born in Ireland in 1798, Patterson was six years old when his father was banished for rebellion. The family sailed to the United States and settled in Pennsylvania where young Patterson began his education in the public schools. At fifteen he entered a counting house in Philadelphia, but his incipient business career was interrupted by the War of 1812 in which he served as the lieutenant colonel, then colonel of the Second Regiment, Pennsylvania militia. His commission in the regular army, slow to keep pace with militia and volunteer commissions of a man on active service, had risen to captain when he was mustered out in June of 1815.

Returning to business life, he remained in the state militia and by 1824 reached the rank of major general. In the meantime, he amassed a large fortune while earning a reputation for business integrity. When the Mexican War began, he was commissioned a major-general of volunteers to serve with Scott's Vera Cruz-Mexico City column; and as a well-known Democrat, he had even been considered by President Polk for command of the Mexico City column before the position was finally given to Scott. At Cerro Gordo he was lifted from sickbed to saddle in order to lead his division into battle, then led the pursuit to Jalapa. While serving as Scott's second in command, he and Scott developed a strong friendship which continued after the war.[14]

In 1861, Patterson felt the supply pinch that plagued all commanders in the first months of the war. None of the arsenals or supply depots would release anything without specific federal orders. His troops had no blankets, clothing, or cooking utensils and very few weapons.

Patterson's principal assignment at the outset was simple and clear: reestablish communication between Washington and the loyal states, open the land routes through secessionist Maryland to Washington for reinforcements, and clear the Harrisburg-Wilmington-Baltimore-Washington road. The day after he was commissioned in the federal service, Patterson notified Scott that he did not have enough troops to open the routes and patrol them.[15]

With the usual land route through Baltimore unsafe, Patterson thought the best way to reach Washington from the Northern states was to travel to Philadelphia by any means, take the train for Havre de Grace, then take ship into Chesapeake Bay.

13 Porter MSS (L.C.) letters dated November 24, 1890, (draft) and November 28, 1892, from Porter to Livermore.

14 National Archives, Pennsylvania Military Files for the War of 1812, for Patterson; *D.A.B.*, 7, pt. 2, 306-307; *Martial Deeds*, 953-954; Elliott, *Scott*, 453.

15 *OR*, 2, 580, 582-583, 586.

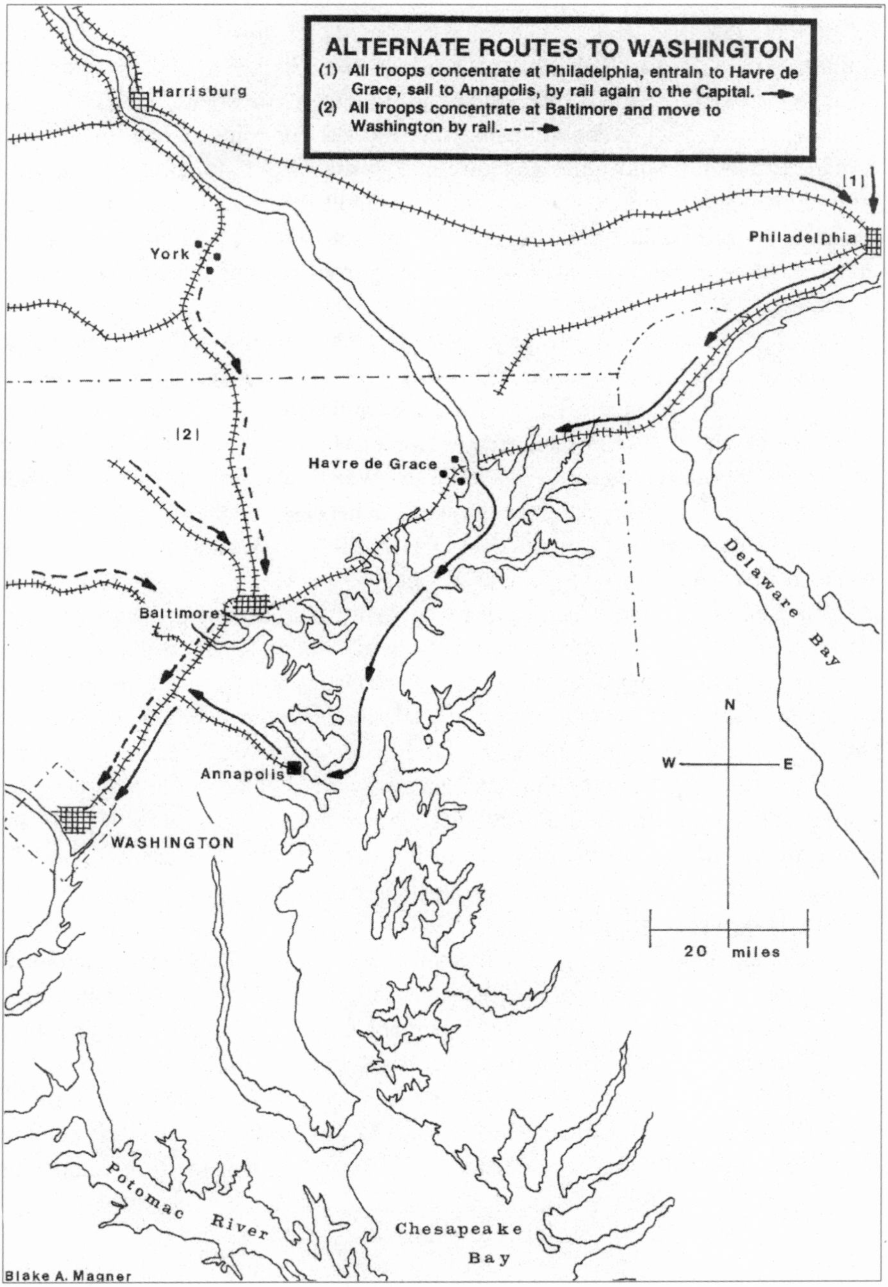
ALTERNATE ROUTES TO WASHINGTON
(1) All troops concentrate at Philadelphia, entrain to Havre de Grace, sail to Annapolis, by rail again to the Capital.
(2) All troops concentrate at Baltimore and move to Washington by rail.
Harrisburg
York
Philadelphia
(1)
(2)
Havre de Grace
Baltimore
Annapolis
WASHINGTON
Delaware Bay
N
W
E
20 miles
Potomac River
Chesapeake Bay
Blake A. Magner

Because the Potomac would presumably be closed by Confederate guns, the ships could not use it to reach the capital;[16] but they could bypass Baltimore and go to Annapolis, where the men could disembark and march overland to Washington. While reinforcements were following this roundabout route to the endangered capital, Patterson could build an army and advance to Baltimore. The railway between Annapolis and the capital would have to be seized and its sabotaged parts repaired; but this would not be difficult, he was sure, because the distance was not great. Scott approved this plan and ordered Patterson to implement it as soon as possible.[17]

While Patterson was preparing his army for its advance on Baltimore and Keyes was sailing toward Annapolis, others were also working to solve the Baltimore part of the problem. On April 18, Major Irvin McDowell with instructions from Secretary of War Cameron searched for Brevet Major Fitz-John Porter, who was serving as an assistant adjutant-general in the War Department. It was after office hours; but Porter, working like Stone, was still at his desk. McDowell told Porter the secretary wanted him to go that day to Harrisburg to hasten the mustering of Pennsylvania state troops into federal service. He was to put them on the Northern Central Railroad, to secure it, and to keep the line from Harrisburg through Baltimore to Washington open. Porter had a brief meeting with Scott, who told him railroad communication with the North was probably broken in Baltimore. If rail communications were shut for ten days, Washington would be on the verge of starvation and likely to be captured by the Rebels. As he had since the turn of the year, General Scott believed the secessionists were plotting its capture. He gave Porter the names of Baltimore men Porter should meet to discuss the state of the public mind and to learn the opinions of influential men in that city. If possible, advised Scott, Porter was to decide whether troops for the capital could pass peacefully through Baltimore.

Scott had no time to prepare written or detailed instructions. General authority had worked with Stone, who saved the capital from internal disruption, and Meigs, who saved Fort Pickens from capture. Scott apparently could see no reason why it would not work here. As far as he was concerned, Porter knew what he wanted. The old general in chief relied, he said, on Porter's judgment and energy to perform his tasks in Baltimore and Harrisburg as quickly as possible and in the best possible way. He authorized Porter to use his name and Cameron's name if in compelling

16 Townsend, *Anecdotes*, 93.

17 *OR*, 2, 580, 582-583, 586.

circumstances he could not communicate with the capital. Like Meigs, Porter was given a one sentence letter.[18] It read:

> War Department
> April 18, 1861
>
> Captain Porter:
>
> Dear Sir: This will introduce to you Hon. Joseph Casey of Harrisburg, who will aid you in any way he can.
>
> Respectfully,
>
> Simon Cameron
> Secretary of War[19]

Armed with this letter of introduction, Porter went to Baltimore, where he spent the night. With several residents and two officers he discussed the passage of Northern troops through the city. If state militia units were preceded by regular army troops and supervised by a Regular Army officer, they said, they would make every effort to control the mob and believed they could do it. Some of the men whose names Scott had supplied were strongly opposed to the passage of state troops at all. Porter argued that, once mustered into the federal service, they were no longer state troops but part of the federal army, a logical argument that failed to convince them. A detailed report to Scott he wrote and sent by messenger that night. Next morning, he set out for Harrisburg.[20]

On the day Patterson established his headquarters in Philadelphia, Major Porter arrived in Harrisburg and reported to Governor Curtin. He told the governor that the secretary of war and General Scott wanted new Pennsylvania troops sent to Washington and the Northern Central Railroad protected. He had been sent to Harrisburg, he said, to muster the troops into the federal service and to give all the assistance he could in hurrying them forward. Curtin replied that he would make every effort.

Working around the clock, Porter had to overcome widespread unpreparedness. He established a close relationship with Thomas A. Scott, general manager of the

18 *OR*, 51, pt. 1, 345; Porter MSS (L.C.), undated memorandum entitled "Copies of Telegrams Referred to in Governor Blair's and Governor Curtin's Letters."

19 *OR*, 51, pt. 1, 328.

20 Porter MSS (L.C.) memorandum dated November 13, 1892, from Wilson.

Pennsylvania Central Railroad, and J. D. Cameron, general manager of the Northern Central Railroad, both of whom gave him access to their telegraph wires and other facilities.[21]

As the situation in Baltimore passed from a simmer to a boil, Governor Curtin convened a meeting in his executive chambers. Telegraphic communication with Washington was impossible. They knew they were acting on their own. They sensed "revolution in the air." No plan assured safety. After everyone had spoken, Porter, the youngest, "his handsome face brightened by the enthusiasm of his patriotism, and his keen eye flashing the fire of his courage," spoke.

"I would march the troops through Baltimore," he said earnestly, "or over its ashes to the defense of the capital of the nation."[22]

Porter was born in Portsmouth, New Hampshire, on August 31, 1822, the son of Captain John Porter and nephew of Commodore David Porter, both of the United States Navy. He was a cousin of Lieutenant David Dixon Porter, now on his way on the *Powhatan* to Fort Pickens. Early in his life he came under the guardianship of Commodore Long, who boarded him with his aunt, then sent him for his early education to Phillips Exeter Academy, perhaps the best of the many extraordinary New England private schools. When he arrived he was a straight limbed, rather slender boy with bright dark eyes, a winning smile, and a frank, open-hearted manner. He enjoyed a good game of marbles, at which he was very skillful and as he grew, came to excel in sports. Just and generous in the settlement of questions or squabbles, his contemporaries regarded his decisions as fair and righteous. He was popular with his schoolmates, an amiable companion, and a lover of innocent fun with an unfailing flow of good spirits.[23] Many years later, his roommate at Exeter described him as "rather retiring and quiet in disposition, rather strong with his prejudices, and warm in his attachments. [He] did not seek the company of everyone, and [was] somewhat diffident on first acquaintance. He was not a boy of many words,—but, in what little he said, you would know what he meant. He was somewhat sensitive, perhaps might be called quick tempered. But, he was not

21 *OR*, 51, pt. 1, 346, 351.

22 Webb MSS (Yale University, Sterling Library) typed article about Porter; McClure, *Lincoln and Men*, 372. Although Webb cites no authority for the conversation, he undoubtedly obtained it from McClure's work if not by word of mouth. The quotations are from Webb but are close to verbatim from McClure. The date of this meeting is not clear. It is not mentioned in Porter's report in *OR*. It must have taken place on this trip because Webb's account mentions a return to Washington after the meeting and a trip back to the Valley to be Patterson's chief of staff, which fixes the meeting during Porter's service in Harrisburg as a mustering officer.

23 Porter MSS (L.C.), letter dated August 22, 1901, from Soule to Mrs. Porter.

vindictive. He was not eminently sociable, but he enjoyed the society of his friends."[24]

Porter's personality when he finished Exeter would continue essentially unchanged to the end of his days. He would always have a narrow selection of close friends, would stand by them, and would enjoy their company. More importantly, his powers of persuasion would give him great influence even with his superiors, who would often seek and follow his advice on the most important matters.

After leaving Exeter, he went for a short time to a private school in Boston, then in 1841 entered the United States Military Academy at West Point, from which he graduated eighth in his class in 1845. Being designated a brevet second lieutenant in the Fourth U.S. Artillery and stationed at Fort Monroe, Virginia, he was commissioned second lieutenant a year later and sent to Taylor's army on the Rio Grande. The following year he was reassigned to General Scott's Mexico City column. During the campaign he was promoted to first lieutenant and awarded brevets of captain and major for gallantry at Molino del Rey and Chapultepec. In the assault on the Belen Gate, one of the main gates into Mexico City, Porter's battery commander and the other officer in the battery were killed. Though wounded, Porter continued to command the guns. Only three of his men were not wounded or killed. By the time he was twenty-five he was a first lieutenant and had two brevets for gallant conduct. He had shown coolness, determination, ability, and bravery in battle.[25]

After the war he was assigned to West Point, first as an instructor in artillery and cavalry, then from 1849 to 1855 as adjutant to the post. Among his fellow instructors were Seth Thomas, John Gibbon, William B. Franklin, John F. Reynolds, Silas Casey, and John G. Barnard, with all of whom he would later serve. His students included John M. Schofield, Oliver O. Howard, Philip M. Sheridan, David McM. Gregg, George Crook, and William W. Averell.

As a grown man he was remarkably handsome and, in form, had a physique of perfect proportions. He moved with unaffected dignity, ease, and grace, whether walking or riding. His courtesy and gentleness were recognized by all who knew him. The cadets at West Point, keen observers of the character and ability of their instructors, regarded Major Porter as an ideal soldier and gentlemen and valued commendation from him.[26]

24 Porter MSS (L.C.), letter dated Aug. 20, 1901, from Gordon to Mrs. Porter.

25 Webb MSS (Y.U.), draft speech of n.d. about Porter; vol. 8 *D.A.B.*, pt. 1, 90.

26 Webb MSS (Y.U.), draft speech by Webb of n.d. about Porter; Averell, *Recollections*, 337-338; Weld, *Diary and Letters*, 53.

When General Albert Sidney Johnston was sent to Utah to deal with the Mormons, Porter was assigned to him as his adjutant-general and his chief of staff. In that capacity, Porter wrote Scott a confidential letter which Scott sent to the secretary of war with the endorsement, "This is a private letter from Johnson's chief of staff—asking the secretary's indulgence toward the capital soldier, the writer—gallant, intelligent and frank—the department cannot fail to profit by its perusal, and so may the Commander of the Utah reinforcements."

In 1860, he was ordered to Charleston Harbor to inspect the defenses and make recommendations to strengthen them and secure the government there. He suggested Major Robert Anderson be put in command of the defenses, and Anderson made the critical transfer to Fort Sumter pursuant to an understanding he had with Porter. He was then sent to Texas to bring away the garrison. By great tact, energy, and decisiveness, he brought out five batteries of artillery and hundreds of the best Regular troops before Twiggs disgraced the Regular Army by his surrender.

During his peacetime service he had established a number of close friendships with his fellow officers. Among them were George B. McClellan, who graduated one year behind him in the class of 1846, who was widely thought to be marked for a great future, and who was deeply attached to Porter;[27] and Irvin McDowell, an older officer who had graduated from the Military Academy before Porter arrived. While he was stationed on the plains, Porter wrote to McDowell often; and when McDowell was in the capital during the earliest days of the war, he showed Porter's letters to Scott and others, "in order," as one of Porter's staff officers later wrote, "to help you forward and bring you into notice as much as possible."[28]

During the 1850s he married Harriet Pierson Cook, who bore him several children.[29] At this stage in his career he was "a Christian soldier—in his family a tenderhearted husband—a loving and beloved father—a true and honest and fearless friend. In his manner he was almost cold but of heart he was warm and sympathizing. He was a Christian man but never paraded this Christian side of his character. He was reflective and only spoke or advised after mature reflection. When giving reproach, he was positive but gentle. To fully appreciate his dazzling influence you had just to win his confidence."[30] Fatalistically, he believed, as he would say or write, "All that is, is right and for the best."[31]

27 Webb MSS (Y.U.), draft speech by Webb of n.d. about Porter at Malvern Hill.

28 Porter MSS (L.C.), letter dated June 14, 1879, from Weld to Porter.

29 *D.A.B.*, 8, pt. 1, 91.

30 Webb MSS (Y.U.), draft speech by Webb of n.d. about Porter at Malvern Hill.

31 McClellan MSS (L.C.), letter dated July 11, 1886, from Porter to Prime.

While Porter was in Harrisburg, Patterson felt great concern about the safety of the forts on Delaware Bay. He asked Porter for authority to put them under Captain A. A. Gibson of the Second United States Artillery and to garrison the forts with volunteers. Once again relying on the general instructions from Scott and the power of Scott's name, Porter replied to Patterson's request, "Lieutenant-General Scott orders you at once to accept the services of a loyal and efficient force and secure the forts on the Delaware."[32]

As he sat in Governor Curtin's telegraph office in the state capital on one of these uncertain, early days, the governor handed him a dispatch from Frank P. Blair, Jr., the younger brother of Postmaster General Montgomery Blair. Curtin suggested that Porter reply to it. Blair's message reported that General Harney, who was in command of the United States forces and equipment in St. Louis, had refused to allow Missouri volunteers to be armed or mustered into the federal service. Local people in St. Louis distrusted Harney and considered him disloyal. Blair urged that Harney be replaced at once. Even though the secessionists wished to seize the arsenal, which had seventy thousand arms, Harney refused to issue equipment to loyal men who wished to defend it.

Porter knew that Captain Nathaniel Lyon of the Second United States Infantry had been requested to be mustering officer, to arm and equip loyal troops, and to command them. He also knew that the problem in St. Louis, "the Philadelphia of the West to the Union at the time,"[33] might become unrecoverable at any moment. Scott had given him blanket instructions to protect the interests of the national government and had made a general statement that Porter knew what the general in chief wanted. The situation in St. Louis could not wait the two days for a round trip courier to the capital. Believing that the circumstances required prompt action and that his conduct would be approved, he decided to use the name and the authority of the secretary of war and the general in chief to solve Blair's problem. He sent the following telegram:

> Harrisburg, Pa., April 21, 1861
>
> General Harney,
> Commanding, St. Louis, Mo.:

32 *OR*, 51, pt. 1, 348-349; Porter MSS (L.C.), memorandum dated November 13, 1893, from Wilson.

33 Porter MSS (L.C.), memorandum dated November 13, 1893.

> Captain Nathaniel Lyon, Second Infantry is detailed to muster in the troops in St. Louis and to use them for the protection of public property. You will see that they are properly armed and equipped.
>
> By order of Lieutenant-General Scott:
>
> F. J. Porter
> Assistant-Adjutant General

He sent similar telegrams to Major Seth Williams and to Captain Lyon.[34]

In Harrisburg, the Regular Army personnel were prepared to muster troops as soon as they could be ready. The state authorities, however, were not prepared to do anything. Within three days, approximately four thousand men, fully organized, were finally reported ready for service; but as Patterson had noted, Porter found them to be without arms, clothing, equipment, and ammunition.

In the name of the secretary of war he called for Major Pike Graham, the commanding officer at Carlisle Barracks, to complete the organization of four companies of Regular cavalry under Major George H. Thomas as rapidly as possible and hold them ready for dispatch to Washington with the volunteers. As the situation in Baltimore deteriorated, he sent train transportation to Carlisle and called the cavalry to Harrisburg.

In Harrisburg, no arms, ammunition, or equipment of any kind existed, not even cooking equipment. For the troops coming from Carlisle Barracks, Porter again used the names of the secretary of war and the general in chief, this time for supplies from arsenals at Governor's Island, Frankfort, and Pittsburgh and from the Quartermaster's Department in Philadelphia. While these facilities busily responded to his calls, he used hotels and restaurants to feed the men until a commissary department could be organized.[35]

In preparation for passing a column through Baltimore, Porter left Harrisburg and traveled to Cockeysville, fourteen miles from Baltimore. There, on the morning of April 21, he unloaded three thousand four hundred men from his trains. With a veritable blizzard of telegrams, and a miraculous effort he had arranged for them to be armed, supplied with ammunition, and issued rations.[36]

During his short stay in Baltimore, he had been warned to have Regular troops with any column passing through the city. When he arrived at Cockeysville, he

34 *OR*, 51, pt. 1, 350.

35 *OR*, 51, pt. 1, 346.

36 OR, 51, pt. 1, 353-355.

intended to move immediately on Baltimore, leaving forces along the railroad to protect it; and to keep the peace he had hoped to have with him Thomas's dismounted Regular cavalry, Sherman's Regular battery of the Third Artillery, and a repair party for the railroad bridges. Major George H. Thomas, he learned, would be in Harrisburg that evening and Sherman would probably arrive that night. Once his troops were properly bivouacked and guards arranged on the adjacent hills, he hurried back to Harrisburg to bring forward the Regular troops and the bridging party.[37]

On April 22, Major Graham at Carlisle Barracks sent forward the cavalry recruits. With them came a single case of cartridges, all Graham could spare.[38] Porter then had to obtain horseshoes, horseshoe nails, shoeing tools, horses, and cavalry equipment, including saddles, bridles, saddlebags, and blankets.[39] Major Thomas's officers, all Southerners, were anxious about their course of action and gloomy about the future. Thomas had been born and raised in North Carolina. His officers looked to him for guidance. Just before boarding the train, which was about to start from Carlisle Barracks, one of them turned to Thomas and said, "What shall we do?"

"We are ordered to Washington," replied Thomas promptly, "and there we go. There will be time enough after getting there for you to decide what to do."[40]

Late in the afternoon, he and his four hundred dismounted cavalry arrived at Harrisburg.

Porter believed the officers would do their duty until they were officially relieved of their commissions in Washington.[41] By dark, his men had been loaded on the cars. A few moments later, the train was in motion for Baltimore, followed by the bridge builders and materials. They reached York near midnight.

There, he and the cavalrymen met a courier from Washington carrying new orders. They were not to proceed past York toward Baltimore. The orders were delivered verbally, a practice that would compromise more than one officer, cause more than one failure, and end in more than one dispute in the next four years. An order from Cameron to reach Washington at all hazards had never been delivered. Nor did Porter have an order from Chase expressing his desire that the troops arrive at the vulnerable capital as soon as possible. Chase became angry at Porter for this

37 *OR*, 51, pt. 1, 351.

38 *OR*, 51, pt. 1, 356-357.

39 *OR*, 51, pt. 1, 356. This left the post with a mere 1,000 rounds for its use.

40 Francis McKinney, *Education in Violence: The Life of George H. Thomas and the History of the Army of the Cumberland* (reprint Chicago, 1991), 96 ("McKinney, *Thomas*").

41 *OR*, 51, pt. 1, 351.

failure and the torture of the next week probably caused him to lose confidence in Thomas.

Now, they were to head for the capital by way of Philadelphia[42] on the Northern Central Railroad. This was a long, time-consuming way around Baltimore. Communication by telegraph was still impossible, and a courier required two days for a round trip. Porter was unable to confirm the genuineness of the orders or their source except to learn that they had come from Washington and that they were peremptory. He put little faith in them. Hoping that an error had been made and that it would be corrected at daybreak, he delayed their execution. At daylight, he received an order from Cameron dated April 21.[43] At the urgent request of the governor of Maryland and the mayor of Baltimore, who feared further bloodshed if troops from Pennsylvania passed through the city, Lincoln directed the troops, specifically the troops at Cockeysville, to take a route around Baltimore. Nevertheless, they were to leave behind sufficient force to keep the railroads safe. The men headed for Washington were to return to Harrisburg, take the route by the Susquehanna, embark on steamers for Annapolis, and continue to Washington from Annapolis. They were not to approach Washington through Baltimore. His worst fears confirmed, Porter returned to Harrisburg that night.

On the morning of April 25, having done his work of mustering Pennsylvania troops and forwarding men to Washington, Major Porter, accompanied by Thomas Scott and Colonel Andrew Porter, left by rail for Hagerstown, Maryland. From there, they traveled by carriage to Washington, which they reached at sunrise the next morning. As soon as possible, Major Porter reported in person to General Scott, who was engaged in a confidential discussion with Treasury Secretary Chase. Scott instructed Porter to wait in a corner of the room while he and Chase sat in another corner on a sofa and finished their discussion. Chase had asked the president to declare martial law from Washington to Havre de Grace along the line of the railroad and through Baltimore. Lincoln had refused. Chase was now trying, unsuccessfully, to persuade Scott to do it. After Chase left, Scott was indignant.

"There goes a bad man, the worst man of all this bad administration."[44]

42 *OR*, 51, pt. 1, 347; McKinney, *Thomas*, 96-97.

43 Cameron MSS (L.C.), letter dated April 21, 1861, from Kellen to Lincoln; orders of April 21, 1861, from Headquarters of the Army signed by Cameron; endorsement by Scott in pencil; letter dated April 24, 1861, from Headquarters of the Army signed by Scott.

44 Cameron MSS (L.C.), letter dated April 21, 1861, from Rev. R. A. Kellen to Lincoln; Order dated April 24, 1861, from Headquarters of the Army signed by Cameron; letter dated November 7, 1879, from Porter to Cameron; Porter MSS (L.C.) letter dated August 20, 1891, from Porter to Townsend.

At Porter's suggestion Colonel Andrew Porter was ordered back to Harrisburg, and Thomas Scott was assigned by Cameron to replace the officer in charge of the railroad to Annapolis.

Having given his verbal reports to the general in chief and to the secretary of war, Porter was ordered by Scott to report to Major General Patterson as his assistant adjutant-general. He passed through Annapolis on April 27 and reported for duty on April 28.[45]

Shortly after assuming his new duties, Porter wrote his friend George B. McClellan a long letter about his activities and his views on the current strife. He and McClellan agreed on many, probably most, things in this new and unique war. "I am with old Patterson," he wrote, "and have all the work to do of which I am not sorry. Only it is getting volunteers ready for duty under most annoying circumstances. Equipping & fitting them out with nothing in store or likely to be, and pushed by the government to send on regiments quickly—but not till fully equipped."

Porter's early hopes for dealing with the South were identical with those of General Scott and several of Lincoln's cabinet officers. Perhaps something other than all-out war and the complete defeat of one belligerent would be possible. He also felt, as did many of his fellow Northern officers, considerable sympathy for the South and the ordinary, intelligent Southerner who was being swept along in the torrent of hot-headed Southern emotion. "I hope this display of force and determination on the part of the Government will bring some of the states to reason and perhaps return to duty," explained Porter, who added,

> I think the schemes of the cessationists are the schemes of madness yet there is much reason in their madness so far as the south is concerned for the elements relied upon there have not failed. But what can they accomplish. They pretend to have given up the attack upon Washington but I doubt it. At Harpers Ferry a larger force is gathering from all parts of the South . . . Am glad to see old Kentucky stick. Some sense left in the South . . . Maryland is safe unless a fight should take place in D.C. and Scott whipped which can never be. So she will hold. Would that old Virginia had not made such a fool of herself. Her ground to be the battleground of such a set of 'frenzy' people as inhabit S. C. Jeff Davis is a damned old scoundrel and is surrounded by the same.

Even before he had real dealings with them, Porter had harsh words for the men who were, in his mind, the cause of the war:

45 *OR*, 51, pt. 1, 348-50.

I have no sympathy for the politicians who have brought this trouble on, but I have for the south generally so much so that I hope we shall have no fighting but if we do I trust this union will not be wiped out. There are thousands of southerners who are innocent and millions who are deceived with the belief that the north is invading their country for the purpose of rising the Negroes, that we are defending a party, a political president. How poorly deceived they are will I fear be never known to them. I do not suppose there is one intelligent human of all this force would not march night and day to crush an insurrection. Their mothers would disown them if it were not so.[46]

46 McClellan MSS (L.C.) letter dated May 10, 1861, from Porter to McClellan.

Chapter 8

"Well, governor, you know Brigadier-General Pierce, and you know me. Isn't this a case where the officer should be appointed who is supposed to be most instructed in affairs with which he is to deal?"

— Benjamin Butler to Governor John A. Andrew

Butler, Keyes, and Lefferts Secure Annapolis

From the moment he assumed command Patterson encountered difficulties that, to him, made the opening of the land route through Baltimore to Washington impossible. All the regiments that could be equipped, he complained, were being sent to Scott. The arms his men received were wholly inferior, the cartridges did not fit them, he had only one artillery battery, and garrisoning important fortresses in Pennsylvania depleted his forces.

The problems of commanding an advancing independent force lay ahead. First, Patterson had to finish the laborious task of building an army. He had a few small Regular units and many three-month regiments. The term of enlistment for new troops, he felt, should be longer than three months; but the war in its early days had a temporary look to it, a walk in the sun, one easy battle, then a renewal of the Union. To Governor Curtin he applied for longer terms of service and recommended that twenty-five more regiments be enlisted by the state.[1]

1 In his *Narrative*, Patterson asserts that the governor refused the request (28, 29); but this is not true. *Pennsylvania Raises an Army*, 94; *Pennsylvania Archives: Papers of the Governors*, series VI, vol. VIII, 375, 378.

Although the federal government had refused Curtin's request for a larger troop quota, the governor grew more and more certain that additional regiments would soon be needed. With foresight, the state legislature granted him the authority to take fifteen more regiments of infantry and cavalry than the federal allocation.[2]

Patterson would seek his course of action in the advice of his subordinates, particularly his new adjutant, Fitz-John Porter. As he had since his youth at Exeter, Porter's reserved but firm, fair, and confident demeanor earned him the immediate trust and reliance of his superior. Scott's early and well-deserved trust in Porter's judgment and discretion added to his stature in Patterson's eyes. The Pennsylvanian greatly respected him and had associated almost constantly with him.[3]

In addition to Porter, Senator John Sherman of Ohio, a volunteer aide, served on Patterson's staff. On April 27, Patterson sent Sherman to Washington in the hope that personal political influence might buttress his requests.[4] Patterson's inability to see beyond his local area was recognized, inadvertently or intentionally, that same day when his department was broken into three departments by General Orders No. 12. Scott wisely removed those areas Patterson could not command in person, leaving him Pennsylvania, Delaware, and northern Maryland as the Department of Pennsylvania. The newly created Military Department of Washington included the District of Columbia and that part of Maryland north of the capital; the Department of Annapolis covered the Baltimore-Relay House-Annapolis-Washington railroad route. These commands went to others.[5]

The Department of Pennsylvania and its army were peculiarly different from their contemporaneous federal counterparts. Although most areas in the early days had few troops, Pennsylvania, through the foresight of its commanding officer and its governor, had many. Because its organization began so early, it eluded the beneficial effects of the Congressional Acts and the General Orders of May. By seeing only half the distance to be covered and not taking later corrective steps, Patterson and Curtin planted the seeds of a fundamental problem: the extra

2 Patterson, *Narrative*, 30; *Pennsylvania Raises An Army*, 97\~ff; *Pennsylvania Archives: Papers of the Governors*, series VI, vol. VIII, 422.

3 Porter MSS (L.C.) draft letter dated November 24, 1890 (draft), and letter dated November 28, 1892, from Porter to Livermore. According to Field Marshall Bernard Montgomery, "By previous thought, by discussion with his staff, and by keeping in close touch with his subordinates by means of visits, a commander should know what he wants to do and whether he can do it. A conference of subordinates to *collect ideas* [Montgomery's italics'] is the resort of a weak commander." *The Memoirs of Field Marshal the Viscount Montgomery of Alamain, K. G.* 76 (New York, 1958).

4 John Sherman MSS (L.C.), letter dated April 27, 1861, from John Sherman to Price.

5 *OR*, 2, 607, General Orders No. 12.

regiments had been taken for a period of only three months. Almost all three-year troops went to Washington and other places in immediate danger. Three-month men would presumably be adequate for Patterson's area because it would not be a regular battleground and it was inhabited by loyal citizens. But Patterson's army did not have longevity.

Immediately after Porter left Baltimore on his first trip to join Patterson, Northern regiments were on their way to Washington through Baltimore: the Seventh New York Militia, an old and illustrious regiment of infantry composed in large part of socially prominent residents of New York City under Colonel Marshall Lefferts, and the four infantry regiments of Massachusetts militia that paraded on July 16 in Boston. The Massachusetts troops were commanded by Benjamin F. Butler, a Massachusetts militia brigadier-general who had no federal commission. Pending federal orders, Governor Andrew had designated Butler's force as the Third Brigade, Second Division, Massachusetts Volunteer Militia. Its regiments, the Third, Fourth, Sixth, and Eighth Infantry, were to ride a train to the North Station in Baltimore, cross through the city to the South Station, then head for the capital.

When the first Massachusetts troops started for the capital, the loyalty of Baltimore was unclear; but everyone knew it was unstable, volatile, and potentially disloyal. Ready first, the Sixth Massachusetts, under Colonel Edward F. Jones, was sent ahead. The Third and Fourth Regiments were put on shipboard for Fort Monroe. Butler followed the Sixth overland with the Eighth Massachusetts.[6]

The morning of April 19, after Major Fitz-John Porter had left Baltimore for Harrisburg, the Sixth arrived at the North Station. Colonel Jones had no federal troops to supervise or accompany his state militia regiment, the most dangerous circumstance according to Porter's informants. Jones ordered ammunition distributed to his men and instructed them to load their weapons. He went through the cars and in each gave the following order:

> The regiment will march through Baltimore in column of sections, arms at will. You will undoubtedly be insulted, abused, and, perhaps, assaulted, to which you must pay no attention whatever, but march with your faces square to the front, and pay no attention to the mob, even if they throw stones, bricks, and other missiles; but if you are fired upon and any of you is hit, your officers will order you to fire. Do not fire into any promiscuous crowds, but select any man whom you see aiming at you, and be sure you drop him.[7]

6 *Butler's Book*, 173-174; Marshall, Jessie Ames, ed., *Private and Official Correspondence of Gen. Benjamin F. Butler During The Period of the Civil War*, 5 vols. (Norwood, 1917), 1, 15 (Marshall, *Butler P.O.C.*); *N&H* 4, 109-111; Nicolay, *Outbreak*, 83-84.

7 *OR*, 2, 7.

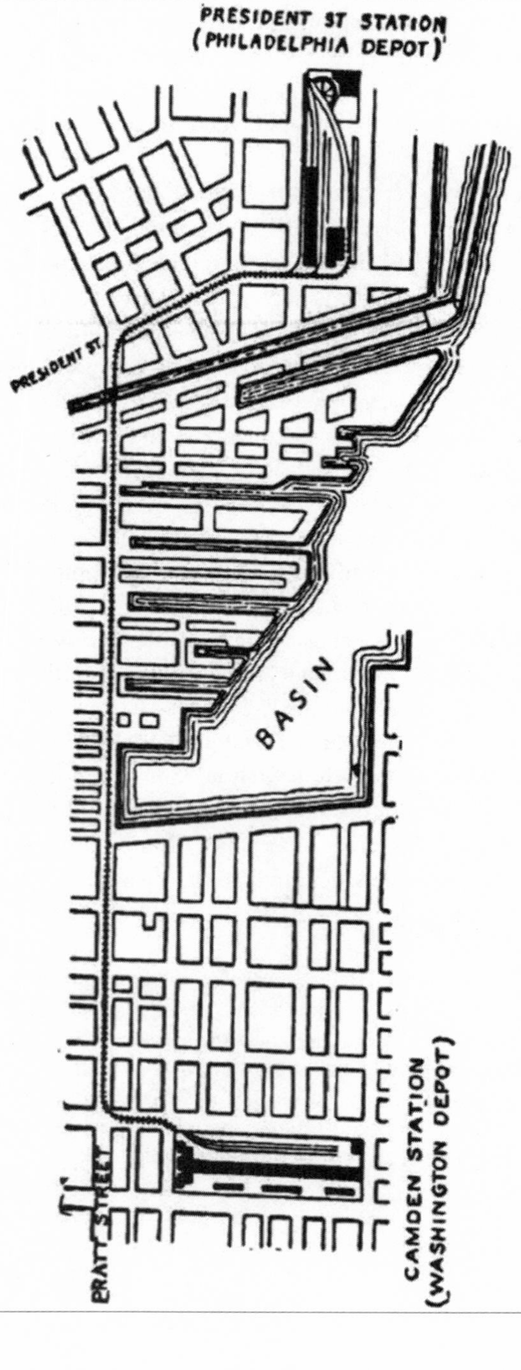

BALTIMORE ROUTE FROM THE PHILADELPHIA TO THE CAMDEN STATION

(from 4 N&H 112)

The cars of the first seven companies were unhitched and with the men still in them drawn by horses over the city tracks between the north and the south terminal. The last four companies and the band found the tracks between the stations blocked. The men dismounted and marched. A mob showered them with stones and pieces of iron. They went to the double-quick. Pistol shots rang out. A soldier fell.

The order went up, "Fire!"

Several of the crowd fell.

The mayor of Baltimore placed himself at the head of the column and begged the captain in command not to fire again. But the crowd did not relent.[8] A moving fight continued through the streets. By the time the Sixth Massachusetts had reached the Washington depot and boarded the train, it had suffered three dead and forty wounded.[9] Many civilian casualties lay in the streets behind them. In an apparent act of treachery, the mayor of Baltimore refused to permit further troops to pass through Baltimore and ordered the railroad bridges north of the city burned.[10] Troops arriving at the north station later in the day were persuaded by civilian authorities to return to Philadelphia.[11] The route to Washington through Baltimore, the only practical land route, was closed.

Butler with the Eighth Massachusetts decided to bypass Baltimore by the water route. He took the train to Perryville and crossed the mouth of the Susquehanna River to Havre de Grace, where he seized the *Maryland*, an old ferry boat. During the beautiful, dark night of April 21, the *Maryland*, carrying Butler and the Eighth Massachusetts, sailed from Perryville down the Chesapeake Bay, arrived in Annapolis Harbor, and headed toward the wharf of the United States Naval Academy. At the wharf lay the revered old frigate *Constitution*, a retired hero of the War of 1812 and now the school-ship of the Naval Academy. She was stuck fast in the mud at the pier and in danger of being seized by disloyal Marylanders.[12] Butler

8 *N&H*, 4, 115-116. According to Colonel Edward F. Jones' report, the Mayor became exasperated, seized a musket from one of the men, and shot a civilian. A policeman with him at the head of the column then shot and killed another citizen. *OR*, 2, 8. In his two accounts, one written three months later and the second in 1887, Mayor Brown mentions no incident like this in the contemporary account and denies it flatly in the post-war account. *N&H*, 4, 116, and fn. 1, 116.

9 *OR*, 2, 7-9.

10 *N&H*, 4, 120-124.

11 *OR*, 2, 10.

12 Swinton, *History of the Seventh New York State Militia*, 2 vols. (New York, NY, 1902), 1, 481-483 (Swinton, *Seventh*); *Butler's Book*, 190-191. Butler wrote many accounts of many events, including this one. None are the same, but all have two common characteristics: Butler is the hero, and he is always right. The various accounts were shaded to the audience at hand; his *Book* was written years later and has only one distorting factor (Butler is the hero). Nor was it

decided to send Captain Peter Haggerty of his staff ashore with a letter to the officer in command of the Academy.

Just as the yawl set out with Captain Haggerty, Butler's brother said: "I will go with him."

He stepped into the boat and handed his pistol to the officer of the deck, saying: "Here, take this. I shall not capture Annapolis with this if I have it, and if they take me, I don't want them to get a good revolver."

An hour passed. Standing at the gangway of his ship, Butler heard the sound of muffled oars and in the darkness saw a boat with four rowers and one passenger.

"What boat is that?" he called out.

"What steamer is that?" was the response.

"None of your business. Come alongside or I will fire into you."

The boat pulled alongside. The passenger, a young man in the uniform of the United States Navy, came aboard and two soldiers seized him.

"Who are you," Butler demanded, "and what are you here for?"

"I am Lieutenant Matthews, sent by Commodore Blake, Commandant of the Naval Academy, to learn what steamer this is."

"Very well. I can tell you that easily. But whether I shall allow you to communicate it to Captain Blake is another question." Having heard that a great many of the naval officers had quit the service, Butler meant to be cautious. "This is the steamer *Maryland*, which plied as a ferry-boat between Havre de Grace and Perryville. I am General Butler of Massachusetts, and my troops here are Massachusetts men, and we propose landing here."

"I am rejoiced to hear it," said the young lieutenant, "and so will be Captain Blake. He is afraid that this boat holds a lot of Baltimore roughs who have come to capture the station."

"Very well. You must remain here. I have sent a boat ashore to Captain Blake—you must have passed it somewhere—with the information that he wants."

At daybreak Captain Haggerty, Butler's brother, and Commodore Blake returned. Butler took the commodore to the quarter-deck where they could speak privately, identified himself, explained his mission, and asked what the commodore needed.

"Thank God! Thank God!" said Blake. "Won't you save the *Constitution*?"

Blake was referring to the old ship stuck at anchor. Butler thought he was talking about the document that was the fabric of government.

written for a particular audience like a regimental reunion, see e.g., the account given at an Eighth Regiment reunion, dated Aug. 2, 1869. *Butler's P.O.C.*, 1, 23-26. The account in *Butler's Book* is accepted in every conflict unless reasons for contrary treatment are stated in the notes.

"Yes, that is just what I am here for."

"Are those your orders? Then the old ship is safe."

Butler could never bear to admit that anyone could tell him what to do. "I have no orders. I am carrying on war now on my own hook. I cut loose from my orders when I left Philadelphia. What do you want me to do to save the Constitution?"

"I want some sailor men, for I have no sailors; I want to let her out, and get her afloat."[13]

Realizing that they were discussing the ship, not the document, Butler replied, "Oh, well! I have plenty of sailor men from the town of Marblehead, where their fathers built the *Constitution*."

"Well, can you stop and help me?"

"I must stop," said Butler. "I can go no further at present, and I propose to stop here and hold this town."

"Oh, well. You can do that as long as we can keep off any force by sea. This peninsula is connected with the mainland by a little neck not half a mile wide, and a small body of troops there posted, can hold off a large force. Now, General, won't you come over with me and take breakfast, and then we can talk of this matter wider."

Butler accepted, assured himself that his force could hold the Naval Academy long enough for reinforcements to arrive, and departed to have breakfast at headquarters with Commodore and Mrs. Blake and their son, also an officer in the United States Navy. At breakfast, Butler started to talk to Commodore Blake about moving the *Constitution* from her dock when Mrs. Blake caught his eye. From her glance he concluded he was about to raise an inappropriate subject, and he changed to the deviled hard-shelled crabs.[14] The two Blake men finished and departed, leaving Mrs. Blake and Butler at the table. Mrs. Blake then raised the issues that had concerned Stone while he created reliable militia forces in the capital and Keyes while he was traveling to New York on his secret mission to reinforce Fort Pickens: loyalty and security.

"General, I observed that you took the hint I tried to give you to keep the conversation upon general topics, and I think it my duty now, however painful it is, to give you the reason. My son, I regret to say, sides with secession; and while I feel certain that nothing you could say would be communicated to the enemies of the country by him, yet we find lately that one cannot be too careful."[15]

13 *Butler's Book*, 193; the colloquy is different in Butler's other accounts, e.g., *Butler's P.O.C.*, 1, 25, speech to the Eighth Massachusetts Regiment, August 2, 1869.

14 Swinton, *Seventh*, 483; *Butler's Book*, 190-93.

15 *Butler's Book*, 193.

In a long, active, and controversial career, Benjamin Franklin Butler was one of the true, lifelong champions of the "little people" in American history. Unlike his contemporaries, he openly sought public office but always in pursuit of his principals, for which he used any party that promised success for them.

Born November 5, 1818, in Deerfield, New Hampshire, his early family were longtime residents of the colonies and the infant Republic. He was a mixture of unsuccessful Irish patriots and English who had settled in America. While sailing as a privateer on the coast of South America under letters of marque from Simon Bolivar, his father died of yellow fever when Butler was but six months old. Left with children and no income, his mother and grandmother moved to Lowell, Massachusetts, where she managed a boarding house for young workers in the bustling Lowell textile mills. Among young Butler's antecedents and acquaintances were a general in the American Revolution, a cavalry officer in the War of 1812, and two neighbors who had served against the British in the Revolution. Fascinated by their accounts of these conflicts, Butler became interested in the military. Having a strong intellect and superb powers of retention, he was granted a scholarship to attend Phillips Exeter Academy some years before Fitz-John Porter but stayed only a short time, finally graduating from Lowell High School in 1834. He wished to attend West Point, but his mother had other ideas: he was to enter the ministry. She enrolled him in Colby College, then Waterville College, in Waterville, Maine, where she believed he would receive a good Protestant parochial education with strong Baptist overtones.

His trip to the ministry ended at an early stage when he petitioned the faculty to be excused from compulsory church attendance, irritated the college president and the nine doctors of divinity on the faculty, and was fortunate to graduate. He began to read law. Over the years he developed a lucrative law practice.

Within a year after completing college, he joined the Fifth Massachusetts militia, in which he rose steadily until in 1852 he was its colonel. Two years later, the American or Know-Nothing Party, a nationwide anti-immigrant, anti-Catholic organization captured Massachusetts; and the new governor attempted to eliminate all men of foreign birth or extraction from the militia. He ordered the Jackson Musketeers, a rifle company of Irish Catholics in Butler's regiment, disbanded. Butler refused, declared the order unlawful, and claimed he could only be discharged for disobedience by a court-martial. The governor tried another tactic, reorganizing the militia in a way that left no post for Colonel Butler. Nothing if not resourceful, Butler retaliated by using the militia election process for his benefit. Under the law the men elected their company officers, the company officers their regimental officers, and the regimental officers their brigade commanders. In 1855, Butler manipulated the system enough to be elected a brigadier general, a post he held from 1855 to 1860. Using the hyper-technical reasoning of a lawyer, he concluded that his attendance at annual "camps" with his regiments had given him command of "a larger body of troops, duly uniformed and equipped than any general of the United States Army then living except General Scott." By his attendance at a gathering of all state militia in 1860, he claimed he had seen a larger body of troops together than even Scott.

In 1859, he opposed the enrollment of blacks in the state militia because they were not, and could not become, citizens. They were, therefore, ineligible for service. He also felt that, if blacks could join the militia, he and other white men would be degraded by training side-by-side with them.

In his law practice, he always had time to represent the little man. He worked for laborers against their employers, supported the secret ballot to protect freedom of the vote, organized support for the ten-hour day, and made speeches on behalf of labor. Active in the machinery of the party, he attended the presidential convention as a delegate in 1852, was elected to the state legislature, ran for governor, and served as a delegate to the tumultuous Democratic Convention in Charleston, South Carolina, in 1860. Throughout his adult life, even when he was in the military, he was a politician and acted like one. Uninterested in theoretical politics he dealt with practical political problems in a practical way.

In personality, he was intelligent, quick-witted, humorous, self-confident, confrontational, courageous, and insatiably curious. His meteoric temper had a microscopic fuse. For Regular Army officers, West Point graduates, and Boston blue-bloods, he enjoyed a thorough distaste. In appearance, his slender frame of youth had been lost. He was fat, uncoordinated but not clumsy, and fair complected with slightly flushed smooth skin. His face had heavy features, clear and bright eyes one of which was wall-eyed, and no hair on top with long white hair hanging down the sides of his head.[16]

As always, he did not let traditional factions or party lines direct his course. As he saw it, this was not a Republican war. It was a national war. And with his "military background," he believed he was as well trained and qualified as any man, West Point graduate or not.

When the Confederates captured Fort Sumter on April 14, Massachusetts was more ready than any other state; and Butler was as ready as any Massachusetts man. Learning about the surrender on April 15 while traveling to Boston, he wired his old political companion Henry Wilson, the Massachusetts senator who was chairman of

16 *D.A.B.*, 2, pt. 1, 357; Howard P. Nash, Jr., *Stormy Petrel The Life and Times of General Benjamin F. Butler*, 1818-1893, 13-56 (Cranbury, 1969); *Butler's Book*, 33-166; Dick Nolan, *Benjamin Franklin Butler*, 1-59.

the Committee on Military Affairs, "See Cameron and have a brigadier asked for, and I will see to it that I am detailed."[17]

On behalf of the secretary of war, Wilson wired Governor Andrew the same day for twenty companies of infantry, the equivalent of two regiments, a few more than two thousand officers and men. Later in the day the secretary of war and the adjutant general of the army telegraphed for two full regiments. Governor Andrew issued a special order calling for the Third, Fourth, Sixth, and Eighth Massachusetts to report to Boston Common at once. All vacancies were to be filled at once. Any left when the regiments reached Boston would be filled from the regiments that were not going to Washington.[18]

On the train downtown Butler saw James G. Carney, president of a large Boston bank. He explained the situation to Carney, asked for financing for the troops, and requested personal support for himself as a brigadier general. Carney gave him a note to Governor Andrew pledging the loan capacity of the bank to fund the initial call for troops until the legislature could be summoned. After Butler departed with the letter, Carney visited other banks and raised a total initial pledge of three and one-half million dollars. Armed with Carney's letter and bursting with martial ambition, Butler went to see Governor Andrew, who wasted no time in proceeding to discuss the commission.

"General, there is a difficulty. We have two brigadier generals in the militia who are your seniors, and one of them, General Pierce, is now outside, I suppose waiting to see me to ask for the detail."

"Well, governor, you know Brigadier General Pierce, and you know me. Isn't this a case where the officer should be appointed who is supposed to be most instructed in affairs with which he is to deal?"

"I suppose I can detail any brigadier," said the governor.

"So do I."

The treasurer of the commonwealth entered the room and greeted the governor. "Governor," he began, "as you requested, I have been examining the condition of the affairs of the treasury since the repeal of the emergency act, and I cannot find a single dollar appropriated for transporting these troops that you have ordered out and other like expenses. You will have to call an extra session of the legislature, and that will

17 Nash, *Stormy Petrel*, 71.

18 Schouler, *Massachusetts in the War*, 1, 49-51; 150-70. In Butler's mind, Schouler tried to suppress everything Butler did, i.e., "Schouler did all he could to have those facts forgotten." *Butler's Book*, 170. In a sense Butler may be correct. He is not mentioned in Schouler's account of Massachusetts's mobilization.

delay matters very considerably, and we understand by the telegram that there is great urgency for haste in getting troops to Washington."

The governor said, "What shall we do?"

"We shall have to call a meeting of the legislature, and get an appropriation, but that will delay matters considerably. Perhaps we can use our current income."

"Governor," interjected Butler, whose shrewd anticipation was about to put him first in line, "I was aware of this condition of things, and I can remedy it. Coming down in the cars, I saw President Carney of the Bank of Mutual Redemption, and he has authorized me to say that fifty thousand dollars of the funds of that bank is at the disposal of the Commonwealth, and that the other banks will answer drafts to that amount, and he recommends that I be selected as the brigadier to take command. Here is his letter."

"Well, Governor," the treasurer said, "As General Butler has found the means to go, I think he ought to go."

"I don't know but he had," said the governor. "I will take it into consideration."

The national capital was well inside Democratic and secessionist territory. Did the governor believe that a Breckenridge Democrat, a compromise man, would be a proper person for this sensitive assignment? Showing the same non-partisan spirit that drove the president, the governor of Massachusetts commissioned Butler a brigadier general and put him in command of the four regiments being ordered to Washington.[19]

Now most of the way there, he was having breakfast with the wife of the officer in command of the Naval Academy. After breakfast, Butler ordered two companies of the Eighth Massachusetts to man the *Constitution*, one as sailors and one as marines. When she had been lightened by removal of her upper deck guns and gun carriages, she was towed to safety by the *Maryland*; but while returning from this task, the *Maryland*, with the remaining companies of the Eighth Massachusetts still aboard, ran hard aground.

Simultaneously, Keyes was sailing with his four regiments from New York City, and the Seventh New York Infantry Regiment under Colonel Lefferts was at sea in the steamer *Boston*. Colonel Lefferts learned from the captain of a schooner on its way north that the Rebels had taken the Norfolk Navy Yard and were capturing all shipping in Hampton Roads. The *Boston* would be no match for any warship from Norfolk. Not knowing whether Fort Monroe was still in Union hands, Lefferts decided to avoid the area altogether and sail up the Chesapeake.[20]

19 *Butler*'s *Book*, 170-73.

20 Swinton, *Seventh*, 1, 481.

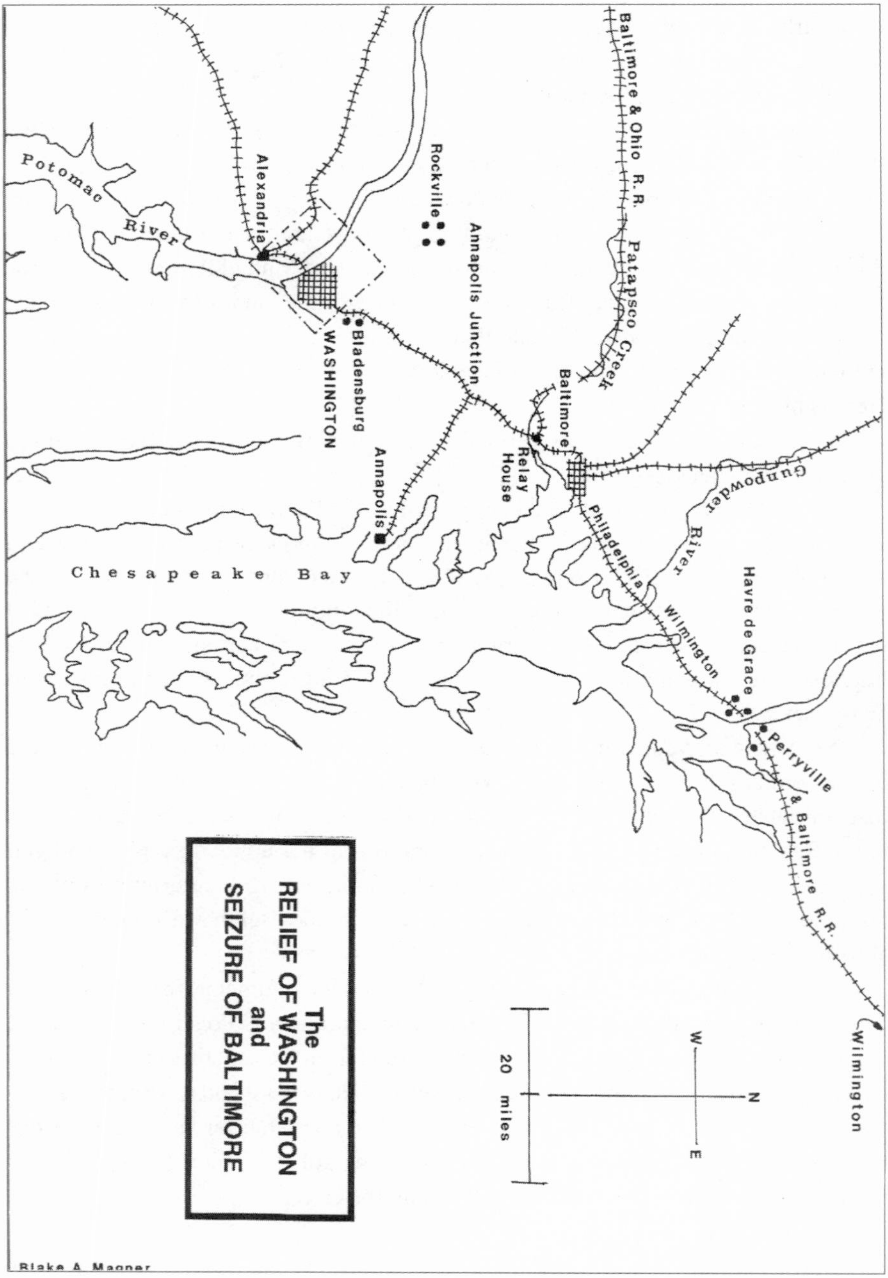
The
RELIEF OF WASHINGTON
and
SEIZURE OF BALTIMORE
Potomac River
Alexandria
Rockville
Annapolis Junction
Bladensburg
WASHINGTON
Baltimore & Ohio R.R.
Patapsco Creek
Baltimore
Relay House
Annapolis
Chesapeake Bay
Gunpowder River
Philadelphia
Wilmington
& Baltimore R.R.
Havre de Grace
Perryville
Wilmington
N
W
E
20 miles
Blake A. Magner

Early on the morning of Monday, April 22, the *Boston* arrived in Annapolis Harbor. Lefferts and his officers went ashore where Lefferts met with the town officials of Annapolis. After the conference he repeated to his officers the information he had been given: the roads were infested with guerillas, the local population was bitterly hostile, ambush along the way to the capital was likely, and large groups of armed secessionists from Baltimore would oppose them at the bridges. The officers unanimously agreed that the Seventh had left New York City to relieve and defend the capital, that it had already been delayed, and that it should push forward at the earliest possible moment along the most direct route, the wagon road from Annapolis to the capital.

Butler approached and requested permission to address the officers. The regiment had already had an unfavorable encounter with his arrogance in Philadelphia. In spite of his "unsoldierly dress, dumpy figure, unprepossessing face," and prior bad conduct, the officers listened with tolerance.[21] Butler wanted the Seventh New York to stay in Annapolis and assist the Eighth Massachusetts in repairing the tracks, bridges, and trestles on the railroad spur from Annapolis to Annapolis Junction on the main line between Washington and Baltimore, then east to Relay House on the main line.[22]

Serving as a volunteer aide to Lefferts was Samuel R. Curtis, an 1831 graduate of West Point and a congressman from Iowa. Curtis was a tall, finely built though heavy-set man with a high forehead, large hazel eyes, and a decidedly grave face adorned with side whiskers. In demeanor, he was serious and deliberate; in speech and action, undemonstrative.[23] Lefferts and his regimental officers relied heavily on him for advice.

After discussing Butler's request with his officers and Colonel Curtis, Lefferts refused. The most direct route to Washington was west along the wagon road. Relay House was east along the main line, away from the capital. Lefferts announced to Butler that "the Seventh Regiment had been ordered by the governor of New York to report direct to General Scott at Washington; that it had not placed itself or been placed by any order of the War Department under the command of any militia officer of the State of Massachusetts; that, while no order from General Butler could be received or obeyed, it was most anxious to co-operate with the troops of

21 Swinton, *Seventh*, 1, 485-86; *Butler's Book*, 199. According to Butler, the Seventh was critical of Lefferts for failing to cooperate with him. Leaving aside the unlikeliness of this as a matter of logic, the more measured and less heroic account in Swinton's *Seventh* seems far more plausible.

22 Marshall, *Butler's P.O.C.*, 1, 25.

23 *D.A.B.*, 2, pt. 2, 619-20; 1 Cullum no. 655, description quoted in *D.A.B.* from Stiles, *Recollection and Sketches*.

Massachusetts or any loyal state in any and every effort designed for speedy relief of Washington or the general welfare of the country; that as the first to land at Annapolis, it was entitled to the advance in the forward movement; and that being a large, well-equipped thoroughly disciplined regiment, it was qualified to meet and overcome opposition, and would be of great service at the capital."[24]

Butler could not bear being refused when he issued an order and had enough military knowledge to believe he was the superior, and in this case the commanding, officer. He already disliked and scorned West Pointers. That must have helped him conclude from Curtis's red nose that Curtis was a drunkard. He also found Curtis to be officious and sometimes discourteous.

Indignant and angry, Butler said, "Colonel Lefferts, war is not carried on in this way. A commander doesn't consult his regiment as to the propriety of obeying his orders. He must judge of what those orders should be. Now, by the Articles of War I am in command as brigadier general of the United States militia called into service and actually in service. I take the responsibility of giving you an order to march and shall expect it to be obeyed."[25]

"General Butler," said Curtis, "you don't appear to be aware that a general of United States militia has no right to command New York State troops."

"No, sir. I am not aware of that, and it is not the law. Have you got a copy of the Articles of War in your pocket?"

"No, sir."

"Have you examined them?"

"No, sir; but I was educated at West Point."

The implication that Regular-Army, West-Point learning represented omniscience and that militia officers who had been very successful in professional and political life knew nothing infuriated Butler.

"What rank does this man hold in your command?" he said to Lefferts.

"None at all."

"Well, then, I have nothing to do with him." With great emphasis Butler asked, "Will you march? I hope you won't refuse to obey my order."

"Well," interjected Curtis again, "What will you do if the Colonel refuses to march?"

Butler had not been a successful lawyer and prominent politician for nothing. He knew how to find the pressure points. "If he refuses to march, I certainly have this

24 Swinton, *Seventh*, 1, 482, 484-485.

25 Under Article 95 of the Articles of War, which were rules passed by Congress for the governance of United States military forces, the officer of highest rank on the scene was in charge unless specific authorization to the contrary had been granted.

remedy: I will denounce him and his regiment as fit only to march down Broadway in gala dress to be grinned at by milliners' apprentices."

He called an orderly and told him to summon Lieutenant-Colonel Edward Hincks of the Eighth Massachusetts. Fortuitously, Hincks was already at the door.

"Colonel Hincks, take two companies of the Eighth Regiment and march out two miles on the Elkton railroad towards Washington, and hold it against all comers until I reinforce you, if necessary, and report to me in the morning. Colonel Lefferts with his whole regiment is afraid to go, Colonel, but you will obey orders."

Butler was already making good on his threat to embarrass the colonel of the Seventh. Curtis said, "Such language as that, General, requires reparation among officers and gentlemen."

Butler took this to be an offer of a duel,[26] which was a Southern, not a Northern, response to a personal insult.[27] He felt he would be justified if he accepted. The Rebels, he thought, did not believe Northerners would fight at all; but if the Yankees could show for now that they were at least willing to fight each other, a good impression would be made.

"Oh, well," he responded, "as far as Colonel Lefferts is concerned, I shall be entirely satisfied with him if he allows a disposition to fight anybody anywhere. Let him begin on me. But as for you," he said to Curtis, "if you interrupt this conversation again and if you do not leave the room instantly, I will direct my orderly to take you out. Good afternoon, Colonel Lefferts."

He mounted his horse and rode with Hincks, taking two companies of the Eighth Massachusetts to seize the railroad depot. They found one building locked. The general asked what was in it.

"Nothing," the custodian replied.

Butler demanded the key, but the keeper said he did not have it. "Where is it?"

"I don't know."

That was enough discussion. His men smashed the doors. Inside was a small, rusty locomotive. Parts had been removed to disable it. Butler turned to his men, who were standing in line in front of the depot and said: "Do any of you know anything about such a machine as this?"

Private Charles Homans of Company E stepped forward, looked at the engine, and replied: "That engine was made in our shop. I guess I can fit her up and run her."

"Go to work, and pick out some men to help you."[28]

26 *Butler's Book*, 197-200.

27 John Hope Franklin, *The Militant South 1800-1861*, 44-58 (Cambridge, 1956).

28 *Butler's Book*, 199-202.

For generations the American infantryman has been imaginative and creative, everything from a scrounger to an inventor.[29] In a short while Private Homans and his assistants found the missing parts and put the engine in working order. Butler's call for all men who knew anything about laying railroad track had collected twenty men. They were ready.

Lieutenant-Colonel Hincks started his reconnaissance, marching his men two miles north along the spur toward the junction with the main line. Meanwhile, before the Seventh could complete its preparations to march, Colonel Frederick W. Lander, a messenger from Scott, arrived with dispatches.[30] Lander was already well known for his exploits in the West, including his participation on the staff of Isaac I. Stevens in the survey of the northern railroad route to the Pacific. There, he had crossed guerilla-infested countryside, been captured and released, and seen armed parties everywhere. He now reported that the trip to Washington would be perilous but believed it should be made at all cost. He added that casualties would be sustained, could not be carried along, and should be left on the road to be treated by the civilian population.[31]

The dispatches proved Lefferts right. They urged the Seventh to advance to Washington as soon as possible because an enemy attack was expected momentarily; but if it could, the regiment should travel the railroad route and repair the rail line as it went. Lefferts now had new, clear orders. He decided not to take the wagon road but to follow Hincks up the spur, then turn west toward Washington on the main line.[32] Lefferts and his men went to bed early that night.

Before midnight the frigate *Constitution*, from its new anchorage, fired three rockets, the pre-arranged signal for the approach of hostile ships. The regimental

29 In 1944, the French countryside west of Paris had numerous small farm fields bounded by hedgerows which were small ridges of packed earth often as high as a tank and topped with a tall growth of trees and brambles. Each field was, in effect, a small defense position with field fortifications for infantry. The dirt ridge would cause a tank to tilt skyward as it climbed, thus exposing its unarmored belly to German antitank weapons that were far more effective than they were against the heavy frontal armor of the tanks. Curtis G. Culin, Jr., a thirty-nine-year-old sergeant from New York City, designed, in effect, a pitchfork to be welded to the frame of the tanks. It had four "tusks" that punctured the dirt ridge, held the tank down, and tore a ground-level hole in the hedgerow. Almost overnight, his gadget was built and attached to a majority of the tanks in the hedgerow area, and was a vital factor in the encirclement of the German Seventh Army in the Falaise pocket. Omar N. Bradley, *A Soldier's Story* (New York, 1951), 296, 342, 369-83.

30 The various accounts imply that Lefferts received two messages from Washington; but the circumstances suggest that he received only one and that, if he received two, they were the same, delivered by two different messengers. Swinton states that two of eight messengers, including Colonel Frederick W. Lander, passed through to Annapolis. *Seventh Regiment*, 189-190.

31 *D.A.B.*, 5, pt. 2, 569; Swinton, *Seventh*, 489-90.

32 Swinton, *Seventh*, 487.

drums sounded the "long roll," a continuous beating that was the signal for "great and immediate danger."[33] Several transports could be seen in the lower Chesapeake Bay, but a sharp look with a night glass showed them to be Lieutenant-Colonel Keyes's ships with his regiments of New York and Rhode Island Infantry on their way to the capital.

At sunrise, the Naval Academy was quiet. Butler had scarcely sent forward the remainder of the Eighth Massachusetts when Lieutenant-Colonel Keyes presented himself, saying he was a member of General Scott's staff, had been sent to the governor of New York to help recruit troops, had finished that work, and was now returning to Washington. Major General Sandford and Governor Sprague had put him in charge of the infantry regiments he had with him. When he had found the way through Baltimore blocked, he came to Annapolis. With no other Regular Army officer present, he said, he deemed it his duty to take command.

Butler now had no troops of his brigade left. He had already unsuccessfully tried the exercise of assuming command of troops from other states. He would try another approach. "Have you any instructions from General Scott to so do?" he asked.

Keyes said he did not but thought his suggestion proper. Under his original orders from General Scott, he was to do anything he thought beneficial to the service of the United States.

Butler had just finished the conflict with Lefferts on his power to command all troops at Annapolis, had lost that struggle simply by being faced down, and had been embarrassed by the result. He decided to humor Keyes until he established communication with General Scott. He thought his troops were close to the Relay House and would be in Washington the next day. Until things had been clarified by the general in chief, he was not ready to risk another affront to his authority.

"Well, I suppose that you will need my services here to press forward these troops as fast as I can," Butler said, referring to Keyes's troops.

"Oh, yes; I only take command to see that everything is done right, owing to your inexperience."

"Very well, give me your orders in writing so that I can be sure exactly what I have got to do."

Keyes wrote out General Orders No. 1, later followed by other general orders. Butler consulted his aide Colonel Schuyler Hamilton about them.

"Don't obey them," Hamilton said. "He has no right to give any such orders."

"Oh, well," responded Butler, "I will take care of him."

33 *Ibid.*, 490.

He gathered the orders together and, as soon as he knew that the route to Washington was open, sent Hamilton on the train to report to General Scott, describe Keyes's conduct, and show the lieutenant general the orders.

To Scott, a senior officer most august, important, sensitive, and egotistical, Keyes had already committed virtually every offense known to military etiquette. While serving as military secretary, Keyes had received and followed orders not given by Scott. He had communicated directly over Scott's head with the president and cabinet members. He had obeyed military orders from a civilian. He had accepted a task not assigned by Scott. He had left Scott without anyone to assist in his burdensome daily affairs. Once gone, he had sent Scott only one report, leaving the lieutenant general to gather information from others. Last, he had stayed away longer than he said he would. Keyes's offenses and his presumptuous conduct in Annapolis ignited the general in chief's fury.

"What!" he exclaimed. "Has Keyes been appointed field marshall? I have not heard of it. Why, nobody but a field marshall could have issued such orders as these while I am lieutenant-general commanding the United States armies. Tell General Butler to order Field Marshal Keyes to report to me forthwith, and I will take care of him."

Every man who came to the capital from the northeast had to pass through Annapolis and would visit Butler's headquarters to be issued a pass for the railroad. As Butler saw it, Lieutenant-Colonel Keyes gave instructions about the art of war, told him what to do, corrected him from time to time, gave the appearance of being Butler's keeper, and made Butler seem ignorant.[34]

If Keyes had observed the cardinal rule, never call attention to a superior's ignorance in front of others, his brief stay in Annapolis might have ended peacefully; but he was enjoying the exuberance of new freedom and was not careful. Besides, he had already taken the measure of General Butler and had formed a low opinion of him. As he would write later, he had found that Butler "possessed phenomenal activity and persistence of brain power, and that he considered himself fit to be the leader of all the pursuits, callings, professions, and occupations of men whether he had studied them or not."

Butler seemed to have the patience to hear a description or account of anything "provided that neither his interest, his vanity, nor his ambition was concerned in it . . . At heart he would have fame, in default of which he is content with notoriety at the expense of abuse and slander. Weighed in the balance his virtues turn the scale

34 *Butler's Book*, 205-07; Marshal, *Butler's P.O.C.*, 35.

against his faults, one of which his accusers call obstinacy. I think it should be called perverseness . . ."[35]

When Colonel Hamilton reported his meeting with General Scott, Butler was freed of any concern about a hostile reaction to his treatment of the lieutenant-colonel and was ready next morning when the first visitor, Senator Wilson of Massachusetts, arrived at headquarters. Wilson and Butler had worked together for several years on political matters and were old acquaintances. Keyes arrived and was introduced. The three men discussed the current situation. Keyes started to instruct Butler about the characteristics of a good officer. Butler pretended to listen intently. Finally, he said:

"Do you think of any other qualification beside those you have described to me and the Senator here, which is necessary to make a good officer of the army?"

"No, I don't think of anything that I need to add."

"Well, Colonel, I think there is one thing more that is necessary, which you have not named and which you evidently don't know anything about."

"Ah, General, what is that?"

"Brains! Colonel Keyes, brains! You haven't any, and you have bothered me here long enough. I have reported you to General Scott, and here is your order to report to him forthwith, and here is a pass for you to go; and if you don't go by the next train, I will send you under guard. Good-morning, sir."[36]

Keyes's order to report was, in fact, a surprising letter from the general in chief:

> Washington, April 19, 1861.
>
> Sir:—Considering that you recently left me on a mission without my suggestion or special consent, and considering that in our late official connection I several times found it necessary to suppress acts of rudeness on your part, and considering that, after the high functions you have recently executed, I should find it still more difficult to restrain your temper, I think it necessary to terminate our official connection without further correspondence or irritation.
>
> I enclose a letter this moment received from his excellency the governor of New York, together with my reply, which you can either use or return to me as you may think proper.
>
> Wishing you and yours all happiness,

35 Keyes, *Fifty Years*, 402, 403, 404.

36 In their post-war memoirs Butler and Keyes give very different accounts of their time at Annapolis, Keyes's account being very brief by comparison. Generally, Butler's account has been preferred.

I remain with much respect,

Yours,
WINFIELD SCOTT.

Lieutenant-Colonel E. D. Keyes, U.S. Army.[37]

Keyes did not regret the loss of his position as military secretary, a job of grueling, unending work governed by the "whims and caprices" of an egotistical and bad-tempered superior. When he reached Washington, he visited the president and "Prime Minister" Seward. They earnestly and warmly thanked him for his efforts. He was cordially received by Secretary of War Cameron and Secretary of Treasury Chase and was invited to breakfast with the latter cabinet officer. As he had been when he was in Scott's favor, Keyes was asked to attend social events with other notable men.

But when he called on General Scott to pay his respects, the old general, an accomplished harborer of grudges, refused to receive him.[38]

37 Keyes, *Fifty Years*, 404. The letter is quoted in full in Keyes's book but cannot be identified with certainty as the one handed to him by Butler. Because neither Keyes nor Butler mention more than one piece of correspondence from Scott to Keyes and the circumstances suggest that no others reached Keyes, the conclusion that they described the same letter seems reasonable and logical.

38 Keyes, *Fifty Years*, 405.

Chapter 9

"In connection with the movement a large force well supplied with artillery should move upon or threaten as the case may be Richmond from Fort Monroe by way of York river operating between York and James River."

— McDowell to Chase describing an overall offensive plan

Halting Offensive Steps Secure the Rear

By April 28 the war was two weeks old. The Virginia shore of the Potomac River, visible from the Capitol Building, was in hostile hands. On it, the Confederates had constructed batteries that might be able to sink transports on the Potomac River. The Union gunboat flotilla made daily examinations of Matthias Point where the channel ran very close to the land. Harpers Ferry had been occupied by the Confederates. Twenty-seven miles from Washington a small force of Rebels held Manassas Junction. Benjamin Butler was still in his equivocal position in Annapolis. The railroad between Washington and Baltimore was still closed; and Baltimore, controlled by secessionists, was the most important point for reinforcements because Baltimore was the focal point of the railroads headed for the capital. It stood clearly as the Baltimore Bottleneck and its most important leg was the forty mile line of track between Baltimore and

Washington. The problem could not be solved without clearing Baltimore and guaranteeing the line to the capital.[1]

In the capital John G. Nicolay described the uncertain and untrustworthy state of affairs to his fiancee, on April 26, "Here we are in this city, in charge of all the public buildings, property and archives, with only about 2,000 *reliable* men to defend it. True we had some 3,000 men in addition, of the District militia under arms. But with the city perfectly demoralized with secession feeling, no man could *know* whom of the residents to trust. We were not certain but that at the first moment when fate would seem to preponderate against us, we would have to look down the muzzles of our own guns. The feeling was not the most comfortable in the world, I assure you. We were not only surrounded by the enemy, but in the midst of traitors."[2]

Although the view from Washington was anything but sanguine, inexperienced men with no judgment but the best interests of the Republic at heart saw stability without danger in condition of the capital. James S. Wadsworth, an older white-haired landowner and patrician of extraordinary wealth and a member of the efficient Union Defense Committee of the Citizens of New York, wrote to the head of the committee from Philadelphia on April 25. "Now that the Capital is safe and the gov't seems to be without a plan for the future," noted Wadsworth, "I think the heavy expenses of our Committee in chartering steamers should be reduced. It is inexpedient to send forward large reinforcements until the organization of the army is completed—or at least made better than it is at present."[3]

Scott knew that Baltimore was the key to Maryland and that he had to occupy it. In his first plan, four overland columns of three thousand men each would converge on it, one each from Washington, York, and Havre de Grace, while the principal effort sailed from Annapolis up the Chesapeake. This plan he quickly abandoned because he had insufficient troops for the Washington column and the defense of the city.[4] Patterson, with his large contingent of short-term troops, reported that he had twenty-six regiments,[5] all equipped, drilled, and trained. In a short time, he felt, he

1 *OR*, 2, 5; *N&H*, 4, 164-67; Swinton, *Army of the Potomac* 26-30; Turner, George Edgar, *Victory Road the Rails: The Strategic Place of the Railroads in the Civil War* (New York, 1952), 48-52; Thomas Weber, *The Northern Railroads in the Civil War 1861-1865* (New York, 1952), 35-36; Edward Hungerford, *The Story of the Baltimore & Ohio Railroad 1827-1927*, 2 vols. (New York and London, 1928), vol. 2, 7-11.

2 Nicolay MSS (L.C.) letter dated April 26, 1861, from Nicolay to Therena.

3 Union Defense Committee MSS (N.Y.H.S.) letter of April 25, 1861, from Wadsworth to Draper.

4 *OR*, 2, 607, 609.

5 *OR*, 2, 615. Patterson had six at York, six at Philadelphia, two at Chambersburg, six at Lancaster, and probably six at Harrisburg.

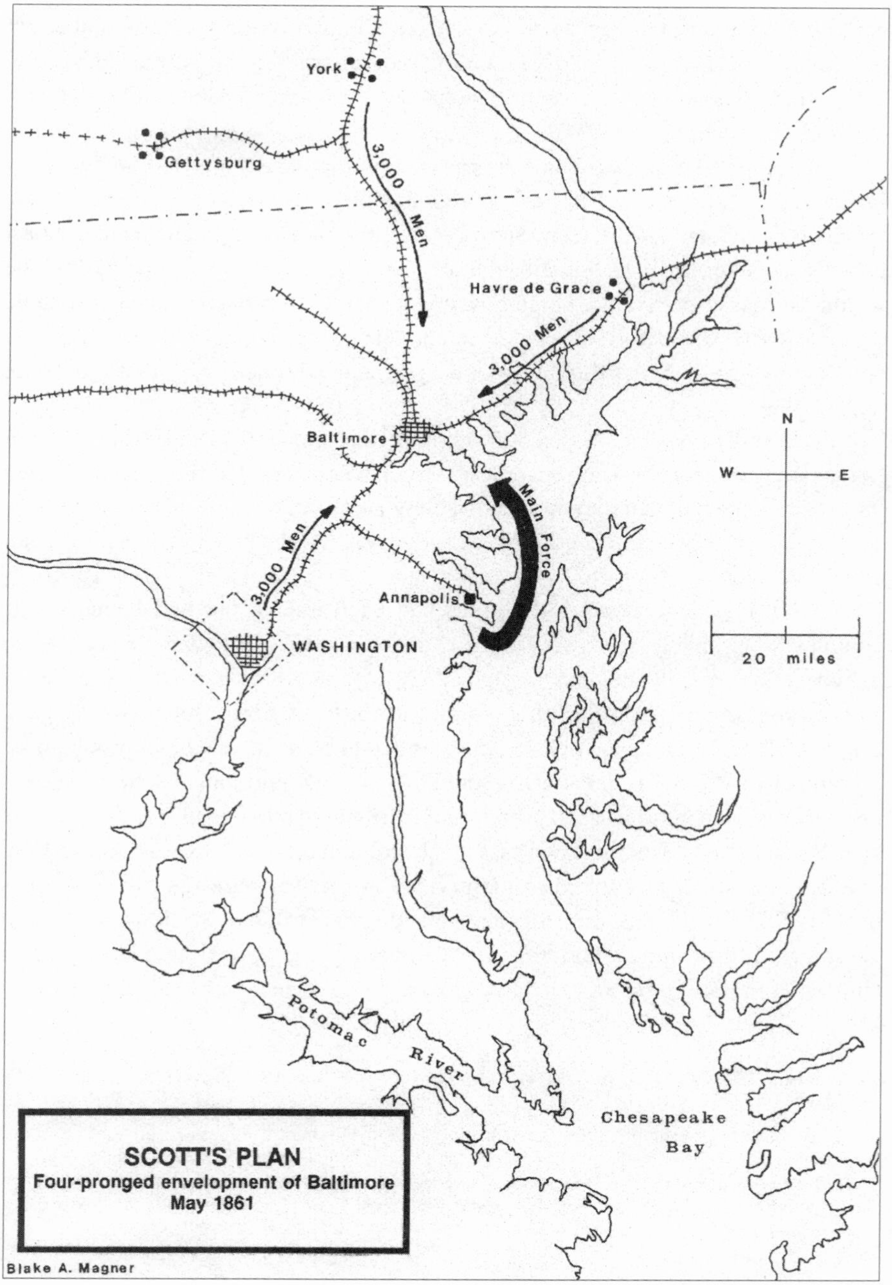
York
Gettysburg
3,000 Men
Havre de Grace
3,000 Men
Baltimore
N
W
E
Main Force
3,000 Men
Annapolis
WASHINGTON
20 miles
Potomac River
Chesapeake Bay
SCOTT'S PLAN
Four-pronged envelopment of Baltimore
May 1861
Blake A. Magner

could put six thousand men on the road from York to Baltimore and another six thousand from Havre de Grace. The problem of controlling the railroads had been successfully overcome by militarizing them and persuading the companies to repair the track destruction.[6]

Patterson had more regiments than any other commander, and his situation was better than most because his area of responsibility was essentially loyal.[7] These factors were evident to Patterson. Though suffering from ill health, he seemed at last to be ready. Pleased with this information, Scott asked him to report the time he would be ready to advance on Baltimore.[8] Patterson discovered insurmountable problems. Always, before he could march, something more had to be done. He consistently saw the best side when prophesying action but only the worst at the time to perform.

In circumstances like those confronting Scott, characteristics like this were not immediately noticeable. They become apparent over a period of time and instructed those with hindsight that they were a disabling part of Patterson's personality. Now Scott could not see a course of conduct over time, and the characteristics were not clearly visible.

More than a week after the order had been issued, the two Pennsylvania columns were finally ready. With Cadwalader's division, Patterson planned to march south from Philadelphia through Havre de Grace and on to Baltimore. Keim, assisted by Porter, would push his division south from York. But first, yet again, supply difficulties had to be overcome, rifles had to be fixed, and other problems *ad infinitum* had to be solved. Patterson sent Scott a long report in which he recited his problems, related his plans, and promised that he would move in two days even if he were not supplied.[9] The two days passed. No column marched. Instead, a new plan: one regiment of artillery armed as infantry, one artillery battery, and five companies of the Third United States Infantry, all Regular troops, would start toward Washington from York.[10] Porter made the necessary arrangements with the civilian authorities in Baltimore to allow the column to pass and helped to ready the troops.

6 *OR*, 2, 616. On May 3, the federal government ordered it reopened to public passengers. *OR*, 2, 618-19.

7 Fremont, for example, serving a short time later in Missouri, had to create an army from nothing, had to arm it with little or no help, had to work in an area that was more hostile to the federal government than not, and had to overcome much hostility within his own organization. Alan Nevins, *Fremont*: *Pathmarker of the West*, 2 vols. (New York, 1955), 474-82 (Nevins, *Fremont*.)

8 Porter MSS (L.C.) memorandum of n.d., n.p., and no author; *OR*, 2, 599.

9 *OR*, 2, 624-25, 626. He would set out on Wednesday, May 8.

10 *OR*, 2, 632.

Then, Patterson changed the composition of the column. Thomas's four hundred dismounted Regular cavalry, three thousand volunteers officered by Regulars, and Sherman's old Regular battery would make the attempt. This was the column prepared by Porter on his first trip to Harrisburg; but just as everything neared completion, a Presidential order had halted the movement before it took the road. Patterson was to use the sea route to send his column to Washington. Days passed. Again, nothing happened.[11]

Butler, still in Annapolis and in command of the Department of Annapolis, decided that the time had come, in the words of Ludwig von Beethoven, "to grasp fate by the throat." He had talked to Scott and Chase in Washington. Rightly fearing that Scott would forbid any advance from Annapolis to Baltimore, he merely obtained confirmation from Scott that Baltimore was in his department but kept his own counsel on his plans.

Calling again on his reliable staff officer, Captain Peter Haggerty, he ordered Haggerty to enter Baltimore undercover and evaluate secessionist military capacity in the city. He was anxious to advance. At the least, he had orders from Scott to seize arms, ammunition, and provisions; and he now knew the locations of the Sixth Massachusetts's survivors who had not reached the South Station.[12]

He decided he would use a decoy train. With three passenger cars loaded with infantry at the head of the engine, flat cars behind with artillery, and an extra engine at the rear ostensibly to aid on the sharp grade before Harpers Ferry, he ran a train north from Relay House at 6:00 a.m. One of his staff officers reported two young men on fast horses heading in the direction of Baltimore.

"Why not arrest them?" asked the staff officer.

Butler refused. "Let them go. Their business is to report at Baltimore. They will report that we have gone to Harper's Ferry, and that may cause their troops, if any there are, to go there, too."

Two miles up the track the train halted. The infantry in the advance cars dismounted to make local arrests for security. The train was reversed. At 6:00 p.m. it reached Baltimore, arriving at a deserted train station. Following a guide the column of troops started toward Federal Hill, an eminence inside the city that commanded the surrounding area. The men were ordered not to fire unless they received fire and suffered casualties, but they were to burn any house from which fire came.

Hardly had they begun the march when pitch darkness and a violent thunderstorm covered their movement. A driving rain fell. Lightning bolts slashed

11 Porter MSS (L.C.) memorandum of n.d., n.p., and n.a.; *OR*, 2, 599.

12 *Butler's Book*, 226-27.

the sky. Bayonets glittered. From horseback at the head of the column, Butler could see the long line of troops in the flashes. It was working its way up the hill behind him. But sheltered from the storm in their houses the civilians did not see them. On the top of the hill, Butler selected a German tavern with a small beer garden for his headquarters. His boots had taken so much rain that the pressure of his foot squirted water in his face when he dismounted.

One of his company commanders arrived with startling news. "General, I have been advised that this hill is mined; and we shall all be blown up."

"Well, Captain, there will be one comfort in that. We shall at least get dry. But I will go with you and reconnoiter."

After he had seen the mine, which he found to be an innocuous, ordinary gravel mine, he settled his troops into their positions.[13]

Once again, a junior officer had bested the general in chief, this time a militia general with no military experience or training. As always when his ego was wounded, his position challenged, or his authority questioned, he was furious. He ordered General George Cadwalader from Philadelphia to take command of Baltimore while Butler was relieved and sent to command Fortress Monroe. Butler considered this a slap for his action, and rightly so. He demanded approval or dismissal, but the government gave its traditional response to demands for vindication by a disgruntled officer: a frustrating dead silence.[14]

Although Cadwalader was given permission to suspend the writ of habeas corpus, declare martial law, and exact a loyalty oath, he decided to pacify the populace with less severe measures.[15] Men caught destroying railway bridges and committing other acts of sabotage were delivered to civil authorities for punishment in the hope that amicable relations with the civilian population could be restored.[16] Baltimore, the focal point of secession in Maryland, had been peacefully "reconstructed" for the moment. If only because Rebel military support was a good distance away, many citizens in Baltimore became "loyal."

In the meantime, during the latter part of April and early May while Patterson temporized with the occupation of Baltimore and Butler provided his unauthorized solution, Scott continued to be concerned about the defense of the capital. The departure of Robert E. Lee had left him without a candidate to command the large, intimidating army he wanted. Many of the other capable higher-ranking officers,

13 *Butler's Book*, 228-33.

14 *OR*, 2, 634 ff.

15 *OR*, 2, 640.

16 *OR*, 2, 642-43.

including Albert Sidney Johnston and Joseph E. Johnston, had resigned to join the Southern army. Applying his rule about promotion of company grade officers to higher ranks, Scott began to make appointments from the junior officers he knew. As a result of the order dividing Patterson's original department, freshly minted Colonel Joseph K. F. Mansfield was made the commander of the Department of Washington. A white-haired, gray-bearded, soldierly looking man, Mansfield had graduated second in the West Point Class of 1822. His career had been marked with distinction, especially while serving as Scott's chief engineer in Mexico; and in that time of crisis his experience had been invaluable to the general in chief. Scott's personal esteem for him, which had begun in Mexico, increased in Washington.[17] Colonel Samuel P. Heintzelman, a cranky, ill-tempered graduate of West Point, also Class of 1822, was made second in command to Mansfield.

On the morning of April 25, Townsend was leaving the office opposite the War Department when Secretary Cameron passed in a buggy. The secretary ordered his driver to step down and asked Townsend to take his place.

Townsend mounted and took the reins. "Where shall I drive, sir?" he asked.

"I wish to go to the railroad depot as fast as possible."

When they arrived, they closed the telegraph office and locked it before the operator could send a dispatch. They found that Colonel Stone was also at the depot, had already stationed a guard there, and was collecting extra rails and material. Cameron directed him to take possession of the depot and all the rolling stock and material and hold it under military control. While they were at the depot a small train from Baltimore arrived and was taken. For the following weeks, Private Homans's reconstructed engine and its cars with some others taken at Annapolis were the only means of land transportation to the capital for troops coming through Annapolis.[18]

Late in the month of April the small force of Regulars and the District of Columbia militia began to receive reinforcements. The Seventh New York militia completed its difficult trip from Annapolis, arriving on April 27. It marched up Pennsylvania Avenue to the White House, where it passed in review before the president, then went to the War Department to be mustered into the United States service.

Major General Charles Sandford, "an energetic and intelligent commander of a fine division of the state uniformed militia," was telegraphed by Scott on May 6, 1861, to forward the entire New York quota by water as soon as possible. With a superb effort, Sandford shortly sent his entire division to the capital. Approximately

17 Cullum, 1, no. 278; vol. 6, *D.A.B.*, pt. 2, 257; Russell, *My Diary*, 211, entry of July 18, 1861; *C.C.W.*, 1, 37 (McDowell).

18 Townsend, Anecdotes, 21-22.

ten thousand men, the division arrived and marched the first grand review past Lincoln, the Cabinet, and Scott, who were seated on a platform on the sidewalk in front of the White House. Local confidence and military enthusiasm turned upward.[19] As the troops arrived, they were immediately put to work on the defenses of the city.

Sandford offered to come in person. Scott replied on May 8, "Nobody more highly estimates your value as a soldier than myself, and you will receive a hearty welcome from me. More than one brigade of your troops are here, and more expected. Your right to follow them and command them is unquestionable, but your presence will be attended with one disadvantage: we are in critical circumstances, and it would take weeks to make you as well acquainted with localities, officers, and men, as Brevet Brigadier General Mansfield, whom you would supersede as the commander of the department."

Sandford was the quintessence of the trouble cured by the General Orders ending the governors' power to appoint general officers, but they had not yet been published. In the meanwhile could a governor's commission give a general power over a regiment recruited under another state's colors? Sandford avoided the problem. He waived rank and followed his division. Scott solved any remnants of the seniority problem by assigning the general to command of all New York troops in the city, two brigades and more, while Colonel Mansfield retained command of the Department.[20]

Now that Baltimore had fallen to Butler and been occupied by Cadwalader, the Maryland side of the capital was safe. In the other direction, directly across the Potomac River from Washington, Virginia, soon to be the home of the Confederate capital and one of the seats of Confederate strength, did not look as if it would be so easy. For the safety of the capital, a foothold on the west bank of the river seemed mandatory.

In the evening of May 2, a group of officers at General Scott's headquarters discussed the heights of Arlington, location of the Lee family mansion. Did they command the capital? The family had long since moved South, but no one knew the geographic relationship of their property to the capital. The next day the meeting reconvened; and Mansfield, having investigated, reported about Arlington Heights.

> We now come to the City and Georgetown and arsenal, exposed to the Virginia shore. Here I must remark that the President's House and department buildings in its vicinity are but two and a half miles across the river from Arlington high

19 Townsend, Anecdotes, 16.

20 *Ibid.*, 15-16.

> ground, where a battery of bombs and heavy guns, if established, could destroy the city with comparatively a small force after destroying the bridges. The capital is only three and a half miles from the same height at Arlington and at the Aqueduct the summits of the heights on the opposite shore are not over one mile from Georgetown.

Mansfield continued:

> With this view of the condition of our position, it is clear to my mind that the city is liable to be bombarded at the will of an enemy unless we occupy the ground which he certainly would occupy if he had any such intention. I therefore recommend that the heights above mentioned be seized and secured by at least two strong redoubts, one commanding the Long Bridge and the other the aqueduct and that a body of men be there encamped to sustain the redoubts and give battle to the enemy if necessary. I have engineers maturing plans and reconnoitering further. It is quite probable that our troops, assembled at Arlington, would create much excitement in Virginia; yet at the same time, if the enemy were to occupy the ground there, a greater excitement would take place on our side, and it might be necessary to fight a battle at disadvantage.[21]

Because he no longer had his military secretary Lieutenant-Colonel Keyes to "harangue" about a plan for the Virginia shore, Scott discussed his ideas with Colonel Edward D. Townsend, his adjutant-general. During numerous conversations he stated his intention to correspond about this subject with Major-General George B. McClellan, a rising young militia general in the West and a former member of Scott's staff in Mexico. Townsend offered to draft a letter to McClellan, and Scott accepted. The final version of the plan was drafted by Townsend, revised by Scott, prepared in final by Townsend, signed by Scott, and on May 3 sent to McClellan.

Because Virginia had not formally seceded, Scott would simply not consider intrusion on her soil; and he did not believe a show of force in Virginia would be useful or appropriate. In spite of the attack on Fort Sumter, his ideas continued to be an odd cross between his clear loyalty to the United States and his overwhelming desire to avoid harm to his beloved Virginia. Postmaster General Blair had been right about the practical effect of Scott's policies. At best, his plans for suppressing the rebellion were unrealistic; at worst, they aided the secessionists by a passivity that allowed the Rebels to organize.

In early May, he wanted a blockade to close the ports of the South while a powerful land and naval force seized control of the Mississippi River including the

21 *Ibid.*, 32-33.

forts at the mouth of the river. The Mississippi and the blockade would "envelope the insurgent states," he thought, "and bring them to terms with less blood-shed than any other plan."[22] He still believed that many Union supporters and many neutral persons in the rebellious states would, if given time, assert themselves and override the hot-heads.[23]

If this program produced results, it would be slow and tedious. He predicted it would be confounded by popular demand for "instant and vigorous action, regardless, I fear, of dangerous consequences."[24] Although some of the thinking stated in his "Views" and the "Supplement" had changed, the core remained intact. His plan not to intrude on Arlington Heights and the Virginia shore sprang from his conclusions about the war, its future course, and the best way to deal with the Rebels.

Others felt differently. To them Manassas Junction, a key to the strategic line of the Rappahannock River, should be taken at once while the price would be low. The land along the east coast was creased by a series of long gashes stretching from northwest to southeast as if they were irregular axe wounds in the face of the countryside. The water in them ran to the Potomac, the Chesapeake Bay, or the ocean. Between two of them, the Occoquan River and Bull Run Creek, was an elevated plateau covered by woods and few decent roads. The beds of the Occoquan and Bull Run were steep-banked, canal-like cuts in horizontal layers of red sandstone.

A railroad trackline headed through this area almost due west from Alexandria to Manassas Gap in the Blue Ridge range. At Manassas Junction it was crossed by the Orange & Alexandria Railroad, which ran south toward Richmond. North of the east-west track and about six or seven miles north of Manassas Junction was the Warrenton Turnpike, a macadamized band of highway that crossed the twenty-two miles between Alexandria and Centerville. A few miles west of Centerville the Turnpike crossed Bull Run Creek on the Stone Bridge.[25] The railroad junction made this an important area.

Salmon P. Chase, a former governor of Ohio, a former senator from Ohio, an aspirant for the Republican nomination for president in 1860, and now secretary of the treasury, believed strongly that Manassas Junction, at the least, should be taken. He expressed this view to Scott.[26]

22 Scott's plan, known contemporaneously as the Anaconda Plan, is printed in Townsend, *Anecdotes*, Appendix D, and *OR*, 2, 1.

23 Townsend, *Anecdotes*, 55, 261-62.

24 *Ibid*.

25 Barnard, *CSA and The Battle of Bull Run*, 43-44.

26 Townsend, *Anecdotes*, 56-57; Schuckers, *Chase*, 365; *C.C.W.*, 1 (Franklin).

On May 3, the day of Scott's letter to McClellan and Mansfield's report on Arlington Heights, Brigadier-General Butler was in Washington, among other things, to confirm that Baltimore was part of his Department of Annapolis. Stopping to see Chase while the general in chief was unavailable, he found the secretary and McDowell hard at work planning an operation to seize the Virginia shore of the Potomac and secure the immediate safety of the capital. McDowell had not been officially designated to command the Potomac River crossing, but he had been positively told that he would.[27] The Chase-McDowell plan involved both the seizure of Alexandria and an immediate advance to Manassas.

"Look here, General," said Chase to Butler, while pointing to the map, "I want your attention to this matter. Here is Manassas Junction, where there is the junction of the system of railroads which must bring the rebels together to make an attack upon Washington. I think that junction should be taken and held by us."

Butler studied the maps for some time.[28]

"Yes," he finally responded, "I think there is the spot which should be fortified and held in order to protect Washington. The Confederates are now assembled at Harper's Ferry. Their plan was to come down from Harper's Ferry to the Relay House and take Washington from that side; but as Maryland will not declare for secession I feel very sure the other point of which they will take possession will be Manassas Junction. They will not do that immediately, but will wait until the vote by the people is taken by Virginia to secede, which is fixed to be on the twenty-third. General Scott, being a Virginian, I know is very anxious not to move on her 'sacred soil' until after that vote. But the rebel government is now coming to Richmond as the capital of the Confederacy, so certain are they of the result of the vote of the people. If they can invade Virginia on their part, I do not see why we may not enter the State on the other. I think we should march to Manassas Junction. Six regiments will be enough to hold it. They could easily be spared from Washington, for they are there now only to defend Washington, and at Manassas Junction they would be defending her all the more surely. For no rebel division will attempt to attack Washington with us behind them at Manassas Junction, cutting off their supplies and communications. Let us go there and form an entrenchment as a nucleus of a very much larger force."

Chase agreed and asked Butler to go with him to see General Scott. Butler believed Scott would do nothing about Manassas Junction and would prefer to wait

27 *C.C.W.*, 1, 134 (McDowell).

28 *Butler's Book*, 222.

but went with Chase and explained the proposition. Scott thought the plan involved too much risk. As Butler had supposed, Scott wanted to wait.[29]

A week later Chase went again to Scott to argue for the seizure of both Alexandria and Manassas. The Confederates had no sizeable force at either point and only a few hundred men at Harpers Ferry. Chase believed that Manassas and its railroad junction had great strategic importance. With Manassas in Union hands the Confederates would be forced to fall back from Harpers Ferry and Winchester. This would clear the Shenandoah Valley, a long length of the Potomac, and the Baltimore and Ohio Railroad as far west as Wheeling. Even more important, Chase believed, this might persuade the citizens of Virginia to vote against secession. Scott acted as if he were impressed with Chase's arguments but "his military prudence decided him against the measures I proposed."[30]

On May 16, a week after Chase's second meeting with Scott, McDowell delivered to Chase a written statement of his own plan. Movements west of the Allegheny Mountains and on the Mississippi River were left to Major-General George B. McClellan. Possession of Manassas Junction by the Confederates allowed them to operate in Maryland and to threaten the capital's communications with the northern and western states. The immediate theater of war, he thought, would be the area between the capital and the Blue Ridge. Its many streams would give both sides the ability to resist an advancing army. In this area possession of the two main railroads, which crossed the streams on wooden bridges ranging from two hundred to one thousand feet in length, was vital. In the end, "the two parties moving upon each other will find themselves in force face-to-face along I think the line of the Rappahannock, near which an important engagement will there take place."

Before that, however, the federal forces had to establish positions beyond the Potomac. "Starting in the beginning we may possess Alexandria. The first object should be to reach as soon as possible the Manassas Junction, occupy it, and the road beyond at the same time occupying the Leesburg Road. The occupation of Alexandria and of the Manassas Junction cuts off communication by rail-road which they have heretofore had with Harpers Ferry." As an alternative he left open the possibility of proceeding to the Rappahannock on the shorter, direct route by way of the Potomac River port at Aquia Creek instead of through Alexandria. In one

29 Chase MSS (U.P.I.) letter dated March 28, 1862, from Chase to Bradford R. Wood; Niven, John, ed., *The Salmon P. Chase Papers*, 4 vols. (Kent and London, 1997); *Correspondence, April 1863-1864*, vol. 4, 345, letter dated March 21, 1864, from Chase to Trowbridge; (Niven, *Chase Papers*); *Butler's Book*, 222-23.

30 Niven, *Chase Papers* (*Correspondence, 1858-March 1863*), 3, 152-153, letter dated March 28, 1862, from Chase to Wood; Shuckers, *Chase*, 365.

continuous movement, McDowell wanted to capture Alexandria, then advance immediately to Manassas and beyond to the Rappahannock River.

Last, he considered other operations in the east. More prescient than he could ever have guessed, he said, "In connection with the movement a large force well supplied with artillery should move upon or threaten as the case may be Richmond from Fort Monroe by way of York river operating between York and James River and as this is the shortest line to Richmond, and a well-grounded one and sustained by Ft. Monroe, it may become the main attack. These operations will not fail to concentrate intensely the whole attention and forces of the South upon Virginia." With Richmond and Charleston in Union possession as a result of these operations, "the back of the enemy will be broken."[31]

For the main part of McDowell's plan, the capture of Manassas Junction, many believed that no more than a simple march would be necessary and that it would fall without a shot. Once the force reached the Junction, it should proceed to Manassas Gap in the Blue Ridge Mountains and to the Rappahannock River, the first natural line of defense after the Potomac. It would then fortify the Rappahannock line, leaving the army free to move up the James and York Rivers to Richmond.[32]

Secretary of the Navy Gideon Welles, like Chase and McDowell, favored active intervention in the seceding states, including Virginia. With Scott and many others, he believed that substantial Union sentiment, if not a majority, existed in certain of the states, including a large part of Virginia. He wanted to give them aggressive, active support by entering their areas with military force. Colonel Mansfield, one of Scott's preferred candidates for significant field command, taking a similar but more restrictive view, said, "We must erect our batteries on the eminences in the vicinity of Washington and establish our military lines. Frontiers between the belligerents, as between the countries of Continental Europe, are requisite."[33]

In spite of Blair's precise and accurate assessment of Scott's attitude, the general in chief remained powerful in the councils of the federal government; and his predispositions dominated the developing plan for the attack on the Virginia shore. The city of Alexandria and Arlington Heights were now held, in all probability, by light Confederate reconnaissance contingents, including a known force of approximately fifty cavalry on the outskirts of Alexandria. Farther inland,

31 Chase MSS (U.P.I.) memo. dated May 16, 1861, unaddressed and unsigned, but noted in the margin of the first page to be from McDowell. The original is in the Chase papers in the Pennsylvania Historical Society; but the most readily available source is the microfilm of all Chase correspondence prepared by University Publications, Inc., a copy of which is in the New York University Library in New York City.

32 *C.C.W.*, 1, 129 (Franklin) and 119 (Heintzelman).

33 Welles, *Diary*, 1, 84, 85.

he believed, a small force of one thousand to fifteen hundred men held Manassas Junction where the Manassas Gap and the Orange and Alexandria Railroads met. Even with no powerful force on the Potomac, he would ignore Alexandria, the railroad, Manassas Junction, and the Warrenton Turnpike. Arlington Heights, a direct threat to the capital, should be occupied; and with little or no bloodshed, it could be. He could tolerate that minimal intrusion on the "sacred soil" of Virginia.

Scott intended to seize Arlington Heights to protect the president and the Capitol from direct artillery fire but was opposed to anything beyond that and was unwilling to advance into Virginia until he knew the outcome of her vote on secession. His policy, a passive, defensive treatment of secession, was supported by other West Point officers in Washington.[34]

Scott's sensitivity toward Virginia and his reluctance to make a military move on her land were not secrets. Adam Gurowski, a clerk in the State Department, had written in his diary for April, "Something seems not right with Scott. Is he too old, or too much of a Virginian or a hero on a small scale."[35] Even closer to home was Gurowski's assessment in May:

> Scott does not wish for any bold demonstration or any offensive movement. The reason may be that he is too old, too crippled, to be able to take the field in person, and too inflated by conceit to give the glory of the act of command to any other man . . . General McDowell made a plan to seize upon Manassas as the center of railroads, the true defense of Washington, and the firm foothold in Virginia. Nobody, or only a few enemies, were in Manassas. McDowell shows his genuine military insight. Scott, and as I am told, the whole senile military counsel, opposed McDowell's plan as being too bold. Do these mummies intend to conduct a war without boldness."[36]

34 Welles, Diary, 1, 84.

35 Gurowski, Diary, 1, 35 entry for April.

36 *Ibid.*, 47, 48 entry for May.

Chapter 10

"We march before daylight for Alexandria. Heaven is my shield of War; to God I commit my self, my regiment, my wife & my darlings."

— *Colonel Orlando B. Willcox to his wife*

Into Virginia at Last

While Scott awaited the outcome of the vote by the citizens of Virginia, regiments continued to reach Washington. The Treasury Department diarist noted on May 10, "One of the most remarkable facts connected with these Northern Regiments is found in their effect upon the morals of this city. This addition of over thirty thousand to the population of the city, instead of increasing crime, actually diminishes it. The old residents all assert that there never was a time when thefts, assaults, incendiaries, and crimes generally were so uncommon as now. These troops avoid the grog shops—the gambling houses are closed for want of patrons, the churches are filled with men in uniforms on Sunday, and military prayer meetings are held almost daily. Civility and military deportment characterize all you meet in the streets, and though a regiment is in camp within 300 yards of where I am now sitting they do not disturb the good order and silence of the neighborhood in the least."[1]

1 Chittendon, *Invisible Siege*, 34-35, entry dated May 10, 1861.

In command of a regiment of Fire Zouaves was a young colonel named Elmer Ephraim Ellsworth. Impetuous, headstrong, uneasy under restraint, modest and deferential in social settings, temperate, a man who never swore, the young twenty-four-year-old Ellsworth had been plagued throughout his life by bad luck and failure. However, he came into his own as war approached. Ellsworth formed companies of Zouaves which he drilled and trained to high proficiency. The nearer the war, the better he became, exhibiting his soldiers at public functions and to paying audiences, preaching preparedness and stirring martial fervor wherever he went. At the outbreak, Ellsworth recruited a regiment of New York City firemen with the help of the fire chief and set out for Washington. The colonel had, at last, succeeded.[2]

After his regiment arrived, a tailor shop and Field's Hotel, adjoining Willard's Hotel, caught fire. The Zouaves ran a full mile from their quarters at the Capitol to the conflagration, Ellsworth at the head of his men. One of Ellsworth's men ran to an engineer wearing a fire hat and carrying a trumpet, seized both, handed Ellsworth the trumpet, and placed the fire hat on his head. The regiment gave three cheers and went to work.

Only a thin brick wall separated Willard's from the burning buildings. The top of the building was three stories high. No ladders were long enough to carry a hose to the roof. One of Ellsworth's soldiers tied the hose around his body, ran to the top of the ladder, climbed by the water pipe and gutters to the front projection at the top, grabbed it, and was pulled the last distance by some of his comrades on the roof. The crowd watching from below cheered his bravery. The men brought the fire under control.

Afterwards the regiment formed on 14th Street. Willard sent a demi-john of liquor to be distributed among the soldiers; Ellsworth, however, smashed it on the pavement, made a short speech complimenting the men on their efficiency and success, and then announced that Willard had set tables for breakfast. He hoped that after eating, "they would go to their quarters and show the people of Washington not only that they were soldiers and firemen but gentlemen." They ate and retired

2 Ruth Painter Randall, *Colonel Elmer E. Ellsworth, a Biography of Lincoln's Friend and First Hero of the Civil War* (Boston and Toronto, 1960), 119-120, (Randall, *Ellsworth*); *The Massachusetts Register of 1862 Containing a Record of the Government and Institutions of the State together with a very Complete Account of the Massachusetts Volunteers* (Boston, 1862), 126-27 (*Massachusetts Register*); *D.A.B.*, 3, pt. 2, 109-110; Knox, Lieutenant-Colonel Edward B., "The Capture of Alexandria and the Death of Ellsworth," in *Military Essays and Recollections: Papers Read before the Commandery of the State of Illinois, Military Order of the Loyal Legion of the United States*, 4 vols. (Chicago, 1894) (Broadfoot edition, 1992, vol. 11), 11, 17 (*Broadfoot MOLLUS Illinois*).

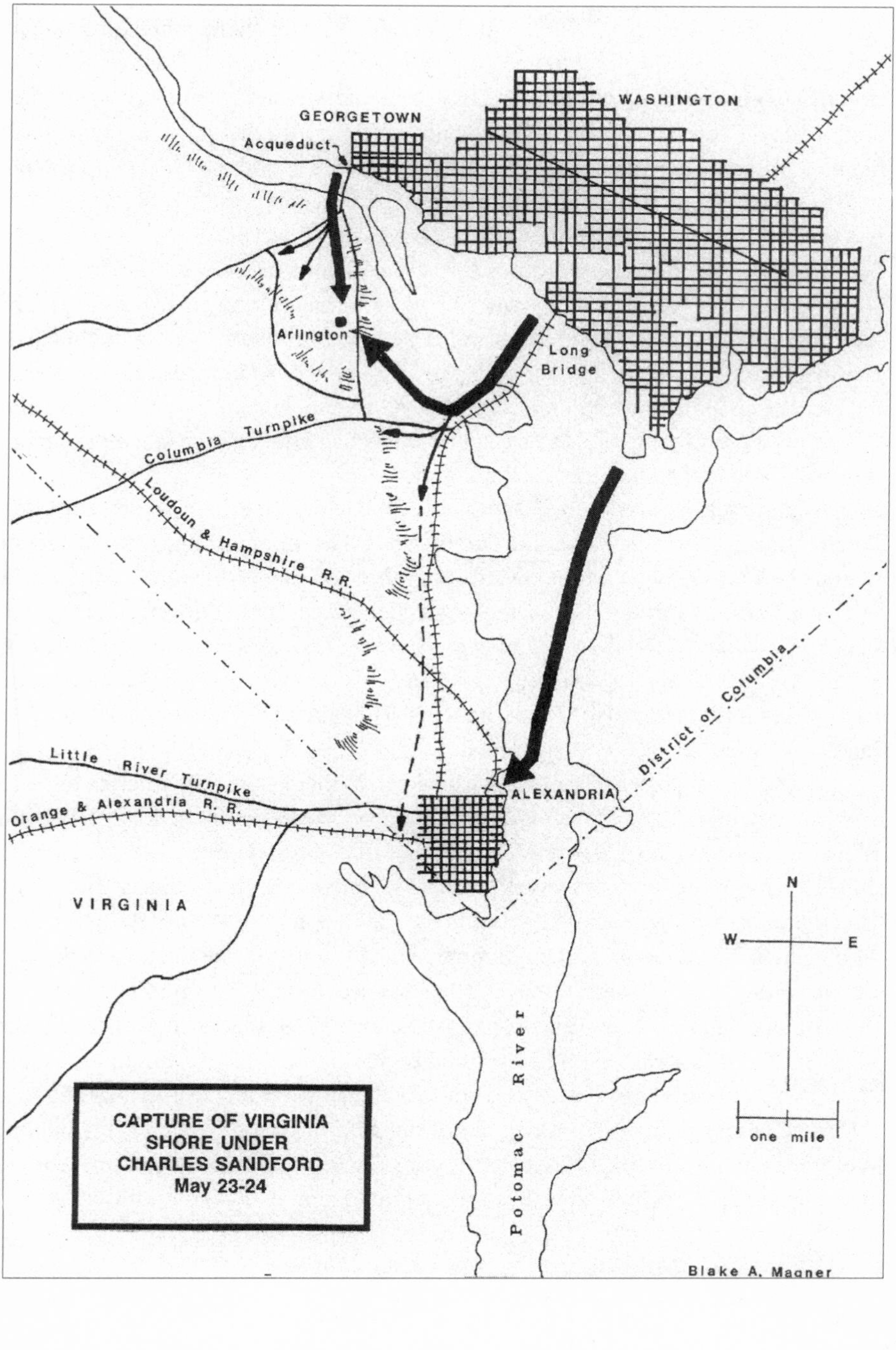
GEORGETOWN
WASHINGTON
Acqueduct
Arlington
Long Bridge
Columbia Turnpike
Loudoun & Hampshire R. R.
Little River Turnpike
Orange & Alexandria R. R.
ALEXANDRIA
District of Columbia
VIRGINIA
N
W
E
one mile
Potomac River
CAPTURE OF VIRGINIA SHORE UNDER CHARLES SANDFORD May 23-24
Blake A. Magner

quietly. As the diarist said, "Ellsworth is just the man for them—they all fear and love him."[3]

Although planning for the Virginia shore operation had taken place in the first half of May, Scott would permit no advance until the citizens of Virginia voted on the ordinance of secession passed by their legislature in April.[4] On May 23, their vote blessed secession. With all hope of reconciliation gone, the federal government had to control the Virginia shore of the Potomac.

On the day of secession, Mansfield explained the plan to Samuel P. Heintzelman, his second in command. Scott had disapproved any plan to capture Alexandria. Only a two-pronged envelopment of Arlington was contemplated. Heintzelman was surprised to learn that no force would occupy Alexandria, which he thought should be the principal object of the movement, and questioned the failure to plan for its capture. His strong inquiries had effect. In the late morning the plan was expanded to include Alexandria.

Three columns would cross the river at the same time, one across the Long Bridge, one on the aqueduct, and one by boat. The Long Bridge and Aqueduct columns, once over, would turn toward each other and converge on the Lee Mansion on the heights at Arlington. On the Aqueduct, three New York regiments, one company of cavalry, and two guns would cross. The column to cross the Long Bridge, half dike, half wooden bridge, included District of Columbia volunteers, one New Jersey regiment, and the First Michigan. The third column would take ship and land at Alexandria.

At noon Ellsworth and Colonel Orlando B. Willcox, West Point class of 1847 and commander of the First Michigan Infantry, were summoned to meet with Mansfield, who explained the new plan to capture Alexandria. Ellsworth by the river and Willcox by land were to work together by signaling each other at Half Way Creek around early dawn, and to coordinate their capture of Alexandria. The First Michigan would turn south after crossing on the Long Bridge, and march to the rear of Alexandria. On steamers, Colonel Ellsworth was to take the Fire Zouaves down the Potomac, land, and seize the town of Alexandria itself. If all went well, the Rebel garrison in Alexandria would be captured by the First Michigan and the Eleventh New York. Once in control, they were to isolate the town from the interior by cutting telegraph wires, destroying railroad tracks, and burning bridges on the track lines of the Orange & Alexandria Railroad as far out as possible. These instructions worked two ways, in effect confirming Scott's continued domination of military thinking

3 Chittendon, *Invisible Siege*, 35-36.

4 *N&H*, 4, 311.

with his concern for Virginia. Their execution would interfere with any Confederate return,[5] but they would also make an advance into the beloved commonwealth difficult.

That evening, the units to take part began massing at their proper positions.[6] The Fire Zouaves under Ellsworth had been told at "retreat" to prepare to move. In the still, clear night with the moon full and lustrous, Ellsworth had the rapt attention of his men as he addressed them in a low, clear voice.

"I will never order one of you to go where I fear to lead. Don't fire without orders. Now, go to your tents and remain quiet until called."[7]

Just before the crossing, the colonel wrote his family, "I am inclined to the opinion that our entrance into Virginia will be hotly contested. . . . Should that happen, my dear parents, it may be my lot to be injured in some manner. Whatever may happen, cherish the consolation that I was engaged in the performance of a sacred duty. . . ."[8]

The emotional intensity wrapped up in this first offensive step in the capital area did not belong to Ellsworth alone. Colonel Willcox wrote his wife in the night, "We march before daylight for Alexandria. Heaven is my shield of War; to God I commit my self, my regiment, my wife & my darlings."[9]

At 11:00 p.m., Ellsworth, on horseback, led his Eleventh in formation to the river. At two o'clock the *Baltimore* and the *Mount Vernon* were ready to be loaded; and two hours later, after being ferried to the ships by small boats, the men were taken down the Potomac to Alexandria.[10]

A clerk in the Treasury Department heard, then saw, the marshaling of the column for the Long Bridge. After midnight, a single horseman galloped to the camps of the Seventh New York and the three New Jersey regiments. "I could hear the clank of his saber and the sharp clatter of his horse's hoofs," he wrote in his diary, "just faint, then clear as he neared the house, then dying away in the distance." Soon he could hear two light taps of the drum at the camp of the Twelfth New York. "The

5 Robert Garth Scott, ed., *Forgotten Valor: The Memoirs, Journals, & Civil War Letters of Orlando B. Willcox* (Kent, 1999), 260-261 (Scott, *Willcox Memoirs, etc.*) Willcox notes a discrepancy between his recollection and Heintzelman's report in *OR*, but the two accounts, both of which sound reasonable, are consistent if Heintzelman's report misrecorded his meeting and complaint as an afternoon event, rather than one in the morning. Reconciling the accounts as much as possible, this error has been assumed.

6 *OR*, 2, 37 ff; *N&H*, 4, 312; Knox in 11, *Broadfoot MOLLUS Illinois*, 17.

7 Knox in 11, *Broadfoot MOLLUS Illinois*, 12.

8 *Massachusetts Register*, 126-27; Randall, *Ellsworth*, 266, quotes the letter in full.

9 Scott, *Willcox Memoirs, etc.*, 255, letter dated May 23, 1861, from Willcox to his wife.

10 Knox in 11, *Broadfoot MOLLUS Illinois*, 12.

full moon shown serenely and soft out of an unclouded sky upon the quiet city." In the distance a dog barked. Then he heard a "regular measured sound which first arrested my attention—growing clearer now as if approaching and regular as the beating of a clock. It comes nearer now, and I am no longer in doubt. *It is the tread of armed men!* I hear it clearer now and the glistening of polished bayonets in the bright moonlight is seen distinctly. There was something indescribably impressive as they came nearer. And I saw the regular ranks and recognized the sharp steps of the New York Seventh Regiment. The men had their knapsacks and blankets and were evidently in regular marching order. They passed down the street and the Twelfth New York filed in behind and moved off with them. After a few minutes I heard another column approaching and immediately the New Jersey Brigade, thirty-five hundred strong, followed after those who had preceded them.

"There was neither music nor conversation, nothing save that heavy regular *solemn* sound which I shall never forget—the tread of armed men."[11]

The Aqueduct column began its preparations shortly after midnight. At 1:00 a.m., the Sixty-ninth New York, Fifth New York, and a squadron of cavalry rose to the drum beats. At 3:00 a.m., they took up their line of march for Virginia across the Aqueduct. "It was a gorgeous moonlight night," wrote a staff officer in a letter home, "the woods deathly silent, except every now and again in advance when there would be a few volleys and random shots as our van drove in the enemy's outposts." Once in position, the units began throwing up entrenchments. The bridges in advance of the new positions were burned to prevent a surprise counterattack.[12]

Meanwhile, Lieutenant Colonel Heintzelman had ordered his regimental commanders to report at the head of the Long Bridge at 1:00 a.m. As dusk deepened into night the commanding officers of the column met in an old, red brick house at the entrance to the Long Bridge to hear the final plan. Heintzelman explained the line of march of each regiment and the position each was to take. When he had finished, he and the regimental commanders sat quietly. Presently, they heard the clump of boots on the stairs outside and the clank of a saber. The door opened and Mansfield entered.

"Colonel Heintzelman, are you ready?" he asked. "Why don't you move, sir?"

"It has not been stated who shall lead, sir."

"Why, Colonel Butterfield's Twelfth Regiment, of course."[13]

11 Chittenden, *Invisible Siege*, 54-55 (emphasis in original).

12 Halpine MSS (Huntington Library) letter dated May 24, 1861, Halpine to his wife.

13 Butterfield, *Butterfield*, 14.

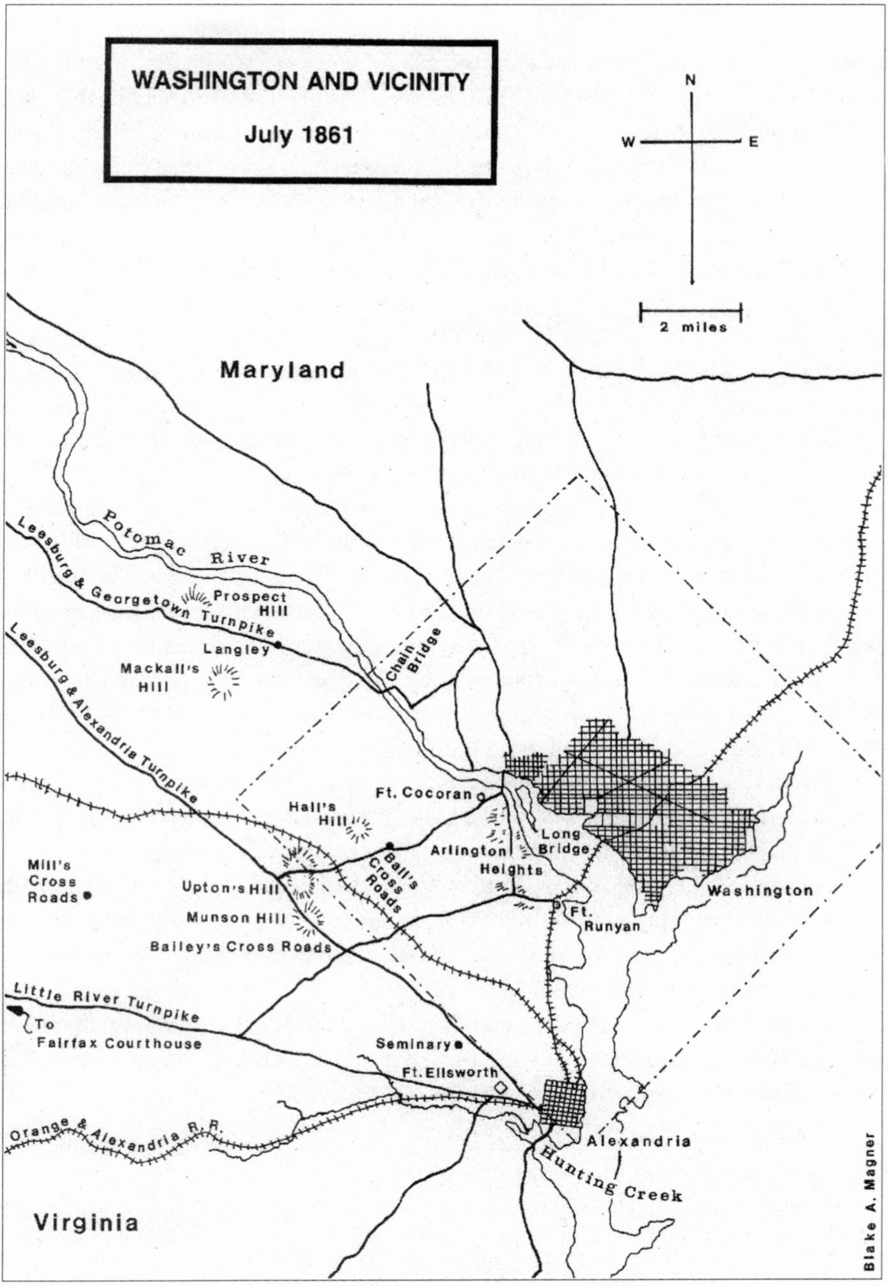
WASHINGTON AND VICINITY
July 1861
N
W
E
2 miles
Maryland
Potomac River
Leesburg & Georgetown Turnpike
Prospect Hill
Langley
Mackall's Hill
Chain Bridge
Leesburg & Alexandria Turnpike
Ft. Cocoran
Hall's Hill
Ball's Cross Roads
Arlington Heights
Long Bridge
Washington
Mill's Cross Roads
Upton's Hill
Munson Hill
Ft. Runyan
Bailey's Cross Roads
Little River Turnpike
To Fairfax Courthouse
Seminary
Ft. Ellsworth
Orange & Alexandria R.R.
Alexandria
Hunting Creek
Virginia
Blake A. Magner

In the warm, beautiful, and serene night, the moon shone brightly overhead, casting reflected light from the surface of the Potomac.[14] At precisely 2:00 a.m. Butterfield's regiment led the Long Bridge column across the river,[15] while the other two columns started on their way, a total force of fifteen thousand men. Heintzelman super- intended the crossing at the Long Bridge, a lengthy structure of rotten timbers and broken planks interrupted by earth embankments. Senator Zachariah Chandler of Michigan accompanied Willcox as a volunteer aide. Colonel George Stoneman with the First United States Cavalry and Colonel Charles P. Stone leading a battalion of his District of Columbia volunteers preceded a column composed of a section of the Fourth Artillery, the Twelfth New York under Colonel Daniel Butterfield, the Twenty-fifth New York, Third New Jersey, Seventh New York, and First Michigan Regiment. On the far side Stone's District of Columbia men took position to cover the bridge. The main part of the column turned right toward Arlington while Willcox, accompanied by Butterfield and the Twelfth New York, turned left and marched together as far as Four Mile Run or Half Way Creek. As the sun peeped over the horizon, they reached the run. There, Willcox looked for Ellsworth's two ships on the river, where they were supposed to "lie to" while they established communications with the land column. The ships were behind; but as they drew even, Willcox looked in vain for the signal. The ships raced on "much faster than our legs could carry us," Willcox wrote after the war. Ellsworth was apparently racing for Alexandria and had the means to win. Willcox could see the Confederate videttes at the run head for Alexandria hurriedly to deliver the alert.

George A. Armes, a guide working under a letter of introduction from Secretary Seward, asked Willcox to allow him to take fifty men and advance into the city to capture Captain Ball and his company of Rebel cavalry, who were quartered in the slave pen near the railroad depot. Willcox ordered a captain to report to Armes with one hundred men. Marching ahead of the command, they slipped around the depot and were just coming to the slave pen when Willcox reached the pen on another street with the regiment. Captain Ball and his men were mounting to depart.

Willcox ordered 12-pounder cannon unlimbered, loaded, and aimed at the small group of Confederate cavalry. They saw at a glance that they had no chance to escape. Some were mounted, some on foot, and some had one foot in the stirrup. All

14 Swinton, *Seventh New York*, 2, 26.

15 Clowes states that Company A of the First Michigan led the advance across the bridge (*Detroit Light Guard*, 40-41); but all contemporary reports and other later narratives (Heintzelman MS Diary (large diary), entry dated May 25, 1861; *OR*, 2, 40 ff; Butterfield, *Memorial*, 14) record the Twelfth New York as the leading infantry unit. From a practical and tactical viewpoint, Nicolay and Hay are probably correct (*op. cit.*, 4, 312): the far ends of the bridges were seized by cavalry followed by the main force, which was infantry.

sat or stood motionless as Willcox dashed forward and shouted, "Surrender or I'll blow you to Hell."

Captain Ball drew his sword and handed it to Willcox.

The colonel said, "You can keep your sword, sir. But who are you and what is your command."

"Captain Ball and company of Virginia cavalry, sir."

The prisoners, including the unfortunate Captain Schaeffer, were ordered into the slave pen under a guard. Willcox's regiment then continued forward to the railroad depot. He had already destroyed the first bridge and torn up the Orange and Alexandria Railroad thus assuring the capture of Confederate stores, which had been loaded on cars for shipment south.

Strong pickets pushed in all directions while Alexandria was occupied.[16] Willcox began to burn bridges further along the railroad track and tear up the track until he discovered that the Confederates retreating up the railroad were burning bridges ahead of him to prevent pursuit.[17]

As Ellsworth's regiment entered Alexandria from the wharves, he took with him two officers, a sergeant, four enlisted men, and a reporter from the New York *Tribune*. The bulk of his regiment he left in formation in the street and headed for the telegraph office. On the way he saw a large Rebel flag hanging motionless on its staff on the roof of the Marshall House, a small hotel two blocks away.

"Boys, we must have that flag," he said.

At the entrance to the hotel, Ellsworth directed the sergeant to return to the regiment and bring forward Company A. Just inside they met a partially dressed man who responded to their questions about the flag.

"I don't know anything about it. I'm only a boarder here."

Paying him little mind, Ellsworth and his companions ran up the stairs, cut the halyards, and dropped the flag. They returned to the landing on the second floor, Corporal Brownell in the lead followed by Ellsworth. The boarder, who was really the proprietor of the hotel, stepped from the shadows and aimed a shotgun at the colonel. Brownell tried to deflect the barrel with his bayonet, but the first blast sent shot and slugs into the colonel. Ellsworth fell forward, the golden circlet worn about his neck and engraved *non nobis sed pro patria* driven into his heart by the blast. He was dead before he hit the floor. The proprietor, James P. Jackson, swung the second

16 Heintzelman MS Diary (large diary) (L.C.), entry of May 25, 1861; *OR*, 2, 40 ff; Clowes, *Detroit Light Guard*, 40-41; *Massachusetts Register*, 126-27; Swinton, *Army of the Potomac*, 30; Armes, *Ups and Downs*, 41-42, letter dated April 20, 1889, from Willcox to Armes; Scott, *Willcox Journal, etc.*, 262-264, 268.

17 Armes, *Ups and Downs*, 36, 38, and 39.

barrel toward Private Brownell; but he was too late. A bullet in the head staggered him, and a bayonet in the body sent him tumbling down the staircase to the next landing.

As the guests began to emerge from their rooms, they were herded into one room. Seven men from Ellsworth's regiment lifted his body and carried it to a bed in a nearby room, throwing the Rebel flag across his feet. His face bore a natural expression except for the pallor of death.[18]

Among the friends Ellsworth had earned on the White House staff, John G. Nicolay wrote his fiancee after he had learned of Ellsworth's death. "I heard of the sad fate of Col. Ellsworth, who, as you already have read, was assassinated at the taking of Alexandria by our troops, last Friday morning; and since that time I had been quite unable to keep the tears out of my eyes whenever I thought, or heard, or read, about him until I had almost concluded that I am quite a weak and womanous sort of creature. I had known and seen him almost daily for more than six months past, and although our intimacy was never in any wise confidential as to personal matters, I had learned to value him very highly. He was very young—only 24 I think—very talented and ambitious, and very poor—a combination of the qualities upon which sadness and misfortune seem ever to prey. He had by constant exertion already made himself famous . . ."[19]

Willcox deployed Ellsworth's regiment to prevent retribution against the town, then rode to meet Mayor Lewis Mackenzie, an old friend from earlier tours of duty in the capital area. The mayor claimed he had arranged a truce with a Lieutenant Rowan.

"Neither hostilities nor military possession," Mackenzie claimed, "could be the thing."

But military possession was precisely what Willcox had been ordered to accomplish. "I cannot recognize your right to bind the military, but you may be assured that nothing shall be done by myself further than to make provision for the security of life and property in a city where I have already so many friends and acquaintances. And how are the Masons, the Fairfaxes, the Benhams, and other old friends? Besides, very dear sir, we have restored you and your people to the Union."

No matter what, Willcox thought Mackenzie was pleased to be under the old flag again. A very wealthy merchant, he had profited from his dealings with Union troops and officers but carried many bad debts of Rebel officers.

18 Knox in 11 *Broadfoot MOLLUS Illinois*, 14-16; *Massachusetts Register*, 126-27.

19 Nicolay MSS (L.C.) letter dated May 26, 1861, from Nicolay to Therena.

From Mackenzie, Willcox went to the slave pen where Ball and his men were prisoners under the guard of the First Michigan. The pen he found to be a sturdy building with artifacts of the "great national problem," including a few slaves, an auctioneer's book showing human sales for prices ranging up from fifty dollars, and one man who had come—unsuccessfully—to claim his "property."[20]

Under a program intended to put Regular Army officers in command of the brigades, Willcox was succeeded in command of Alexandria by Colonel Stone, who kept Willcox's adjutant, surgeon, provost marshal, and military police. When Willcox departed with his regiment for the army forming on the banks of the Potomac, the local citizens in Alexandria asked to have the Michigan men left behind to be its guard. Willcox rightly took this as a high compliment for his regiment and probably for his ability as an officer.[21]

Next morning, May 24, General Sandford and his staff crossed the river to inspect the new positions while the men fortified them.[22] By May 27, the surrounding hills had been occupied, fortifications had been commenced, and artillery was awaited.[23]

At the outbreak of the war, the entire United States Army had one company of engineers, the unit in which Lieutenant George B. McClellan had served in Mexico and the one he later commanded at the military academy at West Point. It had been ordered from the Military Academy to Washington early in 1861, then sent with Meigs, Porter, and Colonel Harvey Browne on the *Atlantic* to Fort Pickens a few days before the attack on Sumter. Without it the army had no trained or skilled engineering troops.[24]

Making do as best he could, Major John G. Barnard, the Chief Engineer, began construction of fortifications on the basis of reconnaissances he directed at daylight.[25] From the center of the capital, the Long Bridge stretched to the Virginia

20 Scott, *Willcox Memoirs, etc.*, 267-268.

21 *Ibid.*, 274, letter dated May 31, 1861, from Willcox to "Chancellor," his father-in-law; 280, letter dated June 30, 1861, from Willcox to his wife.

22 Heintzelman MS Diary (L.C.), entry of May 25, 1861; *OR*, 2, 38-39; Robert G. Athearn, *Thomas F. Meagher: An Irish Revolutionary in America* (Boulder, 1949), 91 (Athearn, *Meagher*); Edward K. Gould, *Major General Hiram G. Berry* (Gould, *Berry*), 91.

23 Halpine MSS (H.L.), letter dated May 27, 1861, from Halpine to his wife.

24 Gilbert S. Thompson, *The Engineer Battalion in the Civil War: A Contribution to the History of the United States Engineers* (Washington, 1910), 1 (Thompson, *Engineer Battalion*).

25 J. G. Barnard and W. F. Barry, *Report of the Engineer and Artillery Operations of the Army of the Potomac from its Organization to the Close of the Peninsula Campaign* (New York, 1863) (Barnard and Barry, *Reports*), 9-10. Although Barnard's reports are in *OR*, e.g., *OR*, 11, 106, the version published by Barnard and Barry has reports that are not in *OR*.

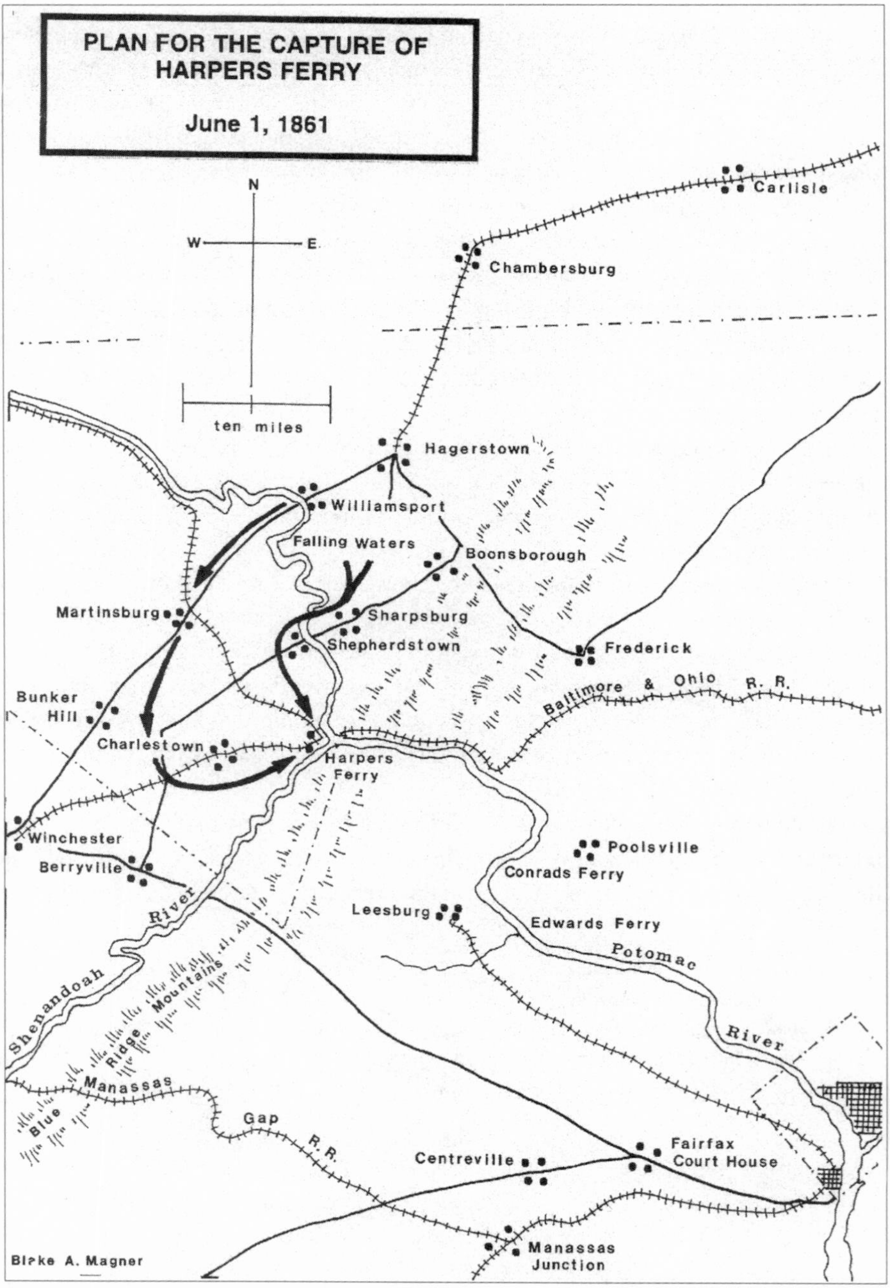
PLAN FOR THE CAPTURE OF
HARPERS FERRY
June 1, 1861
N
W
E
ten miles
Carlisle
Chambersburg
Hagerstown
Williamsport
Falling Waters
Boonsborough
Martinsburg
Sharpsburg
Shepherdstown
Frederick
Baltimore & Ohio R. R.
Bunker Hill
Charlestown
Harpers Ferry
Winchester
Berryville
Poolsville
Conrads Ferry
Leesburg
Edwards Ferry
Potomac
River
Shenandoah
River
Blue Ridge Mountains
Manassas
Gap
R. R.
Centreville
Fairfax Court House
Manassas Junction
Blake A. Magner

shore, crossed a spit and a swamp, and reached high ground.[26] Here, Barnard marked the outline for a huge fortification, Fort Runyon, having a perimeter of almost a mile. At the same time Captain Horatio G. Wright, the engineer officer with the dead Ellsworth's column, found an excellent piece of high ground west of Alexandria to fortify. Two weeks later, Barnard added Fort Albany to protect the Virginia *debouches* from the Long Bridge. All were large, intended to be armed with artillery, constructed to protect infantry, meant to eliminate the need for a continuous line, and were entirely separate from each other. In theory, cannon and rifle fire from the works would sweep the surrounding cleared areas with a deadly volume of fire.[27]

A brigade composed of the Fifth, Twenty-eighth, and Sixty-Ninth New York Infantry Regiments was created and assigned to Colonel David Hunter, whose new aide described him as, "a very distinguished officer [who had] served with credit through the Mexican and other wars." Each morning at 2:00 a.m. and 4:00 a.m., Colonel Hunter and his aide took Colonel Corcoran or Lieutenant Colonel Nugent of the Sixty-ninth New York on a "grand round" to visit the most advanced sentries and pickets. They rode alone over fields and through thick patches of wood, down valleys, and over hills with their revolvers in hand, for a circle of five miles round the camp to see that all the guards were properly stationed and that the men were awake. Occasionally, they would pop into sight of the Confederate outposts and could see Rebel campfires three or four miles away.[28]

"The excitement of this life is intense and most agreeable," the aide found, "though the scouting parties through the woods, or visiting the pickets after nightfall are ticklish."[29]

Sandford was deemed to be inappropriate for command of the troops in Virginia. To replace him, Scott was allowed to choose one of two men, both recently promoted to brigadier general in the Regular Army: Mansfield or McDowell. Once

26 Chase MSS, letter dated [Feb.?] 25, 1862, from Barnard to Chase. Author's collection ("A.C."). Map based on reconnaissances August, 1862, from Headquarters of General Irvin McDowell, Arlington.

27 Barnard and Barry, *Reports*, 10-12. Barnard's report, which was written after he had developed a critical hostility for McClellan, was an early example of his penchant for claiming credit not due him, and compared with other statements he made about the fortifications shows his willingness to lie. In it he implies that he first planned the Torres Vedras style defenses on the west bank without using the name. The letter, written much earlier, does not make the claim even by inference. After the war Barnard and McClellan would both claim credit, but Barnard's many statements about the works, including those before the dispute arose, tend to support McClellan. Given Barnard's penchant for false claims, the implied claim in the report has been rejected; and McClellan's claim, which is consistent with Barnard's letter, is accepted.

28 Halpine MSS (H.L.) letter dated May 29, 1861, from Halpine to his wife.

29 *Ibid.*, letter dated May 25, 1861, from Halpine to his wife.

again, Mansfield's indispensability kept him in the capital and compelled Scott to give the command to McDowell even though he did not want McDowell to have it. Scott was again annoyed that his judgment was thwarted, and Mansfield was annoyed because he had to remain in the Washington defenses without a chance to win distinction with a field command.[30] McDowell assumed this command with envy behind him and annoyance above him.

Irvin McDowell, a man of complex, confusing, and easily misread physical and personal characteristics, was an odd but not illogical choice for the command. The McDowell family had fled religious persecution in Scotland for northern Ireland, then Virginia. From there, the family moved again, this time to Kentucky and finally to Ohio where Abram McDowell, although often much reduced in circumstances remained aristocratic in ancestry, spirit, and thought.

The son born to him in October of 1818 was raised to have these characteristics. In his childhood, young Irvin was warm-hearted, affectionate, and outspoken. His tutor persuaded the family to allow him to be taken to Paris for a year of school. This year abroad was followed by four years at West Point where he was a social standout despite his mediocre academic status at twenty-third of forty-five graduating cadets. The total effect of these five years was repressive. Teenagers being the cruelest age group, his classmates awarded him the nickname "Squash McDowell." He became more reserved and formal although his polish remained unchanged.

Upon graduation in 1838, he began a tour of duty in the First Artillery Regiment and during the following years held a series of staff positions, which rewarded him with the derisive new nickname "Guts" McDowell. In the Mexican War he served as General John E. Wool's adjutant, won a brevet for captain for services at the Battle of Buena Vista, but somehow became the victim of rumors of cowardice. After the close of the war he continued his staff positions and at the outbreak of the Civil War was a major on duty in Washington.

He believed that no reconciliation with the South was possible and that the rebellion should be put down vigorously. Scott had known him since graduation and

30 In *Army of the Potomac*, 6, Stine quotes a statement by Schuyler Hamilton, Winfield Scott's military secretary, that McDowell was chosen because Mansfield had been selected as inspector-general over Scott's son-in-law when Jefferson Davis was secretary of war. All other sources are to the contrary. Whitelaw Reid, *Ohio in the War*, 2 vols. (New York, 1867), 1, 660 (Reid, *Ohio in the War*); Fry, *McDowell and Tyler*, 8 ff; John B. Alley, in Allen Thorndike Rice, ed., *Reminiscences of Abraham Lincoln by Distinguished Men of his Time* (New York, 1888), 588 (Rice, *Reminiscences of Lincoln*); Pease, *Browning Diary*, 537-538, entry dated April 2, 1862; Theodore C. Blegen, ed., *Abraham Lincoln and his Mailbag: Two Documents by Edward D. Neill, One of Lincoln's Secretaries* (St. Paul, 1888), 28; *C.C.W.*, 1, 37 (McDowell). The actions of the authorities in Washington also suggest that Hamilton, and therefore Stine, were wrong.

thought highly of him. Working as an assistant-adjutant-general in the defenses of the capital during April, the major, by his energy and intelligence, attracted the attention of important people in the inner circles of the government. During this time, he met his first real backer, Salmon P. Chase, Secretary of the Treasury. Chase had great influence over early military decisions, earning himself the unofficial title of "General." An ex-governor of Ohio, Chase remembered McDowell as an Ohioan in the Regular Army and sought McDowell's advice on questions of military organization.

Secretary of War Simon Cameron had been overwhelmed with responsibility for the seventy-five thousand militia called by Lincoln. When Chase suggested a call for sixty-five thousand more volunteers, he was given responsibility for the call and an additional number of Regulars. Chase invited three capable officers to assist and guide him: Colonel Lorenzo Thomas, Adjutant-General; Major Irvin McDowell, Assistant Adjutant-General; and Captain William B. Franklin, Topographical Engineer. Under Chase as the "presiding officer," the three men developed uniform federal systems for the enlistment of volunteers and Regulars, which were reduced to General Orders Nos. 15 and 16. Once again, however, the intention to create a centralized system run by the federal government failed. "Great irregularities prevailed," Chase wrote in a letter a short time later. "Regiments were raised under verbal authorities from the President and the Secretary of War and under written Memoranda of which no record was preserved so that the Orders failed to secure the principal objects I had in view beyond the simple provision of force—order and system, and so efficiency and accountability."

Virtually buried by his privacy responsibilities, Thomas could do little for Chase in his role as an adjunct secretary of war. But Chase's fellow Ohioan, Major Irvin McDowell, an officer of growing influence through his association with the secretary, Cameron, and the men he met while responsible for the capitol building, contributed. McDowell earned the support of the secretary for his efforts.[31]

31 John Niven, *The Salmon P. Chase Papers*, 6 vols. (incomplete) (Kent and London, 1997), vol. 4, letter dated March 21, 1864, from Chase to John T. Trowbridge, *Correspondence, April 1863-1864*, (Niven, *Chase Papers*); Townsend, *Anecdotes*, 56-57; Schuckers, *Chase*, 365; Upton, *Military Policy*, 233-235. These facts are based in large part on a letter from Franklin to Upton, dated Nov. 9, 1877. *Upton, supra*, 233, n.a. Correspondence between Upton and Henry S. DuPont is in the DuPont papers in the Winterthur Museum, but this is not a broadscale collection of Upton's papers. The fate of his letters, used by Peter S. Michie in the *Life and Letters*, is unknown. They are neither in the Dupont MSS nor in the West Point Library. Although Chase has long been known to have had an active early role in the war, this particular information appears only in Upton's book, with a comment by another knowledgeable officer, W. T. Sherman, long after the war, that it was new information to him and in a long letter by Chase in his MSS in the Pennsylvania Historical Society and reprinted in Niven, *Chase Papers*, *supra*.

Impressed with his intelligence and poise, the secretary determined that McDowell should be promoted to a higher rank. In addition to support from this powerful source, McDowell was also backed by Governor William Dennison of Ohio, to whom he was related by marriage. Although local political pressure forced the governor to appoint George B. McClellan to command all Ohio troops, Dennison had seriously considered McDowell for the post and even offered it to him.

Known favorably by these men and Simon Cameron, the Secretary of War, McDowell had the assurance of a sizeable promotion if the Regular Army were expanded. Lincoln's call for twenty-two thousand more Regulars in early May provided the opportunity. The cabinet convened to discuss the appointment of three new major generals and several additional brigadier generals. Chase sent the major a note at the War Department telling him to report to the White House as soon as possible. When he arrived, McDowell found the meeting had already begun. He sent his card to notify the secretary of his presence. In a few moments Chase came down the stairs. After describing the purpose of the meeting, Chase said he was about to propose McDowell as one of the three major generals. McDowell was taken aback. He demurred, saying that such rapid promotion would cause jealousy among officers who were bypassed. Further, he had never expected to progress beyond the rank of colonel during his military career. Brigadier general would be fine. He suggested that McClellan, Henry W. Halleck, and John C. Fremont would make excellent major generals. Chase acquiesced and returned to the meeting.

McDowell's promotion to brigadier general did not spare him the discomfort he had hoped to avoid. His first opposition came in the massive form of the general in chief. Although Scott had created the Scott Rule for the promotion of junior officers, he shared the hostile opinion of many in the army toward their rapid promotion. Despite the fact that he liked McDowell, Scott was annoyed, in addition, because his advice had not been sought on the subject of McDowell's promotion. He was also nettled that Major McDowell, West Point '38, should be promoted to brigadier general when Colonel Mansfield, West Point '22, was not. Favoring Mansfield, Scott demanded that Mansfield be promoted to rank from the same day, May 14.[32] In this way Mansfield's commission as colonel would give him seniority.

Although he was tall and strong, McDowell had a torso too long for his short legs, an arrangement that magnified the substantial girth in his middle. His legs were well-proportioned in themselves, but "were attached to his body by brawny rolling

32 McDowell testified (*C.C.W.*, 1, 17) that Scott ordered Mansfield's commission predated a week to his; but if this is true—and no other contemporaneous source mentions it—Scott failed because both commissions for brigadier general bear the same date of May 14. 1, *Cullum*, nos. 963 and 287.

hips that worked up and down when he walked." The short legs and large body, making expert horsemanship an impossibility, often caused him to lose his seat and tumble from his horse. Nevertheless, in spite of his clumsy and ungainly appearance he enjoyed a good dance at which he was light of foot with "elf-like grace." His head, attached to his fat body by a short, thick neck, seemed "bullet-shaped"; and his florid face, fleshy and chubby, was made to appear even more fat by his jaws, which protruded on either side. He wore a brawly, bristling imperial and a bushy, drooping German mustache which emphasized his Teutonic appearance. Nevertheless, his face, through fine features, was remarkably open, sympathetic, and congenial with an air of frankness and kindness. In a hoarse, chest-toned alto voice, he spoke rapidly and fluently in conversation but never loudly.[33]

In his personal habits and demeanor, he had a mammoth appetite, being known to eat an entire watermelon at one sitting. But he complimented the characteristics of a gourmand with those of a *bon vivant*, being highly skilled at the preparation of fine food and likened by one of his subordinates to a Delmonico chef. Hard liquor, wine, and spirits of any other kind he never used, a characteristic for which he was known throughout the army. In fact, he never even drank tea, coffee, or other lesser stimulants. Nor did he use tobacco in any form, a practice he found abhorrent. And he never swore.[34]

A well-spoken, entertaining conversationalist, who spoke French fluently, he enjoyed warm personal relationships with his friends. To them, he was a frank, honest, straight-forward man. But in his military relationships he was formal and reserved, methodical and careful, and a strict disciplinarian. His manner seemed doctrinaire or that of a professor more than a military leader, and he was prone to sharp, impulsive statements, whose effect and consequences he did not always consider. Light or frivolous conversation was not part of his nature, giving him an appearance of haute superiority and creating the impression that he believed his intellect and attainments put him above others. Lacking the vices of ordinary mortals and having but few of their weaknesses, he believed himself to be on a higher plane and affected an air of elevated dignity. All this he made worse by being forgetful of

33 Comte de Paris MS Diary (Archive Nationale de la Maison de France), entry of September 28, 1861; Halpine MSS (H.L.) mem entitled "Rough Notes from an Old Soldier: How the Battle of Bull Run was lost in One Lesson" in the handwriting of Hunter and arbitrarily dated August 1, 1861, by the curator; Tidball MS Mem. (U.S.M.A.) 225, 226, 226A, 229; Pisani, *Napoleon in America*, 116; Averell, *Ten Years*, 284; Schurz, *Memoirs*, 1, 383; Theodore B. Gates, *The Ulster Guard and The War of the Rebellion* (New York, 1879), 140 (Gates, *Ulster Guard*).

34 Comte dé Paris MS Diary (large diary) (A.N. de la M. de F.) entry of September 28, 1861; Tidball MS Mem. (U.S.M.A.), 226A, 227; *OR*, 12, pt. 3, 94 (McDowell Court of Inquiry—McClellan); Gates, *Ulster Guard*, 139; Schuckers, *Chase*, 451, letter dated September 4, 1862, from Chase to Bryant.

the courtesy due his inferiors, thus suffering in his popularity and effectiveness. A cold, distant superior, he lacked the kind of magnetic personality that would have made him a natural leader of men; and he did not evoke great devotion in his subordinates, particularly the enlisted men he would call to do his fighting.[35]

In his attitude toward the war he was dominated by an intense loyalty to the federal government, truly patriotic, devoid of political ambition, and without tolerance for politicians. In fact, he appeared to have no political principles one way or the other but was steadfastly devoted to his country and his career as a soldier. He believed that the war sprang from the influence of slavery and that, wherever slavery stood in the way of its successful prosecution, slavery must step aside.[36]

McDowell had seen battle but had never in his military career held any line position. Now, he was to command an entire army. On May 27, General Orders No. 26 created an unnamed department to include all Virginia east of the Alleghenies and north of the James River "under the command of Brigadier General Irvin McDowell, U.S.A." Late in the afternoon of May 27 he crossed the river to Virginia,[37] where he sought General Sandford in Arlington to learn the state of affairs. Because he arrived late in the day, he decided not to assume command until the next morning. After spending the night with the New Jersey brigade, he rose early and at five o'clock began to inspect the entire position.

During their four days in Virginia, the troops had fortified their positions. Trees had been felled and covered with dirt, trenches dug, forts laid out. The fortifications

35 Tidball MS Rem. (U.S.M.A.) 225, 230; Williams, Frederick, *The Wild Life of the Army: Civil War Letters of James A. Garfield* (Michigan, 1964), 148, 313 (Williams, *Garfield Letters*); Schuckers, *Chase*, 450-451, letter dated Sept. 4, 1862 from Chase to Bryant; Niven, John, ed., *The Salmon P. Chase Papers*, 5 vols. (incomplete) (Kent and London, 1996), vol. 3, *Correspondence, 1858-March 1863*, 213, letter dated June 17, 1862, from Keyes to Chase (Niven, *Chase Papers*). Schurz, *Reminiscences*, 1, 383; Averell, *Ten Years*, 284; Haupt, Herman, *Reminiscences*, 303 (Haupt, *Reminiscences*); George F. Noyes, *The Bivouac and the Battlefield or Campaign Sketches in Virginia and Maryland* (New York, 1863), 24 (Noyes, *Bivouac*).

36 Tidball MS Rem (U.S.M.A.), 225; Williams, *Wild Life of the Army Garfield Letters*, 314; Gates, *Ulster Guard*, 179; Schuckers, *Chase*, 450-51, letter dated September 4, 1862 from Chase to Bryant.

37 McDowell did not leave a manuscript collection that found its way into a public repository and seems to have written hardly any letters. A few survive scattered randomly in various collections of others. In addition, no author has found him a suitable subject for biographical treatment. He was overshadowed by Scott, swept aside by McClellan, and almost erased by bad fortune even though he had his supporters inside the army and out. But he is mentioned or described frequently. Vol. 6, *D.A.B.*, pt. 2, 29-30; Reid, *Ohio in the War*, 1, 656 ff; *C.C.W.*, 37 (McDowell); *OR*, 51, pt. 1, 335; Fry, *McDowell and Tyler*, 7 ff; Stine, *Army of the Potomac*, 2 ff; National Archives, General Staff Files for Irvin McDowell; Haupt, Herman, *Reminiscences of Herman Haupt* (Milwaukee, 1901), 303-04 (Haupt, *Reminiscences*); James Harrison Wilson, *Under the old Flag*, 2 vols. (New York, 1912), 1, 66 (Wilson, *Under the old Flag*).

at the approaches to the Long Bridge, the ferry, and the Aqueduct were progressing well. The Virginia shore position was anchored on the right by Arlington Heights, a series of small hills, and on the left by the town of Alexandria. Between these two was a concave line of redoubts, works, batteries, and infantry obstructions passing through low ground close to the river.[38]

A Confederate breakthrough would leave the Virginia line without much hope of restoration.[39] In addition, no suitable fortifications had been constructed about Alexandria, regiments still had not been brigaded, and supplies were disoriented by the change of base from the capital to Alexandria. Wagons, a constant problem early in the war, had to be taken from individual regiments and pooled for maximum efficiency.

38 Pisani, *Napoleon in America*, 114-115.

39 Comte de Paris MS Diary (large diary) (A.N. de la M. de F.) entry of September 28, 1861, and September 29, 1861; Comte de Paris in *B&L*, 2, 113; 2 McClellan in *B&L*, 2, 161; *M.O.S.*, 69, 73, 95.

Chapter 11

"Attempt nothing without a clear prospect of success, as you will find the enemy strongly posted and not inferior to you in numbers."

— *Winfield Scott's instructions to Patterson*

Scott and Patterson Plan

By May 24, Baltimore had been peacefully occupied; Alexandria, Arlington, and the Virginia shore of the Potomac opposite the capital captured; and forces sufficient to defend the capital accumulated. Patterson's mission to Baltimore now being moot, Scott terminated his orders to support Mansfield in Washington and Cadwalader in Baltimore. Instead, his troops should proceed against Frederick, Hagerstown, and Cumberland in Maryland.[1]

Patterson shifted his headquarters from Philadelphia to Chambersburg.[2] Once there, Generals Patterson, Cadwalader, and Keim, Colonels John Sherman and George H. Thomas, Fitz-John Porter, and Abner Doubleday had dinner at the Chambersburg home of A. K. McClure, a powerful force in Pennsylvania politics. They discussed the war freely. Most believed it would not last three months and would produce two or three battles at most. Doubleday, an aggressive, voluble talker, and Thomas, who required "exhaustive ingenuity . . . to induce him to speak"

1 *OR*, 2, 652.

2 *OR*, 51, pt. 1, 390-342; Patterson, *Narrative*, 31.

on military matters, disagreed, both believing the conflict would be long and bloody.[3]

Patterson had a plan to move from Hagerstown, threaten the enemy at Harpers Ferry, and recapture the town.[4] Scott approved the plan and added to it. He wanted a thrust into the Shenandoah Valley, an idea much the same as his Mississippi River plan but on a smaller scale: Union forces would drive deep into Confederate territory along a natural geographic feature and sever a large section from the rebellious states on the eastern seaboard. If Patterson could force his way south to the head of the Valley around Lynchburg,[5] he would hold a position behind any armies in northern Virginia and directly behind Richmond. If these thoughts did not occur to Scott in their entirety,[6] they found subconscious expression in his emphasis on Patterson's movements during the month of June and his later plans for an advance from Alexandria. To him, the advance into the Shenandoah Valley became the most important movement; and when he added to Patterson's plan to threaten Harpers Ferry, Scott told him to forget Cumberland and prepare to cross the Potomac at Williamsport. He would have support at the opportune moment by a demonstration from Alexandria.

Patterson proposed that, after crossing the Potomac at Williamsport, he push south, cut the Winchester Railroad, and close the area behind Harpers Ferry while another column advanced through Shepherdstown. Caught in a pincers, Harpers Ferry would be captured. His army, once reunited, could then march on Winchester. To execute this plan, Patterson began concentrating his troops at Chambersburg in preparation for the preliminary movement toward Hagerstown. Brigades were created and assigned to capable officers. Supplies and wagons were gathered to support the advance.

On the day of his arrival in Chambersburg, Monday, June 3, Patterson notified Scott that he planned to move through Hagerstown with Colonel George H. Thomas's brigade on Saturday. Part of his troops would capture and picket the Potomac ford at Williamsport while the rest advanced on Boonsborough as a

3 McClure, *Lincoln and Men*, 369-370.

4 *OR*, 51, pt. 1, 390-392; Patterson, *Narrative*, 31.

5 "Up" the Valley was south or southwest to Lynchburg. "Down" the Valley was north to Harpers Ferry. The "lower" end was at Harpers Ferry and Williamsport along the Potomac, and the "upper" end was behind Richmond at Lexington, Virginia.

6 Almost this exact plan was recorded in his diary by Ethan A. Hitchcock, an older officer serving in Washington. He would have had McClellan join Patterson and drive up the Valley, forcing the Confederates to evacuate Manassas because of the threat to their rear and their capital at Richmond. W. A. Croffut, ed., *Fifty Years in Camp and Field* (New York, 1909), 431-432, entry dated July 22, 1861 (Croffut, *Hitchcock Diary*).

blocking force against any Confederate foray from Harpers Ferry. The remainder of his army would advance on these places as soon as possible, but by the next Monday at least fourteen regiments would be beyond Hagerstown.[7] Information had reached him that the enemy at Harpers Ferry could be heard felling trees and fortifying, but his men could not approach near enough to verify this. He feared stubborn resistance.[8]

Meanwhile, Scott did his utmost to augment the Army of the Valley and ordered Patterson not to march until a Regular battery of the Fourth Artillery, five companies of the Third United States Infantry, two Ohio regiments, and the first two regiments to pass through his area from any northeastern states were in hand. By the end of the week Patterson felt he could march with eight thousand troops and support them with two thousand more on the railroad; but as ordered, he waited for the Regulars. Soon, he would have seventeen thousand volunteers and regulars. Everything was in hand except the regulars, who had not yet arrived.[9] Colonel Ambrose E. Burnside with his Rhode Island infantry regiment and artillery battery was ordered from Washington to Pennsylvania; and Brigadier General Charles P. Stone with two thousand five hundred men and two guns had been sent as a supporting expedition from the capital toward Rockville, Maryland, and the ferry near Leesburg.

Colonel Frank Patterson, commanding officer of the First Pennsylvania Infantry and son of Robert Patterson, and General George Cadwalader while in Washington in early June met Cameron and Scott. Cadwalader carried Patterson's perpetual desire for augmentation and asked to have Colonel Patterson's regiment. Cameron responded favorably as he always did to a fellow Pennsylvanian and political constituent.

"Well, I suppose you can take them."

"Mr. Cameron," said Scott, who ceased writing at his desk and looked up, "we are going to send all our best regiments away from Washington. You know we want them here."[10]

By this time in June, Scott was probably already changing his mind about the importance of Patterson's Pennsylvania column and recognizing the obvious. The main effort against the Rebels would originate in the capital area.

7 *OR*, 2, 660-661.

8 *OR*, 2, 661, 669.

9 See Scott to McClellan, *OR*, Series 3, 1, 177-78, 250, for details of the plan. This letter is one of the earliest recognitions by a person in high authority of the industrial and productive superiority of the North and the inability of the South to be self-sufficient. For discussions of Scott's plan, see Elliott, *Scott*, 721 ff, and *N&H*, 4, chap. XVII, 298-307.

10 James C. Biddle MSS (Pennsylvania Hist. Soc.) letter of June 13, 1861, from Biddle to Gertrude.

Scott then laid the unfortunate cornerstone for events to come. "Attempt nothing," he said, "without a clear prospect of success, as you will find the enemy strongly posted and not inferior to you in numbers."[11]

At this point Patterson seemed to be aggressive with a tinge of trepidation. He knew he had enough force to attack, his movement was the principal Union effort against the Confederates, and the nation counted on him for victory. Harpers Ferry was apparently being fortified for great resistance. There, the first great battle of the war would be fought. Scott had enjoined him to do nothing unless he was certain of victory and had warned that the Confederates were at least his equal in numbers.

Action by Patterson's force was necessary but how much and how soon? Should he set out for Harpers Ferry at once or should he leave nothing to chance? Perhaps the Confederates could be maneuvered from the Ferry without a fight.

Scott had long feared for the safety of the capital on the northern flank. To the south where the Potomac was wide he had less concern. From both sides of the river between Edward's and Harpers Ferries, where the land was a luxuriant bread basket, it could be crossed easily, especially in the summer when the water was down.[12]

His fears were relieved once again by his loyal and reliable subordinate Charles P. Stone, now a brigadier general. Promoted on May 14 along with a raft of junior Regular Army officers, Stone commanded a small force on the northern outskirts of the capital, where he provided limited security against any Confederate thrust across the Potomac between Washington and Harpers Ferry.

Stone proposed to Scott that he take a brigade to make a demonstration along the canal toward Harpers Ferry. Large flour mills on which the Union forces depended for bread stuffs were in Georgetown. The owners had told Stone that the wheat harvest in the Leesburg district could probably be brought into Georgetown by a show of force, which would induce the farmers to sell their harvest to their usual customers, the Georgetown millers. Stone thought this sort of demonstration, in addition to protecting the canal, might be continued toward Harpers Ferry, in order to cooperate with Patterson's column and compel the Confederates to evacuate the place.[13]

11 *OR*, 2, 652.

12 *OR*, 2, 107, 110, 114, 116, 117, 119.

13 Townsend, *Anecdotes*, 70. According to Townsend, this arrangement was made in "the Fall of 1861." He implies that it was shortly before the Battle of Balls Bluff and led to the battle; but the correspondence and orders in *OR*, 2, and *OR*, 5, make it relatively clear that it occurred in June and July of 1861 and had nothing to do with Balls Bluff.

Stone's orders were to collect his command, march to Edward's Ferry, seize and hold it, then cross the Potomac and take Leesburg if that were practicable.[14] Like Captain Montgomery C. Meigs and Major Fitz-John Porter, Scott's two subordinates sent on prior independent missions, Stone received great latitude. "The general in chief has left much to your well-known discretion," wrote Colonel Edward D. Townsend, "but he enjoins you to proceed with caution and by no means to hazard the safety of your expedition."

Collecting his available men, Stone marched north. He arrived at Tenallytown on June 10 with four battalions of infantry and one company of cavalry. On the way were another battalion of infantry, another company of cavalry, and one section of artillery from Griffin's Regular battery.[15] The next day he arrived at Rockville, and on June 16 at Poolesville[16] a few miles from the Potomac and due east of Leesburg across the river.

Knowing his man, as Porter had and Keyes strangely had not, Stone sent a stream of daily reports to Scott in Washington. Just as he predicted, he found the areas north, northeast, and northwest filled with cattle and crops. His troops, formerly battalion strength, now included the First Pennsylvania, First New Hampshire, and Ninth New York Regiments of infantry.[17] Harpers Ferry was, according to rumor, empty; but Stone heard nothing from Patterson who would, he assumed, have reoccupied it if he could do it without resistance.

Stone regularly exchanged artillery fire with the Rebels at Edward's Ferry, "a most beautiful place," wrote a staff officer. Stone could see the smoke of fires destroying bridges and other valuable military property on the far side of the river and played cat-and-mouse with Confederate skirmishers at the various crossing points.[18] Having found the area between Poolesville and Harpers Ferry devoid of Rebel troops, he sent the Ninth New York to Point of Rocks, a crossing of the river just south of Harpers Ferry.[19]

Meanwhile, the officers of the Second Battalion, District of Columbia Volunteers, stationed at Seneca Mills, had "forgotten themselves" and requested that the battalion be relieved from duty and sent back to Washington, thus giving substance to the concern that the District of Columbia militia companies would be

14 *OR*, 2, 104.

15 *OR*, 2, 106.

16 *OR*, 2, 108.

17 *OR*, 2, 107.

18 James C. Biddle MSS (PHS) letter dated June 18, 1861, from Biddle to Gertrude; *OR*, 2, 108-113.

19 *OR*, 2, 113.

unwilling to serve outside the capital. Once again shrewder than his "adversaries," Stone took advantage of the old adage, "Be careful what you ask for; you may get it." He chose not to confront the battalion and precipitate a contest of uncertain outcome. Instead, he granted their wish and ordered the battalion's return to Washington with a recommendation that it be mustered out of the service. Of course, this would mean public humiliation for men of all ranks in the battalion. Later in the day all officers in the battalion urgently appealed to him that they not be sent home in disgrace. Again wisely, Stone suspended the order and left the battalion in its position.[20]

The wheat crops in the area north, northeast, and northwest were among the richest ever. Harvest was no more than days away. Particularly productive and largely Union in its sentiments, Loudon County, Virginia, cried for a force of occupation that would protect the crops, especially those of loyal men, from seizure by Rebel forces in the area. Stone's force was small. Its presence and visibility in an area of predictable Confederate activity, were far more important than its negligible ability to defend against an attack. Even though he had been asked for protection by a loyal farmer, Stone felt he could not safely cross the river until he had heard from Patterson at Harpers Ferry.

Baffling it was. Why was Patterson not in the important but unoccupied Harpers Ferry? Perhaps, he suggested, Scott could send up the river a small amount of artillery or order a small part of Patterson's force to Stone's column. With small reinforcements, he could secure Loudon County.[21]

Stone would answer these questions himself. His plan for a reconnaissance he explained to Frank E. Patterson, colonel of the First Pennsylvania Infantry. At midnight June 23, he left Patterson in command, mounted his horse, left his headquarters at Poolesville, and started north to reconnoiter. Stone took with him Captain William S. Abert, his adjutant; an aide, Captain Stewart; and twelve cavalrymen as an escort. Three hours later he passed his extreme pickets about three miles short of Point of Rocks. Entering the village as day broke, the column found the charred remnants of the bridge across the Potomac, which had been burned by the Rebels, and five Confederate pickets on the Virginia side of the river. Here, he learned that no troops were on the Maryland side ahead. With two men on a handcar Captain Abert continued upriver on the Baltimore and Ohio Railroad until he reached Sandy Hook, a tiny village opposite Harpers Ferry. Greeting Abert with enthusiasm, earnestness, and anxiety, the citizens questioned him about the arrival of United States troops and the time they could expect to be relieved of occupation

20 *OR*, 2, 113-114.

21 *OR*, 2, 113, 114, 115.

by Rebel troops. Carefully, Abert examined the ground. He could see that the Confederates, also suffering from rookie blues, had negligently occupied the village somewhat earlier. Then, he met Captain John Newton, an engineer on the staff of General Patterson, on a reconnaissance from the other direction. Abert told[22] Newton, a hard drinking, Regular Army, West Point graduate, second in the Class of 1842,[23] the size of Stone's column; gathered some additional useful information from the local citizens; and started back to Stone at Point of Rocks.

Not until 1:45 in the afternoon did the captain reach Stone to report on his reconnaissance. At Winchester, General Joseph E. Johnston had only about twelve to fourteen thousand Confederate troops. At Leesburg, he had learned from a fugitive, the Rebels had only about sixteen hundred men with supporting troops nine miles away. Foretelling a grave concern of a month and a half later, he told Scott that Johnston might reach Leesburg by the afternoon of the next day, June 25, where he would cross the Potomac into Maryland or move toward Arlington on McDowell's right. He thought both Point of Rocks and Sandy Hook should be occupied, but his present force was too small.[24] For the next week Stone described the things he could do—make the Potomac safe against crossing, stop Confederate correspondence across the Potomac between Point of Rocks and Harpers Ferry, occupy Point of Rocks, protect the canal and railroad, and operate between Johnston and McDowell's right flank—if he had one, two, or three additional regiments.[25]

On June 10 and 11, the organization of the Army of Pennsylvania was published in general orders. By that time all units ordered to Patterson had reached him. Combined in two divisions under Generals Cadwalader and Keim were five brigades of four or five regiments each.[26] Two days later the plan of advance was published. Cadwalader's division, composed of the three brigades of George H. Thomas, Alpheus S. Williams, and Dixon S. Miles, would march from its position between Chambersburg and Hagerstown with three days' cooked rations in haversacks, while Keim's division of Negley's and Wynkoop's brigades followed as fast as possible by rail.[27]

22 *OR*, 2, 115-116.

23 Warner, *Generals in Blue*, 344-345; 1 *Cullum*, no. 112; *D.A.B.*, 7, pt. 1, 473-474.

24 *OR*, 2, 116.

25 *OR*, 2, 116-118.

26 *OR*, 2, 715; *OR*, 51, pt. 1, 397-98.

27 Williams says he left Hagerstown for Williamsport but the army could not have been there on June 13 because the end of the track was at Hagerstown, as he notes himself, thus making progress by rail beyond Hagerstown impossible. *OR*, 2, 679.

In another two days, Patterson's units advanced according to orders. Thomas passed east of Hagerstown and headed toward the river at Williamsport while Miles's brigade followed to his right rear along a stream into the Potomac. Williams, the last brigade of Cadwalader's division, passed through Hagerstown heading due south on the pike for Sharpsburg with heavy pickets deployed across his front, while Keim's pair of brigades came forward by railroad and marched along the turnpike in support. From Chambersburg to Hagerstown, Patterson shifted his headquarters forward.[28]

Scott expected the army to cross the Potomac as soon as it reached the ford; but in the last days before the advance, Patterson determined that his transportation was inadequate. He was, therefore, somewhat surprised when he learned that he was expected across the river on Monday or Tuesday while a demonstration was made from the capital to draw attention from him.[29]

Scott was perfectly justified in expecting his subordinate to ford the Potomac at Williamsport and press forward. This had been the plan, and they had agreed on it. But somewhere between development and execution, the old Pennsylvanian again discovered difficulties that forced him to change his timetable.

Had another man been in command, he might have marched boldly and directly against Harpers Ferry. Scott naturally assumed Patterson would do this. It was, after all, the course he himself would have followed. But a leader of this stripe Robert Patterson was not. He lacked sufficient wagons and horses for his train. Despite constant reports that the Confederates were evacuating Harpers Ferry, Patterson believed the place would be strongly held. Worse yet, he believed that Rebel forces were concentrating there in preparation for a long siege, and that the roads all about it were heavily fortified for defense. Patterson would need siege guns.[30] The day before his advance to the Potomac, Patterson repeated with many embellishments the plan to surround Harpers Ferry—if he could mount a column strong enough to occupy the territory behind it. Once into Virginia, he felt, he would not retreat; but he would need support on all sides and must avoid precipitating a general engagement.[31]

Patterson received reports from Captain John Newton, his engineer officer, that Harpers Ferry had been abandoned and destroyed. He could see long columns of

28 *OR*, 51, pt. 1, 399-400; *OR*, 2, 679.

29 *OR*, 2, 678; *C.C.W.*, 2, 79 (Patterson).

30 Porter MSS (L.C.) memo dated June 7, 1861; *OR*, 2, 684. In a note dated June 14, Patterson echoed Porter's comment that they would not be ready to cross before June 17 or 18.

31 *OR*, 2, 685.

smoke from the break in the mountains which cradled the tiny town.[32] That did not change his mind. He continued firm in his belief that the enemy would not retreat.[33]

Captain Newton had to reconnoiter Martinsburg to learn whether the Rebel retreat was real. If that were the case and the Rebels were abandoning the line of the Potomac, Cadwalader must cross part or all of his division to bolster the reconnaissance, harass the retreat, and occupy Harpers Ferry immediately.[34]

All signs pointed to a Rebel retreat. Camp ruins were discovered. Everything of military value was gone or destroyed. Martinsburg was completely deserted. Its depot and iron works had been razed.[35] This was the opportunity to occupy the lower entrance to the Valley, seize Harpers Ferry, and establish a supply base for operations against Winchester. Although the ferry at Williamsport had been destroyed, the river was low enough for the men to ford it. At last, on June 16, Patterson crossed the Potomac with Cadwalader's division. The men struggled over the rocky, irregular bottom in water to their armpits and pressed unopposed onto Virginia soil. Harpers Ferry was deserted.[36] The rumors and intelligence had been right.

Encouraged by this easy success, Patterson began to plan again. First, he made the mistake that everyone would make until 1864. Harpers Ferry, the least defensible position in the eastern United States, would be his headquarters, base of operations, and supply depot. The Baltimore and Ohio Railroad would be opened east and west. With strong forces at Harpers Ferry, Charlestown, and Martinsburg, he could march against Winchester and Strasburg. As he turned the Valley flank of the Rebel line, he would force it to retire from the line of the Potomac; and he would make secure all Maryland and Virginia along the Potomac. This would be another way to accomplish the result wanted by Chase and McDowell: the Rebels' main line of resistance would withdraw from the Potomac, retire to the Rappahannock, and give the Union a position with depth in Virginia in front of Washington. He would accomplish this by maneuver, not by fighting; and the maneuver would occur in northwestern Virginia, where strong Union sentiment would make everything easier. Harpers Ferry, the scene of John Brown's legendary raid in 1859, a place with

32 *OR*, 2, 686, 687-89. On page 96 of volume 1 Bates in *Penn. Vols.* states it was June 25; but the events and chronology, e.g., camping south of Williamsport after a march, seem to indicate June 15.

33 Jackson quit Harpers Ferry on June 15, 1861, and had begun his withdrawal even earlier. Vandiver, Frank F., *Mighty Stonewall*, 147-48 (New York, 1957).

34 *OR*, 2, 687.

35 *OR*, 2, 689.

36 *OR*, 2, 691; Bates, *History of the Pennsylvania Volunteers*, 1, 87.

emotional and historical significance even if it lacked strategic and tactical value, would serve as an Achilles' heel to the Confederates. To Patterson, the moth, Harpers Ferry became the flame.

The ferry lay at the junction of the Potomac and Shenandoah Rivers in the middle of the Blue Ridge Mountains. It was easily accessible by water from three directions, by railroad from two, and by foot from everywhere. Lofty positions on Loudon Heights, Bolivar Heights, and Maryland Heights loomed overhead on all three sides. Although its river level location made it a perfect east-west railroad pass for the Baltimore and Ohio Railroad through the mountains, the three unconnected heights exposed it to a plunging artillery fire and made it indefensible. Its occupation could be denied if only one of the three heights were held by an enemy force with artillery, but to occupy it safely all three heights had to be held.[37]

For real and practical reasons it could not be defended. In a personal letter Fitz-John Porter described it as a beautiful place to defend and a beautiful one to attack. With a large force, he wrote, it could hold out forever.[38] Under attack, the town was useless to the defender. The heights around it were the key to its defense; if the defender held at least one of them, occupation by the attacker was impossible. Remembering his first look at the heights and the Harpers Ferry area, an engineer officer after the war, wrote that Maryland Heights was "the Soul of the triad of giant mountains and far o'ertops its fellows. Of course, it completely [sic] commands Harpers Ferry into which a plunging fire of even musketry can be had upon it."[39]

From a larger viewpoint, it and the nearby towns on the Potomac, Williamsport, Shepherdstown, and Monocacy, were the doors to the lower or northern end of the Valley. It had no military value as a strategic or tactical location, but to Rebel forces headed north into Pennsylvania and to Union forces headed south into the Valley its occupation was an extraordinary convenience.

In Washington, the importance Scott had placed on the campaign in the Valley waned. The very day Patterson crossed the Potomac into Virginia and began to make grandiose new plans, the general in chief wrote that, if there were to be no pursuit, "and I recommend none specially," all Regular units and Burnside's Rhode Island regiment should be sent to Washington.

Why he recalled the Regulars to Washington, Scott never explained. He had certainly changed his mind about the most important theater of war. Now that Virginia had snubbed the mother country, its citizens had voted to secede, and its

37 Jones, Ray, *Harpers Ferry*, 21-22 (Gretna, 1992).

38 McClellan MSS (L.C.) letter dated May 10, 1861, from Porter to McClellan.

39 Malles, Ed, (editor), *Bridge Building in Wartime: Colonel Wesley Brainerd's Memoir of the 50th New York Volunteer Engineers* (Knoxville, 1997), 86 (Malles, *Brainerd's Memoirs*).

military forces had become a threat, he could no longer afford the luxury of being so sensitive about provoking his old state or about military activity on her soil. The capital of the Confederacy had been moved to Richmond, only ninety miles from Washington. If the primary line of operations were to be from Washington and the Potomac toward Richmond and the James, the Regulars, the most reliable troops, should be on that line.

Although Scott's opinion about the existence of strong loyal sentiment in Rebel territory was shared by others, no one else agreed that the soil of Virginia was sacred and should be spared. His lateness in coming to reality was probably a function of age. Scott was seventy-four years old, his judgment was faulty at times, and he did not have his old powers of discernment.[40] He grew more and more tired. He was at his post night and day, often wrapping himself in his cloak and sleeping on the settee in his office.[41] The mental and physical strain of his duties would have exhausted a much younger man.

Patterson wanted to retain the Regular infantry. Without it, he felt stripped of striking power; and for a change, he had a legitimate complaint, particularly because he would also lose the Regular artillery. His only recourse would be to fall back across the river and entrench. The telegraph wires worked overtime as the two men explained and defended their positions.

Finally, the old general in chief, never known for his patience, ended the discussion when he snapped, "We are pressed here. Send the troops that I have twice called for without delay."

The order could not have been more explicit or peremptory. It contained none of the earlier discretion or discussion. The Second, Third, and Eighth Infantry, the dismounted cavalry, Burnside's regiment, and the two artillery batteries went to Hagerstown to board the train for Washington. Part of Cadwalader's division withdrew north of the river.[42]

As the Regulars prepared to leave, reports began to arrive that General Joseph E. Johnston, the Confederate commander in the Valley, was marching on Martinsburg with an army of fifteen thousand. Patterson was certain that the advancing Rebels intended to take advantage of the departure of the Regular troops. Without artillery, he could not resist a determined attempt to cross the Potomac. He

40 Elliott, *Scott*, 727-28; Russel, *My Diary*, 197, entry dated July 9, 1861; K. P. Williams, *Lincoln Finds a General*, 5 vols. (New York, 1952), 1, 72 (Williams, *Lincoln Finds a General*). When the Regulars arrived in Washington, their weary eyes found a parade and celebration in progress.

41 Seward, *Reminiscences*, 166.

42 *OR*, 2, 696.

ordered the departures from Hagerstown halted. The units bound for Washington must be ready to return to Williamsport at once if necessary. Negley was ordered to reinforce his forward position; and Wynkoop, Keim's other brigade, would follow Negley early the next morning, June 18.[43]

All during the night of June 17, the remainder of Cadwalader's division, seven regiments of infantry and one troop of the Philadelphia City Cavalry, lay somewhere on the Virginia side of the river. The hours passed slowly. The officers prepared to defend.

June 18 dawned brighter. The forward units returned peacefully, Abner Doubleday's battery of Regular artillery arrived, and the expected attack failed to materialize. The Regular troops, except for Thomas's four hundred dismounted cavalry, resumed their trip to Washington.[44]

The withdrawal of the Regular Army units had a profound effect on Patterson. He had regarded them as his striking power, his offensive unit, in effect his Imperial Guard or his Companion Cavalry. When they were withdrawn from his control, he had no artillery, no cavalry, and no infantry with a longer term of service than three months. Great offensive plans ceased to exist in his mind, and his mentality became completely defensive. Patterson's faith in the fighting ability of his soldiers and his willingness to meet the enemy shrank. He needed more regiments, always more regiments. Every time he was given discretion to call any troops to his army, he did it at once. He no longer intended to fight but only to threaten and demonstrate. His independence made him uneasy. He longed to join the forces about Washington.[45]

Two days after the Regulars left, Scott suggested that a column of troops be placed atop Maryland Heights next to Harpers Ferry; that the Army of the Upper Potomac absorb Colonel Stone's brigade, which was stretched along the Potomac River fords from Washington to Point of Rocks; and that Patterson's army cooperate with a thrust from the south against Leesburg.[46] This appealed to him.[47]

Next day, he modified and enlarged the plan. He would occupy and fortify Maryland Heights with a brigade of 2,100 men and Doubleday's battery of artillery, collect a store of provisions sufficient for twenty days, abandon the Williamsport

43 *OR*, 2, 699 ff.

44 *OR*, 2, 698-99, 703.

45 John Sherman MSS (L.C.) letter of June 27, 1861, from Patterson to Sherman; Porter MSS (L.C.) draft letter, November 24, 1890, from Porter to Livermore.

46 *OR*, 2, 709.

47 Patterson, *Narrative*, 39. This seemed the most desirable plan to Patterson in the retrospection of later years, but this statement must be assessed in light of the fact that it was not part of the matured plan.

line, move his base to Frederick, cross the Potomac River at Point of Rocks, and unite with Stone at Leesburg. From there, action could be taken as desired. By shifting his line of operations eastward, he thought, he would strengthen the position of the other Union armies and would keep alive the ardor of the men.[48]

After sending his plan to Scott, Patterson sent Captain Newton to reconnoiter Maryland Heights.[49] Ascending the western slope by a country road to Solomon's Gap, the captain turned south along the crest and headed toward the end. He saw at once that the roads would have to be repaired before artillery could be put in position. The crest was covered with scrub timber and brush, which made movement difficult. The springs, which had been full the week before, were now dry; and the nearest water supply was in Pleasant Valley at the eastern base of the mountain. The roads to the crest, which had been built by the Confederates at Solomon's Gap and Sandy Hook, were choked with huge boulders. To defend the ridge, thought Newton, a two-hundred-yard-wide swath should be cut across the crest and a parapet constructed with a stockade and loopholes. Because the sides of the mountain were very steep, the flank approaches could be blocked by felling trees. If two thousand men worked ten days to fortify the crest, it could hold out indefinitely.[50]

While receiving Newton's reports Patterson also gathered information about the enemy. From deserters, he learned that the Rebels numbered some twenty-five thousand men. Eight thousand, under General T. J. Jackson, were marching on Martinsburg while the main body lay at Winchester.[51] In the days that followed, other reports estimated Johnston at twelve thousand infantry; thirteen thousand infantry with seventeen guns; and fifteen thousand infantry, one thousand cavalry, and twenty to twenty-four guns.[52]

In a personal letter near the end of the month Patterson himself estimated the Confederates at fifteen thousand infantry supported by a large force of cavalry, and twenty-two guns, seventeen of which were rifled. His own strength was only eleven thousand men, four hundred cavalry, and six guns without harness.[53] In truth, the

48 *OR*, 2, 711. This serves as further evidence that Porter dominated Patterson's thought processes. In a letter dated June 21, 1861, Porter described the same plan with the same morale fringe benefit. Who had the idea first? No record shows it, but with the long-term importance of Porter in every decision Patterson made and the view of many others about their interaction, the "credit" should go to Porter.

49 *OR*, 2, 717; *D.A.B.*, 8, pt. 1, 473.

50 Reports of the reconnaissance appear at *OR*, 2, 717, 732-33. The impregnability of Maryland Heights would be tested again, at least twice in one campaign in 1862.

51 *OR*, 2, 717.

52 *OR*, 2, 728, 729-30.

53 John Sherman MSS (L.C.) letter dated June 24, 1861, from Patterson to Sherman.

total force facing him numbered only ten thousand five hundred at the end of the month, of which three hundred thirty-four were cavalry and very few were artillery.[54]

Aided by the fears of his subordinates, who had less information than he did, Patterson persistently overestimated Johnston's numbers. Logically, the Confederacy would have had difficulty building armies and supplying them.[55] It had a smaller population base, the black part of its population was not allowed to serve, and it had little or no industrial capacity.

In spite of the Rebels' "superior" numbers, he said he was willing to cross the Potomac again and drive them back if permission were granted. No more than ten days would be needed to clear that part of Virginia.[56]

On June 25, the day Captain Newton wrote the final report of his Maryland Heights reconnaissance, Scott notified Patterson that he should continue to confront those Confederates who had not left the area since the evacuation of Harpers Ferry. If he felt equal or superior in numbers, he could cross the Potomac and offer battle; and if the enemy retreated on Winchester, he need not follow. If he were to pursue, he must be certain he had superiority. As a second choice, the army could unite with Stone in a movement on Point of Rocks.[57] Both men believed a lost or drawn battle would be disastrous.

This exchange of correspondence highlights the command relationship between the two old friends and Patterson's preferences. Patterson constantly promised immediate action while actually procrastinating. He sought authorization for initiative but placed responsibility for all decisions in Scott's distant hands. His request for permission to cross the river and defeat a "superior enemy" was unnecessary because the "permission" he sought lay well within the latitude already granted by Scott. No doubt, he found independent command lonely and intimidating. By slipping to his left, joining Stone, and operating from Point of Rocks, he would change that. He would increase his force, he would eliminate a range of mountains and a series of rivers that separated him from Washington and the other main army in the east, and he would shorten the distance between them. In effect, he would become little more than an oversized flank guard for McDowell's Army of Northeastern Virginia and would leave the Valley to the Confederates. In

54 Vandiver, *Mighty Stonewall*, 145. Johnston's army, in addition to numbering but 6,500 men of all arms, was acutely short of all equipment. *Id.*, 148.

55 For an account of Floyd's activities, see John Hope Franklin, *The Militant South*, 241-242 (Cambridge, 1956).

56 *OR*, 2, 717.

57 *OR*, 2, 725.

his attempt to give discretion to the field commander while coordinating the movements of separate forces, Scott failed to realize the true mettle of his old friend.

Once Patterson had the reports from Captain Newton about Maryland Heights, he began to think about recrossing the Potomac. To clear the Williamsport Ford, which was well picketed,[58] he decided to cross east and south of it, then strike for the Shepherdstown Road junction with the Winchester Pike to cut off any Rebels in the "neck" of the river. On June 27, he sent Captain Simpson of the engineers to join Newton and reconnoiter the crossings. Speed and secrecy were mandatory in order to insure surprise and keep the Southerners from reinforcing their advance units.[59]

At midnight, Captain Newton reported the enemy in great strength along the river at the intended crossing places.[60] The plan would have to be changed. The entire army would cross at Williamsport and push down the Valley Pike. Two days later the harnesses for Doubleday's battery arrived, and the army was in condition to start in spite of the fact that the Confederates seemed to be crossing the river below his left flank during the darkness of the twenty-ninth.[61]

The next day he received word that Stone's four and a half regiments had been ordered to join him with a battery of Rhode Island artillery.[62] These excellent additions to his command made an advance a certainty. On the last day of June, he telegraphed with dramatic curtness:

> Downsville, Md., June 30, 1861
> Colonel Townshend,
>
> Asst. Adjt. Gen., U.S. Army, Washington City:
>
> I cross at daylight tomorrow morning.
>
> R. Patterson
> Major-General, Commanding.[63]

58 John Sherman MSS (L.C.) letter dated June 24, 1861, from Patterson to Sherman; Bates, *Penn. Vols.*, 1, 97.

59 *OR*, 2, 727.

60 The numbers reported were as follows: 5,000 from Falling Waters to Dam No. 4, 4,500 at Shepherdstown, 5,000 at Bunker Hill, twenty to twenty-four guns, and 1,000 cavalry, yet another example of poor intelligence.

61 John Sherman MSS (L.C.) letter dated June 27, 1861, from Patterson to Sherman; *OR*, 2, 729, 734. The brigades of Negley and Abercrombie were sent to verify the report and defend if necessary, but no Confederates were found.

62 *OR*, 2, 734.

63 *OR*, 2, 735.

Chapter 12

"He repeatedly said that his troops were not sufficiently drilled and disciplined for an offensive campaign and that the politicians were responsible for the premature movement. Nevertheless, he would do his duty to the best of his ability."

— Henry Villard describing McDowell before Bull Run

McDowell Creates an Army

McDowell had hardly assumed command of the Alexandria-Arlington line when he began to encounter problems. Among other things he had difficulty moving the necessary supplies to the west bank of the Potomac. Scott was still annoyed by McDowell's promotion to brigadier general and assignment to command of the Army of Northeastern Virginia. He never said he thought another man would be better, but he did not think McDowell was the right choice. Mansfield had been kept in his lesser command because of his accumulated experience in the District of Columbia. He, too, was not pleased that the battle assignment had been given to a man far younger and less experienced.

Born in New Haven, Connecticut, on December 22, 1803, Joseph K. F. Mansfield began his life not long after the struggle for independence and the maiden voyage of the *Constitution*. After an education in the common schools of the state, he entered West Point two months before his fourteenth birthday, took the five-year course, graduated second in the class of 1822, and was commissioned in the Corps of Engineers. In the years that followed he toiled on the coastal defenses in New York, Virginia, North Carolina, South Carolina, Florida, and Georgia. Chief engineer under General Zachary Taylor during the war with Mexico, he constructed and participated in the defense of Fort Brown, Texas, was awarded a brevet of major for gallant and distinguished services in the defense of Fort Brown, and received a brevet of lieutenant-colonel for gallant and meritorious conduct in several conflicts at Monterey, September 23, 1846. He suffered a painful wound while leading an assault on a redoubt. He was breveted colonel for gallant and meritorious conduct at Buena Vista, February 23, 1847. According to some, he planned the battle; and its success was partly due to his shrewdness and his prompt decisions at critical moments.

From 1848 to 1853 he served on the board of engineers planning coast defenses on the Atlantic and Pacific oceans. On May 28, 1853, Secretary of War Jefferson Davis, who had observed him during the war with Mexico, appointed him inspector-general. Mansfield inspected the Department of New Mexico in 1853, California in 1854, Texas in 1856, Utah in 1857, Oregon and California in 1858 and 1859, and the Department of Texas again in 1860 and 1861. During the last inspection of Texas he became aware of activities that would lead to war. Appreciating the crisis, he hurried to Washington to communicate his observations to the War Department. John B. Floyd, the secretary of war, had just resigned in late December after first sending all the available spare rifles and field artillery to the Southern states. Once in Washington, he received recognition by his assignments. Throughout, he would have preferred, and he continuously tried to obtain, a field command even though in his long service he had never commanded troops.

Although vigorous, his flowing white hair and white beard made him appear all of his years in a war that did not lend itself to older officers. A man of kind disposition he followed with parental interest the careers of his children, an unmarried daughter and a son at West Point. A typical man of the nineteenth century, he showed his deeply religious and patriotic nature in a letter he wrote his daughter on June 17, 1861, ". . . I am now engaged in the cause of my country, and of Freedom, and free institutions: and in a civil war, a most unhappy war, from which there is no escape. I feel that I am right, and I shall do my duty to the full extent of my ability and power. May God help me, & strengthen me with his strong arm, and uphold with his mighty power. If God be with us, who can be against us. My Dear Child I would have you look to God, & do your duty in all things, and you will find in time of need, he is ever ready to help you. Many is the time I have felt that, He from whom there is nothing hid, has stretched out his hand, & plucked me out of evil, & kept me from harm. His special kindness in my behalf has spared me to the present hour; and I trust in him still, with that confidence in the intercession of our Lord &

savior Jesus Christ which calms the troubled heart, and gives me peace & consolation."[1]

Two messages were sent by the old general in chief to induce McDowell to resign. The new brigadier general realized he was young, generally unknown, and recently promoted; but he would not desert a post obtained for him by his good friends as a result of his good work. As politely as possible, he rejected the general in chief's suggestion. The strain was not alleviated by McDowell's plan of action when it was presented.[2]

Regiment after regiment from the Washington defenses now crossed the river to join the Army of Northeastern Virginia, but the lack of cooperation by Washington officers delayed everything because Scott and Mansfield had to approve all movements across the river. They did not openly or consciously thwart McDowell. They were as loyal as any man. Rather, their nettled feelings diminished the prompt willingness that should have helped McDowell. Personal feelings had no place in this work, injured pride should not have reduced efficiency, and balked desires should not have caused delay. Of course, Scott and Mansfield would have agreed with this in a flash; but their conduct did not sharply reflect the things they knew were right. At one point McDowell went to Mansfield for more troops to be sent across the river.

"I have no transportation," Mansfield complained.

In charge of transportation was Montgomery C. Meigs, now a brigadier general, chief quartermaster of the army, and logically, the man to see. Although he had enough wagons, Meigs would not release them until the army was ready to move against the enemy.

"I agree to that," replied the frustrated McDowell, "but between you two, I get nothing."[3]

Visited daily by Henry Villard, a reporter for James G. Bennett's *New York Herald*, McDowell unburdened himself. He "showed anything but confidence in (his Army's) success," wrote Villard later, "and plainly displayed distrust of himself

1 J. K. F. Mansfield MSS (United States Military Academy) letter dated June 17, 1861, from Mansfield to his daughter Mary; Morgan MSS (N.Y.S.L.) letter dated August 22, 1861, from Mansfield to Morgan; *Cullum*, 1, no. 287; Russel K. Brown, *Fallen in Battle: American General Officer Combat Fatalities from 1775* (Westport, 1988), 85 (Brown, *Fallen in Battle*); Ezra J. Warner, *Generals in Blue: Lives of the Union Commanders* (Baton Rouge, 1964), 309 (Warner, *Generals in Blue*); Jack K. Bauer, *The Mexican War 1846-1848* (Easton, 1990), 49-52, 92-101 (Bauer, *Mexican War*); George Gordon Meade, *The Life and Letters of George Gordon Meade*, 2 vols. (New York, 1913), 1, 96 (Meade, *Life and Letters*); *D.A.B.*, 6, pt. 2, 257; Elijah R. Kennedy, *John B., Woodward, a Biographical Memoir* (New York, 1897), 78, 92.

2 *C.C.W.*, 1, 37-38 (McDowell).

3 *C.C.W.*, 1, 38 (McDowell).

and of his soldiery. He repeatedly said that his troops were not sufficiently drilled and disciplined for an offensive campaign and that the politicians were responsible for the premature movement." Nevertheless, he would do his duty to the best of his ability.[4]

The new army produced problems of its own. Some of the regiments were committing depredations against the civilian population. They excused themselves on the ground that the injured were secessionists. McDowell vehemently opposed this. Because the Virginia courts in the area were not functioning, military courts would have to handle the problem. Damage done by Union troops to crops, fields, trees, buildings, and even fences was to be reported with an estimated price by the owner, who could then claim reimbursement from the government.[5]

General Sandford had used the Lee Mansion at Arlington as his headquarters even though it had no furniture. True to his straight-laced, puritanical character, McDowell held his headquarters to the standards he set for his army. When he assumed command, he first refused to use the house, moving his headquarters onto the grounds. He wrote to Mrs. Lee, assured her that the house and grounds would be respected, and said that the family could return under his protection if it wished.

Early in June, George Templeton Strong and a friend, both prominent New York City Republican supporters of the war and both members of the United States Sanitary Commission, visited McDowell's headquarters at Arlington. They found it a splendid place with beautiful surrounding grounds, but the sentinels at the mansion denied them admission. They started back to their carriage when they met McDowell followed by a "tail of staff and orderlies." He hailed them, dismounted, took them through the house, and "was very kind and obliging." Strong found it "a queer place, an odd mixture of magnificence and meanness, like the castle of some illustrious, shabby, semi-insolvent old Irish family; for example, a grand costly portico with half-rotten wooden steps."

A member of the White House staff visited the new fortifications being built around the house before its contents were shipped south. "Arlington House is the old

4 Villard, *Memoirs*, 1, 182.

5 *OR*, 2, 654-55, 659. This was originally intended to apply only to those things that had been destroyed or damaged under proper authority but soon came to apply to all damage as long as the owner could make at least a nominal showing of loyalty. In 1958, the author learned that the local citizen who told McDowell about the roads and fords north of the Stone Bridge over Bull Run Creek had filed a claim for damage to his farm in the area and had used the information given to McDowell to prove his loyalty. The National Archives declared these files unavailable without permission of the local representative to Congress; but the representative's staff said that, because descendants of the claimant still lived in the area and might be compromised if their kinsman were known to have assisted the Yankees, the information could not be made available.

family mansion of the Custis family the relatives and decedents of Washington," he wrote,

> and has one of the most beautiful situations imaginable—just opposite this City on a high sloping hill that rises up from the Potomac. The house looks quite old—I don't know when it was built, but it was evidently in its day a grand affair, and its arrangement, furniture, pictures, etc., at once carry one back to the good old 'first family' days of Virginia before social decay had bred and engendered the treasonous reptiles that now wallow in the slime and mire of her political and moral corruption—in those days plantation grandeur atoned somewhat for their assumptions of family pride. The furniture of the house was evidently 'stylish' in its time. The chambers are filled up with family portraits—most of them very indifferent as works of art, of course. Deers antlers, the trophy of the chase in the old days, are nailed up about the halls and passages and altogether a historic and traditional atmosphere seemed to pervade the house such as I had not stood in for many a day."[6]

McDowell's headquarters never grew very large even with the approach of battle. To many, a large headquarters and staff were ostentatious. In the spirit of democratic egalitarianism, military display indicating rank or prestige was viewed unfavorably. Unfortunately for McDowell, few people knew the difference in military matters between necessity and ostentation. He was even censured by General Scott for being too showy when he paraded eight regiments in one review.[7]

Having a command comparable to that of a major or lieutenant-general, McDowell was in title and support only a brigadier general and had a force far too large for the small staff of a brigadier general, a rank intended for a brigade of three to five regiments. His headquarters establishment never exceeded four small tents and a few men,[8] a handicap that continued from the time he assumed command through the battle.

Added to this was the problem of finding senior officers for the now rapidly growing army. When McDowell arrived in Virginia on the evening of May 27, he had with him a commission as colonel in the Regular Army for Samuel Peter Heintzelman, who was in command at Alexandria. Late that night after he had seen to his other business, he found Heintzelman asleep at his headquarters. McDowell awakened the lieutenant colonel and presented him with his promotion.[9]

6 Nicolay MSS (L.C.) letter dated May 31, 1861, from Nicolay to Therena.

7 Manton Marble MSS (L.C.) letter dated November 27, 1861, from Fitz-John Porter to Marble; *C.C.W.*, 1, 38 (McDowell).

8 Russell, *My Diary*, 207, entry of July 6, 1861; Gurowski, *Diary*, 61-62, entry for July, 1861.

9 Heintzelman MS diary (large diary) (L.C.) entry dated May 25, 1861.

Born in 1805, Heintzelman had been appointed to West Point from Pennsylvania and graduated in the class of 1826. His stern, hardy visage, pinched features which made his nose seem to touch his chin, full beard, long thin hair, and sharp, scowling eyes made his nickname of youth, "grim old Heintzelman," an apt description. Over the years, he had acquired much battle experience. After the war another general described him as "a man of the keenest sense of honor, but captions and querulous oftentimes to such an extent, that, if the junior officers did not seek to avoid him, they rarely sought his society. And yet he was a man of vast and varied acquirements; a great reader, he had the best library in the garrison, and there was no one of the officers who could draw upon so wide a range of reading and study for information upon any point of history, ancient or modern. He was kind hearted in acts, far more so than in words. He was the only officer in the garrison whose pecuniary means had grown beyond his wants, and to those few subalterns who appreciated his real worth, in spite of a repellant manner, he was a true friend, and his purse was always open to aid his less prosperous brother officers."

Manifesting his "captious and querulous" nature when the war began, he complained about his status as a fifty-five year old major, and he would gripe to his sympathetic diary about the promotion of less qualified juniors over his head. Blunt and caustic, he spoke his feelings on this and numerous other points which rankled him. His strange, cranky personal appearance compounded the vitriol in his complaints.[10]

Instead of appreciating the promotion McDowell presented, Heintzelman sputtered that he did not consider it a compliment because all other new colonels in the Regular Army also dated from May 14, thus making him junior to them. McDowell tried to pacify his irate subordinate. Regular Army colonels, he said, would be assigned to command brigades, rather than the normal regiment. This had little effect on Heintzelman's mood or complaints. As McDowell prepared to make an awkward departure, a sudden alarm on the picket lines cut the tension. He and Heintzelman hastened outside to the position of the Eighth New York which was forming with alacrity. When all was once again quiet, McDowell retreated to the New Jersey brigade, where he spent the night.[11]

10 Comte de Paris MS diary (large diary) (A.N. de la M. de F.) entry dated November 7, 1861; Heintzelman MS diary (large diary) (L.C.) entries dated May 26 through 30, 1861; *D.A.B.*, 4, pt. 2, 505-506; *Martial Deeds*, 608; *Cullum*, 1, no. 445; Howard, *Autobiography*, 1, 142; Small, *Road to Richmond*, 14; Jerry Thompson, ed., *Fifty Miles and a Fight: Major Samuel Peter Heintzelman's Journal of Texas and the Cortina War* (Austin, 1998), 3-39 (Thompson, *Fifty Miles*); the quotation is from Hamilton, "Reminiscences of the Old Army," in 46, *Broadfoot MOLLUS Wisconsin*, 41-42.

11 Heintzelman MS diary (large diary) (L.C.) entry dated May 28, 1861; *OR*, 2, 654.

Although the next day dawned cold, McDowell rose to his new tasks with vigor. He issued General Orders, No. 1,[12] for the new Army of Northeastern Virginia. True to his word, the orders established several brigades to be commanded by Regular Army colonels. "Grim old Heintzelman" was among them.[13] Still smarting from his slow advancement Heintzelman wrestled with himself to determine whether he should accept the new colonelcy. His wife, who was in Washington, felt he should decline. He wrote the necessary refusal to the War Department, but wiser counsel from his friends persuaded him not to mail it until they had interceded for him in Washington.[14]

Another of the brigades went to Colonel David Hunter, a native of the capital who had been born at the turn of the century. When he graduated from West Point in 1822, he stood below the middle of his class, twenty-fifth of forty. Among his classmates were George A. McCall, John J. Abercombie, and Joseph K. F. Mansfield. For several years he served on the frontier against the Indians; but marriage brought responsibilities which prompted him to resign his commission. Military habit, however, was in his blood. The year 1842 saw him reenter the army.

As crisis followed crisis in 1861, Hunter concluded that conflict was inevitable. From his post at Fort Leavenworth, Kansas, he communicated this opinion to the newly elected president and was rewarded with an invitation to accompany the presidential train on the inaugural trip from Illinois to Washington. While trying to restrain a crowd during this journey, he suffered a separated shoulder and was forced to remain behind, rejoining Lincoln in Washington after he recovered. There, he organized a force of one hundred gentleman volunteers to guard the White House and its occupants day and night, living himself in the East Wing. Because he was constantly in the eye of the president, Hunter was a natural choice for promotion to full colonel on May 14 when the army was expanded. He brought to his new rank an entirely different attitude than Heintzelman. Handsome and unprepossessing, with died black hair and mustache, he was easy and friendly, almost like an adoptive father to his young staff officers as if they were the children he had never had. As a newly appointed Regular Army colonel, he, too, was a natural to command a new brigade.[15]

12 Heintzelman MS diary (large diary) (L.C.) entry dated May 26, 1861; *OR*, 51, pt. 1, 389-90.

13 It included the Eighth, Twelfth, and Twenty-fifth New York Regiments and any loose regiments in the vicinity.

14 Heintzelman MS diary (large diary) (L.C.) entry dated June 1, 1861.

15 *Cullum*, 1, no. 310; *D.A.B.*; R. C. Schenck, "Major-General David Hunter," *Magazine of American History*, vol. 15, no. 2, February 1887; David Hunter, *Report of the Military Services of General David Hunter, U.S.A., During the War of the Rebellion made to the United States War Department* (New York, 1873); Otto Eisenschiml, *Why Lincoln Was Murdered* (Boston

The afternoon of the day in which the brigades were created, George Armes, Seward's civilian assistant who had guided Willcox's encircling force to Alexandria on May 24, inveigled Lieutenant Charles B. Tompkins, commanding officer of B Company, Second U. S. Cavalry, to request permission for a little cavalry raid on Fairfax Courthouse within the Confederate lines. Hunter agreed. That evening Lieutenant Tompkins headed for Fairfax Court House, Virginia, with fifty men. Armes, with two pistols, served as a guide. They surprised and captured the pickets before they entered the town; but as they rode into the street, they were ambushed from windows and rooftops and confronted by a mounted force at the far end of the main street. With the men firing wildly in the shadowy light, a quick charge drove the Rebel horsemen. Losing only two horses and four wounded men, he returned bringing the Southern pickets as prisoners. This aggressive little action merited the approval and praise of General McDowell. More importantly, it achieved applause from the public.[16]

By the beginning of June, a week after Union troops had occupied the west bank, Scott was ready to plan more aggressive strokes. At last, he had reached the all-too-obvious conclusion he had rejected earlier. He telegraphed McDowell for an estimate of the force needed for an advance in about five days against Manassas Junction and Manassas Gap to support Patterson's expected crossing of the Potomac and attack on Harpers Ferry.[17]

In view of the Confederate strength at Fairfax Station, Fairfax Court House, Manassas Junction, and along the Manassas Gap Railroad to the Valley, McDowell responded that he should have twelve thousand troops, two batteries of artillery, and six to eight companies of cavalry. He thought he should also have a mobile railroad reserve at Alexandria of five thousand men and a heavy artillery battery. In keeping with the lack of faith in volunteers that typified Regular Army officers, he wanted Regular Army colonels to command the troops and Regular Army junior officers to train them.[18] Despite his lack of experienced senior officers, he, like Scott, felt that

1937); Margaret Leech, *Revillie in Washington* (New York and London 1941), 33; Miller, Edward A., Jr., *Lincoln's Abolitionist General: The Biography of David Hunter* (Columbia, 1997), 52, 103-104 (Miller, *Hunter*); Victor Searcher, *Lincoln's Journey to Greatness: A Factual Account of the Twelve Day Inaugural Trip*, (Philadelphia, 1960), 9.

16 Nicolay MSS (L.C.), Meigs MS diary entry dated June 1, 1861; *OR*, 2, 59-61; Stone in *B&L*, 1, 174; Armes, *Ups and Downs*, 44-45. In his diary, Meigs dated this raid on June 1, but contemporaneous reports and Armes all give it the date in the text, May 30; *OR*, 2, 50 ff.

17 Heintzelman says this occurred on June 2, MS diary (large diary), entry dated, June 2, 1861; but the reports dated it May 30 (*OR*, 2, 662).

18 *OR*, 2, 664.

all regiments desiring service should be accepted in order "to overwhelm and conquer as much by the show of force as by the use of it."

From a lifetime of military experience, Scott did not like volunteers any more then McDowell. He would always prefer Regular troops and Regular officers. In Mexico, he had used both with great skill and effect; but he and many of his younger Regular Army officers had finished that war believing in Regulars and skeptical about volunteers. He was armed almost entirely with three-month militia troops. He wanted long-term volunteers with an extended period of training before he undertook a significant offensive movement, and his plans for June and early July reflected that. Holding the Virginia shore opposite Washington, he was content to build an army slowly, train it thoroughly, and take the offense in the fall. This would be a slow, deliberate program. The country might not stand for it, but he was not alone in his views.[19]

Others, too, were uncertain about the volunteers and not simply because they were volunteers. The United States Sanitary Commission, a civilian organization created to oversee the medical and hygienic condition of the country's new military forces, collected information for recommendations.[20] It found the task difficult because its questions were brushed aside by government officials and army officers. But they were good evidence of the inadequate preparation of the army for a great battle and a grave indictment of the government:

> First, a general order requiring a stricter physical examination of recruits? Answer. The volunteers would not submit to it.
>
> Second, a general order placing a limit on the number of absences to be allowed from the camp of each regiment? Answer. The colonels ought to know enough not to grant leave injudiciously.
>
> Third, a general order limiting the hours during which officers and men could have leave of absence from their camps? Answer. It could not be enforced.
>
> Fourth, an order to prevent men from purchasing intoxicating liquor and from bringing it into the camps? Answer. It could not be enforced.

19 *OR*, 2, 664-65; Nicolay, *Outbreak*, 171-172; *N&H*, 4, 302-305; Dix, Morgan, *Memoirs of John A. Dix*, 2 vols. (New York, 1883), 2, 20-24 (Dix, *Memoirs*).

20 Charles C. McLaughlin, ed., *The Papers of Frederick Law Olmstead*, 5 vols. (incomplete) (Baltimore and London 1972), 4, Jane Turner Censer, ed., *Defending the Union: the Civil War and the U.S. Sanitary Commission 1861-1863*, 4-5, 8-11 (McLaughlin, *Olmstead Papers*).

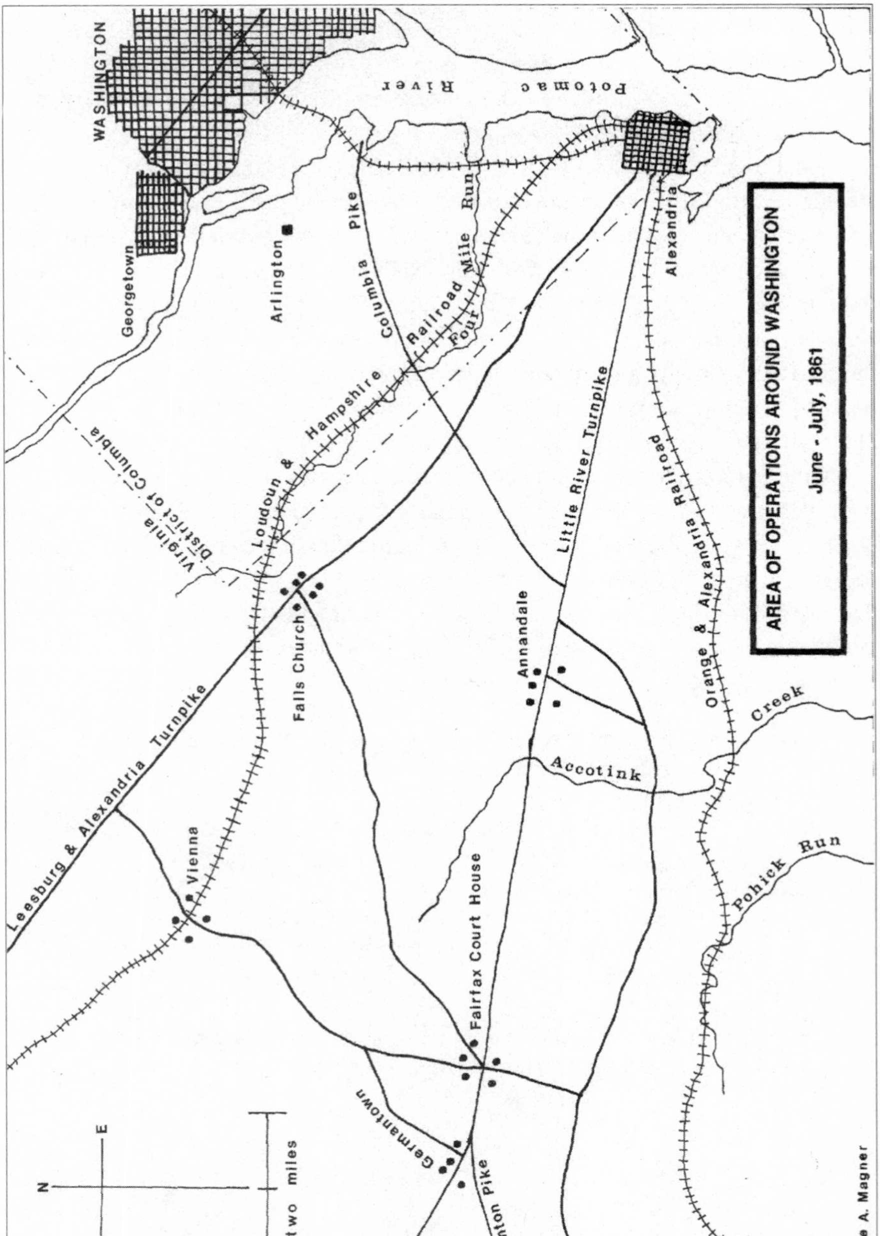
AREA OF OPERATIONS AROUND WASHINGTON
June - July, 1861
WASHINGTON
Georgetown
Potomac River
Arlington
Columbia Pike
Four Mile Run
Alexandria
Loudoun & Hampshire Railroad
Virginia
District of Columbia
Leesburg & Alexandria Turnpike
Little River Turnpike
Orange & Alexandria Railroad
Falls Church
Annandale
Accotink Creek
Pohick Run
Vienna
Fairfax Court House
Germantown
Warrenton Pike
N
E
W
two miles
Blake A. Magner

> Fifth, a general order calling attention to various infractions of the army regulations and of the articles of war, which were then constantly witnessed and which passed without rebuke? Answer. Nothing better was to be expected of volunteers.
>
> Sixth, instructions to captains were "almost universally neglected by them." Answer. The colonels' duty was to instruct them.
>
> Seventh, the issuance of detailed instructions to colonels about duties almost universally neglected by them? Answer. If they did not know the duties of their office, they had no business in it.
>
> Eighth, should certain rules be modified to meet the special difficulties of officers ignorant of their duties? Answer. These rules worked well in the Regular Army.[21]

The points and responses produced by the Commission showed that the leap from peacetime Regular Army to wartime militia–volunteer army was not being made with a mobilization plan, great care, or good success. To some they foretold that the Union military forces were doomed to defeat in the field until the responses on important points of preparation improved. Putting the non-Regulars in the correct condition for arduous fighting, making them into semi-Regulars, would be hard work for all officers, Regular or not. It was not enough to say the volunteers would not do something; they must learn whether or not they were willing.

On June 5, Heintzelman sent information that twenty thousand Confederates were at Manassas Junction, Fairfax Station, and Fairfax Court House.[22] Perhaps they could be bypassed. McDowell and Scott decided that a force from Vienna could march on Centerville leaving Fairfax Court House a few miles to the left.[23] In this way a Union column could strike Centerville, create a diversion, and be gone before it could be trapped by heavier forces. As Patterson dallied with his advance, they dropped consideration of a stroke at Centerville but authorized McDowell to use his own initiative against enemy positions.[24]

21 McLaughlin, *Olmstead Papers*, 4, 176-177, *Report of the Secretary with Regard to the Probable Origin of the Recent Demoralization of the Volunteer Army at Washington, and the Duty of the Sanitary Commission with Reference to Certain Deficiencies in the Existing Army Arrangements, as Suggested Thereby*. This report, prepared by the commission in August and September, was never publicly circulated in its full form. *Ibid.*, 187, n. 187.

22 *OR*, 2, 683; Nicolay, *Outbreak*, 171.

23 Heintzelman MS Diary (large diary) (L.C.) entry dated June 10, 1861.

24 *OR*, 2, 690.

He decided to send a reconnaissance up the line of track toward Leesburg. Brigadier General Robert C. Schenck was to move one of his regiments by train on the Loudon and Hampshire Railroad to the point where it intersected the wagon road from Fort Corcoran. At this junction Schenck was to establish himself and patrol cautiously toward Vienna and Falls Church, paying special attention to the condition of the track and bridges. No trouble was anticipated because Brigadier General Daniel Tyler had been there the day before and left behind the Sixty-ninth New York. Schenck's men were to relieve the Sixty-Ninth.[25] On Tuesday, June 18, Schenck, who had been assigned his brigade less than a week earlier, set out with approximately seven hundred officers and men of the First Ohio Regiment.

Schenck was fifty-one, broad chested, and compactly built. His rugged features were an external indication of the strong will that lay within. The Whig Party had been his early political affiliation after admission to the Ohio bar, but he had later become one of the most ardent Lincoln Republicans and a great favorite of the president himself. In 1861, Schenck was a statesman, a lawyer, a thinker, and an earnest, energetic, forceful, successful man. He had no military education or experience.

On May 17, the president appointed him a brigadier general. Experience and training or not, Schenck was unhappy about his very junior place on the long list of brigadier-generals created that day. Others were also displeased but not because Schenck was very junior on the list. They were unhappy that he was on the list at all. An immediate cry of political favoritism arose in the press, which denounced his appointment as an insult to the troops. One newspaper even said he should be turned over to a sergeant to be drilled for a month. As a political appointee with no military experience, he, no doubt, felt he had to prove himself.[26]

Schenck had not been ordered to go with the column himself but decided that, because the colonels of both his regiments were absent, he would head the column. He knew that Tyler had, two days earlier, passed without event beyond the junction of the Loudon and Hampshire Railroad and the wagon road from Fort Corcoran. According to a local citizen the Confederates were at Vienna but the citizen admitted that he had not actually seen them himself. Schenck and Alexander McCook, the regimental commander, who had just arrived and taken command of the regiment,

25 *OR*, 51, pt. 1, 399. For the orders creating Schenck's brigade, see *OR*, 2, 126, 135.

26 Milroy MSS (Indiana Historical Soc.) letter dated June 3, 1862, from Schuyler Colfax to Milroy; Kiefer, *Slavery and Four Years of War*, 1, 322; Lincoln MSS (L.C.) letter in the form of a printed pamphlet, dated January 4, 1861, from Schenck to Lincoln, and letter dated January 4, 1861, from Schenck to Lincoln enclosing the printed letter. Both the letter and the pamphlet letter must be misdated because the events described in the pamphlet occurred long after January of 1861. The printed letter also discusses many events that occurred much later.

listened to this report together and agreed that it was no more than a rumor.[27] He decided he could exceed his instructions and proceed aboard his train with four companies beyond the crossing of the railroad track and the wagon road.[28] Green and thoughtless as he could be, he rode with no reconnaissance, no advance guard, no skirmishers, and no other attempt to discover what lay ahead. He let his train, engine in the rear pushing the cars, puff its way blindly toward Vienna. This was a far different maneuver than a cautious patrol from the junction toward Falls Church and Vienna.

As the train turned a blind curve, it was suddenly enveloped in artillery fire from unseen batteries. Several of the cars were damaged. The men poured out to the right and left into the trees. The engineer unhooked his engine and hurried toward Washington. Immediate withdrawal was necessary. Gathering up eight dead and four wounded, the column moved back along the line of track. The location of the Confederate batteries was never determined; nor was the Rebel strength, which Schenck claimed at four thousand in his report.

This unfortunate little affair caused a large reaction, both political and military. It was compounded in the critical eye of the public by the background of the officer in command, a man of no military experience wearing a brigadier-general's star granted apparently for political service to the Republican Party and the president. Greeley's *Tribune* participated in the storm of criticism.

On June 21, Captain Don Piatt, a Thirteenth Ohio officer with a political background, great admiration for his political friend Schenck, and a well-known acerbic pen,[29] wrote a hot-tempered letter to Greeley, saying, "I must again protest against the injustice you permit in the *Tribune* to a gallant man and able officer. Is your Washington correspondent so ignorant or is he so vicious that he insists upon holding General Schenck responsible for an expedition in which he simply obeyed orders. He was commanded to post companies along the line of the railway previously as he did—and as was proper for him to do. The talk about masked batteries and troops is all stuff. We have no cavalry to do scout duty and General Scott will give us none. According to wounded men from Vienna, the Confederates

27 *OR*, 2, 125-26; Lincoln MSS (L.C.) unsigned memorandum in an envelope, dated July 15, 1861.

28 Two companies were left at the crossing, two sent to Falls Church, and another pair strung along the track from the crossing toward Vienna.

29 *D.A.B.*, 7, pt. 2, 555-556; Heitman, *Historical Register and Dictionary of the United States Army, 1789-1903*, 2 vols. (Washington, 1903), 1, 790; Adjutant General's Office, *Official Army Register of the Volunteer Force of the United States Army for the Years 1861, 1862, 1863, 1864*, 10 vols. (Washington 1865), 5, 354; C. G. Miller, *Donn Piatt: His Work and his Ways*, (Cincinnati, 1893), 325-344; *Ohio In The War*, 1, 726-27.

did not follow their advantage because of the manner in which the officers rallied the men. The Confederates became satisfied that a heavy force was in the vicinity. Instead of cutting the two companies to pieces, they fell back on Vienna. The self possession of Schenck and McCook you see saved the company or rather two companies in the train at the time of the attack. What is the meaning of this abuse?"[30]

In reality, the military consequences would be more far-reaching than appeared at first. Fear of unseen artillery, the "masked" battery, assumed disproportionate, if not overwhelming, importance to all commanders of advancing infantry columns.

McDowell wanted to attack Vienna with Tyler's entire column at once, but the old general in chief concluded that the damage had been done and that surprise was impossible. Only enough force to extricate the Ohioans was allowed.[31]

After receiving his engineer's reports, McDowell decided that Tyler's position on that flank was too far advanced and that he should withdraw to Ball's Cross Roads. Tyler failed to see any advantage in this; in fact, he saw distinct disadvantages and was perturbed by the failure of the engineers to consult him or to stay more than half an hour. After a trip to army headquarters failed to persuade McDowell, he returned to his camp to make his objections in writing. Camp McDowell,[32] he asserted, was the best observation post in the present lines, in addition to being one of the most defensible positions. In Confederate hands, it would give the Rebels control of Four Mile Run Valley from Vienna to Roachs Mill and would be difficult to retake. With four regiments and one battery, he was certain that against ten thousand attackers he could hold the position at least two hours from the time his pickets sounded the alarm, more than enough time for reinforcement.

Born in Connecticut just prior to the turn of the century, Tyler came from distinguished lineage. His family had direct blood ties to Jonathan Edwards and Aaron Burr. At Plainfield Academy, he received his early education in preparation for Yale from which three elder brothers had graduated; but a visit to one of his brothers in the army so swayed him toward military life that he sought and received an appointment to the United States Military Academy. He graduated fourteenth of twenty-nine, Class of 1819, completing his studies in a year less than the usual time. Artillery was his branch, and in it he soon found distinction. After being assigned a tour of duty in Europe during the twenties, he persuaded the government to award munitions contracts to private firms at better prices; but because this bypassed friends of Andrew Jackson, civilian pressure kept him from being promoted in the

30 Greeley MSS (N.Y.P.L.) letter dated June 21, 1861, from Piatt to Greeley.

31 *OR*, 2, 700.

32 Although the position was described in the dispatch as Shooters Hill, Camp McDowell had the only Union emplacements on School House Hill. *OR*, 1, *Atlas*, plates 6 and 7.

artillery reorganization of 1834. Incensed, he resigned his commission and returned to private life, refusing several efforts to keep him in the service.

By the outbreak of the war he had amassed a sizeable fortune, $91,000 of which he used for loans to support the Union. Someone proposed that he go to Europe to buy artillery for the North; but the governor of Connecticut offered command of a regiment of Connecticut infantry. Scott swayed him by saying that he could do just as much by marching in a good regiment as by sailing to Europe to shop for guns. Tyler took the regiment, and on June 3 received a temporary brigade of three regiments until more Connecticut units arrived to provide him a full strength brigade appropriate for his commission as a brigadier general of Connecticut volunteers. In spite of his sixty-two years, he was fit and active, entirely unimpaired, and ready for battle.[33]

33 *OR*, 51, pt. 1, 396; *D.A.B.*, 10, pt. 1, 86-87; Donald Mitchell, ed. *Daniel Tyler: A Memorial Volume* (New Haven 1883), 1-49 (Mitchell, *Tyler*); *Cullum*, 1, no. 216; NAACP file Daniel Tyler; Keyes, *Fifty Years*, 432.

Chapter 13

"If Johnston joins Beauregard, he shall have Patterson on his heels."

— General Scott commenting on McDowell's offensive plan

McDowell Plans the Army's First Battle

Public pressure for an advance from Washington became irresistible. Lieutenant Tompkins's successful cavalry raid beyond Fairfax Court House had shown what could be done by a competent, aggressive leader; and the skirmish at Vienna had touched the retaliatory nerve of every newspaper and citizen. With his new command at Fort Monroe, where he would presumably not be able to cause trouble, Major-General Benjamin Butler increased the demand for action by a dreadfully embarrassing defeat in a minor encounter at Big Bethel. Although few men had been engaged and negligible casualties suffered, his men had fired into each other and been driven from the field in disorder. The public was incensed. Lincoln simply could not ignore this.[1]

Scott wanted to wait until late fall when the three-year volunteers had replaced the three-month militia and were trained and ready for a major battle, but the circumstances compelled him to make use of the three-month troops. He had

1 Fry in *B&L*, 1, 174.

brought them to Washington to make the capital secure. He had used them to capture Arlington Heights.[2] Patterson was using them to recapture Harpers Ferry. McClellan would use them to secure the western reaches of the Baltimore and Ohio Railroad.[3]

Scott's plan was not much faster than the Anaconda Plan, his earlier vast, slow-moving constriction of the South. He had admitted that his earlier plan was not likely to generate public support.[4] He was right. More than one war in American history has sharpened the focus of the public on the relationship between the press and public opinion. With the Confederate legislature scheduled to meet for the first time in Richmond, its new capital, on July 20, Greeley insisted that Richmond be in Union hands before that date. Was the *Tribune* and its mercurial editor reflecting public opinion or forming it when they ran a headline on June 26, "The Nation's War-Cry, Forward to Richmond. Forward to Richmond." Every issue of the *Tribune* from June 26 to July 20 carried this headline on its editorial page. The message was supported by Congress[5] and not received with hostility by Lincoln or his cabinet. They were mentally prepared to insist on an offensive.[6]

In the last ten days of June, information began to arrive that the Confederates confronting the Army of Northeastern Virginia were not as numerous or as well armed as people supposed. When he estimated the enemy forces confronting him at twenty-three to twenty-five thousand men, with two thousand cavalry and many guns, McDowell was probably over the mark.[7] A preacher who had been in the Manassas Junction area for several days entered the Union lines near Alexandria and reported that the Rebels were not numerous or well-equipped and that they were not ready to attack. Other information reported the Rebels to be scattered over the long northwest to southeast line from Leesburg to Occoquan Creek.[8]

The original intention that Patterson make the principal advance had faded. When a joint thrust at Leesburg was suggested, McDowell was asked for his view. If he were to march up the west bank of the Potomac, he wrote, his army would be forced to rely completely on the railroad for supplies because he lacked wagons. As he moved northward his left flank and rear would be open to attack while he had the

2 Series 3, *OR*, 1, 263.

3 Series 3, *OR*, 1, 263; Nicolay, *Outbreak*, 171; *N&H*, 4, 308-09.

4 Series 3, *OR*, 1, 263.

5 *New York Tribune*, June 26-July 26, 1861; Horner, *Lincoln and Greeley*, 226; Villard, *Memoirs*, 1, 180-181.

6 *N&H* 4, 321-22; Nicolay, *Outbreak*, 171-172.

7 Established on June 24, 1861; *OR*, 2, 718.

8 Heintzelman MS Diary (large diary) (L.C.) entries dated June 21 and 26, 1861.

unfordable Potomac River on his right. To protect his open line of supply, he would be forced to weaken his main force by detachments.[9]

As he had stated in his May memorandum to Secretary Chase, he still believed the Rappahannock River to be the true line of defense for the capital. He also believed that by advancing to the Rappahannock, he would recover northeastern Virginia for the Union. But to accomplish this, he must expel the Confederates from their central position at Manassas Junction. By now, of course, the task would not be as easy as it would have been if Scott had adopted his proposal to march on the Junction immediately after the capture of Alexandria. In retrospect, Scott's unwillingness to intrude on his beloved Virginia had assured a major engagement at Manassas Junction because the Confederates, too, had recognized its importance and reinforced it.

Scott's strategic plan had featured a huge encirclement by land and sea, a combination of blockade on the coast and campaign on the Mississippi. He was reluctant to abandon his plans for the Mississippi, and he still wished to defer an advance into Virginia. Although he remained opposed to an advance on Manassas with inexperienced and untrained militia troops, he knew his young subordinate was correct: he could not avoid waging the war in the east. He asked McDowell to submit a plan for the capture of Manassas along with an estimate of the necessary force.[10]

McDowell promptly prepared a plan for presentation to the cabinet. The maximum Rebel force capable of concentration for battle, he assumed, would not exceed twenty-five thousand to which he added at least ten thousand more that could be brought by rail. Patterson and Butler should occupy their opponents' attention long enough to keep them from reaching Manassas Junction in time for the battle. McDowell could reach the Junction by any of five ways: (1) the Leesburg State Road and the Georgetown Pike; (2) the Little River Turnpike via Fairfax Court House; (3) the line of track of the Orange and Alexandria Railroad; (4) the road running south of and parallel to the line of track; and (5) by ship to Brentsville, then on foot through Dumfries or Evansville.

The last route he eliminated because of the water trip and the march of twenty-two miles. Of the remaining four, no route would carry his entire army at one time. He decided to use several routes, the advance to be concerted, and each column to coordinate with the columns on its flanks. The road network between the Potomac and Manassas was unknown, and no reliable maps existed. Without them, he could not know whether lateral roads would allow one column to assist another under

9 *OR*, 2, 718-19.

10 Elliott, *Scott*, 723 ff; Stine, *Army Of The Potomac*, 86-87; *C.C.W.*, 2, 37 (McDowell); Townsend, *Anecdotes*, 55.

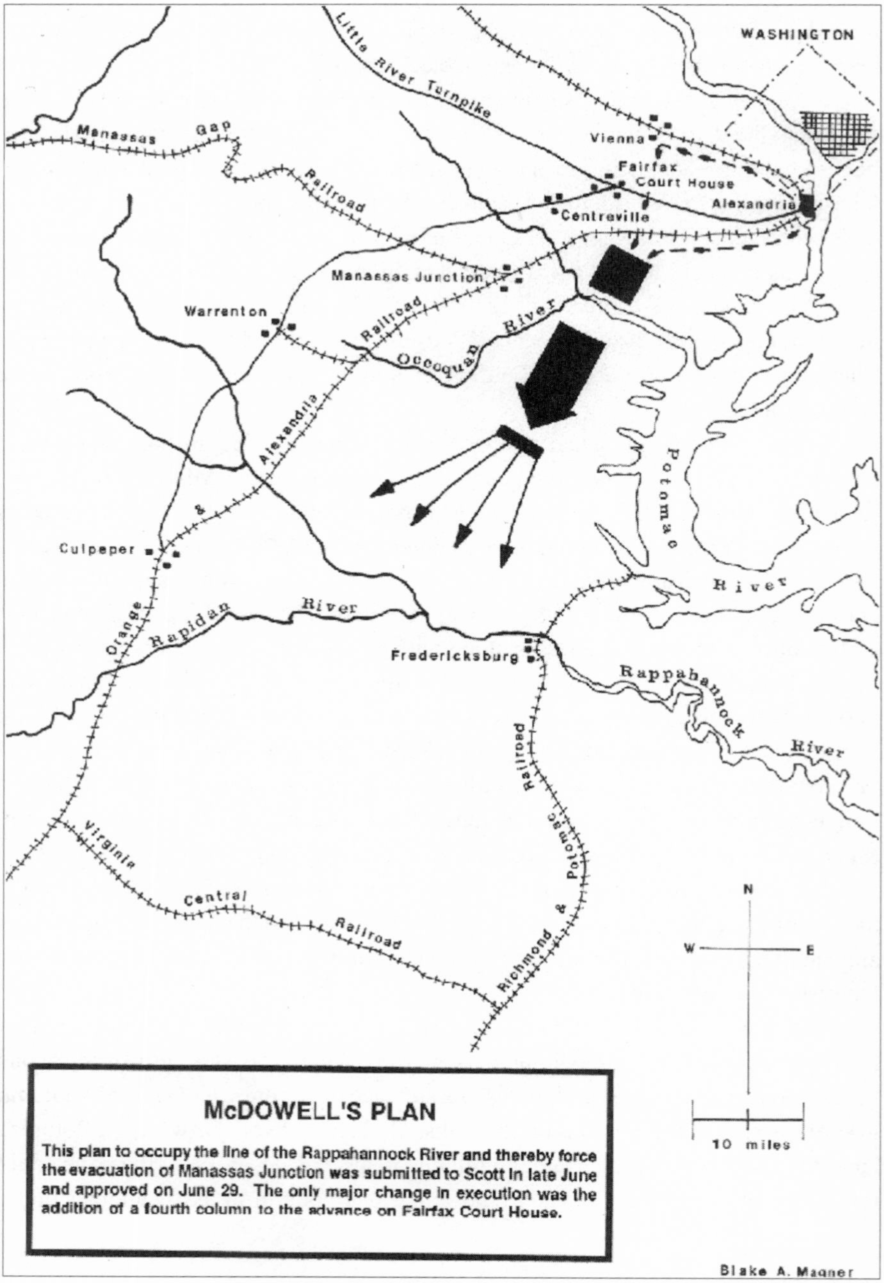

McDOWELL'S PLAN

This plan to occupy the line of the Rappahannock River and thereby force the evacuation of Manassas Junction was submitted to Scott in late June and approved on June 29. The only major change in execution was the addition of a fourth column to the advance on Fairfax Court House.

attack. He concluded that each column, much like the independent Napoleonic corps, had to be large enough to defend itself until one of the other columns could come to its assistance. In a very crude form, this plan of related but separated columns had a very Napoleonic appearance.

Supplying the advancing columns would be a great problem. The best supply route would be the Orange and Alexandria Railroad, but that had been obvious to both sides. In their withdrawal, the Confederates had destroyed track and filled the cuts with boulders, dirt, and fallen trees. Significant repair would be necessary, and a wagon train would be needed in case repairs failed to keep pace with the advance. The recent spring rains had left the unsurfaced Virginia roads deep in mud, rutted, and pot-holed. Wheeled transportation would break down and delay the advance. The number of supply wagons had to be small. Fate had already arranged for a small train because only a limited number of wagons were available.

On the state of his supporting arms, cavalry and artillery, McDowell had little say. With six batteries of artillery, three volunteer and three Regular, he felt he had enough. Like almost all other Union officers at the outbreak of the war, he had no idea how to use cavalry. The country through which the advance was to be made was heavily wooded.[11] He thought his cavalry needs would be small because the unsuitable terrain would make horsemen unnecessary. He had only a few companies of Regular cavalry. In fact, his cavalry was woefully inadequate in numbers, in experience, and in theory.

On June 25, a council of war composed of Lincoln, Scott, Mansfield, Meigs, and the cabinet met to hear the plan; but McDowell, the speaker of the hour, was unavailable. In a prefatory presentation, Scott described the condition of the contending forces. On both sides of the Potomac River at Washington, the federal forces, including the command of General Stone at Poolesville, numbered fifty thousand. In addition, Patterson had about ten to sixteen thousand more, making in all sixty-six thousand. Overall, the Union troops were better armed, equipped, and paid than their adversaries; but they were raw, had less artillery, and had almost no cavalry.

Beauregard had at Manassas Junction, Fairfax, and Centerville nearly twenty-four thousand infantry and two-thousand cavalry, all of whom had no pay, little food, poor clothing, and hostility to discipline. Nevertheless, his men had greater experience in the use of arms and longer drill than the Union troops.

According to Scott, raw troops like the Union forces were liable to sudden panics. Having learned that Jackson had left Harpers Ferry, he explained, he had

11 *OR*, 2, 720-21; *C.C.W.*, 2, 22 (Richardson) and 35 ff (McDowell); Russell, *My Diary*, 194, entry dated July 6, 1861, 208, entry dated July 16, 1861.

ordered the Regulars, originally sent to bear the brunt of Patterson's proposed attack on the Ferry, back to Washington. When they headed back across the Potomac, the volunteers followed them without orders despite the efforts of their officers to prevent a panic. Raw troops could be turned to heroes. In their current state they were individually brave. But they needed to develop confidence in the courage and steadiness of their companions, a characteristic that could only be gained by experience.

Scott said he had at one time intended to order Patterson and McDowell to make a combined movement to occupy the country along the Leesburg Turnpike and the Loudon & Hampshire Railroad. Now he was less clear about this although he still had it under consideration. To this point the capital had not been safe, but as the number of federal troops kept constantly ahead of the Rebels, he thought he had enough strength to undertake expeditions. Taking a page from McDowell's memorandum, he described the routes to Richmond by the York River, the James River, Aquia Creek, and directly from the capital. Someone asked Meigs how many men would be needed to drive Beauregard.

"Beauregard having twenty-six thousand," he responded, "I should ask about thirty-thousand and a full supply of artillery."

"How many batteries," asked Scott.

"I should want ninety pieces—three to the thousand."

"Too many," responded the general in chief.

"Two to the thousand is the ordinary estimate, but with raw troops I would ask more rather than less."

"Fifty would be enough, fifty pieces manned by well drilled men," Scott said.

Mansfield evaded a question about the number of men he would want by requesting more time to think about it. Lincoln expressed a great desire to "bag" Jackson in the Shenandoah Valley; but Scott, more prescient than he knew, thought it could not be done. Meigs described his efforts to collect more transportation, and they were approved. At this point they agreed that nothing more could be accomplished without McDowell, and the conference ended. As everyone departed, the secretary of war asked Meigs to walk with him. Meigs congratulated him on having ordered the three hundred guns and asked him if he had done anything about carriages for them.

Cameron said, "No."

Meigs pressed their importance. This was a time, he said, when someone must act, must take the risk of being blamed, and must acquire guns and the materials of war.

Cameron, no doubt aware of Meigs's sound and successful positions work on the reinforcement of Fort Pickens, said he would do anything Meigs advised.

At once, Meigs advised him to have a gun carriage given to a factory as a pattern or model and to order a large number. Cameron said he would do it.[12]

The meeting with McDowell was rescheduled for Friday, June 29. Early that morning, McDowell telegraphed several of his commanders to report to Washington for a presentation of plans. Meeting Heintzelman, who arrived on the ten o'clock boat from Alexandria, McDowell explained his plans in rough detail and told Heintzelman he would command the left wing along the railroad.[13]

In the afternoon the full group reassembled: the president, the cabinet, Scott, Mansfield, Meigs still ever-present, Tyler, Major General John Charles Fremont, and a number of aides-de-camp. Fremont, the "Pathmarker of the West," a veteran of the Mexican War, and the first Republican candidate for president, had just returned from Europe and was on his way to take command of the western theater, where he was to organize a major command to keep Missouri in the Union.[14] This time McDowell appeared to present the plan for an advance from Washington. During the meeting Scott, Mansfield, Chase, and Seward commented.

Scott explained his position. The outcry for an advance and the public ridicule of his "Anaconda Plan" had not caused him to retreat. He wanted to blockade the coast, interdict the Mississippi by a line of posts, and remain inactive around Washington. In his heart, Virginia was still sacred. Butler's operations at Fort Monroe, he said, did not advance the war. Finally, he did not want the whole responsibility of the war to pass upon him. He was growing old and had begun to distrust his judgment. But if it were put upon him, he would accept it.

As Meigs listened, he concluded that Scott's plan did not show "any definite purpose." Scott said he had called on General McDowell to lead the movement if everyone agreed to it, and the discussion turned to this point.

McDowell expected the Confederate main line to run north and south through Fairfax. Using his map,[15] the young brigadier general began explaining his idea for an advance in three columns. The largest of the three columns would move to Vienna, bypass Fairfax Court House leaving it to the left, drop behind the Confederates at Germantown, and cut off the Confederate flank if it failed to retreat

12 Nicolay MSS (L.C.), to Meigs MS diary, entry dated June 25, 1861.

13 McDowell believed his advance should be made in three columns, a plan he discussed with Heintzelman both before and after the cabinet session. Heintzelman MS diary (large diary), entry dated June 29, 1861, and undated memorandum.

14 Townsend, *Anecdotes*, 57; Nevins, *Fremont*, 457-58; *C.C.W.*, 2, 58 (McDowell); John Charles Fremont MSS (University of California, Berkeley) MS *Memoirs*, 221.

15 According to Townsend, *Anecdotes*, 57, the map was spread on a table; Schuyler Hamilton, quoted in Stine, *Army Of The Potomac*, says it was tacked to the wall and McDowell used a pointer.

promptly. Tyler, the most respected of the brigadiers, had already demonstrated his grasp of terrain and tactics and would be given command of this column. It would be the largest of the three because it would move on the flank toward Patterson, which was exposed. The army would not assault the Rebel positions frontally if that could be avoided. Green troops in a frontal assault on artillery in emplacements would be unreliable, he was sure.

After this initial maneuver, he would not attack Manassas Junction outright but would again accomplish his goal by maneuver. He would drop past his left flank and cross Bull Run Creek to the south of the Confederates around their right flank. This move by his left would be decisive because it would break the Rebel line where it was thinly held, isolate the main battle line, threaten the severed Confederate line with destruction, threaten their new flank, threaten their supply line, and force evacuation of the creek line and the Junction without a battle. The Confederates could do one of two things: evacuate, as he thought they would, or give battle. If they chose to fight, McDowell could take the tactical defensive. A move against their left or northern flank would not break their line, would drive the flank elements onto the main force, would not endanger their supply lines, and would guarantee a battle. Worst of all, movement from the Union right would place the burden of assault on inexperienced federal troops.[16]

McDowell did not limit his plan to the army under his command. Patterson had to cooperate in the Valley. With a rail line to Manassas at his disposal, Joseph E. Johnston, commanding the Confederate forces in the Valley, could join General P. G. T. Beauregard at Manassas Junction without much trouble or time. Several times McDowell emphasized this, noting that, if Patterson were to go to Leesburg on the right of his advancing army, no pressure would be exerted on Johnston, who would be released from the Valley. Patterson had to hold Johnston in the Valley to keep him away from Beauregard and Manassas Junction. The critical word was "hold."

Scott still had faith in his old Pennsylvania friend. "If Johnston joins Beauregard," he said, "he shall have Patterson on his heels."[17]

Only Sandford objected to the proposed movement. He held a peculiar position. Senior to McDowell, not only in age but also in rank and experience, he nevertheless felt far removed from the command picture. They must definitely ascertain, he felt, that Patterson could prevent the junction of Johnston and Beauregard. And he did

16 Heintzelman MSS (L.C.) undated memorandum.

17 Although this statement cannot be definitely fixed at the council of war, McDowell's testimony makes it appear so, *C.C.W.*, 2, 36 (McDowell). For a strange account of this meeting, which is contradicted by all other sources, even those hostile to McDowell, see Schuyler Hamilton, quoted in Stine, *Army Of The Potomac*, 9-10.

not think marching fourteen miles to fight a battle was a good idea. The first point had some merit. The second had none. The Army of Northeastern Virginia could not hope to take the offensive without a march. His objections were not supported by anyone.[18] As Meigs listened to the presentation and the discussion, he concluded that it was not being done very ably. Someone called upon him for his opinion.

"I do not think we will ever end this war without beating the rebels," he said. "They have come near us. We are, according to General Scott's information given to us at the Council of the twenty-fifth, stronger than they, better prepared, our troops better contented, better clothed, better fed, better paid, better armed. Here we have the most violent of the Rebels near us. It is better to whip them here than to go far into an unhealthy country to fight them and to fight far from our supplies, to spend our money among enemies instead of our friends. To make the fight in Virginia is cheaper and better as the case now stands. Let them come here to be beaten, and leave the Union men in time to be a majority at home."

The men decided that a movement should be made as soon as the army could prepare and obtain transportation. When asked how soon he could arrange transportation, Meigs told them to fix the time of the movement; and he would have the wagons and horses. They determined that on Monday, July 8, McDowell with thirty thousand men should march for Manassas Junction to drive out Beauregard.[19]

That evening, after his ordeal with his numerous superiors, McDowell met with Hunter, Heintzelman, Colonel W. T. Sherman, and Colonel William B. Franklin at Hunter's house to discuss the plan. For several hours they remained together until, at last after nine o'clock, the meeting ended.[20]

William T. Sherman, an Ohioan who had graduated sixth of forty-two from West Point in 1840, had been out of the army for some time. During the 1850s, he had been a major general of California militia and at the outbreak of war in 1861 was privately employed in his home state. He constantly refused to accept service in the three-month troops because he would have been forced to resign a civilian job that had been difficult to obtain and because he did not want to command volunteers. Through the efforts of his younger brother, John, who was the United States senator

18 McDowell testified that the only criticism was by Mansfield, *C.C.W.*, 2, 36 (McDowell) but gave no specifics. Sandford testified that he criticized the plan, *C.C.W.*, 2, 55, 62 (Sandford). Sandford had no reason to lie and was describing his own conduct. He is accepted as the critic, and McDowell, who probably had many other reasons to remember Mansfield unfavorably, probably misrecollected.

19 Nicolay MSS (L.C.) tr. Meigs MS diary entry of June 25, 1861; *C.C.W.*, 2, 36 (McDowell).

20 Nicolay MS (L.C.) tr. Meigs MS diary entry of June 29, 1861; Heintzelman MS Diary (large diary) (L.C.) entry dated June 29, 1861; Townsend, *Anecdotes*, 57; *C.C.W.*, 2, 36 ff (McDowell); 53 and 62 (Sandford), and 22 (Richardson).

from Ohio and who was serving as a volunteer aide to Patterson, and his brother-in-law Thomas Ewing, he was given the colonelcy of a new regiment of Regulars which had not yet been recruited. Like McDowell, he, too, had refused higher rank because he felt he should rise through experience. He reorganized his business to leave it in capable hands and away to Washington he went. When reporting to the White House, he met newly appointed General McDowell in a fresh brigadier general's uniform.

"Hello, Sherman. What did you ask for?" asked McDowell.

"A colonelcy," was the short reply.

"What? You should have asked for a brigadier general's rank. You're just as fit for it as I am."

"I know it," snapped Sherman.

Confident of his ability, curt in relationships, and authoritarian in leadership, Sherman was assigned to McDowell until his regiment of Regulars had been recruited. Like other presumably reliable new Regular Army colonels with experience, he was soon in command of a brigade of volunteers in the Army of Northeastern Virginia.[21]

As June became July, the plans for the advance were hastily implemented, but the original date for the schedule, Monday, July 8, saw only the first attempts at army organization. General Orders No. 13 proclaimed brigade, division, and staff assignments for the campaign. The army would be composed of one reserve and three active divisions. Its organization would be as follows:

Daniel Tyler would command the largest division, which would form the right flank advancing from Vienna. Brigades under Colonels Keyes, Sherman, Israel B. Richardson, and Schenck, the only non-West Pointer, would compose his command. David Hunter would have a division of two brigades under Colonels Andrew Porter[22] and Ambrose Burnside, both West Point graduates. "Grim Old Heintzelman," now a division commander, had brigades commanded by William B. Franklin, Orlando B. Willcox, and Oliver O. Howard, all graduates of the Military Academy.[23] The fourth division, to be led by Colonel Dixon S. Miles, contained brigades under Colonels Lewis Blenker and Thomas A. Davies. It would serve as the

21 W. T. Sherman MSS (L.C.), letters April 22 to June 28; *D.A.B.*, 9, pt. 1, 93-94; *OR*, 51, pt. 1, 406; *Cullum*, 1, no. 1022; Lloyd Lewis, *Sherman: Fighting Prophet*, 2 vols. (Norwalk 1991), 1, 162 (Lewis, *Sherman*) for the McDowell incident.

22 Regular Army officers Andrew Porter and Fitz-John Porter should not be confused. They were not related. Both were Regular Army officers and both would become ardent supporters of McClellan. There, the similarities ceased.

23 Heintzelman MS Diary (large diary) (L.C.) entry dated July 8, 1861; *OR*, 51, pt. 1, 413-414. Miles stood twenty-seven in a class of thirty.

immediate reserve. Three columns and a reserve division would advance on the enemy, not four and a reserve as he had originally planned.

Miles, the commanding officer of the fourth division was a fifty-seven-year-old Marylander who, like the others, had graduated from West Point but, unlike the others, stood near the bottom of his class. During his years in the army, he had served in the Florida War; in Mexico, where he was breveted for gallantry; and in numerous Indian campaigns between the end of the Mexican War and the fall of Fort Sumter. In April of 1861, he was a full colonel serving at Fort Leavenworth, Kansas, but was immediately brought to Washington to aid in its defense. After brief duty with Patterson in the Shenandoah, he had brought the Regular troops and the Rhode Islanders to the capital. General orders of July 6 created a command for him to the south of Heintzelman. He was "a soldier of the old school, joining by his own life two widely distant and differing periods" and over a long career in the war could probably not be expected to fare well with the standard issue American volunteer. In personality he was "punctilious, pompous, and quick-tempered, blazing up like a straw fire at the slightest provocation,"[24] an inveterate, heavy drinker. He probably had as much battle experience as any officer in McDowell's army.[25]

On July 8, the day of the proposed move, Colonel Andrew Porter examined his brigade outposts and the pickets of the army. Taking a squadron of cavalry as an escort, Porter and his staff officer, First Lieutenant William W. Averell, rode about a mile beyond the outer pickets. They passed over a gentle hill and saw a small column of a dozen or so horsemen approaching along the road about five hundred yards away. One of the horsemen carried a white flag. Their uniforms were grey. Without halting, Porter turned his head and gave the command, "Draw sabres." One hundred twenty sabres flashed into the sunlight, and every trooper gathered his reins for a charge. When a hundred paces separated the two columns, the officer at the head of the Confederate column raised his right hand, palm to the front, and came to a halt. Porter halted his squadron and ordered Averell to ride forward to learn what they wanted. Averell exchanged salutes with a tall officer at the front of the group.

"Sir, I am Colonel Taylor of the Confederate States Army, bearer of dispatches from President Davis of the Confederates States of America to President Lincoln of the United States."

24 Drake, Samuel A. "The Old Army in Kansas," in 52, *Broadfoot MOLLUS Massachusetts*, 150.

25 National Archives: Transcript of Court of Inquiry—Dixon S. Miles ("MS CI Miles"); Record of Harpers Ferry Commission, September, 1862, *OR*, 19, pt. 1, 799-800; *OR*, 51, pt. 1, 441; *Cullum*, 1, no. 387; Willson, Arabella M., *Disaster, Struggle, Triumph: the Adventures of 1000 Boys in Blue from August, 1862, to June, 1865*, 45-76 (Albany, 1870).

In the Tombs in New York City sat the crew of the captured privateer *Savannah*, threatened with indictment and sentencing as pirates. Jefferson Davis wrote President Lincoln asking for an exchange of the crew as prisoners of war and deploring their treatment as common pirates. Taylor carried Davis's letter, dated July 6, 1861, in his dispatch pouch. Averell had strange feelings of amazement, indignation, sorrow, and incredulity at this meeting, his first with a Confederate in uniform.

"Sir, you will please dismount your escort and stand to horse until I return," replied Averell.

The Confederates dismounted.

Averell repeated the message to Porter, who ordered his men to return their sabres to their scabbards, then dismounted them. Averell asked the officer to approach. The Confederate officer came on foot to a position about ten paces from Porter, who stood, handsome, powerfully built, with wavy black hair, in the middle of the road to receive him. After saluting, the Confederate officer repeated his message.

"I know of no President nor government in this country except that of the United States," replied Porter, "and I cannot receive any dispatches from you without instructions from the government. You will go into bivouac where you are and a portion of my command will remain here until instructions are received." The entire interview had proceeded with chilly dignity.

The Confederate officer then asked, "Does this conclude our official interview?"

Porter responded, "It does until further orders."

Both men walked easily, almost eagerly, toward each other and shook hands.

Taylor said, "Andrew, old fellow, how do you do?"

Porter responded, "Tom, how are you?"

They sat on a bank by the roadside, where Porter produced a flask of whiskey from his saddle bags. They chatted about old times as comrades in arms in the Mexican War.[26]

For the rest of the army, July 8 passed without a move; and it appeared as if some time would elapse before any advance could be made. The earliest day,

26 Averell MS Diary vol. 1, entry dated July 8, 1861 (Gilder Lehrman MSS, Morgan Library); *Papers of Jefferson Davis*, 8 vols. (incomplete) (Baton Rouge and London (1971-1995)), vol. 7, 221-225, esp. 223 nos. 2 and 5, letter dated July 6, 1861, from Davis to Lincoln; Averell, *Ten Years*, 285-86. The original of the letter is in the Lincoln MSS (L.C.). In note 5, 223, the editors of Davis' papers state the Confederate officer was Thomas H. Taylor. The editor of Averell's MS incomplete memoirs identifies him as John G. Taylor. Given the colloquy in Averell's memoirs and other evidence, the Davis editors seem to be correct.

McDowell estimated, would probably be Saturday, July 13. In the meantime, reconnaissances were revealing few signs of any enemy confronting the army. Perhaps the advance would be unresisted. Perhaps it would be ambushed.[27]

On Saturday, Scott called Tyler to headquarters and told him that the army would set out next day and that his division would concentrate on Vienna the first night. In spite of his previous resistance to an early battle with the Rebels, "Old Fuss and Feathers" was confident of the result. He noted McDowell's superiority in numbers. He could see no excuse, he said, for a bad result.

"Suppose General Joe Johnston should reinforce Beauregard. What result should you expect then, General?" asked Tyler.

Scott, predictable when his judgment was questioned, became irate. "Patterson will take care of Joe Johnston."

Cowed by this outburst, Tyler replied meekly, "I know them both and will be agreeably surprised if we do not have to go against both."[28]

The next day dawned pleasantly but the forward movement failed to materialize. McDowell collected his officers at Arlington to review the plans. He set the move for the following day; but like Patterson, he, too, was presumptuous about his ability to start his army forward.

July 15 was cool compared to the day before, but once again no movement occurred. Units were still crossing to the west bank to be brigaded. Supplies were not yet ready. The commander of the Army of Northeastern Virginia called a last meeting of his division officers, this time in Washington. Heintzelman would follow the track line of the Orange and Alexandria Railroad, swinging south of Sangster's Station and marching by his left for Brentsville. Miles would march on the Little River Turnpike, but at Annandale he would turn to the left and follow the Old Braddock Road, which paralleled the Pike. Hunter's division would follow directly behind Miles but would continue on the Pike after Miles slipped to the left. Tyler on the right flank would march to Vienna and turn south toward Germantown behind Fairfax Court House, thus cutting off and capturing the advance Confederate brigade. If the Confederates stood firm, McDowell expected to fight along the Fairfax-Germantown line. Tyler, Hunter, and Miles would move at 2:00 p.m.; Heintzelman at 2:30.[29] The meeting adjourned, and the division officers returned to

27 Heintzelman MS Diary (large diary) (L.C.) entry dated July 10, 1861; *C.C.W.*, 2, 23 (Richardson); Curtis, *Bull Run to Chancellorsville*, 34-35.

28 Tyler, *Biographical Memorial*, 48-49, with the last sentence converted from indirect discourse to direct discourse. Tyler constantly referred to the Confederate Valley Commander as Joe Johnson.

29 In his testimony (*C.C.W.*, 1, 40), McDowell did not mention Miles; but because Miles was to precede Hunter on the Little River Turnpike, he would have to march at the same time, at least.

their brigade commanders to explain the plans.[30] At 4:00 p.m. the written orders for the advance reached the components of the army. They would march at 3:00 p.m. the next day.[31]

July 16 would see movement, no doubt to be followed promptly by a battle.

30 Heintzelman MS diary (large diary) (L.C.) entries dated July 14 and 15, 1861; National Archives: General and Special Orders for the Department of North Eastern Virginia; *C.C.W.*, 1, 37 ff (McDowell).

31 Averell MS Diary vol. 1, entry dated July 15, 1861 (Gilder Lehrman MSS, M.L.).

Chapter 14

"Our forces must not be defeated nor checked in battle or meet with reverses. 'Twould be fatal to our cause.'"

— Patterson to his senior officers in a council of war

Patterson Temporizes

As usual, Patterson's performance fell short of promise. On the last day of June, he had written the dramatically curt note that he would cross the Potomac the following day. On the projected day of crossing, he merely issued his order of march for July 2. Tired of constant inaction and stagnant waiting, his army readied itself happily.[1]

At four in the morning of July 2, the Army of the Upper Potomac started down the banks of the ford at Williamsport. Keim's division led the way with Abercrombie's brigade, supported by Hudson's section of artillery and a squadron of cavalry, in front. First into the water were McMullen's Philadelphia Rangers, a cavalry unit, and one hundred and fifty men of the Eleventh Pennsylvania Regiment. As they fought the swift, knee-deep to armpit-deep water rushing over the rocky, irregular bottom, enemy picket fire opened with great volume but little accuracy.

1 Bates, *History of the Pennsylvania Volunteers*, 1, 97; Mary W. Thomas, and Richard A. Sauers, eds., *The Civil War Letters of First Lieutenant James B. Thomas, Adjutant, 107th Pennsylvania Volunteers* (Baltimore, 1995), 13, letter dated June 30, 1861, from Thomas to Theora (Thomas, *Thomas Letters*).

The men scrambled up the steep opposite bank and cleared the opposition. The main force followed.[2] Able to hear infantry fire of the advance units in the distance, the remainder of Patterson's army crossed by regiment with a company front on the double quick. The wagons crossed, as many as fifty at a time, the driver applying the whip and the three-man guard yelling. When an occasional wagon stalled, men reentered the water to push it out, until all two hundred twenty-three had crossed.[3]

Behind Abercrombie came Thomas, followed by Negley, with Cadwalader's division bringing up the rear.[4] Many of the farms along the road ahead already showed the inevitable traces of war—fences gone, crops damaged, buildings deserted.[5]

After marching one mile in a single column, Patterson sent Negley, the rear brigade of his leading division, to the right to parallel the advance of the army and protect its open flank from attack.[6] Under a clear sky, the column marched south unopposed. Three enemy horsemen atop a hill studied the column carefully, then galloped up the road. Enemy pickets posted in a strong natural position at a mill and along the mill run withdrew without resistance. About five miles from the crossing, the road turned through a series of wheat fields. Beyond the fields stood enemy breastworks of fence rails and logs along a tree line.[7] At 9:15, Company B of the First Wisconsin, the advance picket unit, opened fire on the enemy. The regimental commander at once sent a company to reinforce his forward line while Abercrombie deployed the rest of the regiment to the left and the Eleventh Pennsylvania to the right of the road. Hudson's guns swung into battery on a knoll with the Philadelphia Cavalry in support.[8] The artillery, shelling Rebels from a barn, set the barn afire.[9] On

2 *OR*, 2, 184, 704; *Wisconsin in the War*, 218; Bates, *History of the Pennsylvania Volunteers*, 1, 78; William Henry Locke, *The Story of the Regiment* (Philadelphia, 1868), 21-22 (Locke, *Regiment*).

3 Thomas, *Thomas Letters*, 15-16, letter dated July 8, 1861, from Thomas to Theora.

4 Locke, *Regiment*, 21-22.

5 Bates, *History of the Pennsylvania Volunteers*, 1, 97.

6 *OR*, 2, 160.

7 *OR*, 2, 160; Thomas, *Thomas Letters*, 36, letter dated July 8, 1861, from Thomas to Theora; Locke, *Regiment*, 23; James O. Pierce, "The Skirmish at Falling Waters," *Glimpses of the Nation's Struggle. Military Order of the Loyal Legion of the United States*, 5 series (St. Paul, 1887-1903), series 2, 293 (*Broadfoot MOLLUS Minnesota*).

8 The various accounts disagree. According to General Patterson, *OR*, 2, 160, they deployed in the road; and Hudson agrees, *OR*, 2, 184. *Life of David Bell Birney, Major-General, U.S. Volunteers*, (New York, 1867) 22 (*Birney*) says to the left of the road. Pierce in *Broadfoot MOLLUS Minnesota*, 27, 305, says in the road. Hudson, the account most contemporaneous and by the person most involved, is accepted.

9 Thomas, *Thomas Letters*, 16, letter dated July 8, 1872, from Thomas to Theora.

the right, three companies[10] drove a flanking force of Rebel cavalry while the artillery fired on the Confederate line and a large white house on a hill behind. The Twenty-third Pennsylvania swept behind the Wisconsin regiment and onto its flank to prolong the line, but Abercrombie felt they needed more striking power. He called for help from the brigade in his rear. George H. Thomas obliged by signaling that he would swing left to outflank the Confederate position. Twenty-five minutes from the first firing, it had ended. Thomas's men far overlapped the Rebels' flank. They withdrew precipitously.[11]

"The brigade on the right seems to be hotly engaged," commented one of his officers, noticing the rattle of musketry from Abercrombie's troops.

"I hear no return fire," snapped Thomas.[12]

Exuberantly, the men pressed across the undefended barricades; past the white house, now partially destroyed by artillery fire; and into the Rebel camp, which was almost intact. Neither Keim nor Patterson reached the field in time to influence the outcome. A neat little action it had been, executed with skill, finesse, initiative, and perception.

The encounter at Falling Waters had a good effect on the morale of Patterson's army. After weeks of boredom the glory of war had seemed as near as the farthest star, and the men had begun to despair of ever seeing battle. The exhilaration and confidence they felt after twenty-five minutes of fire and maneuver was a tonic. They were anxious to press the "fleeing" foe, who had been "ignominiously routed" from prepared defenses. The fact that the Confederate troops had been under orders to give way if attacked in force was not known, nor did the possibility cross any man's mind. The flood of victory ruled.[13]

Patterson's Army of the Upper Potomac, a peculiar organization, had no Union counterpart then or later in the war. Composed almost entirely of Pennsylvania militia regiments, the officers at the regimental level were militiamen of Pennsylvania. Patterson had no West Point men among his colonels but the percentage of veterans of the Mexican War was much higher than it was in McDowell's army. In addition, all but one or two men had served long in the state

10 Companies A, B, and C of the Eleventh Pennsylvania Infantry Regiment.

11 Jackson's orders were not to hold in the face of a determined attack but to retire on the main body. Van Diver, *Mighty Stonewall*, 150.

12 The encounter is variously called Falling Waters, Hoke's Run, and Gainesville. *OR*, 2, 160, 180 ff; Locke, *Regiment*, 23 ff; *Birney*, 21; Pierce in *Broadfoot MOLLUS Minnesota*, 2, 239ff, Cleaves, *Thomas*, 134; *D.A.B.*, 9, pt. 2, 434; *Cullum*, 227, 1028; Daniel H. Strother, "Personal Recollections of the War," *Harpers News Weekly*, vol. 33, July-November, 1866, 153 (Strother, *Recollections*).

13 Pierce in *Broadfoot MOLLUS Minnesota*, 27, 298.

militia. Thus, in spite of the lack of Regulars or ex-Regulars in command of his regiments, the colonels brought a considerable amount of military experience to the field.

The division commanders reflected the Pennsylvania origins of the army. They had been appointed before the federal government's decree ending the governors' power to appoint general officers. Keim and Cadwalader were the doing of Andrew Curtin, not Lincoln or Scott. When the May order was issued, numerous practical reasons made it too late to remove them even if such an action were desirable; and no record of pressure to do that exists. By the first of June, Patterson's army needed complete reorganization; but it could not be done until the three-month terms of its officers expired.

Brigades, on the other hand, were divided equally between West Pointers and militia veterans. George H. Thomas, John L. Abercrombie, Charles P. Stone, and Dixon S. Miles were Academy alumni, while Alpheus Williams, George Wynkoop, Daniel Butterfield, James Negley, and George Starkweather had served in the military forces of their respective states.[14] Only Butterfield, the New Yorker, had not fought in Mexico. Because of its peculiar antecedents, Patterson's army was not on paper officered as well as McDowell's, but neither was his command structure deficient.

Patterson and his army suffered from the same disadvantages that plagued their Washington counterpart: no cavalry, lack of wagons, and general inefficiency of supply due to the crush of large, new, unanticipated demands. Patterson felt that McDowell had all the available wagons. McDowell felt the reverse. Both complained about restricted movements because of the lack.[15] Unlike McDowell, Patterson lacked artillery.

For the remainder of the day Patterson was content to allow the enemy a headstart in withdrawing, rest on his laurels, and remain with his army about Falling Waters. He had been notified that McDowell would be on the road to capture Fairfax Court House and Manassas Junction in less than a week. He felt secure in his ability to keep Johnston in the Valley for that length of time. The next day he set out for Martinsburg, marching unopposed the entire way. Soon, led by Colonel Birney's

14 Butterfield, *Butterfield*, 7 ff, points out that he was the lone New Yorker in command of a brigade under Patterson; in fact, he was the lone non-Pennsylvanian with the exception of Regulars like Thomas.

15 An interesting parallel occurred during World War II, when the Allies were faced with the problem of supplying landing craft to the Pacific and European theatres and could satisfy neither theater and their commanders. Harrison, Gordon A., *The United States in World War II*, 91 vols., *The European Theater of Operations*, 9 vols., *Cross-Channel Attack*, 1, 12-13, 100-105, 126-127 (Washington, 1951). Both felt undersupplied and retarded.

Twenty-third Pennsylvania, the Army of the Upper Potomac entered the town amid cheers from the loyal population.[16] As a precaution he sent a patrol of infantry and cavalry beyond the town on the Pike toward Winchester.[17] In the vicinity of Berkeley School House, it encountered Confederates who were more anxious to rejoin their friends than fight; but in spite of their haste, they managed to leave one dead and two wounded men behind. The enemy, then, was neither aggressive nor resistant to the advance of Patterson's army. They had been "driven" from their position at Williamsport. Their scouts would not face Union patrols. They seemed inclined to withdraw when confronted with any aggressive movement.

In almost two months of campaigning, Patterson had not suffered a reverse. Nor had he met stout resistance. At Martinsburg, he found the train depot a smouldering ruin. The track to Harpers Ferry was destroyed, and scattered about lay the remains of forty-eight locomotives. Everything was propitious for him to strike a blow before the enemy could be reinforced and find its courage.

But he failed to march.

Instead, he decided that he should wait until he could bring forward more supplies for a supply depot. The country, he asserted, was short of provisions. He could not cut himself loose from his supply lines.[18] The ripe wheat and produce[19] could not have escaped his eye, but Patterson would not choose to live off the country. That would come later under a much different man. He would wait at Martinsburg until his trains were ready again. Meantime, he called for more troops.[20]

In the first week of July, Stone was ordered to join Patterson while he engaged in his elaborate encircling movement on an unoccupied Harpers Ferry. He was to march to Charlestown, then join Patterson's left flank at Martinsburg. By July 6, his three regiments and one battery of artillery, minus scratch forces of two companies left to occupy Point of Rocks and one at Sandy Hook to close the river, were on their way to join Patterson.[21]

Dissatisfaction with Patterson had already arisen in Washington. Active elements in the cabinet sought to have him removed, "General" Chase urging

16 *OR*, 2, 157; *Birney*, 22.

17 The units involved in the patrol were B Company, Tenth Pennsylvania Regiment, and the City Troop Cavalry.

18 Bates, *History of Pennsylvania Volunteers*, 1, 97. In 1864, after four years of ravages, the Shenandoah Valley still served as a breadbasket for the Confederate border states causing Hunter and Sheridan to spend considerable time burning the entire Valley from top to bottom.

19 Henry Hall and James Hall, *Cayuga in the Field* (Auburn, 1873), 58 (Hall, *Cayuga*).

20 Porter MSS (L.C.) letter dated July 4, 1861, from Porter to Stone; *OR*, 2, 158.

21 The First New Hampshire, Ninth New York, and Twenty-fifth Pennsylvania Infantry Regiments and the First Pennsylvania Artillery. *OR*, 2, 122.

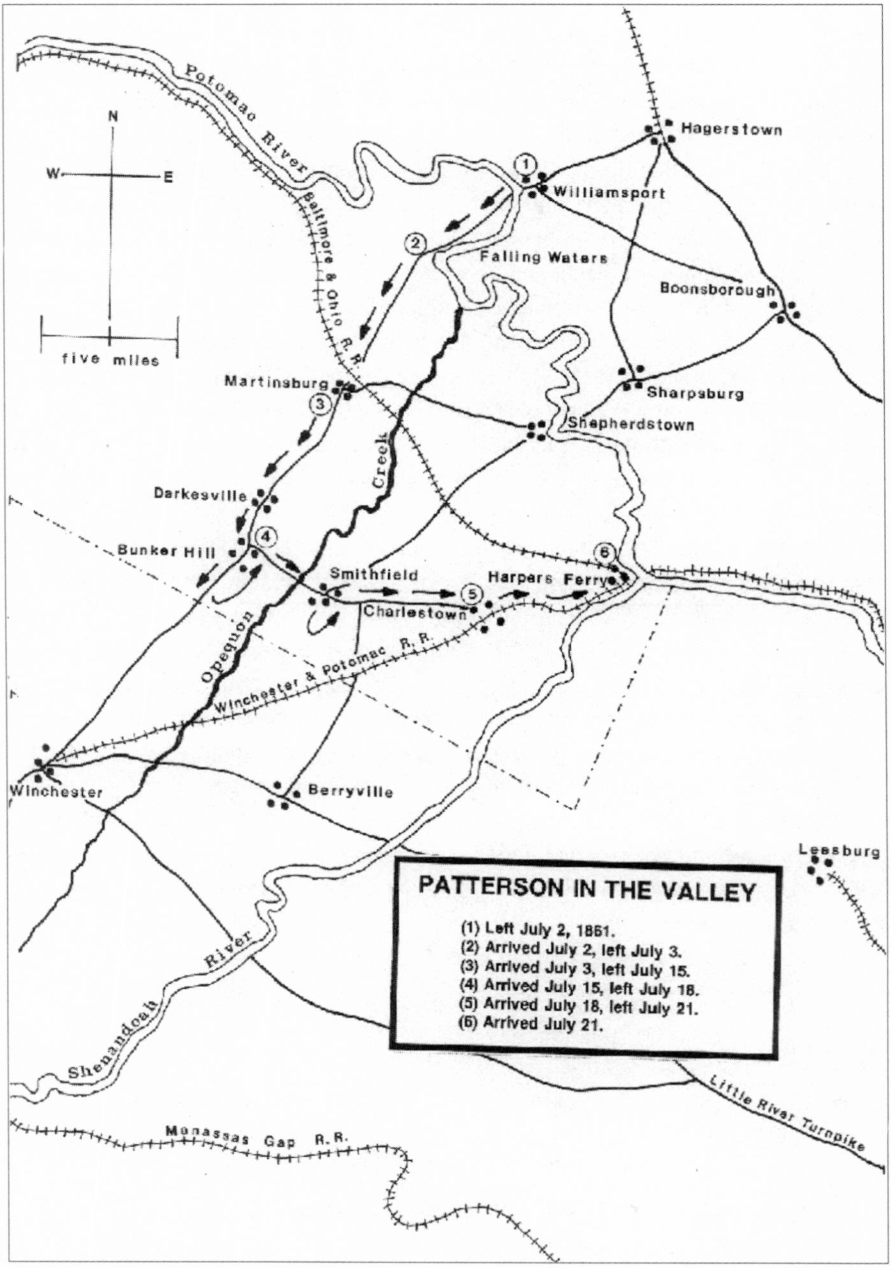
N
W
E
five miles
Potomac River
Baltimore & Ohio R. R.
Hagerstown
Williamsport
Falling Waters
Boonsborough
Sharpsburg
Martinsburg
Shepherdstown
Darkesville
Bunker Hill
Opequon Creek
Smithfield
Charlestown
Harpers Ferry
Winchester & Potomac R. R.
Winchester
Berryville
Leesburg
Shenandoah River
Little River Turnpike
Manassas Gap R. R.
PATTERSON IN THE VALLEY
(1) Left July 2, 1861.
(2) Arrived July 2, left July 3.
(3) Arrived July 3, left July 15.
(4) Arrived July 15, left July 18.
(5) Arrived July 18, left July 21.
(6) Arrived July 21.

specifically that he be replaced by John Charles Fremont.[22] Scott did not share these concerns. With some difficulty, he succeeded in mollifying them, suggesting that Sandford be assigned to the Valley, where he would waive rank. Persuaded for the moment, the politicians hoped Sandford would put some aggressiveness into the Valley leadership. Sandford received the orders with pleasure. He was more than happy to rid himself of his anomalous Washington position, where he had no troops, and to exchange it for an opportunity to engage the enemy.[23]

In the meantime, Scott notified Patterson that Sandford's New York troops had departed for the Shenandoah and gave him permission to assume command of Stone's force at Harpers Ferry, Wallace's Indiana regiment at Chambersburg, and a regiment at Frederick, Maryland. Two Wisconsin regiments were also on their way to join him.

If Patterson defeated the enemy, said Scott, he could move toward Alexandria by way of Leesburg but must watch the passes in the Blue Ridge Mountains. Scott then declared himself satisfied with the movements of the Army of the Upper Potomac, a statement which, if somewhat twisted, could be taken as approval for inaction at Martinsburg.[24]

Bivouacked there, Patterson turned from advancing to telegraphing. By the time he had rested four days, he had on route to reinforce him Stone's force of three and one half regiments, Wallace's Indiana regiment, the two Wisconsin regiments, the Second Massachusetts regiment, and General Sandford's four New York regiments.[25] From its position guarding the Williamsport Ford, Doubleday's battery was brought forward with his infantry support. His three guns were of exceptionally heavy caliber,[26] and the horses were new to harness. To surmount the steep southern bank of the ford, the gunners were forced to help the inexperienced horses pull the

22 Chase MSS (U.P.I.) letter, of July 23, 1861, from Chase to William P. Mellen; *C.C.W.*, 2, 55 (Sandford). On the basis of the evidence available to him at the time he wrote (1890), Livermore suggests that no dissatisfaction had been expressed about Patterson's performance and discounts Sandford's testimony. *PMHSM*, 1, 21. But the private letter by Chase, dated July 23, confirms the testimony by Sandford about his conversation with Seward.

23 Livermore in *PMHSM*, 1, 21-22; on the evening of July 6 the Nineteenth and Twenty-eighth New York set out and were followed next morning by the Fifth and Twelfth New York Regiments, *C.C.W.*, 2, 55 (Sandford).

24 Patterson's MS Orderly Book (Pennsylvania Historical Soc.), letter dated July 5, 1861, from Scott to Patterson (Patterson's MS OB); *OR*, 2, 158-59; Porter, *Stone*, 7-8.

25 Patterson MS Order Book, notation for July 7, 1861, referring to a Massachusetts regiment; but the regimental histories of the Second Massachusetts make it clear that it was the regiment.

26 The three-gun battery was composed of one eight-inch howitzer, one 24-pounder, and one 30-pounder.

heavy guns onto Virginia soil; but in a short while they reported for duty at the army's bivouac area.[27]

By the eighth day of the month, after lying idle at Martinsburg for five days, Patterson had gathered ten days' rations. In spite of the fact that he did not consider his supply problems solved, he began to feel the need for a forward movement. He still wished heartily that he could go to Charlestown and establish a convenient supply depot at Harpers Ferry, but he knew that McDowell must be, if not actually advancing on the enemy, at least preparing to march at any moment. The Army of the Upper Potomac had to hold Johnston.

Subconsciously, he continued to hold the false belief that he, not McDowell, was the main effort. If he were lured into a trap, he could be cut off by forces from Manassas Junction and destroyed by the united Rebel armies. To him, the enemy forces were superior in number; their retreat was nothing but a deception.[28] Yet he had to advance. He wrote an order for an advance the next morning.[29]

That night, the first of the reinforcements arrived. Stone's troops from Harpers Ferry were followed by two of Sandford's New York regiments, which had covered the distance from Washington to Martinsburg by way of Williamsport in two days.[30] In spite of the evident exhaustion of his latest arrivals, Patterson felt he had to move forward to fulfill his part of Scott's plan; but Fitz-John Porter clearly and forcefully resisted an advance. As a youth in school and a junior company grade officer, Porter had been persuasive. People had valued and sought his opinions. He still had that power, particularly with Patterson. He did not intrude his views unsolicited. That was not his style. But he certainly gave them when he was asked and in any emergency. With or without high rank, he commanded the attention of his superior. Although Patterson also valued advice from John J. Abercrombie, a West Point graduate, Class of 1822, and his son-in-law, and George H. Thomas, he was most influenced by Porter.[31]

Officers outside the chain of command had no difficulty recognizing the questions facing Patterson and resolving them. A junior staff officer in Stone's column wrote home two days after Stone arrived in Martinsburg, ". . . I hope they have good reasons for not pushing us on, our time is nearly out, most of the troops

27 Bates, *History of Pennsylvania Volunteers*, 1, 78.

28 *OR*, 2, 161, 162-63.

29 *OR*, 2, 162-63.

30 Patterson's MS OB (P.H.S.), letter of July 5, 1861 from Scott to Patterson; *OR*, 2, 158-59.

31 Porter MSS (L.C.) draft letter of November 24, 1890, from Porter to Livermore; Cecil D. Eby, Jr., *A Virginia Yankee in the Civil War—The Diaries of David Hunter Strother* (Chapel Hill, 1961), 206, entry dated September 20, 1863 (Eby, *Strother Diaries*).

here are 3 months troops. [Y]esterday there was very little firing, which looks as if the Secessionists had retreated, we have quite a number of prisoners, a great many of them giving themselves up . . . McLellan [sic] is not the great ways off. Genl. Scott wants to finish this rebellion with as little bloodshed as possible & I think they are completely cornered."[32]

With aid from several of the generals Porter succeeded in persuading Patterson to delay the movement. Patterson knew he was to support McDowell but was reluctant to march into a trap. The following morning, he yielded to pressure to give the recently arrived regiments time to rest. Then, he supplanted necessity with personal predilection by calling a council of war.[33]

Just as he had earlier, he allowed himself to be misled about the strength of the enemy. Before Stone's arrival, his forces numbered fourteen to seventeen thousand men. On the fourth of July, the day after he had entered Martinsburg, he wrote Scott that the enemy must include some fifteen thousand to eighteen thousand men, twenty-two guns, and six hundred fifty cavalry.[34] A few days later, he reported Rebel reinforcements which raised his estimate to twenty-six thousand men supported by twenty-four guns, many of which were large caliber and rifled.[35] Even so, many of the Confederates were reportedly raw militia.[36] D. H. Strother, a noteworthy private citizen in the Valley, joined the army the same day Patterson called the council of war. From personal observation, he reported to Porter and Newton that the Confederates were only fifteen thousand strong, of which many were sick. Rebel impressments had stirred a spirit of desertion which would reduce their numbers even further. They brusquely rejected Strother's information as untrue and probably never gave it to Patterson. Many men sought to report other information. Some felt strongly that the enemy was at least two thousand men inferior to the Army of the Upper Potomac.[37]

But Patterson's intelligence service failed him continuously. His tendency to accept reports of Rebel superiority was compounded by an obstruction that kept much accurate information from him. Few people were able to penetrate the wall of staff officers who had turned away Strother; and no one managed to pass McMullen's Rangers, the Philadelphia cavalry troop. Captain McMullen, the

32 James C. Biddle MSS, letter dated July 10, 1861, from Biddle to Gertrude.

33 *C.C.W.* 2, 194-95 (Biddle); Patterson, *Narrative*, 52.

34 *OR*, 2, 158.

35 *OR*, 2, 159.

36 *C.C.W.*, 2, 166 (Birney) and 67, 68 (Doubleday).

37 Ibid.; Strother, *Recollections*, 152.

company commander, had a reputation in Philadelphia as a disrespectful, belligerent bully. He and his men, serving as Patterson's escort, were certain that the enemy far outnumbered the Union forces in the Valley. They did not allow trifling tales to the contrary to bother the general.[38]

On the afternoon of July 9, therefore, Robert Patterson, commander of the Army of the Upper Potomac, which was cooperating in an overall plan to capture Manassas Junction as the first step in an advance to the Rappahannock River, listened to his subordinates tell him what his army should do. He never wondered how they could make proper judgments when they lacked correct information about their own forces, the enemy's forces, and the orders and plans from the capital. According to an old military axiom, "councils of war don't fight." In this small Virginia town, the old maxim was reaffirmed.[39]

When all the officers had gathered, Patterson gave vent to the fears which had burdened his thoughts in ever-increasing intensity as he marched farther into Virginia and closer to the enemy. The nearer he approached the main body of the Confederate Valley army, the larger they seemed to grow. He began by referring to plans long outdated and long unrelated to the current circumstances.

"This force was collected originally to retake Harper's Ferry," he said. "That evacuated, it was directed to remain so long as Johnston remained in force in this vicinity. Threatening, as he was, to move to the aid of a force attacking Washington and annoying the frontier of Maryland, the army was directed to cross the Potomac and offer battle. If accepted, so soon as Johnston was defeated, to return and approach Washington."

Briefly, he had outlined the overall plans and purposes of the army. Now, he turned to the misgivings which plagued him.

"The enemy retires," he continued. "For what? Is it weakness or a trap?

"Can we continue to advance and pursue if he retires? If so, how far?

"When shall we retire? Our volunteer force will soon dwindle before us, and we may be left without aid. If our men go home without a regular battle, a good fight, they will go home discontented and will not reenlist and will sour the minds of others.

38 *C.C.W.* 2, 166 (Birney) and 225 (Spates and Stake).

39 Patterson claimed in *C.C.W.*, 2, 84 ff, and later in his *Narrative*, 52-53, that Scott told him to "make good use of your engineers and other experienced staff officers and generals." That Scott meant this to justify inaction is clearly contradicted by his actions during the month of July, Elliott, *Scott*, 723 ff. That Patterson really believed it as he later explained it is more than questionable. More likely, it became a later rationalization for his actions.

"We have a long line to defend, liable at any moment to be cut off from our base and depots and to a blow on our flank. A force threatens Washington. If we abandon our present position, Johnston will be available to aid. The command has been largely reinforced to enable us to clear the Valley to Winchester, to defeat the enemy if he accepts battle, and to be in position to aid General McDowell or to move upon Washington, Richmond, or elsewhere as the general in chief may direct.

"General Sandford with two rifled guns and three regiments will be up tomorrow. Our force will then be as large as it will ever be. Under the prospect of losing a large part of our force in a few days by expiration of service," he concluded, "what shall be done?"[40]

According to a custom based on the principle that an officer should not be intimidated by his superiors when he spoke, the junior officers generally spoke first at meetings of this sort. Quartermaster Colonel Grossman described the condition of supplies. He thought nine hundred wagons would be enough. At that moment the army had five hundred operational, with two hundred more expected shortly.

Following him, Captain Beckwith,[41] the commissary officer, felt that subsistence was a question of wagons. One day's march would force the army to live off the country, which he felt could not be done.

Because the Confederates could move twelve thousand men round trip by rail between Manassas and the Valley in one day, the topographical engineer officer, Captain Simpson, felt the army should combine with the Washington forces.

The last of the staff, Captain John Newton, the army's engineer officer, said the present position was abominable. The supply lines could be cut at any time. The proper course was to march the army to Harpers Ferry, Charlestown, or Shepherdstown to flank Johnston.

The brigade commanders except Negley all wanted to march by the flank to Charlestown. General Keim agreed. Negley was for following Newton's advice about a better position from which to flank Johnston, and General Cadwalader merely expressed opposition to any forward movement.[42]

40 Patterson MS OB (P.H.S.), memo dated July 9, 1861. Either the speech was read from the memorandum or recorded during delivery. Some of the punctuation has been changed for clarity.

41 Both the minutes in *OR*, 2, 163-164 and the Memorandum of July 9, 1861, from which the minutes were probably taken, put the men in this order in spite of military custom.

42 *OR*, 2, 163-164. According to Cadwalader's testimony, *C.C.W.*, 2, 236-237, he proclaimed that since Johnston remained in the Valley as long as he wished and could depart at any time, he should be attacked, and the army could then march to Washington to join McDowell. The notes after the meeting are probably more reliable then the later statement of an officer trying to distance himself from a highly censured and publicly denounced movement. Cadwalader's testimony may be rejected as untrue.

These opinions were valid and the advice logical if they applied to Patterson's army operating in a vacuum. None of them considered the army's orders or the circumstances. Patterson was, it was true, in a comparatively bad position and had less supply facilities than he needed; but his mission was to hold Johnston in the Valley and prevent him from joining the Confederates at Manassas. This was vital to the success of McDowell's advance from the capital. To withdraw, march to Charlestown, or re-establish at Harpers Ferry would release Johnston to move toward Washington—just as Patterson had said in his preliminary remarks to his officers before he asked their opinions. None of the officers were in Patterson's position. None saw the necessity of remaining at Martinsburg, and none saw an overall need to advance on Winchester. Many decades earlier, Napoleon had written, "The same consequences which have uniformly attended long discussions and councils of war will follow at all times. They will terminate in adoption of the worst course, which in war is the most timid, or, if you will, the most prudent. The only true wisdom in a general is determined courage."[43]

After the meeting, Patterson continued to temporize. He would await Sandford's arrival. At daybreak the next day, Sandford with the Fifth and Twelfth New York Regiments reported to Patterson and delivered orders from Scott. He added his own personal urging for an aggressive forward movement.

Two brigades, each with a battery, were created from the newly arrived troops and assigned to Colonels Schwartzwalder and Stone,[44] with Sandford as their division commander. In a few days, however, Schwartzwalder was forced to resign because of ill health and Colonel Daniel Butterfield of the Twelfth New York assumed command of Schwartzwalder's brigade.[45] Patterson now had approximately twenty thousand men with several batteries. He would not grow stronger.[46]

43 D'Aguilar, Lt. Gen. Sir. G. C., C. B., trans., *Napoleon's Art of War*, (New York, 1995), 87-88.

44 To Schwartzwalder were assigned the Fifth, Twelfth, Nineteenth, and Twenty-eighth Regiments. The Ninth, Seventeenth, and Twenty-fifth New York and First New Hampshire went to Stone.

45 The date of change was July 13.

46 *C.C.W.*, 2, 228 (Butterfield) and 56 (Sandford); Butterfield, *Butterfield*, 25; *Cayuga in the War*, 52; Jacques, John W., *Three Years Campaign of the Ninth New York State Militia during the Southern Rebellion* (New York, 1865), 30 (*Ninth N.Y.S.M.*). The Second Massachusetts was still on the way. Estimates range from 18,000 to 20,000 with some as high as 26,000 for Patterson, *C.C.W.*, 2, 56 (Sandford) and 225 (Stoke and Spates); Biddle MSS (PHS) letter dated July 9, 1861, from Biddle to Gertrude. In his *Narrative*, 63-64, Patterson manages to reduce his force to 18,000 men ready for action; but having started the campaign with that many and been vigorously reinforced as it progressed, his number is not plausible.

During the delay at Martinsburg, which lasted from July 3 to July 15, other problems required solutions. Colonel Clark of the Nineteenth New York Infantry had earned the animosity of his regimental officers by his strict discipline. With the kind of personal irregularities that often characterized good officers, Clark rode a huge horse and wore a red shirt. His courage and aggressiveness were not enough to lift him above criticism, and his subordinates reported him incompetent. Patterson ordered him relieved and arrested and delayed decision on the matter until he had free time. Good officers were not to be wasted. Patterson handled this matter in an unfortunate manner.[47]

The men, too, provided difficulties, sometimes humorous. A few of them had hidden a huge whiskey jug in one of the wagons, imbibing away the vicissitudes of military life during their free time until an officer discovered the location of the jug. He "captured" it in their presence and bracing the men, poured its contents on the ground. An Irishman watched mournfully as the spirits seeped into the dirt, turned to his comrade, and said, "Dennis, if I'm kilt in the next battle, bring me back and bury me here."[48]

For Patterson, the problems did not relent; and Scott did not help. The dispatches from the Valley gave an invalid picture of Patterson. They showed him to be a horse with the bit in his teeth, charging hard and fast on the enemy. Scott's letters and telegrams constantly stressed the value of caution but always left Patterson latitude as long as he kept to the overall plan. Unmistakably, Scott pressed for action. In his own mind, Scott merely guided the stroke of the sword; but in actuality, if the sword, Patterson's army, had ever left its scabbard, it dangled irresolutely by his side.

The misunderstanding continued between the two men. After the negative response from the council of war, Patterson's doubts were enhanced by a dispatch from his old friend in the capital enclosing a note about Johnston's intentions. Scott portrayed the enemy as drawing Patterson's Army of the Upper Potomac too far south for it to retreat. It would defeat him, unite with Wise to beat McClellan, then join the forces about Manassas Junction to march against the capital.

Any anxiety this may have aroused was vitiated by news received on July 13. McClellan had soundly beaten his opponents at Rich Mountain. "My determination is not changed by this news," wrote Patterson, "I would rather lose the chance of accomplishing something brilliant than, by hazarding this column, to destroy the fruits of the campaign to the country by defeat. If wrong, let me be instructed." Later

47 *Cayuga in the War*, 55-56.

48 Abner Doubleday, MS Reminiscences (New York Historical Soc.), *Some Experiences in Wit, Humor, and Repartee in Army and Navy Life*, 4.

that day, he said, "This force is the keystone of the combined movements and injury to it would counteract the good effects of all victories elsewhere."[49]

The view that his column was too important to the national military effort for Patterson to risk a defeat seemed to square directly with Scott's views. Shortly after McClellan's victory in the mountains of West Virginia, Porter received a letter from Colonel E. D. Townsend in Washington that said everyone was delighted with Porter's position, force, and caution. They hoped Patterson did not misunderstand Scott's objective when he sent news of McClellan's success in West Virginia. "It was done to give you all a share in our rejoicing. Genl. P. knows the state of affairs. But not to hurry him, or to *hint* a modification of his plans or movements." In an aside, Townsend added, "The General enjoys your off-hand notes to me fully as much as I do."[50] As always, Porter had reported in writing with regularity.

This note seemed to validate Porter's continuous restraint on Patterson and Patterson's halting, cautious movements. Whatever it did to Patterson's state of mind, it could only have reinforced Porter's view about the correctness of the advice he was giving Patterson. It also gave the highest approval to Porter's conduct. He would repeat the conduct in the future with a dramatic effect on his career.

The troops, however, were anxious for a fight. The glory of soldiering was in battle, not in drilling and marching. The longer they waited without fighting the more discontented they became. Finally, Patterson issued an order that the army would advance on Monday, July 15. The men were ready. Sunday, the day before the advance, saw solemn religious services as the men prepared;[51] and late Sunday evening the army received orders to be ready to march at 5:00 a.m. The orders gave no destination.[52]

49 *OR*, 2, 164, 165.

50 Porter MSS (L.C.) letter dated July 14, 1861, from Townsend to Porter.

51 *C.C.W.*, 2, 226 (Stake), 52 (Morell), and 166 (Birney); Butterfield, *Butterfield*, 26.

52 Dwight, *Letters*, 52, letter dated July 18, 1861, from Dwight.

Chapter 15

"I look upon that dispatch as a positive order from General Scott to attack Johnston wherever you can find him. And if you do not do it, I think you will be a ruined man."

— Major Russell to Patterson while delivering a note from Scott

Patterson Stumbles

Monday dawned clear and warm to find Patterson's army on the march. The main column of ten thousand pressed up the Valley Pike preceded by skirmishers which were heavily reinforced on their center and flanks. With the vanguard were Tompkins's four hundred cavalry and a battery. Behind the main column stretched the trains, while marching out to the left on parallel roads was Sandford's division hoping for a chance to strike the flank of the enemy.

The country was verdant and lush, the grain crops ripe, and the farm yards surrounded by neat, white, picket fences. Traces of the enemy, deserted bivouacs, overturned wagons, and dead horses, speckled the countryside. Crackling small arms fire to the front announced continuous contact with opposing cavalry pickets. Tompkins finally succeeded in dispersing his foe with a bold charge about one mile south of Parkesville.

As the day wore on, the sun beat down, scorching everything and releasing huge quantities of dust.[1] By afternoon the army had covered the fifteen miles to Bunker Hill, where they encountered the main body of enemy cavalry. In a twenty-minute fight Patterson's artillery drove the Rebels, who left behind one dead and five prisoners.[2] The Army of the Upper Potomac bivouacked. Patterson rode about the lines. The First New Hampshire opened ranks to allow Patterson through toward the front units, faced inward and presented arms. On the left he found Sandford and a staff officer laying out the division area after pushing the Rebel pickets back across a stream three miles above. Patterson complimented his aggressive subordinate on his pickets and layout, adding that the position looked quite comfortable.

"Very comfortable," confirmed Sandford. "When shall we move on?"

Patterson hesitated. "I don't know yet when we shall move on. And if I did, I would not tell my own father."

Sandford smiled, thought the remark a bit odd, and said, "General, I am only anxious that we shall get forward, that the enemy shall not escape us."

"There is no danger of that. I will make a reconnaissance tomorrow and we will arrange to move at a very early period."

The position about Bunker Hill was, indeed, a comfortable one.[3] The town itself was a quiet little village of three or four mills and several houses surrounded on all sides by the ever-present, ripe wheatfields.[4] But Patterson was not meant to occupy this pleasant spot. He was to hold Johnston in the Valley while McDowell fought the Confederates at Manassas Junction.

Scott and Patterson had arranged a code for information about McDowell's advance. Scott would send, "Let me hear of you on——." The blank space would be filled by a day of the week, the day McDowell was to attack and Patterson was to have Johnston in the Valley. On Friday, July 12, Scott telegraphed Patterson, "Let me hear of you on Tuesday."[5] That was July 16.

If the Confederates retired, Patterson was determined that he would not follow. He wanted to withdraw to Charlestown where he could reinforce the capital or march toward Winchester. His fixation on Charlestown as a refuge had almost

1 *C.C.W.*, 2, 56 (Sandford) and 50 (Morell); Strother, *Recollections*, 154; Wallace, Lewis, *Lew Wallace: an Autobiography*, 2 vols. (New York, 1905), vol. 1, 318 (Wallace, *Autobiography*).

2 *OR*, 2, 166; *C.C.W.*, 1, 56 (Sandford); Strother, *Recollections*, 154; Wallace, *Autobiography*, 1, 318.

3 *Ninth N.Y.S.M.*, 30; Livermore, *Days and Events*, 16.

4 Roebling MSS (RU), letter dated July 19, 1861, from Roebling to his sister; *Cayuga in the War*, 58. Roebling described it as three houses and the same number of pig pens, probably a somewhat hyperbolic description.

5 *OR*, 2, 162-163, 164; *C.C.W.*, 1, 164 (Birney).

overwhelmed any comprehension of his part in the overall plan. On the designated day, Patterson assumed, McDowell would begin his march, reach the Confederate army, and fight his battle. He decided he needed information for his own advance and sent out a reconnaissance. Tuesday, July 16, was a perfect day, except for the red dust which roiled about everything that moved.[6]

Lieutenant Colonel David Birney, commanding the Twenty-third Pennsylvania during the illness of its colonel, was selected to lead a combined arms force of infantry, cavalry, and artillery toward Winchester.[7] He moved down the pike until he met a body of cavalry. Quick fire dispersed the Confederate horsemen. The column continued until it was slowed by fallen trees and fence rail barricades. Birney's instructions were to make the enemy think the army was coming. He decided that he had fulfilled his assignment. Believing that to proceed farther would endanger his men, he returned to Bunker Hill and reported to Patterson, who telegraphed the gist of the events to Scott. The barricades, he felt, indicated "no confidence in the large force now said to be at Winchester."[8]

At 3:00 p.m. a cavalry column of eight companies under Captain R. W. Johnson was sent forward toward Winchester to see if General Johnston's Confederates remained in their front. He advanced without meeting a picket until he found himself on the edge of the camp occupied by the Rebels forces. The long roll sounded. Great confusion prevailed. Horses created a dense dust cloud which the captain, having satisfied himself that the entire Confederate army was still in front, used to cover his withdrawal.

But a cavalry scout commanded by Second Lieutenant Thomas M. Anderson ranged far to the front of Patterson's army. Anderson saw the clouds of dust raised by columns of men, but they were headed from Winchester toward the fords over the Shenandoah and the gaps in the Blue Ridge. When he reported this information to Thomas, the colonel, his uniform coat unbuttoned and no hat, hastily left his quarters for Patterson's tent to report.[9]

The report by Captain Johnson seemed satisfactory to Patterson. Only a captain, he did not know the general movements. But in conversations with Thomas, he learned that Scott had said the Washington column would fight its battle that day and

6 Wallace, *Autobiography*, 1, 319; Strother, *Recollections*, 154.

7 According to Birney's testimony, *C.C.W.*, 1, 163, six companies of infantry, two sections of artillery, and one squadron of cavalry. Sandford mentions only cavalry and artillery, *id.*, 56.

8 *OR*, 2, 166; *C.C.W.*, 1, 163 (Birney).

9 Anderson, Thomas M., "General George H. Thomas: His Place in History," in *Broadfoot MOLLUS California*, 60, 431; *Heitman*, 1, 165.

that Patterson was expected to hold Johnston in his front until after that date, then take a position at Charlestown.[10]

During the day, however, the lack of confidence seemed to belong more to Patterson than to the Confederates. Deserters were arriving in fair numbers. A talkative citizen of the Bunker Hill area arrived. The Rebels had twenty thousand men at Winchester, he said, and were determined to make a stand. They had felled trees to block the road and built a strong battery across it a mile and a half north of Winchester.[11] From his statements, Captain Simpson made a map of the strong Winchester defenses, signed it, and gave it to Patterson. A young boy of thirteen or fourteen, whose father owned a Bunker Hill store which had been protected by Yankee sentinels, said he knew this man and his brother to be shiftless and lazy. A major on Patterson's staff said he was sure the man was lying about the great numbers of Rebel troops and fortifications. Nevertheless, as would so often be true about logically implausible information inflating the numbers of the enemy, Patterson accepted the report as true.[12]

Two brothers who had deserted the Rebel army reported an entirely different story. Sickness and desertion, according to them, were daily depleting the strength of Johnston's regiments. D. H. Strother, the civilian who had joined the column at Martinsburg, said that this information fit perfectly with his personal observations. The Confederates could not have the force described by the citizen, could not supply it if they did, and would never have retreated so far if they had it. A heated argument erupted over this report, but its veracity was not doubted.[13]

According to Patterson's intelligence, measles, dysentery, and typhoid were widespread in the Confederate army; but this did not alter his firm belief that he was now confronted by a forty-two-thousand-man army with more than sixty guns, including several 32-pounders pulled by twenty-eight horses each. Winchester itself was defended by fortifications on high ground all about the city. Logs, barrels filled with earth, and barricades of earth were fronted by deep trenches which

10 Porter MSS (L.C.) letters of December 3 and 11, 1890, from Johnson to Porter. There was some controversy about the date of the afternoon cavalry reconnaissance, but it seems to be the one led by the captain even though in his 1890 letters to Porter he was insistent that it took place on July 18. The analysis by Livermore in 1 *PMHSM* e.g., 24-27, especially n. 4 on 25-26, seems sound, clear, and dispositive.

11 Francis Channing Barlow MSS (M.H.S.) letter dated July 18, 1861, from Barlow to his brother Edward.

12 *C.C.W.*, 2, 229 (Russell).

13 Strother, *Recollections*, 155; Thomas, *Thomas Letters*, 21, letter dated July 16, 1861, from Thomas to his father.

communicated with the inside by tunnels. All artillery was masked by evergreen thickets.[14]

Patterson and his staff had instantaneously accepted one report and hurriedly rejected contradictory information. He made little effort to do more than believe the information that fit his perceptions. His nerve was weakening, but he realized that he must continue. He told Birney he expected to hear that McDowell had fought a battle that day. After that, the Army of the Upper Potomac would attack. An order was prepared for an advance on Winchester the following morning. Word spread through the bivouac area that tomorrow would be the day. The army was anxious to fight.[15]

When Sandford heard this, he was overjoyed. He thought he could cut Johnston's line of retreat in three hours by driving from the Bunker Hill left flank, crossing Opequon Creek, and turning to the right when he was behind Winchester. Or he could march to the Shenandoah River and take blocking positions between Winchester and Manassas.[16]

Colonel Morell had already been sent with forty men to prepare the road east of Winchester for artillery. The bridge over the Opequon was placed under a guard of two or three hundred men. Sandford had decided to make his own move to force the issue if Patterson failed. His men had a full supply of ammunition and a day's cooked rations in their haversacks.[17]

Patterson rode through the camps of his regiments. When he reached the Nineteenth New York, he said he expected to engage the enemy next day and asked if the men would support him. A vociferous "Yes" was followed by three thunderous cheers.

"I can trust that regiment," he said as he rode off. "A soldier who cheers well fights well."[18]

The mental state of his army was apparently not unanimous, however; and he received different reactions from other regiments. Once again, his negative view that the glass was half-empty dominated. The three-month terms of service of his regiments were beginning to expire, and during the next week he would lose more than half his army. Worse than unwillingness to fight, he even had fearful questions about willingness to advance.

14 Patterson MS OB (P.H.S.), memoranda. Johnston did not begin constructing earthworks until he drew back to Winchester about July 15, Van Diver, *Mighty Stonewall*, 152. Patterson, *Narrative*, 57 ff.

15 *C.C.W.*, 2, 164 (Birney), 56 (Sandford), and 226 (Stake). Livermore, *Days and Events*, 16.

16 Livermore, *Days and Events*, 17.

17 *C.C.W.*, 2, 56 (Sandford).

18 *Cayuga in the War*, 60.

At regiment after regiment he talked to the men. "He appealed to their pride as men, as soldiers entrusted with the Flag and its honor, not to desert them at their expiration of service." At one regiment, after the speech he called for the men willing to stay to "shoulder arms." Not one man in twenty raised his rifle. He concluded he did not have enough reliable troops to hold any position in the face of the enemy.[19]

The colonel of a western regiment went to Porter and said that "he knew many regiments were in almost the state of mutiny and would not go into action and that, while he knew his men were very discontented and would probably revolt if ordered forward, he would like to do what he could to down any expression of such feeling and would bring forward his regiment and offer its services for any duty, even to moving on the enemy, if General Patterson would receive and address them thanking them for firmness and courage and sense of duty. But knowing that General Patterson had decided not to attack the enemy he would want the general to give the men some assurance that they were not likely to be called upon except in absolute necessity and for defense." Patterson received the regiment and addressed the men, who returned to camp in good spirits and envied by others.[20]

But news of a proposed advance set Fitz-John Porter to work at once. Strongly opposed to a forward movement because he was certain the Rebels were too strong, Porter believed the army would march right to the grave or to Richmond prisons. As soon as he could find his commander, he argued against an advance, asking Patterson to talk to Abercrombie and Thomas.

"No, sir, for I know they will attempt to dissuade me from it," answered the old Pennsylvanian, standing firmly for the course he knew to be right.

Porter persisted. Finally, he persuaded Patterson to discuss the best way to accomplish the task with them. They were summoned and told about the plan for the next day. The order itself was written and ready to be issued.[21] Should he attack? Should he demonstrate against the Winchester position? Should he remain in position at Martinsburg? Should he withdraw to a safer position? What would happen if he were defeated? He could be pinned against the Potomac, and he had no reserves. No army would remain to oppose a Confederate advance into Washington.

19 Chase MSS (L.C.) letter dated July 19, 1861, from Patterson to Sherman; letter dated July 19, 1861, from Russell to Sherman.

20 Porter MSS (L.C.) draft letter dated Nov. 24, 1890, from Porter to Livermore. The date of the event is unclear but it seems to have occurred at Bunker Hill.

21 Patterson MS OB (P.H.S.) letter dated July 31, 1861, from Porter to Patterson; *C.C.W.*, 2, 191 (Price).

Still deluded that his army was more important than McDowell's and had the most important mission, he could not attack without the certainty of victory.[22]

Scott had told him not to attack without a force larger than Johnston's. His intelligence services, especially their most recent reports, showed him to have little more than half the troops Johnston had in Winchester. He was certain that Johnston had recently been reinforced. This confirmed, among other things, that the Confederates recognized his efforts. His campaign was successful.

His army was nearing the end of its period of service, was unreliable, and would not fight. The characteristic that had created it so early and so fast now made it liable to overnight dissolution. His campaign, begun as early as possible, had absorbed most of the earliest three-month men. He knew they would not serve a day beyond their time. In his mind this also meant they would not fight as they drew near the end of their time. They were becoming, in modern parlance, "short-timers."

If he attacked the Confederates in position, he would cause the very result he was meant to prevent: he would drive Johnston to Beauregard and Manassas. Outnumbered, he could never destroy Johnston; and with a railroad at its back even a defeated Rebel army could board a train and take refuge with its counterpart one hundred miles away. A marching army, even an army flushed with victory, could not keep pace with a retreating, defeated army aboard a train.[23]

According to the code he had arranged with Scott, "Let me hear from you on Tuesday," the engagement between McDowell and Beauregard should have taken place on Tuesday, July 16. He had heard nothing to the contrary. With the main Confederate force in the Valley still intact and in front of him in Winchester, it was two days plus travel past the time that McDowell was to have fought his battle. An attack, therefore, was no longer necessary.

Last, when Scott ordered away the only reliable troops Patterson had, the Regulars, the cavalry, and most of the artillery, the general in chief had indirectly said he did not intend or want an attack by Patterson's army. All this in Patterson's mind made a demonstration, a threatened attack, sufficient.

These reasons meant he need not do more than he had. His course of inaction had the explicit support of his staff officers and the higher ranking officers of his army. More importantly, it was the course recommended by his able and reliable adjutant-general, Fitz-John Porter, the man with the greatest influence on his thinking. Porter had advanced two of these considerations primarily and vigorously:

22 Patterson, *Narrative*, 64.

23 Porter MSS (L.C.) letter dated November 28, 1892, and a draft letter dated November 20, 1890, from Porter to Livermore; John Sherman MSS (L.C.), letter dated July 26, 1862, from Porter to Sherman; Patterson, *Narrative*, 66; *OR*, 2, 177.

even a victory would have the undesired effect of "driving" Johnston to join the forces of Beauregard at Manassas, and removal of the Regulars, Patterson's only real striking force, was an indirect assertion by Scott that Patterson should not attack.[24] In half an hour Patterson's officers convinced him not to follow his "determination." He would avoid Winchester and march east to Charlestown.

Why did the commander of the Valley army do this? He knew McDowell had advanced on July 16. He knew McDowell would carry Manassas Junction on July 17. Johnston, now at Winchester, could not march to his railhead at Strasburg and ride to the Junction in time to take part. The reconnaissance had struck the enemy. It would certainly suffice as a demonstration. The enemy was superior in numbers, position, and supply. Patterson's officers, with the exception of Sandford, were anxious to retreat. Scott had approved the move to Charlestown once Patterson had completed the Valley part of the plan. He would, therefore, be justified in marching from Bunker Hill to Charlestown, instead of advancing on Winchester. From there, the army could outflank Johnston by marching down the Shenandoah or reinforce Washington by crossing the Blue Ridge and marching through Leesburg.

During the month of July, the task of the Army of the Upper Potomac was—first, last, and always—to keep Johnston from joining Beauregard. Patterson had two ways to do that. First, he could hold Johnston in the Valley. Second, he could prevent him from going to Manassas. One way or the other, this would probably result in a battle for Patterson's army.

In spite of Patterson's fear about the reliability of his short term troops in battle, his men were anxious to fight. They were annoyed at the constant inaction and the apparent indecision. A core of Patterson's troops were well-trained and in good order. Although eighteen regiments of Pennsylvania infantry would end their three-month commitments by approximately July 25,[25] his army was composed of excellent officers with battle experience, West Point training, or Regular Army service, including Fitz-John Porter, John Newton, Simpson, and Orville E. Babcock on his staff; Cadwalader and Sandford at the divisional level, Thomas, Stone, Negley, Abercrombie, and Wynkoop at the brigade level; and Gordon, Andrews, Wallace, and Starkweather at the regimental level.

A number of his regiments were already well-trained, well-disciplined, and reliable. The Second Massachusetts Infantry, the First Wisconsin Infantry, the Eleventh Pennsylvania Infantry, the Philadelphia City Troop of cavalry, and a

24 A footnote to fully explain the derivation of these unstated conclusions about Porter's points would require a chapter or an appendix. Instead, they will be left to develop themselves as the story unfolds.

25 *OR*, 2, 730.

section of Battery F., Fourth U.S. Artillery had all performed well at Falling Waters when Patterson crossed the Potomac at the beginning of the month. Other units showed potential, the Ninth New York and First New Hampshire Infantry regiments, two batteries of Regular artillery, and two troops[26] of Regular cavalry.[27]

Writing years after the war, Thomas L. Livermore, who ended the war as a colonel in command of the Eighteenth New Hampshire and who served with Patterson as a company grade officer in the First New Hampshire, wrote of Patterson's army deployed for battle at Bunker Hill: ". . . his men, inspired by the martial array, the many fluttering banners, the career of horsemen, and the consciousness that the eyes of the country and the world were upon them, in happy ignorance of the actualities of battle, were preparing themselves for the clash of bayonets. Never was an army more willing to fight, and never was one more disappointed and dispirited by the refusal of the opportunity."[28]

The most reliable way to hold Johnston in his position was to attack him, forcing him to stand and fight where he was. The Confederates simply could not move to Manassas, or anywhere for that matter, while they were deployed and fighting. It would not be enough to advance and "offer battle," a phrase that appeared repeatedly on both sides of the correspondence between Patterson and Scott. To keep the Confederates from going to Manassas he had to make their departure impossible by fighting them.

If he chose the other alternative—prevent Johnston from going to Beauregard—his best course was to march south on the road paralleling the Shenandoah from Charlestown and take a blocking position between Millwood and Berryville.[29] There, he would be between the Rebel forces at Winchester and their railheads at Strasburg and Front Royal. He would also block the main road from Winchester, through the Blue Ridge at Ashby's Gap, to Fairfax Court House. The considerable benefit of this maneuver was the reverse of McDowell's difficult tactical offensive with inexperienced troops. Patterson would have the strategic offensive by marching and maneuvering but the tactical defensive by forcing Johnston to fight through his position or bypass it with an exposed flank.

26 In the cavalry a troop was the equivalent of a company in the infantry and a battery in the artillery although the three basic units had different numbers of both enlisted men and officers.

27 Livermore in *PMHSM*, 1, 55-57.

28 *C.C.W.*, 2, 50 (Patterson); quotation from Livermore in *PMHSM*, 1, 58; Livermore in *Days and Events*, 17, says he never heard that any regiment was unwilling to stay and fight. If the discrepancy is a function of memory (unlikely), the *PMHSM* article was submitted in December, 1890, and his memoirs were copyrighted in 1920 but written over a number of years much before that.

29 Livermore in *PMHSM*, 1, 23-24, 53-54, 57-58.

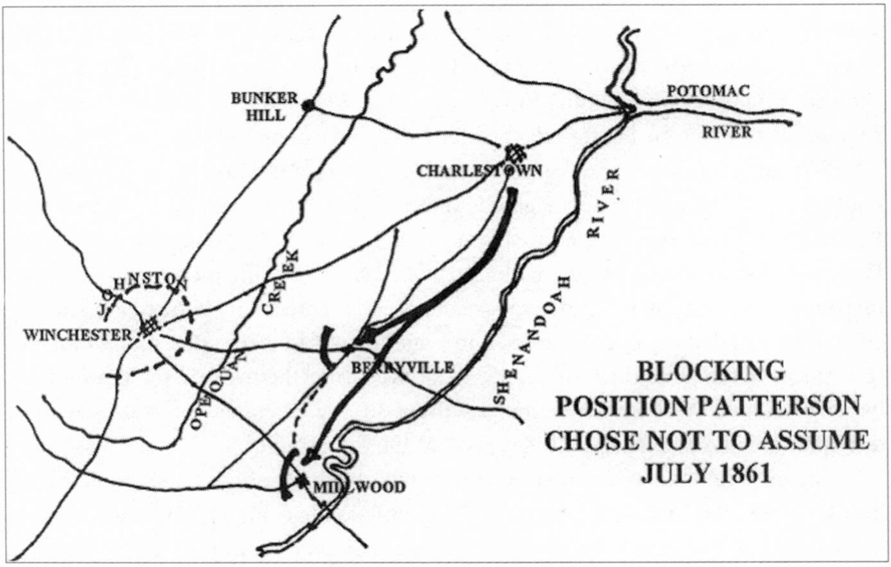

Patterson seems never to have considered more than a direct attack and "offering battle." But if he only "offered" battle, he would achieve nothing if Johnston did not accept.

If Patterson fought and lost while McDowell fought and won, the old veteran would have left the field with glory. If he fought a drawn battle while McDowell won, he would have been a hero. And if, tactical offensive or defensive, he fought and won at the same time that McDowell did, he would have been a lionized early leader of the war. All these alternatives were available to him when he chose his course of action. In fact, he decided to turn away from Johnston, march from Bunker Hill to Charlestown, and come to rest at Charlestown. This enlarged the distance between his army and Johnston from thirteen to twenty miles and more.

At midnight, a three-page order was circulated for the army to march toward Charlestown in three hours. To avoid angering the men because he avoided a fight, he told them this was an "advance" on Wizard's Cliff, after which they would turn south and cut off the Rebels. At 3:00 a.m., July 17, when the army left Bunker Hill, everyone supposed they were heading for Winchester.[30] When they learned their true destination, they were disappointed. All had expected an advance to Winchester

30 Francis Channing Barlow MSS (M.H.S.) letter dated July 18, 1861, from Barlow to his brother Edward.

and an encounter with the enemy. ". . . [I]ndignation was outspoken on all sides. General Patterson was called a traitor and the men felt the disgrace that this withdrawal, without an engagement, implied."

Colonel Dudley Donnelly, commanding the Twenty-eighth New York, ordered his regimental colors rolled and put in a wagon.

Colonel Daniel Butterfield asked why he did not carry his colors.

"I will not," replied Donnelly, "show my flag in a retreat."

The rising sun lit tall columns of smoke from Winchester as if the Confederates were burning buildings or bridges. The day was almost unbearably hot as the column covered the twelve miles to Charlestown.[31] One of Patterson's colonels had spent the night under a tree anxiously awaiting battle the next day and thought he heard the sound of trains on the Manassas Gap Railroad. The light rattle—that would be the empties—seemed to be coming; the heavy rattle—the full trains—was apparently leaving. When he reported this to headquarters next morning, his information was cavalierly rejected—and the plan for withdrawal was executed.[32]

While Sandford held fast on the left and guarded the roads by which the Confederates might attack, the other two divisions passed behind him toward Charlestown.[33] At Smithfield, one brigade feinted toward Winchester while the main column continued rearward. Rebel cavalry was close on the flank keeping the entire movement under constant watch. Sandford attempted to cut them off with the Twelfth New York and a battery of artillery, but they escaped by taking down fences and heading cross-country.

At the ruin of an old Episcopal church, the main column halted while detachments went around Charlestown, which was supposedly defended by Virginia militia. Charlestown, a slovenly, wretched village with an occasional large, old, pleasant looking house, was only seven miles from Harpers Ferry. The Union forces encountered no resistance. The army continued into the town with drums beating and flags flying, but the sight which greeted them there was far different from the victorious entry into Martinsburg. All houses were tightly shuttered. The streets were empty except for a few children and some blacks who stared curiously. After

31 Roebling MSS (R.U.), letter dated July 19, 1861, from Roebling to his sister; *C.C.W.*, 2, 57, 60 (Sandford), 50, 52 (Morell), and 226 (Stake); Dwight, *Letters*, 51, letter dated July 18, 1861, from Wilder Dwight; Strother, *Recollections*, 155; Butterfield, *Butterfield*, 27; Wallace, *Autobiography*, 1, 319-320; C. W. Boyce, *A Brief History of the Twenty-Eighth New York State Volunteers, First Brigade, First Division, Twelfth Corps, Army of the Potomac* (Buffalo, 1896), 18 (Boyce, *Twenty-Eighth New York*).

32 Wallace, *Autobiography*, 1, 319-320.

33 In 1864, Lieutenant-General Ulysses S. Grant would make this movement continuously famous as he marched southward without ever truly disengaging himself from the Confederates.

the Rebel flag atop a storehouse had been replaced by the Stars and Stripes, the troops were posted; and Patterson established his headquarters in the house of former United States Senator R. M. T. Hunter, now a member of the government of the Confederate States of America. Inhabitants, reassured about their safety, began to appear slowly, quietly on the streets.

Long after Patterson and most of his staff had retired, a special messenger accompanied by one of Patterson's aides arrived at the Hunter house with a dispatch. Major Russell, sitting alone on the porch, received it. He took the note to Fitz-John Porter, who opened and read it. Porter rose, showed it to Captain Newton, and discussed it briefly with him, then asked Russell to take it to General Patterson and awaken him. Russell, who had just joined the staff, was reluctant to disturb his commanding officer's sleep. He believed the message was a matter of great importance and would be better delivered by Porter. But the adjutant was adamant.

"You better take it," he affirmed.

"I will do so."

Taking the dispatch, the major climbed to Patterson's room and rousing him from his sleep, presented the note:

> Headquarters of the Army July 17, 1861—9:30 p.m. Major General Patterson, U.S. Forces, Harpers Ferry.
>
> I have nothing official from you since Sunday July 14, but I am glad to learn from the Philadelphia papers that you have advanced. Do not let the enemy amuse and delay you with a small force in front whilst he reinforces the junction with his main body. McDowell's first day's work has driven the enemy beyond Fairfax Court-House. The Junction will probably be taken tomorrow.
>
> Winfield Scott.[34]

After he read it a second time, Patterson looked up and asked Russell if he had read it. The major replied that he had.

The dispatch was clear proof that Scott and Patterson had misunderstood each other. The general in chief had no idea that the Valley commander and his army were at Charlestown.[35] In fact, he expected him to be marching on Winchester. Patterson realized this only too well. McDowell was already a day late as far as Patterson was

34 *OR*, 2, 167-68; *C.C.W.*, 2, 230.

35 Livermore in *PMHSM*, 1, 44, n. 1; *C.C.W.*, 2 (Russell). The content is the same in both but much different in details. The message in the text is a composite of both, preserving the content but using the standard form of a military dispatch.

concerned. The advance was Tuesday, July 16; and McDowell's battle should have been fought on that day or July 17, the day the Army of the Upper Potomac marched away to Charlestown. Unfortunately, the battle had not been fought. What should be done now? Johnston may have escaped already. He surely knew from his cavalry that the Union forces were no longer pressing him and that he could turn all his energies to reaching Manassas.

When Patterson asked the major what he thought of it, Russell reminded him that he was new to the staff. Fitz-John Porter was the man to ask.

"I desire your opinion, sir," demanded the white-haired old general.

"I will give you my opinion honestly and without hesitation. I look upon that dispatch as a positive order from General Scott to attack Johnston wherever you can find him. And if you do not do it, I think you will be a ruined man. It will be impossible to meet the public sentiment of the country if you fail to carry out this order. And in the event of a misfortune in front of Washington, the whole blame will be laid to your charge."

"Do you think so, sir?"

"That is my honest conviction!"

"I will advance tomorrow, but how can we make a forced march with our trains?" queried Patterson.

"Sir," replied Russell dramatically, "if you cannot send them across the river into Maryland, we can make a bonfire of them." The major paused, then continued, "General, have you positively made up your mind to this advance?"

"I have."

"Then I hope you will allow no one to influence you tomorrow in relation to it."

By nine o'clock the next morning, Patterson had assembled all his officers and revealed his determination. "Gentlemen, I have sent for you not for the purpose of consulting you as to the propriety of the movement I intend to make, but to ask the best mode of making it."

As soon as plans were made, the troops were assembled on their parade grounds.[36] Because some of the three-month regiments had served their term, they would have to be discharged if they could not be persuaded to stay. Beginning with his son's regiment, Patterson delivered impassioned speeches requesting the regiments to remain. At his son Frank's regiment, the Seventeenth Pennsylvania Infantry, almost every man agreed to stay.[37] As he moved from unit to unit, his success diminished. At the Second Pennsylvania, every man of Company H stepped

36 Barlow MSS (M.H.S.) letter of July 18, 1861, from Barlow to his brother Edward; *C.C.W.*, 2, 329-331 (Russell).

37 Bates, *History of Pennsylvania Volunteers*, Broadfoot ed., vol. 1, 1861.

forward at the call . . . but very few others emulated them; and the regiment was discharged.[38] Many of the men were wearing trousers patched with pieces of their tent flaps, and their shoes were literally falling off their feet. At many regiments he was greeted with cheers followed by cries of "shoes and pants." Nor had his army been paid.

In spite of the privations the men had borne, they would have remained if they had faced an enemy; but the continual promises of a battle on the "next day" had been unkept; and the appetite whetted at Falling Waters had died a hungry death on the road from Bunker Hill to Charlestown. The army believed they had marched to Bunker Hill to await the arrival of George B. McClellan's army from his recent victories on the Ohio line.[39]

While haranguing his troops, Patterson appealed to their patriotic senses, asking them to stay ten more days. Even now, he made no promise of the battle he had finally decided to fight; but if he had mentioned it, more than likely no more than a few of the troops would have stayed. The army's enthusiasm had lasted all the way to Bunker Hill—but no farther. Now that there seemed no chance they would ever fight, the troops thought of their physical comfort, which had been neglected for so long.

It was obvious that Patterson could not fight a battle with the army left after discharges; but at 1:30 a.m. on July 18, he telegraphed Scott the question, "Shall I attack?" Later in the day he ordered his troops to prepare for a march of two days with two day's rations[40] in haversacks. They were to march without baggage. When Colonel George H. Gordon and Lieutenant-Colonel Wilder Dwight of the Second Massachusetts saw Patterson and Major Fitz-John Porter, they found it evident that "no vigorous move was to be attempted, and that this column awaited the news from Manassas."[41]

Scott was at last beginning to have some true understanding of the situation. He had, he replied, expected a victory or at least an attempt to delay Johnston because Patterson was the equal if not the superior of his opponent. "Has he not stolen a march and sent reinforcements to Manassas Junction?" Patterson indignantly

38 Allen Albert, ed., *History of the Forty-fifth Regiment Pennsylvania Veteran Volunteer Infantry, 1861-1865* (Williamsport, 1912), chap. 1 by James A. Beaver, 13 (Albert, *Forty-Fifth Pennsylvania*); Bates, *History of Pennsylvania Volunteers*, 1, 24.

39 Barlow MSS (M.H.S.) letter of July 18, 1861, from Barlow to his brother Edward; Roebling MSS (R.U.) letter dated July 19, 1861, from Roebling to his sister.

40 *OR*, 2, 169; *C.C.W.*, 2, 230-231 (Russell), and 195-196 (Biddle); Wallace, *Autobiography*, 1, 322-323; Locke, *Regiment*, 33-34; Quint, Alonzo H., *Record of the Second Massachusetts* (Boston, 1867), 38 (Quint, *Record*).

41 Dwight, *Letters*, 52, letter dated July 19, 1861, from Wilder Dwight.

replied that Johnston had stolen no march but rather had been reinforced. He felt he had done more than Scott had asked—in the face of vastly superior forces.[42]

Patterson sent Major Russell to Washington on July 18 to tell Scott why Winchester had not been attacked, and later in the day he sent part of his army to Harpers Ferry.[43] On July 20, Patterson reported that Johnston had left for Manassas with all his force except five thousand militia and fifteen hundred sick.

On July 21, McDowell crossed Bull Run.[44]

42 *OR*, 2, 168.

43 Dwight, *Letters*, 53, 76, letter dated July 19, 1861, from Wilder Dwight; *C.C.W.*, 2, 232 (Russell).

44 *OR*, 2, 171.

Chapter 16

"I have made arrangements for the correspondents of our papers to take the field under certain regulations, and I have suggested to them they should wear a white uniform to indicate the purity of their character."

— *McDowell to William Howard Russell*

McDowell Advances to Battle

On Tuesday, July 16, the sun shone from high in the sky with intense heat. In his recently acquired uniform of a brigadier-general, McDowell strode from his headquarters at Arlington. He was wearing a white helmet with a lance head on top and was followed by a well-dressed staff officer. Knowing they were headed for important operations, they had an appearance of gravity. The general collected his tiny staff, mounted, and rode down the shady drive.[1] While his army began its advance on parallel routes, he worked on last minute details, ordinarily the duties of a staff. But with the limited available support, he did them himself. McDowell never had enough staff officers for the task of assembling and organizing an army.

He had arranged for two batteries of artillery to be ordered to Washington and anxiously went to the railroad station himself to see if they had arrived. At the station

1 Averell, *Ten Years*, 289-90; *Ohio in the War*, 1, 726-27, 738.

he met the English war correspondent William Howard Russell. He asked Russell if he had seen the two batteries and commented that they had "gone astray."

Russell, who knew nothing about them, replied that he was surprised to find the general chasing lost batteries.

"Well, it is quite true, Mr. Russell; but I am obliged to look after them myself as I have too small a staff, and they are all engaged out with my headquarters. You are aware I have advanced?"

"No!"

"You have just come in time, and I shall be happy, indeed, to take you with me. I have made arrangements for the correspondents of our papers to take the field under certain regulations, and I have suggested to them they should wear a white uniform," he finished, probably with sarcastic intent, "to indicate the purity of their character."[2]

Although many diverse sources produced the regimental commanders who marched with McDowell on July 16, they could be divided into a small number of categories based on their military experience: West Point graduates, veterans of the war with Mexico, militia officers, and veterans of foreign armies. Six regimental commanders were United States Military Academy alumni, of whom two had been on active duty continuously since graduation. Both of these men, George Sykes, the commanding officer of the Regular battalion, and Alexander McD. McCook, colonel of the First Ohio, had served in Mexico or against Indians and had been tested before the campaign began. The remaining three men, Isaac F. Quinby, colonel of the Thirteenth New York; John S. Slocum, commanding the Second Rhode Island; Henry W. Slocum, the commander of the Twenty-seventh New York; and Henry Whiting, the colonel at the head of the Second Vermont, had all resigned their commissions to enter civilian life although Quinby had become a militia officer when he quit the Regular Army. In spite of the fact that these men had not passed beyond the rank of first lieutenant, they gave no reason to suspect that they would be incapable of handling their duties as regimental commanders. The commissioning authorities took for granted that their West Point education had taught them the basics of command, regardless of the size of the unit. Of the forty-three regiments that marched in the Army of Northeastern Virginia, five, more than ten percent, were under the control of Regular or former Regular Army officers. These men could be expected to lead their regiments well and to behave well under fire.[3]

2 Russell, *My Diary*, 207-208, entry dated July 16, 1861.

3 See *Cullum*, 2, 1033, 1149, 1172, 1542, 1565; for additional information on Slocum see his biography and for a hostile sketch of McCook with details see *Ohio in the War*, 1, 807ff.

A second group of regimental commanders was composed of Mexican War veterans. The ranks held by this group during the 1846 war ranged from non-commissioned officer to full colonel;[4] but the important fact was that they had battle experience in command positions. In some cases members of this group had continued in the militia after Mexico. In 1861, they were able to step into regimental command with relatively little difficulty. Thus, persons selecting regimental commanders could consider this to be a source of dependable men.

Militia officers formed the third and largest source of regimental leaders under McDowell. Despite the decrepit condition of some state militias and the ineffective training given the officers, the experience they gained in these units made them dependable regimental and company leaders. The peacetime soldier trains for an eventuality which may never occur in his lifetime. For militia leaders, the arts they learned during peacetime might never be tested. At the same time they were not bound to the military like a Regular Army officer. Yet, in the end, many of these men were just as qualified for regimental command as their West Point counterparts. The experience of commanding a body of troops on a parade ground made them valuable as leaders;[5] and because many of them had been members of militia units for a number of years. The mechanics of command had become known to them. If the peacetime militia would not produce a large number of high-ranking officers, it would certainly be a source of dependable regimental and company officers.

The last group of McDowell's regimental commanders with previous military experience had served in European armies before coming to the United States. The revolutions of 1848 had forced many men, because of their political views and their unsuccessful assaults on the crown, to leave their homelands for America. The tendencies toward homogeneous enlistment, by geography or ethnicity, produced regiments that were primarily Irish, German, Italian, and Scottish. Of course, these ethnic units wanted their countrymen in command. Although these appointments occurred because of ethnic origin and standing in the ethnic community, in most cases the men brought with them experience which exceeded that of many of their American born counterparts. In this way, Adolph Wilhelm August Friedrich Baron von Steinwehr, a Brunswician nobleman who had been raised to be an officer and who had served in the Prussian army, found himself at the head of the Twenty-ninth New York, a regiment of Germans he recruited.[6]

4 John Henry Hobart Ward had been a non-commissioned officer; Willis A. Gorman had been colonel of the Fourth Indiana.

5 See Appendix I.

6 Lonn, *Foreigners in the Union Army*, 193ff.

Though they might have been somewhat peculiar and incongruous with the American military system, these men had experience in actual warfare, a fact not to be overlooked in granting commissions; and they would add to the cohesiveness of the group supporting the war, something Lincoln sought at every level in the early months of his administration. Prospectively, they would be dependable in battle and good leaders of higher rank.[7]

Whether by president, cabinet, governor, or electing troops, the choice of officers for any grade was made with one eye on the man and the other on his record. If he had military experience without stigma, he would be considered a valuable candidate. No one could tell with certainty how each would perform in bivouac or under fire. Each man had potential which might be realized and might not. In general, the higher the potential, the higher the rank. The fact that several men advanced under lofty expectations but failed to honor this hope in no way reflected upon the perspicacity or wiseness of the choices.

Of the total number of regimental commanders who marched with McDowell from Washington, less than twenty percent and probably closer to ten percent, had no previous military experience. This was a small portion considering the conditions governing the creation of the Army of Northeastern Virginia. Presumably, then, the leadership at the regimental level would be reliable in the ultimate test of battle. While nothing spectacular could be predicted, McDowell would not have been justified in fearing that, at the crucial moment, his army would buckle and give way through faulty direction. McDowell's regimental commanders before the battle, appeared "dependable."

Of the eleven brigade commanders all but three had graduated from West Point, and all but two had served in the Regular Army. In spite of his incompetence, Robert Schenck, a political appointee, was "protected" and would serve. While the governors were still appointing general officers, Daniel Tyler had written to the governor of Connecticut, his state, about political appointments. His letter showed wise foresight:

> . . . If political, not patriotic considerations, are to impose on the new Army incompetent generals, men who have to learn the profession of commanding and handling troops, you will have to pay an awful penalty in blood before these gentlemen will have learned their profession.
>
> We suffered awfully in the Mexican war from this terrible calamity but with General [Winfield] Scott in his vigor and a whole army of West Point officers to extend their influence and example to a small army of 20,000 men, we got there,

7 Lonn sketches all foreign officers who served with the rank of colonel or above in the Union Army with the exception of Max Einstein. Lonn, *Foreigners in the Union Army*.

> but when you have to raise any army of 75,000 men and West Point influence reduced twenty-five to thirty-three percent, you will see the great necessity of making every army appointment with great care.

Lewis Blenker, the other brigade commander without Regular Army experience and a member of the foreign officer group, was as well qualified for his post as anyone. Born in Hesse Darmstadt, Germany, Blenker had been a wine merchant with a skill for motivation but not for organization. He had risen from private to lieutenant in the Bavarian army, a substantial accomplishment for a commoner in the socially stratified armies of Europe. Like many other Germans, Blenker, a "Forty-eighter," had fled his homeland after participating in an abortive revolt. When war erupted in the United States, he was a businessman in New York City and a natural choice to lead an ethnic regiment. The four regiments in his brigade were predominantly, if not totally, German.[8]

Andrew Porter, the last of the three brigade commanders without a West Point degree, nevertheless had a Regular Army commission and part of a West Point education at the outbreak of war. In 1836, Porter, then only sixteen, entered the Military Academy but resigned a year later. When war erupted with Mexico a decade later, he obtained a commission as a first lieutenant in the Mounted Rifles, won a promotion to captain, and was awarded a brevet to lieutenant colonel. After the war he remained in the army until the fall of Fort Sumter. In the expansion of the Regular Army officer corps he was promoted to colonel of the Sixteenth Infantry, one of the new regiments created by Lincoln but not yet in existence. Like Sherman and Keyes, he was assigned to the Army of Northeastern Virginia to command a brigade until his regiment was recruited.[9] He could be considered a fully qualified officer.

Of the remaining eight brigade commanders, all West Point graduates, Keyes, Franklin, and Howard were on active duty in April 1861. The five others had been civilians for as many as thirty and as few as four years; but all eight had battle experience of one sort or another in Mexico or against Indians, an important factor in their qualifications.

The brigade leaders, experienced, capable men, were chosen for their potential more than anything else. With the army scattered over the United States, many men who would later become officers of note were geographically disqualified from the

8 Warner, *Generals in Blue*, 37; Sperber, Jonathan, *Rhineland Radicals: The Democratic Movement and the Revolution of 1848-1849* (Princeton, 1991), 296, 307; James S. Pula, *The History of a German-Polish Civil War Brigade* (San Francisco, 1976), 10.

9 Warner, *Generals in Blue*, 377-378; *Heitman*, 1, 798; *D.A.B.*, 8, pt. 1, 82-83.

campaign; but the most important factor in judging the selection of McDowell's brigade commanders is that they all had definite, prospective qualifications for command. Before the fall of Fort Sumter none had commanded a brigade, but in 1861 almost no one alive in the United States had commanded a brigade in war. General Scott himself had never led more than fifteen thousand troops. Commissions had to be awarded on the basis of potential. With the exception of Robert Schenck, the brigade leadership had been well chosen.

All more than fifty years of age and considerably older than their commanding officer, the division commanders, Tyler, Hunter, Miles, and Heintzelman were respected officers with long experience. Of the four only Dan Tyler was not on active duty when the war began, but he had earned himself such an outstanding reputation during his service that he was a natural choice for division leadership. Before the campaign, no one could complain about the selection of these four men to command McDowell's divisions. In the final analysis, division commanders who marched to Manassas had been well chosen. Criticism of the leaders in the battle, even the criticism of hindsight, pales under the circumstances of the moment: little time available, no organized federal officer training program, no rudimentary officer training program anywhere, and no general staff school. With a few exceptions, all the officers, from company to general grade, were among the best available under the circumstances.

The country before McDowell on July 16 was typical of northeastern Virginia. Although some mansions and farm buildings were pretentious, earlier years of grandeur and prosperity had not protected them from dilapidation. And the surrounding countryside had gone to seed. West from the capital the terrain was uneven and rough. Heavily timbered ridge-lines ran close together in a north-south direction. Creeks flowed through the valleys between the ridges. Many trees were original growth hardwoods, but old pines had grown plentifully in abandoned farm fields. Running east and west, the main roads crossed these obstacles. Small farms, none profitable, provided no more than a grudging existence for their owners because the thin soil had been exhausted by years of careless planting.[10]

On July 16 the divisions marched to their positions for an advance on the enemy works known to be along the Fairfax Courthouse–Sangster's Station line, where McDowell expected to fight his battle.[11] Many, of course, thought their approach to

10 Henry M. Blake, *Three Years In The Army Of The Potomac* (Boston, 1865), 8 (Blake, *Three Years*); Major John M. Gould, *History of the First-Tenth-Twenty-Ninth Regiment* (Portland, 1871), 57 (Gould, *First-Tenth*); R. I. Holcombe, *History of the First Regiment Minnesota Volunteer Infantry* (Stillwater, 1916), 39 (Holcombe, *First Minnesota*).

11 Scott, *Willcox Memoirs, etc.*, 283, letter dated July 16, 1861, from Willcox to his wife.

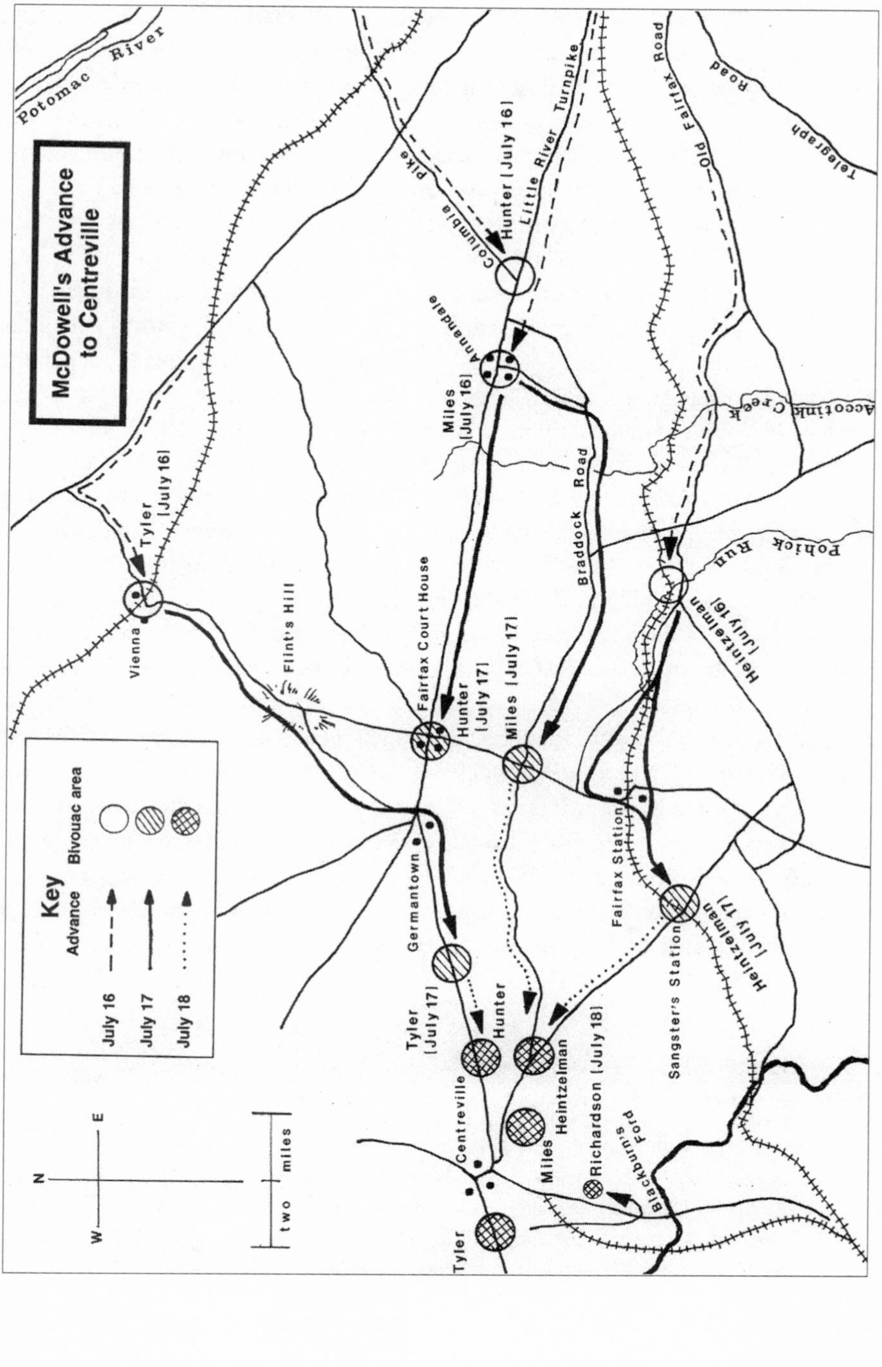
McDowell's Advance to Centreville
Key
Advance
Bivouac area
July 16
July 17
July 18
N
W
E
two miles
Potomac River
Columbia Pike
Little River Turnpike
Old Fairfax Road
Telegraph Road
Accotink Creek
Pohick Run
Braddock Road
Hunter [July 16]
Annandale
Miles [July 16]
Tyler [July 16]
Vienna
Flint's Hill
Fairfax Court House
Hunter [July 17]
Miles [July 17]
Heintzelman [July 16]
Fairfax Station
Germantown
Sangster's Station
Heintzelman [July 17]
Tyler [July 17]
Hunter
Heintzelman
Richardson [July 18]
Centreville
Miles
Blackburn's Ford
Tyler

the Confederates would be a "walk in the park." Zachariah Chandler, a radical abolitionist senator from Michigan who accompanied the army on its march, wrote his wife that day, ". . . today the column is marching from Washington. Thirty thousand men are at this moment approaching Borreguard's [sic] column and you may expect startling news before this letter reaches you. I think [illegible] column will be captured though a man of Borreguard will run like cowards as they are. Not much winning will occur in my estimation until the army reaches Richmond which will I trust not be long now."[12] At the end of the day a wiser man, Colonel William T. Sherman, wrote his family, "I still regard this as but the beginning of a long war."[13]

The marching distance for each division, approximately five miles, would not tire the men, an important consideration because they were new to marching. McDowell expected to pass the Fairfax defenses before he followed his plan to veer south by his left flank. The designated positions were to be reached by nightfall,[14] by which time Tyler was at Vienna.[15] Hunter's division marched at 2 o'clock in the afternoon. After short progress along the Columbia River Turnpike, it reached its bivouac area just short of the Little River Turnpike.[16] Just in front of Hunter camped the brigades of Dixon Miles's division, which marched along the Little River Turnpike to its junction with the Old Braddock Road.[17]

On the left of the advancing army, Heintzelman had been given permission to push his division to Accotinck Creek or beyond to the Pohick if he could. Held up initially by the late arrival of these instructions, the crotchety old colonel was delayed further by a heavy rifled gun, which had been attached to his division but had not yet arrived. Not until 5 o'clock did the artillery piece join the column and then with worn-out horses. McDowell, who appeared a few minutes before the gun arrived, was anxious to begin the advance. With no fresh horses available the gun was left behind along with the usual infuriating administrative paperwork, a requisition for six fresh horses from the Alexandria supply depot. Determined to reach Pohick Creek before camping, "Grim old Heintzelman" pushed across the

12 Chandler MSS (L.C.) letter dated July 16, 1861, from Chandler to his wife.

13 Howe, *Sherman Home Letters*, 200, letter dated July 16, 1861.

14 Russell, *My Diary*, 158, entry dated July 18, 1861; Holcombe, *First Minnesota*, 40; *OR*, 2, 303 ff; Barnard, John G., *The C.S.A. and the Battle of Bull Run, a Letter to an English Friend* (New York, 1862), 47 (Barnard, *Bull Run*).

15 Sherman MSS (L.C.) letter dated July 19, 1861, from W. T. Sherman to John Sherman; *C.C.W.*, 2, 19 (Richardson); Captain D. P. Conyngham, *The Irish Brigade and its Campaigns* (New York, 1867), 28 (Conyngham, *Irish Brigade*).

16 *OR*, 2, 303; Haynes, *Second New Hampshire*, 19; Augustus Woodbury, *The Second Rhode Island Regiment* (Providence, 1875), 28 (Woodbury, *Second Rhode Island*).

17 *OR*, 2, 303 ff.

Accotinck with the head of his division.[18] The creek was only twenty yards wide and knee-deep, but the two leading brigades crossed it on two parallel logs, each taking two hours. When the last brigade reached the banks, its young commander, Colonel Oliver O. Howard, was shocked at the delay. The instructions of his old teacher at West Point, "Do not imperil the success of the campaign from fear of wetting the soldiers' feet," flashing in his mind, he forded the stream and closed rapidly on the units ahead. Night had long since fallen when the division reached its bivouac area along the Pohick.[19]

Not before 3:00 a.m.[20] the next morning did the Eleventh Massachusetts finally reach its bivouac area and join its brigade. It had found the heavy 32-pounder mired at the Accotinck, manhandled it across the creek, and dragged it all the way to the bivouac area. Heintzelman decided that the horses he had sent to this gun could not be spared from his artillery ammunition wagons and that it slowed the advance too much. By 5:00 a.m. the next day his brigades were on the road for Sangster's Station, without the big gun and two 20-pounders left behind under an infantry guard from the Fourth Maine Regiment.[21]

Unlike the Accotinck, Pohick Creek was too deep and swift to ford even though it, too, was twenty-five feet wide. The division lost several hours while it crossed single file on one tree in spite of the fact that pioneers and engineers were present.[22] Heavy forests of scrubby pines and larger oaks came to the edge of the road, which was unsurfaced, narrow, and rutted. The usual, few, dilapidated farms dotted the way. To impede the advance, the Confederates had blocked the road by felling trees, which had to be cleared. The axmen, fifty soldiers from the First Minnesota and the Fifth Massachusetts, rifles slung across their backs, moved behind the skirmishers chopping away the obstructions.[23]

In response to Heintzelman's constant orders for the column to hurry, Colonel William B. Franklin, commanding the leading brigade, responded that he could not move any faster.[24] Behind him in the road stood the brigade under Colonel Orlando

18 Heintzelman MS Diary (large diary) (L.C.) July 18, 1861; *OR*, 2, 303 ff.

19 Howard, *Autobiography*, 1, 148; Gould, *First-Tenth*, 57; Small, *Road to Richmond*, 18.

20 Heintzelman MS Diary (large diary) (L.C.) entry dated July 18, 1861, says 3:00 A.M.; and Blake, *Three Years*, 8, says 3:45 A.M.

21 Heintzelman MS Diary (L.C.) entry of July 18, 1861; Gould, *First-Tenth*, 59; Blake, *Three Years*, 8.

22 Blake, *Three Years*, 10.

23 Heintzelman MS Diary (large diary) (L.C.), entry dated, July 18, 1861; Alfred S. Roe, *The Fifth Massachusetts Volunteer Infantry* (Boston, 1870), 65 (Roe, *Fifth Massachusetts*); Gould, *First-Tenth*, 57; Holcombe, *First Minnesota*, 40; Blake, *Three Years*, 8.

24 Gould, *First-Tenth*, 50.

B. Willcox, West Point Class of 1847. Impatiently, Willcox waited to pass Franklin and swing to the right for Fairfax Courthouse. Deeply in love with his wife and devoted to his family, Willcox had, no doubt, long forgotten the beautiful young woman for whom he had suffered an intense infatuation but who had married Franklin.[25]

At last they reached Elzy's Fork to Sangster's Station and Fairfax Courthouse. The pickets surprised an enemy outpost which escaped westward. Heintzelman hastened forward. He divided his force to flank and cut off any enemy engaged with the remainder of the army to the north at Fairfax. Franklin turned north toward the Courthouse while Willcox continued to Sangster's and three companies of Zouaves went to Barnes' Mill to capture eighty Rebels reportedly posted there. When Howard arrived, he was posted at Elzy's as a reserve for either brigade. The guns left behind arrived a short time after, drawn by brute force.[26]

The Zouaves soon returned to report that the eleven soldiers and two cavalrymen who had been at the mill had left earlier in the morning. As Willcox approached Fairfax Station, he could hear firing to the front. He hurried his men forward but found Miles and his division in possession of the Station. The firing had not been an encounter with the Rebels but foraging for turkeys by the ill-disciplined Garibaldi Guard, the Thirty-ninth New York, of Blenker's brigade. Large numbers of infantry and some cavalry could be seen retreating in the distance.[27]

In a short while Willcox reported his occupation of Fairfax Station and the retreat of one thousand Confederates toward Sangster's Station up the railroad. The other thousand headed for Fairfax Courthouse. Heintzelman forwarded this information to Franklin with orders to continue toward the Courthouse while he marched with Howard to join Willcox at Sangster's. On the way he passed through Fairfax Station where he found numerous signs of a hasty retreat. The much-vaunted fortifications were poorly made and large enough for only about eight hundred men. Clouds of smoke rose from partially destroyed supplies, and two bridges were still smoldering. Some supplies were taken intact, but most were useless. Not until five o'clock did Howard's brigade, accompanied by Heintzelman, finally rejoin Willcox at Sangster's Station.[28]

25 Scott, *Willcox Memoirs, etc.*, 284, letter dated July 20, 1861, from Willcox to his wife.

26 Gould, *First-Tenth*, 50.

27 Scott, *Willcox Memoirs, etc.*, 287.

28 Heintzelman MS Diary (large diary) (L.C.) entry dated July 18, 1861; O. S. Barrett, *Reminiscences, Incidents, Battles, Marches, and Camp Life in the War of the Rebellion, 1861-1864* (Detroit, 1888), 58-59 (Barrett, *Reminiscences*); Holcombe, *First Minnesota*, 40; Roe, *Fifth Massachusetts*, 66.

In the meantime, Franklin advanced his command unopposed along the road to Fairfax Courthouse. The enemy fled, leaving a sergeant, a corporal, and nine men captive plus two bivouac areas which had been so hastily evacuated that fires were still lit and one regimental flag had been left behind. Here, as they had at the Station, the Confederates had set fire to the bridges. When his troops made contact with Colonel Miles on the Old Braddock Road to the north, Franklin returned to Fairfax Station.[29]

Having now reached the destination set for him in the general orders for the march, Heintzelman established his headquarters in the county poorhouse, ate a sparse dinner, and awaited further orders from McDowell. Detailed plans for the movement to the left across the Occoquan had not been circulated.[30]

Miles, in the meantime, had started as early as Heintzelman, half past eight, on the Old Braddock Road. With Davies's brigade in the lead, the command proceeded westward at a slow pace. Here, too, the Confederates had felled trees across the road, leaving a few pickets at each one. Resistance was negligible, the Rebels firing, then pulling back; but the little spurts of flame from behind the logs, trees, and brush slowed the advance. Light fire from concealed positions never conclusively showed the strength of the defenders. Were they a few riflemen or a strong force screened by a few skirmishers? Would the main force of the enemy be developed here? A marching column was not suited for attack. It simply could not plunge ahead on the assumption that a small number of Rebel skirmishers would fire a few rounds and retire. Davies did the only thing he could. He kept enough force in front, four companies of skirmishers,[31] until he reached the main body of the enemy. Deploying the Sixteenth New York right and the Eighteenth New York left, he swept forward and drove the enemy with little difficulty. In a short while he had captured a prepared position of log and earth barricades, but the purpose of the few men left behind had been achieved.

A rear guard was generally intended to create time for the main column to withdraw at its leisure or to reach a better position to receive an attack. By resisting from time to time, especially when its numbers and strength could not be known, it would force the pursuing column to deploy, slow the pursuit, and allow the main column to escape.

29 *OR*, 2, 309-10; Gould, *First-Tenth*, 58-59.

30 Heintzelman MS Diary (large diary) (L.C.) entry dated, July 18, 1861.

31 Companies A and K of the Eighteenth New York and A and B of the Sixteenth New York. *OR*, 2, 433.

When he reached a point about half a mile south of the Courthouse, Miles halted his division and bivouacked.[32] While Miles was suffering four casualties on the Old Braddock Road, Burnside's regiments, which had only been brigaded that day[33] led Hunter's division along the Little River Turnpike directly toward the enemy works around Fairfax Courthouse. Although the same obstructions blocked the pike, no defenders resisted the advance; and the column was able to advance rapidly. The road passed through a deep cut. The Confederates had felled a huge tree, its branches projecting into the cut and its mighty trunk pointing skyward. Burnside led his brigade off the road and over the ridge. When the column had drawn close enough to attack the works around the Courthouse, the colonel delivered a few words about duty and honor, then led his men gallantly against the emplacements—which were deserted except for a newsman and two Rhode Island skirmishers who had already entered the town. A wretched, dirty, straggling little village, Fairfax Courthouse was almost deserted. All men and most of the well-to-do women were gone. The best houses were empty. Poor, ill-fed, dirty looking women stood in doorways.

The pioneers cleared the last obstructions from the road, and the troops cheered as the band struck up the *Star Spangled Banner*. Around 1:00 p.m. the column marched down the main street. They replaced the Rebel ensign over the courthouse with the Union flag to notify Tyler to the north that friends were in occupation. The troops halted, stacked arms, and rested in the main street. As soon as they broke ranks, the men entered the large houses, destroying pianos and pictures, ransacking wardrobes, and carrying furniture into the street. They appeared wearing tall hats, women's bonnets, and dresses. Many were loaded with plunder.[34] They killed the pigs and poultry for fresh food and robbed beehives. As best they could, the officers tried to stop the plundering and ordered all property returned.[35] About noon when the Regulars arrived, a number of officers went to McDowell and reported the misconduct saying they would tender their resignations if it were not stopped.[36]

32 *OR*, 2, 423; *C.C.W.*, 1, 177 (Miles); Francis A. Walker, *History of the Second Army Corps in the Army of the Potomac* (New York, 1891), 325-327 (Walker, *Second Corps*).

33 *OR*, 2, 303; Haynes, *Second New Hampshire*, 19; Woodbury, Augustus, *The Second Rhode Island Regiment* (Providence, 1875), 28 (Woodbury, *Second Rhode Island*).

34 Favil, *Diary*, 28; Benjamin Perley Poore, *The Life and Public Services of Ambrose E. Burnside-Soldier-Citizen-Statesman* (Providence, 1882), 109 (Poore, *Burnside*); Woodbury, *Second Rhode Island*, 28-29; Augustus P. Woodbury, "Narrative of the Campaign of the First Rhode Island Regiment in the Spring and Summer of 1861," in *Personal Narratives of Events in the War of the Rebellion Being Papers Read Before the Rhode Island Soldiers and Sailors Historical Society* (Providence, 1878-1890), series 1, 17 (Woodbury in *PNRISSHS*).

35 Rhodes, Robert H., ed., *All For The Union: The Civil War Diary and Letters of Elisha Hunt Rhodes* (New York, 1985), 24-25.

36 Carter, *Four Brothers In Blue*, 11.

On the northern flank, Tyler with twelve thousand men[37] left his bivouac around Vienna for his encircling movement to Germantown at half past five. McDowell had intended him to cut the line of retreat of the Confederates occupying the Fairfax Courthouse position; but although his march was unopposed and less obstructed than the others, he failed to cover the few miles to Germantown before noon. The Rebels had long since evacuated.

Schenck's brigade, part of the division, had the Irish Sixty-ninth New York in it. Resting with his right hand on his hip, Captain Thomas Francis Meagher, a famous Irish revolutionary leader who had moved to New York City,[38] held a cocked pistol in his right hand. Henry Villard, a passing newspaper reporter, called out, "Well, Captain, are you ready for the fray?"

"Yes. There is nothing like being always ready for the damned rebs." Meagher's eyes and his unsteadiness in the saddle showed plainly that "he had braced himself up internally for the fight."[39]

As the division marched through the village, flames raged among the buildings while the townspeople frantically tried to save their belongings. By four in the afternoon, Meagher reached a position on the pike just short of Centerville, where he received an order to halt and await further orders.[40]

Wednesday, July 17, had been the first full day of marching. The inexperience of the Army of Northeastern Virginia and its officers was clear. The weather was intensely hot and the roads dusty. The men had not yet acquired march discipline.[41] They drank water whenever it suited their fancy. Soon without, many were ready to refill their empty canteens with fresh water at every pond or creek or to empty the tepid contents of their canteens for a refill. The countryside abounded with berries; and they, too, distracted the marching soldiers. The constant, irregular stopping and starting caused the troops to break ranks. The advance was slow and erratic due to obstructions, resistance, ignorance of proper water crossing procedures, and lack of engineers with bridging equipment.[42] But greater than these, two other factors

37 Jackson, Lieutenant H. B., "From Washington to Bull Run and Back Again," *Broadfoot MOLLUS Wisconsin*, 49, 234.

38 *D.A.B.*, 6, pt. 2, 481-482; Warner, *Generals in Blue*, 317-318.

39 Villard, *Memoirs*, 1, 183-184.

40 W. T. Sherman MSS (L.C.), letter of July 19, 1861, from W. T. Sherman to John Sherman; Crotty, D. G., *Four Years Campaigning in the Army of the Potomac* (Grand Rapids, 1874), 20 (Crotty, *Four Years*); Tyler, *Memorial*, 50-51.

41 *C.C.W.*, 39 (McDowell); Holcombe, *First Minnesota*, 38; Roe, *Fifth Massachusetts*, 68; Blake, *Three Years*, 10; Haynes, *Second New Hampshire*, 20.

42 Heintzelman MS Diary (large diary) (L.C.), entry dated July 18, 1861; *C.C.W.*, 2, 39 (McDowell); Blake, *Three Years*, 10.

slowed the march: the memory of Schenck's rebuff at Vienna in June and the lack of effective cavalry.

The Vienna affair had involved hidden artillery, not infantry contact. In the era of the Civil War and for centuries before, artillery had been a direct fire arm. The men at the guns could see their targets and had a clear line of sight. The great fear after Schenck's debacle was the "masked battery," one which could not be seen until, and sometimes could not be seen even while, it was firing. The lesson was simple: no column should advance on a position without first learning its characteristics and defenses. An observant, thoughtful critic had noted this in his diary in June after Schenck's embarrassment. ". . . [T]here is a new bug bear to frighten the soldiers; this bug bear is the masked battery . . . The stupid press resounds the absurdity. Now everybody begins to believe that the whole of Virginia is covered with masked batteries, constituting, so to speak, a subterranean artillery which is to explode on every step and humbug is rather welcome to Scott, otherwise he would explain to the nation and to the army that the existence of numerous masked batteries is an absolute material and military impossibility . . . The terror prevailing now may do great mischief."[43]

McDowell had reflected this lesson in his general orders for the advance. "To come upon a battery or breastwork without a knowledge of its position,"[44] would not be "pardonable in any commander." Commanders of leading brigades did not move ahead blindly. They halted their columns and deployed their leading regiments at the slightest provocation. When, as Heintzelman did throughout the day, the division commander figuratively kicked his leading unit to hurry it, he met outright refusal.

By the middle of the nineteenth century cavalry had long been the eyes and ears of an army on the march. It was the equivalent of the armored cavalry regiment, the HU-1 helicopter reconnaissance unit, or the L-19 observation plane. The day of the great cavalry charge against infantry in battle array, like the charge of ten thousand French horseman boot to boot at Eylau, was gone.[45] Cavalry would scout, bring information about the enemy, and clear minor resistance. But the Army of Northeastern Virginia had little cavalry and made no use of it, even for these limited purposes. In July 1861, the trained Regular cavalry were almost entirely on the frontier. McDowell had but one battalion of Regular cavalry, no volunteer cavalry, and no experience in the use of cavalry anyway. His one battalion was attached to an

43 Gurowski, *Diary*, 1, 58.

44 *OR*, 2, 305.

45 Chandler, in *Napoleon*, 1, 543-544, characterizes it as "one of the greatest cavalry charges in history." *Ibid.*, 544.

infantry brigade, which was in the rear of its division on the march. Unable to scout, the advancing divisions were forced to rely on caution.

These two factors, inability to see ahead and concern about the unseen, caused most of the delay in the advance of the divisions and much of the straggling from the ranks. McDowell had expected to fight his battle at Fairfax Courthouse, but the enemy had retreated to the Manassas–Bull Run Creek area. In effect, his army had just thrown a mighty punch only to find no opponent to receive it. And now that the position had been taken without a fight, the roads had converged. The right wing and right center were on the Little River Turnpike between Fairfax Courthouse and Centerville with the left center, Miles, a short distance away. The coordinated advance along parallel routes had become impossible.

Chapter 17

"Tyler's 'faux pas' has made a delay which is very dangerous. . . ."

— Lieutenant W. W. Averell to his family

McDowell Closes on the Enemy

Whatever McDowell may have wanted to do after he reached the Fairfax Court House line, he could not pursue.[1] He halted his troops for the night and began to plan the next day's operations, the shift past the left flank. He had to know the location of his divisions. Marching an inexperienced green army on four separate roads was a difficult task, made harder by the inadequacy of his staff. He had lost track of Tyler on the right until the division was seen on the skyline crossing Flint Hill;[2] and he had no idea where Heintzelman was on the left.

Around nine in the evening of July 17, McDowell called Tyler to headquarters and ordered him to take Centerville the next day. Two howitzers would be attached

1 According to Johnston, *Bull Run*, 123, McDowell's "early intuition had been to push on another four or five miles to Centerville," but he cites no source for this assertion, nor does it seem likely that McDowell could have intended to reach Centerville that day when he expected to fight a major battle at Fairfax Court House.

2 Johnston, *Bull Run*, 121.

to his division for the purpose.[3] Early the next morning, McDowell scrawled a note in pencil to Heintzelman. Where was his division and would he report to headquarters more often?[4] Then, he headed for the left flank to find Heintzelman and to study the roads for the movement to sever the Confederate line south of Manassas. On the way he passed his chief engineer, Major John G. Barnard, and asked him to go along. Thinking that McDowell was merely riding to find Heintzelman, Barnard thought he should accompany Tyler through Centerville.[5] McDowell made the reconnaissance without his chief engineer officer.

By eleven, he had found his left division at Sangster's Station and met its commander. The few roads in this area, indescribably bad, were incapable of bearing large bodies of troops or artillery. Movement there would be slow and vulnerable. He would abandon his plan to move south of Manassas. The Warrenton Turnpike, the main road east, bore off the Little River Turnpike and passed through Centerville. He would make it the main route of advance. In the spectrum of Virginia roads, the pike was excellent; and the surrounding terrain was much less difficult than usual. While McDowell scouted to the left, he heard distant firing from the direction of Tyler's advance and started at once for Centerville, ordering more troops forward to that place.[6]

At 7:00 a.m. while McDowell was still trying to find his left flank units, Tyler marched for Centerville.[7] Major James S. Wadsworth, an aide on McDowell's staff, delivered McDowell's note:

> Hdqrs. Department Northeastern Virginia,
> Between Germantown and Centerville, July 18, 1861—8:15 a.m.
>
> General: I have information which leads me to believe you will find no force at Centerville, and will meet with no resistance in getting there.
>
> Observe well the roads to Bull Run and to Warrenton. Do not bring on an engagement, but keep up the impression that we are moving on Manassas.
> I go to Heintzelman's to arrange about the plan we have talked over.
>
> Irvin McDowell, Brigadier-General

3 *C.C.W.*, 2, 120-121 (Tyler).

4 *C.C.W.*, 2, 39 (McDowell); the original is in the Heintzelman MSS, Fry to Heintzelman, July 19, 1861.

5 *OR*, 2, 312, 328-29.

6 Heintzelman MS Diary (large diary) (L.C.) July 19, 1861; *C.C.W.*, 1, 39 (McDowell); *OR*, 2, 307.

7 *C.C.W.*, 1, 120-21 (Tyler); Tyler, *Memorial*, 51.

Diligently, Major Wadsworth called Tyler's attention to McDowell's order that Tyler not provoke an engagement while the commanding general gathered information on the left.[8]

Just as McDowell had said, Tyler's leading brigade, under Colonel Israel B. Richardson, found Centerville undefended when he arrived at around 9:00 a.m. Centerville was a small, squalid, wretched, country village at the crossroads of the Warrenton Pike and the Sudley Springs road, an insignificant north-south road running along the crest of one of the long, north-south ridges. Situated on rising ground, it gave a good view of the surrounding countryside in many directions. The few houses were constructed almost entirely of stone, which abounded in the countryside. Most of them were perched on the slope of the ridge west of the north-south road. The surrounding countryside, rolling and picturesque, was to a great extent covered with original growth hard woods and field pine that had grown in abandoned farm fields. "Some of the mansions showed pretensions from the days of their owners' prosperity, [but] the farm buildings were generally rickety and the countryside looked as if it had gone to seed,"[9] wrote an artillery officer after the war. It had the typical look of "Old Virginia."

Tyler's column turned right and left forming a line of battle facing almost west, stacked arms, and lay down.

While he waited for orders, Tyler sent a cavalry unit to collect respectable local civilians still in the area and sent Richardson beyond the town to find water. In thirty minutes the cavalrymen returned with half a dozen citizens, who were thoroughly questioned. The Rebels had apparently divided, part retreating across the Stone Bridge on the Pike and the larger force toward Blackburn's Ford south of the Stone Bridge. Tyler continued to wait. By half past ten, he had been in Centerville an hour and a half without further orders. He decided to make a reconnaissance. Three regiments of infantry he sent forward to reconnoiter. About a mile in front they exchanged fire at long range with Confederate pickets. They advanced, initiating a little fight. An aide returned for reinforcements, and Tyler sent forward two more regiments.

Tyler rode to Richardson's brigade, which had found water in an abandoned enemy camp and was now resting.[10] The Rebels had been falling back for two days.

8 Pearson, *Wadsworth*, 69. No sources fix the time when Tyler received this note; but it was created after Tyler began his march and was received, according to Tyler's report, *OR*, 2, 312-13, before he reached Centerville.

9 The quotation is from Tidball MS Rem (U.S.M.A.) 218; Favill, *Diary*, 29; Holcombe, *First Minnesota*, 41; Howard, *Autobiography*, 1, 146.

10 *C.C.W.*, 2, 199-200 (Tyler); *OR*, 2, 313; Tyler, *Memorial*, 51-52; Favill, *Diary*, 29.

Tyler could see no reason why they would stop now. He was certain that a bold front would continue their retreat and that the Junction could be occupied without effort.[11] The man who accomplished this would win the laurels of the day.

Taking Richardson with him, Tyler rode toward Blackburn's Ford[12] with four companies of infantry, one company of cavalry,[13] and Major Barnard. They proceeded some distance and were about to stop when he received word from the forward elements that the ford was in sight. Hurrying forward, he saw a gratifying sight. Before him stretched a broad, unobstructed open field leading to Bull Run Creek. The banks of the creek were covered with heavy clumps of trees and underbrush. Confederate artillery and a few skirmishers could be seen but no bodies of troops. Keeping his force under cover, Tyler called forward Richardson's brigade and the battery of artillery commanded by Captain Romeyn B. Ayers.

When the artillery had deployed, Second Lieutenant Emory Upton, a recent graduate standing eighth of forty-five in the five-year West Point class, aimed and fired the first gun.[14] Benjamin's two 20-pounder guns banged away. Nothing on the far side of the stream showed Rebels in large numbers. The skirmishers entered the trees on the far side of the open field. Firing began. Richardson sent three more companies forward and went to Tyler to see if he could put all four regiments of his brigade into action. Barnard and Captain James B. Fry, McDowell's adjutant general, who had just arrived, sent an aide to remind Tyler about the order not to bring on an engagement;[15] but Tyler was determined to cross if he could. He granted Richardson's request, told him to scour the woods by the stream, and sent an aide to bring forward Sherman's brigade.

11 Swinton, *Army of the Potomac*, 47-48; Barnard, *C.S.A. and Bull Run*, 47.

12 Fray, in *McDowell and Tyler*, 23, 39, notes that Blackburn's Ford had long since fallen into disuse and that most of the fighting took place at Mitchell's Ford. Blackburn's Ford fell under fire often and was mentioned (incorrectly) frequently in the reports. For convenience the frequent references in the reports to Blackburn's are retained. In addition, few of the maps properly represent the sharp hook in the creek in that area.

13 In his report, *OR*, 2, 312-13, Tyler stated that he took two companies with him; but he gave the composition used in the text in both his *Memorial*, 52, and his testimony, *C.C.W.*, 2, 119.

14 Peter S. Michie, *The Life and Letters of Emory Upton, Colonel of the Fourth Regiment of Artillery and Brevet Major General U.S. Army*, 41 (New York, 1885), 53 (Michie, *Emory Upton*).

15 In *C.S.A. and Bull Run*, 47-49, Barnard claims that he urged Tyler to make a drive for Manassas but that Tyler merely deployed his men and allowed them to be shot up. This is not consistent with his report, submitted a few days after the battle while events were fresh in his mind, *OR*, 2, 328-29. According to the report, he and Fry twice warned against the push. His testimony before the Joint Committee, *C.C.W.*, 2, 162, is consistent with the report; he cautioned against an advance. Johnston, *Bull Run*, 136, notes that McDowell was greeted with recriminations by Barnard and Fry when he arrived.

Leading the Twelfth New York in column of companies down a ravine where it was protected, Richardson deployed it on the left of the guns. He complimented the regiment, said it would do well, then ordered the colonel to charge the woods to his front and clear them.[16] He went to the right of the battery to deploy his remaining three regiments. Captain Romeyn B. Ayres brought two guns close to the tree line and opened fire. Sudden heavy volleys proved that the Confederates held the creek line in force. In Mexico, Richardson had earned the nickname "Fighting Dick." Moving among his three right regiments, he steadied them by his indifference to the Confederate fire. But the left flank of the Twelfth New York was unprotected. The Confederates struck the regiment in front and on its uncovered left, rolling it up. Two companies held formation and retreated in order; but when Richardson crossed to the left, he found the rest of the regiment in flight.[17]

"What are you running for?" he shouted. "There is no enemy here. I cannot see anybody at all. Where is your colonel?"

The fugitives were too frightened to know or care. A supreme effort on Richardson's part rallied them for a short while, but they broke again. He called Tyler forward and asked for permission to charge the enemy with his three intact regiments. But Tyler knew he had already overstepped his instructions. He refused and ordered the brigade back.[18]

In a foul humor no doubt caused by the way Tyler had misused his brigade, Richardson approached the Second Michigan, his old regiment, and suggested "in a scornful sort of manner" that the regiment withdraw before it was cut off by Rebel cavalry. Major Williams took the regiment well into the woods and formed a large, hollow square to receive the expected cavalry charge. Everywhere about his brigade, Richardson reappeared. When he saw the position of the regiment in the woods and recognized the useless square formation, he gave Major Williams a pithy criticism of his efforts.

A lieutenant lay under a tree, his skin pale and his body limp. When Richardson saw an assistant surgeon try to load him in a wagon headed for the rear, he was not touched by the lieutenant's condition. The brigade commander obviously disagreed with the assistant surgeon's diagnosis. They could both see the lieutenant was not wounded, and Richardson did not believe he was ill. He apparently believed the

16 The Tyler *Memorial*, 54-55, claims Richardson charged without orders; but this is after-the-fact rewriting of history and is contradicted by Richardson's report, *OR*, 2, 313, Richardson's testimony, *C.C.W.*, 1, 20, and Tyler's own report, *OR*, 2, 311, in which Tyler states that he ordered Richardson to advance to the Run.

17 *OR* 2, 310-313, 328-30; *C.C.W.*, 2, 199-200, 205 (Tyler), 19-20 (Richardson); *Four Years*, 21-22; Tyler, *Memorial*, 51 ff; Howard, *Autobiography*, 150.

18 *C.C.W.*, 2, 20 (Richardson).

man, even though a Mexican War veteran, was a malingerer, a coward, or worse. Harshly, he ordered him from the wagon; and turning to his brigade, he started for the rear.[19]

Meanwhile, Sherman's brigade could hear the firing at the ford. Unflappable, Sherman sat under a tree while he and the aide from Tyler had a short conversation. He assembled his brigade. It ascended the hill east of Centerville, passed through the village, and followed the road taken by the rest of the division, covering about one and one-half miles at the double-quick. Finally, it reached a position behind the artillery, still firing at the Confederates, and deployed in support.[20]

Numerous Confederate shells flew overhead while Sherman anxiously brought forward his brigade. When he saw his men pulling in their heads at the sound of firing in the distance, he ordered them to be cool and not duck. Just then a large shell crashed through the trees overhead. He flattened himself on his horse's withers, then raised himself. A smile creased his stony face.

"Well, boys, you may dodge the big ones," he said.

Once extricated, Richardson was redeployed by Tyler—a safe distance from the ford. Sherman he placed to the left.[21] McDowell arrived to be greeted by his two staff officers, Barnard and Fry, with complaints about Tyler's conduct. The commander ordered a report of the affair, then tried to forget it, but he was rankled;[22] and his army was "greatly depressed" by it.[23]

Colonel Andrew Porter's adjutant general, Lieutenant William W. Averell, wrote in his diary that night, "Heavy firing. Tyler engaged with the enemy at Bulls Head Run, was shipped. 12th NYV acted badly."[24] The next day he wrote his brother, "Yesterday Tyler's division had a brisk affair with the enemy in which our loss was six killed and twenty-three wounded. He disobeyed his orders in going where he did—his engineers protested against it—we were whipped—the 12th NY broke & ran with the exception of three companies. The enemy have finally halted behind their entrenchments and masked batteries and tomorrow we shall probably have to storm them. Tyler's 'faux pas' has made a delay which is very dangerous. . . .

19 Lyster in *Broadfoot MOLLUS Michigan*, 50, 119-120.

20 Jackson in *Broadfoot MOLLUS Wisconsin*, 49, 237-238.

21 W. T. Sherman MSS (L.C.), letter of July 19, 1861, from W. T. Sherman to John Sherman; William Todd, *The Seventy-Ninth Highlanders New York Volunteers in the War of the Rebellion 1861-1865* (Albany, 1886), 25 (Todd, *Highlanders*).

22 Johnston, *Bull Run*, 136.

23 Tidball MS Rem (U.S.M.A.), 241.

24 Gilder Lehrman MSS, M.L; Averell MS Diary vol. 1, entry dated July 18, 1861.

Tyler ought to be disgraced with the N.Y. 12th. Had he done as ordered the position (Bull's Head Run) would have been won today."[25]

McDowell's army had concentrated at Centerville; but even in the presence of the enemy, it was still forming. Some of his larger units assembled on the march to the Vienna Line and even on the continuation to the Bull Run Creek line. Units and officers were still joining the army. Major William F. Barry was not appointed chief of artillery until July 19.[26] The marine battalion did not leave the capital to join the army until July 16.[27] And a battery of field artillery under freshly minted Captain John C. Tidball joined him about five miles short of Centerville.

Tidball had left Fort Pickens on shipboard, arrived in New York harbor on July 14, arrived in Washington by train a day or so later, learned that McDowell was already on the march, and received a note McDowell had left for him to hurry forward or he would miss the fight. Tidball went to the arsenal, where he spent the remainder of the night filling his ammunition chests, drawing horses from the depot quartermaster, and learning that wagons, forage, and provisions simply were not available. He set out to catch the army without them. When he arrived, he learned he had been assigned to Blenker's brigade.[28]

Having left Washington with no supplies or rations, Tidball sent men to find some; and when they failed, he went himself. The night was quite dark. By asking the "Dutchmen" he met along the way, he shortly found his way to the headquarters of his brigade commander, Colonel Louis Blenker, in a clump of pine trees. As he neared the clump, he heard a din of voices very uncharacteristic of the quiet that usually surrounded a headquarters camp at night. He hesitated a moment; but seeing an opening into the thicket he proceeded, found a pathway cut into the pines, and saw that it terminated in a small space in the center of the clump. He thought he had come unaware upon a group of disorderly soldiers.

The cleared space was lighted by a flickering torch which cast intermittent glows on the pine branches and deepened the shadowy spots in the foliage into gloomy holes. From this strange cavern came the sound of voices. He could see the speakers gesticulating wildly and talking.[29] Resting on stakes driven crosswise into

25 W. W. Averell MSS (N.Y.S.L.) letter of July 19, 1861, from Averell to his brother. In his diary, vol. 1, entry dated July 19, 1861, Averell recorded that Tyler reported losses of nine killed and thirty wounded.

26 *OR*, 2, 345.

27 *N.O.R.*, 4, 589.

28 Tidball MS Rem (U.S.M.A.) 206, 215, 216. "An out and out captain!" he wrote in his memoirs. "A rank that a year before I could not even see with the aid of a powerful field glass."

29 Tidball MS Rem (U.S.M.A.), 232-33.

the ground was a keg of beer. A table improvised from cracker boxes served as a convenient place for mugs and glasses when they were not in use. "Standing around, drinking and talking excitedly, but talking either in German or in such broken English that I could scarcely make anything out of what was said," wrote Tidball after the war, "was a group of officers, most of whom I recognized to be colonels and other field officers of Blenker's brigade. When not drinking they were talking and all talked at once, each endeavoring to gain attention by elevating his voice above the rest and gesticulating more violently. But one of them seemed to have a little more of the floor than the rest acquired evidently from a glamour of prestige which he had acquired through his bullness in having ridden, as he averred, down to the very edge of Bull Run and from there had looked over upon the enemy on the further side. This bold feat had apparently inspired him with great contempt for the foe, for he asserted with tremendous emphasis that if only permitted he would take his regiment down and 'clen dem fellows out quiger than von streak of lightning.' And then the way would be opened for the army to Richmond."

No man was silent except when he was drinking. They banged the table with their swords and shook their fists in the air "as though striking at Jeff Davis in person." Not much time was lost between drinks "and as they drank, the more eager did they become for the fight." Tidball went forward and asked where he could find Colonel Blenker. One of them stepped forward and saluting with the military precision characteristic of European officers, asked his business. Tidball realized that it was Blenker. Glancing around the group before him, he stated his business.

Blenker expressed his regrets at having given Tidball so much trouble. He conferred with his commissary and informed Tidball that all the provisions had been issued. Only a few boxes of crackers, kept as a reserve, remained. He pointed to them. After considerable negotiation in which Tidball threatened to take the issue to General McDowell, Blenker allowed Tidball to have the cracker boxes and ordered them delivered to the men Tidball had brought with him. While collecting the crackers, Tidball discovered some bacon hidden in the bushes and took a share. Blenker then invited him to take a glass of beer, which he did, and swore that Tidball need not fear he would lose any guns as long as he was attached to their brigade.[30]

Supplies for the army arrived that night and the next morning, removing a great burden from McDowell's mind. The army had eaten the last of its provisions.[31] Practically, the men could live off the country. Heintzelman had even wisely begun to gather cattle from nearby farms when he thought the supply wagons might not

30 Tidball MS Rem (U.S.M.A.), 232-38.

31 *OR*, 2, 336 ff; Johnston, *Bull Run*, 137 ff.

arrive in time.[32] The Orange and Alexandria Railroad had proven to be so thoroughly damaged that wagons, readied as a precaution, were used. Although the railroad would have been faster, the unusable track was in reality a blessing because, once the movement to the left had been abandoned and the army concentrated around Centerville, the tracks lay more than five miles off the open flank to the south. By noon of the nineteenth, the army was well supplied for the next two or three days.[33]

By the evening of July 18, McDowell had decided against moving to his left. The terrain was too difficult, and Tyler had probably caused the Confederates to concentrate there. That evening he discussed new ideas with his staff.[34] During the night a thunder shower cooled the intense heat which had made the three days of the advance so tiring, but the nineteenth dawned with a promise of more high temperatures.[35] While the remaining supplies were distributed, McDowell began to gather information to see if he could outflank the Confederates from his right wing.

Here, his staff was important to him; but no one had any experience in operations this large. Certainly none of his officers had planned a maneuver as complex as the one he had selected or participated in a battle as large as the one that would take place. On the only test McDowell could apply, prior Regular Army experience, promise of good performance in a new role, and skill in his bureau service, his staff was as good as he could have found below the superannuated survivors of the war with Mexico. His chief engineer, Major John G. Barnard, and his chief of artillery, Major William F. Barry, would be the most important.

The Stone Bridge and the fords below were important. The Confederates had not left them undefended. The bridge was protected by several thousand men, artillery, and an abatis.[36] It was also rigged with explosive charges to be detonated if the Yankees tried to use it;[37] but men and vehicles could cross at the Sudley Springs Ford, a few miles up the Run and lightly picketed. In addition, another ford midway between the Sudley Ford and the Stone Bridge was reported to be usable. According to rumors, both these crossings could be reached by a road which turned north from the Pike just beyond Cub Run and which roughly paralleled Bull Run Creek. By following this road, then marching across farm fields, both fords could be reached. To verify this information, Barnard, Captain Daniel P. Woodbury of the engineers,

32 Heintzelman MS Diary (large diary) (L.C.) entry dated July 19, 1861.

33 See the reports by the supply train commanders, *OR*, 2, 336 ff and the analysis by Johnston, *Bull Run*, 138.

34 *OR,* 2, 330.

35 Heintzelman MS Diary (large diary) (L.C.) entry dated July 19, 1861.

36 Heintzelman MS Diary (large diary) (L.C.) entry dated July 19, 1861.

37 John G. Nicolay MSS (L.C.) partial draft for "Outbreak of the Rebellion," n.p.

Governor Sprague of Rhode Island, who was serving as a volunteer aide, and a company of cavalry rode north up Cub Run Valley. After some distance they turned left across country until they reached the road which apparently went to the fords, then continued along that road until they detected enemy patrols.

Barnard was certain this road led to the fords; but he was also certain that, if he continued, he would come upon the enemy and alert them to the plan. He assumed the fords could be reached from the road and returned to Centerville; but to be sure, he accepted Captain Woodbury's proposal to investigate under cover of darkness by returning that night with a few Michigan woodsmen from Sherman's brigade.

That night two groups set out to reconnoiter: Captain Woodbury with two other engineer officers to the Sudley Ford, and Captain Whipple and Lieutenant Prime to the area between the Stone Bridge and Blackburn's Ford. Finding strong enemy pickets on the east bank of the Run, both groups returned with no positive information.[38] McDowell now knew that a way to the fords did exist. But where were they located? No one could say. The lack of adequate maps made it necessary for him to create his plan without definite information.

While these two reconnaissances were turning back, the troops in their bivouac areas could hear the whistle of trains and the clatter of cars in the distance. The Confederates were apparently bringing reinforcements to face the Army of Northeastern Virginia. And among the trees along the banks of Bull Run, the rattle of musketry pinpointed by muzzle flashes told of uneasiness among the pickets on both sides. The night air was quiet except for the lowing of one or two unforaged cows.[39]

The troops had anticipated an early start that morning but been surprised when they did not leave camp. To protect themselves from the intense heat, many had built bush huts. In the evening the countryside was marked by hundreds of campfires visible on all sides as McDowell rode among his troops. When he came upon the camp of Burnside's brigade, he found the chaplain of the Second Rhode Island Infantry conducting a service which included the Lord's Prayer, the Doxology, and singing by the men.[40]

On Saturday, July 20, the sun once again rose to beat with intensity on the army clustered about Centerville. Curious crowds bringing picnic baskets and liquor for their excursion from Washington poured through the camp. "Many of the visitors,"

38 *OR*, 2, 330-31; *Heitman*, 1, 1056; Warner, *Generals in Blue*, 570-571.

39 Since he mentioned the trains in a letter to his brother dated July 19, 1861, Sherman must have heard them during the night of July 18. W. T. Sherman MSS (L.C.); Warren H. Cudworth, *History of the First Regiment* (Boston, 1866), 52 (Cudworth, *First Regiment*); Tyler, *Memorial*, 56; *C.C.W.*, 1, 23 (Richardson), 34 (Franklin), 162 (Barnard), and 207 (Tyler).

40 Aldrich, *A*, *First R.I.*, 1; Woodbury, *Second Rhode Island*, 30-31..

wrote Tidball later, "were of such prominence that McDowell could not ignore their presence and much of precious time was consumed in giving them audience."[41] The heterogeneous crowd included important officials like Simon Cameron, the able politician but incompetent secretary of war. When he approached McDowell at army headquarters, the secretary's face was marked with apprehension; but the youthful commander was filled with confidence.[42] Accompanied by Governor William Sprague, Cameron said he had intended to stay in camp overnight but Sprague and others had reconnoitered as far as possible and determined that the Rebels had at least seventy-five thousand men. Their position, he thought, was almost impregnable. Cameron had decided to return to Washington where he would send forward the fifteen-deep reserve regiments to support the main army.

McDowell said heartily he was grateful to have Governor Sprague's information. He was very glad the secretary had learned this information from the governor. If not, Cameron would have told him, "You want everything."[43]

Once again, McDowell toured the camps of his men; and once again, he found himself in the midst of Burnside's brigade where he watched the Regulars perform a dress parade for the First and Second Rhode Island regiments. He knew that Burnside's brigade was part of Hunter's division, that it would be one of the front elements in the turning column, and that it would probably be one of the first to strike the Rebels.

McDowell and Senator Henry Wilson, chairman of the Senate Committee on Military Affairs, were talking when Colonel Ambrose Burnside interrupted, saying he would not advance and fight if it were his choice. The senator stared at him as if he were a coward while McDowell patiently replied.

"If I do not fight them tomorrow, I cannot do it in six months."

"Better wait that time than hazard a battle now," said Burnside.

"Colonel," he said, "I shall depend upon your brigade whenever we meet the enemy."[44]

41 Tidball MS Rem (U.S.M.A.), 246.

42 Fry in *B&L*, 1, 183; Holcombe, *First Minnesota*, 42-43.

43 Robert Hunt Rhodes, ed., *All for the Union: the Civil War Diary and Letters of Elisha Hunt Rhodes* (New York, 1985), 35, memorandum entitled "Historical Notes on 1st Bull Run," dated September 9, 1892, in the papers of Governor William Sprague (Rhodes, *All for the Union*); Aldrich, *A*, *First R.I.*, 18. These two incidents ("wait to fight" and "count on your brigade") are reported separately in Rhodes and Aldrich but logically probably occurred during the same conversation.

44 Aldrich, *A*, *First R.I.*, 18.

Perhaps Burnside was right. Certainly McDowell was right. To a smaller degree McDowell suffered from Patterson's problem. If he waited, the terms of his three-month militia would expire without sufficient trained volunteers to take their place. If reorganization did not actually require the six months estimated by McDowell, it would certainly take the rest of the summer. Already the terms of several regiments had expired. Burnside's First Rhode Island had reached the end of its service that very day, but volunteered to remain until no longer needed.[45] Some soldiers, however, were not as willing as the Rhode Islanders. Both the Fourth Pennsylvania Infantry and the battery of artillery attached to the Eighth New York were due to be released the next day. In spite of McDowell's request, both units refused to remain and passed to the rear the next day while the army marched to battle.[46]

McDowell knew that the Rebel railroad was active and that reinforcements were being brought forward. He had expected this. The general in chief had firmly stated on numerous occasions that Patterson would keep Johnston, the other major enemy force, in the Valley. McDowell assumed that this would be done and that the army he would meet would be Beauregard's with any troops that could be spared from Richmond and other places.[47]

He now had information from Barnard and the reconnaissance parties and would find it difficult, if not impossible, to learn more. He began to devise his plan of attack. The same tactics used on July 16 would be employed: the troops would march to assembly areas early in the evening, camp for the night, and march early the next day. The march to the battlefield would be as short as possible. Several officers opposed this. Burnside complained that two marches would tire his men, who had the farthest to go. Sherman, too, was against the two marches for reasons he did not state. Deferring to his subordinates, McDowell canceled the six o'clock evening march.[48]

The division and brigade commanders were ordered to assemble at army headquarters at eight o'clock that night. Not until ten o'clock were they called into the headquarters tent, a large tent lit by lanterns and candles, to be told the detailed plan developed during the day. Sherman arrived early and used the opportunity to

45 Poore, *Burnside*, 110, 122.

46 *OR*, 2, 745.

47 *OR*, 2, 308; *C.C.W.*, 2, 39 ff (McDowell).

48 Heintzelman MS Diary (large diary) (L.C.) entry dated July 20, 1861; *C.C.W.*, 1, 39 (McDowell); Mark DeWolfe Howe, ed., *Home Letters of General Sherman* (New York, 1909), 202, letter dated July 19, 1861 (Howe, *Sherman Home Letters*). In his "Home Letters" he would state that "night marches with raw troops are always dangerous."

write a letter to his wife while he waited.[49] As the officers arrived, they talked among themselves and with the numerous civilians, politicians, and regimental commanders also around headquarters at the time. McDowell's staff officers, Major John G. Barnard, his chief engineer; Captain Amiel W. Whipple, an engineer; Major Albert J. Meyer, his signal officer; and Major William F. Barry, his chief of artillery, attended. The staff officers of the division and brigade commanders and the regimental commanders waited outside. Willis A. Gorman, colonel of the First Minnesota, was certain that Johnston had arrived. Opposed to any attack until the ground could be thoroughly examined by reconnaissance, Gorman believed the army should retire to Centerville, entrench, and await reinforcements. He and others believed the Union army was not large enough. But his opinion mattered little. In fact, McDowell held councils of war in low regard and intended to solicit no opinions. He would explain his plans. The meeting was not to be a council of war. It was a briefing.[50]

Both McDowell and Scott had opposed the campaign, but they had been overruled by their political superiors in the capital if not ultimately by the mindless press led by Horace Greeley. Whatever the merits or faults of opening the war with this movement, McDowell could not shy from battle now. Too many factors outside the purely military sphere dictated the events transpiring in northeastern Virginia and the Shenandoah Valley.

Tyler, still self-confident despite his fiasco two days before, asked McDowell, "General, what force do we have to fight tomorrow?"

"You know as well as I do."

"General, we have got the whole of Joe Johnston's army in our front, and we must fight the two armies."

He began to speak about the trains he had heard all afternoon and the night before. McDowell was already well aware of them, ignored his outburst, and began to describe his plans.

Pitched at the foot of a long slope east of Centerville, McDowell's headquarters tent had no flooring. His maps were spread on the dirt and were viewed by the

49 Gilder Lehrman MSS, M.L., Averell MS diary, vol. 1, entry dated July 20, 1861; Robert Garth Scott, ed., *Forgotten Valor: The Memoirs, Journals, & Civil War Letters of Orlando B. Willcox* (Kent and London, 1999), 289 (Scott, *Willcox Memoirs, etc.*); *Lewis*, 1, 172.

50 Heintzelman MSS (L.C.) letters dated Aug. 15, 1861, from Wilkinson and Aldrich to Heintzelman and Aug. 23, 1861, from Heintzelman to Aldrich and Aug. 13 or Sept. 13, 1861, from Heintzelman to Aldrich. The last letter, its date unclear, was probably not written as early as Aug. 13 because of the wound on his writing arm. His diary entries did not resume until much later; MS Diary (large diary) (L.C.) entry dated Sept. 1, 1861; Averell, *Ten Years*, 293.

flickering light of the lanterns and candles as he explained in detail the events to take place the following morning.[51]

The Rebels were obviously prepared to defend the Stone Bridge, one of the most important means of access to their position. If this position could be turned and the defenders of the bridge cleared by a flanking column, the army could cross to drive the Confederates from Manassas Junction.[52]

From its camps around Centerville, Tyler's division, which would consist of the three brigades under Schenck, Sherman, and Keyes, would march at 2:00 a.m.; proceed west on the pike to the Stone Bridge; and demonstrate to hold the Rebels at the bridge. McDowell believed they had mined the bridge to destroy it if necessary. For this eventuality a trestle bridge would be ready and would be installed by the engineers at the earliest possible moment in order to facilitate the crossing of artillery and troops after the defenders had been driven away.

Hunter, who was camped on the pike behind Centerville, would set out at the same time and follow Tyler. Just beyond Cub Run he would turn north on the road that ran parallel to Bull Run to the Sudley Springs Ford, where he could cross easily. Once over, he would turn south and strike the exposed flank of any defenders along the Run.

Heintzelman's division, camped on the Sudley Springs Road leading south from Centerville to the Old Braddock Road and Sangster's Station, would start half an hour behind Hunter. He would pass through Miles and Centerville and follow Hunter. Once up the road to Sudley's, he would turn left to the ford between Sudley's and the Stone Bridge. If Hunter's crossing were contested, Heintzelman's crossing below him would outflank the defenders and force them to withdraw. Deployed perpendicular to the Run and moving south parallel to it on the Confederate bank, the two divisions would uncover the Stone Bridge for Tyler and his division. By slipping to their right, Hunter and Heintzelman would make room on the line for Tyler, a third division, and present a broad front to the Rebels, a front that would far outflank their creek-line defenses.

Miles's division, augmented by Richardson's brigade from Tyler, would stand in reserve around Centerville. Demonstrations might be made with artillery around Blackburn's Ford; but sensitized by Tyler's indiscretion there, McDowell explicitly ordered that any action to be taken there be limited. McDowell assumed from the

51 Averell, *Ten Years*, 293, says the maps were spread on a long table, but he was outside the tent; Poore, *Burnside*, 10, said McDowell arrived late, 10:00 p.m. and distributed the orders to his officers without comment or explanation.

52 For the plan, see *OR*, 2, 317. For the part played by the engineers, see Barnard, *OR*, 2, 330 ff, and *C.C.W.*, 1, 39 ff (McDowell).

repulse at Blackburn's Ford on July 18 that the main enemy force would be concentrated there. Using the many fords below Blackburn's the Confederates could cross, turn north, and strike the rear of the army while the turning column was on the march.[53] Miles's reinforced division would be at Centerville to prevent this.

Excellent in its conception, the plan would achieve unopposed stream crossings by the ever increasing strength of the turning column, it would continuously add fresh troops to the battle line as it closed with the enemy. Heintzelman would march half as far as Hunter and Tyler the short distance to the Stone Bridge and across.

The demonstration at Stone Bridge was not wise.[54] A major demonstration of troops and artillery there would shift Confederate attention from Blackburn's Ford toward the turning column and perhaps bring enough reinforcements to resist Hunter and Heintzelman while preventing Tyler from crossing Bull Run. If the feint or a pinning attack had been assigned to Miles's division at Blackburn's Ford, Rebel attention might have remained fixed on the federal left wing while the right wing crossed with irresistible strength. The worst effect of the repulse at Blackburn's Ford was not its impact on the morale of the troops, but on McDowell's decision to stay as far away from it as he could.

A second problem was inherent in any offensive McDowell could design. He had to cross a defended stream with one wing while the other remained behind. This divided his army while the Rebels remained unified on one bank. Also, the Army of Northeastern Virginia would have exterior lines forming an obtuse angle which would require too much time for one wing to reinforce the other. The corollary was also true. The Confederates would have a central position with short, interior lines.

The meeting ended around eleven o'clock,[55] and the officers left headquarters for their bivouac areas. McDowell's background was not unknown to the older officers in attendance. Hunter and others were conscious of his lack of experience as a line officer, his career in staff positions, and the ugly rumors that followed Buena Vista. In their view Secretary Chase and the other politicians could legislate his rank but they could not legislate confidence in him.[56]

53 This was, in fact, the Confederate battle plan for July 21, but its execution was so poor that the Union troops defined the events of the day by their column on the other flank. Freeman, *Lee's Lieutenants*, 1, 48-49.

54 Confederate troops were massing at Blackburn's Ford for their own attack. When General McDowell attacked from his right flank on July 21, Beauregard was trying to do the same thing from his right flank at Blackburn's Ford. Freeman, *Lee's Lieutenants*, 1, 48-49, 55.

55 Heintzelman MS Diary (large diary) (L.C.) entry dated Sept. 1, 1861.

56 Halpine MSS (H.L.), "Rough Notes from an old Soldier: How the Battle of Bull Run was lost in One Short Lesson" in the handwriting of Hunter and arbitrarily dated August 1, 1861, by the curator.

At some point Dick Richardson said to Tyler, "It is impossible, General, to move an army of Regular troops under two hours; and you will take at least that time to move volunteers. And if reveille is not beaten before two o'clock in the morning, you cannot get into action at daylight. If you beat reveille at twelve with volunteer troops, you may get into action at daylight but not before. That is the best you can do."[57]

The night was cool and beautiful. The moon shone full casting long shadows through the still air. As the officers left McDowell's tent to brief their subordinates, the only sounds were the occasional shouts of a soldier in the distance and the intermittent lowing of cattle.[58]

McDowell retired to sleep away the uncomfortable feeling of a badly upset stomach.[59] What thoughts crossed his mind as he attempted to sleep? He must have hoped that neither the stomach nor a late start would plague him the next day. Despite the somewhat humble circumstances of his family, he had been raised in the tradition of the patrician. He had been taught not to complain about circumstances or events, and finger-pointing "I told you so" would never have entered his mind. The truth was, however, that he was about to fight a battle that would have been unnecessary if his advice had been followed in May. When the crossing to Alexandria had occurred on May 24, less than two months earlier, he and others had urged on Scott an immediate march to Manassas Junction, then held by a tiny force of Rebels, and a continuing advance to the line of the Rappahannock. This would have been an unopposed tactical maneuver with strategic advantages. But Scott's unfortunate sensitivity for his native state of Virginia and his short-sighted hope that hostilities could be avoided, had limited the objectives to Arlington and Alexandria on the Potomac River.

Now, McDowell was most of the way to the Junction, was facing a line of defense behind a water barrier, was confronted by an alert and growing enemy, had suffered first blood at Blackburn's Ford, and was compelled to take the offensive with an inexperienced army officered at virtually all levels by inexperienced men. In one way or another superior and subordinate officers had imposed these adverse conditions on him against his advice or his orders. A march to a defensive position was one thing. An offensive march was another altogether. Consistent with his

57 *C.C.W.*, 2, 24 (Richardson).

58 *C.C.W.*, 2, 42 (McDowell); J. Cutler Andrews, *The North Reports The War* (Philadelphia, 1955), 87-88 (Andrews, *North Reports*); Jackson in *Broadfoot MOLLUS Wisconsin*, 49, 241-242.

59 *C.C.W.*, 2, 42 (McDowell).

upbringing, he did not complain. He prepared himself for a turning point in his career.

While McDowell tried to sleep, the last of his officers, a shiny new second lieutenant from the Military Academy was on the road from Washington to Centerville. After graduating last in his class on July 18, 1861, and finishing a nasty little court-martial for the kind of boyish conduct that would characterize him for life, he set out to report for duty at Washington, D.C., the home of the Second United States Cavalry, his first unit. Early Saturday morning, July 20, he arrived at the nation's capital, made his way to the Ebbit House to see if any of his classmates were registered there, and found the name of his old roommate and tent-mate, James P. Parker, a Southern sympathizer who had stayed to graduate. Rather than send up his card, the lieutenant went straight to Parker's room where he found his comrade still in bed.

Parker told him that McDowell's army was confronting Beauregard's and that a general engagement was expected hourly. Parker's future plans? He directed the lieutenant to a document lying on the table. It was an order from the War Department dismissing Parker from the service for tendering his resignation in the face of the enemy. The two young subalterns talked for an hour. Finally, the lieutenant bid his friend a fond and reluctant farewell. They had struggled with the same academic problems, eaten day-by-day at the same table, marched side-by-side year after year, and shared blankets in camp. Parker was headed to Richmond to take a commission in the Confederate army. The lieutenant was on his way to the adjutant-general's office to report for duty in the United States Army.

Not until two o'clock was he able to report formally to the adjutant-general. Messengers with huge envelopes scampered from room to room bewildering the lieutenant with the air of important military events. He presented his orders to an officer who seemed to be in charge. A quick glance at them, and the officer said perhaps he would like to be presented to General Scott.

The lieutenant had often seen the towering form at the Military Academy during summer visits; but the gulf between officers, especially such august officers, and cadets was far wider even than that between officers and enlisted men. Personal conversation with anyone above the rank of lieutenant or captain simply did not occur. He was overjoyed with the opportunity. To young graduates of West Point, including this one, Winfield Scott was an idol barely second to Napoleon in the military art and to Wellington in patriotism.

He followed the officer to the room in which the old general in chief received official visitors. Scott, seated at a table covered with maps and other documents, was with several senators and representatives. The officer introduced him as a lieutenant of the Second Cavalry.

"He has just reported from West Point, and I did not know but that you might have some special orders to give him."

The general looked at the lieutenant a moment, shook his hand cordially, and said, "Well, my young friend, I am glad to welcome you to the service at this critical time. Our country has need of the strong arms of all her loyal sons in this emergency." He turned to the adjutant general and asked the lieutenant's assignment.

"To Company G, Second Cavalry, now under Major Innis Palmer with General McDowell."

Scott turned back to the young officer.

"We have had the assistance of quite a number of you young men from the Academy, drilling volunteers and so on. Now, what can I do for you? Would you prefer to be ordered to General Mansfield to aid in this work, or is your desire for something more active?"

This was not a choice. Train volunteers? Reject a chance for battle, leadership, promotion, glory? As a brand new second lieutenant he had all this ahead of him; and he at any rank craved it all. Awestruck by the great presence he stammered that he earnestly desired to join his company with General McDowell at once because he was anxious for active service.

"A very commendable resolution, young man." The lieutenant would have orders directing him to proceed to his company at once. Scott asked if he had been able to obtain a mount for the field.

Not yet, he responded, but he would set about it at once.

"I fear you have a difficult task before you because, if rumor is correct, every serviceable horse in the City has been bought, borrowed, or begged by citizens who have gone or are going as spectators to witness the battle. I only hope Beauregard may capture some of them and teach them a lesson. However, what I desire to say to you is go and provide yourself with a horse if possible and call here at seven o'clock this evening. I desire to send some dispatches to General McDowell and you can be the bearer of them. You are not afraid of a night ride, are you?"

In fact, he was delighted at the prospect of being immediately on active service and perhaps participating in a great battle. Best of all, a fledgling in the service, he was to bear important dispatches from the general in chief to the general commanding the most important army in the field.

But first he had to obtain a horse. Every place he went he received the same answer—he was too late. As he paced about the capital, he met on Pennsylvania Avenue a man in uniform who had been one of the enlisted men called from West Point to Washington at the time of the inauguration. The lieutenant asked him about his duties. He was serving with Captain Charles Griffin's battery which was with

McDowell's army. Griffin had ordered him back to Washington to retrieve a horse the battery had left behind. The horse problem was solved.

This was "old home week" for the lieutenant. The horse he recognized as "Wellington," a mount he had ridden many times as a cadet during cavalry exercises. The lieutenant and his benefactor took the horse and crossed Long Bridge at nightfall. They spoke occasionally, the enlisted man doing most of the talking. The description of the brief encounter at Blackburn's Ford fascinated the lieutenant.

Between two and three o'clock in the morning, they reached the army at Centerville. The men had already arisen and had their breakfast. They were formed in columns in the roads, but most were lying on the ground napping, smoking, and chatting. Others sat or stood in small groups. Knowing the location of army headquarters, his enlisted man took him to a group of tents with a large log fire throwing a bright light. As the lieutenant rode toward the tents, a white-haired officer emerged from one of them and asked whom he wished to see. He replied that he had dispatches for General McDowell from General Scott.

"I will relieve you of them."

The lieutenant hesitated. He had already met the general in chief and was anxious to meet the officer in command of the largest army in his country's history.

"I am Major Wadsworth of General McDowell's staff."

Reluctantly, the lieutenant put the documents in Wadsworth's hand. Through the flaps of a tent a few paces away, he could see Wadsworth give them to a large, portly officer, whom he rightly surmised to be McDowell.

Wadsworth returned and asked for the latest news from the capital. The lieutenant replied that everyone was waiting for news from the army.

"Well, I guess they will not have to wait much longer. The entire army is under arms and moving to attack the enemy today."

Sipping hot coffee with his classmate, Lieutenant H. W. Kingsbury, another aide to McDowell, Lieutenant George Armstrong Custer philosophized privately about his situation. Three days earlier he had been on the plains of the United States Military Academy at West Point high above the mighty Hudson. Now, with long flowing hair, a hat and plume like that of the great Napoleonic cavalry leader Joachin Murat, and a royal purple silk and velvet jacket with gold trimming, attire that would deteriorate in the next year, he was about to participate in the first major battle of the American Civil War.[60]

60 Frederick, Whittaker, *A Complete Life of Gen. George A. Custer, Major-General of Volunteers, Brevet Major-General, U.S. Army, and Lieutenant-Colonel, Seventh U.S. Cavalry* (New York, 1876), 49-57 (Whittaker, *Custer*); Bvt Brig-Gen'l Thomas S. Allen, "The Second Wisconsin at the First Battle of Bull Run," in *Broadfoot MOLLUS Wisconsin*, 4, 382.

After seeing the puffs of smoke from testy Confederate pickets along Bull Run, Lieutenant James E. Smith returned from the picket line to the headquarters tent of his unit, Varian's battery of New York Light Artillery. Because its period of enlistment had expired on July 17, a vote to stay or leave had been taken during Smith's absence.

Smith was expected to cast his vote. He asked if it would change the result.

It would not.

Smith said he would not vote.

"And I, sir," said Captain Varian sharply, "order you to vote."

Smith had great respect and affection for Varian, but he held his view about service strongly.

"Very well, then I wish it to be distinctly understood that I vote to remain."

Smith's vote was "ungraciously received and the chilly atmosphere of the tent became decidedly unpleasant," he recalled after the war.

About 10:00 p.m. Lieutenant Price, McDowell's ordnance officer arrived and called for Captain Varian. He delivered an order for Varian to surrender the battery equipment and take his men to the rear.

Smith had been attempting to obtain a position on Keyes's staff. Having heard about Smith's vote to remain, Keyes had tried to reward Smith by arranging for him to command the battery. Smith was stunned. He was not certain he had enough experience to perform the duties of battery commander in the battle next day. He knew nothing about Keyes's role in this and was uncertain about the effect his acceptance would have on a staff position with Keyes. He also felt his acceptance would compromise Varian and he would not do this to a man he greatly respected.

Seeing Smith's embarrassment, Varian suggested that he consider it for half an hour. A number of men gathered and suggested that they would stay if Smith would take the command. Flattered, Smith finally said he must refuse the battery.

At 1:00 a.m. on July 21, the men started to the rear. When the role for muster-out had been prepared and signed, Smith became the unlucky man to deliver it to McDowell. A very cool reception preceded McDowell's review of the documents. In the rude and abrupt manner for which he would become well known, McDowell dismissed the hapless lieutenant.

"Your discharge will be attended to, sir!"

McDowell ended the discussion by turning his back.[61]

61 James Smith, *A Famous Battery and its Campaigns, 1861-1864* (Washington, 1892), 19-22; *Official Army Register*, 2, 751. The chronology of these events is unclear from the narrative, e.g., the discussion with McDowell could have occurred earlier; but all things taken into account, the order in the text seems most logical.

Chapter 18

"Victory! Victory! The day is ours."

— McDowell to his troops as they advanced up Henry House Hill

A Hot Sunday Afternoon

A cool breeze brushed Centerville as the moon sank in the west.[1] By the time the new West Point lieutenant sat to contemplate the beginning of his new life, the artillerymen of Varian's battery started their march to the rear; and the columns had begun their approach marches on the Warrenton Pike.[2]

Carlisle's battery of artillery had been ready to march since 2:00 a.m.; but Tyler, no more adept than he had been at Blackburn's Ford on July 18, was

1 Woodbury, *First Rhode Island*, 87.

2 Bull Run has attracted writers for reasons different than other American Civil War battles. John G. Barnard, *The C.S.A. and the Battle of Bull Run: A Letter to an English Friend* (New York, 1862); Russel H. Beatie, Jr., *Road to Manassas: The Growth of Union Command in the Eastern Theatre from the Fall of Fort Sumter to the First Battle of Bull Run* (New York, 1961); William C. Davis, *Battle at Bull Run: A History of the First Major Campaign of the Civil War* (Garden City, 1977); Charles E. Heller and William A. Stafft, eds., *America's First Battles 1776-1965*; esp. W. Glenn Robertson, "First Bull Run 19 July 1861," Chap. 4, 81-108 (Lawrence, 1986); John Hennessy, *The First Battle of Manassas: An End to Innocence, July 18-21, 1861* (Lynchburg, 1989); James B. Fry, *McDowell and Tyler in the Campaign of Bull Run* (New York, 1884); R. M. Johnston, *Bull Run: Its Strategy and Tactics* (Boston and New York, 1913); Robert Patterson, *A Narrative of the Campaign in the Valley of the Shenandoah in 1861* (Philadelphia, 1865). Having stood the test of time for almost a century, Johnston remains the best all around work by far.

validating the prophesy of the night before. His troops were difficult to organize. He had not roused them early enough to put them on the road at the appointed hour. Half an hour or more late, his brigades began the short march to the Stone Bridge,[3] Schenck's brigade in the lead, followed by Carlisle's battery of Regulars, Lieutenant Haines's massive 30-pounder gun, then Sherman and Keyes in the rear.[4] His column advanced slowly, constantly patrolling and probing with skirmishers. Once again, lack of cavalry closed the eyes of the army to everything beyond the sight of the leading units; and the resulting fear of ambush aggravated the slowness of the advance.[5]

Cub Run came in sight. The ford had been obstructed with trees by the Southerners, and the rickety little bridge did not look strong enough to bear the immense weight of the 30-pounder. With trepidation the officers watched the huge gun roll slowly onto the planking. It stuck. The men struggled to clear it. For a while it looked as if the bridge would collapse, but at last after mighty efforts the wheels rolled to the road beyond.

The march was quietly resumed. In the meantime, realizing that the pike must be cleared for the turning column, Tyler ordered Keyes's brigade, the rear unit, off the road and rode back to see that his order was carried out.[6]

When Sherman and Keyes reached the vicinity of the Stone Bridge, they halted behind a ridgeline. Schenck deployed to the left of the Pike, and Sherman strung his regiments to the right. Then they advanced to the crest of the ridge, from which Bull Run was clearly visible.[7] Carlisle brought his battery into position between the two brigades where he had a clear field of fire across open ground and across the stream.[8] By half-past six the division was in position with its artillery almost in place. In the

3 The accounts disagree about the time Tyler started. Carlisle says, *OR*, 2, 362, that the march began at 3:00; Burnham of Keyes Brigade says 2:00 a.m., Adj't Gen'ls Rpt Conn 12; Tyler in his report, *OR*, 2, 349, and his testimony, *C.C.W.*, 1, 200, 2:30; and his time is corroborated by both Schenck, *OR*, 2, 357, and Sherman, *OR*, 2, 368. In his post-war MS Memoirs, Tidball blamed Tyler for both a late start and a slow advance. Tidball MS mem (U.S.M.A.) 249. Apparently, Tyler managed to move his volunteers on time, but the crucial time was the hour he cleared the junction of the Warrenton Turnpike and the Sudley Springs Road for the flanking column. In this, he failed. His rear brigade was at least one hour and probably two late clearing the turn and delayed the flanking column by that much. Thus, he was probably not guilty of the charge levied against him by most historians (late start), but it did not matter. He was guilty of a culpably slow advance.

4 *OR*, 2, 357.

5 *C.C.W.*, 2, 201 (Tyler).

6 *C.C.W.*, 2, 202-203 (Tyler) and corroborated by McDowell, *id.*, 43.

7 *OR*, 2, 357-358, 360.

8 *OR*, 2, 362, 364.

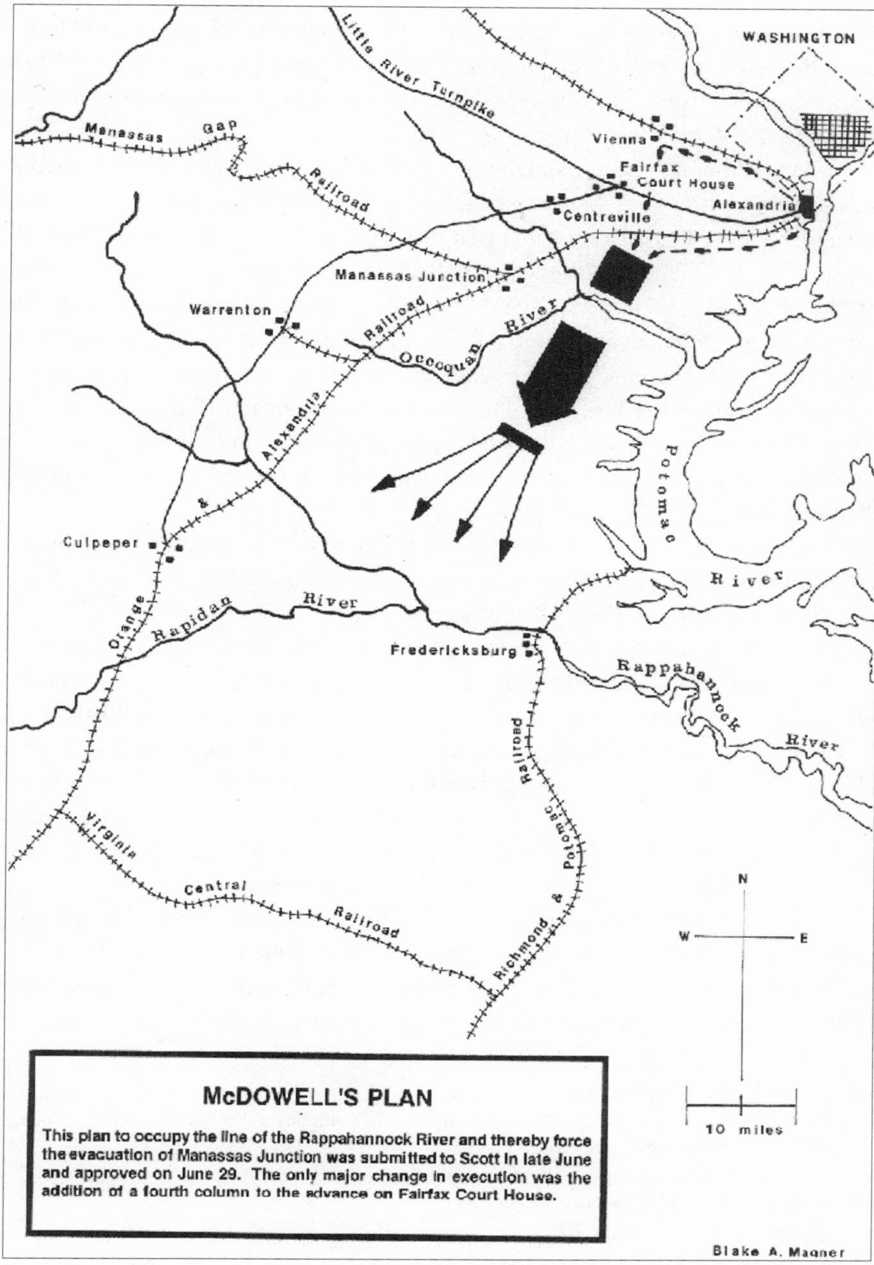

McDOWELL'S PLAN

This plan to occupy the line of the Rappahannock River and thereby force the evacuation of Manassas Junction was submitted to Scott in late June and approved on June 29. The only major change in execution was the addition of a fourth column to the advance on Fairfax Court House.

Pike behind the infantry, Lieutenant Thomas Jefferson Haines was ordered to fire the signal with his Parrott gun to notify McDowell that Tyler was ready.[9] Three tremendous booms told the army that its leading division stood in position to begin the battle.[10]

Major William F. Barry, McDowell's staff officer in charge of artillery, arrived at Haines's position about half-past eight while Hunter and Heintzelman toiled north toward Sudley's Ford. Barry suggested that Carlisle fire on the abatis across the bridge. In a short while shells began to fall about the obstruction and the brush huts of the defenders with good effect, but no enemy batteries were seen. The Confederates offered no return fire. One section of two guns was sent to the Run to cover the site for the trestle bridge while the remainder maintained a more or less continuous fire on the far bank. The two guns close to the Run received heavy counter battery fire as soon as they opened. Fighting hard to keep their position in front of Schenck's brigade, the gun crews expended their entire ammunition supply, then withdrew.[11]

On Tyler's right, Sherman spent the early hours quietly waiting. One of his men pointed to a flag flying in the trees across the stream and called out to him.

"Colonel, there's a flag, a flag of truce."

"No, it is no flag of truce," one of the men answered, "but a flag of defiance!"

The colonel paid little attention. He had other things on his mind. About half an hour after the artillery opened fire, he rode over to his pickets near Bull Run. From that point Sherman could see two mounted Confederates, one of whom was an officer. They descended the ridge toward the stream, rode their horses across it, and came up the east bank. The officer waved his pistol and shouted, "You damned black abolitionists, come on!" along with several other uncomplimentary vituperations. Union pickets fired at them but only sent them back to their own side.[12]

Tyler's slow movement on the pike and the consequent delay of the flanking column upset McDowell. He still felt the ill effects of the bad watermelon he had eaten, and the tension caused by Tyler's dilatory march increased his discomfort.[13] Hunter had been ready to march since 2:00 a.m. and Heintzelman, who was to follow

9 Wilson says, *OR*, 2, 362, that Tyler opened fire at 5:00 a.m.; Johnston accepts this. In his report, Tyler says 6:30 a.m., *OR*, 2, 349; and in his testimony 6:15 a.m., *C.C.W.*, 2, 200. McDowell confirms 6:30 a.m., in *OR*, 2, 318.

10 Van L. Naisawald, "Bull Run, The Artillery and the Infantry," *Civil War History*, vol. III, no. 2, June, 1957, 164 (Naisawald, *Bull Run*).

11 *OR*, 2, 362-364; Naisawald, *Bull Run*, 164.

12 *OR*, 2, 368; Howe, *Sherman Home Letters*, 206, letter dated July 28, 1861; Todd, *Seventy-Ninth Highlanders*, 33.

13 Henry E. Clement, *The Bull Run Rout* (Cambridge, 1969), 13.

Hunter, since 2:30 p.m.; but when they reached Centerville the road was choked with Tyler's regiments, which seemed to be making no progress.[14] Not until 5:30 a.m. was the junction of the Pike and the road to Sudley's cleared by the last of Tyler's men. At last, Burnside could lead the flanking column north.[15] As the Second Rhode Island turned right, McDowell watched from the blacksmith shop at the intersection. The sight pleased him. He saw power in the men and strength in the officers leading them. A little toughening of the legs, a little discipline, and a little privation would make them all good soldiers.[16]

By the time Hunter passed with Heintzelman following, Tyler had been firing for some time but had received no return fire. McDowell could hear this plainly, and it worried him. Fearing the Confederates might be preparing to assault from Blackburn's Ford while his flank march hung in the balance,[17] McDowell decided to detain Howard's brigade, the rear unit of Heintzelman's division, at the crossroads to reinforce Miles on the left if necessary.[18] The task complete, McDowell allowed the pride he felt for his army to overflow and break the silence as the soldiers filed past.

"Gentlemen," he said, "that is a big force."[19]

McDowell mounted his horse and turned its head in the direction of Sudley's Ford.[20] The route to Sudley's was little more than a dirt track, with deep ruts and rocks littering its route. Trees had been felled across it by the Confederates. The Second Rhode Island dealt with the trees while the artillery struggled over the "road."[21]

Progress was slow and was worsened by the intense heat. Already the sun promised a scorching July Sunday. Although the route was covered by trees most of the way and was somewhat shaded, the trees also kept out the breeze.[22] With the permission of Secretary of War Cameron, numerous civilians in carriages

14 *OR*, 2, 383, 402; *C.C.W.*, 2, 30 (Heintzelman).

15 *OR*, 2, 334, 383, 416.

16 Fry in *B&L*, 1, 187; Small, *Road to Richmond*, 20; Woodbury, *Second Rhode Island*, 31.

17 In fact, he was right. Beauregard had convinced Johnston to attack across the three southern fords (McLean's, Blackburn's, and Mitchell's) at daybreak on July 21 before Patterson could join McDowell. Freeman, *Lee's Lieutenants*, 1, 45-60.

18 *OR*, 2, 319, 418; Howard, *Autobiography*, 1, 153.

19 *OR*, 2, 368; Howe, *Sherman Home Letters*, 206, Sherman letter dated July 28, 1861; Todd, *Seventy-Ninth Highlanders*, 33.

20 Fry in *B&L*, 1, 187.

21 *OR*, 2, 334; Woodbury, *Second Rhode Island*, 31.

22 Dangerfield Parker, "Personal Reminiscences: The Battalion of Regular Infantry at the First Battle of Bull Run," *Broadfoot MOLLUS District of Columbia*, 43, 210.

accompanied the column; but their joy ride impeded the troops.[23] Senator Henry Wilson sat by the roadside in his carriage while his attendant passed out sandwiches.[24] The farms in this area, like those on the advance from Arlington and Alexandria, were poor and ramshackle. Most of the able-bodied men were gone. As the brigades passed one old log hovel, an unkempt woman hollered that enough Confederates were ahead to whip them all and her "old man" was among them so they had better watch out.[25]

On the Sudley Road, McDowell's plan was again disrupted. First, the route to the ford forked. Mathias C. Mitchell, Hunter's guide,[26] knew that both routes reached Sudley's. The left road, he said would be close to the Run, would disclose the movement to the Confederates, and would expose the column to artillery fire.[27] Hunter took the safer, more cautious—and longer—route to the right. No longer did the march parallel the stream. To the right the route was twelve rather than six miles. Delayed by Tyler and extended by the route, the column would arrive at the ford late and would give the Confederates time to respond to the federal movement. They could mount an offensive of their own across Blackburn's Ford while the Union army was extended over the countryside. Worse yet, they had apparently deciphered the plan and were taking steps to oppose the turning column because dust clouds on the far side of the Run could be seen moving to meet it.

Second, because Heintzelman's guide failed to find any route to the ford between the Stone Bridge and Sudley's Ford, Heintzelman simply followed Hunter all the way to Sudley's Ford,[28] thus removing the center of the three attacking prongs. Hunter might be forced to fight his way from Sudley's to the Stone Bridge to clear a crossing for Tyler. Having started from a bivouac east of Centerville, Heintzelman would now have the longest march of all McDowell's divisions; and his troops would not be as fresh as planned. His men would move at the double quick to catch Hunter once they had crossed to the west side of Bull Run. These circumstances would have taxed veterans. Green troops pushed to such physical

23 Blake, *Three Years in the Army*, 14; Woodbury, *Second Rhode Island*, 31; Albert G. Riddle, *Recollections of War Times* (New York, 1895), 45 (Riddle, *Recollections*).

24 Bennett, Edwin, *Musket and Sword or the Camp, March, and Firing Line in the Army of the Potomac* (Boston, 1900), 16 (Bennett, *Musket and Sword*).

25 Haynes, *Second New Hampshire*, 23-24.

26 Carter, *Four Brothers in Blue*, 22.

27 *C.C.W.*, 2, 161 (Barnard).

28 Howard, in his *Autobiography*, 1, 153, claims McDowell ordered Heintzelman to march all the way to Sudley's Ford; but in his report, *OR*, 2, 402, Heintzelman said he went to the Ford because the guide could not find the road to the intermediate ford, a fact he confirmed in his testimony, *C.C.W.*, 2, 30.

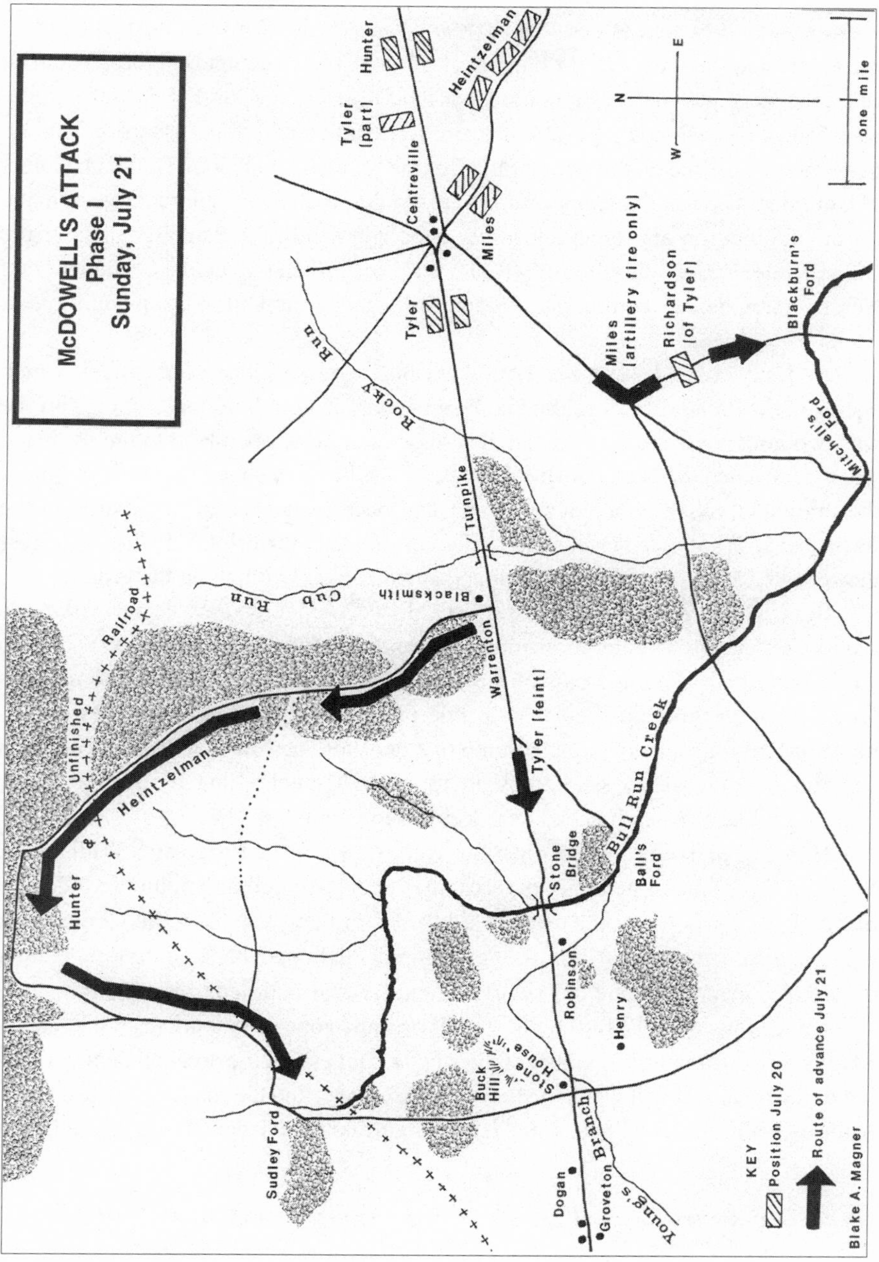
McDOWELL'S ATTACK
Phase I
Sunday, July 21
Hunter
Tyler
(part)
Heintzelman
Centreville
Tyler
Miles
Rocky Run
Miles
(artillery fire only)
Richardson
(of Tyler)
Blackburn's Ford
Mitchell's Ford
Turnpike
Warrenton
Blacksmith
Cub Run
Unfinished
Railroad
Heintzelman
Hunter
Tyler (feint)
Bull Run Creek
Stone Bridge
Ball's Ford
Robinson
Henry
Stone House
Buck Hill
Sudley Ford
Dogan
Groveton
Young's Branch
N
W
E
one mile
KEY
Position July 20
Route of advance July 21
Blake A. Magner

exertion would be less effective in battle.[29] Perhaps the Confederates, if they had extra time and no threat to their flank from Heintzelman's center crossing, would be able to stop Hunter before he could clear the Stone Bridge for Tyler. McDowell's plan had been designed around his desire to avoid frontal attacks until he had an overwhelming force on the flank of the Confederate position along Bull Run Creek. The elimination of Heintzelman's crossing would, in effect, require Hunter to make a frontal attack on any blocking force without the aid of a flanking force. If the Confederates could hold Bull Run, they could mass against Hunter and Heintzelman, defeat them in detail, then turn against the Union troops on the east bank.

At last, Burnside and his Rhode Islanders broke clear of the trees which enclosed the road north from the blacksmith shop. Through no fault on his part, he was two hours or more late. Ahead, he crossed a mile of open land to the ford; and when he reached the banks of Bull Run Creek, he halted his men to rest them before the imminent action. Once again, water had been exhausted on the march in the intense heat. He allowed his men to refill their canteens and drink.[30] In the shade near the springs, he and Hunter sat to rest and spread an early lunch on the ground.

But Captain William W. Averell, an aide to Colonel Andrew Porter, arrived to report Confederate counter movements. He and others had seen a low dust cloud to the left and rear. Taking a pair of binoculars, Averell had climbed to the top of a fence. About a mile away on the far side of Bull Run, he saw mounted officers, glistening bayonets, and a long column of troops among low wooded hills across a cultivated valley. They were moving to block Hunter's line of march. Porter immediately sent Averell ahead to report this to Hunter.

Hunter received the information calmly. He asked Captain William D. Whipple, his adjutant general, to verify the report. Averell and Whipple rode to a place clear of woods on the crest of a hill. From there they saw the Confederate column advancing with flags flying. Whipple galloped back to report, Hunter ordered his men to resume their march,[31] and Averell returned to Porter.

On the far side of Bull Run, the woods extended one mile south from the Sudley Springs Ford. Captain Woodbury suggested to Hunter that the division deploy to the left of the road, where it would be between the colonel and the road and close enough to the crossings to coordinate with Heintzelman and later Tyler. Hunter agreed, then

29 Late in the war, after many lessons had been learned, tired troops would not be given pivotal roles or positions in battle.

30 *OR*, 2, 319, 395, 413; *C.C.W.*, 2, 161 (Barnard); Woodbury, *Second Rhode Island*, 31; and Barnard, *C.S.A. and Bull Run*, 51.

31 Averell, *Ten Years*, 295.

went forward to direct the formation of the skirmish line. While the rest of the column waited, Hunter led Burnside's artillery battery and Burnside's leading regiment, the Second Rhode Island, south toward the Stone Bridge.

"We expect a great deal of Rhode Island troops today," he called.

"You shall not be disappointed, sir," replied Colonel John S. Slocum, the regimental commander. Turning to his men Slocum shouted, "Now show them what Rhode Island can do."[32]

The fighting began when, at 9:45,[33] the leading units of Hunter's division emerged from the trees. The country ahead was rolling fields open to the Warrenton Pike. Near the intersection of the Pike and the Sudley Springs Road, Young's Branch, a small tributary to Bull Run, wandered along beside the Pike and crossed it. A battery of Rebel artillery was posted near a stone house at the crossroads with infantry in the trees around it.[34]

Averell rejoined the Second Rhode Island Infantry and Captain Whipple. The two captains suggested to Slocum that he send two companies forward and helped him deploy them.[35]

Riding rapidly up the road from the blacksmith shop to Sudley's, McDowell had seen through a break in the trees the clouds of dust on the far side of the run. The Confederates must be moving reinforcements to halt the Union turning column. The column must not be caught on both sides of the stream. The general reversed his orders to Howard, calling him forward from the blacksmith shop to strengthen the turning force. At Sudley Springs Ford, McDowell found Burnside with three remaining regiments of his brigade only half across, moving slowly, and stopping to drink.[36]

"The enemy is moving heavy columns from Manassas," said McDowell. He urged Burnside to hurry.

After he reached the front, he sent an aide to the rear to tell Heintzelman to send forward two regiments at once and to tell the regimental commanders to bring their regiments forward independently and as fast as possible. The aide was to continue, find Howard's brigade on the route north, and tell it to increase its pace to the

32 Rhodes, *All for the Union*, 40. The chronology of all events involved in the march of the flanking column is nowhere stated with precision, and has been arranged here, as usual, on the basis of logic and relationship.

33 Allen in *Broadfoot MOLLUS Wisconsin*, 46, 385.

34 Parker in *Broadfoot MOLLUS District of Columbia*, 43, 211, 213.

35 Averell, *Ten Years*, 296.

36 *OR*, 2, 319.

double-quick.[37] As he passed the Second New Hampshire, McDowell called for Colonel Gilman Marston, the regimental commander.

"Tell him to have his men ready," he said, "for we shall soon meet the enemy in large force."[38]

Farther to the front the Second Rhode Island and the Rhode Island battery had passed the Sudley Church. In great excitement, McDowell rode to Captain Reynolds.

"Forward your light battery!" he shouted.

The six guns, already moving at a trot, had more than enough speed to advance in a rapid but orderly way to the support of the infantry. At a gallop, they raced ahead of the infantry, in fact too far ahead, stopped, unlimbered, and opened fire at the puffs of smoke from a Confederate battery to the right front and at a good-sized clump of trees with a group of Rebels in front of it.[39]

John Slocum's Second Rhode Island, the first Union infantry on the field, had been led forward by Captain Whipple, Captain Averell, and its commanding officer. As they rode toward the Confederates, Averell saw a gap in the trees that would allow Porter and his brigade to leave the column and deploy. He halted his horse. Lighting a cigar, Slocum continued forward. To the left and south open fields with an occasional clump of trees sloped gently down for half a mile to the Warrenton Pike. Beyond the pike the ground rose to a wooded plateau, the Henry House Hill. The Confederates were already well deployed in force among the shrubs and fences along the pike.[40]

Slocum called out, "By the left flank—MARCH!" His men turned. Through infantry and artillery fire Slocum and his regiment crossed a rail fence into a field to the left of the road. For approximately forty minutes the battery and the Second Rhode Island regiment held the advanced position alone. Slocum then went closer to the brow of the hill than the regiment.

37 Oliver Otis Howard MSS (Bowdoin College) letter dated July 24, 1861, from Howard to his wife. McDowell does not mention these orders in his report in *OR* or his testimony in *C.C.W.*, but both are recited in accounts by recipients. The orders are presumed to have been carried by the same aide.

38 Haynes, *Second New Hampshire*, 24.

39 *OR*, 2, 395, 334; Woodbury, *Second Rhode Island*, 32; PNRI, series 1, 14 ff; Theodore Reichardt, *Diary of Battery A, First Regiment Rhode Island Light Artillery* (Providence, 1865), 12-13 (Reichardt, *Btry A, 1st R.I.*). The order of events is not clear. McDowell was coming from the rear of the column; and because the Second New Hampshire was to the rear of the artillery and the Second Rhode Island in the marching column, it would have been passed first by McDowell.

40 Averell, *Ten Years*, 296.

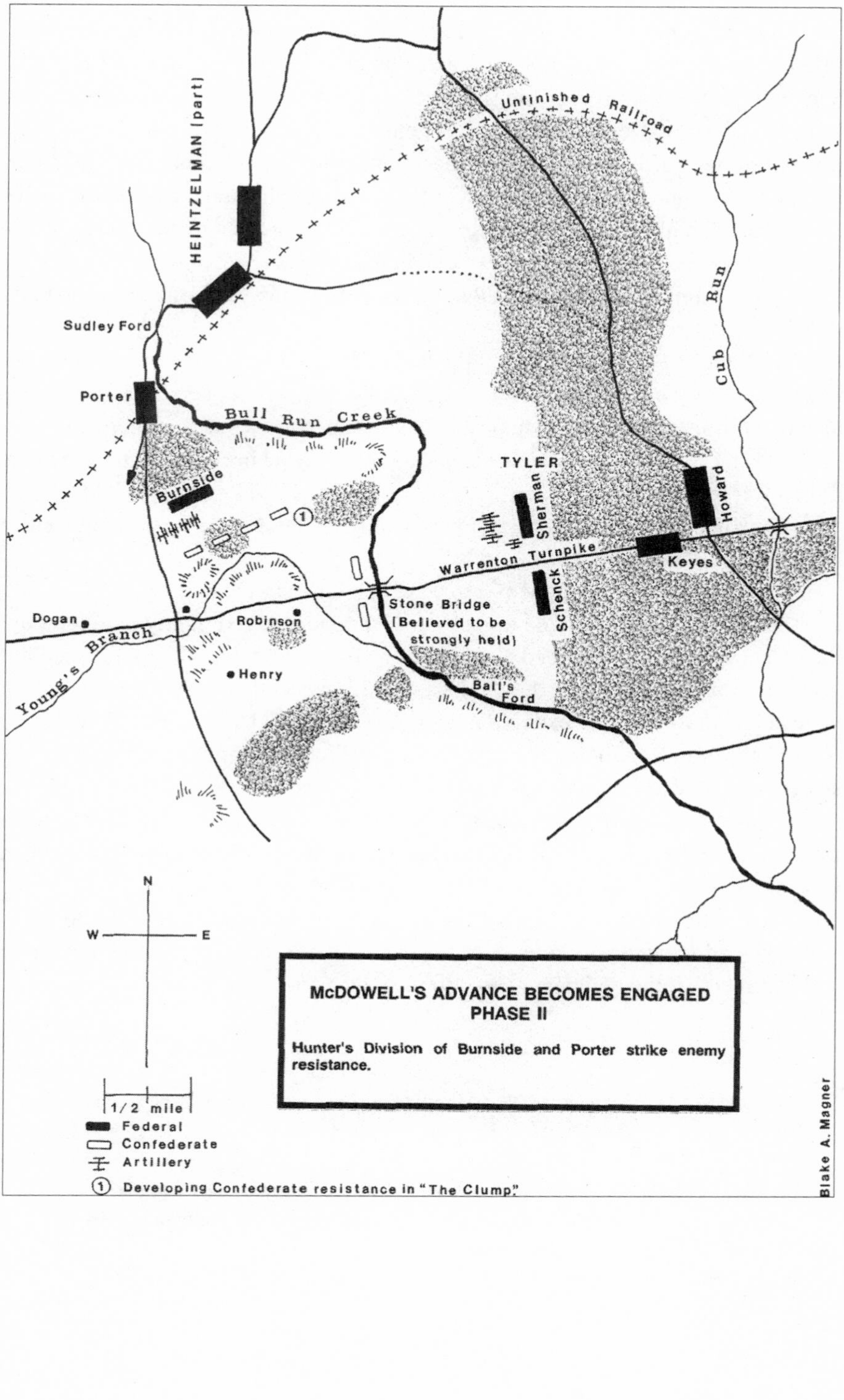
HEINTZELMAN (part)
Unfinished Railroad
Sudley Ford
Porter
Bull Run Creek
Burnside
1
TYLER
Sherman
Howard
Cub Run
Warrenton Turnpike
Keyes
Schenck
Stone Bridge
(Believed to be strongly held)
Dogan
Robinson
Young's Branch
Henry
Ball's Ford
N
W
E
McDOWELL'S ADVANCE BECOMES ENGAGED
PHASE II
Hunter's Division of Burnside and Porter strike enemy resistance.
1/2 mile
Federal
Confederate
Artillery
1 Developing Confederate resistance in "The Clump."
Blake A. Magner

Private Thomas Parker brought back a Rebel prisoner. Taking the prisoner's rifle, Slocum fired it at the Rebels and climbed the fence to rejoin his men.[41] Suddenly, he fell forward. Private Elisha Rhodes ran to his side. Slocum's prediction had been accurate. He had three wounds, one in the head and two in one ankle. He was conscious but helpless; and Rhodes, young and slight, could not move him. Private Parker answered his call for help. They carried Slocum to a house on the left of the regimental line and laid him on the floor. The regimental surgeon, the chaplain, and the assistant surgeon of the First Rhode Island decided to send him to the rear in an ambulance. Rhodes took the door off its hinges to carry Slocum to the ambulance.[42]

Meanwhile, Burnside hastened the last of his men across the ford and pushed down the road toward Matthews Hill where Slocum was engaged. He met Hunter bleeding profusely all over his tunic and being helped to the rear.[43] While urging the Second Rhode Island forward in a bayonet charge, he had been struck in the neck by a shell fragment.

"Burnside, I leave the matter in your hands. Slocum and his regiment went in handsomely and drove the scoundrels."

Trying to staunch the flow of blood, he continued to the rear.

At last, Burnside deployed the rest of the brigade, three infantry regiments and the two boat howitzers attached to the Seventy-first New York, and joined the fight. The First Rhode Island relieved the hard-pressed Second. The two boat howitzers were added to Reynolds's battery on the left of the road. The line held. The Second New Hampshire Regiment, in support of the artillery but directly behind the guns, suffered particularly because all Rebel "overs" landed on it.[44]

Colonel Gilman Marston called the regiment to attention to move them. As the men rose, the colonel was struck in the shoulder and knocked down. His adjutant bent down to help him up, inadvertently grasping the injured arm. "The air was burdened with choice selections from the old colonel's matchless vocabulary." When he had regained his composure, he allowed himself to be helped to the rear; and command of the regiment passed to its lieutenant-colonel.[45]

41 Rhodes, *All for the Union*, 40; Elisha H. Rhodes, "The First Campaign of the Second Rhode Island Infantry," in *Broadfoot MOLLUS Rhode Island*, 32, 15.

42 *Ibid.*, 27-28.

43 *OR*, 2, 334; Hunter, *Report of Services*, 8; Woodbury, *Second Rhode Island*, 32-33.

44 *OR*, 2, 346, 395-396; Haynes, *Second New Hampshire*, 26; Rhodes in *Broadfoot MOLLUS Rhode Island*, 32, 15 ff.

45 Haynes, *Second New Hampshire*, 29.

The situation had changed considerably in the half hour that the lead regiment and battery had advanced alone to Matthews Hill. Hunter had been hit and gone to the rear. Colonel Slocum was wounded and dying. The regimental sergeant major was down, his horse and both his legs crushed by a cannon ball.[46] The Second Rhode Island and the other units in Burnside's brigade were low on ammunition and were suffering severely.

About 9:00 a.m. Porter's brigade, suffering from the Virginia heat and lack of water, passed Sudley's Church. It could hear lively firing in front. Porter sent an aide to hurry the brigade forward as the Twenty-seventh New York under Colonel Henry W. Slocum, West Point class of 1852, emerged from the trees. Delivering the Civil War equivalent of the more modern five paragraph field order in writing, Porter's aide ordered Slocum to move forward and waved his hand in a general direction.

"You will find the enemy down there somewhere," he said with exquisite precision.[47]

With two of four colonels and many of the field officers disabled, Burnside found himself in an exposed position and sorely tried by the Confederates, who were firing from the cover of trees. Coming forward as fast as possible, Porter and his brigade reached the spot where Captain Averell was waiting to show them a break in the trees that would allow the brigade to leave the column and deploy. From left to right, the Twenty-seventh New York, the Battalion of United States Marines, the Fourteenth New York, the Eighth New York, and the Regular Infantry Battalion went into line. The Regular cavalry extended from the right flank to the rear with Griffin's Regular artillery battery in front of the center firing. Just as Porter and Averell were putting out the skirmishers to screen an advance, Captain Whipple arrived with news that Hunter had been wounded and carried from the field. Porter was now the senior officer of the division. None too soon had Porter arrived on the field and deployed his brigade to the right of the road. Senior in rank, he assumed command of the division.

Griffin's artillery battery galloped to Burnside's left flank to augment the fire of Reynolds's guns and the two howitzers. In a short while Ricketts, too, arrived and went into position next to Griffin.[48] Soon the fire of these guns silenced the Rebel artillery. The Confederate line began to give way. A lucky hit on a caisson or a

46 *OR*, 2, 395-396; *P.N.R.I.S.S.I.*, Series 2, 19; Poore, *Burnside*, 114-115; and Woodbury, *Second Rhode Island*, 33-34.

47 C. B. Fairchild, *History of the 27th Regiment N.Y. Vols. being a record of its more than two years of Service in the War for the Union from May 21st, 1861, to May 31st, 1863* (Binghamton, 1888), 11 (Fairchild, *27th New York*).

48 *OR*, 2, 383-384, 346.

magazine caused an explosion in the Rebel position. Feeling the elation of success, McDowell raised his headgear and shouted.

"Soldiers! This is the great explosion of Manassas."

Burnside's left flank remained shaky even after Porter had deployed. Galloping to his right toward Porter's brigade Burnside came first to the commanding officer of the battalion of Regulars. Excited about his crumbling left flank and fearing collapse of his brigade, he shouted, "Good God, Major Sykes, your Regulars are just what we want. Form on my left and give aid to my men, who are being cut to pieces!"[49]

Major George Sykes would hardly have been at liberty to leave his position in the brigade line without an order from his brigade commander. A stiff, crusty, Regular Army officer with continuous service since his graduation from West Point in 1842, Sykes had become known in the old army for his clean, pressed white shirts and spotless white gloves. He was unimaginative and uninspired.[50] At his best he was a "by the book" officer. Whatever he may have thought about the condition of Burnside's brigade, he was not about to leave his position without an order from one of his superiors, either Porter, his brigade commander, or Hunter, his division commander.

Burnside galloped again, this time finding Colonel Andrew Porter at the left of his brigade and the center of the division. Astride his foaming horse, Burnside blurted his problems with "hysterical excitement."

"Porter, for God's sake let me have the Regulars. My men are all being cut to pieces."

Porter, always calm and clear-headed, responded coolly, "Colonel Burnside, do you mean to say that the enemy is advancing on my left?"

"Yes, and you will be cut off if you can't stop him."

Reluctantly, Porter directed Averell to carry an order to Major Sykes to take his battalion to the left of the line. Then he said to Averell, "Look after this brigade yourself."[51] The experienced Regulars marched left and stabilized the flank.

Porter began to think of offensive action. The Confederates were deployed from a farmhouse surrounded by haystacks on their right to a house on their left. All along their line the puffs of smoke and spurts of flame gave no indication of any intention to retreat.[52]

49 Carter, *Four Brothers In Blue*, 13.

50 Warner, *Generals In Blue*, 492-93; Heitman, *Historical Register*, 1, 941-42.

51 Averell, *Ten Years*, 297.

52 *OR*, 2, 319, 383, 387, 390, 393-394; Woodbury, *First Rhode Island*, 99; Haynes, *Second New Hampshire*, 29; Woodbury, *Second Rhode Island*, 35.

This was exactly the situation that McDowell had hoped to avoid. The Southerners had detected his turning column on the march, halted it north of the Stone Bridge and the Warrenton Pike by forcing it to deploy and fight, and prevented the Union troops from controlling the Stone Bridge area by maneuver. He now had two alternatives.

First, by adding Heintzelman, he could enlarge his force and drive the enemy south with a frontal attack before they could match his force. Howard was already on the way to Sudley's to join Heintzelman, which would put five brigades on the field. Marching on shorter, interior lines, the Southerners had a clear advantage. It was a question of legs.

Second, Tyler could force the bridge in his front or cross the Run by any other means, just so long as he reached the west bank and joined the turning column. If Tyler were able to cross the Run with his three brigades, he would, in effect, produce the flanking intended for Heintzelman. Either alternative would be fine. But he had to have one of them before the dust clouds rolling north were transformed into Confederate infantry. McDowell sent his aide, Lieutenant Henry W. Kingsbury, to order Tyler to press the attack on the bridge with all vigor.[53]

The front of Heintzelman's column was emerging from the trees extending south from Sudley's Ford while troops from Hunter's division charged on the Stone House by the Warrenton Turnpike. Dismounted, Colonel Henry Slocum of the Twenty-seventh New York ordered his color guard to position itself left and rear of the Stone House to allow formation of a battle line on it. A Rebel battery found the range with cannister. Several men fell. Slocum moved his men some distance to the left with the colors in the lead.[54]

Both sides had regiments in gray. Making signs as if they were friendly, infantry with gray uniforms and colors furled marched south from the grove of oak trees on the left and rear of Slocum's regiment. Some men yelled, "Fire," while others countered, "Don't shoot! It is a Massachusetts regiment or the Eighth New York!"

A Rebel straggler managed to reach Colonel Slocum to tell him that the "regiment yonder wanted to surrender." Slocum would not believe it. He drew his sword and threatened to strike. The fugitive insisted he was right. Slocum sent John P. Jenkins, his adjutant, toward the force to identify it. Jenkins waved a havelock as a flag of truce while he rode to the unknown infantry.

53 *OR*, 2, 337; *C.C.W.*, 2, 42 (McDowell).

54 Fairchild, *27th New York*, 12; Blake, *Three Years*, 16. He was probably referring to Buck Hill, south of their position and just north of the Warrenton Turnpike.

"What regiment are you?" he called.

A tall infantryman in the line of the Twenty-seventh demanded in a voice like a foghorn, "Show your colors."

The column shook out the Confederate flag and opened fire.

Jenkins galloped his mount back to his regiment shouting, "Give it to them, boys!"

Uncertainty gone, the Twenty-seventh returned fire. Lieutenant-Colonel Joseph J. Chambers rode behind the line to keep it firm.

"Ne-ne-ne-never mind a f-f-few shells, boys," stammered Chambers behind an unsteady company. "G-G-G-God Almighty is m-m-merciful."

He passed along, coming to another company that was maintaining a destructive fire on the withdrawing Rebels. "G-g-g-give it to 'em, b-b-boys. God l-l-loves a cheerful g-g-giver."

Slocum fell with a bullet through the hip and was replaced by Chambers. Part of the regiment withdrew followed by the colors but a number of the men covered by haystacks or positioned in the streambed of Young's Branch remained to continue a hot fire on the passing Confederates.

As the Eleventh Massachusetts and the First Minnesota, the first regiments from Heintzelman's division to emerge from the trees, neared the fields where Burnside and Porter were heavily engaged, McDowell and Heintzelman pointed in the direction of the firing and called, "They are running! The day is ours! They are on retreat!" One of them added, "Men, I pledge you my word of honor that there are not three hundred Rebels upon that hill!"

The added infantry forces, the Union artillery fire augmented by Griffin's and Ricketts's batteries, and a resolute charge by Burnside's brigade supported by Porter broke the Confederates. They deserted the clump of trees. Overcoming determined resistance, Porter's men captured the stone farmhouse.[55]

The retiring Confederates crossed Young's Branch, the tiny tributary of Bull Run Creek, crossed the Warrenton Pike, and took up a position near the Robinson and Henry houses on Henry House Hill. After some regrouping, the Union forces, regiment by regiment, and not by brigade or division, advanced toward the enemy-occupied hill. Lieutenant Colonel Chambers fell with a bullet through the

55 *OR*, 2, 384, 388, 396; Woodbury, *Second Rhode Island*, 35; Fairchild, *27th New York*, 12-13; H. Seymour Hall, "A Volunteer at the First Bull Run," in *Broadfoot MOLLUS Kansas*, 15, 155 (1892). The account of the activities of the Twenty-seventh New York is a composite of Fairchild and Hall, which vary in details but are not inconsistent and probably differ because the two writers had different vantage points.

leg, and Major Joseph J. Bartlett assumed command of the Twenty-seventh New York.[56]

McDowell knew the men of Hunter's and Heintzelman's divisions would be tired. They had marched long in the hot weather and fought hard on Matthews Hill and at the Pike. He expected Tyler, with his three fresh brigades, almost ten thousand men, to carry the fighting and to brush the beaten and equally exhausted Confederates from Henry House Hill.[57]

While Hunter's men were wading through the water at Sudley's Ford, Tyler was continuing his demonstration at the Stone Bridge. He took a position next to a tall pine tree and sent Lieutenant O'Rourke, one of his aides, high up the tree with a glass. When Hunter's first troops emerged from the woods, they could be seen easily; and when the flanking movement had stalled an hour later, Tyler knew it. He began to ponder his course.[58] Three days before he had been aggressive. In the process he had figuratively received a bloody nose in more ways than one. Should he try again? McDowell had been irate the last time he over-reached. What would he say this time? And, more important, what would happen if he tried to force a crossing? Tyler mounted his horse and rode to Sherman's brigade. The colonel also knew that Hunter had stalled because he could hear the firing and it was not drawing closer. The two officers talked briefly. He might have to send a regiment, Tyler explained, to aid the column if something did not happen soon. The battlefield meeting at an end, Tyler returned to his tree.[59] There, at about 11:00 a.m., Lieutenant Kingsbury delivered the order from General McDowell to press the attack on the Stone Bridge.

"What does he mean?" asked Tyler. "Does he mean that I shall cross the stream?"

"I give you the message exactly as it was given to me," replied Kingsbury.

"I have a great mind to send Sherman across the stream," Tyler thought aloud but directed to no one.[60]

56 Adjutant General's Office, *Official Army Register of the Volunteer Force of the United States Army for the Years 1861, '62, '63, '64, '65*, 10 vols. (n.p., n.d. reprint Gaithersburg, 1987), 2, 462 (A. G., *Official Army Register*); Hall, General H. Seymour, "A Volunteer at the First Bull Run," 155-156.

57 Fry, *B&L*, 1, 187.

58 *OR*, 2, 349; Tyler, *Memorial*, 60.

59 *OR*, 2, 368; Howe, *Sherman Home Letters*, 206; Fry in *B&L*, 1, 187.

60 *C.C.W.*, 2, 43 (McDowell).

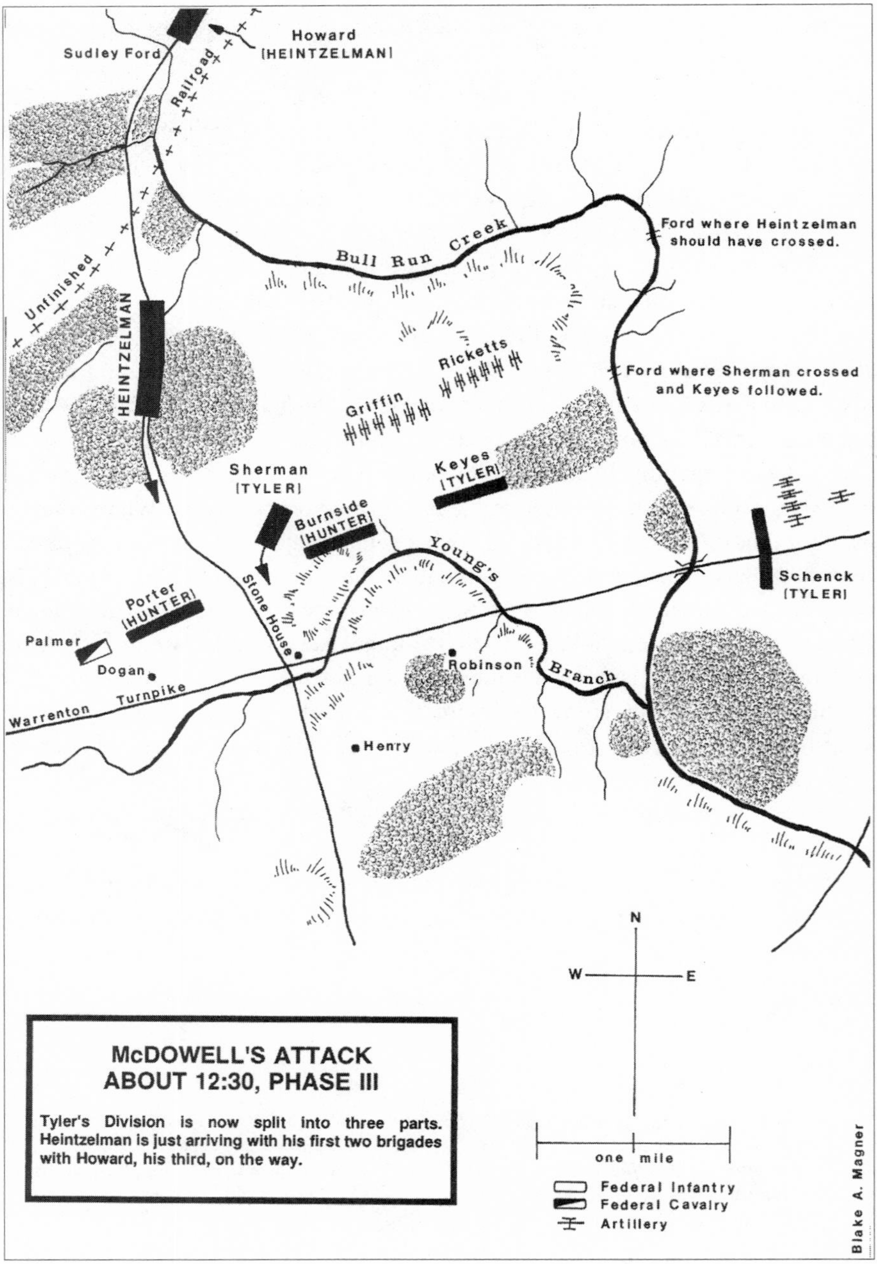

McDOWELL'S ATTACK ABOUT 12:30, PHASE III

Tyler's Division is now split into three parts. Heintzelman is just arriving with his first two brigades with Howard, his third, on the way.

But nevertheless he temporized. Not until noon did he order Sherman to cross Bull Run. He would bring Keyes's brigade, still in the rear from the delay, forward himself.[61]

Sherman needed no engraved invitation to join the fight. He remembered the two Rebels who had forded the Run to taunt him. Now he could use their crossing to whip them. With Ayres's battery close behind and Keyes's brigade closing up rapidly, he started toward the stream. A company of skirmishers crossed, then the rest of the brigade splashed into the water single file, clambered up the steep far bank, and advanced onto the field. He made certain that his colors were well displayed and that his men marched slowly because he had a regiment with gray uniforms in his command. Friendly fire at the wrong moment could turn the day. When Ayres reached the Run behind the last regiment, he found the banks too steep for his horses and guns. Sherman put him on his own to handle his pieces as he saw fit,[62] passed his men behind Burnside's brigade and turned south on the road that ran from Sudley's across Henry House Hill.

Thinking that his brigade had been roughly handled and had borne the brunt of the fighting for more than an hour, Burnside decided he should withdraw his soldiers from the line, rest, and resupply with ammunition. He approached McDowell, said his brigade had no ammunition, and asked permission to withdraw to refit and resupply. Reluctantly, McDowell consented to the request. At Burnside's order the brigade marched back up Matthews Hill where it halted again and broke ranks. Talking happily about their victory and exchanging stories of feats at arms, the troops built fires to boil their coffee. The battle moved away from them, across Young's Branch, and up the gentle slope of Henry House Hill. Burnside was oblivious to all this.[63]

McDowell had survived the first crisis of the day by adjusting to the miscarriages and failures in the execution of his plan. He now had three divisions across Bull Run and a front of three brigades to drive the Confederates from their position below the Pike on the Henry House Hill. Keyes followed close behind

61 *OR*, 2, 319, 349; Fry, *B&L*, 1, 187. Johnston, in *Bull Run*, 193, says Tyler did this on his own initiative. Tyler's report, *OR*, 2, 349, is misleading because it does not mention Lieutenant Kingsbury; and Sherman observes only through his own eyes, attributing motivation to Tyler without knowing all the facts; but when Tyler testified a second time, he corrected his former statement by saying that he received an order through an aide around 11:00 a.m. to press the attack; and he corroborates this in his *Memorial*, 60.

62 *OR*, 2, 369, 372; Howe, *Sherman Home Letters*, 206, letter dated July 28, 1861, from Sherman.

63 Fry, *B&L*, 1, 187; Brigadier General Thomas M. Vincent, "Battle of Bull Run, July 21, 1861," *Broadfoot MOLLUS District of Columbia*, 44, 216-217.

Sherman. As the brigade reached the Run at the double-quick, it found Tyler waiting for it in good spirits.

"Ha! Ha!" Tyler exclaimed. "Here comes my Connecticut boys."

He ordered one of the brigade bands to stop and play "Yankee Doodle." A Confederate band began to match the tune while the men crossed in the shallow water and worked their way up a gorge to an open plain where they formed a line of battle.[64]

Tyler then put Keyes's brigade on the very left of the line.[65] Heintzelman's two leading brigades, Franklin and Willcox, were immediately behind Sherman on the road from Sudley's Ford. Howard, the third brigade of that division, was marching at the double-quick on the road to the ford and would soon be across.

McDowell rode along the rear of the line with his staff waving his hat and shouting, "Victory! Victory! The day is ours."

"Give us a chance at them, General, before they all run away," called one of Sherman's men.

An old British veteran snapped, "Shut up your damned head. You'll get chances enough, maybe, before the day is over."[66]

As he neared the Second Wisconsin, McDowell met Sherman. They exchanged salutes. McDowell cheerfully instructed Sherman to "join in the general pursuit."

McDowell's bearing gave an air of proudness. More plainly than his words about pursuit, his demeanor showed that he believed he was a victorious military leader; and at the moment he was. Figuratively, he was already wearing the laurels of success.[67]

On the far left James B. Fry, McDowell's adjutant, stood by a fence shouting to Tyler jubilantly, "Victory! Victory! We have done it!"

They had only to drive the Rebels from Henry House Hill, and the day would belong to the North.[68]

64 Frinkle Fry, *Wooden Nutmegs at Bull Run: a Humorous Account of some of the Exploits and Experiences of the Three Months Connecticut Brigade, and the Part they Bore in the National Stampede* (Hartford, 1872), 57 (Fry, *Wooden Nutmegs*).

65 Vincent in *Broadfoot MOLLUS District of Columbia*, 44, 216.

66 Todd, *Seventy-ninth Highlanders*, 34.

67 *OR*, 2, 349; Jackson in *Broadfoot MOLLUS Wisconsin*, 49, 243.

68 *C.C.W.*, 2, 201 (Tyler).

Chapter 19

"I will go, but mark my words, they will not support us."

— Griffin to Barry after being ordered to Henry House Hill

The Struggle for Henry House Hill

But Andrew Porter had been greeted strongly by the Southerners. Two of his regiments were in confusion. Colonel Henry W. Slocum had been wounded, leaving the Twenty-seventh New York without a leader; and the Eighth New York had taken such a pounding that it was temporarily demoralized.[1]

If Porter's men had been treated with a heavy hand, Howard's men had suffered doubly but in a different way. Early in the day, McDowell had retained them at the blacksmith shop. Again at McDowell's order, they had marched north on the road to Sudley's Ford, then another order whipped them to the double-quick. For almost a mile the brigade ran, shedding packs, blanket rolls, and canteens. When it became obvious that such a killing pace could not be maintained in the broiling sun, the column was slowed to quick time. Although McDowell's orders had called for the

1 *OR*, 2, 384, 387-388.

shorter route,[2] the aide followed the only course he knew—the long way around the ford. By the time they reached it, the road was strewn with equipment; and many of the men had fallen. They waded into the shallow water, the veins on their heads and necks standing out like whipcords. A staff officer on the far side echoed McDowell's sentiments.

"You better hurry if you want to have any fun."

Toward the Pike and the Henry House Hill they hurried, the signs and sounds of battle growing ever more distinct. Major Fry met them at the edge of the trees with orders to place the brigade on the right. Aching from the incredible race up the Sudley Road, the men pushed nervously forward into a hollow. Howard formed the brigade in a double column of regiments, two columns of two regiments each, just north of the Dogan House.[3]

At this point, confusion prevailed on the battlefield. No one exercised overall command, no one knew where to look for his next order, and no one knew who was to the right or left. Coordination was lacking. Heintzelman could find no staff officer or commander to tell him where to go. Finally, he found McDowell; but McDowell left the placement of Heintzelman's two brigades, Franklin and Willcox, to his discretion. He decided that the best place to deploy was on the right flank in hopes that he could overlap the Rebel left.[4] Barry had already brought the Rhode Island battery five hundred yards forward.[5]

To give his men a chance to rest, Porter allowed Heintzelman's brigades to pass through his line and form a line in front of him. Keyes still held the left flank. On his right was Sherman's brigade in a column of regiments, thus presenting a front of only one regiment. Then came Willcox, and to his right the brigade under Franklin. Palmer's cavalry battalion prolonged Franklin, and on the extreme right was Howard's much fatigued brigade. Porter's weakened brigade supported Howard.[6]

On his own initiative, Griffin had already come forward two hundred yards from his first position to a place where he was blasting away at the Confederates across the pike.[7] There, Barry found him and delivered an order for the two batteries, his and Ricketts's, to go forward. Griffin looked across the valley to Henry House

2 *OR*, 2, 319.

3 *OR*, 2, 419, 421; Howard, *Autobiography*, 1, 157-58; Small, *Road to Richmond*, 21; Gould, *Berry*, 62; Holcombe, *First Minnesota*, 44; J. N. Searles, "The First Minnesota Volunteers," in *Broadfoot MOLLUS Minnesota*, 27, 84.

4 Heintzelman MS Diary (large diary) (L.C.) entry dated September 1, 1861.

5 *OR*, 2, 346-347.

6 *OR*, 2, 319-320, 370.

7 *OR*, 2, 394.

Hill. From the spot he was to occupy, he had shortly before driven a Confederate battery. Surely that was not where he was to go. He could almost spit into the Confederate lines from there, and he would be a good distance in front of his own troops. Barry assured him he would have infantry support.

A ball was lodged in the barrel of one of his guns. With substantial misgivings, he limbered the other five and started forward. He could not clear his mind of the doubts he felt about the position he was to occupy. It was too far advanced. He would have no support to defend his guns against direct infantry attack. He searched out Barry and explained his concerns.[8]

Barry had selected the Eleventh New York, the Fire Zouave regiment which had belonged to Ellsworth before his death, as one of the two to act as artillery supports.[9] He had seen it march smartly under fire and cross obstacles with the proper procedure. It looked like an excellent unit. The major said the Zouaves were ready to double quick to a position right behind the batteries.

Griffin wanted them to go first and deploy on the hill as a screen while the guns were unlimbered behind them. He was also still opposed to any position on Henry House Hill. A better place, he felt, would be Buck Hill about five hundred yards north of his present destination and slightly north of the Pike.

Barry reaffirmed his faith in the Zouaves. He added that the choice of position had been made by McDowell, which placed it beyond their authority anyway.[10]

Although reserved, Griffin had a cynical bent, a hot temper, and a sharp tongue.[11] He was nearing his boiling point as he repeated his convictions about the supporting units Barry had chosen. They would not hold. He was certain of it.

"Yes, they will. At any rate it is McDowell's order to go there."

"I will go, but mark my words, they will not support us."

Once again he started his guns toward the Pike and the hill beyond.[12] The Eleventh Massachusetts broke down a rail fence for them as the horses trotted toward the ridge. The gunners were confident and cocksure. They were Regulars, their weapons were excellent, their condition superb, and they had just finished driving a Rebel battery from the position they were approaching.[13]

8 *C.C.W.*, 2, 168-169 (Griffin).

9 *C.C.W.*, 2, 143 (Barry).

10 *C.C.W.*, 2, 168-169 (Griffin).

11 *Cullum*, 2, no. 1353.

12 *C.C.W.*, 2, 169 (Griffin).

13 Blake, *Three Years In The Army*, 20. Blake's account does not specifically identify Griffin, but it must have been his battery because Ricketts, in *C.C.W.*, 2, 243, testified that he took his own fence down.

When Ricketts received the order to move forward, he demanded that the officer designate the exact spot "so that there should be no mistake about it. I saw at a glance," he testified later, "that I was going into great peril for my horses and men."[14] Lieutenant George W. Snyder, an engineer officer who carried a brevet for gallant service at Fort Sumter, joined him. Ricketts explained the order.

"Snyder, I have such an order to move forward," he said.

"You have the best position in the world," replied Snyder. "Stand fast and I will go and see General McDowell."

Snyder departed. Ricketts waited and in a few moments Snyder returned. General McDowell would comply with Barry's orders, he reported.[15]

When Ricketts's battery, some distance behind Griffin, reached the Young's Branch ravine, it came under Rebel artillery fire.

"We cannot pass that ravine," said one of Ricketts's lieutenants.

At the head of his battery, Ricketts heard him. They had to do it, he assured his subordinate. Under fire, any countermarch would produce such confusion that they would surely be destroyed. The horses were whipped and at a gallop they went down the slope, across the stream, and up the far side amid bursting shells. A wheel shattered on the rough ground. Rapidly it was replaced. The cannoneers rushed forward to tear down a fence blocking their advance.[16] In short order the six guns reached the top of Henry House Hill and went into battery. Horses went down. Men fell at their pieces. It seemed to Ricketts as if the fire were coming from the Henry House, which was very near. He turned his guns on the building and opened fire. Shingles, plaster, and wood splinters flew as he riddled it before returning his attention to the Confederates in his front.[17]

A few minutes later Griffin arrived. Leading his battery up the hill he had mistakenly turned left, allowing Ricketts to pass into the lead. With his five guns, he swung into battery on Ricketts's left. In the trees rimming the southern side of the hill, palls of smoke drifted lazily in the hot air.[18] Shortly eleven guns were firing at the Confederates on the far side of the ridge.[19]

14 *C.C.W.*, 2, 243 (Ricketts).

15 *C.C.W.*, 2, 172 (Griffin); *Cullum*, 2, 1,711; *Heitman*, 1, 907.

16 Although Ricketts does not specifically mention Young's Branch, this ravine was the only one rough enough to break a wheel and he next speaks of taking down a fence, probably along the Warrenton Turnpike, to ascend the Henry House Hill.

17 *C.C.W.*, 2, 243 (Ricketts).

18 Blake, *Three Years in the Army*, 17.

19 *C.C.W.*, 2, 169 (Griffin).

Barry arrived with the Eleventh and Fourteenth New York to support the guns in their precarious position.[20] An officer of the Fourteenth approached Griffin.

"I have been ordered to support you. Where shall I go?" he asked. He headed for a fence in Griffin's rear.

"Don't go there in rear of us, for you will stand a chance of being hit. If their batteries fire at me and don't hit me, it will pass over us and hit you."[21]

The Fourteenth marched into the woods on the right. The Zouaves and the battalion of marines deployed behind the guns. Franklin's brigade, augmented by one regiment from Porter, moved to the left of the batteries and lay down to protect itself.[22]

McDowell rode to the Henry house, dismounted, and clambered to the second story for a better look at the battlefield. The Confederates, generally in woods and trees, held the southern edge of the plateau.[23] So far, he had succeeded in executing his design. He had four batteries of artillery and seven brigades of infantry on the west bank of Bull Run. He was on the Henry House Hill below the Warrenton Pike and the Stone Bridge, and he was about to drive the enemy off the last defensible position before Manassas Junction. The day was progressing well. He had already concluded how the battle would end. The elation of victory coursed through his veins. It was probably only a matter of time.

Keyes's brigade had assumed a disconnected position on the left of McDowell's line. With it was General Tyler. Atop Henry House Hill were two houses, one its namesake and the other farther east and closer to the Pike, the Robinson house. When the action resumed around two o'clock, Tyler sent Keyes's brigade forward to capture a Confederate battery firing destructively from a position near the Robinson farmhouse.[24] Up the steep slope at a run went two of Keyes's regiments, the Second Maine and the Third Connecticut. After about one hundred yards, Keyes ordered them to drop behind a slight rise in the ground and load. Then, up they went again. From the farm buildings and from behind the hedges and fences in the farm yard came a hail of fire from Rebel infantry supporting the battery. The two regiments captured a small shed and a garden adjoining the house with great gallantry. Now the

20 Barry testified that he ordered a change from the first position of the guns, *C.C.W.*, 2, 144; but neither Griffin nor Ricketts, in their reports or their testimony, verify the fact. Griffin did move two guns to the right while Barry was with Ricketts.

21 *C.C.W*, 2, 175 (Griffin).

22 *OR*, 2, 384-385; *C.C.W.*, 2, 144 (Barry).

23 Fry in *B&L*, 1, 188.

24 Johnston has Keyes attacking the Van Pelt house, but terrain analysis and the reports of Tyler and Keyes show this to be inaccurate. Tyler, *Memorial*, 61, says the brigade attacked the Henry House Hill but this is no more than a slip of memory after a long period of time.

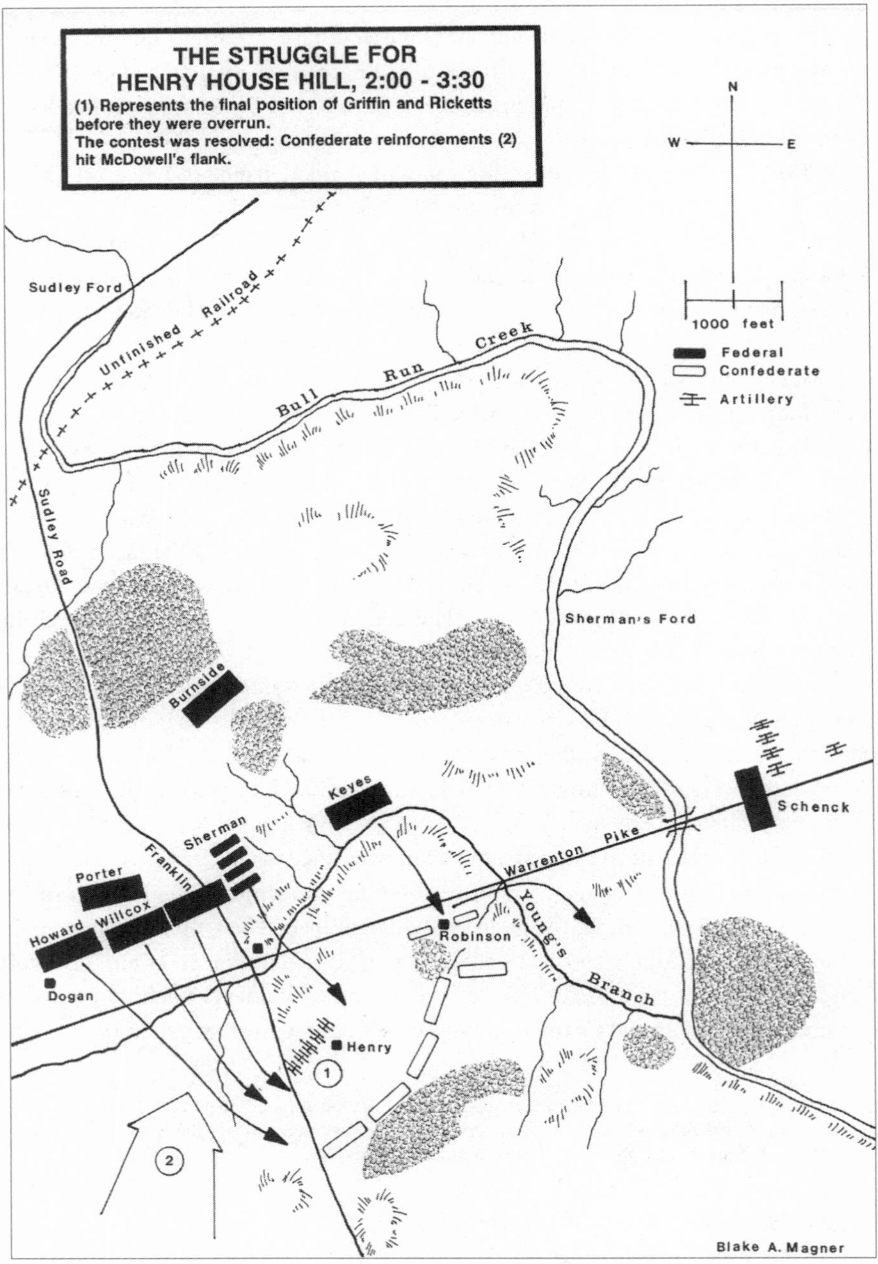
THE STRUGGLE FOR
HENRY HOUSE HILL, 2:00 - 3:30
(1) Represents the final position of Griffin and Ricketts before they were overrun.
The contest was resolved: Confederate reinforcements (2) hit McDowell's flank.
N
W
E
1000 feet
Federal
Confederate
Artillery
Sudley Ford
Unfinished Railroad
Bull Run Creek
Sudley Road
Sherman's Ford
Burnside
Keyes
Schenck
Sherman
Franklin
Porter
Warrenton Pike
Howard
Willcox
Robinson
Young's Branch
Dogan
Henry
1
2
Blake A. Magner

Third Connecticut was badly disorganized. An officer seized the regimental flag and stood waving it on the roof of the shed. The men rallied, then fell back fifty feet to the Warrenton Pike where they lay down.

Tyler had followed them up the hill. Now, he went to Keyes and began to harangue him excitedly. He wanted the men to take the battery with the bayonet. The men of the Third Connecticut could see their colonel try to dissuade him. Knowing the colonel to be an exceptionally brave man, they knew the assault would be futile. Turning from the officers, Tyler addressed the men directly.

"Men! Can't you take that bayonet at the point of the battery."

The verbal error in the excitement of the moment did not escape Keyes's men. They called back.

"No, sir. We can't take it, and there ain't no use of trying."

The intensity of the Southern fire made their position untenable. The regiments could not capture the batteries, but neither did Keyes want to retreat. He dropped to his left, and Tyler brought the remainder of the brigade around the base of the hill to reunite the regiments in a patch of woods.[25]

Here, Tyler in practical effect abandoned his position as a division commander and lost control of his line of battle. Sherman had preceded him and, operating independently, placed his brigade on the left end of Heintzelman's division. Schenck had remained behind on the Warrenton Turnpike facing Bull Run and the Stone Bridge in support of Carlisle's battery.[26] Carlisle and his guns were in line in a field to the left of the turnpike. In the woods along the pike, Sherman's old battery was in position. A group of officers gathered. Captain Romeyn B. Ayres, now in command of Sherman's old battery, sat astride his horse next to his flank piece. Joining Ayres were Schenck, with orders from Tyler to hold his position in support of the artillery; Captain B. S. Alexander, staff engineer officer to General Tyler; and the ubiquitous Captain Montgomery C. Meigs, who had just arrived from Washington as a spectator.

Alexander reported that he and his engineer troops had just finished building a bridge over the Run and clearing the abatis created by the Rebels. The road, now open, could be used by Schenck to cross to the battle on the far side of the creek or by the flanking column if recrossing became necessary. Artillery could be heard to the southwest for half a minute.

Alexander said, "Meigs, if you go forward there, they will shoot at you. They have shot at me every time I have done so."

25 *OR*, 2, 349, 354; Tyler, *Memorial*, 60; Fry, *Wooden Nutmegs*, 67-68, 70-71.

26 *OR*, 2, 359.

"Well, as I have no business there but to look on," replied Meigs, "and can do nothing but satisfy curiosity by going forward, I have no desire."[27]

The original plan had called for three consecutive crossings as the fords and bridges were cleared by the advancing flank column, Tyler to be the third and last; but Tyler had left no orders for Schenck to cross under any circumstances. Because he attended the meeting at which McDowell explained the plan, Schenck must have known what was expected of the division and his brigade. But he had no military knowledge, no military training, no military skill, and no military instincts. Worse yet, he had been humiliated in June at Vienna by a minor failure to follow orders. With no orders from Tyler and no military judgment of his own, Schenck sat uselessly on the peaceful east bank while the flanking column fought without him on Henry House Hill.

After the unsuccessful effort to capture the artillery at the Robinson House, Tyler led Keyes's brigade farther left toward Bull Run, pushing ever southward in the hope that he could find a place to outflank the Confederate batteries. After he sent word to McDowell of his intention, he became engrossed in his own little maneuver. A Rebel battery deployed to enfilade the brigade but its inaccurate initial rounds allowed the regiments time to evade its fire. At long last Tyler found a place from which he could strike the Confederates on their flank. More than an hour had passed from the time he first attacked the Robinson house. He was "leading" Keyes brigade. He had no idea what Sherman was doing. And he apparently never gave any thought to Schenck, who inexplicably never crossed Bull Run at all. He never considered a concerted attack by his entire division of three fresh brigades, which might have carried the day whether or not the Confederates received reinforcements. His staff officers felt the isolation of their position and their lack of any contribution to the fighting. Vainly, they hoped to make contact with Sherman or the other divisions. He had nothing in sight or mind beyond his immediate, personal vicinity. But other events had occurred on the crest of Henry House Hill.[28]

His aide, Lieutenant Emory Upton, wounded in the left arm and side on July 18 at Blackburn's Ford but keeping his position in spite of the pain, reined his panting horse and blurted, "The army is in full retreat towards Bull Run!"

27 Nicolay MSS (L.C.) tr. Meigs MS diary, entry dated July 21, 1861; *OR*, 2, 359.

28 *OR*, 2, 350-54; *C.C.W.*, 2, 201 (Tyler); Villard, *Memoirs*, 1, 189; *Adj't Gen'l Rpt Conn*, 12-13; Michie, *Emory Upton*, 53, 55; Stephen E. Ambrose, *Upton and the Army* (Baton Rouge, 1964), 18 (Ambrose, *Upton*). Tyler on the field and McDowell overall had not taken advantage of, or foreseen the possibility of, a stroke like the great assault of Soult on the Heights of Pratzen at Austerlitz, discussed *infra*, chapter 19, Chandler, *Napoleon*, 1, 422-426.

Tyler was skeptical. After all, he was about to complete a brilliant, perhaps decisive, tactical maneuver.

"Ride with me to the rear a hundred yards, and I will show you I am right," affirmed Upton.

Tyler went. An amazing sight materialized before his eyes. The lieutenant had been truthful except he had understated the situation. The army was in flight. He sent Upton to Keyes with orders to withdraw across the Run because the right wing had been routed.[29] As Keyes's men emerged from the woods, Tyler arrived with new orders.

"Halt! Fix bayonets! And prepare for a charge of cavalry!"

Confederate cavalry from the left charged and delivered a volley of carbine fire—but aimed too high. The Connecticut men fired low laying dead and wounded on the field.[30]

How had all this occurred? At the time Griffin and Ricketts moved from their positions on Matthews Hill and McDowell straightened his infantry line as best he could, a lull of half an hour occurred. On Matthews Hill, where the Rhode Island troops had first deployed, the James guns of the battery under Captain William H. Reynolds, which was attached to the Second Rhode Island Infantry, were firing rapidly, randomly, and aimlessly at Confederate artillery and infantry positions on Henry House Hill. William Sprague, young, handsome, fabulously wealthy, a Democrat who strongly supported Lincoln, governor of Rhode Island, a volunteer aide to Burnside, and a man of "very limited moral capacity," rode with Captain Reynolds toward Second Lieutenant J. Albert Monroe, commanding the guns still in battery and firing.

"Monroe," said Sprague, "Can't you get your guns over on the hill there?"

Without a moment's thought Monroe started his remaining piece and one of Lieutenant Vaughan's to the position held by Griffin and Ricketts. On the way the guns passed a pool of muddy water in which lay a dead man and a dead horse. The afternoon sun was scorching, and Monroe later remembered, his thirst was "almost unendurable." Unable to resist and undeterred by the flotsam in the water, he dismounted, drank, remounted, and took his guns up a lane on the side of the hill to a position between Griffin and Ricketts.[31]

29 Tyler, *Memorial*, 61; *Cullum*, 1, no. 8; Keyes, *Fifty Years*, 434.

30 Fry, *Wooden Nutmegs*, 74-75.

31 *C.C.W.*, 2, 169 (Griffin); Villard, *Memoirs*, 1, 115, PNRI, series 1, 20 ff; *OR*, 2, 315, n. 3; *C.C.W.*, 2, 69 (Griffin); *D.A.B.*, 9, pt. 1, 475-476; Lieutenant Colonel J. Albert Munroe, "The Rhode Island Artillery at the First Battle of Bull Run," in *Broadfoot MOLLUS Rhode Island*, 1, 28, 40-41. The battery seems to have begun with four guns although Barry in his report, *OR*, 2, 346, records six 13-pounder James rifles. One was damaged. A second had fired away its unique

Thirteen guns, an excellent small concentration, were now in line on the hill. At last at about 2:00 p.m., the guns in position, the supports in place, and the brigades deployed in line, the battle resumed. McDowell was confident of victory. Ricketts and Griffin were pouring their combined fire through clouds of smoke into the Confederates across the ridge. Ricketts's position had not been carefully chosen. The ground in front of him rose to a broken line of second growth pine trees, not giving his guns a clear and direct field of fire for any distance. The trees were within small arms range, especially on the right. Union infantry struggled valiantly to control the woods to the right of the two batteries. In the heavy growth, the regiments became broken and lost their formations, the men fighting individually or in small groups. The crucial struggle, it became clear, would develop around the two batteries near the Henry house. Officers on both sides knew it.

For a better field of fire, Griffin pulled two of his guns from their position and directed them behind Ricketts to the right of the gun line, where they went into battery. Clearly, both batteries would remain on the ridge whether or not they wanted to leave, because Confederate rifle fire had killed or incapacitated most of their horses. Hardly enough were left to pull one caisson let alone two full batteries.[32]

On the right, Franklin watched with anticipation as the gallant artillerymen moved into place. He was equally impressed with the spirit of their supporting units, particularly the Eleventh New York Fire Zouaves Regiment.

"There goes a gallant regiment," he said, "but it ought to be supported."

Colonel S. C. Lawrence, pacing about his regiment where it lay on the brow of the hill, responded. "It can have support, General. The Fifth Massachusetts will go anywhere you order it."

"Move your regiment by the right to their support."[33]

At the same time Major Barry, who had been observing from Ricketts's battery, rode to Griffin's two guns on the right.[34] Half an hour had passed since the Regulars first opened fire. The effect of their fire was noticable in the smoke-wreathed trees across the ridge.

ammunition, for which battlefield resupply was impossible, and had been ordered to the rear for safety.

32 *C.C.W.*, 2, 243 (Ricketts); Scott, *Willcox Memoirs*, 290.

33 Roe, *Fifth Massachusetts*, 71, 81.

34 *OR*, 2, 347; *C.C.W.*, 2, 146 (Barry) and 169 (Griffin).

Griffin's sharp eyes detected a regiment to his right front even though it was almost obscured by a fence. It climbed over the rails, dressed its ranks, and waited for its colonel. Shortly, he stepped in front. Griffin could see the colonel exhorting his men to some great feat of arms. They were Confederates. He was positive. He ordered the section leader to change front and give them a taste of canister. The powder was rammed home, then the payloads. Major Barry reined his horse next to Griffin.

"Captain, don't fire there. Those are your battery support."

"They are Confederates. As certain as the world, they are Confederates."

"I know they are your battery support. It is the regiment taken there by Colonel Wood."[35]

"Very well."

Griffin raced to his guns and ordered them not to fire at the irregularly clad troops. The two muzzles swung again to the front and splattered their canister loads across the field.[36]

Intent on the woods, Heintzelman did not notice the unidentified regiment scale the fence and march toward Griffin. Lieutenant Averell saw them.

"What troops are those in front of us?" he called.

Heintzelman was still looking in another direction.

"Here, right in front of the battery." Averell dropped the reins across the pommel of his saddle and raised his field glasses.[37]

Heintzelman reined his horse with a jerk and looked forward. They must be Confederates. He looked for the supports. In the Fire Zouaves he could see four men rolling the colors as if they were on a parade ground, one on the spearhead, one on the shaft, and two on the outside corners of the flag. He spurred his huge, coal black horse toward them.

"What are you about?" he demanded.

"We are going home."

"I'll be damned if you are. Unfurl the flags and march to the support of your comrades."

35 The name is represented with a blank in the published transcript. The only support regiment in that position was Colonel Wood's Fourteenth New York.

36 *C.C.W.*, 2, 169 (Griffin), 220 (Reed). Barry denied this entire colloquy, *C.C.W.*, 2, 145; but Lieutenant Reed confirmed Griffin's account, *C.C.W.*, 2, 220, as Griffin said he would, *C.C.W.* 2, 169, 175.

37 Scott, *Willcox Memoirs*, 290; Roe, *Fifth Massachusetts*, 72.

While the color guard unfurled the flag and displayed it,[38] he rode among the Zouaves. In the woods to the front were disorganized but still dangerous remnants of several Confederate brigades.

"Here they are! Here they are!" he shouted and waved the Zouaves forward. Willcox, still with the Zouaves, his leading regiment, also ordered them forward. "Charge them," he shouted to the Zouaves.

At this moment Lieutenant Adelbert Ames, a newly minted 1861 graduate of West Point, arrived at his section of Griffin's battery on the right side of the line of guns. Wounded in the thigh at the first fire after crossing Sudley's Ford, Lieutenant Ames had gallantly refused to leave his post for safer ground in the rear. But his leg stiffened, and unable to walk on it, he had his men drive him from position to position on a caisson. The caisson with Ames aboard halted at the new position of his section.[39]

After Griffin had restrained his guns, the mysterious regiment faced left, marched fifty yards, faced right, and marched forty yards closer to the guns. As Willcox and the advancing Zouaves reached the crest of the rising round, the mysterious regiment suddenly raised its rifles to shoulder, aimed at the Union guns; and to everyone's horror, fired.[40] The effect was disastrous. The few remaining horses were slain. Gunners fell on all sides. Ricketts was knocked from his saddle, desperately wounded. Lieutenant Ramsay, one of Ricketts's section officers, fell to the ground dead. The batteries had no chance to withdraw. To be saved, they had to be defended.[41]

In *War and Peace* Leo Tolstoy theorized that an order is not an order unless it is obeyed. If his theory is accurate, Heintzelman and Willcox gave the Fire Zouaves no

38 John C. Robinson and John Watts de Peyster, "Obituaries of Major General Samuel P. Heintzelman, first Commander of the Third Army Corps, and Major General Joseph Hooker," 8-9 (New York, 1881) (pam.); *C.C.W.*, 2, 216 (Averell). In his incomplete memoirs, written many years later, Averell managed to confuse all this; put Heintzelman in the place of Barry, even in the conversation; gave Heintzelman his arm wound in the valley; and added himself to a conversation that included no-one but Barry and Griffin (Averell, *Ten Years*, 298-99).

39 Military Historical Society of Massachusetts MSS (Boston Univ., Mugar Library) John Codman Ropes letters, letters dated April 19, 1894, May 14, 1894, May 17, 1894, and May 20, 1894, from Ames to Ropes; *Heitman*, 1, 162. Ames firmly stated and restated that the gun crews suffered the crushing volley just as he arrived but does not state (nor does Griffin in his report) that he commanded the section moved to the right. In fact, he states that Ricketts's guns were to his right even though he could not see them. His repeated statements to Ropes about the terrain, the undergrowth, his position not being near the Henry House, and many other circumstances put him with the two guns on the right. United States Department of the Interior, National Park Service, *Battle of First Manassas, Third Phase, noon to 2 p.m., Troop Movement Map 4.*

40 The regiment was the Thirty-third Virginia.

41 *C.C.W.*, 2, 169 (Griffin); Fry in *B&L*, 1, 189.

order when they called for a charge. Instead of charging, the regiment fired,[42] then broke, and finally disintegrated when thirty or forty Rebel horsemen poured through its ranks firing their pistols and slashing wildly with their sabers. Once the cavalry had passed, the Zouaves fired after them. Three horses fell with a crash. The clearing smoke revealed five empty saddles. The Rebel cavalry, now through the main line of Union troops, had reached a precarious position. Part of Palmer's Regular cavalry battalion turned on them from the right, smashed what formation was left, captured several, and scattered the rest. Among the prisoners was Rebel Brigadier General George Stewart.[43]

Collecting a detachment of Zouaves, Willcox entered the woods on the right, the source of the heaviest Confederate fire. His men took a few prisoners, killed or wounded twenty Rebels, and cleared the woods. Willcox put the men in a holding position and rode back for reinforcements.

While Heintzelman was leading the Eleventh New York forward, a bullet, which he concluded had been carelessly fired by one of the Zouaves, struck his arm just below the elbow.[44] Doctor King, still on his horse, tried to cut the bullet out, but found it impossible. While Heintzelman fumed and swore from his saddle, he dangled his damaged arm so the doctor, who had dismounted, could cut the ball out and bandage the wound.

Heintzelman then led Colonel Willis A. Gorman's First Minnesota into the fray. Gorman's men drove the Southerners back and retook the guns; but instead of pulling them toward the pike, they began to re-form and reload. The few men who tried to drag the guns found them encumbered by dead horses. They would not budge. Griffin managed to start three to the rear, but a Rebel counterattack recaptured all eleven and drove the regiment back in "tolerably good order."[45]

Heintzelman snatched the next regiment he could find, the First Michigan of Willcox's brigade, to throw it forward. Willcox, too, joined the First Michigan, his old regiment. Now holding Ricketts's guns, Confederate infantry received them. Willcox snatched off his hat, went to the front of his men and shouted, "Charge bayonet." He knew he could not be heard. Nor would it have mattered if he could be. Some of his men at once demonstrated their fleetness of foot—to the rear—but others attached themselves in small groups to other regiments trying to retake the guns. Barry,

42 Heintzelman MS Diary (L.C.) entry dated September 1, 1861; *C.C.W.*, 2, 30 (Heintzelman); Fry in *B&L*, 1, 189.

43 *OR*, 2, 347, 385, 402-403; *C.C.W.*, 2, 30 (Heintzelman).

44 Heintzelman MS diary (L.C.) entry of September 1, 1861; C. S. Hamilton, "Reminiscences of the Old Army," in *Broadfoot MOLLUS Wisconsin*, 47, 43; *OR*, 2, 403.

45 *OR*, 2, 403.

Heintzelman, Wadsworth, and Willcox rode among them, pleading, shouting, and swearing in an effort to hold them together—all to no avail. A bullet badly wounded Willcox's horse.[46]

The marine battalion, composed entirely of green recruits, ceased to exist as an organized unit.[47] Colonel Lawrence, on the way to reinforce the Zouaves with his Fifth Massachusetts, went down wounded; and his regiment fell into confusion.

Still on horseback, Willcox rode to Ricketts's position, dismounted, and went to one of the guns. A lone gunner, loading his piece, greeted him.

"Colonel, I'm the only man left here."

Willcox fired the piece toward the hot fire coming again from the woods on the right.

Heintzelman could see the Fourteenth Brooklyn at the base of the plateau. He rode down the slope, had the commanding officer call the regiment to attention, and "addressed a few words" to it. He was about to lead them into battle, he said, and hoped they would do their duty. They answered with an encouraging cheer and followed him up the slope in good order. At the crest they saw a Confederate regiment. Both sides raised their weapons, fired high, and broke for the woods.

Willcox proposed to enter the woods he had already taken and turn the Rebel left flank. Heintzelman told him to "push on & he would send me another regiment," Willcox recalled a short time later. By mistake the right wing of the First Michigan fell back in confusion, but the left wing cleared the field.

"Colonel!" shouted Willcox to Heintzelman, "The First Michigan has retrieved the day."

The Thirty-eighth New York, also of Willcox's brigade, recaptured Ricketts's guns and repulsed a Confederate attack. Meanwhile, Willcox led the steady left wing of his old regiment through the woods and into a gully. He could see Confederate soldiers taking deliberate aim at him, but he had already survived such "hot work" that he did not believe they could hit him.

He felt a severe shock in his right arm. Faintness swept over him. Everything began to "spin like a top." He could barely hold the reins in his left hand and guide his horse. Captain William H. Withington of his old regiment delivered the disturbing news that the Rebels were in their rear. Withington took the reins and led the horse into the nearby woods. Willcox dismounted. Withington bound the arm with a handkerchief above the wound. Willcox's horse, severely wounded, followed him like a child.

46 Scott, *Willcox Memoirs*, 290-292; *OR*, 2, 393.

47 *OR*, 2, 385.

A party of Confederate skirmishers approached on a road in the woods. Two or three men had gathered with Willcox. He ordered them to fire and as loud as he could shouted, "Bring up the whole regiment!" The Confederates retreated.

With Withington's assistance, Willcox started for the rear, hoping his men would not know he was disabled. They scaled a fence and headed across an open field on foot. A Confederate colonel brandishing a pistol, swearing, and calling for their surrender galloped toward them. In a loud, gruff voice he demanded to know who they were. Willcox identified himself.

"You're just the man I've been looking for."

"I am an officer and a gentleman, sir," replied Willcox, "and expect to be treated as such."

Chastened by the sturdy response, the colonel told them to keep their swords.[48]

While Willcox was being captured, chaos reigned in the batteries. All eyes were riveted on the position. The two Rhode Island guns had miraculously escaped[49] the several Confederate regiments which captured the immobilized Regular batteries. Every effort was made to recapture the lost guns. Willcox had fought his regiments one at a time. Heintzelman had thrown one regiment after another into the fray. They captured and lost the guns three times.[50] Sherman attacked with his regiments one at a time. His troops struggled up the slope past dead and dying artillery horses. The ground around the Henry house changed hands several times. Here, within a few yards of the house, Secretary of War Cameron's brother fell in a hail of small arms fire, leaving his regiment, the Seventy-ninth New York Highlanders, without a colonel. Gallantly leading their troops, officers fell in droves. In a short time many units lost cohesion.[51] Sherman failed to muster sufficient force at any one time to hold what he captured and became an unstable left wing in need of support.

Separated from McDowell, James B. Fry went to Burnside on his own. In the American army, staff officers did not order line commanders. He suggested that Burnside form his brigade and march it back into the fight. Burnside did nothing. Fry

48 Scott, *Willcox Memoirs*, 291-296.

49 PNRI, series 1, 20 ff.

50 *OR*, 2, 403. The chronology of events from the time the thirteen guns took position on Henry House Hill until the retreat remains utterly confused. Many personal anecdotal accounts exist, but the only serious attempt at chronology based on firsthand knowledge appears in Heintzelman's report, *ibid.* The numerous direct and hearsay anecdotes used here have been ordered in the most logical way with attempts to confirm their place in the narrative on the basis of details. Footnotes describing the process of organization would require a small book. Disagreement is fully justifiable and cannot be conclusively refuted. Someone could provoke the footnotes with the right—or wrong—criticism.

51 *OR*, 2, 370; Howe, *Sherman Home Letters*, 208, letter dated July 28, 1861.

then joined Major Barnard, McDowell's chief engineer. Barnard knew that two of Tyler's brigades had crossed the Run and entered the fight. He assumed, as McDowell did, that the third brigade had come across as well. The Stone Bridge, if things went badly, was a vital route for any retreat that might become necessary. Something had to be done to protect it from the Rebels. He discussed this with Fry and after assuming responsibility for it, persuaded Fry to send an order to Miles to come forward to the Stone Bridge with two brigades and to telegraph Washington to send forward all possible troops.[52]

McDowell committed Howard, deployed in his double column of regiments near the Dogan House, to the gun position while Sherman struggled for the Henry house. The first two regiments swept up the ridge through scattered trees. On the run they passed one of Ricketts's lieutenants bringing off one caisson. His face was covered with blood from a head wound and his horse spouted blood from its wounded nose. Struggling through thickets and trees at the crest, the two regiments delivered a crashing volley while Howard hastened back to bring up the remaining regiments. In a short time he had three regiments in action with one in reserve[53] in the woods to the right of the fatal artillery position. Down went the colorbearer of the Fourth Maine; but the colonel, Hiram G. Berry, snatched up the flag and spurred his wounded horse to the front. Miraculously, the many bullet holes in his clothing produced no wounds of the flesh.[54]

The brunt of the fight to hold the plateau and the guns fell to Franklin's brigade of three regiments.[55] Franklin had sent forward two Massachusetts regiments, the Fifth and Eleventh, while Ricketts and Griffin were still firing. By the time they arrived, the critical contest for the guns was in full sway. The two regiments opened fire while still in column, some men shooting their compatriots ahead of them.[56] In a short while the intense fire had "used them up," and they began to break.

52 *OR*, 2, 332; Fry in *B&L*, 1, 190.

53 *OR*, 2, 418; Howard, *Autobiography*, 1, 158-159.

54 Gould, *Berry*, 64.

55 The Fourth Pennsylvania, its term expired, had demanded its discharge that morning.

56 In the hysteria and criticism of the war in Vietnam, casualties suffered from friendly fire caused public furors as if they had never happened before. In fact, numerous instances of this occurred during the Civil War. Casualties from friendly fire would even occur when Alonzo Cushing captured eternal fame by taking his guns to the stone wall at Gettysburg on July 3. These incidents are recorded as far back as the wars of the ancient Greeks. Richard Townsend Bickers, *Friendly Fire: Accidents in Battle from Ancient Greece to the Gulf War* (London, 1994).

A disorganized body of federal troops had gathered on the north slope of the Hill. Accompanied by his aide Major Wadsworth, McDowell found the Twenty-seventh New York passing forward at this place. They rode to Major Bartlett, now commanding the regiment. The general said Bartlett's regiment was so steady and reliable he wanted it to move to the crest of the ridge to be the foundation for a new line and a firm front until they were relieved. The Twenty-seventh went forward. Others followed, forming on its right and left. To the west columns of troops could be seen coming toward the flank and rear of their position.[57]

By this time, McDowell had moved to Sherman's brigade, which was trying to steady the line, while Heintzelman, freshly bandaged, and Barry tried desperately to save the guns.[58] The attention of everyone on the field had been drawn to the struggle for control of the hill, particularly the area about the Henry house and the guns. All eyes were glued to the surging lines. Sherman, from the left, had angled into the gun position while Willcox and Howard, on the right, drifted left into the trees on the western edge of the plateau. The Union right flank and rear had been almost completely forgotten.

While the struggle about the Henry house hung in the balance, fresh Confederate reinforcements struck the right flank and rear of the attacking Northerners. Nothing could stop them when they hit. The preoccupation of every Union officer and man with the two batteries had so uncovered that wing that no one paid any attention to the open flank. The right of the federal line disintegrated.

57 Hamilton, "Reminiscences," in, *Broadfoot MOLLUS Wisconsin*, 46, 43; Hall in *Broadfoot MOLLUS Kansas*, 15, 156. Hall believed, years afterward, that McDowell said they would be relieved "by General Patterson, who will soon be here." In all the many accounts of July 21, none but this one suggests that McDowell expected Patterson and his army on the field that day. Of course, Scott had said that, if Johnston reached Beauregard, he would have "Patterson on his heels;" and McDowell believed that Johnston, at least in part, had reached the field. Because he could have expected Patterson for this reason, this account cannot be brushed aside. However, the lack of confirmatory evidence, the apparent lack of certainty in the account ("I have always thought he added . . ."), and the number of years between the event and the article (1861 and 1892, almost thirty-one years) make it unreliable.

58 *OR*, 2, 320, 270, 385, 402-403, 406-407; *OR*, 51, pt. 1, 21ff; *C.C.W.*, 2, 146-147 (Barry); Blake, *Three Years in the Army*, 20ff. These are the major, contemporaneous, primary, official sources prepared on behalf of the units that sought to hold the two batteries on Henry House Hill. They govern the narrative from the time the Rebel regiment fired until this point. The numerous anecdotal sources are cited as their content has appeared in the text. The overall chronology recorded by Heintzelman in his official report, July 31, 1861, *OR*, 2, 402-403, has been accepted. The anecdotal and personal accounts add more confusion than clarity on chronology and only prove the accuracy of Professor C. C. Gillespie's statement to the author when he learned that the author's topic for his senior thesis included an account of the battle, "I served in the army in the European theater, and I could not give a reliable account of my own activities even the day after."

McDowell, with Sherman and his men, knew the day was lost but acted as if he expected a battlefield cure from heaven.

"What is to be done?" asked Sherman.

McDowell simply could not face the ugly truth that had replaced his visions of victory. "Wait a while," he temporized and rode off. McDowell was "a picture of despair," Sherman recalled.

A few moments later with the Union position on the hill collapsing, Sherman's subordinate in charge of the brigade wagon train asked what he should do.

The question was a proper one. Sherman thought for a moment and recalled that the commanding general had ordered him to "wait a while." He would do just that. He turned to his subordinate, looked him squarely in the face, and in a stern, almost savage voice said, "I give you no orders at all, sir!"[59]

Men in flight covered the slope behind the two batteries. The Twenty-seventh New York re-formed on the first position of the brigade and acted as a nucleus for the regrouping and gathering of other regiments. Sykes's Regular battalion was sent from the left back to its original position on the right.

Expressing the desperation of the moment and his own loss of control, Major James S. Wadsworth, revolver in hand, said to two of Porter's aides, "Gentlemen, I am ready to lead any regiment against the enemy that will follow me."[60]

No infantryman wanted to subordinate himself to an unknown officer on a confused and unfavorable battlefield. Twelve thousand men on the field had "lost their regimental organizations" and could no longer be handled. The officers and men were no longer together. Even if not in flight, they certainly were not manageable as fighting units.[61] None of this was lost on McDowell, who met with several of his senior officers on the left of his crumbling army. "Waiting a while" was no longer a reality.

"Gentlemen," he said, "it seems evident that we must fall back on Centerville. Colonel Porter, will you please cover the withdrawal with your division."[62]

The Regular battalion took a position on the Chain House Hill and formed a square when Rebel cavalry threatened. Then, with the "whole field . . . covered with panic-stricken and flying men" the battalion formed a line of battle in the face of the fresh Southerners. The seasoned troops blunted the onslaught enough to give the Army of Northeastern Virginia time to withdraw across Bull Run. Only the extreme

59 Jackson in *Broadfoot MOLLUS Wisconsin*, 49, 241, 243-45.

60 Averell, *Ten Years*, 299.

61 *OR*, 2, 334.

62 Averell, *Ten Years*, 299.

right flank elements were leaving the field when the order to retreat was given. Regiments and brigades in the center and the left of the line, that were in good order, "were surprised when the order came to retreat, and for a time considered it as merely an order to change position for another general advance." When they received the order to retire, some officers "warmly remonstrated—too warmly perhaps," they admitted shortly after the battle.

McDowell had a chance here to save the day, arrest the Confederate attack, and resume the offensive. If Tyler had fulfilled his orders, he would have had a division of three brigades, relatively fresh, concentrated on the lightly engaged left flank of the turning column. One brigade, either Keyes or Schenck could have formed a line perpendicular to the main line of battle; marched behind the line to the right; and formed a return on the steady Regulars.

On the left the remaining two brigades, Sherman and either Keyes or Schenck could have made a strong attack in column to break the Confederate hinge between the Henry House Hill position and the remainder of the Rebel line stretched along Bull Run Creek.

This had been done under much worse conditions by General von Bülow and his Prussian infantry at Waterloo. Beaten, they regrouped, marched, then counterattacked to crush the flank of the French. This would have been too much for green volunteer regiments. Whatever the practicality of this maneuver might have been, it never seemed to occur to McDowell and was well beyond his mental capabilities at the moment. The mentality to repair a line of battle after a classic flanking assault, then resume the offensive, would be years in the coming and require different men.

The men did not race from the field in individual flight but rather moved slowly in groups. Some went by way of Sudley's Ford to collect their blankets and packs. Others forded the stream in various places and moved across country toward Centerville.[63]

63 Frederick L. Olmstead, Secretary, United States Sanitary Commission, "Report of the Secretary with Regard to the Probable Origin of the Recent Demoralization of the Volunteer Army at Washington and the duty of the Sanitary Commission with Reference to Certain Deficiencies in the Existing Army Arrangements as Suggested Thereby" (Pamphlet) (Washington, 1861) reprinted in Charles Capen, McLaughlin, ed., *The Papers of Frederick Law Olmstead*, 5 vols. (incomplete) (Baltimore and London 1977-), 4, 163-166 (McLaughlin, *Olmstead Papers*); Jane Turner Censer, ed., *Defending the Union: the Civil War and the U.S. Sanitary Commission, 1861-1863*, 4, 163-166; Dangerfield Parker, "The Regular Battalion in the First Battle of Bull Run," in *The United Service: A Monthly Review of Military and Naval Affairs*, xiii, no. 5, 528-529 (November, 1885). In the Wilderness in 1864, James Wadsworth would redeploy his division from a position facing front (west) to a position facing left (south) after his division had been mauled by the Rebels, Pearson, *Wadsworth*, 268-282; and Sheridan would in the late summer of 1864 return a severely defeated army with some men in flight to a

Major Barry, the unfortunate chief of artillery who had delivered the order to Griffin to move forward, then ordered him not to fire on the unidentified regiment, spurred his horse at a gallop down the north slope of Henry House Hill to escape the victorious Confederates. An officer galloped behind him shouting, "Halloo, Barry, is that you?"

"Yes."

"Where is Griffin?"

"I am afraid he is killed," answered Barry.

"That battery is lost," said the officer, stating the all too obvious fact. "I am afraid we are gone up."

"I am to blame for the loss of that battery," said Barry assuming responsibility. "I put Griffin there myself."[64]

Barry rode down the slope until he came to Young's Branch, where he allowed his jaded horse to water. Beside him appeared two other officers who also reined their horses to let them drink. It was Griffin and one of his lieutenants. All the bitterness and personal enmity which Griffin had felt toward Barry long before the battle welled up inside him and burst forth in sarcasm.

"Major, do you think the Zouaves will support us?"

"I was mistaken," replied Barry, chagrined.

This confession was not enough for the sharp-tongued Griffin. He pressed the attack. "Do you think that was our support?"

"I was mistaken," repeated the major.

"Yes, you were mistaken all around," snapped Griffin fiercely.[65]

McDowell headed for Mathews Hill and the Mathews house, where he, his staff, and various officers tried to form a line of battle to arrest the slow, steady

victorious counterattack at Winchester. George E. Pond, *The Shenandoah Valley in 1864* (New York, 1883), 220ff; Jeffrey D. Wert, *From Winchester to Cedar Creek: The Shenandoah Campaign of 1864* (Carlysle, 1987), 197ff. On June 15 in the early fighting of the Waterloo Campaign, the Prussians on the allied left were badly beaten by part of the French right wing and driven from the field in near flight. General Blücher, the commanding officer, lay pinned under a dead horse and was twice ridden over and back by French *cuirassiers*. Instead of retreating toward Liege, as any ordinary officer would, Blücher's chief of staff, August Wilhelm von Gneisenau, made the decision himself not to withdraw to Liege. He decided that he was not "defeated" and that he should maintain contact with the English to the west. He withdrew his "horribly mangled Prussians" to Wavre. Two days later they showed the power of recovery by delivering the crushing attack on Napoleon's right wing and flank. Goerlitz, *German General Staff*, 46; Chandler, *Napoleon*, 2, 1046, 1058, generally, 1034-1057. *OR*, 2, 320-321, 385, 350; *OR*, 51, pt. 1, 21; *C.C.W.*, 1, 33 (Franklin), 120 (Griffin), and 146-147 (Barry).

64 *C.C.W.*, 2, 1216, 1217 (Averell).

65 Heintzelman MS Diary (large diary) (L.C.) entry dated September 5, 1861.

departure of the army's infantrymen.[66] The ubiquitous Fry halted Arnold and his Rhode Island Battery and asked him to go into battery as a rallying point for a stand.

Arnold responded that his unit was still in fair condition and ready to fight as long as there was any fighting to be done. But all to no avail. The men continued to drift toward Sudley's Ford, the route they knew, to collect the equipment they had doffed as they prepared to enter the battle. A few rounds of canister and shell scattered a feeble attempt at pursuit by the Rebels.[67] Recognizing that nothing more could be done on the battlefield McDowell headed his horse for Centerville with the intention of rallying his army on the heights at the village.[68]

The army, meanwhile, was having difficulties on the road back. Covering the retreat, the Regular battalion drew the attention of several Confederate batteries. Avoiding the road in his own retreat, Sykes kept his battalion from raising dust and marched them, still in formation, out of the Rebel artillery fire and through some woods.

Once in the woods, Lieutenant Dangerfield Parker turned to Sykes and, with his infinite inexperience, asked, "What do you make of this major?"

In the "dry . . . nasal tone" habitual to him Sykes replied laconically, "Looks very much like a rout, lieutenant."[69] Confederate cavalry crossed the Run south of the Stone Bridge and harassed the retreating soldiers, adding to the disorganization.[70] Everywhere, fear of cavalry was rampant. The picture of Allied cavalry sabering the fleeing remnants of Napoleon's army after Waterloo[71] was in everyone's mind. Rebel artillery from the western bank of Bull Run had been firing for some time on the pike and disrupting the retreat. Now it concentrated on the ramshackle little bridge across Cub Run where a train of wagons was crossing. A direct hit on a vehicle in the middle of the bridge blew off a wheel and overturned the vehicle. It could not be moved. Colonel A. M. Wood of the Fourteenth New York and Captain O. H. Tillinghast, an artillery officer serving as McDowell's quartermaster were too severely wounded to be carried across the bridge. While helping Griffin with his guns Tillinghast had suffered a mortal wound in the body. When his ambulance reached the bridge, he said nothing could be done for him and he would not recover. As soon as he had been taken from the ambulance and laid by

66 *C.C.W.*, 2, 169 (Griffin).

67 Fry in *B&L*, 1, 191.

68 *OR*, 2, 316.

69 Dangerfield, "The Regular Battalion at the First Battle of Bull Run," no. 5, 529. *United Service* gives Parker's name as "Dangerfield" but *Heitman*, 1, 769, gives it as "Daingerfield."

70 *OR*, 2, 404, 320 ff.

71 Russell, *My Diary*, 229, entry dated July 21, 1861.

the roadside, a solid shot smashed the ambulance to pieces. Both had to be left by the road. Confusion reigned. Little could be done. The Cub Run Bridge was blocked. The pike, clogged with smashed and abandoned wagons, guns, and equipment, was under artillery fire.[72]

Would McDowell's army be destroyed or scattered to the winds? Could a line of defense short of the capital be arranged? Was the capital again in danger of capture?

72 Military Historical Society of Massachusetts (John C. Ropes letters) (M.L., B.U.) letter of August 8, 1861, from Bache to Ropes; *OR*, 2, 374, 394.

Chapter 20

"General Patterson directed me to say to you that he understood your orders to him were to make demonstrations. To hold Johnston, not to drive him."

– Major Russell reporting from Patterson to Scott

Collapse

As McDowell and his army advanced from their Alexandria–Arlington line toward Centerville, Bull Run Creek, and Manassas, the officers who remained behind in the capital were every bit as tense as those headed into battle. To Scott, his staff, Mansfield, and the War Department, all seemed to go well in the beginning. On July 17, they received a report from McDowell about the capture of Fairfax Courthouse and the retreat of the Confederates toward Centerville and Manassas. They must have been encouraged by McDowell's July 17 assertion that, "the enemies' flight was so precipitate that he left in our hands a quantity of flour, fresh beef, entrenching tools, hospital furniture, and baggage."[1]

The following day, July 18, he described the next advance of his troops, saying that the Confederates "left in such haste that they did not draw in their pickets, who

1 *OR*, 2, 305.

came into one of our camps, thinking, as it occupied the same place, it was their own . . . [M]uch flour, some arms, forage, tents, camp equipage were abandoned by them."[2]

Having been extended to an improvised facility at Fairfax Courthouse, the telegraph permitted direct communication with McDowell's headquarters; and as his army marched beyond Fairfax, McDowell maintained communication with the telegraph line by a group of mounted couriers organized by Andrew Carnegie, the civilian employee in charge of telegraphic communications.[3]

During the morning of July 18, General Mansfield, in his headquarters in Washington, received word about Tyler's ill-fated encounter at Blackburn's Ford on Bull Run Creek. Dashing excitedly from his office, he met William H. Russell, an English war correspondent famous for his coverage of the Crimean War and now covering the United States Civil War as the war correspondent for the London *Times*.

"Mr. Russell, I fear there is bad news from the front."

"Are they fighting, General?"

"Yes, sir. That fellow Tyler has been engaged, and we are whipped."

A short time later Charles Sumner, a Radical Republican abolitionist from Massachusetts and an influential member of the United States Senate, announced on the floor of the Senate, "We have obtained great success. The Rebels are falling back in all directions. General Scott says we ought to be in Richmond by Saturday night."

Russell then met two more officers on horseback. One of them called, "You have heard we are whipped. These confounded volunteers have run away."

In a shop the proprietor and his wife greeted the correspondent with the assertion, "Have you heard the news? Beauregard has knocked them into a cocked hat?"

"Believe me," said the proprietor's wife, "it is the finger of the Almighty in it. Didn't he curse the niggers, and why should he take their part now with these Yankee Abolitionists against true white men?"

"But how do you know this?" asked Russell.

"Why, it's all true enough. Depend upon it. No matter how we know it. We've got our underground railway as well as the Abolitionists."[4]

2 *OR*, 2, 306.

3 *OR*, 2, 306; Bates, *Lincoln Stories*, 17; Paul J. Scheips, *Albert J. Meyer, Founder of the Army Signal Corps: A Biographical Study*, 2 parts (unpublished Ph.D. dissertation) (U.M.I. Dissertation Services), pt. 1, 342-365 (Scheips, *Ph.D. MS Bio. of Meyer*).

4 Russell, *My Diary*, 211-12, entry dated July 18, 1861.

On Saturday, July 20, Senator Sumner announced again, "McDowell has carried Bull's Run without firing a shot. Seven regiments attacked it at the point of the bayonet and the enemy immediately fled. General Scott only gives McDowell till midday tomorrow to be in possession of Manassas."

When John Hay, one of Lincoln's private secretaries, appeared on the floor of the Senate to deliver a message from the president, he was asked about this news of a victory. He said, "All I can tell you is that the President has heard nothing at all about it, and that General Scott, from whom we have just received a communication, is equally ignorant of the reported success."[5]

That same day Major Russell, the messenger from Patterson, arrived in Washington. It was two days after Tyler's misadventure at Blackburn's Ford and the day before McDowell was to cross Bull Run Creek to strike Beauregard. The major called on Scott in his private quarters, presented Captain Simpson's sketch of the Winchester fortifications, and explained the motives for the movement from Bunker Hill to Charlestown. Never one to conceal his displeasure from subordinates the old general was only too obviously annoyed.

"Why did not General Patterson advance?" he demanded.

"Sir," replied Russell, "General Patterson directed me to say to you that he understood your orders to him were to make demonstrations. To hold Johnston, not to drive him."

Scott spun in his chair and snapped fiercely, "I will sacrifice my commission if my dispatches will bear any such interpretation."[6]

That day a telegram arrived from Patterson confirming the bad news:

> Headquarters, Department of Pennsylvania
> Charlestown, Virginia, July 20, 1861
>
> With a portion of his force Johnston left Winchester by the road to Millwood on the afternoon of the 18th; his whole force 18,200.
>
> R. Patterson
> Major-General, Commanding
>
> Colonel E. D. Townsend,
> A.A.G., U.S.A., Washington, D.C.

5 Russell, *My Diary*, 215, entry dated July 20, 1861.

6 *C.C.W.*, 2, 232 (Russell).

When the president learned about this telegram, he hurried to Scott's offices to suggest that McDowell wait until Patterson could join him before attacking. The old general's petulance was at a high level. Originally opposed to the early offensive and to the appointment of its commanding officer, he had come to believe in the fledgling army and its commander. As far as he could see, McDowell did not need any help.[7] The following day, July 21, Scott notified McDowell that "a strong reenforcement left Winchester on the afternoon of the 18th, which you will also have to beat?" To Major-General McClellan he noted scathingly that Johnston had "amused Patterson and re-enforced Beauregard."[8]

That same day McDowell reported to the capital over his new telegraph lines that five efforts to find places to cross Bull Run Creek and flank the Confederates from their position had been unsuccessful. Because the Confederates were in force on the federal side of the Run, thorough reconnaissances along the creek had been impossible. McDowell intended to drive the Confederates across the creek in order to get the information, adding his voice to the chorus of those who doubted the steadiness and reliability of volunteers, especially green volunteers. "If it were needed, the experience of the 18th instant shows we cannot, with this description of force, attempt to carry batteries such as these now before us." He also reported rumors that Johnston had joined Beauregard at the Manassas Junction–Bull Run Creek position.[9]

On Sunday, July 21, while Tyler was delaying the march of McDowell's flanking column toward Sudley Ford, a beautiful morning broke calmly and quietly in Washington. Scott spoke with confidence and predicted success. The president, who could do nothing to influence the upcoming battle, was impatient to know the course of events. No one knew more than the reports coming over the telegraph wire;[10] but because the wires stretched only as far as Fairfax,[11] on-the-scene information had to be relayed by courier from the battlefield to the telegraph.

At 11:00 a.m., the president, maintaining his outer calm, went quietly to church. A short time after noon, telegrams from Fairfax to the War Department and army headquarters were delivered to him at the White House. They reported the things the

7 *Cong. Globe*, February 15, 1862, debates of Ingham, Chicago; Patterson, *Narrative*, 77-80; William B. Wilson, *A Leaf from the History of the Rebellion: Sketches of Events and Persons* (Philadelphia, 1888) (pamphlet), 7 (Wilson, *A Leaf*).

8 *OR*, 2, 746.

9 *OR*, 2, 308.

10 Nicolay MSS (L.C.) letter dated 12M. July 21, 1861, from Nicolay to Therena; Russell, *My Diary*, 217, entry dated July 21, 1861.

11 *OR*, 2, 746.

telegraphers at Fairfax could hear far from the battlefield, but they gave no certain or reliable information. In the middle of the afternoon, the messages from the men at the telegraph station, becoming more frequent, reported considerable fluctuation in the artillery fire.[12]

Lincoln went to Scott's quarters where he found the general in chief asleep. He woke him to discuss the information. Applying his extensive experience to the reports, Scott said they gave no information one way or the other. In his view, changes in wind currents and echo variations prevented a distant person from assessing the course of a battle by sounds. Still, his confidence in a favorable outcome continued. The president left, preparing himself for a nap of his own.

The dispatches continued to arrive about every ten or fifteen minutes. Still, they did not report concrete information based on direct observations; but the information grew more heartening and more definite: the battle now seemed to extend along the entire line, and the Confederate lines seemed to have been driven back two or three miles.[13] As the inconclusive dispatches grew in number, so did the group gathered in the telegraph office in the War Department. Lincoln was joined by William H. Seward, Simon Cameron, Salmon P. Chase, Gideon Welles, and Attorney General Edward Bates of his Cabinet. Also present were Colonels E. D. Townsend, Van Rensalear, Hamilton, and Wright of General Scott's staff. General Mansfield, commanding the defenses of Washington, and Colonel Thomas A. Scott, an assistant secretary of war, watched. Comparing the telegrams with large maps of the field, they maintained a desultory conversation. The president, quietly dignified, told none of his usual stories. Confidant that his prophesy of a thirty-day war would be substantiated, Seward sat complacently puffing on the usual cigar. Equally confidant in the outcome for the day but not agreeing with Seward's prediction of brevity, Cameron gave forcible, practical expressions of his views. The officers huddled to agree on various messages to Scott, who was confined to his quarters by his infirmities. The others watched with great interest as, from time to time, the officers explained the movements described in the telegrams.

12 Lincoln received at least thirty-one telegrams in this manner on July 21, all of which are in the Lincoln MSS in the Library of Congress.

13 Nicolay MSS (L.C.) letter of 12M. July 21, 1861, from Nicolay to Therena; *N&H*, 4, 352; Wilson, *A Leaf* (pam.), 8. *N&H* imply that Scott was in his office, vol. 4, 352; but Nicolay's letter to Therena is not clear. Wilson, *op. cit.*, 8, states that he was in his quarters because of his infirmities. The Wilson account, because of the importance of those present to him, is accepted.

At half past three the telegraph key fell silent and the dispatches stopped. As the men waited, they speculated on the reason for the silence, finally agreeing that McDowell was too busy pressing his victory to send more dispatches.[14]

The ever-present John G. Nicolay, one of Lincoln's secretaries, had begun a letter to his fiancee at noon. "Even while I write this," he explained, "dispatches come which indicate that a considerable part of the forces are engaged, so that we may know by night whether we are to be successful in this fight or not. We shall therefore have to discontentedly satisfy ourselves with being impatiently patient until we get reliable news of either success or defeat. Of course," he concluded, "everybody is in great suspense."

One of Scott's aides brought a telegram sent by an engineer officer from Centerville at 4:00 p.m., and forwarded to Washington from Fairfax Courthouse at 5:15 p.m. McDowell had driven the Confederate army and had ordered his reserves to cross Bull Run Creek. He wanted "all the troops from Washington to come here [Centerville] without delay."[15] The aide reported that General Scott was satisfied with the truth of the report. In Scott's opinion, McDowell would attack and capture the Junction at once, probably that evening, but certainly by noon of Monday, July 22.

Here at last was substantiation for Scott's early optimism. It was also concrete, favorable information to relieve the president's inner, but well-concealed, turmoil. His doubts resolved, Lincoln ordered his carriage and took his customary evening drive.[16]

Meanwhile, units at Centerville and infantry from Runyan's deep reserve division at Vienna were straining on the march to reach the battlefield in time to participate.[17] Leading Runyan's column were the First New Jersey and Second New Jersey Infantry. By seniority, Colonel William R. Montgomery, an 1825 Military Academy graduate who had served for thirty years and been cashiered for participating in irregular land transactions in a military reserve, was in command.[18] With Montgomery at the head of the two regiments, command of the First New Jersey had passed to its lieutenant-colonel, Robert McAllister, a prominent civilian

14 Wilson, *A Leaf* (pam), 7-9.

15 Nicolay MSS (L.C.) letter dated 12 M. July 21, 1861, from Nicolay to Therena; *OR*, 2, 747.

16 *N&H*, 4, 353.

17 Tidball MSS Mem (U.S.M.A.), 271; James I. "Bud" Robertson, ed. *The Civil War Letters of General Robert McAllister* (New Brunswick, 1965), 43-46, 50, letters dated July 18, 1861, from McAllister to his daughter; July 19, 1861, from McAllister to his wife; July 21, 1861, from McAllister to his wife; July 25, 1861, from McAllister to Wiestling (Robertson, *McAllister Letters*).

18 Robertson, *McAllister Letters*, 32-33, fn 14.

with little or no military experience.[19] They could hear the artillery firing in the distance. As they passed Germantown, the firing grew louder. Several miles before reaching Centerville, a civilian heading toward the capital passed them. He reported that all was well and that the Confederates were being driven toward Manassas Gap. The New Jerseyans felt elated. Some time later, the sound of artillery ceased. The battle had apparently ended. But who had won?

Late in the afternoon Captain Tidball had been ordered by an excited Major Wadsworth to rush his battery down the Warrenton Turnpike toward the Stone Bridge. Because Wadsworth told him nothing else, Tidball assumed that the flanking column had succeeded and that he could now cross the Stone Bridge to take part in the battle. He went through Centerville, passed Miles on the porch of the village inn, and pressed toward the bridge. The road was clogged with ambulance wagons bringing the wounded from the field. The farther he went, the heavier the traffic became. Cut into a hillside, the road now had steep banks on both sides. Finally, he came to a standstill.

A man wearing a heavy brown overcoat, no visible insignia of rank, and a broad brimmed hat that flopped up and down with his energetic motions approached him. His face was red; and his hat having failed in its mission to protect him from the sun, his nose was peeling from sunburn. The oppressive heat of the day made his overcoat seem bizarre.

"Whose battery is this?" he demanded.

Tidball replied that he was the battery commander.

"Reverse and immediately get out of here. I have orders from General McDowell to clear this road." He added that the army was defeated and retreating.

Tidball asked a young officer accompanying the red-faced man who the man was. The officer replied that it was Colonel Sherman. Turning back to Sherman, Tidball begged his pardon and explained his orders to go forward.

Sherman responded that Tidball's orders made no difference. The road must be cleared. And the battery could do no good at the Stone Bridge.

Tidball ordered the guns unhitched, turned, and started toward the rear. When he found a place with less steep banks and a handy knoll, he turned off the road, put his guns in position, and surveyed the scene in the direction of the battlefield. He could see Cub Run and a line of Regulars in skirmish order marked by periodic puffs of smoke as they covered the rear of the broken army.[20]

19 Robertson, *McAllister Letters*, 42, 50, letters of July 17, 1861, from McAllister to his daughter; July 25, 1861, from McAllister to Wiestling.

20 Tidball MS Mem (L.C.), 273-276.

The battle wing of the army was doing its best to put distance between itself and the spiteful Confederates. Heading toward Cub Run, Captain Reynolds and Lieutenant Monroe of the Rhode Island battery became entangled in the mess accumulating beyond the blockage at the bridge. A siege gun was overturned in the neighboring ford. They abandoned the guns. Doing his utmost to leave the field to the Confederates, Monroe was puzzled by the serious attention he and Reynolds were receiving from Confederate artillery across Bull Run. A shot struck the ground a few feet away.

"What do you suppose they are trying to do?" he asked Reynolds naively.

"They are trying to kill every mother's son of us. That is what they are trying to do."[21]

On Henry House Hill all but one of Griffin's and Ricketts's guns had fallen to the victorious Confederates. Surrounded by dead horses and men Captain James B. Ricketts, the battery commander, lay critically wounded between two of his guns. He had been struck by a shell fragment in the forehead, had a terrible shrapnel wound in one arm, had buckshot in the breast and shoulders, and had taken a bullet near the knee shattering the bone. Knowing he could not be taken from the field, he had ordered his sword and sash cut from his belt by a lieutenant.

"I will never surrender my sword," he said. "Take it to my wife, tell her I have done my duty, and my last thoughts are of her and our child."[22]

The femoral artery in his leg was intact or he would already have been dead but his wounds were probably fatal. Confederate Lieutenant-Colonel William H. Harman approached the position and recognized his old Regular Army acquaintance.

"Why, Ricketts, is this you?"

"Yes, but I do not know you, sir."

"We were in the Mexican War together. Harman is my name."

Ricketts recognized him. They reached across the bodies and shook hands.[23] The battery position was swarming with Confederate infantry infuriated at the heavy casualties they had suffered from the guns. In danger of being pinned to the ground, Ricketts saw his West Point schoolmate Pierre Beauregard ride into the area where he lay helpless on the ground. Ricketts asked for protection.

"You will receive the same treatment," replied Beauregard, "that our privateers in New York received."

21 Monroe, *Broadfoot MOLLUS Rhode Island*, 32, 45-47; Reichardt, *Btry A, 1st R.I.*, 14.

22 Hunt MSS (L.C.) "Notes for a biographical sketch of Ricketts" (n.d., n.p.).

23 John N. Opie, *A Rebel Cavalryman With Lee, Stuart, and Jackson* (Chicago, 1899), 35-36.

He ordered his men to put Ricketts in a wagon. Next to him, a Confederate soldier, wounded in the head and delirious, rolled and "fought" over Ricketts in his dying agonies. Twice, Ricketts was pitched from the wagon. When it arrived at the hospital, he was laid on the porch, where he was surrounded by the dead and dying.

While Ricketts was being taken to the rear, Colonel Willcox and Captain Withington were delivered by the Confederate colonel to some of his men, who took them to a hollow in the Confederate rear. Under a tree a Rebel surgeon introduced Willcox to combat medicine, style of 1861. First, a swallow of rotgut whiskey, a severe treatment for Willcox who apparently did not drink, smoke, or swear . . . saving his only war time oath at the slave pen in Alexandria in May. Then, off with a piece of cloth from his sleeve to plug the large bullet hole, which was three inches by four inches. Then a piece of a corn cob off the ground to serve as a compress, and a handkerchief tied round to hold everything in place.

The wounded prisoners were started to the rear. After ten paces Willcox's head began to swim. His surroundings turned black. To the ground he fell, no doubt faint from the shock of the wound. The Rebels carried him, semiconscious, back to the tree. After a while he struggled to a sitting position against the trunk and suffered more "vile whiskey." A passing enemy officer asked if he were the Colonel Willcox who had commanded in Alexandria. He was. "He said I should be taken care of," Willcox wrote a short time later "as I had been kind to his friends in Alexandria."

When the officer somehow produced a blanket, Captain Withington and five Confederate soldiers carried Willcox on it toward "Portici," the Lewis House, to the right and rear of the battlefield. After a long and painful ride, Willcox had almost reached the house when another Rebel doctor identified him and stopped the party to examine his wound. He commented that the colonel "had shown some kindness to friends or relations of his in Alexandria." To ease the pain of the ride, the doctor sent for a litter; and while they waited for it, he replaced the battlefield dressing with cotton bandages. A Confederate colonel asked if he should remove the large topographical map stuffed in Willcox's tunic. The wounded man nodded and away it went. Willcox's spurs and watch disappeared in the same manner. The surgeon who had first dressed the wound had taken Willcox's sword with a promise that he would return it, but it never reappeared. At "Portici," the surgeon who had redressed the wound assigned him a small room to himself on the second floor.

The wounded of both sides filled every room and corridor. Withington noticed Ricketts lying on the floor in the hall at the foot of the stairs and had him carried to Willcox's room.[24] Next day the surgeon for Wade Hampton's Carolina regiment

24 The two most important narratives about Willcox and Ricketts after they fell wounded and into the hands of Confederates are the Hunt MS biography of Ricketts, and *Willcox Memoirs*,

applied a clean, new dressing that was more comfortable. The bullet had grazed but not broken the bone. It had struck Willcox while his arm was raised. If his arm had not been raised holding the bridle rein, the projectile would have penetrated his side causing a mortal wound.

Various distinguished guests came daily, all Southern gentlemen of standing, until a surprise visit by the "most distinguished visitor" of his prison tour, Fanny Ricketts.[25]

From a Confederate officer under a flag of truce, Major Wadsworth of McDowell's staff had learned that Ricketts was still alive though dangerously wounded and a prisoner. By telegram he sent the information to Ricketts's wife Fanny in Washington.[26]

Only twenty-three years old, no great beauty, and taller than her husband, she was a strong-willed woman thought by many of Ricketts's subordinates to have been capable of commanding a corps.[27] She went to Scott to request a pass through the lines to join her husband. The general in chief received her request with considerable hesitation. She pleaded.

"You're a woman of good judgment," Scott said to her finally, "I have known you from infancy, and held you in my arms when you were christened. I cannot well refuse you."[28]

A pass was soon prepared; Captain Beckwith brought her a light double team; and leaving her children behind, she started for the battlefield. She took no clothing or necessaries with her.

Under a flag of truce and with an escort commanded by Captain Alexander S. Webb, she passed through the Union lines.[29] When she reached the Confederate lines, she asked to see General Johnston from whom she sought a parole for her husband. Not showing any "Southern hospitality," Johnston refused the request for an informal exchange and confiscated her carriage.[30]

296-298. They have many insignificant disagreements. In general, Willcox is preferred because the writings were contemporary and firsthand.

25 Scott, *Willcox Memoir*, 295-299.

26 Hunt MSS (L.C.) "Notes for a biographical sketch of General Ricketts."

27 J. Warren Kiefer, *Slavery and Four Years of War*, 2 vols. (New York, 1900), 2, 106 (Kiefer, *Slavery and Four Years*); Eby, *Strother's Diary*, 286, entry of August 6, 1864.

28 Stine, *Army of the Potomac*, 21.

29 Hunt MSS (L.C.) "Notes for a Biographical Sketch of Ricketts"; Webb MSS (Y.U.) letter dated July 25, 1861, from Webb to his wife.

30 Kiefer, *Slavery and Four Years of War*, 2, 106.

In the small, crowded room with barely enough room for each of the wounded to stretch out on the floor, Ricketts was tended by his wife for several weeks without prepared food and with only rations of raw bacon and hardtack captured at Centerville.[31] As Willcox recorded it in the narrative he wrote while in prison, she had encountered "great trouble & some insults after leaving our lines, but was equal to any danger. But she did not confine her nursing cares to her husband, but administered those sick room blessings to me which a lady only knows how to confer, sharing the duties with Capt. Withington."[32] Finally, the wounded were taken to Richmond; but when Ricketts and his wife arrived, Ricketts was still in such bad condition that he was taken to an alms house being used as a hospital, rather than a prison.[33]

In the capital, while Ricketts was receiving his initial care and being removed from the battlefield, the president had not yet returned from his drive. Pale and haggard, Seward entered the White House.

"Where is the president?" he asked hoarsely.

Lincoln's private secretaries, John Hay and John G. Nicolay, answered, "Gone to drive."

"Have you any late news?" Seward asked.

Nicolay began to read him the telegram which announced apparent victory.

"Tell no one," said Seward. "That is not true. The battle is lost. The telegraph says that McDowell is in full retreat and calls on General Scott to save the capital. Find the president and tell him to come immediately to General Scott's."

After an absence of about half an hour, Lincoln returned from his drive. His secretaries repeated Seward's message, the first suggestion to the president that the battle had ended unfavorably. He listened in silence. Neither his features nor his expression changed. He walked to army headquarters, where he found the following telegram:

> July 21, 1861
>
> General McDowell's army in full retreat. The day is lost. Save Washington and the remnants of this army. All available troops ought to be thrown forward in one body.

31 Hunt MSS, "Notes for a Biography of General Ricketts"; Stine, *Army of the Potomac*, 22.

32 Scott, *Willcox Memoirs*, 299.

33 Hunt MSS, "Notes for a Biography of General Ricketts"; Stine, *Army of the Potomac*, 22.

General McDowell is doing all he can to cover the retreat. Colonel Miles is forming for that purpose. He was in reserve at Centerville.
The routed troops will not reform.

B. S. Alexander
Captain, Corps Engineers[34]

In the first telegram, McDowell had reported his army west of Bull Run and driving the enemy. He was mounting the pursuit of a demoralized foe by ordering his immediate reserves forward and by requesting that the deep reserves be sent to Centerville. The second report suggested that McDowell's army was three miles east of Bull Run, in full retreat, and deplorably demoralized. Although the two telegrams had been prepared some time apart, they had been sent from Fairfax but fifteen minutes apart.

The men in the telegraph office, outwardly composed, showed only a brief and feeble "ripple of excitement." Whatever their real feelings, they kept them inside. Seward continued to puff on his cigar, secure in the new knowledge that he was not an immediate prophet but salvaging something by knowing that, if he could extend the time, he could make his predictions come true. Colonel Thomas A. Scott turned quietly to Mansfield.

"General, it would be well to man your fortifications and stay this retreat."

Scott and Cameron left for the general in chief's quarters to discuss the next measures.[35]

Scott considered the second telegram an impossibility and refused to believe it. But the bad news simply could not be brushed aside. Lincoln and the Cabinet gathered in Scott's office where they awaited further news in great suspense.[36] They received the first of three reports from McDowell about the loss of the battle and the events that followed.

Crammed into Scott's quarters with a revolving collection of senators, representatives, and governors, Lincoln, Scott, and members of the Cabinet began to discuss ways to recover control of the situation. The crowd showed a great deal of trepidation.[37] Accurately sensing the tenor of the crowd in his apartment, Scott announced his usually calming judgment to Lincoln about a Confederate pursuit.

34 Nicolay MSS (L.C.) letter dated 12M. (3½ p.m. continuation) from Nicolay to Therena; *OR*, 2, 747.

35 Wilson, *A Leaf* (pam), 9-10.

36 *N&H*, 4, 353-354; *OR*, 2, 316.

37 *N&H*, 4, 354; Schuyler Hamilton in Stine, *Army of the Potomac*, 29.

"There is terror in my quarters. It is needless. With the aid of the gunboats stationed in the Potomac and the troops under General Mansfield, which I have reserved here for just such a contingency, the enemy cannot cross either the Chain Brigade or the Long Bridge. I would get into my cabriolet and head the troops myself if that were necessary. But, Mr. President, the enemy have not wings, and I am assured that they have no transportation."[38]

Now fully convinced that McDowell's army had been soundly beaten, he wrote and gave to William Wilson, the telegraph operator from the War Department, an order suppressing all news of the disaster. Wilson drove his carriage down Pennsylvania Avenue to the American Telegraph Office where he gave the manager Scott's directive. The telegraph tables were piled with "Specials" from the war correspondents. Language suggesting the actual events was carefully excised from the waiting "copy," leaving only the "rose colored" parts of the accounts.

All available troops were hurried forward to McDowell. On his own Colonel Scott sent a short telegram to the governor of his home state, Andrew Curtin of Pennsylvania, ordering him to prepare all his available regiments for immediate shipment to the capital. The Pennsylvania Reserves, once destined to have George Brinton McClellan as their commanding officer, were readied and forwarded at once.[39] Baltimore was alerted. The recruiting stations of the nearest Northern states were ordered to send their organized regiments to Washington at once.[40] Scott ordered Major General McClellan to enter the Shenandoah Valley with all the men he could spare from western Virginia and take any steps he could "against the enemy in that quarter." Banks and Dix were to remain at Baltimore "which is liable to revolt."[41]

At 1:00 a.m. on July 22, Scott canceled his orders to McClellan to enter the Shenandoah Valley, instructing him instead to remain in his present position. The extraordinary change in McDowell's army, shown by telegrams forwarded only fifteen minutes apart, puzzled Scott. Perhaps he was still dubious that the change had happened at all. In his second telegram to McClellan, he referred to "a most unaccountable transformation into a mob of a finely-appointed and admirably-led army."[42]

38 Schuyler Hamilton in Stine, *Army of the Potomac*, 29.

39 Wilson, *A Leaf* (pam), 10-11.

40 *OR*, 2, 746, 747, 749-52; Wilson, *A Leaf* (pam), 10.

41 *OR*, 2, 749.

42 *OR*, 2, 752-53.

While these problems were being considered, one of the high-ranking visitors said, "Our soldiers behave like cowards."

Scott released an immediate but unresponsive outburst. "That is not true! The only coward, Mr. President, is Winfield Scott. When I was urging that this untoward battle should not be fought, I should have insisted that my resignation be accepted rather than the battle should be fought."[43]

The immediate steps having been determined and taken, Lincoln left Scott's office and returned to the White House for a rest. From about 1:30 a.m. and through the small hours of the morning, he received callers.[44] In no special order, they were civilians of all kinds, newspaper correspondents, senators, and representatives who had followed McDowell's army to the battlefield. As day broke, the president was still on his lounge in the Executive Office hearing accounts from these people and making his own notes for the immediate future.[45]

While Lincoln, Scott, and the Cabinet were meeting to decide how to reestablish order, protect the capital, and reconstitute the army, McDowell headed toward Centerville, where he attempted to deal with the chaos of his retreating army and to arrange a defensive line along the Centerville ridge.[46]

The Warrenton Pike was choked with baggage wagons and clusters of men.[47] The retreating mass did not show fear, just overpowering fatigue. "They were footsore, lame, hungry, and tired but seemed to be in good heart . . ."[48] In good order, Blenker's brigade deployed, one regiment across the pike, one to the right rear, and one in reserve.[49]

McDowell learned that Colonel Miles was not in condition to command his division. According to Captain James B. Fry, his adjutant, the army's left wing was in confusion. McDowell sent one of Tyler's aides to tell Richardson to take command of the left wing. McDowell would go there as soon as possible.[50]

Regiments from Runyan's reserve division began to arrive. In front of the Centerville position, McDowell put the First New Jersey, Second New Jersey, and

43 Schuyler Hamilton in Stine, *The Army of the Potomac*, 29.

44 *OR*, 2, 752-53; *N&H*, 4, 355; Wilson, *A Leaf* (pam), 11.

45 *N&H*, 4, 354-55.

46 *OR*, 2, 321.

47 *OR*, 2, 427.

48 *OR*, 2, 380.

49 *OR*, 2, 427, 380.

50 MS Court of Inquiry in the case of Dixon S. Miles, NA ("NACIM") (Alexander and McDowell). In each citation to the court of inquiry manuscript, the name of the witness is at the end of the citation in parentheses.

DeKalb Regiments in line. The position on the Centerville Ridge became stable. "The retreating current passed slowly through Centerville to the rear." By sundown, most of the men were behind Centerville Ridge.[51] They had passed through a number of full regiments not employed in the battle. Those who had fought and were able to pay attention were disturbed by this. Why had fresh troops not been committed to the fight? They were "very severe in their comments upon the ability and loyalty of the commanding general" and concluded that McDowell's incompetence was the "primary cause of the defeat."[52]

When Robert Schenck reached Centerville, he halted his two Ohio Regiments on the ridge as a reserve, and reported to McDowell. He offered his men; but although he had never crossed the Run, he whined that his men had been seventeen hours without food, were weary, and had marched and fought on the battlefield. He believed they "might not be very effective," and should, therefore, probably be held as a reserve. McDowell ordered them east to the foot of the Centerville Ridge.[53]

Richardson's brigade of Tyler's division had been posted to block the road from Blackburn's Ford to Centerville to insure the safety of the left wing. These troops now had the vital task of preventing the Confederates from reaching and severing the turnpike, the main route of retreat. From the direction of that flank, McDowell could hear much firing, see great activity, and see columns of dust. He feared that the line of the creek might be forced or that the flank might be turned. If that happened, "the whole stream of our retreating mass would be captured or destroyed," he wrote in his report.[54]

51 *OR*, 2, 321.

52 Blake, *Three Years in the Army*, 29.

53 *OR*, 2, 360.

54 *OR*, 2, 321.

Chapter 21

"Circumstances make your presence here necessary . . . come hither without delay."

– Telegram from Lorenzo Thomas to McClellan

A Precedent for Change

What had happened during the day to the left wing of the Army of Northeastern Virginia under Colonel Dixon S. Miles? Why was Richardson withdrawing? The three brigades under Miles's command had been uninvolved until the retreat from Henry House Hill. When the flanking column set out early that morning, Miles's division, augmented by Richardson's brigade, was to demonstrate against Blackburn's Ford to hold the Confederates's attention on that flank, and to protect the army against attack from that direction. Richardson, originally in Tyler's division and a battered participant in the ill-fated encounter at Blackburn's Ford on July 18, was west of Centerville in position to advance toward the fords. The two brigades which originally made up Miles's division, Davies and Blenker, were bivouacked east of Centerville on the road from Sangster's Station.

When the hour arrived to march to the positions of the day, Richardson started down the road to the fords;[1] but the remaining two brigades, headed out the pike,

1 *OR*, 2, 374.

were forced to wait at Centerville because of the congestion caused by Tyler's dilatory advance.[2] Miles decided that Davies should support Richardson while Blenker remained at Centerville.[3] To reach Richardson, Davies turned off the road, marched through farm fields until he was far enough south to ensure that his route would be free of the turning column, and re-entered the road. As he approached the scene of Tyler's fiasco on July 18, he passed a road to the left.

"There is a road that leads around to the enemy's camp direct," his guide said casually.

"Can they get through that road?" asked Davies.

"Oh, yes, they can."

Davies realized that an enemy force could cross the Run south of them, march up that small road to the route between Centerville and Blackburn's Ford, and place itself directly across the only line of retreat for two of Miles's three brigades. He halted, detached two regiments and two guns to guard against this, then resumed his march. Richardson he found deployed across the road.[4] Because Davies ranked Richardson by ten or eleven days,[5] he assumed command, sent the remainder of his brigade to the left, and at Richardson's suggestion posted his artillery near a barn.

As planned, the artillery opened fire after the signal from Tyler. By ten o'clock, however, ammunition began to dwindle. Davies requested authorization to cease firing. If the enemy attacked and the artillery ammunition had been fired away, the infantry would be forced to fight without artillery support.[6] Miles denied it. Greene and Hunt continued to fire their guns though at a much slower rate.

During the morning, Miles's brigades busily strengthened their positions with log revetments and felled trees toward the enemy to form an abatis. Blenker added to the Confederate works about Centerville, improving and enlarging them for his own men.[7] He found himself the heir of six unmanned artillery pieces left behind when the gun crews demanded recognition of their discharge date that morning. Among his units were men who had served as artillerymen in European conflicts. In a short while he had collected enough experienced volunteers from the Eighth and Twenty-ninth New York Infantry Regiments to man them.[8]

2 *OR*, 2, 428-29; *C.C.W.*, 2, 178 (Davies).

3 *OR*, 2, 424.

4 *OR*, 2, 429; *C.C.W.*, 2, 178-79 (Davies).

5 Richardson's report says ten days, *OR*, 2, 374; and his testimony eleven, *C.C.W.*, 2, 25.

6 Hunt would find himself in this position in July two years later, but his responsibilities and the risks would be much greater.

7 *OR*, 2, 374, 424.

8 *OR*, 2, 427.

Meantime, Miles rode toward Blackburn's Ford. When he learned about Davies's two regiments and two guns on the side road, he was annoyed. This did not comply with his orders. Without attempting to learn the reason for the detachment, he hurried forward to find Davies.[9] A hard-drinking man of violent temper and harsh speech, he was worse than usual on this particular Sunday. Dysenteric diarrhea had plagued him all the way from Washington. Early in the advance his doctor had prescribed opium and quinine pills without beneficial effect. Finally, to treat some of the discomfort, the physician authorized brandy. Miles found this prescription a welcome one. Remedy or not, he was on the day of the battle uncured, quite ill, and happy to apply the new prescription.[10] When he reached Davies at the front, he was drunk, was disinclined to be reasonable, and swore at his brigade commander profusely. The units on the side road were to be called back and placed in line. Miles turned his horse to the right to see Richardson. After Miles left, Davies[11] sent pioneers to fell trees in the undefended side road.

It was almost noon when Miles reached Richardson. Across the Run, the clouds of dust indicated that the Confederates were moving north toward the flanking movement. Richardson handed Miles a glass to verify the fact.[12] There was not much danger here. Satisfied with what he had seen, Miles brought his temper under control and returned to Centerville to check Blenker's position again.[13]

He reappeared at Richardson's brigade when the enemy appeared to be falling back before the flanking column.[14] Perhaps it would be possible to force the ford here and capture some of the laurels of the day for his division. At the council of war the night before, he had expressed his displeasure at being designated the army reserve, but orders were orders.[15] He could do nothing then. Now, he had a chance. They had better try to force the Run, he said to Richardson.[16]

But "Greasy Dick's" brigade had borne the brunt of Tyler's violation of orders on July 18. He did not care to be misused a second time in the same place. Outspoken

9 *C.C.W.*, 2, 179 (Davies).

10 NACIM (Mendell and Dr. Woodward) Halpine MSS (H.L.) letter dated August 1861, from Hunter to Halpine.

11 *OR*, 2, 429; *C.C.W.*, 2, 179 (Davies). The order of these events is not given anywhere, but they have been reconstructed, as usual, on the basis of logic and could hardly have happened any other way.

12 *C.C.W.*, 2, 25 (Richardson).

13 *OR*, 2, 424.

14 *OR*, 2, 374, 424; *C.C.W.*, 2, 25 (Richardson). Miles's movements are confirmed by the account of his adjutant, Vincent, in *Broadfoot MOLLUS District of Columbia*, 44, 222-223.

15 *C.C.W.*, 2, 25 (Richardson).

16 NACIM (Ricketts); *C.C.W.*, 2, 25 (Ricketts).

to inferior and superior alike, Richardson was sharper than usual here because he had disliked Miles for almost a decade. From 1851 to 1853 both men had served in the Third Infantry Regiment at Fort Fillmore, New Mexico, Richardson as a captain, Miles as the regimental lieutenant colonel. They had become embroiled in a personal quarrel which led to harsh words and strong animosity. Unrelated to the quarrel, both men were transferred; and in 1855 Richardson resigned his commission.[17] After almost ten years, Richardson's old animosity was still alive and well, especially since Miles's behavior and appearance showed that he had been drinking far beyond the doctor's prescription.[18] When Miles told Richardson to force the Run, Richardson refused.

"Colonel Miles, I have a positive order for this brigade not to attack at all." He reached into his pocket, pulled out the orders for the day, and showed it to his division commander.

"That is positive," replied Miles.

He could probe the Rebels if nothing else.[19] He ordered both brigades to feel the enemy along the Run. Davies sent forward several companies from the Thirty-first and Sixteenth New York Regiments. Richardson sent two from the Third Michigan and Brethschneider's Light Infantry Battalion as a support. Down the slope and into the trees they went where they were almost immediately greeted by a heavy fire. They recoiled and, covered by artillery fire from Greene's battery, returned to their original positions.[20]

Miles's adjutant Captain Thomas M. Vincent rode to an exposed position from which he could see the Confederates better and drew their fire. Bullets whizzed past his head. They fell around his horse and landed near the division commander.

"Gentlemen," said Miles, "take cover!"[21]

He turned his horse toward Centerville.

The Thirty-ninth New York had been divided between Centerville and a position on the road to Blackburn's Ford. Major George E. Waring, Jr., received an order to bring the Centerville part to Blackburn's Ford to unite the regiment. On the road he met Colonel Miles, who was swaying drunkenly in his saddle.

17 When he testified before Miles's Court of Inquiry, Richardson denied he threatened to harm Miles "at the first opportunity" but made no effort to deny that he and Miles traded personal animosities. See *Cullum* 1, nos. 387 and 1,096 for the time in Mexico when their periods of assignment overlapped, a fact not mentioned in NACIM.

18 Greene, Locke, and Ritchie all testified they saw Miles drink alcohol. Numerous other witnesses testified that he appeared to be drunk. NACIM.

19 *C.C.W.*, 2, 25 (Richardson).

20 *OR*, 2, 375, 424-25, 430; Curtis, *Bull Run to Chancellorsville*, 40-42.

21 Vincent in *Broadfoot MOLLUS District of Columbia*, 44, 223-224.

"Halt! What have you got there?!" called the division commander.

"The left wing of the Garibaldi Guard," answered Waring.

"Where are you going?"

"To join the Colonel and the rest of the regiment."

"'Bout face and march to the battlefield. Damned quick, too!"

From his earlier position, Waring had been able to see the road from Centerville fork somewhat to the west. He galloped ahead to overtake Miles.

"General, which road shall I take?"

Miles's disposition had not improved. "Follow your nose, God damn you."

Waring explained about the fork in the road. Miles was already too drunk to focus on a logical question.

"Follow your nose, God damn you."

Waring pressed onward, passing Centerville and turning toward the Stone Bridge. A very young officer arrived at a gallop, shoved a cocked pistol into Waring's face, and cried, "Halt! Turn your men into this field and form a line of battle."

"Put up your revolver," said Waring. "Who are you anyway and what is the matter."

"I am General Miles's aide!" said the young officer, proving that the apple does not fall far from the tree. "Our whole army is beaten and retreating. We must rally them here."[22]

By the time Miles reached his headquarters at the village inn, he had altogether lost control of his faculties, the tide of battle had turned beyond recovery, and the Union troops were in retreat across Bull Run. On the steps of the house in which he had established the division headquarters, he met Chauncy McKeever, the assistant adjutant general of Heintzelman's division. McKeever reported the disaster and asked that Blenker's brigade be sent out the pike to block the fugitives and stop the retreat.

Miles pushed him away, saying curtly, "I know all about the fight. You can't give me any information. I have something else to attend to."[23]

22 George E. Waring, Jr., *The Garibaldi Guard*, 573-575 (New York, 1893).

23 NACIM (McKeever); Tidball MS Mem. (U.S.M.A.), 272; *OR*, 2, 425.

Around 4:00 p.m., the order from Fry to advance arrived. The gravity of the situation penetrated to his submerged consciousness, and he began to act. He ordered Blenker west along the pike to do as McKeever had requested. Davies and Richardson were recalled to Centerville.[24] Richardson started as soon as he received the order.[25]

In a foul humor, Richardson approached his old regiment, the Second Michigan, and suggested, "in a scornful sort of manner," that the regiment withdraw before it was cut off by Rebel cavalry. Major Williams took the regiment well into the woods and formed a large, hollow square in preparation to receive the expected cavalry charge. Richardson, who was everywhere about his brigade, reappeared, saw the position of the regiment in the woods, recognized the useless square formation, and gave Major Williams a pithy criticism of his efforts.

When the assistant surgeon, Dr. Henry M. Lyster, tried to load a lieutenant lying under a tree in a wagon headed for the rear, the lieutenant's pallor and limp body did not touch Richardson's heart. The brigade commander and the doctor could both see that the lieutenant was not wounded. Nor did Richardson think the man was ill. Richardson obviously disagreed with the assistant surgeon's diagnosis. Believing the man, Mexican War veteran or not, was malingering, a coward, or worse, he ordered him from the wagon.[26]

At once, Richardson began to collect his brigade. Once again, he found the regimental assistant surgeon, who had just performed his first battlefield amputation. Once again, he was not in a good humor, this time probably because his brigade was being misused by Miles, who was, unlike Tyler, drunk rather than incompetent. Worse yet, he was in the same predicament that had confronted him on July 18: he had to retreat in the face of the enemy.

"You had better be getting out of here," he said to Lyster, "or the enemy's cavalry will cut you off."

Lyster packed his equipment and his patient, minus one arm. Richardson realized that he should remove his wife, suspected by some of being the real commander of the brigade, from the battlefield area. She had lost her horse with its side-saddle. Richardson asked Lyster if he would be obliging enough to allow Mrs. Richardson to use his horse because she could not find hers and was about to be sent back to Alexandria under escort of Captain Brethschneider and his two companies.

24 *OR*, 2, 425.

25 *OR*, 2, 376.

26 Lyster in *Broadfoot MOLLUS Michigan*, 50, 119-120.

Lyster expected a charge from the "Black Horse Cavalry" and wanted the horse for his own escape but felt he must comply with the colonel's request.

"I consider it a privilege," he said with some sarcasm, "to render any service to either the male or female commander of our brigade."[27]

Davies did not receive the order to retreat at the same time Richardson did. The Confederates, probably trying to intercept the retreat of the defeated right, had crossed the Run on this flank, too. Just as Davies had feared, they had advanced up the side road Davies had blocked with trees after Miles recalled the two regiments. When they reached the trees, the Rebels turned into a valley which led toward Davies's left flank. As he was turning Hunt's guns toward this force, Davies received the order from Miles to withdraw. If he started back now, organized Confederates would be breathing down his neck. He waited, carefully arranging his artillery with his infantry lying under cover in support. The Southerners moved farther into the valley. He held his fire until their last rank had emerged from the cover of the trees, then:

"FIRE!"

The first round hit a horse and rider, sending them flying into the air. The rest of the battery fired canister, driving the Confederates pell-mell back into the trees. In a postwar letter Henry Hunt waxed hyperbolic on this earliest demonstration of the power of the federal artillery over infantry in the open, a scene to be repeated with great magnification in the future.

"The fighting was at close range. [The gunners] used only canister, and the enemy was promptly defeated and put to flight . . . Centerville was thus saved, and by its safety secured the retreat of our army, and I do not hesitate to say, saved Washington from capture from the Rebels."[28] Now, Davies started his troops toward Centerville, went to see if Richardson had received the order, and found to his dismay that he was the only force on the field. He hurried his men.[29]

Miles had here demonstrated just how intoxicated he really was. The movement of Blenker's brigade, although ineffectual,[30] was sound but hardly his idea. The retreat from Blackburn's Ford was not only contrary to specific orders given by McDowell the previous day[31] but also ill-advised for the very reason that had caused McDowell to caution against it: a retreat would open the rear of the Union army at

27 Lyster in *Broadfoot MOLLUS Michigan*, 50, 113, 122-124.

28 Benedict, *Vermont in the Civil War*, 87, n. 1, letter of no date from Hunt to Platt.

29 *OR*, 2, 430.

30 *OR*, 2, 427; *C.C.W.*, 2, 76-77 (Blenker).

31 *C.C.W.*, 2, 26 (Richardson).

Centerville. If the Confederates could reach the Pike to Washington, McDowell's retreat could be intercepted and his army destroyed. McDowell realized this. In better condition, Miles would surely have known it.

Instead, Miles had committed a fundamental error which almost cost him an entire brigade and had created an opportunity for destruction and disaster, not just defeat. Davies commanded the two brigades at Blackburn's Ford; but when the time to retreat came, Miles sent separate orders to each one. They retreated independently without the coordination of one leader. As a result, Richardson marched rearward to the music of firing which could have destroyed Davies. Fortuitous circumstances and Davies's own foresight had saved his men from annihilation.[32]

Pushing his men, Davies soon overtook Richardson. Both were puzzled by the actions of their division commander. Richardson asked Davies why the retreat had been ordered.

He did not know.

Well, did the enemy attack from the left?

Yes, but they had been handsomely repulsed. And he had no idea what was happening.

Three-quarters of a mile from Centerville, the aide from McDowell intercepted them with orders to block the road from Blackburn's. McDowell was only too well aware of the danger to his rear from the lower fords.[33] The two officers began to deploy their brigades. Richardson put his men in a ravine across the road, placed his artillery on a crest to the rear, and put one regiment in column as a reserve behind the guns.[34]

When he saw Richardson's position, Miles was again displeased. The shadows of late afternoon were beginning to lengthen and blur into dusk, but the passage of time had done nothing to sober the division commander. He was worse. First, he ordered the Twelfth New York to change position; and when this had been done,[35] he rode his big bay horse to check on it. He was wearing two straw hats, one on top of the other, a ludicrous sight on a battlefield. The New Yorkers, now lying behind the fences, saw this caricature unsteadily riding his horse along their lines and talking monotonously. Miles knew the Twelfth had broken and run on July 18.

32 In his report, Miles stated that he received word from Davies that he was under attack and could not retreat, which caused the order to be canceled for both brigades; but this is not confirmed in Richardson's testimony in *C.C.W.*, NACIM, or his report in *OR* , nor does Davies confirm it in his report in *OR*, or his testimony before the Committee.

33 *OR*, 2, 376; *C.C.W.*, 2, 25 (Richardson); NACIM (McDowell).

34 *OR*, 2, 376; *C.C.W.*, 2, 25 (Richardson); NACIM (McDowell).

35 In NACIM, Walrath says an "unidentified colonel."

"You are now where I want you," he said almost incoherently. "Stay there, damn you, and die there."[36]

Next, he spied a regiment lying in column behind the artillery. He rode to it, asked for the regimental commander, and was told that it was Colonel Daniel McConnell.[37]

He called out for O'Donnell.

Someone corrected him; it was McConnell.

Again he called for O'Donnell.

McConnell reported to his flushed superior. With thick-tongued speech, Miles ordered him to deploy his regiment in line of battle to the front to protect the vulnerable ambulances. Cursing freely, Miles continued to mumble unintelligibly for several moments before riding away. The perplexed regimental officers did not know what to do. The regiment had been placed in its present position by Colonel Richardson, their brigade commander. The division commander, who was obviously deep in his cups, had now ordered it somewhere else. Someone must see Richardson.

In spite of the fact that he had been sick the entire day, McConnell had refused to yield his post at the head of his regiment. Instead of going himself, he agreed with his officers that Lieutenant Colonel Stevens should make the trip. Stevens set out and found Richardson.

Why did Colonel Miles order the regiment deployed into line of battle, Stevens wanted to know. Whose order should be obeyed?

Richardson replied that any direction for a move must come from him. Why had this move been ordered?

"I do not know," answered Stevens, "but we have no confidence in Colonel Miles."

"Why?" demanded Richardson with intensity.

"Because Colonel Miles is drunk!"[38]

Alexander, the aide sent by McDowell, found Richardson a few moments later. The brigade commander complained about the drunken interference by his superior

36 NACIM (Todd and Walrath). No account provides a sequence of events. The most logical progression is used here. The two hats are confirmed by Tidball in his MS Mem (286-287), where he explains that this was a common custom in very hot climates, where Miles had served, and that the weather in Virginia in July 1861 was hot enough to justify its use here.

37 *OR*, 2, 376; NACIM (McConnell, Stevens, Judd).

38 *OR*, 2, 376; *C.C.W.*, 2, 26 (Richardson); NACIM (Stevens). The description of the conversation is a logical synthesis of all three accounts, with emphasis on the *OR*, and NACIM accounts because they are similar and contemporaneous.

officer. The aide told him he was now in command, not Miles.[39] Richardson set out to fix the "corrections" made by Miles.

He and Lieutenant Alexander agreed that the present position was unmanageably long. He must correct the position of the brigade as a whole. The flanks must be drawn back to rest on clumps of trees to their rear to protect against cavalry. Major Barry would mass all the artillery he could find along the ridge to their rear.[40] Richardson led the Third Michigan in its change of position. They had gone a short distance when Colonel Miles rode toward them. He was hardly able to keep his saddle.

"Colonel Richardson, I don't understand this. You should march that regiment more to the left."

Exercising his new authority, "Fighting Dick" replied curtly, "Colonel Miles, I will do as I please. I am in command of these troops."

"I don't understand this, Colonel Richardson."

"Colonel Miles, you are drunk," he snapped and turned away to take care of the regiment.

"I will put you in arrest," called Miles.

Richardson knew that would not happen. "Colonel Miles, you can try that on if you have a mind to."

Miles fell silent. He watched his former subordinate tend to the Michigan regiment[41] then turned his horse up the ridge to Barry, who was posting the guns.

"What is going on here," he demanded in angry tones. "Who was moving those guns?"

Barry said he was.

Miles demanded that his arrangements not be changed, but Barry also had a mandate from McDowell. He calmly ignored Miles's vehement protests.[42]

39 The exact position that Richardson was to assume or the one McDowell wanted him to assume was never clear, either at the time or later. Certainly, McDowell wanted Richardson to be free of Miles, NACIM. But was he to continue in command of his brigade independent of Miles, or was he to assume responsibility for the division. When he delivered the message, Alexander told Richardson to take command of the division troops around the fords. NACIM. That is what Richardson did. *OR*, 2, 377; *C.C.W.*, 2, 26 (Richardson). In his report McDowell said he himself took "in person, the command of this part of the Army," *OR*, 2, 321, which is probably accurate for that moment. Davies said McDowell ordered him "to take command of the left wing," *OR*, 2, 432, which is probably also true.

40 *C.C.W.*, 2, 26 (Richardson); NACIM (Barry).

41 *OR*, 2, 377; *C.C.W.*, 2, 27 (Richardson); NACIM (Richardson). While these accounts are generally the same, they have slight variations. The Committee testimony is used here. The conversation was confirmed by both Walrath and Ritchie in the Court of Inquiry.

42 NACIM (Barry).

Meantime, McDowell had covered his main line of retreat by advancing Blenker and had sufficient control of the situation in front of Centerville to inspect the Blackburn's Ford front. He headed in that direction, leaving Porter's Regulars to withdraw last.

When he arrived, he found Miles and Richardson in a heated argument. Miles was giving orders, and Richardson's expression showed clearly to all that the orders were inappropriate.

"I will not obey your orders, Sir! You are drunk, Sir!"

Miles turned pitifully to McDowell for support. But McDowell had long since decided on a solution for the problem.

"Colonel Miles, I find you have everything here in great confusion. You are relieved from the command of your troops."

Crestfallen and silent, Miles gave a sullen salute and rode to a nearby point where he waited stolidly for half an hour. Then he left the field. McDowell ignored the obvious lack of respect and rode to see Richardson.[43]

"Great God, Colonel Richardson," he exclaimed, at last able to find out why his flank had been so endangered, "Why didn't you hold onto the position at Blackburn's Ford?"

"Colonel Miles ordered me to retreat to Centerville, and I obeyed the order."

McDowell replied that Richardson should take command of the troops in that area now and put them in the best position he could find on the Centerville Ridge. When the colonel protested the unfitness of his superior for command, McDowell told him Miles had been relieved.[44] In a short time the new line was stabilized, and the mass of artillery in its rear easily broke a body of enemy cavalry approaching from the ford.[45] Leading the disorganized mass headed rearward on the Warrentown Pike was the Sunday afternoon civilian picnic group, which found proximity to the advancing Confederates distasteful.[46] Many of the regiments would be fractured into

43 Tidball MS mem. (U.S.M.A.), 285-287. McDowell in his report makes no mention of relieving Miles, *OR*, 2, 324 ff; and he testified in NACIM that he did not relieve Miles but merely ignored his presence. Vincent testified that Miles was definitely relieved, NACIM. Richardson confirmed this in his testimony before the Committee (*C.C.W.*, 2, 26). See fn 39, *supra*. Tidball, generally confirming this in his MS Memoirs (285-286), has a slightly different arrangement of events; but because his account was written years later, the contemporary reports and testimony are adopted.

44 *OR*, 2, 321; *C.C.W.*, 2, 26 (Richardson).

45 *OR*, 2, 177.

46 John C. Ropes Letters, in Military Historical Society of Massachusetts MSS (M.L., B.U.), dated August 8, 1861, Bache to Ropes; Don Pedro Quaerendo Reminisco, *Life in the Union Army by a Two Years Volunteer: A History in Verse of the Fifteenth Regiment N.Y.V. Engineers, Col. John McLeod Murphy* (New York, 1864), 67 (Reminisco, *Life in the Union Army*).

small parts by this flood of people and would not meet again as units until they found their camps about the capital. But the majority of McDowell's brigades kept their organization. Those led by Keyes, Schenck, Burnside, Richardson, Davies, and Blenker, six of his eleven brigades, were essentially intact. Half his army, then, remained in firm condition about Centerville; and reinforcements were coming forward. But at least one of the still organized brigades operated under the senior officer present and without its brigade commander. Henry Villard, reporter for the *New York Herald*, was on his way back to Washington to report the battle when he heard a galloping horse behind him. He could see an officer approaching on a black stallion. Without hat, cap, overcoat, sword, or aides the officer neared quickly. He did not stop or slow his horse. It was Ambrose E. Burnside.

"I am hurrying ahead to get rations for my command," he exclaimed as he galloped past.

Villard was puzzled. This was hardly a mission for a brigade commander. And why was he galloping to the rear without hat or sword. Villard "conceived a natural prejudice against [Burnside's] trustworthiness as a general officer."[47]

As the First and Second New Jersey Regiments approached Centerville on the pike from Washington, they began to encounter the confused mass of retreating troops pressing to the rear. McAllister appealed to their patriotism, to their honor, and to the flag, urging them to return and fight. But the retreating flow was too powerful. The appeals were ignored. McAllister advanced his regiment with bayonets, and the officers drew swords and pistols. For a moment only the wounded were allowed to pass, and about five hundred men were taken into his ranks. The New Jersey troops and their "recruits" continued their steady march toward Centerville through the flotsam and jetsam of McDowell's retreating army.[48]

A fleeing civilian appeared on the road. Earlier, he had clambered over an old worm fence; but the top rail had broken, pitching him into brambles. His short legs and stout body were covered with dust and sweat. His round chubby face, enshrouded with mutton-chop whiskers, was pale as death. He was heading rapidly toward Washington. McAllister ordered him to halt. Agitated and frightened, the man exclaimed, "I am a civilian and must pass on."

"No, you cannot pass," McAllister replied. "My orders are to stop everybody, and you are included in that number."

The civilian responded, "I am a bearer of dispatches from Washington and must pass."

47 Villard, *Memoirs*, 1, 1971-198, 208.

48 Robertson, *McAllister Letters*, 47, 50, letters dated July 24, 1861, from McAllister to his wife; July 25, 1861, from McAllister to Wiestling.

McAllister was not persuaded. "You cannot pass until this panic has stopped, for everyone who passes helps to increase the stampede."

The civilian pulled a document from his pockets saying, "Here are my papers. Look at them."

"I have no time to examine papers now. Wait until we are through with this job, and we will consider your case."

In a pitiful tone showing he was frightened out of his wits, the civilian began to plead.

McAllister finally pointed to Colonel Montgomery. "There is my commander. Go to him."

The civilian went to the colonel and pleaded his case. Disgusted with the civilian's cowardice, Montgomery raised himself in his stirrups and exclaimed at the top of his voice, "Let that man go!"

The civilian put spurs to his horse and made the stones of the turnpike fly. William Howard Russell, the terrified British war correspondent, would not set foot on another American battlefield; and before the end of the war his antics would still be unfavorably recalled by the quirky historian of the Fifteenth New York, who told his story and vented his spleen in verse:

> . . . mercenary penny-a-liners, conceited and pedantic,
> With "Bull Run Russell" at their head, have crossed
> the broad Atlantic,
>
> And, by vile, malicious lying, and misstating what they saw,
> Have thought to bring discredit on our troops,
> then new and raw.
>
> Yet the motives of these hirelings, contemptible and mean,
> Though dark and dirty, in each line were plainly to be seen.
> The scoundrels at the head of the concerns for
> which they wrote;
>
> Pandered to aristocracy and wealthy men of note;
> They sympathized with all of those who dealt and
> wrought in cotton,
>
> And, consequently, in their columns they would daily issue
> Of slanders, on our country and ourselves,
> the blackest tissue.
>
> What wonder, then, that Russell, with his followers and peers,
> For everything republican should have such hates and fears;
> And that our gallant soldiers should receive from them abuse,

> For which, 'tis hoped, they yet may make them bring a flag
> of truce![49]

McAllister and his troops, cheered by some as they advanced up the slope toward Centerville, were greeted by others with cries of, "Go up yonder hill and you'll get it! You'll be cut to pieces!" When the regiment reached the summit of the hill, Montgomery conferred with McDowell, who had now returned from his encounter with Miles on the left flank. Montgomery urged the army commander to make a stand on the Centerville heights. The men could prepare breastworks and hold the position, argued Montgomery. McDowell agreed. He ordered Montgomery to take his command to the other side of Centerville, form a line of defense, and make a stand.

The First New Jersey passed Centerville and took a position on the hill to the west with its right resting on the pike. The regiments under Blenker were nearby. The Second New Jersey was expected shortly.[50] Montgomery and McAllister talked with the colonel of one of Blenker's New York regiments and agreed to stand together and fight. An hour or two passed in silence. McAllister sat his horse in the darkness awaiting developments. He expected an attack at any moment. Then he learned the Second New Jersey had never come forward but had joined the retreat. Montgomery sent the regimental adjutant to bring Colonel McLean and his regiment back to the ridge.[51]

Around midnight, Montgomery and McAllister thought they heard movement nearby. Blenker's regiments were moving to the rear. When the officers rode to see what was happening, they were told that McDowell had ordered them to withdraw.[52] The First New Jersey was about to be left alone with the Confederates. They decided to take position on either side of the turnpike, which would probably serve as the Confederates's main route of pursuit. Montgomery ordered McAllister to march his men down to the village, deploy them on both sides of the Warrenton Pike, and open fire if attacked. McAllister obeyed, deploying the men where they would have raking flank fires on any pursuers, but left the road itself unoccupied.[53]

49 Reminisco, *Life in the Union Army*, 67.

50 Tidball MS (U.S.M.A.), 281-282; *OR*, 2, 321; Robertson, *McAllister Letters*, 47, 50-51, letters dated July 24, 1861, from McAllister to his wife; July 25, 1861, from McAllister to Wiestling.

51 *OR*, 2, 438.

52 *OR*, 2, 427; Robertson, *McAllister Letters*, 47, 52, letters of July 24, 1861, from McAllister to his wife; July 25, 1861, from McAllister to Wiestling.

53 Robertson, *McAllister Letters*, 52, letter dated July 25, 1861, from McAllister to Wiestling.

Montgomery and Major David Hatfield rode to find McDowell and clarify their orders. Again, McAllister sat his horse in silence in the darkness. Most of his men fell asleep. McAllister crossed the road to his left wing, where one of his captains asked if he knew the danger they were confronting.

"Certainly," McAllister replied.

The captain then asked, "Why don't we retreat?"

McAllister told him their orders were to hold the position and they would do it.

"We may as well surrender at once as we will be cut to pieces," said the captain.

McAllister responded that he would not surrender and that he would give the Confederates a terrific fight. He returned to his central position to wait for the return of Major Hatfield from the visit to McDowell, then toured the pickets. Dr. Taylor, the regimental surgeon, came to him.

"Colonel, come in and see these poor fellows, many of whom are officers."

McAllister replied, "I am alone and know not the moment we are to be attacked. To go in and see the wounded might destroy the whole command."[54]

After returning from his left, McDowell had taken stock of his position. He could defend the line on the Centerville ridge with his organized units or establish a new position on the Fairfax Court House line. When Major Barry, his chief of artillery, arrived, McDowell ordered him to post artillery to cover the retreat. Barry collected on Centerville ridge batteries under Hunt, Ayres, Tidball, Edwards, and Greene, with guns from the departed New York regiment manned by volunteer crews[55] from the Eighth and Twenty-ninth New York Regiments.[56] In a short time he had a line of twenty guns, a better concentration than he had managed at any point in the battle. The artillery, its ammunition supply low, was not in good condition. A number of guns had been lost on Henry House Hill. Many others with much of the ammunition had been lost at the bridge over Cub Run.

Nor were his men any better. They were exhausted from lack of food and drink. Of the supplies issued on July 20, the day before the battle, most had been abandoned, thrown away, or eaten. Many had not eaten since the evening of July 20; and the rest, probably a minority, had not eaten since breakfast at 2:30 in the morning on July 21. They had been awake since 1:00 or 2:00 a.m.; been on the march since 2:00 or 2:30; been exhausted by the double-quick march; and been

54 Robertson, *McAllister Letters*, 48, 52, letters dated July 24, 1861, from McAllister to his wife; July 25, 1861, from McAllister to Wiestling.

55 *OR*, 2, 347.

56 *OR*, 2, 427, 347. Barry says they were served by volunteers from Wilcox's brigade, *OR*, 2, 347, but Blenker and Davies, more likely to know because the guns and regiments were under their command, *OR*, 2, 427, give the statement in the text.

under fire for five to six hours. A large part of the army was hopelessly disorganized. All division, brigade, and staff officers told McDowell he should retreat.[57] When Barnard reached Centerville, McDowell asked about defending the Centerville ridge or retreating. Barnard was categorical and clear: the army should make "a prompt retreat." He believed the Rebels to be far superior in numbers. He believed that, in the elation of victory, they would pursue. In fact, they had already been seen at the bridge over Cub Run. He believed that a defeated army, driven back on Washington by a pursuing enemy, would "endanger the safety of the capital."[58]

The decision, although doubtless unpalatable, could not have been difficult. Blackburn's Ford was in Confederates hands. The Rebel pursuit was at least as close as Cub Run.[59] The men were exhausted and hungry. They had no food. A large part of the army was already voting with its feet.

If part of the terrain covered by the advance from the Alexandria–Arlington line on the Potomac River could be retained, some of the embarrassment of the defeat could be avoided. McDowell decided to form a line at Fairfax Court House. Around midnight or earlier, he circulated orders to withdraw and departed himself.[60]

Once at Fairfax Court House, however, he found that nothing had changed. Once again, the consensus of his men's feet left him no choice. Many of the organized units had already passed along the turnpike toward Washington. The men could not be prepared for action by the next morning. A prisoner reported that twenty thousand men from Johnston had joined the Rebel army the night before and that the Confederates intended to begin their pursuit that evening.

McDowell pondered. Should he hold the heights about Fairfax Court House with his reduced army or continue to Washington? He recognized the inevitable and ordered a retreat to the Potomac line. McDowell also established direct telegraphic communication with Scott in the capital. Always able to handle the situation, the old general in one of his messages said, "We are not discouraged," and in another advised McDowell that he had no choice but to return to the line of the Potomac.[61]

57 *OR*, 2, 321.

58 *OR*, 2, 332.

59 Olmstead's "Report of the Secretary," in McLaughlin, *Olmstead Papers*, 4, 155- 157; *OR*, 2, 311.

60 *OR*, 2, 316, 320, 321, 325-26, 347, 404; Villard, *Memoirs*, 1, 196, claims the decision to withdraw was made at 10:00 p.m.

61 *OR*, 2, 747, 748. Fry, in *B&L*, 1, 193, states the message about not being discouraged was received by McDowell at Fairfax Courthouse; but it was addressed to McDowell at Centerville. Because the end of the telegraph line was at Fairfax Courthouse and messages addressed to people like McDowell beyond there were carried on horseback by orderly, McDowell could have received it in either place.

McDowell sat on the ground and took his pencil in hand to prepare a dispatch of his own. He had been in the saddle working at a feverish pitch for many hours, not to mention the exhausting emotional cyclone he had ridden. He was encased in gloom and so tired that, midsentence, pencil in hand, he fell asleep. Captain Fry awakened him, and he completed the dispatch.[62] Wearily, he mounted and turned his horse toward the rear. At the fork where the Little River Turnpike and the Columbia Turnpike came together to form the Warrenton Turnpike he halted to send stragglers and fragments of regiments to Arlington or Alexandria. There, he received the welcome information that Richardson, the rear guard, had left Fairfax Court House, was in good order, and had not been attacked by any pursuing Rebels. After two hours he headed for Arlington, leaving his aide, Major James S. Wadsworth, behind at Fairfax.[63] As she would so many times after a battle, Mother Nature showed her emotions about this brothers' war in the early hours of the morning. She began to cry a torrential downpour.

Everyone that dark and unhappy night feared a slashing cavalry pursuit, just as Wellington's cavalry, they believed, had mercilessly pursued Napoleon's beaten and disorganized infantry after Waterloo.[64] But McDowell had confirmed the wise judgment of his president about the comparative characteristics of the fighting men on both sides. The Union and Confederate armies were so evenly matched in equipment, temperament, determination, and fighting quality that the victor in any battle would never be in much better condition than the loser.[65] Not until the last few days of the war would the winner be able to defeat, pursue, and destroy his adversary.

After the order to retreat had been received by the New Jersey regiment and McAllister had communicated it to Taylor, the doctor came to him again.

62 Fry in *B&L*, 1, 193. The dispatch was probably the one sent from Fairfax Court House to Scott in *OR*, 2, 316.

63 *OR*, 2, 316-17; Hall in *Broadfoot MOLLUS Kansas*, 15, 158.

64 According to Chandler in *The Campaigns of Napoleon*, the cavalry pursuit by the Prussians under von Gneisenau has been overstated, vol. 2, 1090. Still, it was a powerful historical event in the minds of the Union officers.

65 The controversy among senior Confederates about the failure to pursue McDowell began almost at once. See Lynda C. Crist, ed., *The Papers of Jefferson Davis*, 10 vols. to date (Baton Rouge, 1992), 7, 383-384, ed. note, 384-385, letter dated October 30, 1861, Davis to Beauregard (Crist, *Davis Papers*), and continued after the war. In his memoirs, General Joseph E. Johnston commented on the criticism he received for his failure to pursue McDowell and capture Washington: "The Confederate army was more disorganized by victory than that of the United States by defeat." Joseph E. Johnston, *Narrative of Military Operations during the late War between the States* (New York, 1872), 59, 60.

"Colonel, will you let me stay with the sick and wounded? All the other surgeons have left. I can't think of leaving them here to die."

McAllister replied, "I should like to do so, but you would be taken prisoner. Besides, we may want your services within an hour. But whatever Colonel Montgomery says will be alright."

"Where's the colonel?"

"Half a mile ahead of us."

The doctor rode to Montgomery, obtained permission to stay, and returned. McAllister bid him goodbye thinking he would not see him again. The orders to retreat were issued in a low tone, almost a whisper. At 2:00 p.m. Monday afternoon, exhausted and hungry, McAllister reached Fairfax to assume a new position. His men had not eaten for thirty hours.[66]

Others were still straggling through Fairfax singly and in small groups. Trains, wagons, equipment, and officers' property were strewn about everywhere. Arriving on foot with one of his sergeants after a peaceful sleep on the grass at Centerville, Lieutenant H. Seymour Hall of the Twenty-seventh New York Infantry recognized McDowell's volunteer aide, Major James S. Wadsworth, the great landowner of Geneseo, New York, where the Twenty-seventh had been recruited.

"Sir," said Hall approaching Wadsworth, "we belong to the Lima Volunteers from your county. Can we be of service?"

Working entirely alone, Wadsworth replied that they could help by collecting enough men from those passing through on foot to gather horses and wagons, hitch them together, make a train, and take everything to Alexandria. In a short while, Hall had a huge train on its way toward the Potomac for redistribution of the contents to the appropriate regiments.[67]

Around three in the morning of July 22, the first remnants of McDowell's army began to arrive at Fort Runyan on the Potomac, the wounded in ambulances and wagons. They were followed by the stragglers arriving singly and in small groups, most of whom were also wounded. After twenty-seven miles, one man, his left arm shot off above the elbow, still had his rifle slung over his shoulder. "The entire remnant of regiments and batteries came in together, and in good order,—all accounted for," wrote a regimental historian years later.[68]

66 Robertson, *McAllister Letters*, 48, 52, 53, letters dated July 24, 1861, from McAllister to his wife; July 25, 1861, from McAllister to Wiestling.

67 Hall in *Broadfoot MOLLUS Kansas*, 158-159.

68 J. Harrison Mills, *Chronicles of the Twenty-first Regiment New York State Volunteers, embracing a full History of the Regiment, from the enrolling of the first Volunteer in Buffalo April 15, 1861 to the final mustering out May 18, 1863* (Buffalo, 1887), 93-95 (Mills, *Twenty-first*).

McDowell's position on the Potomac River was worse than it had been before his advance. It was essentially high ground on both ends, Arlington and Alexandria, connected by inadequate field fortifications in the low ground between.[69] It had always been a poor defensive position because it was too shallow in the center. With no depth for maneuvering behind the front units, he would be unable to isolate a breakthrough or move reserves.[70] Unlike the earlier period when Washington was insecure, the capital was about to face a victorious enemy in pursuit. Seven thousand men were mingling about in Alexandria without officers.[71] Thousands of others were scattered along the road between Centerville and Alexandria. McDowell had lost control of his army.

Arriving at Arlington in the late morning of July 22, McDowell had been more than thirty-two hours in the saddle. He was soaked and exhausted. Not surprisingly, he was also demoralized by the events of the preceding day. Around the Arlington House the birds twittered in the branches. A few untied horses, their heads drooping with ground hitches, stood nearby. He went to the portico of the house and sat his large frame in the lone rocking chair. Soon he was sound asleep, his arm hanging over the back of the chair and his bare head bowed. His face was flushed. He breathed the deep, heavy sleep of an exhausted man. The spike broken off, his helmet lay on the floor next to him. In his pocket diary Lieutenant Averell wrote, "Genl McD used up."

Finally, he awoke to gather his staff and a few other officers for breakfast. He spoke little and then in a broken, effeminate voice. For a change his appetite was indifferent. Lieutenant W. W. Averell raised a spectre of immediate danger by saying that a corporal's guard of Confederate troopers riding across country could have captured him and his escort. McDowell began to recover. He put Colonel Andrew Porter in charge of the immediate defenses in front of Arlington. Pickets were sent to Bailey's Crossroads to cover a line from there to the Chain Bridge above Georgetown. Outposts were established, abatis and additional field works constructed, and new regiments brought over the Potomac to join the forces already there.[72]

The scene in the capital was "of such confusion and panic as required no ordinary nerve to encounter. General Scott was firm and unwavering as a rock." When reports were delivered to him that the Confederates were advancing

69 Pisani, *Letters*, 114-115, letter dated August 10, 1861.

70 George B. McClellan, *McClellan's Own Story*, 67-69 (Norwalk, 1995)(*M.O.S.*).

71 *OR*, 2, 753.

72 Gilder, Lehrman MSS, Averell MS diary, 1, entry dated July 22, 1861; Averell, *Ten Years*, 304; Fry in *B&L*, 1, 193.

unopposed on the capital and would soon be on the Long Bridge, Scott denied any threat in his blunt, caustic way.

"It is impossible, sir! We are now tasting the first fruits of a war and learning what a panic is. We must be prepared for all kinds of rumors. Why, sir, we shall soon hear that Jefferson Davis has crossed the Long Bridge at the head of a brigade of elephants and is trampling our citizens under foot! He has no brigade of elephants. He cannot by any possibility get a brigade of elephants!"[73]

He took personal control of the situation. He would strengthen the garrisons of Forts Albany, Corcoran, Ellsworth, and Runyan on the far side of the Potomac. They must be held under all circumstances. He ordered the retreating army to be halted at the river.[74] McDowell was to stay on the Virginia side, keep fifteen regiments, retain "such field batteries as you deem necessary, . . . [and] send over to this side all the remaining troops and all the wagons and teams not absolutely needed for your purposes." With the equipment being sent across to Washington,[75] McDowell's former command, a fully equipped army of forty-five thousand men, had been stripped to an immobile defensive force of less than fifteen thousand infantry with scant artillery and no wagons. Under the departmental rule, command of the men withdrawn to the east side of the river would pass to Mansfield, Scott's original choice to command the Army of Northeastern Virginia.

Reconsidering a short time later, Scott told McDowell he could take until July 23 "if the enemy will permit" or the following day to comply with his orders. As soon as possible McDowell was to designate the regiments to remain on the west bank, but they were to be long-term volunteers only. All but two companies of cavalry were to be sent to Washington to report to Mansfield, yet another diminution of the command and certainly a lessening of his abilities because he would now have insufficient cavalry for scouting and advance picket duty.[76]

To begin the process of reestablishing order, one rallying point was fixed for each regiment wherever a part of it could be found. By issuing rations at that point to the members of that regiment but no one else, the soldiers would be induced to find their units. When an Ohio volunteer reported that he had walked from Centerville to the capital without seeing any Confederates, Scott knew the area of pursuit was clear and ordered McDowell to send back for the wounded and stragglers.[77]

73 Townsend, *Anecdotes*, 58-59.

74 *OR*, 2, 753, 754-55.

75 *OR*, 2, 755.

76 *OR*, 2, 758.

77 *OR*, 2, 756, 758.

By his steadiness, Scott kept others from panic. The leaders in the capital soon learned that the brigade of Regulars, the brigade commanded by Colonel Keyes, and other units had maintained their organization and had already occupied positions guarding the approaches to the capital.

Scott's aides busily attempted to press order from the chaos. Signs were posted in obvious places designating the rendezvous points for various organizations and commanding all officers and men to go to their rendezvous points. Some of the general's staff officers went to the hotels where they ordered all officers to join their regiments immediately or be arrested. The names and regiments of the officers were taken. "In this way, by nightfall things assumed a more orderly shape, and patrols, kept up throughout the day and night, soon suppressed all fear of disorders."[78]

Although a system had been established to guide the men to their units as they arrived,[79] thus keeping stragglers from crossing the Potomac into Washington,[80] the system was not completely effective. The capital had enough loose stragglers to convince any observer who saw only this part of the army that McDowell had lost control completely.[81] Lieutenant William H. Harris wrote his father, Senator Ira Harris, the day after the battle that the army was "disorganized, routed, demoralized."[82] And in a letter written a short time after the battle, a West Point cadet who had served as a volunteer aide in the battle said, "I think that our defeat is completely owing to the fact that our troops were not properly officered and the soldiers had no confidence in their abilities."[83]

Willard's Hotel, well known as a gathering place for notables, Lincoln's residence before he was inaugurated, and a place where general impressions formed easily, attracted many of the officers separated from their units. This must have proven, even more, that McDowell no longer controlled his army.[84]

78 Townsend, *Anecdotes*, 58-59.

79 *OR*, 2, 756.

80 *OR*, 2, 754-55.

81 By July 22, 1861, enough of the Army of Northeastern Virginia had been collected to determine that the losses, i.e., the men missing from the colors, were only two thousand five hundred to three thousand, far less than originally believed, *OR*, 2, 756-57. Because the actual losses in killed, wounded and missing were 1,176, *OR*, 2, 327, only about one thousand five hundred to two thousand were loose in the capital; but less than one hundred would have made a huge crowd in the bar at Willards.

82 William H. Harris MSS (U.S.M.A.) letter dated July 22, 1861, from William Harris to Ira Harris.

83 Crary, *Dear Belle*, 105.

84 Emerson, *Lowell's Life and Letters*, 217, August 5, 1861; Lowenfals, *Walt Whitman's Civil War*, 24-25; Dwight MSS, letter of July 28, 1861, from Dwight to his mother; McLaughlin, *Olmstead Letters*, 4, letter of August 3, 1861, from Olmstead to his father, *M.O.S.*, 62.

Senator Benjamin Wade received a letter immediately after the battle from one of the gadfly, civilian spectators, saying, "I witnessed much of the battle. Our troops behaved with great bravery but our officers in my mind just were very stupid."[85]

And a few days later William Dwight, who had left the Military Academy without finishing and was now one of the many aspirants in Washington seeking a commission, wrote to his parents, "McDowell showed himself unequal to the command of so large an army. Americans show themselves green at war. Colonels show themselves incompetent. Line officers cowards. The men showed want of trust in their officers, that want of trust made them think they were hurt when no harm was near them."[86]

An even greater problem for McDowell in the minds of his superiors, military and civilian, was the disappointment they had suffered. No one could charge him with culpable conduct that caused the failure; but they did know that, even though he had opposed the campaign, he had been extremely optimistic when he marched on July 16. Infected with his optimism, they certainly suffered, probably as much as he did, when he was defeated and deep down must have blamed him for their disappointed expectations.

And the numerous negative comments about the performance of the officers in the battle? They came from politicians, men with experience, men without, men with military training, and men with none. But how could any of them have evaluated the company grade, field grade, and general officers? These officers were a first cut, and their performance at the moment of truth could not have been predicted with any certainty. The best available criteria had been used to select them, but the evaluation process now followed the selection process. Those who had failed had to be identified and deprived of their shoulder straps. McDowell had no authority or structure for that. With little or no control over the selection process, he had marched on July 16 with the men given him by Lincoln, Secretary of War Cameron, Lieutenant-General Scott, various members of the House and Senate, and the governors of the states. Over the lower-level appointments, Lincoln, the Cabinet, and the federal government had been involved only in haphazard, individual cases that caught their attention.

The command of the Army of Northeastern Virginia was not a subject that eluded the attention of the civilian authorities. After he left Scott's apartment and returned to the White House, Lincoln met with his Cabinet to discuss this very subject. All present knew that "Patterson's misconduct in suffering Johnson [sic] to

85 Benjamin Wade MSS (Library of Congress), letter of July 22, 1861, from Frant to Leer Cab.

86 Dwight Family MSS (M.H.S.) letter of July 26, 1861, from William Dwight to his mother.

get away from him and join Beauregard was the first cause of the disaster." "General" Chase could say "I told you so" because he had urged two weeks earlier that John Fremont be sent to take command of the Valley army. If his suggestion had been adopted, Chase believed, "we should now be rejoicing over a great victory." Now, Nathaniel Prentiss Banks was being sent to take command. Relying on the inapplicable, even silly, historical example of Cincinnatus and "plowshares to swords" for identifying qualified material for command positions, Chase believed Banks lacked only "experience . . . to make a very able general."[87] As it progressed, the war would show how much nonsense this approach to high command had become by the middle of the nineteenth century.

George B. McClellan, a young major-general in Ohio, had attracted a great deal of attention by winning a small but emotionally important victory in the mountains of the Virginia–Ohio line a week before the disaster at Bull Run. Before the war while McClellan was a young, promising vice-president of the Illinois Central Railroad Company and Lincoln served as one of the lawyers for the company, the two men had met more than once in "out-of-the way county seats, where some important case was being tried." With sleeping accommodations unavailable, they would spend the night in front of the stove where Lincoln would, as McClellan recalled it, release his neverending "flow of anecdotes," which were "seldom refined, but always to the point."

George McClellan apparently listened well enough to impress his lanky raconteur.[88] Scott had known McClellan favorably since he graduated from the Military Academy at West Point number two in the extraordinary Class of 1846,[89] had dealt with him personally during the Battle of Cerro Gordo on the way to Mexico City,[90] and had corresponded with him on important matters of strategy since the early days of the war.[91] Two or three times during the night, Scott sent Schuyler Hamilton, his military secretary, to the White House to answer questions

87 Chase MSS (U.P.I.), letter dated July 23, 1861, from Chase to Mellen.

88 *M.O.S.*, 162.

89 See, generally, John C. Waugh, *The Class of 1846: From West Point to Appomattox: Stonewall Jackson, George McClellan and their Brothers* (New York, 1994) (Waugh, *Class of 1846*).

90 William S. Myers, ed., *The Mexican War Diary of George B. McClellan, A Campaign Journal Written in Camp and Field in 1846-47* (Princeton, 1917), 70, entry of [March] 25, 1847, 86, 87, narrative for April 16-17 (Myers, *McClellan Mexican War Diary*).

91 Sears, *McClellan's Correspondence*, 7-10, 12-13, 16-18, 28-31, letters of April 23, 1861, from McClellan to Scott; April 27, 1861, from McClellan to Scott; May 9, 1861, from McClellan to Scott; May 30, 1861 from McClellan to Lincoln; June 1, 1861, from McClellan to Lincoln; and June 5, 1861, from McClellan to Scott.

and convey information. Among other things, Hamilton carried Scott's messages recommending McClellan for the command in the east. Although he knew few officers in the army, Lincoln did know McClellan. He agreed with Scott. McClellan was the man for the job.[92]

The Cabinet seemed to be somewhat divided in its opinions about McDowell. But the "best informed" had not lost confidence in him. He had done "all that could have been done in his circumstances," but he had not won. They "felt that on this important line it is needful that the lead be confided to one having the prestige of victory as well as military talents." Together, the president and the Cabinet decided to replace McDowell as commander of the major military force in the east with McClellan. McDowell was not to be demoted, banished, or ostracized. He would continue to serve as an important officer under McClellan.[93]

Having already received orders to come to the rescue, followed by orders canceling the rescue mission, McClellan must have been puzzled when he received the following telegram:

> Adjutant General's Office
> Washington, D.C. July 22, 1861
> General George B. McClellan, Beverly, Va:
>
> Circumstances make your presence here necessary. Charge Rosecrans or some other general with your present department and come hither without delay.
>
> L. Thomas
> Adjutant-General[94]

92 Schuyler Hamilton in Stine, *The Army of the Potomac*, 99.

93 Little about this meeting is known except that it occurred, that Scott sent messengers to it, and that the events described in quotation marks took place. *N&H*, 4, 354, describe the meeting in one laconic sentence. Only Schuyler Hamilton quoted in Stine, *The Army of the Potomac*, 99; and one Chase letter, Chase MSS (U.P.I.), letter dated July 23, 1861, from Chase to Mellen, say anything about the meeting. Neither of the diarists in the Cabinet (Bates and Welles) recorded this meeting. During the period from January to October, 1861, Chase did not keep a diary. David Donald,ed., *The Civil War Diaries of Salmon P. Chase*, 46 (New York, 1954). Nor did the letter writers (Blair, Seward, and Chase) mention it. Elliott, Scott's diligent and superb biographer, says nothing about it and presumably found nothing. Nor does the blank record delineate the factors that tipped the scales against McDowell. Mentioned in the text are the factors that would have, and probably did, come to Lincoln's attention and to the attention of his Cabinet officers during July 22, the day after the battle. These factors would be things a civilian official without military training (Lincoln and his Cabinet were highly qualified for this position) would be likely to recognize and take into account.

94 *OR*, 2, 753.

Chapter 22

"Don't cheer, boys. I confess I rather like it myself, but Colonel Sherman here says it is not military; and I guess we had better defer to his opinion."

– Lincoln to the men of Sherman's brigade

Interregnum

On the morning of July 23, with the ugly events of Sunday fresh in everyone's mind, Lincoln, Cameron, and Scott met four members of the House of Representatives at the White House. In the discussion the "universal chagrin and fault-finding" was more than Scott could tolerate.[1] Without intending any criticism of the president but, no doubt, with a strong desire for vindication, exoneration, or "self-justification,"[2] Scott repeated himself as he often had in his older years.

"Sir, I am the greatest coward in America."

At once, one of the representatives rose from his chair as if to speak.

1 *N&H*, 4, 358; *Congressional Globe*, July 24, 1861, 246, 37th Cong., House of Representatives debates, Series No. 15. *N&H* say the conversation took place "a few days after the battle," but the indisputable dating in the *Globe* and the content of the speech make July 23 clear.

2 *N&H*, 4, 358; *Congressional Globe*, Aug. 1, 1861, 387.

"Stop, sir," continued Scott, "I will prove it. I have fought this battle, sir, against my judgment. I think the president of the United States ought to remove me today for doing it. As God is my judge, after my superiors had determined to fight it, I did all in my power to fight it. I deserve removal because I did not stand up when my army was not in condition for fighting and resist it to the last."

Lincoln had heard this before and had, no doubt, thought about it carefully and been puzzled. On the day of the battle he had questioned the advisability of fighting if the information about Johnston's escape from Patterson was accurate, but Scott had persuaded him to go forward with the plan. Now, the old general in chief was playing the role of the warrior who had reluctantly fought at the orders of his political superior. Notwithstanding Scott's lack of intent to blame the president, Lincoln could be forgiven for thinking that Scott was trying to direct criticism away from himself and refocus it on the chief executive.

"Your conversation seems to imply that I forced you to fight this battle," he said.

Scott had served under Andrew Jackson, James K. Polk, and James Buchanan, all difficult taskmasters, and had survived controversies with all of them. Skilled at extricating himself from a presidential predicament, he responded promptly.

"I have never served a president who has been kinder to me than you have been."[3]

After the retreat from Bull Run, most of the regiments resumed their old positions along the Potomac River and began working to restore their fighting trim. Although Scott, McDowell, and Mansfield had done much to return the officers and men to their colors and although the percentage of troops absent from the colors was not large, those who failed to return were highly visible proof that McDowell had lost control of his army. Worse yet at this time of disorder, the three-month troops, which had at least some training, had to be replaced with the new three-year men, who had none.

Sherman's brigade, like other cohesive units after the retreat, had returned to its old bivouac; and Sherman, a man who never lost sight of his goal, was hard at work bringing them back to order. He believed his men were in as good condition as any in McDowell's army. Nevertheless, some of his three-month men, near the end of their time, were ready to depart and had become mutinous. The Sixty-ninth New York behaved so badly that he put Ayres's battery in firing position and told the regiment he would order it to open fire if the men dared to leave camp.[4]

3 *Congressional Globe*, July 24, 1861, 246, 37th Cong., House, Series No. 18.

4 Sherman, *Memoirs*, 1, 188.

After reveille and roll call on July 23, Sherman found himself in a crowd of men going about their early duties. One of the officers, mistaking his man, said to him, "Colonel, I am going to New York today. What can I do for you?"

"How can you go to New York?" queried Sherman. "I do not remember to have signed a leave for you."

"No. I do not want a leave. I engaged to serve three months and have already served more than that time. If the government does not intend to pay me, I can not afford to lose the money. I am a lawyer and have neglected my business long enough and am going home."[5]

Sherman saw that a number of soldiers had gathered round them while they were talking. If they realized that a junior officer could defy him, he would lose all authority. Sharply, he turned on the officer.

"Captain, this question of your term of service has been submitted to the rightful authority; and the decision has been published in orders. You are a soldier and must submit to orders till you are properly discharged. If you attempt to leave without orders, it will be mutiny; and I will shoot you like a dog. Go back into the fort *now*, instantly," Sherman continued, "and don't dare to leave without my consent."

Sherman and the officer exchanged hard looks, Sherman with his hand stuck inside his overcoat implying that he had a pistol and would shoot, the officer probably trying to determine whether he really had a pistol. The officer took the course of discretion and returned to the fort.[6]

A short time later while a cold drizzling rain fell, Sherman entered a barn looking for a place to stable his horses. Inside, he found a group of the Seventy-ninth Highlanders, cold, hungry, wet, and demoralized. In a gruff and unsympathetic tone he asked what they were doing there. He knew they would be far better mentally and physically if they began to look after themselves at once. Continuing his gruff demeanor, he said, "Well, you had better go down into the woods and build bush huts. I want to put my horses in here." The men left, quickly collected a few tents and rations, and began to build a temporary camp.[7]

Later that morning McDowell received a telegram saying, the "general in chief directs that you have a suitable escort at the Georgetown Ferry at 1:00 p.m. today to meet the president of the United States and accompany him throughout the lines to visit the troops."[8]

5 Although the words are in quotes in the text, the language is given as indirect discourse.

6 Sherman, *Memoirs*, 1, 188-89.

7 Todd, *Seventy-ninth Highlanders*, 52-53.

8 *OR*, 2, 758, July 23, 1861.

When Lincoln reached McDowell's side of the Potomac, he and the general met for the first time since the July 21st battle. McDowell had resumed his headquarters at the Arlington House and was engaged in restoring order to his army, sending the ninety-day men home, and replacing them with three-year regiments. With his superb instinct for human relations and for preserving productive value in subordinates, Lincoln confided to McDowell, "I have not lost a particle of confidence in you."

"I don't see why you should, Mr. President," replied McDowell, expressing in his reserved way his deepest feelings about the outcome of the battle and the execution of his plans by his subordinates.[9]

Lincoln and McDowell reviewed a number of units. Passing down the lines of the Regular battalion, he paused in front of the colors.

"Mr. President," said McDowell, "these are the men who saved your army at Bull Run."

Lincoln looked keenly up and down the line. "I have heard of them!" he replied.[10]

Without any cavalry escort, President Lincoln and Secretary Seward left to see some of the other troops. The president was "full of feeling and wanted to encourage our men," Sherman explained later. Standing by the road that crossed the river on the aqueduct at Georgetown was a man examining a blockhouse built to defend the aqueduct. The figure hurried to a place on the roadside, where he could observe the occupants of the approaching carriage. As the carriage drew nearer, Lincoln and

9 Russell, *My Diary*, 247, entry of August 26, 1861. Although Russell does not place or date the meeting and describes it in a late August diary entry, the circumstances strongly suggest that it occurred on July 23 on the west bank of the Potomac during Lincoln's visit to the army. According to the timing in the order from Scott, the president must have met McDowell before he reached Sherman's brigade and presumably preferred to visit the troops without a cavalry escort. After the battle, McDowell had returned to his old headquarters on the grounds of the Arlington House and apparently remained there. Averell, *Ten Years*, 302-305; Russell, *My Diary*, 237, entry dated July 23, 1861. The first and only time Lincoln went to the west bank in the period after the battle was July 23. Miers, Earl Schenck, *Lincoln Day by Day*, 1861, 55-58.

10 Carter, *Four Brothers in Blue*, 15-16; Dangerfield, "The Regular Infantry in the First Bull Run Campaign," *The United Service*, 531. The visit is not dated in the letter from the brother serving in the Regulars, nor is the letter, but the writer was transferred to the east bank on August 2, *ibid.*, 16, so it had to have occurred before that. He merely says it occurred "a few days after the battle" and the letter is unhelpfully dated July, 1861. Todd, *Seventy-ninth Highlanders*, 53, says, in a somewhat confusing chronology of events that the visit occurred on the afternoon of July 23. That the event could have occurred on any other day than Lincoln's visit to the west bank of the Potomac on July 23 seems impossible. According to Meirs, *Lincoln Day By Day*, 1861, 56-57 no other visit was made to the west bank in the week after the battle. In fact, he visited only one other infantry regiment on any day in the week after the battles, the Twenty-seventh New York on July 27, 1861.

Seward recognized Colonel Sherman, who inquired whether they were going to his camps.[11]

"Yes," replied the president, "We heard you had gotten over the big scare, and we thought we would come over and see the boys."

The roads being rough and having changed, Sherman asked if he might give directions to the coachman. Lincoln agreed and invited him to ride in the coach.[12]

To begin on one flank of his brigade and continue to the other, Sherman turned the driver into a side road that led up a very steep hill. He saw a soldier on foot, called to him, and sent him ahead to announce that the president was coming. Slowly, the carriage ascended the hill.

"Do you intend to speak to them?" Sherman asked.

"I would like to."

"Please, discourage all cheering, noise, or any sort of confusion. We have had enough of it before Bull Run to ruin any set of men, and what we need are cool, thoughtful, hard-fighting soldiers—no more hurraying, no more humbug."[13] The president accepted Sherman's remarks in "the most perfect good-nature."

As they approached the first camp, they could hear the drum beating the assembly and see the men running for their tents. In a few minutes the regiment had formed in line, presented arms, come to order, and settled at "parade rest."

Lincoln rose in the carriage and made "one of the neatest, best, and most healing addresses I ever listened to," recalled Sherman later, "referring to our late disaster at Bull Run, the high duties [that] have still devolved on us, and the brighter days yet to come." At one or two points the men began to cheer. The president checked them.

"Don't cheer, boys. I confess I rather like it myself, but Colonel Sherman here says it is not military; and I guess we had better defer to his opinion."

At the end Lincoln explained that, as president, he was commander in chief and that he wanted his soldiers to have everything the law allowed. He called on them, one and all, to appeal to him personally in case they felt wronged. The effect of his speech was "excellent."

The three men rode in the carriage to the camps of the other regiments in the brigade. Lincoln complimented Sherman on the order, cleanliness, and discipline he saw in the camps. It was the first bright moment he and Seward had experienced since the battle.

11 According to Sherman, *Memoirs*, 1, 189, the president's visit occurred on July 26; Meirs, *Lincoln Day by Day*, and *OR*, 2, 758, date the visit July 23. See also note 10, *supra*.

12 Sherman, *Memoirs*, 1, 189.

13 Indirect discourse has been converted to direct.

When they reached the Second Wisconsin, they repeated the performance. Speaking from the carriage both Lincoln and Seward encouraged the men. Captain Gabriel Bouck, commander of Company E, eccentric enough to speak his mind at all times, turned one of his private's backside to the front, exposed a large tear in the rear of his trousers, and, therefore, a large "flag of truce," saying, "Lincoln, look here! Here is a specimen of the soldiers. Give us good guns and respectable clothing and there will be no trouble."

He then showed Lincoln an unsatisfactory firearm. Lincoln and Seward promised the men that they would be better armed and clothed and that they would be "healed."[14]

They also visited the Seventy-ninth Highlanders. When the carriage stopped, the men again gathered to hear "a few words of sympathy and encouragement."

"Now, boys," he concluded, "keep up a good heart and all will yet be well."

He motioned the driver to proceed; but the day had apparently become "All Complaints Day." One of the men decided to tell the president about his brigade commander's inhumanity in the barn.

"Mr. President," he began, "We don't think Colonel Sherman has treated us very well;" and he continued with the story. Lincoln listened patiently to the end.

"Well, boys, I have a great deal of respect for Colonel Sherman, and if he turned you out of the barn, I have no doubt it was for some good purpose. I presume he thought you would feel better if you went to work and tried to forget your troubles."

He bowed, waived his hand, and told the driver to head for the next camp.[15]

Finally, they reached Fort Corcoran, where the carriage could not enter the fort. Sherman ordered the regiment to come outside without arms and gather round the president. Lincoln made the same address, but with more personal allusions because of the special gallantry the regiment had shown in battle under Colonel Corcoran, now a Rebel prisoner. He concluded with the same general offer to hear any man feeling aggrieved.

In the crowd was the officer Sherman had braced at reveille that morning. His face was pale, his lips compressed. Sherman anticipated an incident but sat quietly while the officer forced his way through the crowd to the carriage. "Mr. President I have a cause of grievance. This morning I went to speak to Colonel Sherman, and he threatened to shoot me."

Still standing at the edge of the carriage, Lincoln said, "Threatened to shoot you?"

14 Goff, Alan, *The Second Wisconsin Infantry* (Dayton, 1994), 20, 30 (Goff, *Second Wisconsin*).

15 Todd, *Seventy-ninth Highlanders*, 53-54.

"Yes, sir, he threatened to shoot me."

Lincoln looked at the officer, looked at Sherman, then stooped his tall form toward the officer and said to him in a loud whisper easily heard for some distance, "Well, if I were you and he threatened to shoot, I would not trust him; for I believe he would do it."

The officer turned and disappeared into the crowd, the enlisted men laughing at him. While the carriage drove down the hill, the president asked why the man had spoken so violently. Sherman described the earlier event.[16]

"I told him, Mr. President," he added, "that if he refused to obey my orders, I would shoot him on the spot. And I here repeat it, sir, that if I remain in command here and he or any other man refused to obey my orders, I'll shoot him on the spot."[17]

The president responded, as his comment to the officer had suggested he would, "Of course, I didn't know anything about it; but I thought you knew your own business best."

The colonel thanked his commander in chief for his confidence and assured him that the president's response would go far to maintain good discipline. He was right. The visit by the president "with his grave, serious, yet kindly face . . . a sympathetic friend . . . worked a magic cure for the demoralized men." Now, the day was spent. The colonel took his leave, and Lincoln and Seward drove back to Washington.[18]

Superseded at the head of the army but in command until McClellan's arrival, McDowell now had to deal with his equivocal state during the interim. He received the usual unfair and inaccurate treatment from the press, one Philadelphia newspaper stating that he was drunk during the battle and that he had stayed awake all night before the battle drinking, smoking, and playing cards.[19] Others charged him with incapacity, disloyalty, and general drunkenness.[20] Even some of his subordinates thought he had been drunk.[21]

In the campaign and the events surrounding it, the seeds of a much greater problem for McDowell were sown. During the advance, plundering had taken place. The Regular Army officers had reacted harshly to it, and McDowell had issued a circular denouncing the marauders in strong terms. The men in the ranks were indignant. In the minds of many, Rebel civilians were villains, had no rights, and

16 Todd, *Seventy-ninth Highlanders*, 54; Sherman, *Memoirs*, 1, 189-190.

17 Russell, *My Diary*, 236-237, entry dated July 23, 1861.

18 Todd, *Seventy-ninth Highlanders*, 54; Sherman, *Memoirs*, 1, 189-190.

19 Russell, *My Diary*, 241, entry dated July 27, 1861.

20 Allen in *Broadfoot MOLLUS Wisconsin*, 46, 392.

21 Robertson, *McAllister Letters*, 57-58, letter of July 30, 1861, from McAllister to his wife.

should not pass unscathed. Stringent orders against plundering their property were no different than orders of protection and safe conduct. Many of the men believed these orders should not have been issued, should not be tolerated, and should not be obeyed. The officers who were responsible for them provoked a strong hostility among the enlisted men, a hostility established early in McDowell's case.[22]

During the retreat from Henry House Hill, most parts of the shattered army passed through Centerville. The full, unblooded regiments from Miles's division and Runyan's division caused much excitement among the men who had marched and fought in the broiling sun and had left comrades behind on the bloodsoaked field. They were "very severe in their comments upon the ability and loyalty of the commanding general." They and others concluded that McDowell's incompetency—or worse—was the primary cause of the defeat. Initially, these beliefs simmered; but a hearty boil was only a short time and a few incidents away.[23]

On the morning of July 24, two gentlemen of the press visited McDowell at headquarters. He was seated at a table under a tree at the Arlington House. Using maps and plans, he explained the battle to them. In his diary one of them summarized McDowell's position and his mood, "Cast down from his high estate, placed as a subordinate to his junior, covered with obloquy and abuse, the American General displayed a calm self-possession and perfect amiability which could only proceed from a philosophic temperament and a consciousness that he would outlive the calumnies of his countrymen. He accused nobody . . ."[24]

Consistent with his upbringing, McDowell maintained his dignity and reserve. He spoke of his defeat, said another European, "without bitterness or complaint, with an accent of sincerity and elevation of mind truly to his honor."[25] But in his explanation even a layman without military training could identify the failures of his subordinates. Nor could they help but conclude that, victimized by an unfortunate coalescence of these failures, he was without fault.

But he was not superhuman. On Friday, August 2, he and George Templeton Strong had a long talk about the defeat. He could not conceal his depression and mortification. As he had to the president, he confirmed to Strong that he had no reason to doubt himself, that he had "nothing to reproach himself with."[26]

22 Blake, *Three Years in the Army*, 11-12.

23 *Ibid.*, 29.

24 Russell, *My Diary*, 237, entry dated July 24, 1861.

25 Comte de Paris MS Diary (large diary) (A.N. de la M. de F.) entry of September 28, 1861; *Pisani Letters*, 116, letter dated August 10, 1861, from Pisani in Washington.

26 Nevins, *Strong Diary*, 3, 174, entry dated Aug. 2, 1861.

During this period of reduction, criticism, lies, and vilification, McDowell undertook the unenviable task of preparing his report of the battle. He had sustained the supreme human disappointment. Galloping headlong across the battlefield, he had shouted, "Victory," to his advancing troops. He had stood on Henry House Hill at the head of his turning column with no more needed, so it seemed, than a flick of his wrist to brush the last organized resistance off the hub of the Confederate position. In moments, the Rebels would be defeated and in retreat if not in flight. He would achieve the object of the campaign. He would move the Capital's main line of defense from the Potomac River to the line of the Rappahannock River, Manassas Gap, and Strasburg. An exalted, honorable place in the military history of his country was in his grasp. While the taste of victory was strong in his mouth, the cup was snatched from his hand at the very last moment by cruel quirks of fate—over which he had no control—and he was "cast down." No man in these circumstances could have escaped the vicious flights of fancy, the emotionally crushing might-have-beens. If only this subordinate or that leader had . . . Whatever McDowell might say for the rest of his life, whatever he would write in his report, he could not have been unmindful of the crown that had been snatched away from him.

Under date of August 4 he forwarded his report, as proper military etiquette and procedure required, to Lieutenant-Colonel Edward D. Townsend, the assistant-adjutant-general of his immediate superior Winfield Scott at the headquarters of the army.[27] He had kept manfully to the work. The two weeks required to prepare it had been caused by the delay of subordinate commanders who submitted accounts for their commands late. Having already reported the nasty affair at Blackburn's Ford,[28] he began with the events of July 20 and laconically traced their fateful course through the battle to the retreat to the Potomac. Occasionally, he described the operations of his mind, his own thoughts. About all others he merely recounted their actions as he understood them from their reports, from others' reports, and from his own observations. The unfortunate Miles's drunkenness he never mentioned or implied. When Miles's subordinate units maneuvered on orders given by others because Miles was disabled, he described their activity in the passive voice, "Orders had been sent back to Miles's division for a brigade to move forward and protect this retreat, and Colonel Blenker's brigade was detached for this purpose and was ordered to go . . ."[29]

27 *OR*, 2, 317, 325.

28 *OR*, 2, 307.

29 *OR*, 2, 321.

In the usual manner he listed those worthy of recognition, giving their name, rank, unit, and position. This long list of twenty-eight names included almost his entire staff, every brigade commander, and every division commander save Miles, the only officer of higher command left unmentioned. Among the staff officers, who, he said, "did everything in their power, exposing themselves freely when required and doing all that men could do,"[30] he even included Major Barry, though Barry had been responsible for the beginning of the disaster on Henry House Hill. On the most determinative event—the failure to hold Johnston in the Valley—he merely said, "From causes not necessary for me to refer to, even if I knew them all, this was not done, and the enemy was free to assemble from every direction."[31] Not a word in criticism did he pen.

When the report was finished, McDowell laid aside his pen and hoped he had put his Bull Run experience behind him forever. To give its submission complete finality, he kept no copy. He would be willing to describe, without opinion or editorial comment, the events. But criticize his comrades in arms? Refight the battle and treat them as the enemy? Unthinkable. As he later described this bleak, unhappy period in his life,

> When I wrote my report of that battle I endeavored to do so in such a way that I should not, in any case, have to touch the subject again. Whatever shortcomings there were, in my judgment, on the part of others concerned in, or connected with that event, which I did not mention, I cannot mention now, and the load as I have carried it, I must continue to carry to the end!
>
> I have no reason to complain of the view generally expressed by the most thoughtful and candid writers as to my own part, as the general in command, and I have not, myself—except in the case of the testimony I was called on to give before the Congressional Committee—attempted to controvert the statements, or combat the opinions of others—when I have thought them erroneous or unfounded as to the merits or demerits of anyone in the matter. Therefore I have said all that I had, or have, to say—such certainty is to my present feeling—and I trust nothing may occur to require me to do more than I have already done![32]

McDowell's plan of battle had been excellent. It took into consideration all aspects of his army, militia, volunteers, lack of experience, too brief training, lack of inter-unit service. But in the end he was compromised at every turn. He expected to fight at Fairfax Courthouse, but he could not. He planned to move by his left flank,

30 *OR*, 2, 322-23.

31 *OR*, 2, 325.

32 Misc. Civil War MSS, Huntington Library, dated April 20, 1869, from McDowell to Henry B. Dawson.

but he could not. He decided to flank the enemy from his right, but his subordinates delayed the accumulation of information, then improperly executed the flanking march. His artillery was prepared to blow the Confederates off Henry House Hill, but its fire was changed to the wrong target. Strong Rebel forces were to be held in the Valley, but they were not. Through all these subversions of his intentions he managed well, dealing flexibly with each in its turn. Until the problems passed beyond his capacity, he was a problem solver, not a man who stopped because he saw a problem. At the last, however, he failed to win the victory his government wanted and needed so badly.

How much did he contribute to his own defeat? In comparison with Patterson's easily accomplished fifteen miles of marching a day—when he marched at all—McDowell never covered more than five or six. He did everything in his power to hasten the columns on their way but to no avail. The inexperience of the troops, the rough and wooded terrain, the wretched roads, the many unbridged streams, the shortness of his military sight because he had no effective cavalry, and the constant fear of the "masked battery"[33] frustrated all his efforts to increase the speed of his army. In addition, his inadequate staff and communications system could not overcome lack of coordination for the four divisions each marching on a separate road.

His most culpable act was the delay at Centerville. Every day he allowed to pass brought more Confederates to Manassas, and he knew it. Peculiarly enough, he eventually fought the number of troops he had earlier predicted. July 20 was a day uselessly wasted, and the arrival on Sunday of the last units from the valley turned the tide of battle. When the reconnaissance ended in failure to reach the fords on Friday afternoon, he should have used the knowledge he had. Absolutely nothing was added to his intelligence through the efforts made that night, but the net effect was to force him to wait another full day in order to complete his plan, brief his officers, and strike at early dawn.

Second, he yielded his determination to marshal his forces with a short march on Saturday evening. The result was delay and disorientation of his approach march. When he left the banks of the Potomac on Tuesday, he used only the latter half of that day to march his troops, who moved from their entrenched positions to what were, in effect, "jump-off" areas for the planned assault on the Fairfax Courthouse line. Without attempting to strike a blow, the divisions marched a short, easy distance in one to three hours. Next day, the columns were rested, had little distance to march, and were easily coordinated for the attack. The reason Burnside opposed the

33 Lyster in *Broadfoot MOLLUS Michigan*, 50, 115; Gurowski, *Diary*, 1, 78-79, entry of August, 1861.

movement on July 20—that it would tire the infantry more to make two short marches than a single long one—directly contradicted experience less than one week old. McDowell acquiesced, and the result was the unrecoverable delay and confusion in the early hours of July 21. Tyler was to blame, but the army commander made the initial decision, and made it incorrectly.

In the battle he allowed his focus to be captured by individual units, which he often directed himself. The army needed overall direction, and he should have provided it as the coordinator of all units. At some times, he was little more than a company commander. One major cause of this, aside from the fact that no Union officer on the field had ever commanded a regiment and few, if any, had ever commanded a company in battle, was the inadequacy of his staff. It was too small, and it lacked experience. Tasks which should have been done by staff officers remained to plague him and divert his attention.

Much blame was placed on McDowell for sending Ricketts and Griffin to Henry House Hill.[34] In retrospect, whatever might have been said about selecting the position and who actually did it, two things were true. First, visible support by artillery was good for infantry and probably more so for inexperienced infantry. Close support by direct artillery fire was a Napoleonic tactic that had worked marvelously well at the turn of the century and would continue to work well through the end of the Civil War.[35] Its emotional value for infantry would be sharply debated by two brilliant officers at a critical moment later in the war. Second, the position of the two batteries was not to blame for their loss. The move itself was tactically sound, and the batteries would have been safe if Barry had allowed Griffin to fire at the Confederate regiment.

The retention of Howard's brigade at the blacksmith shop was indefensible under any circumstances. Twenty percent of the striking power of the flanking column was removed and no advantage was gained. On the east bank he kept six brigades in two divisions, more than half his army, to defend the creek line against Confederate assaults. Why strengthen the safest wing and weaken the most

34 The origin of the order is unclear. Barry claimed at the time that McDowell gave it, *C.C.W.*, 2, 144, (Barry) and stated that in his report. *OR*, 2, 347. In his testimony before the Joint Commitee, Griffin gave a hearsay account of a conversation between Ricketts and Lieutenant Snyder suggesting that McDowell merely acquiesced in Barry's order; *C.C.W.*, 2, 172 (Griffin). Snyder died of disease in November without ever confirming or denying the conversations. *Cullum*, 2, no. 1711, and Ricketts never had any reason in his testimony to address the issue, *C.C.W.*, 2, 242-246 (Ricketts). On the basis of the colloquy quoted, *supra*, Chap. 18, p. XX, Barry probably gave the order on his own.

35 Chandler, *Napoleon*, 1, 360-367; the predominance of indirect fire, i.e. the men at the guns could not see their targets, awaited developments in communications for feasibility and in long range accurate infantry weapons for necessity.

vulnerable? On a very small scale this decision foretold the fate of the Schlieffen Plan for the initial German assault on France in the early nineteenth century. The German General Staff, prior to World War I, modified the plan until the ratio of the flanking column to the defensive line had been cut in half.[36]

The basic concept of McDowell's original plan was sound. After he advanced, a movement by the left to cut the Confederate line would have forced the severed wing to retreat by itself or fight its way home, a classic strategic offensive and tactical defensive. It was also sound because, among other things, it would avoid two developments that would help the Confederates. The movement by the right would only have been decisive if the Rebels chose to stand and fight, and even a victory would present no opportunity to destroy the Rebel army. Instead, as the Confederate units were driven back by the flanking column, they would continuously gain reinforcement and strength because they would be driven onto the remainder of their army. At the same time, as the battle progressed and McDowell was increasingly successful, the rear of his flanking column was forced to march farther and farther. Once across the Run, the Army of Northeastern Virginia had to make a frontal attack on a Rebel force which lay between the Federals and Manassas Junction, the very tactic McDowell had tried to plan away.

Next, where should he have stood on the battlefield, particularly once the fighting had made Judith Henry's hill the focal point of the battle? Natural instinct, which he followed, identified the turning column as most likely to need him in the early going on July 21. Although he did not manage to cure Tyler's negative contribution and he did arrange to exhaust Howard's brigade, he prodded the column, hurried it along, and exercised the kind of overall supervision that none of the division commanders thought to do. Once the column had begun its deployment south of the trees on the far side of Sudley Springs Ford, the division commanders, Hunter and Heintzelman, should have managed the tactics on Matthews Hill, Buck Hill, and Henry House Hill—not the commander of the army.

Putting the lie to suspicions and rumors of cowardice, McDowell exposed himself freely as he moved from brigade to brigade on the hill;[37] but he could have

36 Gunther E. Rothenberg, "Moltke, Schlieffen, and the Doctrine of Strategic Envelopment," in Peter Paret, ed., *Makers of Modern Strategy from Machievelli to the Nuclear Age* (Princeton, 1986), 318, 322-323 (Paret, *Makers of Modern Strategy*). This was not the classic battle of annihilation by the double, flanking encirclement that was made famous by Hannibal at Cannae and that captivated theorists and planners in the late Nineteenth Century. However, by forcing the severed wing to take the offensive and fight its way free under adverse conditions, especially without the freedom to choose the ground for battle, it had the potential for many of the same beneficial aspects.

37 Military Historical Society of Massachusetts MSS (John Ropes letters) (M.L., B.U.) letter dated August 8, 1861, from Bache to Ropes.

done more if he had followed the example of Napoleon at Austerlitz. Although Napoleon had no fixed rules for battle,[38] one tactic he used often was a powerful attack on an important part of the enemy line, followed by enough delay for the enemy to send reinforcements from adjacent positions, then an attack by the *masse de decision* or the *schwerpunkt* on the position weakened by the departure of the "reinforcements."[39] At Austerlitz, Napoleon did not position himself on either of his embattled flanks, where heavy fighting took place at the beginning of the battle. Watching the Heights of Pratzen in the center, he could see forty thousand enemy troops marching toward the French right to "save the day" for the Austrian army. When the reinforcements from the center had gone too far to return in time, he ordered Marshall Davout to launch the assault that shattered the weakened center.[40]

If McDowell had taken position with Tyler, he might have been able, like Napoleon, to launch Tyler's division in a single assault by a column of brigades, a classic Napoleonic stroke that would have shattered the Confederate line.

The Stone Bridge, a critical tactical position, had originally been strongly guarded by the Confederates. When they realized that Tyler's desultory demonstration was a bluff and that the turning column was the main effort, they left the Stone Bridge area of the creek undefended and rushed north to delay the flanking force. Just above the bridge Sherman crossed without opposition. Keyes followed without opposition. For no reason other than military incompetence, Schenck never crossed at all. With three fresh brigades in column, a single resolute charge, even

38 Burnod, Lieutenant-General Sir G. C. D'Aguilar, C. B., trans., *Napoleon's Art of War*, 2-4 (New York, 1995).

39 Chandler, *Napoleon*, 1, 188-191, 424-428.

40 Chandler, *Napoleon*, 1, 422-428. Officers who knew no better and were aligned with the group disposed to criticize McDowell would have been critical of this and would have thought his personal efforts on Henry House Hill were the correct choice. McClellan would face this problem in 1862: the choice between the critical position for the army commander and the "public relations" position. The days of Hannibal and Alexander the Great were long gone and the presence of the commander of the army in the heaviest fighting was no longer so important. See generally, Keegan, *The Mask of Command*. But in a conversation with the author, a well known writer on McClellan implied that McClellan should have stayed with his troops and guns when he said that McClellan "deserted" his army after it reached Malvern Hill and Harrison's Landing by going aboard the *Galena* on the James River. He should have known better for two reasons. First, all McClellan's subordinates were unanimous about his personal courage, especially the staff officers who served with him most closely. Second, the reasons for his *Galena* trips are described in a letter in a manuscript collection the writer used (he cited the collection, and his use of it has been confirmed by the curator), Military Historical Society of Massachusetts MSS (John C. Ropes letters) (B.U.) letter dated March 27, 1895, from Biddle to Ropes. No one else has given any reason for the boat trips except that a few superficial writers infer he was a coward because he took them. The explanation given by Biddle to Ropes is consistent with many other statements by McClellan about the quality of his subordinates and his unwillingness to delegate, a characteristic of his idol Napoleon.

with green regiments, would have broken the hinge between the Henry House Hill position and the Bull Run line and flanked the Rebel line on Henry House Hill before the counterattack on McDowell's right flank and rear.

Last, McDowell showed that he lacked continuous battlefield visualization, an important characteristic for a man in his position. As the war progressed, many others would prove that they, too, had this deficiency, McClellan at Ball's Bluff and Sickles at Chancellorsville and Gettysburg being two excellent examples. During the battle, his concentration on the Henry House Hill position intensified; and his awareness of the entire field waned. His flanking column had turned the Rebel line so effectively that, when he had doubled it into a hairpin, his own forces had the same shape. Unfortunately, however, McDowell's own flank and rear were directly exposed to forces coming from the Confederate left on the Sudley Springs Road and other roads that ran behind and parallel to the Confederate front line—and to forces coming, as they did, from Manassas Junction. Having become a regimental and company commander, McDowell's concentration on the success of his flanking force made him unaware that his own right flank was exposed to nearby Confederates. While he failed to maintain his overall visualization, a Confederate force attacked his flank without warning.

McDowell never received credit, even from his friends and supporters, for the miracle he accomplished between May 24 and July 21: from nothing he created an army capable of a complicated offensive battle in less than two months. Ten years later, while Otto von Bismarck completed his creation of the modern German state, the contrast presented by Prussia and France showed McDowell's achievement to have been outstanding.

Operating under a unified system, Prussia and the independent states of the North German Confederation required universal military service for three years, followed by four years in the reserve, then five years in the Landwehr, the equivalent of a militia. Thus, at any time the Prussian army had more than seven years of trained men available immediately and a large militia pool behind them. Because the Prussian Regular Army supervised the reserve and the Landwehr throughout the North German Confederation, these forces had the equivalent of national uniformity. The reserve and the Landwehr were organized according to geographic home areas, each one independent, self-sufficient, and the equivalent of a military corps. The princes of the North German Confederation, like Lincoln's governors, had particularistic but only superficial powers. Unlike the president of the United States, the king of Prussia had virtually all the important powers; and he, also unlike Lincoln, held these powers unsupervised by the states or the Reichstag.

When war with the French appeared likely in 1870, the Prussian General Staff already had a plan for full mobilization. Even the French, in their traditional haphazard, disorganized, and arrogant way, had a plan. In July of 1870 the king of

Prussia ordered mobilization of the Confederation against France. Eighteen days later the small Regular Army had been transformed into one million two hundred thousand trained men on the march to battle the French.[41] With the same information, the French, too, mobilized for a war they had expected and set their army moving west to meet the Germans.

McDowell could draw on none of this. Lincoln, the Republican government, their Regular Army, and the kaleidoscopic state militias had no pre-existing organization or plan like the Prussians or even the inept French. The federal government had tried so hard to avoid provoking the hot-headed Southerners that it had reduced itself to military impotency. A few state governors, Banks and Andrew of Massachusetts and to a lesser degree Curtin of Pennsylvania, had shown some foresight. Not so the other leaders, state and federal. Staff planning for mobilization of the militias to supplement the Regular Army? Not a glimmer. Into this well of confused ineffectiveness, McDowell plunged his burly arms and drew forth an army with offensive capability in less than two months. Little wonder that his artillery lacked any structure or theory beyond the individual battery, that his cavalry had no

41 Howard, *Franco-Prussian War*, 20-21, 27, 58-60; Craig, *Politics of the Prussian Army*, 140-179; Otto Pflanze, *Bismarck and the Development of Germany*, 3 vols., (Princeton, 1990), *The Period of Unification, 1815-1871*, 1, 342-346. Unfortunately, Hans Delbruck, perhaps dismayed at the humiliating outcome of World War I, changed his mind and ceased his thoughtful, incisive labors with the end of Napoleon in 1815. At the end of volume four, he said, ". . . the phenomenal rise of Prussia and its final collapse . . . must be undertaken by others." *op. cit.*, 455. According to Michael Howard, the general staffs of most armies were "no more than a collection of adjutants and clerks for the commander in the field." The German General Staff had developed into much more:

> the Prussians at least studied their errors, and readjusted their training and organisation accordingly. They did so, not because the Prussian generals were more intelligent or harder-working than their opponents, but because the Prussians possessed, in their General Staff, a body whose object was to fulfil exactly this function: applying to the conduct of war a continuous intelligent study, analyzing the past, appreciating the future, and providing the commanders in the field with an unceasing supply of information and advice. (Howard, *Franco Prussian War*, 25.)

Even the horrible example presented by the United States in 1861 did not teach the rest of the world. Teetering on the brink of war with Prussia ten years later, France finally mobilized an army with outmoded doctrine, confused military plans, and inept leaders. According to Michael Howard, ". . . neither the faults of the French strategic planning nor the incompetence of French commanders, nor even the total numerical inferiority of the French army . . . gave the Germans so overwhelming an advantage when the war began. It was the chaos of the French mobilization." *Ibid.*, 66, 8E. Working almost singlehandedly, facing the same problems, and suffering uncooperative interference by the general in chief, McDowell came within an eyelash of winning his country's first major battle of the war.

strength or purpose, and that his staff amounted to a handful of men without even classroom experience at the needs of Napoleonic-sized armies.

In April, Lincoln had a Regular Army of approximately seventeen thousand officers and men scattered over a huge continent, and he called for militia of seventy-five thousand, altogether less than one hundred thousand men. On July 16, McDowell met with his staff and commanding officers, then marched with a polyglot army of forty-five thousand. From virtually nothing he had created an army capable of effective offensive action and led it in a battle he lost because others failed to perform. The critical point for McDowell was not that his army failed its task or that it exemplified this or that deficiency. That it stood manfully to its task and performed as well as it did marks the merit of his performance and the extraordinary, inherent capability of his countrymen.

A balanced assessment of McDowell was written soon after the battle by a young staff officer with the turning column. He said in early August, "McDowell is a gallant soldier & did his best the other day at the Run, but *I* do not think him a great general. He exposed himself gallantly the other day, but was not *the great general* we should have had on that field. We wanted a man with a reputation. He had none."[42] Only the passage of time would tell whether McDowell would recover from the loss at Bull Run Creek or sink into oblivion. By the last days of July both developments were possible, but the most likely one could not be identified.

Meanwhile, on July 27, Patterson's commission as a major-general of volunteers expired; but before the battle west of Bull Run his future services had already been deemed unnecessary. He had been tested, had been found to lack offensive spirit, had resisted repeated orders to carry out his mission, and had offered repeated excuses for his failure to make any assertive movement. As a military leader, he had disappointed everyone.

A good subordinate needed certain characteristics. The successful independent commander required all those and more. Both flanks were his responsibility; he could not look to other forces to deploy on them for protection. His line of supply, line of advance, line of retreat, and tactical objectives were his responsibility. Nor would the independent commander have anyone to make his daily decisions for him. Patterson's handling of these responsibilities had been poor.

But Patterson had a powerful voice in the background, his Regular Army, West Point Adjutant Fitz-John Porter. At the critical moment on July 18, the failure to attack Johnston was undoubtedly Porter's work, not an independent decision, as it should have been, by the commanding officer.

42 Military Historical Society of Massachusetts MSS (John C. Ropes letters) letter of August 8, 1861, from Bache to Ropes.

Quite simply, the burden of independent command lay heavy on Patterson; as the commander of an independent army, he was a failure in every respect, especially as the commander of an independent army with an offensive mission. His timidity, his domination by Fitz-John Porter, and all the by-products of this unhealthy, ineffective combination made him utterly unsuited for the command he had.

Patterson's mission had been simple and stated to him repeatedly. He was to keep Johnston in the valley until McDowell fought Beauregard. Whether it was by a pinning attack that forced Johnston to deploy and fight, by interposition between Winchester and Manassas, or by some artifice, Patterson was to hold Johnston while McDowell fought Beauregard. Dominated by thoughts from his first days in command when his army was the principal force in the east and its survival the most important consideration, Patterson lost track of his assignment. By July, the complete destruction of his army was less important than a victory by McDowell at Manassas; but Patterson continued to believe that defeat of his army spelled doom for the cause of the Union.

In the final event, Patterson's failure to hold Johnston in the valley had allowed some nine thousand troops to be added to Beauregard's army behind Bull Run, the last of these being the fresh units which hit the naked right flank and rear of the Union army on Henry House Hill during the struggle for the guns of Griffin and Ricketts. Although he was misguided by Scott, he reciprocated. Prevarication in his reports and dispatches coupled with minimal action sufficed to allow the Confederates to escape; and Scott was not able to notify McDowell of Johnston's departure until July 21—after the Army of Northeastern Virginia had attacked the reinforced enemy.[43] From his subordinates, Patterson sought confirmation of decisions he knew to be wrong. He ignored reality. He grasped authority but failed to use it. He certainly lacked the capacity for a large independent command. Under the circumstances he had committed an absolute blunder. His removal from command was necessary, if not mandatory.

On July 19, the adjutant-general's office in Washington issued General Orders No. 46. Paragraph one "honorably discharged" Patterson from the service of the United States on July 27, the date his commission expired. General Cadwalader, his fellow Pennsylvanian, fellow veteran of the Mexican War, and ineffective division commander, was also discharged.[44] As was so often true, the order found its way into the hands of the press before it reached either of them.[45]

43 *OR*, 2, 746.

44 *OR*, 2, 171.

45 *OR*, 2, 173.

Unaware that his Washington superiors anticipated the expiration of his commission with relief, if not gratitude, Patterson continued to recommend maneuvers after the defeat at Bull Run, this time for a march to Washington with his entire force. In a short, icy reply Scott told him he was not needed or wanted in Washington. He should occupy and hold Harpers Ferry.

The press, looking everywhere for a victim, published false statements about him. The vast majority of the blame for the disaster at Bull Run was laid at his door. He was drunk. He was unfit for command. He was disloyal, a secessionist, a Confederate sympathizer.[46] Whatever could be said about his military competence, the factual inventions about questionable loyalty had not a glimmer of truth in them.

Before he received the frosty order to occupy Harpers Ferry, Patterson read the newspaper article that published General Orders No. 46 relieving him and Cadwalader. Neither of them, he thought, could march to Washington without appearing to be thrusting themselves on the administration.[47]

He knew that publication of his reports and his correspondence would violate orders, and he was unwilling to do that. He believed publication would be "detrimental to the interests of the service." The facts, the correspondence, and his opinions he kept to himself except for his family, his former adjutant-general, Major Fitz-John Porter, and his former volunteer aide, Senator John Sherman.[48] He was, he wrote a few years later, "quite satisfied . . . to await the returning sense of the people, and to abide by their decision, when the natural passion and disappointment of the hour should pass away and a full knowledge of the facts should enable them to form an intelligent and dispassionate judgment."[49] But he was willing to use Sherman and Porter for an indirect approach. Major Porter should write to Senator Sherman.

"At the request of General Patterson," Porter wrote, "I send you copies of letters and telegrams received and issued relating to the campaign with which he was connected. He is confident that you, and the country also, when the facts are known, will do him justice and be thankful that he conducted all his operations in compliance with orders and expectations and with good judgment and that the government should be thankful for his prudence." Patterson authorized Sherman to use the letters and telegrams according to his judgment.

"A Court of Inquiry," Porter continued, "should be granted if justice is not done him. I believe when the facts are known and reason is restored to the public mind, it

46 *OR*, 2, 177.

47 *OR*, 2, 173.

48 Porter MSS (L.C.) letter dated November 8, 1861, from Patterson to Porter.

49 Patterson, *Narrative*, 10.

will be acknowledged he has done the country a great good, that he effected all and more than could be reasonably expected and had he done more or less he would have been greatly blamed and held up to censure."

Having dominated Patterson and been the real source of the decisions for Patterson's army, a fact that had not escaped attention, Porter became one of Patterson's most fervent defenders. In practical effect, he was defending himself; but it only looked that way to people who knew what had happened and who understood the personalities at work.

"The General," continued Porter, "performed his duty and he should have the credit, not opprobrium. Had success crowned McDowell's efforts General Patterson would have been glorified. History will do him justice. Defection of which he is accused forms no part of his composition. I will add that every officer here (except General Sandford to whom many operations were unknown and also much information) approved and advised his caution."[50]

The general consulted some of his former Regular Army officers about the attacks on him and the silence of the Washington authorities he considered responsible for Johnston's escape. At the end of August, George H. Thomas said to John Newton, Patterson's chief engineer, that he would, if put in Patterson's predicament, send a statement of the facts to Scott or Cameron with copies of the critical correspondence and orders. If Patterson did not receive "justice at their hands," he should "demand a court of inquiry." But, Thomas noted, ". . . time will set the general all right, as I see the papers are much more favorable to him than at first."

Newton and Porter agreed that a newspaper controversy was "improper and unsoldierly." During September and October, Patterson suffered quietly. Finally, he could stand it no longer. On November 1, a day of great change for his old friend from the Mexican War, he wrote to his fellow Pennsylvanian, Simon Cameron, the secretary of war, to defend his conduct, request a court of inquiry, or seek permission to publish his correspondence with Scott.[51]

His request had been pending a week when he wrote to his former adjutant-general, Fitz-John Porter, expressing his heartfelt opinion about the valley campaign:

> "If a Court is granted I have no fear of the result. I doubt if the government will grant me a court or have the candor to say that my loyalty was never doubted and that after a careful examination of my orders I could not have done better.

50 John Sherman MSS (L.C.) letter dated July 26, 1861, from Porter to Sherman.

51 Patterson, *Narrative*, 10-14, and letter of August 25, 1861, from Thomas to "Colonel," 11, and letter dated November 1, 1861, from Patterson to Cameron, 12-14.

> This is my due but I will not get it. The government will not take the trouble to examine the orders."[52]

In response to his request he was told that the secretary was out of town but that the letter would be forwarded to him "for instructions."[53] He waited. Again, nothing happened. Again, he could stand it no longer. Near the end of the month he wrote a second time to the secretary of war, this time "respectfully" referring to his earlier letter and renewing his request for a court of inquiry.[54]

On the last day of the month, Cameron responded. He had received the original letter after Scott had retired and left for Europe. A request for review of the conduct of an officer who had been honorably discharged was unprecedented, he felt. In addition, it would require the involvement of the late general in chief, who was no longer in the United States and could not, as fairness would demand, participate. "The respect I have always entertained for you, as well as the friendly relations which have long existed between us, would claim for any personal request from you the most prompt and favorable attention; but in my public capacity, in the present condition of affairs, I cannot convince myself that my duty to the government and to the country would justify me in acceding to your request. I must, therefore, reluctantly decline the appointment of a court of inquiry at this time."[55]

Patterson packed the necessary documents and boarded a train for Washington. He would make his case in person. After a long interview with Cameron and Assistant Secretary of War Thomas A. Scott, in which he showed the correspondence and orders to them, he was told by both that they now saw the case "in a very different light from their previous understanding of it."

Patterson insisted on a court of inquiry. The assistant secretary agreed that he should have a court "in order that justice might be done" to all.

The secretary, however, felt bound by larger issues than simple justice. He agreed that a court was justified but thought it would throw the blame on Scott. To this, he would never agree. Scott had retired from the service "full of years and full of honors." Cameron wanted him to pass his remaining years peacefully enjoying the gratitude of his country. He deserved that. Nothing on earth could make him put a "thorn in General Scott's pillow."

Patterson, of course, agreed with Cameron. He and Scott had been friends for a many, many years. He "honored and venerated" the general as much as any man; but

52 Porter MSS (L.C.) letter dated November 8, 1861, from Patterson to Porter.

53 Patterson, *Narrative*, 15, letter of November 3, 1861, from Thomas A. Scott to Patterson.

54 *OR*, 2, 176.

55 *OR*, 2, 176-177.

he, too, had larger issues than personal justice. He had children, grandchildren, and warm friends. He had been an officer of Pennsylvania, Secretary of War Cameron's home state. He represented the troops he had commanded. The truth was due them all. A trial, an official order, or a letter referring to his services and approving them would suffice. Cameron agreed and promised a letter or an order. Cameron also said he would like President Lincoln to see the orders and correspondence. Patterson, naturally, wanted that greatly.

Scott said he would see the president at once, returned shortly, and announced that Lincoln would see them at half past seven that evening in the White House. After Patterson's recitation, which Lincoln heard attentively, they discussed the events. Five hours passed.

"General Patterson," his tall host said in the frank, candid manner that would disarm many men before the war ended, "I have never found fault with or censored you. I have never been able to see that you could have done anything else than you did do. Your hands were tied. You obeyed orders, and did your duty, and I am satisfied with your conduct."

Very pleased and gratified, Patterson thanked the president for the fair hearing he had received and the time he had been given. As far as the chief executive and the War Department were concerned, he was satisfied. But only a court and a trial would stop the public abuse.

"I will cheerfully accede to any practicable measure to do you justice, but you need not expect to escape abuse so long as you are of any importance or value to the community. I receive infinitely more abuse than you do, but I have ceased to regard it, and you must learn to do the same."[56]

The former commander of the Army of the Upper Potomac bore well the plentiful scorn of his countrymen. In a war whose comrades in arms would endlessly refight battles in newspapers and politics, white-haired old Robert Patterson maintained a manly silence until the war was almost won. Refused a court of inquiry as "incompatible with the public interest,"[57] the general finally published, at the end of 1864, his *Narrative of the Campaign in the Shenandoah*, a work marked by weakly defended assertions, badly copied correspondence, and misleadingly arranged dispatches and orders.[58] After his misadventures in the early months of the

56 Patterson, *Narrative*, 16-19. The final quotation has been converted from indirect to direct discourse.

57 Details of this are in *Narrative*, 1 ff; and Patterson's MS OB.

58 Porter MSS (L.C.), draft letter of November 24, 1890, from Porter to Livermore; Livermore in *PMHSM*, 41-42, 1, fn. 3, which notes that correspondence is filed with the paper. This note refers to the letters in the Porter MSS including those between Porter and Johnson, the cavalry officer.

war, Patterson would never re-enter the military lists. He lived the remainder of his lengthy life in great usefulness characterized by an honorable financial wizardry rarely found in reconstruction industrialization and expansion.[59]

The General Orders that relieved Patterson replaced him with Nathaniel Prentiss Banks,[60] a major general with vast political but no military experience. Forty-five years old, able and skilled at the delicate balancing of conflicting political forces, Banks was another Massachusetts example of the self-made man. On July 22, 1861, he was relieved in Baltimore by Major General John A. Dix, another prominent Democrat, and assigned to command the new Army of the Shenandoah, which he had to recreate after the dissolution of Patterson's force by the discharge of the three-month regiments.[61]

On the day Lincoln was crossing the Potomac to see the "boys" on the Virginia side, Scott ordered Banks to hold Harpers Ferry in spite of an expected Confederate attack; and one day later, Banks assumed command in Harpers Ferry. He found a force of three thousand militia in Winchester and a small force, far too small in Patterson's view, in the Ferry. Two to four regiments of three-month militia were leaving per day as their periods of enlistment expired.[62]

One of the regiments in Harpers Ferry was the Second Massachusetts, which carried the Bay State flag but had been recruited and mustered into the service under federal auspices for "the war," not three months. It boasted two, not one, West Point graduates as field grade officers, Colonel George H. Gordon and Lieutenant-Colonel George L. Andrews. The major was Wilder Dwight, a Harvard graduate of 1853 and one of seven sons from a socially prominent, well-to-do Massachusetts family of long lineage.[63] On July 25, when Patterson received the newspaper announcing that President Lincoln had appointed Nathaniel P. Banks, former governor of Massachusetts, to replace him in the Shenandoah Valley, he summoned the flinty, often disagreeable Colonel Gordon to his headquarters.

59 *D.A.B.*, 7, pt. 2, 306-307.

60 *OR*, 2, 171.

61 Harrington, *Banks*, 56-59; *D.A.B.*, 1, pt. 577-79; Nevins, *Strong Diary*, entry dated July 1, 1861; Roe, *10th Massachusetts*, 8.

62 *OR*, 2, 173-174.

63 George H. Gordon, *Brook Farm to Cedar Mountain in the War of the Great Rebellion 1861-62* (Boston, 1883), 29 (Gordon, *Brook Farm*); Wilder Dwight, ed., *Life and Letters of Wilder Dwight, Lieutenant-Colonel Second Massachusetts Infantry Volunteers* (Boston, 1868), 1, 3, 14, 42-43, 44, letter dated April 28, 1861, from Simon Cameron to Dwight and George L. Andrews (Dwight, *Life and Letters*). The originals of Wilder Dwight's letters without the nineteenth century deletions have recently been deposited in the Massachusetts Historical Society along with letters of other members of the family.

"What do you think of the truth of this report?" Patterson asked.[64]

"It has no foundation. I have a slight acquaintance with Mr. Banks—Governor Banks, as we call him—and I think I can assure you that he has too much good sense and good judgment to assume the responsibilities of such rank until he has fitted in subordinate positions to know something of a soldier's profession . . ." Gordon was about to complete his thought by saying, "in which he is now totally inexperienced," when he heard a knock on the door.

A messenger entered. He delivered General Banks's compliments and said the general would present himself in a few minutes to relieve Patterson of his command.[65]

Late on the afternoon of the following day a train from Philadelphia chugged into the Washington train station.[66] Among the debarking passengers was a broad shouldered, muscularly built, short young man, perhaps five-feet-eight-inches tall. Although he appeared quiet and modest, his movements, active and graceful, showed no lack of confidence. He had a shapely head, dark hair and mustache, blue eyes, and a fine face, all resting on a short, thick neck.[67]

Major General George B. McClellan left the platform and headed at once to present himself to General Scott.

64 Converted from indirect to direct discourse.

65 Gordon, *Brook Farm*, 29-30.

66 Sears, *McClellan's Correspondence*, 67, telegram dated July 22, 1861, from McClellan to his wife; *M.O.S.*, 66; *N&H*, 4, 440.

67 Comte de Paris MS Diary (large diary) (A.N. de la M. de F.) entry of September 28, 1861; *Pisani Letters*, 107, letter dated August 10, 1861, from Pisani in Washington; Howard, *Autobiography*, 1, 167; Nevins, *Wainwright Diary*, 109, entry dated October 2, 1862; Cox, Jacob D., *Reminiscences of the Civil War*, 9.

Chapter 23

"The plain truth of the matter is, that the war horse can't stand quietly by when he hears the sound of the trumpet . . . Life is too short to waste in bickering about cross ties and contracts—I cannot learn to love it."

– McClellan to S. L. M. Barlow

McClellan, The Enigma

Brevet Lieutenant-General Winfield Scott was seventy-four. Brevet Major General John E. Wool was seventy. Brigadier General Edwin Vose Sumner was sixty-four. Brigadier General Joseph King Fenno Mansfield was fifty-seven. Colonel Samuel Peter Heintzelman was fifty-five. Colonel Erasmus Darwin Keyes was fifty-one. Brigadier General Irvin McDowell was forty-two. When he stepped onto the platform in the Washington train station, Major General George Brinton McClellan, born December 3, 1826, was thirty-four years old.

McClellan probably paid little attention to his relative youth. A well-educated student of history, he would have known about Alexander the Great, conqueror of the known world when he was assassinated by his officers at the age of thirty-three; and Henry V, king of England at twenty-six and victor at Agincourt and conqueror of France, all before his early death at the age of thirty-five.[1] If he thought about

1 Fuller, Maj. Gen. J. F. C., *The Generalship of Alexander the Great* (Norwalk, 1990), 143; Peter Green, *Alexander of Macedon, 356-323 B.C. A Historical Biography* (Berkeley, 1991). Fuller believes Alexander died of a fever, probably malaria. Seward, Desmond, *Henry V, Scourge of God* (New York, 1987), 40-43, 70-83.

these men, predecessors as youthful military chieftains, he would have noted their deeply religious nature, a relatively new but very powerful part of his being.

In his own country youth had played a significant role. Alexander Hamilton had been chief of staff to Washington during the Revolution, leader of the critical infantry assault at Yorktown, and secretary of the treasury, all by the time he was thirty-two.[2]

McClellan's father, Dr. George McClellan of Philadelphia, could trace his Scottish ancestors back to the thirteenth century through a series of active and noteworthy antecedents. In the early eighteenth century three McClellan brothers emigrated to the American colonies, one of whom served in the military in the French and Indian Wars and rose to brigadier-general of Connecticut militia during the Revolution. Major-General George McClellan was one of his great grandsons.

Devoted to and extraordinarily successful at a most demanding profession, Dr. McClellan provided well for his family but did not have much time for his children. The third child and second son to the doctor and his wife, young George was raised primarily by his mother, a woman of "gentle refinement and unselfish disposition."

A happy childhood, a penchant for the pranks of children, devoted family relationships, and numerous educational advantages from private tutors through private schools to two years as an undergraduate at the University of Pennsylvania qualified him for appointment to the United States Military Academy. When he reported in 1842, he was found to be under the minimum age; but the age requirement was suspended to allow him to enter. In his studies, he benefitted from a broad classical education, including Latin and Greek; had great facility for his lessons; and was a "good student making steady progress."

A vigorous young man who appreciated order and discipline, McClellan fit well the rigors of West Point student life; and his sturdy frame made the outdoor aspects of cadet life easy. In academics he fluctuated among the highest rankings in his class, finally finishing second of sixty in a class that had begun with one hundred twenty-two, the largest in the history of the academy to that point.[3]

2 *D.A.B.* 4, pt. 2, 171-174.

3 William Starr Myers, *General George Brinton McClellan: A Study in Personality* (New York, 1934), 1-18 (Myers, *McClellan*); General Peter S. Michie, *General McClellan* (New York, 1915), 1-13 (Michie, *McClellan*); Sears, Stephen W., *George B. McClellan: The Young Napoleon* (New York, 1988), 1-8 (Sears, *McClellan*); H. J. Eckenrode and Bryan Conrad, *George B. McClellan: The Man who Saved the Union* (Chapel Hill, 1941), 1-4 (Eckenrode and Conrad, *McClellan*); James Havelock Campbell, *McClellan: A Vindication of the Military Career of General George B. McClellan, A Lawyers Brief* (New York, 1916), 9-11 (Campbell, *McClellan*); Keyes, *Fifty Years*, 440; *D.A.B.*, 6, pt. 1, 581.

Among his classmates were John Gibbon, Jesse L. Reno, Darius N. Couch, Truman Seymour, John G. Foster, Samuel D. Sturgis, George Stoneman, and George H. Gordon, all of whom would become major-generals in the Union army. As corporals in the Corps of Cadets, he and William W. Burns had stood side by side. Later, he would see most of these men among his subordinates. Classmates he would see somewhat differently were Thomas Jonathan Jackson, Ambrose Powell Hill, George Edward Pickett, D. R. Jones, and Dabney Maury, two of whom would die as lieutenant-generals in the Confederate service and the rest of whom would become major-generals for the South. Among his schoolmates in the classes of 1843 to 1849 were William B. Franklin, John J. Peck, Charles S. Hamilton, Rufus Ingalls, Alfred Pleasonton, William F. Smith, Charles P. Stone, Fitz-John Porter, John W. Davidson, Gordon Granger, David A. Russell, Orlando B. Willcox, Ambrose E. Burnside, Romeyn B. Ayres, Charles Griffin, Thomas H. Neill, John C. Tidball, John Buford, and Milton Cogswell. These men, slightly younger to slightly older, would serve with him as his subordinates in the great campaigns in the East in 1862.[4] While a cadet he earned a reputation as a gentleman and had strong attachments to his friends. Years after graduation and after McClellan himself had died, one of his schoolmates in the Class of 1847 would write, "The most popular, if not the most prominent, cadet in the corps during my four years at West Point was George B. McClellan. He stood next to the head and was first captain in his class. His was one of the most faultless personalities I have ever known. He was full of life and enthusiasm, had charming address and manners, was void of pretension, and a steadfast friend . . . He was a leader and organizer, natural born."[5]

A member of a substantial family and by upbringing something of a patrician, he was attracted to the aristocratic ways of his Southern schoolmates. "Somehow or other I take to the Southerners," he wrote home. ". . . I am sorry to say that their manners, feelings, & opinions are far, far preferable to those of the majority of the Northerners at this place." Among his roommates and close friends were Ambrose Powell Hill, appointed from Virginia; Cadmus Marcellus Willcox, appointed from Tennessee; Dabney Maury, appointed at large but born in Virginia; and James Stuart, appointed from South Carolina.[6]

4 McClellan MSS, memorandum dated October, 1885, (by the curator) entitled "Coincidences of my Life without Genl Geo. B. McClellan" by Burns; *Cullum*, 2, nos. 1279, 1284, 1290, 1303, 1304, 1309, 1314, and 1358 and 1266, 1330 and 1167, 1174, 1192, 1198, 1212, 1234, 1237, 1238, 1257, 1265, 1268, 1338, 1348, 1350, 1352, 1353, 1357, 1379, 1384, 1417); and Waugh, *Class of 1846*, xiv-xv.

5 Scott, *Willcox Memoirs, etc.*, 55.

6 *Cullum*, 2, nos. 1310, 1345, 1325, 1308; Sears, *McClellan*, 6.

Like almost all graduates with high rank in their class, McClellan received a commission in the prestigious engineers corps, something of which he was intensely proud.[7] After graduation he began active duty with the Engineer Company, which was assigned to General Zachary Taylor's column along the Rio Grande River. After inconclusive and frustrating service of no consequence, McClellan, the engineers, and other units were reassigned to Winfield Scott's Vera Cruz–Mexico City column, a dramatically different enterprise.[8] Beginning with a simple landing, made possible by superb cooperation with the navy, the siege of Vera Cruz gave McClellan, a fledgling, immediate responsibility for construction of a mortar emplacement.[9]

One of the ten engineer officers with the column, McClellan was assigned the typical work of a nineteenth-century engineer officer in war. He scouted enemy positions and fortifications closely; he determined their strengths and weaknesses; if he did not decide on, he at least recommended, the best points of attack; and he supervised the construction of bridges and other structures. During this service he had direct contact with General Scott on several occasions, demonstrated comfortable skill with his science, proved his ample personal bravery, had two horses shot under him in one battle, was struck by grapeshot, had temporary command of an artillery battery, and strengthened his already deeply felt self-confidence.[10] Through all of this, he worked with many of the senior officers in the column, few of whom would survive to the Civil War and even fewer of whom would side with the North. He also came to know well his fellow officers in the Engineer Company, Gustavus Woodson "G. W." or "Legs" Smith; Simon B. Buckner; Robert E. Lee; and Zealous B. Tower.

Sharing the opinion of his fellow Regular Army, West Point officers, he quickly came to detest the untrained, uncontrolled, and unreliable volunteer infantry and their officers, saying in a letter to his mother, "The people . . . hate volunteers as they do old scratch himself . . . you never hear of a Mexican being murdered by a Regular or a Regular by a Mexican. The volunteers carry on in a most shameful and disgraceful manner; they think nothing of robbing and killing the Mexicans." To his diary he confided, "I have seen enough on this march to convince me that Volunteers and Volunteer Generals won't do. I have repeatedly seen a Second Lieutenant of the

7 *Cullum* 2, no. 1273; Keyes, *Fifty Years*, 440.

8 Sears, *McClellan*, 6; McClellan MSS (L.C.), letters dated January 21, 1842, and January 21, 1843, from McClellan to J. H. B. McClellan.

9 Bauer, *Mexican War*, 242-244 (Bauer, *Mexican War*).

10 Michie, *McClellan*, 14-23; Sears, *McClellan*, 15-25; Myers, *McClellan*, 22-45.

Regular Army exercise more authority over the Volunteers—*officers and privates*—than a Mustang General."[11]

By the end of the war with Mexico, McClellan had received two brevets, first lieutenant and captain, had declined another that would have been unfair to his superior and friend, Gustavus W. Smith, and was well and favorably known to General Scott. He must have been on everyone's list of young officers headed for bigger things in his career—and he knew it. He returned to the United States and to the Military Academy, this time as the commanding officer of the Engineer Company.[12]

Once there, he found everything to be routine, repetitious, and without originality or adventure. Certainly, it did not match the ruggedness of his outdoor life in Mexico or its occasional bursts of heady excitement. In the back of his Mexican War diary he noted in September of 1849 that he was "booked for an infernally monotonous life for the remainder of my natural existence."[13]

While at the head of the Engineer Company, he had numerous rounds of fractious correspondence about matters of command with Colonel Totten, the chief of engineers and his titular commanding officer, many miles away in Washington, and with Captain Henry Breverton, superintendent of West Point, who attempted without success to assert command over McClellan and the Engineer Company while it was stationed at his post.[14] In one prickly exchange he received a response from the Engineer Department categorically rejecting his request to move the company off the grounds of the Academy with the prefatory statement, "If I am ever to have the disposition of the members of the Corps, I shall put you and John Barnard in the questioning department—and make sure of having the duty well performed. You and he can ask more questions on one sheet of paper than any other six men I know, and the worst of it is you always expect answers."[15] In the midst of this bickering he wrote a family member, "I don't think I am of a quarrelsome disposition—but I do have the luck of getting into more trouble than any dozen other officers I know."[16]

While at West Point in command of the Engineer Company he became a devoted member of the Napoleon Club, a group of officers who studied the

11 Myers, *McClellan Mexican War Diary*, 43, entry of January 4, 1847; and letter dated Nov. 14, 1846, from McClellan to his mother.

12 Michie, *McClellan*, 22-23; Sears, *McClellan*, 27; Myers, *McClellan*, 47.

13 Myers, *McClellan's Mexican War Diary*, entry dated Sept. 22, 1849.

14 Myers, *McClellan*, 55-56, 63-68.

15 McClellan MSS (L.C.) letter dated Sept. 19, 1850, from F. A. S. to McClellan.

16 McClellan MSS (L.C.) letter from McClellan to Maria, quoted in Myers, *McClellan*.

campaigns and methods of the Emperor Napoleon Bonaparte.[17] The great exponent of Napoleon, known to all nineteenth century students of the military art, was the Baron Antoine-Henri Jomini, a Swiss-born officer who had served under Bonaparte in the early days of the emperor's rise to fame.[18] McClellan studied Jomini's works with care but did not learn the things he might have if the works of the great Clausewitz had been known to him.[19] The presiding genius of the Napoleon Club was Dennis Hart Mahan, head of the Department of Civil and Military Engineering, one of McClellan's former teachers and a fast personal friend.[20]

After brief consideration of Frederick the Great, the club concentrated on Napoleon's campaigns, members being assigned by Mahan to deliver papers. McClellan was assigned Napoleon's Austrian War, which ended with the Battle of Wagram in 1809, the emperor's last great victory and in the view of at least one writer of today the first truly modern battle.[21]

17 Michie, *McClellan*, 24-25.

18 Shy, John, "Jomini," in Paret, *Makers of Modern Strategy*, 146-153.

19 Although one of von Clauswitz's first pieces had been published in English as early as 1815, *Vom Kriege*, his major work, had not been translated into English at the outbreak of the American Civil War, the first English edition not appearing until 1873. Bassford, Christopher, *Clausewitz in English: the Reception of Clausewitz in Britain and America* (New York, 1994), 35, 37 (Bassford, *Clausewitz in English*). As a military thinker and writer, Clausewitz was known to a few men in British military circles before 1861, Bassford, *Clausewitz in English*, 35-46; but in America, Clausewitz was essentially unknown. His major work was savaged in the bibliographical note to the widely read Winship / McLean translation of Jomini's major work *Precis de l'art de la Guerre*; he was cited in bibliographies of Halleck's works, Bassford, *Clausewitz in English*, 50-51; and he might have been known to Dennis Hart Mahan, Bassford, *Clausewitz in English*, 51; Thomas Everett Griess, *Dennis Hart Mahan: West Point Professor and Advocate of Military Professionalism 1830-1871* (MS Ph.D. dissertation, Duke University, 1969), 317-326 (Griess, MS *Mahan*.) Nothing suggests that the writings of Clausewitz came to McClellan's attention during his travels before and after the Crimean War or at any other time before the end of the Civil War.

20 Griess, MS *Mahan*, 236-238; Michie, *McClellan*, 24-25.

21 Robert Epstein, *Napoleon's Last Victory and the Emergence of Modern War*, 3-7, 176-183 (Lawrence, 1994). Epstein noted the contrary thinking of many of the best military writers of today, American and European, Michael Howard, Russel F. Weigley, Edward Hagerman, and Matthew Cooper, who generally select the Franco-Prussian War (1871) on the basis of technology and industrialization (*op. cit.*, 4). He then defined modern war by the following characteristics: "a strategic war plan that effectively integrates the various theaters of operations; the fullest mobilization of the resources of the state, which includes the raising of conscript armies; and the use of operational campaigns by opposing sides to achieve strategic objectives in the various theaters of operations. Those operational campaigns are characterized by symmetrical conscript armies organized into corps, maneuvered in a distributed fashion so that tactical engagements are sequenced and often simultaneous, command is decentralized, yet the commanders have a common understanding of operational methods. Victory is achieved by the cumulative effects of tactical engagements and operational campaigns." (p. 6). The application of his test to nineteenth and twentieth century warfare is explained in his final chapter (*op. cit.*, 171-183).

To escape the monotony and quarrels of his assignment to the Engineer Company, McClellan applied for a professorship at the West Point of the South, the ten-year-old Virginia Military Institute. He was not alone. Jesse L. Reno, William S. Rosecrans, and his old friend from the engineers in Mexico "Legs" Smith also applied. But the job went to his classmate from West Point and companion from Scott's Mexico City column, Thomas Jonathan Jackson.[22] At last, in 1851 he was reassigned to Fort Delaware, south of Philadelphia, for a simple engineering job. Less than a year later, he was assigned to Captain Randolph B. Marcy's expedition to explore the sources of the Red River in Arkansas.[23] During that completely successful venture he met and became well known to Captain Marcy's family, including the captain's beautiful daughter, Ellen.

After another southwestern expedition, in which he was the commanding officer, he was sought by Isaac I. Stevens, a former army officer and Mexican War veteran, and now governor of the Washington Territory, to assist in finding a northern railroad route through the rugged Cascade Mountains. McClellan's friend from the Mexican War, P. G. T. Beauregard, recommended that he accept, and he did.[24]

With his usual fastidious care and attention to detail, he over-thought and over-prepared for his assignment, which had been given to him with wide discretion by Governor Stevens and Secretary of War Jefferson Davis.[25] After his first unsuccessful efforts he realized that his party was too large, lacked the necessary mobility, and should be reduced in size and equipment. When this had been done, he began his field work in earnest. During the months of July, August, and September, 1853, he searched for passes through the Cascades.[26]

McClellan himself examined the Snoqualmie Pass, the only apparently practicable pass for a railroad other than the Columbia River basin. From reports by Indians and tree marks that he presumed indicated snow depth, he concluded that the Snoqualmie would be blocked by twenty to twenty-five feet of snow in the winter.

22 Myers, *McClellan*, 61; T. J. Arnold, *The Early Life and Letters of General Thomas J. "Stonewall" Jackson* (New York, 1916), 173-174; James I. Robertson, Jr., *Stonewall Jackson: the Man, the Soldier, the Legend* (New York, 1997), 99-108 (Robertson, *Stonewall Jackson*).

23 Sears, *McClellan*, 32-33.

24 Myers, *McClellan*, 79.

25 McClellan MSS (L.C.) letters dated May 9, 1853, from Governor Isaac I. Stevens to McClellan and from Secretary of War Jefferson Davis to McClellan; Sears, *McClellan*, 36-37.

26 Myers, *McClellan*, 81-83; Michie, *McClellan*, 29-33; Sears, *McClellan*, 38-39; and Stevens, *Life of Stevens*, 1, 394-395.

Even crossing the pass on snowshoes, he reported to Stevens, was "positively impracticable."[27]

Not persuaded by this report, Stevens ordered Lieutenant Tinkham, a member of his own party, to cross the pass from the other side. Only ten days after McClellan had declared it impossible, Tinkham started on horseback with two Indians, switched to snowshoes, and crossed the mountains on foot in seven days. He measured the snow periodically, finding it to be five feet deep on average and never more than seven feet deep.[28]

Taking Stevens's action as a personal affront, McClellan cooled toward him. On two other lesser tasks McClellan also failed, again finding impossibility in the assignment when another accomplished it at almost the same time.[29] At the approach of the ferocious Rocky Mountain winter, he and his party joined Governor Stevens's party, which was then leaving the mountains.

In spite of McClellan's failure to find the pass, Stevens complimented McClellan's work when he returned east to make his report to the secretary of war. In fact, McClellan's work and his incorrect reports benefitted him. Secretary Davis preferred a southern route that would connect his native southern region to the west coast. He was perfectly happy to hear that no northern route was practicable.[30]

A series of brief but responsible assignments from the secretary of war, promotion to captain, and transfer to a new cavalry regiment followed. Then came, in 1855, the most important assignment of his brief career. McClellan and two older, more senior officers were appointed a military commission to study the Crimean War and report on it. They traveled to London, Paris, Berlin, Warsaw, St. Petersburg, and Vienna to obtain the necessary permissions to enter the combatants' lines. He and his companions arrived on the Crimean peninsula in time for the siege of Sebastopol. As usual, his relations with his two higher ranking colleagues became inharmonious, both personally and professionally.

In 1856 he returned to the United States, making leisurely stops in Constantinople and Vienna on the way and filing his report late in the year. Throughout all this traveling, he met, and was entertained by, royalty, nobility, and important citizens. Combining his strong preference for the aristocratic Southerners at the Military Academy and their way of life, an American equivalent of the landed

27 Stevens, *Life of Stevens*, 1, 394-395, 406-407.

28 Stevens, *Life of Stevens*, 1, 408. In reality, the snow in the Columbia River Pass was and is worse than it was in the Snoqualmie. *Ibid.*, fn, 495. Today, both are railroad passes.

29 *Ibid.*, 409-410.

30 Myers, *McClellan*, 81-83; Stevens, *Life of Stevens*, 1, 428-429.

gentry of Europe, with these new European associations enhanced his patrician sentiments.

In the laconic, dry style, devoid of adjectives and adverbs, that was to be his for the rest of his days, his report summarized the war, then described the engineer troops, the infantry, the Russian army, and the cavalry. An odd, eclectic selection of topics it was; and having had a relatively brief career of ten years, most of which had been spent in the engineers, his descriptions lacked the kind of penetrating analysis and comparisons that experience as an older officer who had seen more of the military might have made possible. Although the reporting had to be based on judgments and critical conclusions, McClellan's final report was primarily a careful, encyclopedic word photograph of the armies of several nations. At the beginning of it, he proudly compared the sophisticated Allied armies and his infant American Army, noting on the second page that the experienced Allies had required seven days to complete their line of investment at Sebastopol while the rookie Americans had needed only two at Vera Cruz. In addition, the Americans had opened fire on the thirteenth day, the allies after twenty-seven.[31] As the report showed, he had acquired an extraordinary depth of knowledge about army organization.

But the peacetime army had lost its luster. Always restless in old familiar surroundings and wishing a secure income because of his struggle to repay the debts he inherited from his father, who had incautiously guaranteed the borrowings of a kinsmen, McClellan was looking carefully at new, civilian horizons.[32]

When he broached his intention to seek civilian employment to his former commanding officer, Captain Marcy gave him an unequivocal response. "I was truly rejoiced to hear from you the other day, and I was equally pleased to learn that you had made the wise resolve to leave the army as I am satisfied you can make yourself much more distinguished in civil life as an engineer than by doing garrison duty or hunting Indians in time of peace. You are young and with your talents, acquirements and application you cannot fail to succeed and without any friendly bias I should venture to predict for you a brilliant future . . . This is infinitely better than plodding along in the Army where in peace you might drag out a tolerable existence but your best energies would be expended without any marked results."[33] With varied advice in hand from his old army friends, Joseph E. Johnston, Gustavus W. Smith, and W.

31 McClellan, George B., *The Armies of Europe: comprising Descriptions in Detail of the military Systems of England, France, Russia, Prussia, Austria, and Sardinia adopting their Advantages to all Arms of the United States Service; and Embodying the Report of Observations in Europe during the Crimean War, as Military Commissioner from the United States Government in 1855-1856*, 10 (Philadelphia, 1861).

32 Myers, *McClellan*, 104-108.

33 McClellan MSS (L.C.), letter dated April 24, 1857, from Marcy to McClellan.

Raymond Lee, among others, McClellan resigned from the army in November to become chief engineer of the Illinois Central Railroad at a huge increase in annual income.

Taking a residence in Chicago for his new job, he was, in 1858 while still in his early thirties, elected vice president of the company with practical control of the railroad operations in Illinois. His home in Chicago became a roadhouse for his friends from the Old Army.[34] The Great Creole, Louisiana-born Pierre Gustave Toutant Beauregard, West Point, number two in the Class of 1838, and a distinguished fellow engineer of Mexican War renown, stayed with him when he was traveling in the North.[35] His old schoolmate at the Military Academy, Ambrose E. Burnside, Class of 1847, had invested all he had in a company developing and manufacturing a repeating cavalry carbine. When the company failed and Burnside was without means of support, he wrote to Chicago to ask for assistance. McClellan arranged for him to be employed as cashier in the land department of the railroad; and when Mr. and Mrs. Burnside moved into his spacious quarters, he acquired many of the social advantages of marriage.[36]

McClellan and Burnside had become close personal friends during their days at the academy at West Point. In Chicago their friendship continued in a boyish, demonstrative way, addressing each other as "Mac" and "Burn." No one outside McClellan's own family knew his inner thoughts as much as Burnside, who was sufficiently ingenuous to be unable to distinguish between the official and the unofficial sides of the relationship. In fact, few people knew McClellan's innermost, personal thoughts or feelings at any time on any subject.[37]

At this time in Utah, it began to look as if a war would erupt between Federal forces and the Mormons. All the childhood desires for a military career were rekindled.[38] Writing in January 1858 to his friend Samuel Latham Mitchell Barlow, a wealthy California lawyer his age, McClellan said, "It is a little more than a year ago that I asked your help in leaving the army, now—with admirable consistency—I want you to help me get back. The plain truth of the matter is, that the war horse can't

34 Myers, *McClellan*, 101-107.

35 William F. Biddle, "Recollections of McClellan," in vol. xi, *The United Service: A Monthly Review of Military and Naval Affairs* (May, 1894), 466; *Cullum* 1, no. 942; Pisani, *Napoleon in America*, 109.

36 Myers, *McClellan*, 104.

37 Jacob D. Cox, *Military Reminiscences of the Civil War*, 2 vols. (New York, 1900), 1, 376, 545 (Cox, *Reminiscences*).

38 Myers, *McClellan*, 110-114.

stand quietly by when he hears the sound of the trumpet . . . Life is too short to waste in bickering about cross ties and contracts—I cannot learn to love it."[39]

McClellan was also considering an adventure in South or Central America. In the opinion—and advice—of his trusted friend Fitz-John Porter, then serving in Utah, the Mormon confrontation was no more than a "guerilla" war without dignity; and anything south of the Rio Grande was at best a "Filibuster expedition."[40]

Instead of returning to the army, McClellan added another success to his civilian career. Through the efforts of Barlow and other wealthy businessmen, he changed jobs to become president of the Eastern Division of the Ohio and Mississippi Railroad at an extraordinary salary of $10,000 per year—a far cry from the pay of a cavalry captain. To assume his new responsibilities he moved to Cincinnati and rented a large home, but he was so certain about war with the South and determined to participate that he negotiated a cancellation clause in his lease.[41]

After his tour of duty with Captain Marcy in Texas, McClellan maintained a careful and dignified correspondence with the Marcys, father and mother, and with their daughter Nellie. His progress in assignments, his trip to the Crimea, his change to substantial businessman were all carefully recorded in his many letters to them.[42] His correspondence with Nellie eventually evolved into a courtship, which proceeded slowly from long distance friendship to deep love throughout the decade of the fifties. As McClellan's pursuit neared marriage and became known to the world, his old friends of the army wrote to congratulate him. "Dr. Mc," wrote Gustavus Woodson Smith, "I wanted a chance to congratulate you upon your approaching marriage. Well old fellow, of the Bull Head fraternity here's to you and yours forever, and ever. May happiness and joy attend your steps through this life and into the next. I suppose when we get there alright, we are safe."[43]

Among those who had pursued Miss Marcy and fallen by the wayside were John G. Barnard, chief engineer for McDowell and about to become chief engineer for McClellan; Ambrose P. Hill, a rising star about to serve in the Army of Northern Virginia under Lee[44] and McClellan's roommate at the Military Academy; and

39 McClellan MSS (L.C.), letter of January 5, 1858, from McClellan to S. L. M. Barlow.

40 McClellan MSS (L.C.), letter dated February 28, 1958, from Porter to McClellan.

41 Myers, *McClellan*, 118-119.

42 Many of these are discussed and quoted at length in the only good account of the courtship, which appears in Myers, *McClellan*, Chap. V, 123-156.

43 McClellan MSS (L.C.), letter dated April 2, 1860, from "G. W." to "Mc."

44 McClellan MSS (L.C.) from A. P. Hill to R. B. Marcy; from John G. Barnard to Nellie Marcy; and from Gordon Granger to Nellie Marcy discussed in Myers, *McClellan*, 134-138, 148.

Gordon Granger, a classmate McClellan would want for his staff and a future corps commander under Grant and Sherman in the West.

On May 22, 1860, McClellan's courtship of Ellen Marcy ended in marriage in New York City. In this union McClellan found a steady, devoted, supportive mate to whom he could unburden himself, to whom he could without apprehension express his innermost hopes, desires, uncertainties, and fears—but always with his characteristic maleness. Through the influence of his wife and her mother, McClellan became a deeply religious man.[45] Even before the couple married, he wrote, "If I can ever feel that I am a Christian (and I do not despair it) I shall ever feel that you did it—that your dear influence has directed my mind in the right direction."[46]

In the early fall of 1860 McClellan was traveling on business. He and several other men were to have dinner in the hotel dining room. As they entered, one of them stopped to talk to a guest at one of the tables while McClellan and the others continued into the room. When asked who it was, the conversant said it was Captain John Pope of the Engineers. That having been McClellan's branch, William F. Biddle, McClellan's assistant, asked if he had never met Captain Pope.

McClellan replied that he *had* known him some years earlier.

McClellan so invariably spoke well of people that Biddle thought he had inadvertently touched a sore spot. Passing the subject Biddle commented that Pope had a fine head.

"He has plenty of brains," responded McClellan. "He graduated high."

This response differed so greatly from McClellan's "invariably cordial and hearty tone towards army men" that Biddle was surprised. A short awkward pause followed.

As if he had breached some social custom of gentlemanly conduct and must therefore explain himself—something he never did—McClellan hesitatingly continued. "The truth is that all his old set in the army found that we couldn't get along with him."

That ended the subject. This was the only time Biddle ever heard McClellan speak poorly of another officer in four years of work with him on railroad business and the years as an aide to McClellan throughout his military career in the war. The event stood in bold contrast to the many reminiscent moments about Joe Johnston, Randolph Marcy, Pierre Beauregard, Fitz Porter, Mansfield Lovell, Baldy Smith,

45 Myers, *McClellan*, 123-129, 143-144, 151, 153.

46 McClellan MSS (L.C.), letter from McClellan to Nellie, quoted in Myers, *McClellan*, 151.

Alex McCook, G. W. Smith, and others who were "the flower of the *ante-bellum* army."[47]

As war seemed more and more imminent, McClellan involved himself more and more in preparations for it. The city leaders of Cincinnati, his new home town, sought his advice on organizational issues, and recommended him to Governor Dennison. His reputation in the "Old Army" was exceptionally high, his report on the Crimean War being one of the few truly important pieces published by the American military before the war. Great things were expected of him.[48]

In the eyes of many, McClellan had long stood above all other company grade soldiers. In the early 1850s, a group of officers assembled at the officers' mess at West Point. All had served in the Mexican War, and most were at that time instructors at the Military Academy. Present, among others, were George H. Thomas, Fitz-John Porter, Delous B. Sackett, John M. Jones, Cadmus Wilcox, Milton Cogswell, and others who would become prominent during the war. They tried to decide who would be the general in chief after the retirement of Scott. They agreed to give their answer without regard to personal like or dislike by writing the name of the candidate on a piece of paper and putting it in a ballot box. Some expressed their own view and others their understanding of the feeling throughout the army. When their ballots were opened, they had unanimously selected McClellan.[49]

Among others, Dennis Hart Mahan, McClellan's instructor in tactics at West Point and founder of the Napoleon Club, foresaw war with the South. To Secretary of War John B. Floyd he wrote in 1858 about officers for an expanded army, and in a way he anticipated the Scott Rule. "In the event of the increase of the Army by the additional regiments called for in your Report, and under the supposition that these will be, in part, officered as were the last raised, by appointments from civil life, I would respectfully direct your attention to George B. McClellan, Esq., late of the U.S. Army, as a gentleman eminently distinguished by those acquirements, both scientific and military, which, in my opinion, would render him an invaluable acquisition to the service in any grade however responsible." Mahan had known McClellan when he was a student, he wrote, and also when he was assigned to command the Engineer Company. While on duty at the Military Academy, he

47 Webb MSS (Yale University), typewritten MS review by Webb of Michie's biography of McClellan; William F. Biddle, "Recollections of McClellan," in *United Service*, May 1894, pp. 466-467.

48 Cox, *Reminiscences*, 1, 9.

49 Porter MSS (L.C.), letter dated April 18, 1861, from McClellan to Porter; *M.O.S.*, 40. This letter, one of two from McClellan of this date to Porter appears in Sears, *McClellan's Correspondence*, 4-5. Another copy of it is in the Nicholson MSS (Huntington Library).

became prominent "in a group of most promising young officers who, from the direction which they voluntarily gave to their private studies, showed a settled purpose to make themselves masters of the highest branches of their profession, and thus qualify themselves for any post in which their Country might ask for their services."[50]

Having left the military with a long list of fine credits and become very successful as a leader in the corporate world, he was only naturally a candidate for many positions during the helter-skelter commissioning before Bull Run. He was, in fact, bombarded and pursued. His old Mexican War friend William F. "Baldy" Smith wrote to "Mac" to report that McClellan had been suggested to the Cabinet for a brigadier-generalcy if the army were expanded. This was consistent with Scott's early view that the North would be forced to rely on the large number of loyal, young, but exceptional company grade West Point graduates. Smith said, "As the row is upon us & you will probably take a hand in it, would it not be advisable for you to get the same or a higher commission in the Volunteers either from Ohio or Pennsylvania?"[51] Smith had received word from friends in New York, he added, that Governor Morgan wanted McClellan's services.[52] Major-General Robert Patterson offered the position of chief engineer in the Valley army.[53] He also learned that he was being proposed as commander of the Pennsylvania Reserve Division, the extra Pennsylvania forces being collected by Governor Andrew Curtin.[54]

A division of Pennsylvania troops ought to have a major general, the highest rank available in the United States at that time. Of all the possibilities this one sounded best; and his connections with Pennsylvania, where he had been born and raised and where his family was established and recognized, were far deeper than his new relations with Ohio. He sent a letter of acceptance. It would help, he said in a short note to "My dear old Fitz," if a little support could be given by General Scott. All fondness for the Southern aristocracy and its way of life had fallen away. From his association with able, admirable officers of Southern birth, he knew the war would be severe and bitter. "Say to the General that I am as ready as ever to serve under his command; I trust I need not assure him that he can count on my loyalty to

50 Dennis Hart Mahan MSS (United States Military Academy) draft letter dated January 1, 1858, from Mahan to Floyd.

51 McClellan MSS (L.C.), letter dated April 15, 1861, from Smith to "Mac."

52 *M.O.S.*, 40.

53 Porter MSS (L.C.), letter of "18th" (n.m., n.y.) from McClellan to Porter. Given its content, the letter could only have been written in April of 1861.

54 Porter MSS (L.C.), letter dated April 18, 1861, from McClellan to Porter; *M.O.S.*, 40. This letter, one of two from McClellan of this date to Porter appears in Sears, *McClellan's Correspondence*, 4-5. Another copy of it is in the Nicholson MSS (Huntington Library).

him & to the dear old flag he has so long upheld. I throw to one side here all questions as to the past—political parties, etc.—the Gvt. is in danger, our flag insulted[. W]e must stand by it." Although he had been told he could have a position with the Ohio troops, he much preferred, he wrote, the Pennsylvania service.[55]

He arranged his business affairs to allow a brief absence while he went to Pennsylvania to accept the new command. On the way he would stop in Cleveland to give advice to the governor of Ohio. Wearing a dark business suit and soft felt hat and looking like any young American businessman, he boarded a train in Cincinnati for Cleveland, where he planned, at the request of several Cincinnati men,[56] to tell Governor Dennison about the conditions in Cincinnati. He intended to remain only a few hours, then proceed to Harrisburg.[57]

At the station in Columbus he was met by Jacob D. Cox, who took him directly to Governor Dennison. The governor described the utter embarrassment of the state in military equipment, personnel, and experience. He wanted someone on whom he could rely to assume the details of military work. McClellan showed he understood the organizational problems and said that no one could master them at once. He said he was confident that, if given a few weeks, he would be able to put the Ohio division into reasonable form for taking the field.[58]

The laws of Ohio required that the command of Ohio militia and volunteers be given to general officers of Ohio's existing militia establishment. McClellan did not qualify, but the legislature was in session when he arrived. That day the governor presented a bill which would permit him to appoint any resident of the state as the major general commanding the Ohio militia. Intended specifically for McClellan's benefit, the bill was passed by both houses within a few hours; and the appointment was offered to McClellan the same day. He accepted at once, began his duties within an hour, and abandoned his trip to the east.

While all this was happening, others were recognizing him at an even higher level. The day before his trip from Cincinnati to Columbus, April 22, William H.

55 Porter MSS (L.C.), letter dated April 18, 1861, from McClellan to Porter; Biddle, "Reminiscences of McClellan," in vol. xi, *The United Service*, 464 (May, 1894).

56 *M.O.S.*, 39-41; Cox, *Reminiscences*, 1, 8-9. Cox holds that McClellan had not been offered the Pennsylvania command when he met with Governor Dennison; but the correspondence in both McClellan's and Porter's papers show this is not accurate. Because the facts described in *M.O.S.*, 41, show McClellan in a less favorable light, are generally confirmed by the correspondence, and are also inferentially confirmed by the gap between the letters and the trip (almost a week), McClellan's narrative seems to be the more accurate. Cox's supposed conversation in which McClellan said he would have accepted the Pennsylvania command over the Ohio offer if he had had it in hand must have involved another set of circumstances.

57 *M.O.S.*, 39.

58 Cox, *Reminiscences*, 1, 9.

Aspinwall, a successful and wealthy New York City businessman, wrote to Abraham Lincoln that leading citizens of Cincinnati thought the appointment of McClellan would help keep open the Ohio and Mississippi Railroad and that the people of Cincinnati wanted McClellan to be appointed to organize their forces and take command of the city.[59]

Within a few days of his appointment McClellan, the bright new star, and Scott, the brevet lieutenant-general, were exchanging large plans for bringing the rebellion to its knees; Scott his Anaconda Plan based on a naval blockade, and McClellan his personally heroic plan for marching to the rear of Richmond, seizing it, and destroying the Southern army "if aided by a decided advance on the Eastern line."[60] With the assistance of the general in chief, McClellan's plan found its way promptly into the hands of the president. Governor Dennison also brought McClellan and his plan to the president's attention, suggesting that Lincoln review the plan himself. It met with Lincoln's approval, Dennison thought. The forces west of the Alleghenies should be under one officer; and he recommended that McClellan be the man. "His military character is well-known to Gen. Scott and your military advisers at headquarters . . ."[61]

When McDowell refused Chase's offer of a major-generalcy, the candidacies of others were not impeded by such diffidence. John Charles Fremont, Henry Wager Halleck, and George Brinton McClellan were all promoted to major-general in the Regular Army.

Like so many of Lincoln's coterie in 1861, Salmon P. Chase was devoted almost as much to his home state of Ohio as he was to the federal nation. Recognizing McClellan as an Ohioan with great promise, Chase became at once an ardent proponent of high rank for McClellan, to such an extent that he later deemed himself responsible for McClellan's promotion and his appointment to command in the West. As an introduction, the secretary of the treasury wrote him:

> Though I believe we have never met, I feel as if we were personal friends. Your being called to the command of the Ohio troops inspired the first strong interest I felt in you. I could not help feeling deeply interested in one so connected with men and a State to which I was bound by so many close ties. Then the accounts I heard of your character and qualities, from those who knew you, and the reports of your policy and action that came from Ohio and especially the close circumstances . . . I naturally gave your dispatches to the noble old commanding

59 Lincoln MSS (L.C.), letter dated April 22, 1861, from Aspinwall to Lincoln.

60 Sears, *McClellan's Correspondence*, 12-13, April 27, 1861, from McClellan to Scott.

61 Lincoln MSS (L.C.), letter dated April 27, 1861, from Dennison to Scott.

> general, from whom I sometimes differ but whom I always revere, confirmed that interest and mingled with it respect and confidence. In the result the country was indebted to me—may I say it without too much vanity?—in some considerable degree, for the change of your commission from Ohio into a commission of major-general of the army of the Union, and your assignment to the command of the Department of the Ohio.[62]

As it was for the majority of his adult life, McClellan's reputation and status were not without controversy. Those who did not find him able and decisive were men who had seen him function in the practical day-to-day world. When McClellan was selected to organize the forces in the field and commissioned a major general, one of his directors on the Ohio and Mississippi Railroad learned that another director had recommended him for the appointment.

"How did you come to recommend McClellan?" he asked his fellow board member. "You know he can never make up his mind under two or three weeks on any matter and when he has made it up, is by no means certain about his decision."

"Well, it is certain that we don't want him anymore and that it is a favorable opportunity to get rid of him. He has a military education and if he isn't fitted for that, what is he fit for?"[63]

A short time after McClellan had been called east from West Virginia, a midwestern businessman asked his friend Steven S. L'Hommedieu, president of the Cincinnati, Hamilton & Dayton Railroad, what sort of person McClellan was.

"As a soldier," came the answer, "I do not know what he will prove to be. As a railway president, he is constantly soliciting advice, but he knows no more about a situation and has no more confidence in his own judgment after he has received it, than before."[64]

In the early months of the war while McClellan was holding significant command responsibility in the West, the political and military condition of Kentucky, a border state with a confused position on secession, was uncertain at best. Governor Beriah Magoffin had refused to respond to the president's call for troops, would probably have pushed for secession if he had controlled his legislature, and had declared neutrality for his state. Confederate forces were

62 Schuckers, *Chase*, 427, letter dated July 7, 1861, from Chase to McClellan.

63 T. C. H. Smith MSS (Ohio Historical Society), "Account of the Second Battle of Bull Run," 49-50.

64 Porter MSS (L.C.), letter dated Jan. 30, 1862, from Hoadly to Porter. The quoted statement is given in quotes in the letter but is also described in the text of the letter as L'Hommedieu's substance, not necessarily his exact words.

collecting along the border outside the state. Confederate intrusions were expected.[65]

In charge of the Kentucky State Guards, a weak and inefficient militia organization but the only military force of the state, was Simon Bolivar Buckner, McClellan's schoolmate from the Academy at West Point and a fellow engineer with General Scott's Mexico City column. Buckner made several requests for personal interviews with McClellan, but without success. Finally, on June 7 Buckner telegraphed that he and Samuel Gill, an older graduate of the Military Academy and superintendent of the Louisville and Lexington Railroad, would like to meet with McClellan in Cincinnati and asked when he would be home.[66] Thinking that Buckner, whom he regarded as "an old & intimate friend," was awakening to the absurdity of the policies of Breckenridge and Magoffin and might be reclaimed to the Union cause, McClellan instructed his aide Thomas M. Key, who was heading for Louisville on unrelated business, to tell Buckner and Gill that he would meet with them at his residence.[67] That evening, June 8, the pair arrived at McClellan's home about 10:00 p.m. McClellan intended that he and Buckner, as old friends, would "compare views and see if we could do any good." The meeting was to be personal.

McClellan had no power to guarantee the neutrality of Kentucky, he said; but although the state was not part of his domain, he would not tolerate Confederates in it. Buckner claimed Kentucky was the most loyal state in the Union. McClellan countered that the positions taken by the state were inconsistent with true loyalty.[68]

In McClellan's view, Buckner tried to learn what McClellan would do if the Confederate forces collecting on the Kentucky border invaded and was anxious for McClellan's federal forces in Ohio to respect Kentucky's neutrality. Probably to keep McClellan's troops from entering Kentucky, he promised he would do his best to drive away any encroaching Rebels.

"You had better be very quick about it, Simon," responded McClellan, "for if I learn that the rebels are in Kentucky I will, with or without orders, drive them out without delay."

65 Chase MSS (U.P.I.) letter dated June 26, 1861, from Key to Chase; *N&H*, 4, 227-231; and Myers, *McClellan's Mexican War Diary*, 77, entry dated April 16, 1847.

66 *M.O.S.*, 48.

67 Chase MSS (U.P.I), letter dated June 26, 1861, from Key to Chase; Sears, *McClellan's Correspondence*, tel rec. June 26, 1861, by Scott from McClellan.

68 Chase MSS (U.P.I.), letter dated June 26, 1861, from Key to Chase. Key's letter, not based on his participation in the meeting, varies in minor respects from McClellan's contemporaneous accounts and *M.O.S.*. The accounts by McClellan are preferred.

Far into the morning hours the meeting lasted, finally ending at 5:00 a.m. McClellan found it inconclusive, unsatisfactory, and fruitless.[69]

A few days later McClellan and Buckner met accidentally in Cairo, but this time McClellan was not alone. Accompanied by John M. Douglas, a lawyer with the Illinois Railroad, he confirmed the substance of the earlier meeting, including his unwillingness to tolerate Rebel troops or the Rebel flag in Kentucky. Buckner reported on his recent conversation with the commander of the Confederate forces gathering on the Kentucky–Tennessee border.[70] They seemed to have a clear understanding and agreement about the situation.

Nevertheless, Buckner had sent a much different report of the first meeting to Governor Magoffin; and two weeks after the conversation in Cairo his letter found its way into the press. According to Buckner's report, McClellan had agreed, among other things, to respect the neutrality of Kentucky.[71]

Both McClellan and Key believed Buckner to be a man of honor, a gentleman who would not purposefully misrepresent McClellan's statements. They decided that Buckner was a good soldier, knew nothing about politics, and might have misconceived the conversation. Or unscrupulous public men with whom Buckner associated had attempted to spring a trap on McClellan using Buckner as an unconscious instrument.[72]

Whatever Buckner's motivations or role might have been, McClellan, Key, and Douglas believed the publication of Buckner's letter placed McClellan in a potentially awkward position with Scott, Lincoln, and the cabinet. They took steps to repair any damage.

Douglas wrote McClellan an account of the chance meeting with Buckner in Cairo. McClellan sent Scott a terse telegram describing the first meeting and the position he had taken. He followed this the same day with a longer letter that provided details about the meeting. Later in the day he wrote an even longer letter enclosing the account from Douglas. Key, a quiet but powerful listener, a shrewd politician, and a man of growing political influence over McClellan,[73] wrote a very

69 *M.O.S.*, 48-49; *OR*, 52, pt. 1, 183-184.

70 McClellan MSS (L.C.) letter dated June 26, 1861, from Douglas to McClellan; Sears, *McClellan's Correspondence*, 38-39, letter dated June 26, 1861, from McClellan to Scott; *M.O.S.*, 49.

71 Chase MSS (U.P.I.) letter of June 26, 1861, from Key to Chase; *M.O.S.*, 49; Buckner's letter to Magoffin is also printed in Frank Moore, ed., *The Rebellion Record*, 12 vols. (New York, 1862), 2, 163.

72 Chase MSS (U.P.I.), letter of June 26, 1861, from Key to Chase; *OR*, 52, pt. 1, p. 184.

73 Donn Piatt, *Memoirs of the Men Who Saved the Union* (New York, 1887), 291-295 (Piatt, *Memoirs*).

lengthy letter to his fellow Ohioan, Secretary of the Treasury Salmon P. Chase. All dated the same day and interrelated by text, they must have been written by prearrangement among the three men and circulated among them by hand. Each acknowledged the sensitivity of the event and the potentially prejudicial effect of Buckner's account. All vindicated McClellan. He had not agreed to respect the neutrality of Kentucky.

"This letter" wrote Key to Chase about the Buckner missive,

> fills me with surprise, and its contents are as new to me as they will be to yourself. I was in Kentucky at the time of the interview, but I have supposed that I had full knowledge of the facts . . . The letter [from Buckner to Magoffin] expressed the views presented by General Buckner and represents them as an agreement by General McClellan. Nothing could be more incorrect. General McClellan never imagined that his authority extended to any arrangement or stipulation or concession by which the action of the General Government would be abridged or embarrassed: he never desired to limit in any way the exercise of his own discretion. He never conceived that the neutrality doctrine of Kentucky was either constitutional or practical: he never considered that the people or soil of Kentucky were or should be in any respect exempt from the military powers of the Government . . . he never dreamed of assuming in the smallest degree the discretion of determining the policy of the Government towards Kentucky, and he always supposed that policy would be, and ought to be, the making of the rugged issue of union or succession at the first favorable moment, after opportunity had been given to leaders of the union party to complete its organization & consolidate its strength . . . May I beg as an act of justice to General McClellan, and as a favor to myself, which I will consider as the greatest that I have ever received from any one, that you will not permit this unaccountable & unfortunate conduct of General Buckner, to prejudice General McClellan . . ."[74]

"I was amazed," commented Douglas in his letter to McClellan, "to read the published correspondence touching an agreement which was not of importance enough to mention at Cairo. You distinctly disclaimed any authority to act except as might be ordered by the government."[75]

In his telegram to Scott, McClellan echoed the surprise of Key and Douglas. "I can scarcely believe what he wrote . . . May I ask that you explain this fully to the

74 Chase MSS (U.P.I.), letter dated June 26, 1861, from Key to Chase; *OR*, 52, pt. 1, 184. McClellan wrote in his first letter to Scott, ". . . recognizing as I do his character for veracity, I am constrained to believe that the letter was written for him by some unscrupulous secession Confederates." Chase was born in New Hampshire but built his career in Ohio.

75 McClellan MSS (L.C.), letter dated June 26, 1861, from Douglas to McClellan.

president & the cabinet . . ."[76] And in his second, long letter of the same day, he enclosed the letter from Douglas and referred Scott to the president for Douglas's veracity, which was well known to Lincoln. Then he dwelt on the personal implications of the incident. ". . . [M]y chief fear has been that you, whom I regard as my strongest friend in Washington, might have supposed me to be guilty of the extreme of folly. My personal relations with Buckner, my high regard for his character, have led me to be more chary in my expressions than my own interests would warrant—I know that you will appreciate & respect the feeling which has dictated this course. I shall be fully satisfied if I hear from you that you are not displeased with me, & I trust to my actions of the coming week to show to the people that you have not made a mistake in placing me in the position I now occupy. I am General whatever the result may be your obliged, sincere & respectful friend . . ."[77]

This little imbroglio, which, at least for the moment, went quickly to the inattention it deserved, had an apparent lasting effect on McClellan; and it showed the administration something significant about the man arriving to assume the most important field command in the nation. They learned that, without attempting to cross the civilian-military boundary, McClellan had been willingly drawn into the potentially compromising penumbra between the two. He would have been better served if he had chosen not to meet Buckner at all or had, instead, called for direct advice from Washington or for a presidential designee to attend the meeting. Perhaps this was an incident born of his inexperience, having leaped from a captain of cavalry, who could never have had a meeting of this sort, to one of four Regular Army major generals, who could not move without brushing the skirts of the political demon. Whether this incident and the scrambling to explain it when Buckner's distorted account was published would be a lesson to him remained to be seen. The confused nature of civil war promised that future events would again blur the sharp line between responsibilities as a military leader and the unsorted mass of political considerations confronting Lincoln, his Cabinet, and the Congress. The war that had vaulted McClellan overnight to fame, especially in its early days when no experience was available for guidance, made identification of the line difficult.

Although a strong Democrat devoted to the policies of Stephen A. Douglas, McClellan was really apolitical, having voted only once in his life. In the leap from captain to major-general, he had skipped the slow, instructive years of gradual intertwining between the military and the political. As far as his personal desires were concerned, he now had everything he had always wanted. If the idea of seeking

76 Sears, *McClellan's Correspondence*, 38, telegram dated June 26, 1861, from McClellan to Scott.

77 Sears, *McClellan's Correspondence*, 39, letter of June 26, 1861, from McClellan to Scott.

political office crossed his mind on the train ride east, it found no reception. His ambition would be satisfied if he were given command of the army waiting for him on the banks of the Potomac River.

Of course, he had opinions on clearly political issues, but they were his views about the best course for his country and its people. They were not a platform for a political career. The first and foremost object of the war to him was the restoration of the Union. Matters of politics, whatever they might be, should be put aside except for those few entangled in military issues.[78] But politics and civil war have never been simple to separate. It would only be a matter of time before he took positions on political issues. And these expressions would raise more than the usual risk because the dominant political party was not a simple monolith. It was still composed of many disparate parts driven to assemblage by political necessity rather than political kinship.[79]

McClellan's scrape with a political issue that intruded into the military sphere should have proven to him how unpredictable, if not how untrustworthy, the players in this area could be. He lacked the experience that had made Winfield Scott adept at managing difficult political questions, but his certainty that his judgments were right would make him accept the risks. A short time later an older, wiser, and more experienced officer would write, "As a soldier holding a commission, it has always been my judgment that duty required I should disregard all political questions and obey orders."[80] After his entanglement with his friend Simon Buckner, McClellan should have known to watch closely for political question, deliver the question to the politicians at the earliest moment possible, and accept the political ruling without audible disagreement. He should have, but he did not.

The men waiting for him in Washington also knew, at least indirectly, that many of McClellan's best friends in the army had been Southerners and that the outbreak of war had not changed his attitude toward them. He would work with them when he could. In a subtle, imperceptible way, the Buckner incident flagged another facet of McClellan's personality: his attitude toward and his relations with his superiors. His second letter to Scott had closed with the fairly standard nineteenth century expression, ". . . your obliged, sincere, and respectful friend . . . ." but was he any of these things to any superior?

78 *M.O.S.*, 32-35.

79 See William E. Gienapp., *The Origins of the Republican Party* (New York, 1987), 103-166, 240-271 (Gienapp, *Republican Party*); Tyler Anbinder, *Nativism and Slavery: The Northern Know Nothings and the Politics of the 1850's* (New York, 1992), 220-265 (Anbinder, *Nativism*); see also, Allan G. Bogue, *The Earnest Men: Republicans of the Civil War Senate* (Ithaca, 1981).

80 Meade MSS (PHS) letter dated September 7, 1861, from Meade to Joshua Barney.

He had a lifetime critical eye for all his superiors. In Mexico, he had harsh comments for Patterson. Commanding the Engineer Company at West Point, he had an endless, acrimonious war with Breverton, the superintendent of the Academy. In the Crimea his two superior officers quickly became personal and professional enemies. Superior judgment and performance by Stevens he had taken as a personal affront. The people he did not respect, he just simply did not like; nor could he work well with them.

A bad portent this was. Of course, it was unknown in Washington and certainly unknown to Scott, toward whom McClellan had repeatedly protested his loyalty and willingness to serve in the recent months. In all this he and Scott had been hundreds of miles apart and connected only by the slow mails, the tenuous telegraph, and the interminable messenger. Now he and Scott were to be side by side in the presence of the powerful leaders of the civilian government, an aged, experienced, crippled, highly sensitive brevet lieutenant-general and a young, independent, fractious, inexperienced, self-confident major general.

The seeds of future conflict with the protocol-minded general in chief had already been well-sown, and any moderately astute politician experienced in the "Washington establishment" knew it.[81] Before he ever reached the capital, McClellan had participated in conduct Scott would have considered "disloyal" as he had the prewar conduct of Keyes. When Chase first wrote to his new protégé, he quickly passed from the "introduction" to his new semiofficial military responsibilities which, in his mind, involved national strategy. McClellan replied to Chase.[82] More importantly, he had corresponded directly with the president of the United States to describe the delicate condition of Kentucky and to request assistance in assignments to his staff.[83]

He did not feel any compunction about direct communication with civilians who could help on military matters. Of course, military protocol required that his communications be sent to Scott, who would forward them if he deemed it appropriate and necessary. The critical point of all this was the ease felt by McClellan when he corresponded directly with civilian authorities rather than through Scott, his superior.

Friction with superior officers over matters of protocol and etiquette was one thing; failure to obey orders, insubordination, or disobedience were altogether

81 Moore, *Buchanan Works*, 11, 213-214, letter of July 26, 1861, from Stanton to Buchanan.

82 Sears, *McClellan's Correspondence*, 50-51, telegram dated July 10, 1861, from McClellan to Chase.

83 Sears, *McClellan's Correspondence*, 28-30, letters dated May 30, 1861, and June 1, 1861, from McClellan to Lincoln.

different. Only a clairvoyant could have known McClellan's attitude on this subject when the president and the Cabinet met on the evening of July 22 to consider the question of command in the east. They would have taken for granted McClellan's prompt obedience to orders from his political superiors, whether Dennison or Lincoln. In Mexico, McClellan had been too junior to flash this kind of problem. His contemporaneous diary, however, confirms his attitude early in his career toward orders from superior officers when he disagreed with them, even in battle.

As Scott's army approached Cerro Gordo, where the Mexican forces were in battle position, Lieutenant Zealous B. Tower, McClellan, and ten of their men from the Engineer Company were attached to the column of General Gideon Pillow. At Pillow's approach to the Mexican positions, Tower recommended a route that Pillow rejected. Tower's route would have been concealed from sight, would have been screened from enemy fire, and would have emerged on the flank of the Mexican position. Pillow's route arrived in an exposed position from which he could make only a direct frontal assault on troops behind field fortifications. Pillow's assault was repulsed and at least one of his regiments "scattered."

In McClellan's view, he told his diary, "The fault of the erroneous selection was General Pillow's except that Lieutenant Tower should, as the Senior Engineer with the column, have taken a firm stand and have forced General Pillow to pursue the proper path. It was certainly a fine opportunity for him to show what stuff he was made of—but unfortunately he did not take advantage of it at all."[84]

Different than ordinary military "stuff" it would have been for Captain Tower to "force" General Pillow to take the route Tower recommended. How should it have been done? Would it rise to the level of direct insubordination, mutiny, a court-martial offense? Did McClellan consider any of this when he decided in favor of the much junior Regular Army lieutenant over the volunteer general and when he chose, without regard for rank, the man who was right over the man who was not. McClellan's mountainous self-confidence, his belief in the rightness of his own judgment, and his peculiar view of orders when they conflicted with his "correct" judgment would produce unfortunate relationships after he assumed command in Washington.

His campaign in West Virginia had told much about his characteristics as a field leader. In a brief time, he had organized and trained a force of Ohio and Indiana regiments. In June, he marched for western Virginia, his force numbering in the neighborhood of twenty thousand men and vastly outnumbering the Confederate forces confronting him. The Rebels had two bodies of troops, the main body at a pass

84 Myers, *McClellan's Mexican War Diary*, 81-82, narrative for April 16, 1847.

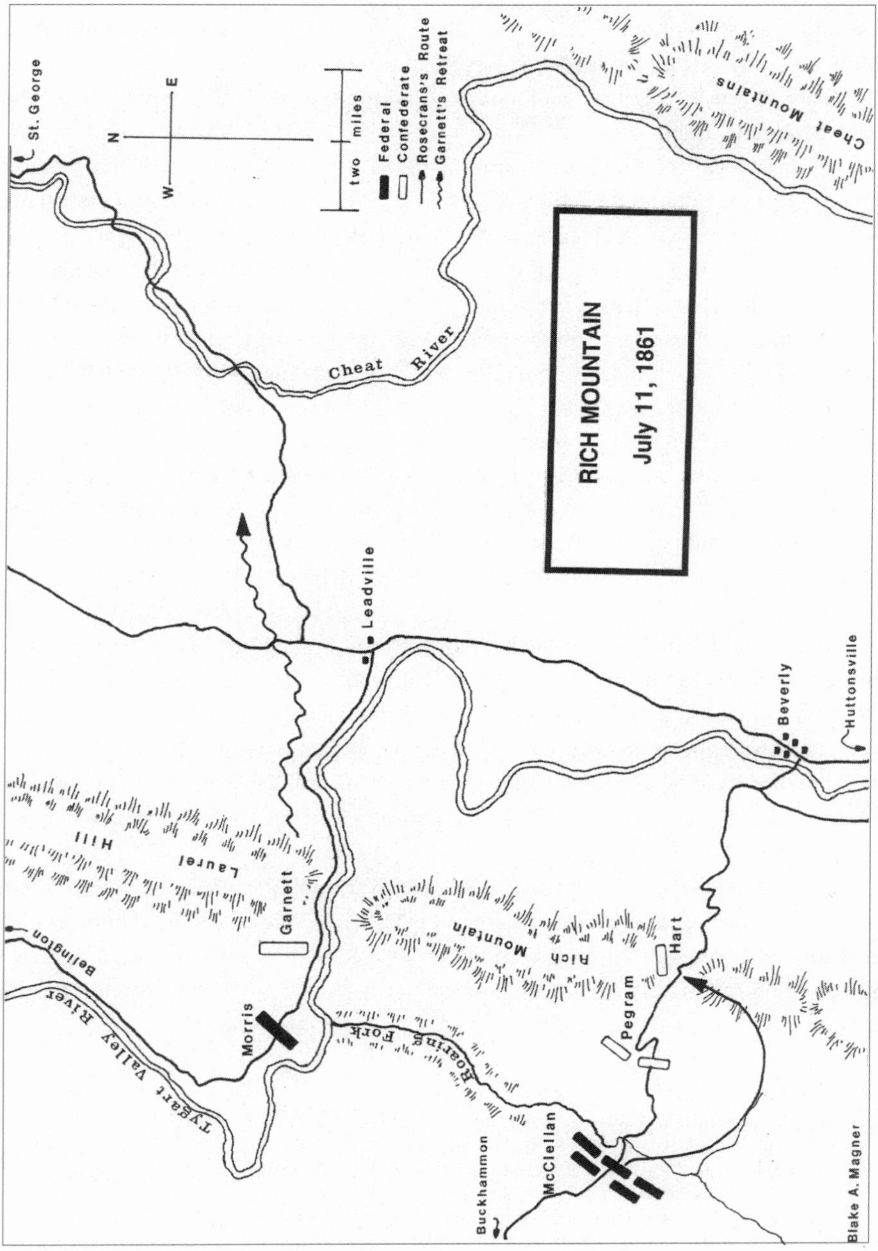
RICH MOUNTAIN
July 11, 1861
St. George
N
W
E
two miles
Federal
Confederate
Rosecrans's Route
Garnett's Retreat
Cheat Mountains
Cheat River
Leadville
Beverly
Huttonsville
Laurel Hill
Garnett
Belington
Tygart Valley River
Morris
Roaring Fork
Rich Mountain
Hart
Pegram
McClellan
Buckhammon
Blake A. Magner

through Laurel Mountain and a smaller body defending a pass through Rich Mountain. McClellan divided his forces, sending one brigade to hold the main Confederate force at Laurel Mountain and taking the remaining three toward the Rich Mountain position.

From a local man serving in one of his regiments McClellan learned that a rugged path, unsuitable for artillery, coiled south around the Confederate left flank to a small farm. He decided to send William S. Rosecrans, his most trusted subordinate, with a flanking column to that place. When Rosecrans reached the position on the Rebel flank, he would attack the enemy; and when McClellan heard his fire, he would launch a frontal assault with the main force. But the Confederate commander was not blind. Although he expected problems on his right flank, he had detached a small infantry force with one gun to the farm on his left. After a long flank march, Rosecrans met the Confederate force at the farm.

The encounter was heard in McClellan's camp, and he formed for the main assault. But the cannon fire—it could only have been Confederate artillery—continued too long; and the Rebels in his front appeared to be exulted. Rosecrans's column must have come to no good. McClellan delayed. Then, he decided not to attack.

Meanwhile, Rosecrans at the head of the flanking column had done more than his job. In a severe rainstorm, he defeated the small force sent to hold the farm and drove it back on the main Confederate position on the mountain. That night, the Confederates slipped around him in retreat. Confused pursuits by both the Laurel Hill and the Rich Mountain forces followed, the Confederate commanding officer was killed while withdrawing his skirmishers at a ford, and his subordinate decided to surrender.[85]

McClellan issued a bombastic, laudatory, Napoleonic address to his small army.[86] The press, having found a hero, praised him to the skies.[87] The Union, which had lost Fort Sumter, suffered humiliation at Big Bethel, and endured a series of minor embarrassments around Washington, was ready for anyone who could bring it a victory.

85 Michie, *McClellan*, 84-92; Sears, *McClellan*, 86-93; Jacob D. Cox, "McClellan in West Virginia," in *B&L*, 1, 128-137; Cox, *Reminiscences*, 1, 50-53. For the American Civil War, nothing is ever the last word; but for every possible word on this campaign, see Newell, Clayton R., *Lee vs. McClellan: The First Campaign* (Washington, 1996),esp. 116-132. In *M.O.S.* McClellan gave no account of the West Virginia campaign, instead stating that he was reserving that for the history of the Army of the Potomac he was writing (p. 52), a history he never finished. McClellan's official report is in *OR*, 2, 205-208.

86 Michie, *McClellan*, 92.

87 Sears, *McClellan*, 93.

The battle was small, the military consequences insignificant, and the numbers inconsequential. Nevertheless, it had a great deal of romantic attraction: a campaign in the mountains, a concealed flanking column, a fight in a driving rainstorm, a pursuit, and the death of the opposing commander in a rear-guard action. A study of the battle, if one had been made at the time, might have shown much about the man and the future.

For such a small force with such numerical superiority, McClellan's plan was elaborate. He had divided his force not once but twice in order to pin the enemy at Laurel Mountain and flank the secondary force at Rich Mountain.

No heroic, casualty-ridden frontal assault had taken place. Not once but twice, first as a cadet and later as a member of the Napoleon Club, McClellan had been educated by Dennis Hart Mahan, a devotee of field works, defensive positions, and limited or controlled frontal attacks. To Mahan—and to McClellan—American volunteers and the tiny Regular Army could not, for very different reasons, be launched on frequent massive frontal assaults.

Politically, they believed, it was simply not possible. A democratic nation like America could not have a large standing army; and the small, trained force of Regulars would rapidly disappear in repeated assaults on strong defensive positions. By now in its history, the country's mainstay in a major war was the volunteer, who would not stand to the mark for destructive assaults.[88] In his letter to Washington before he advanced on the Confederates, he said, ". . . no prospect of a brilliant victory shall induce me to depart from my intention of gaining success by maneuvering rather than by fighting; I will not throw these men of mine into the teeth of artillery and entrenchments, if it is possible to avoid it."[89] McClellan would not, except in a case of absolute necessity, assault the enemy in a prepared defensive position.

When he heard the fire of Rosecrans's flanking column and the small Rebel force sent to protect the left flank on Rich Mountain, he drew a series of adverse inferences. Under almost any military circumstances, the first stroke of a flanking force must be immediately followed by the major attack, even a frontal attack against defensive works, or the flanking force will be destroyed and the plan aborted. McClellan should have done as he had agreed and launched his main force when he heard the firing of Rosecrans's column. Instead, he drew negative conclusions from inconclusive and incomplete facts that supported both negative and positive

88 Edward Hagerman, *The American Civil War and Origins of Modern Warfare: Ideas, Organization, and Field Command* (Indianapolis, 1988), 8-13, 15 (Hagerman, *American Civil War and Modern Warfare*).

89 Sears, *McClellan's Correspondence*, 45; quoted in Michie, *McClellan*, 91; *OR*, 2, 199.

inferences; he decided to do nothing; and he left Rosecrans to deal with his own situation as best he could.

Few decisions in warfare can be made on the basis of complete and accurate information. In the American Civil War, the successful military leaders, as they had in all other wars, were able to "fill in the blanks" by the exercise of sound judgment and make a wise decision. Not every set of circumstances required a negative conclusion. Each required independent treatment. Unable to make a conclusive decision because he did not have clear, complete, and indisputable facts, McClellan chose to make no decision at all. In effect, he chose to do nothing. On the train chugging east he must have known he was leaving the world of twenty-thousand-man engagements and heading for Napoleonic-sized armies. They would deny him the luxury of such an unwillingness to decide.

Divided columns, a minor violation of the rule of concentration, have always had a place in military affairs. Custer did it at the Battle of Washita and tried it again at the Little Big Horn.[90] When the components perform according to plan, no matter how many variations or surprises the enemy present, the division of a force can achieve desirable results. In his greatest victory, the Battle of Emmans, Judah the Maccabee divided his army into four groups for a surprise attack. Two under Judah attacked the Seleucid camps from the east, a third struck from the north at the sound of Judah's battle. As he moved forward in the darkness, a huge phalanx was found in position outside the camp. He would not have the element of surprise and could not enter the camp while the enemy was at rest. The Seleucid phalanx substantially outnumbered him. Judah divided his own force three more times and attacked the flank of the phalanx. North of the camp, the other group, fifteen hundred men, heard the sounds of Judah's battle and performed their part of the plan: they attacked an army of ten thousand foot and two thousand horse. The phalanx broke and fled. After hand-to-hand fighting amongst horses and elephants in the camp, the Seleucid forces in the camp broke and fled, leaving three thousand dead.[91]

The critical fact here—especially for a night battle—was the execution of the plan by separated parts, no one of which knew whether the others had accomplished their missions. McClellan had devised a plan in which he could not see the flanking column and knew his active part would begin on sound. In short, he did not carry out his role as he should have because he refused to make a frontal attack when circumstances demanded it.

90 Jay Monaghan, *Custer: The Life of General George Armstrong Custer* (Boston, 1959), 315, 384-390; Edgar I. Stewart, *Custer's Luck* (Norman, 1955), 164-165, 316-331, esp. map facing 336.

91 Chaim Herzog and Gichon Mordecai, *Battles of the Bible* (London, 1997), 276-280.

Chapter 24

"General, anything that you indicate as necessary shall always be acted upon favorably by our committee; and if you do not feel that you are today king of this country, you do not appreciate your position."

– *Representative Frank Blair to McClellan*

McClellan Takes Center Stage

As he came east, he was the conquering hero. The mayor of Wheeling asked if the town could arrange a demonstration "indicative of the high respect and honor in which they hold you."[1] Secretary Chase wrote to confirm that he would arrive on Saturday, July 27.[2] Another asked to discuss important matters with him at once.[3] Henry W. Benham, a West Point graduate and staff officer he had left behind in West Virginia, tried to convince him he was wrong not to bring him east.[4]

1 McClellan MSS (L.C.) letter dated July 24, 1861, from A.S. Sweeney, Mayor of Wheeling, to McClellan.

2 McClellan MSS (L.C.) telegram dated July 25, 1861, from Chase to McClellan.

3 McClellan MSS (L.C.) letter dated July 26, 1861, from Fry to McClellan.

4 McClellan MSS (L.C.) telegram dated July 25, 1861, from Henry W. Benham to McClellan.

A member of the House of Representatives sent him a resolution of thanks for his services in West Virginia.[5]

After he arrived in Washington, he received laudatory advice from many unsolicited and unknown sources. One well-wisher asked that God endow him with wisdom for his important mission.[6] The secretary of Cassius M. Clay's Washington Guards told him that John Fremont had demanded plenipotentiary powers before he accepted the command in the west, hoped that McClellan would make a similar demand, and added that others considered this essential to the safety of the government.[7] Encomiums were not the only contents of his mailbag. One correspondent warned, "Bets have been made here by strangers to the city, that Washington will be taken within two weeks. You have many traitors among you—look to your own cannon—be careful that the most of them are not spiked just before any attempt is made. Look out for traitors in the army as well as among civilians."[8]

On July 25, the day before McClellan reached Washington, an order created the Division of the Potomac. A geographic command rather than a military unit, it would be composed of the Department of Northeastern Virginia under McDowell, commanding all troops in front of Washington on the Virginia bank of the river, and the Department of Washington, under the command of General Mansfield, who commanded all troops in Washington and its vicinity on the Maryland side.[9]

Next day, July 26, Nicolay wrote again to his fiancee, "Things remain here almost as they were—there has been no further fighting and the gloom and oppression of the late disaster is somewhat wearing off."[10]

5 McClellan MSS (L.C.) letter dated July 24, 1861, from Rep. Edwards to McClellan. This is probably the "thanks of Congress" mentioned in Sears, *McClellan's Correspondence*, 70, letter dated July 27, 1861, from McClellan to his wife.

6 McClellan MSS (L.C.) letter dated July 24, 1861, Hall to McClellan; and e.g., letter dated July 23, 1861, from Moss to McClellan.

7 McClellan MSS (L.C.) letter dated July 26, 1861, from McCoy to McClellan.

8 McClellan MSS (L.C.) letter dated July 29, 1861, from illegible to McClellan.

9 *M.O.S.*, 66-67; the order is in *OR*, 2, 763. The use of geographic, rather than unit, commands dated without interruption from the War of 1812 when the army had no general in chief and the secretary of war served as commanding officer of the army. This system, cumbersome and ineffective, continued until it was abolished by General Order No. 50 of the War Department on August 20, 1920. Elaine Everly, et. al. (National Archives), *Preliminary Inventory of the Records of United States Army Continental Commands, 1821-1920, Record Group 393*, 4 vols. (Washington, 1973), 1, *Geographical Divisions and Departments and Military (Reconstruction) Districts* (Everly, *Preliminary Inventory*).

10 Nicolay MSS (L.C.) letter dated July 26, 1861, from Nicolay to Therena.

For his first morning in Washington, July 27, McClellan reported to Adjutant General Lorenzo Thomas who gave him orders to call on the president. With cordiality Lincoln received him and said he had placed him in command of Washington and all the troops in the vicinity. The president asked him to return to the White House in the afternoon to attend a Cabinet meeting.

McClellan then called again on General Scott, his immediate superior as general in chief of the armies of the United States. For some time they discussed the state of affairs. Scott seemed to know very little about the defensive condition of the city and to have thought very little about it. More concerned about appearances, he was disturbed by the disorganized stragglers in the city.

When McClellan casually remarked that he had to leave because the president wished him to attend a Cabinet meeting at 1:00 p.m., the general became indignant. It was highly improper, he complained, for McClellan to be invited to such a meeting without him. Irritated and offended, the general in chief kept McClellan until it was too late to attend the meeting, then ordered him to ride around the city and send stragglers back to their regiments. He would embarrass McClellan by making him miss a presidential appointment. For now, that would be sufficient punishment for violating, with or without fault, military etiquette.[11]

As McClellan left Scott's offices, he met Colonel E.D. Townsend, Scott's adjutant general, waiting in the anteroom. "I want to give you a hint about the state of things here," Townsend said. "You will find splendid material for soldiers sadly in need of discipline. You will be beset on all sides with applications for passes, and all sorts of things, and if you yield to the pressure your whole time will be taken up at a desk writing. You can from the outset avoid this. Another officer can do it as well in your name. The troops want to see their commanding general, and to be often inspected and reviewed by him. Another thing. There is here a fine body of regulars. I would keep that intact, as a sort of Old Guard. It may sometime save you a battle."[12] In his own way McClellan would adopt all this advice.

McClellan left headquarters and rode toward Tennallytown on the northern outskirts of the city, where he examined some of the camps. He did not personally perform the provost marshal's job of detaining drunken stragglers, but he did learn about the existing preparations for defense against an attack.

Everything was chaos. He did not see troops in military positions. No avenue of approach was guarded. No regiment was properly encamped. The number of troops was insufficient. Their quality was low. The period of service of many regiments had

11 *M.O.S.*, 66.

12 Townsend, *Anecdotes*, 60-61.

expired or was about to expire. Men and officers left their camps at will. He saw the streets, hotels, and bars filled with drunken officers and men.

Finally, he finished and rode back. At some time on that day he managed to publish his own orders assuming command;[13] and hours late, he reported to the president at the White House. When he explained the cause of his apparent lack of courtesy and his failure to attend the Cabinet meeting, Lincoln did not seem annoyed. He had not been dealing with Scott since March for nothing. No doubt recognizing the general in chief's sensitivity and vanity at work, he seemed to be amused by the incident.[14] During this meeting the president asked McClellan to submit his views on an overall strategy for bringing the war to a successful conclusion. He already had Scott's plan, which was impractical at best, and nowhere else to turn for guidance. And he must have requested a list of recommendations for promotion to major-general and brigadier-general in both the Regular Army and the volunteer service.[15]

The next day, Sunday, July 28, McClellan rode the lines on the Virginia side, beginning his tour at Sherman's position opposite Georgetown. He found the Virginia side no better.

Believing the Confederates to be close at hand, Sherman nervously attempted to dissuade McClellan from passing outside the pickets; but the location of the Rebel lines was precisely what McClellan wanted to know. He rode some distance beyond the pickets but found no Confederates.

The troops were on the river banks or on high ground next to the river, but few were in condition to fight. Little had been done to entrench the approaches. The only

13 *OR*, 2, 766; *OR* 5, 11; *M.O.S.*, 67.

14 *M.O.S.*, 66-69; Ed Emerson, *Life and Letters of Charles Russell Lowell* (Boston, 1907), 217 (Emerson, *Lowell*), letter dated August 5, 1861, from Lowell to his mother.

15 The request by the president for views on strategy is noted both in the memorandum that responded to it, Sears, *McClellan's Correspondence*, 71, memorandum dated August 2, 1861, by the editor, from McClellan to Lincoln; and the endorsement on McClellan's copy in his MSS, *ibid.*, 75, n. 1. The date Lincoln made the request is not specified in Lincoln MSS, McClellan MSS, *OR*, Sears, or any other likely source. According to Miers, *Lincoln Day by Day*, year 1861, 56-58, the two meetings on July 27 were the only times McClellan and Lincoln met before the memorandum was delivered on August 2. One must be very careful in relying on *Lincoln Day by Day* and on *Lincoln's Works* when trying to prove the negative. A number of incidents and documents appear in these pages that do not appear in Miers or Basler. Nevertheless, both were monumental undertakings, were done with great care and professionalism, and are invaluable to the student of the period. The same reasoning applies to the request for recommendations for general officer but not even the request, let alone the date of it is recorded. National Archives, Records of the Adjutant General's Office, Letters received, Commission Branch file (Record Group 94) 746-M (CB) 1863, Memorandum dated July 29, 1861, from McClellan to Lincoln. At this time McClellan would not likely have been presumptuous enough to submit a document like this unsolicited to the president.

completed works were Fort Ellsworth near Alexandria, Forts Runyan and Allen at the end of the Long Bridge, Fort Corcoran at the head of the Aqueduct Bridge, and one or two adjacent batteries. Two or three small entrenchments had been commenced on Arlington Heights, but under all circumstances the position on the Virginia side was too shallow. His problems were the same as those that had faced McDowell: if the Confederates attacked and broke into the position, he could not maneuver, and he could not seal the breakthrough because the space between the river and the main line was too shallow. To create depth, the lines had to be pushed away from the Potomac. A small battery at the eastern end of the Chain Bridge was the only entrenchment on the Washington side of the river. No organized defensive line had been established anywhere.

As McClellan saw it, McDowell's army did not amount to an organized force. It was no more than a collection of undisciplined, uninstructed, and poorly officered men who were demoralized by the defeat and ready, in McClellan's opinion, to run at the first shot.

McDowell did not disagree. On July 30, he reported the condition of the regiments under his command on the west bank of the Potomac: "Those who were in the last movement are not yet recovered, and the others are raw. Such as they are, about twenty regiments could be set in motion in two or three days. But few would have any organization with which they would be at all acquainted, and would have but little confidence in themselves or each other."[16]

Positions from which Confederate artillery could fire into the capital were unoccupied. Materiel did not exist in sufficient quantity. A determined attack, he concluded, would carry Arlington Heights, placing the city under direct artillery fire; and a small cavalry force could ride directly into the city. Lincoln and the Cabinet expected an attack from hour to hour.[17]

One of the most immediate problems was the straggling and drinking by the few men who had never rejoined their commands after the battle and the men who were absent from them. After the retreat the officers and men had gradually returned to their regiments, but absence to visit the "sinks" in Washington was little controlled. The members of the Sanitary Commission met in Washington on July 27. The sight that greeted their eyes and that must have been seen by the president and the Cabinet was appalling.

As Frederick Law Olmsted wrote in the Commission's Report in September:

16 *M.O.S.*, 73-74, letter dated July 30, 1861, from McDowell to McClellan.

17 *M.O.S.*, 69.

> Groups of men wearing parts of military uniforms, and some of them with muskets, were indeed to be seen; but upon second sight, they did not appear to be soldiers. Rather they were the most wo-begone rabble, which had, perhaps, clothed itself with the garments of dead soldiers left in a hard-fought battlefield. No two were dressed completely alike; some were without caps, others without coats, others without shoes. All were alike excessively dirty, unshaven, unkempt, and dank with dew. The groups were formed around fires made in the streets, and burning boards wrenched from citizen's fences. Some were still asleep at full length in the gutters and on doorsteps, or sitting on the curbstones resting their heads against the lamp-posts. Others were evidently begging for food at housedoors. Some appeared ferocious, others only sick and dejected; all excessively weak, hungry, and selfish. They were mainly silent, and when they spoke, it humiliated a man to hear them. No pack of whining, snarling, ill-fed vagabond street dogs in an oriental city ever more strongly produced the impression of forlorn, outcast, helpless, hopeless misery. There was no apparent organization; no officers were apparently among them, seldom even a non-commissioned officer. At Willard's Hotel, however, officers swarmed.[18]

The competent brigade and regimental commanders, controlling all but the few who had not rejoined the colors, were taking their own steps to correct the situation. Colonel William B. Franklin, after assuming command of all troops in Fort Ellsworth and in advance of Fort Ellsworth, issued on August 1 an order which restricted the movement of officers and men between the bivouac area and Washington, D.C. No more than two officers from a regiment and two men from a company could be absent from camp at the same time. All passes were to expire at 5:00 p.m. on the day of issue. Franklin strictly enforced these orders.

On August 3 the men of the Sixteenth New York Infantry Regiment were paid for their service from May 15 to June 30. Most of the men wanted the money sent to a local bank in upstate New York, but that could only be done by taking it into Washington and forwarding it by bank draft. They selected Captain Newton M. Curtis for this task. Previously, men who had sought passes for private business in Washington had been returned under arrest. As Curtis set off for Franklin's headquarters, several officers and men created a pool on the time he would return under arrest. Curtis presented his pass to the regimental commander, Colonel Davies, who signed it and expressed the hope that Franklin would approve it. Curtis then went to Alexandria and presented the pass to Colonel Franklin's adjutant, who

18 McLaughlin, *Olmsted Papers*, 4, 164-165, pamphlet entitled "Report of the Secretary with Regard to the Probable Origin of the Recent Demoralization of the Volunteer Army at Washington, and the Duty of the Sanitary Commission with Reference to certain Deficiencies in the Existing Army Arrangements as suggested thereby."

took it to the colonel's room and returned with the endorsement, "Disapproved by order of Colonel Franklin."

Curtis said, "This is not what I want. Will you please procure for me an interview with Colonel Franklin?"

Knowing Franklin's sharp temper, the adjutant replied carefully, "If you are very anxious to see Colonel Franklin, I will present your compliments and state your wishes, but if you will take a suggestion from me, you will not attempt to see him. He is in no mood to discuss the subject of passes, and you will probably be ordered to your regiment."

Curtis thanked him for his interest and asked him to arrange the interview anyway. The adjutant complied. Curtis entered to find Franklin intently studying a map. After a pause, Franklin looked up.

"I desire to explain to you," Curtis said, "the necessity of my going to Washington."

"You state that you have important private business," Franklin replied. "No soldier should have private business to take him away from his official duties, but if you will be brief, you may state why you wish to go to Washington."

Curtis said he had approximately three thousand dollars in coin which the members of his company wished to send home. He said he had given each of his men a check for the amount of their pay on a local bank in upstate New York, wished to deposit the money with the United States Treasury, and wanted a draft sent to the bank upstate to cover the checks that had been given.

Franklin responded, "An officer should have no financial dealings with the men of his company."

"I have no other transactions beyond that of getting them to send all the money possible to their friends," Curtis replied. "The less they have in camp, the better off they will be. I have also commissions to execute for the officers of the regiment who were not able to go to Washington."

Franklin responded, "That is a good reason. Return to your regiment and get all the commissions that the officers desire to have executed. I will pass you or any other officer to Washington to attend to them."

Curtis then said he had as many commissions as he could execute in one day and that he did not wish to remain in Washington overnight. He added that his own business could not be transacted by any other person.

"What can that be?" asked Franklin.

"I have on my best uniform, which as you see, is not suitable for an inspection, and I know of no other person who can represent me at the tailor's in being measured for a suit of clothes."

An officer's appearance was important. Franklin approved the pass and when he returned it executed said, "Whenever you need new clothes, I will give you a pass to the tailor."[19]

McClellan's overall solution for the problem was swift, simple, and effective. He appointed Andrew Porter temporary provost marshal of Washington and assigned him the Regular Army units, the Second United States Cavalry, the few companies of infantry, and two batteries of artillery.[20] Just as Franklin had, McClellan imposed strict limitations on absence from one's unit and visits to the capital. The administrative burdens, as Townsend had suggested, were not retained at army headquarters. Permits were to be issued by the brigade commanders and were to state the "object of the visit." No one was to "absent himself from his camp and visit Washington except for the performance of some public duty or for the transaction of important private business."[21]

Porter was to report directly to McClellan's headquarters, an arrangement that would not change as long as Porter served with McClellan. Within a few days the unauthorized military street traffic disappeared along with the vast majority of the military personnel in the capital, a step that had a powerful, beneficial effect on the morale of the army and the peace of mind of the civilians.[22] By the fourth of August, the capital was quiet.[23]

The enlisted men disappeared from the city almost at once, but a few officers lingered in the saloons. Willard's was no exception. Neither were full colonels. Nor was assignment to the provost marshal's units a guarantor of good conduct. On August 7, 1861, First Lieutenant Robert Finley Hunter, an abysmal forty-sixth in the West Point Class of 1853, Second United States Infantry, in command of a provost guard, found Colonel John H. McCunn of the Thirty-seventh New York Infantry probably severely drunk in Willard's.[24]

19 Curtis, *Bull Run to Chancellorsville*, 52-55; also, F. Colburn Adams, *Story of a Trooper*.

20 *OR*, 2, 769, General Orders No. 2, dated July 30, 1861; *M.O.S.*, 69-70; Howard, *Autobiography*, 1, 168-171.

21 *OR*, 2, 769.

22 Heintzelman MS diary (diary, L.C.) entry dated Sept. 5, 1861; Sears, *McClellan's Correspondence*, 75, letter dated August 2, 1861, from McClellan to his wife; *M.O.S.*, 70; Howard, *Autobiography*, 1, 169.

23 *M.O.S.*, 70.

24 NA, RG 393, pt. 1, no. 3964, Register of outgoing correspondence of the Army of the Potomac (vol. 1 of 8), 1, 6; Heitman, *Historical Register*, 1, 558; *Cullum*, 2, no. 1624; Thomas Lowry, M.D., *Tarnished Eagles: The Courts-Martial of Fifty Union Colonels and Lieutenant Colonels* (Mechanicsburg, 1997), 47-48 (Lowry, *Tarnished Eagles*).

McCunn was not alone. Hunter had made several trips through Willard's bar during the day and had not passed without partaking. His face was flushed. In the infuriating and ever-so-superior manner of the modern-day military police, Hunter asked McCunn to show him his pass or authority for being in the hotel.

The colonel became "abusive, ungentlemanly, and unofficerlike" according to the charges and specifications that followed. He refused to show his pass.

"Go to hell, by God, sir," he fumed. "By what authority do you demand my pass."

Hunter knew he was on sound ground. General Orders No. 2, issued July 30, specifically said, ". . . no officer . . . will be allowed to . . . visit Washington except for the performance of some public duty . . . for which purposes written permits will be given by the commanders of brigades . . ."[25]

Proceeding by the book the lieutenant replied that he demanded McCunn's pass by authority of Colonel Porter, the provost marshal.

The colonel remained unconvinced and disrespectful. "By God! I do not recognize your authority."

Maintaining his composure, Hunter repeatedly asked for the pass. McCunn stuck his hand in his pocket, pulled out a piece of paper, and handed it to the lieutenant.

"There, damn you, will that do."

Hunter saw that the paper was "not a sufficient pass." The colonel must go to his quarters in arrest, Hunter said. Would the colonel give him his name and regiment.

The colonel cursed at the lieutenant and in an "insulting manner" said, "I will see you damned before I will obey your arrest. You and all your guards are drunk."

McCunn was quickly charged with "conduct unbecoming an officer and a gentleman" and with "conduct prejudicial to good order and military discipline," tried, convicted, and sentenced to be "reprimanded in General Orders from the Headquarters of the General Commanding the Army of the Potomac."[26] When he approved the finding of the court martial, McClellan said, "The General commanding . . . desires to express the hope that this instance will be a sufficient warning to him and all other officers who may feel disposed to place themselves in opposition to the constituted military authorities." He considered the sentence lenient but declined to remand for reconsideration of it "partly because the time of many valuable officers would thereby be consumed, and partly because he is willing

25 NA, RG 393, pt. 1, no. 3964, Register of outgoing correspondence of the Army of the Potomac (vol. 1 of 8) charges and specifications and review of court martial result by McClellan.

26 Lowry, *Tarnished Eagles*, 48, quoting the verdict and sentence of the court martial.

to attribute Col. McCunn's misconduct mainly to the fact of his being an inexperienced soldier."[27]

McClellan's adoption of the advice not to involve himself or his headquarters in the business of passes simplified the process, made it more readily accessible, and created unexpected complications. Five junior officers of the Ninth Massachusetts obtained forty-eight-hour passes for leave to Washington from their colonel. A captain designated by the group to obtain brigade approval took the passes to find General Sherman in Fort Corcoran. As he entered the fort, he came upon a tall workman with one trouser leg carelessly stuck in his boot. The captain, resplendent in a new uniform, raised his hand and beckoned with one finger.

"Come here, my man," he said. The workman stepped forward.

"Can you direct me to General Sherman's headquarters?"

"What do you want of General Sherman?"

Newly promoted and impressed with his new station in life, the captain became indignant at being required to explain his purpose to a workman.

"What in hell and damnation is it your business?" he snapped.

The workman was no fool. He would have the better of the encounter. He gave the captain circuitous directions to brigade headquarters. Picking his way carefully through the Virginia mud to avoid soiling his shiny shoes or his trousers, the captain found his way at last to the brigade adjutant and asked him to sign the passes.

"Oh, no, captain, the general is right inside there. You go right in and he will sign your papers." The adjutant smiled.

The captain entered the inner tent. Sitting at the desk was the workman. The captain was dumbfounded.

"Well, captain," said the "workman" in a cheery voice, "what can I do for you?"

The captain struggled, finally found his voice, and stated his business—meekly. The "workman" took the passes and examined them. He would teach the shiny new captain a lesson in humility he would not soon forget.

"How long is it, captain, since you were in Washington?" The workman, General Sherman, did not wait for a reply. "But what in hell and damnation is it my business?"

27 NA, RG 393, pt. 1, no. 3964, Register of outgoing correspondence of the Army of the Potomac (vol. 1 of 8), 8, McClellan's endorsement of the verdict and sentence of the court martial. McCunn led a regiment of poor quality with weak officers who he described by General Richardson as "of low character and can never make anything of themselves." Nevertheless, the officers petitioned to have McCunn removed for incompetence; and he resigned. Lowry, *Tarnished Eagles*, 51, quoting from unidentified letters in McCunn's service file. But McCunn would have his revenge. On November 19, Hunter was cashiered for "drunkenness on duty," *Cullum*, 1, no. 1624, and would not return to the war.

He took his pen, signed the passes, and returned them to the crestfallen captain.[28]

In West Virginia, where he had been victorious, McClellan had faced raw troops with his own raw troops. Although his opponents knew the ground, had taken up strong positions, and were deployed in a country adapted to the defensive, he had attacked and gained success. He felt that, when he was to attack troops who had never been under fire and who were not particularly well commanded, the offensive offered great advantages.

In Washington everything was different. He was not facing inexperienced troops; and the Confederates had the advantage of position, entrenchments, and morale. Their discipline and drill were far better. Thinking it would be madness to renew the attack until a complete change had been made, he decided he could attack victorious and well-drilled troops in entrenchments only with a well-organized and well-drilled army with a good supply of artillery.[29]

A few days after McClellan reached Washington, Scott asked him about the organization of the troops under his command. What did he intend to do? McClellan replied that he wished the force under his command to be organized as an army and called an army instead of a geographic division. At this time all major commands were defined geographically, not by military unit.[30] As commanding officer of the Division of the Potomac, McClellan commanded all troops within the Division and would automatically command any other military force that entered the Division. If he entered another geographic command with his army, for example, the Department of Fortress Monroe, he would, under ordinary circumstances, be subordinate to its commanding officer.[31]

His infantry divisions he intended to organize into corps once the division commanders had acquired experience in the field and demonstrated their abilities. He believed that a mistake by a division commander could be overcome but that a mistake by a corps commander, who should be able to operate independently, could not. He intended a corps to have its own cavalry and artillery and, in the style of Napoleonic warfare, survive several hours of fighting against many times its number until reinforcements could arrive.[32] Within his army he would first form brigades,

28 Daniel G. MacNamara, *History of the Ninth Regiment Massachusetts Volunteer Infantry, Second Brigade, First Division, Fifth Army Corps, Army of the Potomac, June 1861 to June 1864* (Boston, 1899), 54-56 (MacNamara, *Ninth Massachusetts*).

29 *M.O.S.*, 71-72.

30 See footnote 9, *supra*, in this chapter.

31 Everly, *Preliminary Inventory* introduction, 4.

32 Chandler, *Napoleon*, 1, 154.

then divisions. For now, he would postpone the formation of corps and would make no recommendations for major-general because he did not wish to appoint men to such important positions without first testing them in actual campaigns and in battle.

Scott objected to everything McClellan proposed except the formation of brigades. The system of geographic divisions and departments, he felt, was an absolute necessity. In Scott's view, the American system and regulations made administration of the affairs of an army impossible. Scott objected to the formation of infantry divisions on the ground that it was unnecessary because he had used only brigades in Mexico.

McClellan responded that all fighting forces throughout the world were organized as armies and that he had used this format in West Virginia. He also noted that Scott's force in Mexico was "a very small affair in comparison with that soon to be collected in front of Washington." Probably annoyed by the slighting comparison, Scott was unconvinced.[33] Finding the general in chief resistant to his plans of campaign and most of his plans for organization, McClellan decided to proceed according to his own views and not discuss them with Scott.

When they arrived in the capital, McClellan had the new levies of infantry formed into provisional brigades and placed in camps in the Washington suburbs for equipment, instruction, and discipline. As soon as the regiments were in condition to be transferred across the river they were assigned to brigades in Virginia. First assigned to command the provisional brigades was Brigadier General Fitz-John Porter. His old friend "Burn" was assigned to this duty after Porter and was later relieved by Silas Casey, who continued in charge of the new regiments until the Army of the Potomac departed the Washington area in March of 1862. Artillery troops reported to Brigadier William F. Barry, the chief of artillery, and cavalry to George Stoneman, the chief of cavalry.

When the organization of brigades was well-established and the troops disciplined and instructed at the basic level, divisions of three brigades would be formed. McClellan told Lincoln and Representative Schuyler Colfax he did not want to be swallowed by eastern regiments and would like to have some regiments from the midwest. A number of Indiana regiments were to be selected as well as some regiments from Michigan. McClellan expressed a preference for Robert H. Milroy's regiment from Indiana, and for Milroy as a regimental commander.[34]

33 Chandler MSS (L.C.) letter dated March 8, 1862, from Gurowski to Chandler; *OR*, 5, 13, McClellan's final rpt, dated August 4, 1863; *M.O.S.*, 113; *N&H*, 5, 169-170; McClellan in *B&L*, 2, 166.

34 Milroy MSS (Indiana Historical Society) letter dated September 6, 1861, from Colfax to Milroy; *M.O.S.*, 7-8, 61, 71.

On July 29, McClellan delivered to Lincoln a terse memorandum listing the men he recommended for promotion to general officer in both the volunteer and Regular Army. It gave no more than a list and one request. "I would respectfully suggest that the number of Major Generals of Volunteers now appointed be limited, in order that the capacity of the Brig. Genls be tested before giving them the higher command." The list for Regular Army promotions was small, only six altogether. McDowell and George Wright, a graduate of the class of 1822, comprised the entire list for major general, with four more, Hunter, Franklin, Sherman, and Buell, for Regular Army brigadier general. The list for volunteers stood at twenty-six, Heintzelman being the only candidate for major general.

The list expressed McClellan's prior service and his knowledge of the West Point, Regular Army officer corps. All were or had been Regular Army. Only Andrew Porter had not graduated from the Military Academy, but he had attended the institution for one year. The classes reached from 1818, Harvey Browne in apparent exile in Fort Pickens, Florida, to 1854, Oliver Otis Howard. Only a few classes had more than one representative, 1822, 1839, 1841, and 1845. McClellan's class, 1846, had only one other representative, George Stoneman. Of course, his friends, to whom he was always loyal, appeared in the form of Fitz-John Porter, Andrew Porter, William B. Franklin, William F. Smith, A. E. Burnside, and Don Carlos Buell. Missing from the list was his chief engineer, John G. Barnard, although other men like Sacket, Edmund Shriver, Barry, Hunt, and Stoneman, who were also all headed for staff duty, found places on it.[35] Surprisingly, it was not heavily concentrated in his schoolmates from the eight classes while he was a cadet or his classmates even though his own class would produce a number of general officers over the war.[36]

The night of July 29, McClellan worked past midnight and on to three o'clock in the morning on his response to the president's request for a statement of overall policy for the war;[37] and on August 2, the finished version was delivered to the president. It was an important statement of McClellan's strategic thinking and gave

35 NA, Records of the Adjutant General's Office, Letters Received, Commissions Branch File (Microcopy M 1064) 1746-M (C.B.) 1863), memorandum dated July 29, 1861, from McClellan to Lincoln. This document, assumed to exist, eluded the author for more than thirty years until he spoke to Michael Musick, who labors diligently as keeper of the American Civil War at the National Archives, who knows more than any other human about the vast reservoirs of information available there, and who is never too busy to be helpful and pleasant.

36 Jesse L. Reno, John G. Foster, Samuel Sturgis, and numerous brevet brigadier generals. 2 *Cullum* entries for the class of 1846.

37 Sears, *McClellan's Correspondence*, 71, letter dated July 30, 1861, from McClellan to his wife.

an accurate insight into his motivational forces. In the ordinary war, he wrote, the primary goal was to defeat the enemy, their army, their people, and their country in order to extract the most favorable peace terms from them.[38] Taking a sociological page from the book of his not-so-distant youth, he noted a significant difference in this war: an aristocratic class was the real enemy. But the initial successes of the "landed gentry," the plantation owners, had consolidated the "mass of their people" behind them and had expanded the enemy class from a sparse aristocracy to "a population sufficiently numerous, intelligent, and warlike to constitute a nation." Confronting a nation in arms, not merely an outlaw class, the Union must crush the field armies of the South and must show "overwhelming strength" to the civilians. Unlike the ordinary war, however, the defeated enemy must then be re-incorporated into the victorious body politic.

Although his memorandum could have been a model of clarity no more to Lincoln and the Cabinet than it is to the reader of later years, McClellan was apparently saying that the aristocracy was to be crushed; but the remainder of the South, innocent of political guilt, should suffer as little as possible. He was also implying that the final peace would be by negotiation, not by capitulation after defeat. "By thoroughly defeating our enemies, taking their strong places, and pursuing a rigidly protective policy as to private property and unarmed persons, and a lenient course as to common soldiers, we may well hope for the restoration of permanent peaceful Union."

After philosophizing about the planter aristocracy, he described the army required to defeat the Southern forces. It would exceed in men and guns any field army ever commanded by Napoleon. All other Union forces would be shadows of the size and capability of the "main Army of Operations," which he was to create, train, and command. Other forces need only be large enough to keep local peace. For example, Harpers Ferry would have almost no troops because the large force under McClellan would stand on the rear of any Rebel force threatening it. He needed "no very large additions to the troops now in Missouri" and "not more than 20,000 troops . . . together with those that can be raised in [Kentucky] and Eastern Tennessee" for that region. Even smaller bodies would be adequate for western Virginia, Baltimore, Fort Monroe, and the rest; ". . . and not more than 20,000 will be necessary, at the utmost, for the defense of Washington."[39]

38 After World War I the French would learn that the most favorable terms of surrender are not always worth the postwar price.

39 Sears, *McClellan's Correspondence*, 71-72, memo dated Aug. 2, 1861, by the editor, from McClellan to Lincoln; *D.A.B.*, 1, pt. 1, 626-627.

McClellan staunchly believed the vast majority of the Union forces should be concentrated in his "main Army of Operations" around Washington, and he did everything he could to accomplish this end. Daniel Sickles's imaginative and constructive plan for creation of a Federal officer pool had predictably failed, largely because of resistance by the states' governors. By September, President Lincoln had learned that he should decline every recruiting effort independent of the states and their inertia-driven governors. One proposal he endorsed for Governor Morgan of New York, "While I am grateful to Mr. Harrison for his generous offer, what he proposes is precisely what we have been compelled to decline on pain of the States Governors declining all efforts to raise troops for us. They say they cannot and will not continue the effort with this individual competition constantly thwarting them."[40]

Sickles reverted to his original plan to recruit a regiment, but now his plan had grown to recruiting a brigade.[41] He had regiments in the process of formation. McClellan wanted to add them to his growing army even though they were unarmed and undrilled.

In mid-August, he asked Sickles, "How many men have you, General, on Staten Island in the two regiments there?"

"Seven hundred in one and five hundred in the other."

"Send them orders to come to Washington at once. I want every man."

Reports of this and other forming regiments moving to Washington would show the Confederates that he intended to defend the Virginia shore positions to the utmost. Later, these men would be part of the irresistible advance by his "main Army of Operations."[42]

Small, peacekeeping garrisons would be sufficient away from Washington because the "main Army of Operations" would move irresistibly on its one campaign, fight and win its major battle, and end the rebellion. Two hundred seventy-three thousand men, six hundred guns, and twenty-five thousand cavalry would suffice for that army. Almost as an afterthought but foretelling the future, he said, "Its general line of operations should be directed that water transportation can

40 Edwin D. Morgan MSS (New York State Library) letter dated September 6, 1861, from Joshua Harrison to Lincoln with endorsement dated September 9, 1861, from Lincoln to Morgan.

41 Swanberg, *Sickles*, 115-121.

42 Dwight Family MSS (M.H.S.) letter dated August 18, 1861, from William Dwight to his father; William B. Jordan, ed., *The Civil War Journals of John Mead Gould: 1861-1866* (Baltimore, 1997), 55, entry dated August 19, 1861 (Jordan, *Gould Journals*). Although he would have had no firsthand knowledge, Gould noted that the president had ordered all forming regiments to Washington.

be availed of from point to point by means of the ocean and the rivers emptying into it."[43]

A master plan for defeating the South? This was a far cry from the duties of a captain of cavalry, his rank when he resigned from the regular army in 1857. The assignment could not have failed to buttress his belief in himself. In spite of his little scrape with the general in chief about protocol and military etiquette, McClellan found Scott, Lincoln, and the Cabinet deferring to him.[44] Others did as well. In early August, McClellan met at army headquarters with his friend William B. Franklin, and congressman Francis P. Blair, Jr., brother of the postmaster general and chairman of the House Committee on Military Defense. McClellan described certain questions he wanted speedily and favorably resolved. No doubt, they included the appointment of aides and the restructuring of the engineers. Blair promised the issues would be settled at once. And, he added, they would be done as McClellan wished.

"General, anything that you indicate as necessary shall always be acted upon favorably by our committee; and if you do not feel that you are today king of this country, you do not appreciate your position."[45]

McClellan concluded that he had, indeed, become "*the* power of the land." Unfortunately, this put other things in his mind as well. His boundless self-confidence was transformed into unlimited self-importance. Ideas that ought never to have occurred to him he discussed in letters to his soulmate, Ellen.

"I almost think that were I to win some small success now I could become Dictator or anything else that might please me—but nothing of that kind would please me—*therefore* I *won't* be Dictator. Admirable self-denial."[46]

The subject had to be fascinating for a renowned person in a country so hostile to titles, to any pretense of nobility, and to intrusions on democracy. While riding

43 Sears, *McClellan's Correspondence*, 71-72, memorandum dated August 2, 1861, by the editor, from McClellan to Lincoln; *D.A.B.*, 1, pt. 1, 626-627.

44 Sears, *McClellan's Correspondence*, 70, letter dated July 27, 1861, from McClellan to his wife.

45 Major General William B. Franklin, "The First Great Crime of the War," in A. K. McClure, ed., *The Annals of the War Written by Leading Participants North and South* (Philadelphia, 1879), 73 (McClure, *Annals of the War*); *D.A.B.*, 1, pt. 2, 333. Franklin describes Blair in August of 1861 as a "General" and head of a House Committee on Military Affairs. According to *D.A.B.* and other sources, Blair had refused a commission as a general, did not accept one until 1862, was Chairman of the Committee on Military Defense (the committee mentioned by Franklin was the Senate Committee of which Henry Wilson of Massachusetts was chairman). Warner, *Generals in Blue*, 36; Heitman, *Historical Register*, 1, 222.

46 Sears, *McClellan's Correspondence*, 70, letter dated July 27, 1861, from McClellan to his wife.

with General George A. McCall, an old and respected acquaintance from the Mexican War, McClellan commented again on the subject.

"I understand there is a good deal of talk of making a dictatorship."

"Ah, Mr. Lincoln, I suppose," responded McCall.

"Oh, no. It's me they're talking of."[47]

He wrote his wife in the wee hours of August 10, "I receive letter after letter—have conversation [sic] calling on me to save the nation-alluding to the Presidency, Dictatorship. As I hope one day to be united with you forever in heaven, I have no such aspirations—I will never accept the Presidency—I will cheerfully take the Dictatorship & agree to lay down my life when the country is saved."[48]

Others also thought that the leadership vacuum they perceived should be filled with the same person in the same way. Lieutenant-Colonel William Dwight wrote his father in Massachusetts shortly after McClellan arrived in Washington, "McClellan has to combat daily the old notions of Scott, he is sent for by Prest—Cabinet to do a thing political rather than military & he has to visit outposts & he works nights. He is very independent. At what moment he will throw up all because Scott and the Cabinet won't let him have his way I don't know, but when he does, shall we not take a stride towards the greatest blessing this country could now enjoy—a military despotism. Someone must have absolute power."[49]

Civilians familiar with McClellan's problems shared this view. Frederick Law Olmsted, secretary of the Sanitary Commission, wrote his wife a few days after McClellan arrived in Washington, "Tell all our friends to stiffen themselves for harder times than we have yet thought of. Unless McLellan [sic] is a genius as well as a general & unless he becomes a military dictator & rules over our imbecile government, we should & must have a revolution before we can do anything with the South."[50]

47 Cox, *Reminiscences*, 1, 364.

48 Sears, *McClellan's Correspondence*, 81-82, letter of August 9 (redated to August 10 by the editor), 1861, from McClellan to his wife.

49 Dwight Family MSS (M.H.S.) letter of August 15, 1861, William Dwight to his father.

50 McLaughlin, *Olmsted Papers*, 4, 130, letter of July 29, 1861, from Olmsted to Mary Perkins Olmsted.

Chapter 25

"You are aware that you are talking with the next president of the United States?"

– The British ambassador, referring to McClellan

Growing Pains

Meanwhile, problems born under McDowell bubbled to the surface. The units most demoralized by the disaster at Bull Run had been brought to the Washington side of the Potomac. For the newly arrived regiments steps were taken to expedite instruction, discipline, and equipping on the Washington side before they were assigned to brigades across the river. Among the regiments demoralized by the battle and repositioned in the capital, the Seventy-ninth New York Volunteers, the "Highlanders," became highly visible.[1]

The regiment suffered from problems that would probably have passed quietly had it not been for the death of the regimental commander on Henry House Hill. Before the battle the regiment had no colonel. The officers met Secretary of War Cameron's brother John at a reception given by the secretary's wife. At the suggestion of the secretary, John Cameron was "elected" to, and offered, the colonelcy of the Highlanders. He accepted. Killed by a volley from the unidentified

1 *M.O.S.*, 70.

Rebel regiment in Griffin's sights on Henry House Hill, his tenure was short-lived.[2] The Seventy-ninth suffered severe casualties, losing almost two hundred men.

Having arranged for the first regimental commander, Secretary Cameron undertook to fill the vacancy caused by his brother's death. He offered it to McClellan's old superior on the West Coast, Isaac I. Stevens.

Born in Andover, Massachusetts in 1818, Stevens attended Phillips Academy, another superb New England preparatory school, where he excelled in mathematics, then entered the United States Military Academy. Graduating first in his class in 1839, he received the usual commission as a second lieutenant of engineers, followed by the usual assignments. In the next fifteen years he fought with distinction in the Mexican War, in which he served on Scott's staff, received severe wounds in the assault on Mexico City, and won brevets to major. Service with controversial distinction in the Washington Territory followed, where he worked on the coast survey and published a defense of the conduct of Scott and Taylor in the Mexican War. In 1853 he resigned his commission and, an active Democrat, was appointed by President Franklin Pierce as governor of the territory, a post he held to the end of the decade.

Slightly built and short, Stevens had great dignity of bearing and speech, clarity and breadth of thought, and sound practical judgment. In personality, he was intensely serious; and he suffered from not the slightest trace of a sense of humor. Although a Democrat, his loyalty was never in question.[3] A junior company grade officer in the Seventy-ninth wrote home after Stevens assumed command, "He means to be a first class man. His advent among us was inaugurated by an order for us young officers to leave the pleasant rooms we occupied . . . and to return to our tents. This was as it should be; and other strict measures toward officers and men show that he is the right sort of commander for a Regiment like ours, requiring a strong, firm hand to govern it."[4]

With his West Point education, Mexican War record, and West Coast service against Indians, Stevens had sought and expected more than a regiment. But he was a Democrat in a time of Republican domination. Nor did he have the unqualified support of the lieutenant-general or the major-general commanding the army.

2 W. C. L., ed., *War Letters of William Thompson Lusk, Captain, Assistant Adjutant-General, United States Volunteers, 1861-1863 afterward M.D., LLD* (New York, 1909), 72, letter dated August 17, 1861, from Lusk to his mother (Lusk, *War Letters*); Todd, *Seventy-ninth Highlanders*, 13, 38.

3 *D.A.B.*, 9, pt. 1, 612-613; see also, generally, Hazard Stevens, *The Life of Isaac Ingalls Stevens*, 2 vols. (New York, 1901), esp. vol. 1 (Stevens, *Life of Stevens*).

4 Lusk, *War Letters*, 70-71, letter dated August 11, 1861, from Lusk to his mother.

Scott had objected to his promotion to general because of his "drinking and desired me to say so to you," wrote Stevens's brother Oliver. "He expressed himself desirous of having you in a higher position and also said that many unfounded rumors were bruited about and for that reason he hoped you would exercise great circumspection."[5] For McClellan, the circumstances surrounding the failure to find a pass for the railroad in the Cascades had left sour memories of Stevens.

The colonelcy Stevens accepted as a matter of honor because he had offered his services unreservedly to the national government; but he intended to have more. "I will show those men in Washington that I am worthy of something better than a regiment," he wrote to a friend, "or I will lay my bones on the battlefield."[6]

Meanwhile, having suffered severely in the battle, the officers and men of the Seventy-ninth petitioned the secretary of war for permission to return to New York to recruit while the army was being organized for the next campaign. Taking into account the "gallant services of the Seventy-ninth," its "losses in battle," and "the special consideration of their country," Cameron, an old time politician with no experience or aptitude for the job of secretary of war, endorsed the request with approval. The men were told their request had been granted.

The events that followed resulted from the disorganization that characterized the early months of the war. The status of the Seventy-ninth as a three-month or three-year regiment was unclear. The selection of a new regimental commander was a matter of conflict within the regiment. The absurd grant of a "furlough" by Cameron provoked a widespread hostile reaction outside the regiment.

The regimental officers became a mass of conflict and confusion. Some resigned. Of course, Cameron had no power or authority to appoint Stevens to replace his dead brother, appointments in state regiments being by the states, not the federal government. Major-General Charles W. Sandford, commander of the militia of the State of New York, directed the regimental lieutenant-colonel to convene the officers to elect a new colonel.[7] Seeing the ugly reaction he had caused, Cameron revoked the furlough.[8]

On the selection of a new regimental colonel neither Cameron nor the regimental officers seemed to know about the activities of the other until Stevens presented himself to assume command of the regiment on August 10. At the same

5 Stevens Family MSS (University of Washington) letter dated August 15, 1861, from Oliver Stevens to Stevens.

6 Stevens Family MSS telegram dated June 20, 1861, from Stevens to Senator Nesmith; Stevens, *Life of Stevens*, 2, 320.

7 Todd, *Seventy-ninth Highlanders*, 58-59; Stevens, *Life of Stevens*, 2, 322-23.

8 Todd, *Seventy-ninth Highlanders*, 57-61.

time a group of resigned officers circulated rumors among the men: they would not be sent home on furlough, they were being unlawfully converted to three-year men, an officer was being paid ten thousand dollars to agree that they were three-year men, their services and sufferings were being ignored, they were to be assigned to a new brigade commanded by Daniel E. Sickles, a man of unacceptable past. With resignations and casualties, the Seventy-ninth was in a state of poor discipline.[9]

After a day of observation, Stevens decided he knew enough to make judgments. He called the major and several company grade officers to his tent, where he demanded and received their resignations. On the following day he issued an order at dress parade for the regiment to strike camp next morning and be prepared to march to a new encampment.[10]

That night, with the complicity of disgruntled officers, some of the men smuggled whiskey into the camp. Other men went into the city and returned drunk.[11] Next day, the men refused to strike their tents. Stevens appeared and repeated his order. The men remained obstinate. Stevens went among them addressing them as a whole, by company, and individually, telling them about the articles of war governing mutiny and trying to solve the problem without appealing for help outside the regiment. The drunken men refused to obey.

Stevens ordered the officers to strike the tents. As they did, the men, now an infuriated mob, jeered, taunted, and insulted them. Some threatened the officers with their weapons while others put the tents back up. The officers walked the delicate line between showing fear, which they simply could not do, and responding violently, which would have been worse.[12] Stevens joined a group of officers who had just been stopped when the men threatened to shoot anyone who touched the tent.

"Then I will take it down myself," said Stevens.

Struck by his bravery, an old sergeant said, "Doona mind, Colonel, we'll take it doon for ye this ance."[13]

In a situation set to explode, a new provocation appeared. The worst drunks, many of them Scotsmen from the old country, began to fight among themselves over historic Protestant-Catholic issues. In the late morning, Daniel E. Sickles, the new

9 Lusk, *War Letters*, 73, letter dated August 17, 1861, from Lusk to his mother; Todd, *Seventy-ninth Highlanders*, 62.

10 Stevens, *Life of Stevens*, 2, 323.

11 Stevens, *Life of Stevens*, 2, 323-324.

12 Lusk, *War Letters*, 73-74, letter dated August 17, 1861, from Lusk to his mother; Stevens, *Life of Stevens*, 2, 324.

13 Stevens, *Life of Stevens*, 2, 324.

brigade commander, arrived in camp.[14] He was greeted by jeers and hisses. An acquittal for murdering his wife's lover did not make him acceptable to the men of the Seventy-ninth. They strongly opposed serving under him.[15]

As the day passed into afternoon, exhaustion and some sobriety began to take hold.[16] While his junior officers were being roughly handled by his drunken men, Stevens demanded in a private conversation that Lieutenant-Colonel Elliott explain his role in the events. Elliott tried his best to defend himself, but Stevens was not satisfied. He gave Elliott half an hour to resign or stand court-martial, then described the problems to Sickles.[17]

When Sickles reported to McClellan, the major general wasted little time. He ordered Andrew Porter, his provost marshal, to take a battery of Regular artillery, two companies of Regular cavalry, and as much Regular infantry as he deemed necessary to the Seventy-ninth's camp and separate those who were willing to serve from those who were not. The ringleaders, instructed McClellan, were to be put in double-irons.[18]

About an hour before dark Porter arrived at the camp. His men surrounded it. Ostentatiously, his infantry loaded their weapons, the cavalrymen drew sabres, and the cannon were loaded with cannister. They were ordered to shoot any man attempting to pass through their lines.[19]

Standing in the middle of the camp, Stevens addressed his men in the florid oratory of the nineteenth century:

> I know you have been deceived. You have been told you were to go to your homes when no such orders had been given. But you are soldiers, and your duty is to obey. I am your colonel, and your obedience is due to me. I am a soldier of the Regular army. I have spent many years on the frontier fighting the Indians. I have been surrounded by the red devils, fighting for my scalp. I have been a soldier in the war with Mexico, and bear honorable wounds received in battle, and have been in far greater danger than that surrounding me now. All the morning I have begged you to do your duty. Now I shall order you; and if you

14 Todd, *Seventy-ninth Highlanders*, 62.

15 Todd, *Seventy-ninth Highlanders*, 62; for Sickles, see generally, Warner, *Generals in Blue*, 446; *D.A.B.*, 9, pt. 1, 150; Swanberg, W. A., *Sickles the Incredible* (New York, 1956); Edgcumb Pinchon, *Dan Sickles, Hero of Gettysburg and Yankee King of Spain* (New York, 1945).

16 Lusk, *War Letters*, 73-74, letter dated August 17, 1861.

17 Todd, *Seventy-ninth Highlanders*, 62.

18 *OR*, 5, 561.

19 Todd, *Seventy-ninth Highlanders*, 62.

> hesitate to obey instantly, my next order will be to those troops to fire upon you. Soldiers of the 79th Highlanders, fall in!"[20]

The righteousness and importance of their claims evaporated, probably less because of Stevens's oratorical skills than the lethal hardware in the hands of the merciless Regulars. Hastily, the men formed ranks. With Regulars on both flanks and regimental weapons in wagons, they marched to McClellan's headquarters on Fourteenth Street. McClellan's General Order dealing with the regiment was read to them. It suggested that the mutiny might have been prompted by cowardice. Then it said that those who did not lay down their arms and return to duty "will be fired upon." In the group that returned to duty, "the mutinous ringleaders alone will be punished." Last and most humiliating of all, "The regiment will be deprived of its colors, which will not be returned to it until its members have shown by their conduct in camp that they have learned the first duty of soldiers—obedience—and have proven on the field of battle that they are not wanting in courage."[21]

The handsome, heavy-set Porter repeated the order to obey officers' commands or suffer the consequences. He ordered the color-bearers to step forward and surrender the regimental flags. An officer of the guard drew a piece of paper from his pocket, ordered all men whose names were read to take two steps forward, called thirty-five names, then ordered the rest of the regiment to close on the center. The ringleaders, the men who had stepped forward, would be imprisoned and would be tried by court-martial. In the dusk they were marched to prison. A much more sober group, the regiment was ordered to "right face" and was marched to its new camp near the Maryland Insane Asylum, a touch of irony that did not pass unnoticed.

After further investigation fourteen of the thirty-five ringleaders were released and returned to the regiment. The rest were shipped to Dry Tortugas, America's equivalent of Devil's Island, on the Florida coast.

McClellan had acted promptly and decisively when confronted with the mutiny of the Seventy-ninth. Because its conduct was unfortunately not unique, the major-general could not afford to allow the problem to spread. At the time of the Highlander problem McDowell reported that sixty-two non-commissioned officers and men of the Second Maine, claiming their period of service had ended, refused to

20 Two apparently verbatim quotations of Stevens's speech are given in the sources, Todd, *Seventy-ninth Highlanders*, 65; Stevens, *Life of Stevens*, 2, 325; in minor respects they are different. The Stevens account, based on the personal knowledge of Stevens's son and the possibility of notes or a predelivery copy in the son's possession, recommend the quote in the biography rather than the one in the regimental history, even though Todd had access to more memories.

21 Todd, *Seventy-ninth Highlanders*, 62-63.

do further duty. McClellan and McDowell agreed that this was insubordination "if not open mutiny."[22]

The problem was solved the same way. The sixty-two men of the Second Maine were sentenced to the Dry Tortugas to serve out the war at hard labor. The mutineers of the Seventy-ninth were to be tried by court-martial and, McClellan hoped, shot. The colors of the Seventy-ninth Highlanders he put on the main floor of his headquarters building. They would be returned when the men "earned them again by good behavior." He knew that he had mortified and embarrassed the regiment and expected it to rise to the challenge.[23] "An example is necessary to bring these people up to the mark, and if they will not fight and do their duty from honorable motives," he wrote to Ellen, "I intend to co-erce them and let them see what they have to expect if they pretend to rebel."

"Heartsick and much depressed," the young company grade officer of the Highlanders wrote home, "I am eager for another battle in order that we may have an opportunity to regain our colors, yet dread to risk it now that our men are much demoralized."[24] Outsiders believed that discipline in the army would be destroyed "if these mutineers [of the Highlanders] are not promptly shot if guilty and I think the exigencies of the service require their trial more than anything else . . ."[25]

A few days later, the Twelfth New York, already marked for bad conduct by its flight at Blackburn's Ford, refused an order from its brigade commander, "Greasy Dick" Richardson, to appear for company drill, then refused an order to appear for brigade drill. Richardson did not need Porter's Regulars, nor did he need any other help. He turned to his old regiment, the Second Michigan, marched it to the camp of the Twelfth New York, formed it in front of the tents, then ordered the men to load and cap their weapons and to fix bayonets. Richardson was not using experienced, reliable Regulars to overawe green, unreliable volunteers. It was volunteer against volunteer, but he knew what he was doing. He called for the New Yorkers to fall in.

22 *OR*, 5, 561.

23 Sears, *McClellan's Correspondence*, 84-85, letter dated August 15, 1861, (redated August 14 by the editor) from McClellan to his mother. Loss of unit colors is still a significant punishment for inappropriate conduct and a grave embarrassment for loss in battle. The author served in the United States Army (field artillery) from 1959 to 1961, the period 1960-1961 in the forces of occupation in Korea. Among the war stories being circulated at that time were two involving the loss of colors, one having them taken away for breaking badly in combat and losing its artillery, another form of embarrassment; and the other losing them outright when the Chinese intervened and overran unit headquarters. Both circumstances were regarded as humiliating.

24 Lusk, *War Letters*, 75, letter dated August 17, 1861.

25 Dwight MSS (M.H.S.) letter dated August 22, 1861, from Wm. Dwight to his father.

The recalcitrant regiment formed, marched to the brigade parade ground, and under the quiet scrutiny of two 12-pounders loaded with cannister began drilling.[26]

Once he had accomplished his two basic tasks—built a disciplined army capable of crushing the Rebels and fortified Washington to a condition of independent security—McClellan would turn to the offensive. He had planned to do this as early as the moment he alighted from the train from western Virginia. But the mistake of attacking Manassas he did not intend to make a second time.[27] First, he would move his lines forward to give depth to the positions along the river.[28] From time to time after he arrived in Washington, he would ride the lines with McDowell and say in the vicinity of Alexandria that he would begin his forward movement with a march across the Occoquan southwest of Alexandria. He did not describe the first stage of a great campaign to end the war. At best, these statements were made without the benefit of the long thought he would give to the subject after he cured the immediate crises. More than that he had not decided during his early days in the east.[29] General offensive plans McClellan had discussed with Scott after his arrival; but the old general in chief, still unable to accept Virginia as a battleground and opposed to any significant offensive, resisted.[30]

Nevertheless, McClellan kept a close watch on the Occoquan area south of Alexandria. In August, he ordered a cavalry unit to scout the road to Mount Vernon and the vicinity of Accotink and, if possible, to capture Rebel cavalry known to be in the area. Captain William H. Boyd and forty-six men of Company A of the First New York Cavalry, the only company of the regiment stationed in the capital, set out from its camp at the seminary on the finger ridge running west from Alexandria. Over the hills Boyd's column wound after it left the Little River Turnpike. An advance guard of three men and flankers protected the main column. As they approached each clump of woods and heard the "Advance" on the bugle, they asked themselves was that clump or the next one the hiding place for a Confederate ambush?

Deaf in one ear, Boyd turned his good ear to every black man carrying a bundle and fleeing toward freedom. These men, who came to be known throughout the army and among the intelligence gatherers as the "intelligent contraband," presented "a storehouse of knowledge," including all Rebel secrets, information from his

26 Sears, *For Country, Cause and Leader (Haydon Journal)*, entry dated August 15, 1861.

27 McClellan MSS (L.C.) letter dated October 19, 1861, from McClellan to his wife.

28 *M.O.S.*, 69, 73, 95; McClellan in *B&L*, 2, 161.

29 Swinton, *Army of the Potomac*, 69, fn.

30 Comte de Paris MS diary (large diary) (A. N. de la M. de F.) entry dated November 2, 1861; Comte de Paris in *B&L*, 2, 112-113.

acquaintance Jefferson Davis, and the latest from Pierre Beauregard's breakfast table. Each of these men and every local farmer who stopped his work in the field to lean on his fence caused the column to halt while Captain Boyd's good ear collected information about the roads ahead, the presence of Rebel troops, and anything else helpful, true or not, believed or not. Unionist today, loyal Confederate tomorrow, these civilians had no place to go to avoid the armies of either side. To protect themselves and their paltry possessions, they knew much they could never have known and imparted that knowledge freely to anyone who wanted it. As one officer of the First New York Cavalry would write in the middle of the war, " . . . no greater misfortune can befall a man than to live on ground separating the fronts of contending armies during war." The charred ruins of their buildings "mark the spots where good Union men as well as rebels once had happy homes." Most generals fully appreciated that the "intelligent contraband" was "a very uncertain person." From one of these sources, Boyd learned that a body of Confederate cavalry of uncertain size had been at Pohick Church that morning. The captain passed through the village of Accotink, splashed across Accotink Creek, and headed toward Pohick Church.

Emerging from a large patch of woods near the church, the company rode in a column of fours. Boyd could see the church and a crossroad behind it. The flankers closed on the column. One of the advance guard returned at a gallop, signaling danger to the front. A feeling of alarm spread among the men. The guard, intent on reaching the safety of the seminary, reined his horse only long enough to report a regiment of Rebel cavalry, "a whole army," waiting to spring a trap.

Boyd thought for a moment. The company stood in the road, still in a column of fours. Cavalry succeeded by prompt shock action. Boyd's brief hesitation led one old cavalryman in the ranks to seize the moment.

"By fours! Left about, wheel! Forward!" he shouted.

In considerable confusion, the troop began to reverse its direction, some trotting, some moving at a gallop. A second member of the advance guard also approached on a galloping mount, waiving his hat in a signal to "be off." Oliver B. Knowles, the third and last of the advance guards, halted his horse on the side of Boyd's good ear.

"Captain, the enemy is not in large force. It is a troop of cavalry, not stronger than we are . . . if as strong. They are halted." He commented that the other member of the advance guard was short sighted. "There is cattle grazing near them, and these he took for cavalry in reserve."

Boyd well knew he had seen nothing to cause retreat, let alone abject flight. Instantly, he galloped after his column, gained its disorderly head, jerked out his pistol, and commanded the men to halt. When they had quickly formed in order, he appealed to their courage and honor. He pointed to his nephew, Sergeant W. H.

Boyd. He was willing to sacrifice himself and his nephew, he said, rather than he and his company be known as cowards. He had more to lose than they did. But if they would stand by him and meet the enemy, he would lead them. He told them the information Knowles had given him. The men replied they had only followed orders and would follow him where he led. He ordered the company about and put himself, Knowles, and Sergeant Boyd at their head. "Forward!" he called. When they had wheeled by fours and reversed direction again, they proceeded cautiously until Knowles pointed to the position the Confederates occupied. They were already deployed in line.

From a column of fours, Boyd formed his troopers into a line of battle and advanced them with a steady hand. Each cavalryman pulled out his revolver and prepared himself. When they reached firing range, Boyd shouted, "Charge and cheer!"

Away they went at the gallop, yelling and firing. Taken by complete surprise, the Rebels fired one volley, broke in confusion, and precipitously fled. Two saddles appeared empty. At the crossroads the Confederates divided into three groups. Boyd's troop, too, divided in pursuit, reloading and firing as it advanced. Within a short time Boyd could tell the Rebels were approaching infantry reserves. Showing that he had already reached a high level at his new profession, he ordered the "Recall" on the bugle, a practice of reorganization for a second charge that had given Cromwell and his Ironside cavalry a decisive advantage in their battles with the king.[31] Boyd's troopers withdrew in reasonably good order and returned to their camp victorious. Boyd and his men—and many others—learned the value of "sudden and impetuous charges . . . and were always quick to charge whenever they met the enemy."[32]

They had, however, learned nothing about the differences among pistols, sabres, and long guns except that pistol fire from a galloping horse was remarkably inaccurate. Knowledge about their weapons would come in good time. Both Boyd and General William Franklin, for whom Company A served as his escort,

31 *OR*, 5, 113-14; Adams, *Story of a Trooper*, 120-126; James Stevenson, *Boots and Saddles: A History of the First Volunteer Cavalry of the War . . .* (Harrisburg, 1879), 41-43 (Stevenson, *Boots and Saddles*); Antonia Fraser, *Cromwell: The Lord Protector* (New York, 1973), 108, 131-132; Delbrück, *History of the Art of War*, vol. IV, *The Dawn of Modern Warfare*, 189-190. This account is a composite of all three sources, with the differences resolved in favor of the person with the best knowledge: Stevenson was a lieutenant in the company, Boyd wrote his report that same day; Adams worked with hearsay from unidentified sources. Knowles would rise to colonel of the Twenty-first Pennsylvania Cavalry and end the war a brevet brigadier general, but would die in 1866 at the age of twenty-four. Hunt and Brown, *Brevet Brigadier Generals in Blue*, 340.

32 Adams, *Story of a Trooper*, 126.

complained in their reports about their own company horses and the swiftness of the Rebel mounts. McClellan saw the company a few days later in a review, complimented it highly, and promised the men new horses. Stoneman condemned almost every horse in the company a short time later and supplied the men with better mounts.[33]

The collection of intelligence and the restoration of discipline were not McClellan's only functions. Others, whether he liked them or not, commanded his presence and attention. On August 3, he dined at the White House with Prince Napoleon Jerome, the nephew of the great emperor and an outspoken friend of the United States.[34] The prince's staff, a number of important diplomatic persons,[35] members of the Cabinet, men from the diplomatic corps, and selected members of Congress added bulk to the group while the representatives of the military provided the spice, the rank, and the most interesting element for the Europeans.[36]

Scott, severely crippled by his gout, entered the room leaning on McClellan's arm. The young major-general could see many of the guests mark the contrast between the towering but infirm general in chief and, as McClellan already saw it, his successor. Over the years Scott had been an icon when McClellan was a teenage cadet, his commander in the Mexican War when he was a junior subaltern, and now his superior officer. His feelings, rank, and station could be easily offended.[37] McClellan probably already regarded him as an obstacle. To his European military colleagues, however, Scott provided the flavor of another estimable generation. "He is a real gentleman," wrote the aide to Prince Napoleon, "a type of old British general, well educated and well bred, and perfectly acquainted with the military history of Europe."[38]

Wearing a white vest with a red ribbon and decorations, the prince stood on the hearth rug with his hands behind his back. Given his new nickname in the press, the "Little Napoleon," McClellan may have noticed that the prince's features, hair, and attitude showed a startling resemblance to the first Napoleon.

33 *OR*, 5, 113, 114; Stevenson, *Boots and Saddles*, 43; Beach, *First New York Cavalry*, 37.

34 Nicolay MSS (L.C.) letter dated August 2, 1861, from Nicolay to Therena; Pisani, *Letters*, preface, 5; Seward, *Reminiscences*, 184.

35 Pisani, *Letters*, 110-111, letter dated August 10, 1861, from Pisani to Colonel de la Franconière.

36 Pisani, *Letters*, 103, letter dated August 10, 1861; Seward, *Reminiscences*, 184.

37 Sears, *McClellan's Correspondence*, 79, letter of August 4, 1861, from McClellan to his wife.

38 Pisani, *Letters*, 103, letter dated August 10, 1861, from Pisani to Colonel de la Franconière.

The Marine band was stationed in the vestibule. The band master wished to play some appropriate French airs but was German and therefore ignorant of the politics in Paris. Instead of the imperial air *Pratant Pout La Syrie* he struck up the *Marseillaise*, the revolutionary air which had become taboo in Paris during the empire. The guests began to smile. They looked at the prince. He took it with good humor saying, "*Mais, oui, je suis republicain-en Amerique*." Throughout the dinner he spoke of his belief in the ultimate success of the Union.[39]

Fluent in French and Spanish, McClellan was perfectly at ease with his dinner companions, Lieutenant-Colonel Pisani, who spoke no English, and a member of the French legation, who spoke it badly. Although McClellan found the evening tedious and not especially interesting,[40] his "conversation with the Lieutenant-Colonel was animated."

Seeing this Lord Lyons, the British ambassador to the United States, leaned toward Pisani and made a thought-provoking comment.

"You are aware that you are talking with the next president of the United States?"

Pisani smiled and repeated the comment to the major-general.

Predictably, McClellan said nothing. He would always wish to receive offers he could never accept, but he had his own goals in mind. A "fine, modest, silent smile" creased his countenance. Turning the conversation to a different personal subject, McClellan began to speak about his old friends, some now his subordinates, others his enemies, Lee, Beauregard, Johnston, McDowell, and Jefferson Davis. Dinner ended, and the after dinner conversation waned.

Pisani perceived a remarkable similarity between the West Point trained Regular Army officers of the United States, especially McClellan, and the officers from the Ecole Polytechnique, the world famous French military school created by Napoleon at the beginning of the century. As they left the table, he gave McClellan a subtle but large compliment.

"General, I have known you for a long time. Twenty years ago I was with you at the Ecole Polytechnique."[41]

The confidence expressed in McClellan was increasingly shared by others as McClellan's efforts began to show results. "It is now remarked that the darkness of Bull's Run was but the darkness which precedes the day," wrote a friend to Postmaster General Montgomery Blair. "It is evident that General McClellan has

39 Seward, *Reminiscences*, 184.

40 Sears, *McClellan's Correspondence*, 79, letter dated August 4, 1861, McClellan to his wife.

41 Pisani, *Letters*, 113-114, letter dated August 10, 1861.

done more in ten days towards organizing the advance than Scott did in ten weeks. I have not seen Wall Street more comfortable, than on Saturday. The gall and wormwood in the money reported in the Journal of Congress on Saturday betrays the chagrin with which the Secessationists regard the complete success of the financial measures of the Government."[42]

And Count Gurowski noted in his diary, "For the first time since the armaments, enjoyed a military view. McClellan, surrounded as a general ought to be, went to see the army. It looks martial. The city, likewise, has a more martial look than it had all the time under Scott. It seems that a young, strong hand holds the ribbons. God grant that McClellan preserve his western vigor and activity and may not become softened and dissolved by these Washington evaporations."[43]

42 Chase MSS (L.C.) letter dated August 5, 1861, from James W. Riggs to Blair.

43 Gurowski, *Diary*, 1, 76 entry dated July 1861.

Chapter 26

"[Banks is a] wonderful man. There is no-one in the Army who has struck me as he does . . . you never hear him evil spoken of as you do every other General, I mean you don't hear his soldiers speak ill of him."

– John M. Gould to his diary

More Uncertainty in Maryland and the Valley

On July 25, 1861, Major-General Nathaniel Prentiss Banks issued General Orders No. 34, assuming command of the Department of the Shenandoah including the forces in the vicinity of Harpers Ferry.[1]

The first of seven children born to the superintendent of a Massachusetts cotton mill, Banks spent only a few years in common schools before, still a boy, the family's economic circumstances compelled him to abandon his education and begin work in the cotton mill. He taught himself some Latin and much Spanish, thinking the latter would be an important language for the wide contacts he projected in the future with Spanish-speaking peoples. He read voraciously and took every opportunity to practice public speaking, using a local debating society and town

1 *OR*, 2, 175, General Orders, No. 34, dated July 25, 1861.

meetings to sharpen his skills. After aligning himself with the Democratic Party, he became an effective spokesman for the working man in a state then dominated by the Whigs, the party of wealth and class. Dabbling in acting, reading law sufficiently to be admitted to practice, marrying, and becoming an exceptional ballroom dancer, but always verging on poverty, he entered public service as an inspector in the Boston customs house, published a local newspaper supporting the working man, and at last in his thirties began a career in politics. Not until his seventh campaign was he finally elected, in 1849, to the Massachusetts assembly.

Two years later he showed the characteristics that would dominate his political and military life, an ability to avoid doctrinaire positions and to harmonize conflicting forces. He formed a coalition between his Democratic Party and Henry Wilson's Free-Soil Party. Always in danger of exploding but always held together by Banks, the coalition gave Wilson the presidency of the state senate and made Banks speaker of the assembly.

In 1853, he was chosen to be president of the Massachusetts constitutional convention, a difficult job he performed with tact, patience, and self-control. That year he was also elected to the United States Congress, where he served sporadically for ten terms, representing over time no less than five political parties. His willingness to identify and pursue issues that attracted voter support and his need for the income of political employment, his sole means of support after the age of thirty-five, made him the perfect politician, a man who would support any issue that would provide gainful employment as an officeholder.

Slavery and abolition were among these issues. He did not much care about the plight of the black man; but a successful politician in Massachusetts, the national caldron of abolition, needed a strong position on the issue. From time to time, he rose from the political confusion of the 1850s to reveal an ardent abolitionist, which helped his alignment with the Free-Soiler Henry Wilson. He opposed the Kansas-Nebraska Bill and supported restrictions on the expansion of slavery in the Missouri Compromise.

Changing with the political currents, he was reelected to the House as the candidate of the American or Know-Nothing Party, which was anti-foreigner and anti-Catholic. The Pope and his American followers were intent, the Know-Nothings believed, on making America a Romish fiefdom. More important for Banks, the Know-Nothings were home to a growing number of abolitionists and in a peculiar turn of American political history became one of the unpredictable elements of the fledgling Republican Party in 1856. In Congress that year Banks was put forward as an ardent antislavery candidate for Speaker of the House. The campaign was long and bitter but finally successful after a record-setting 133 votes. Knowing his roots and the well-spring of his success, he gave antislavery members majorities on the important committees, appointing many of his political enemies to chairmanships. His abilities, perhaps it was his lack of any fixed principles, made him one of the most able and efficient speakers in the history of the position.

In 1856, Banks became involved in a complex plan to arrange the Republican Presidential nomination for John Charles Fremont by fusion of many political splinter groups like the North American Party, the Temperance Party, the Free-soilers, and the outright abolitionists. The carefully balanced plan to have Banks nominated for president by the Know-Nothings then resign in favor of Fremont failed for unanticipated reasons. Although the delicate maneuvering was to no purpose, the final result occurred as hoped; and Fremont was nominated by both parties. During the campaign Banks was selected to speak for the candidate from Maine to Illinois, giving him national exposure and creating significant personal national aspirations.

In 1857, he left the Congress and the Know-Nothings to become the candidate of the Republican Party for governor of Massachusetts. Breeching all campaign rules, he personally stumped the state and was elected by a landslide. After the end of his term, he replaced George B. McClellan as president of the Illinois Central Railroad and moved to Chicago.[2]

According to the biographer of the early Republican Party, Banks had been "a blatant opportunist who joined the secret society in 1854 in order, as his biographer so aptly puts it, to 'save his political skin.' Bank's anti-slavery principles were equally shallow. Prior to 1854 his position on the slavery issue fluctuated widely as he assumed whatever stance he believed would best promote his political career. Evidencing an 'utter unconcern for principles,' Banks's record was one of 'shifting stands and exploitation of anti-slavery feeling for personal gain.' He was, he once confessed to a friend, 'neither . . . pro-slavery nor anti-slavery.' Slow to oppose the Nebraska Bill and deserting his colleagues on one very crucial vote, the Massachusetts representative became a leading tactician of the anti-Nebraska forces during the last stages of the struggle in the House. The publicity he received gave him a largely undeserved reputation as a firm opponent of the extension of slavery, which he exploited along with his well-advertised nativist affiliation in order to gain the speakership. Those who knew him perceived his true character. Acknowledging

2 James G. Hollandsworth, Jr., *Pretense of Glory: The Life of General Nathaniel P. Banks* (Baton Rouge, 1998), 3-44 (Hollandsworth, *Banks*); Fred Harvey Harrington, *Fighting Politician: Major General N. P. Banks* (Philadelphia and London, 1948), 1-53 (Harrington, *Banks*); *D.A.B.*, 1, pt. 1, 577-578. For the political parties, Banks's roles in them, and his part in complex political events like the nominations for the Republican campaign of 1856, William E. Gienapp, *The Origins of the Republican Party*, 1852-1856 (New York, 1987), 92-93, 136, 180, 242-243; 261-263, chap. 10 at 305-346; 368-369 (Gienapp, *Origins of Republican Party*); Tyler Anbinder, *Nativism and Slavery: The Northern-Know-Nothings and the Politics of the 1850's* (New York 1992), 162-163 (Anbinder, *Nativism*).

that personally he liked Banks, a former congressional associate added that 'he is very ambitious & has always left the impression on my mind that he was not 'nice' as to how he 'stayed himself up'—so [long as] he stood. I deem him cold-hearted—& inclined to be scheming & sinister.' Banks' close association with Israel D. Andrews of Massachusetts and Colonel Charles James of Wisconsin, lobbyists with well-deserved reputations for shady dealings, also disturbed many members.

"For all this well-aimed criticism, Banks enjoyed several advantages in the speakership contest. Exceptionally personable, he was well liked even by his adversaries, and as a one-time actor the handsome Bay State politician possessed a fine speaking voice and a dignified manner, and displayed, in the words of a hostile journalist, 'a genius for being looked at.' In addition, he was a skillful parliamentary tactician and an experienced presiding officer. As a former Democrat, he had particular strength among anti-Nebraska Democrats in the House."

When Fort Sumter surrendered, Banks tendered his services to Lincoln. Although he had served briefly in the Lowell militia, had been a member of the House Committee on Military Affairs, and had been governor during the farsighted, effective reorganization of the Massachusetts militia, he knew nothing about military affairs, a fact he conceded freely.[3]

His military and leadership characteristics would reflect his humble origins and his natural reluctance to adopt the aristocratic superiority and exercise the power of high military rank. He would not insist on the perquisites of a major general. Unlike Scott, he did not demand as one of his hallmarks punctilious military etiquette. Having come from "the people," he would remain one of them; and he would exercise his leadership as a "first among equals," not as a member of a sacred superior caste. His willingness to associate with his enlisted men would put him in a category of "democratic leaders" like James S. Wadsworth. Although he dressed well, wore expensive military clothing, and presided over an officers' mess that cost his military family dearly,[4] he would wear the uniform of a common soldier and work at menial tasks with his men. At one point he worked alongside his men building a dam necessary to save his army.

"General Banks is around the dam doing all he can," wrote one of his junior officers in his diary. "He takes hold and shovels, chops, lifts, or does whatever he can and doesn't claim a whiskey ration either. Being in a uniform of private cloth and

3 The description is quoted from the definitive account of the origins of the Republican Party. Gienapp, *Origins of the Republican Party*, 242-243; *D.A.B.*, 1, pt. 1, 577-578; Harrington, *Banks*, 54; Roe, *Tenth Massachusetts*, 8.

4 Hollandsworth, *Banks*, 50.

without insignia of any kind the boys don't always know when he is around but his presence certainly adds life to their movements."

A member of an infantry regiment working on the dam dropped the log he was lifting and began to curse the general. Wearing a slouch hat, cavalry trousers, and a flannel shirt was a man standing behind him "shoveling dirt or something of that kind." The verbal abuse was too much for him. He dropped the shovel, went to the enlisted man, and took hold of the log. "Keep your temper, my good fellow," said Banks, "Keep cool! Old corporal Banks has been in many a tighter place than this. He'll get you all out right."

To the diary keeper, this kind of familiar conduct made Banks "a wonderful man. There is no one in the Army who has struck me as he does . . . you never hear him evil spoken of as you do every other General, I mean you don't hear his soldiers speak ill of him."[5]

Strict military discipline, which drew the sharp line between officers and enlisted men, he would not enforce. In fact, he had difficulty enforcing discipline at all. The Nineteenth New York had been recruited for two years but mustered for three months. In July after Bull Run, the federal government faced the manpower problem caused by expiration of militia terms of service. It called for the three-month muster–two-year-enlistment regiments to serve two years. The call swept the Nineteenth into the longer term. By political oversight the men, not being told, expected a departure date of August 22, the end of the three-month muster term, and began to anticipate it. Colonel John S. Clark, who had been relieved by Patterson because of complaints by some of his men about severe discipline, foresaw mutinous conduct by at least some of the men. At nine in the morning, August 22, the drums beat the signal for dress parade; and the adjutant and Major James H. Ledlie formed the regiment in two lines facing each other.

While the formation began, the Twenty-first Pennsylvania came up the slope to one side of the regiment on the run. Men of the Second United States Cavalry dismounted on the other side, halted, and loaded their carbines. Perkin's Rhode Island battery unlimbered and aimed its guns down the lines. Other regiments in nearby camps took arms. Between the two lines stood Colonel George H. Thomas, arms folded, impassive, stern, watching. His staff, Colonel Clark, and several reporters stood nearby. Major Ledlie and his staff walked between the two lines.

"Soldiers of the Nineteenth Regiment, New York Volunteers, this is the twenty-second of August, the day on which the term of three months expires. But the president has made requisition for the further services of the Nineteenth Regiment,

5 William B. Jordan, Jr., ed., *The Civil War Journals of John Mead Gould, 1861-1866* (Baltimore, 1997), 345-346, entry dated May 11, 1863 (Jordan, *Gould Journals*).

and the Governor has transferred you to the United States for the remainder of the term of two years, for which you enlisted into the state service, which will be one year and eight months."

The adjutant read two articles of war and a special orders. The men stacked arms then resumed position in line a few paces from their guns. Ledlie ordered those loyal to come forward and take their rifles. Every officer, two companies, and all but a handful of three other companies responded. Two hundred eighty did not move. In one company, only one man took his weapon. Still in a state of suspension from Patterson's order, Clark tried to reason with the company. The men stood fast.

"Well, they show their true Irish grit," said Clark as he turned away.

Thomas put the recalcitrants under arrest. Later in the day he spoke separately to the commanders of the two steadfast companies to congratulate them and ask for an explanation. In addition to poor weapons, worn out shoes, and poor uniforms, the men morally wounded by the decision to show force before an explanation of the two-year period. They would have responded, they said, if anyone had appealed to their loyalty and pride.

"There is something wrong here, Captain," said Thomas. "These men are not to blame. They have not been treated right."

Stewart mentioned that Thomas had put him in charge of the guard for the recalcitrants. "This is the hardest thing I have ever done in my life," he said.

"I only did it," responded Thomas, "to try your pluck."

Unable to accept the severity of army discipline, Banks visited the recalcitrants the next day and the day after that. Speeches and remonstrations, even Banks's excellent public-speaking skills, produced no effect. They would rather go to Dry Tortugas than serve. Again on a third day Banks tried. They began to waiver. More than one hundred returned to camp. After intercession by a chaplain, all but twenty-three had returned to the colors.

McClellan had little patience for the mutineers. His adjutant wrote Banks to say, "the Major Gen'l. Comdg . . . desires you to submit to these men a final alternative either to consent to return to duty and in the future to submit to the orders of the military authorities, or to go to Tortugas." They refused and were put aboard ship.

The problem with the regimental commander remained unresolved. Clark was a good officer, and the complaints were more a product of the disorderly element in the regiment than a defect in leadership. Still relieved from command by Patterson's order, Clark repeatedly asked Banks for a court-martial. Banks rightly perceived the charges to be frivolous and refused.[6] Uncertain about the correct way to deal with

6 Hall, *Cayuga in the Field*, 70-76.

Clark's case, Banks wrote to Scott for guidance on August 2. A few days later headquarters replied, ". . . an act of Congress quite recently past [sic] refers to Department Commanders the subject of Boards to Examine Volunteer Officers so that the matter will be within your competency."[7]

Clark fell ill.[8] Delay followed. Banks thought well of Clark as did many of his men. When an opening developed on his staff, he wrote to Clark: "I have the pleasure to inform you that you are hereby relieved of any official disability in connection with your regiment and free to act on your commission as you may desire. If it should not be your purpose to join your regiment again, I should be pleased to offer you a position upon my staff as may be acceptable to you and to your friends."[9]

"As to assuming command of the regiment," responded Clark the following day, "I can say I have not the slightest desire to do so." Several days later, Clark accepted a staff position with Banks as a colonel and resigned his position in the Nineteenth New York Regiment. He would reappear later under important circumstances.[10]

In the early days of the war, Lincoln was the leader of a nation composed of widely splintered constituencies. Drawing them together was almost as important as appointing competent, effective men. Banks, difficult to label at any time in his long political career, represented the kind of unifying appointment Lincoln wanted to make. A former Democrat, a spokesman for labor, an opponent of slavery, and a successful Republican candidate for political office, Banks's advancement appealed to many groups beyond the Radical, Republican, antislavery men of the president's party.

Banks represented a large and, in Lincoln's mind, perhaps somewhat involuntary source of senior officers, the Democratic Party. Everything about Lincoln's presidency in the first year smacked of divisiveness. Struggles for primacy were everywhere. Every man near the seat of government wished to be the leader in his area, if not the leader overall. In the Cabinet Secretary of State Seward, Secretary of the Treasury Chase, and Secretary of War Cameron had all been strong but unsuccessful candidates for the Republican nomination in 1860 and felt their opinions were entitled to more weight than others. The slave-holding border regions, Maryland, Missouri, Kentucky, eastern Tennessee, and western Virginia, had to be

7 NA RG 393, General in Chief's Ledger of Documents Sent, 223, dispatch dated August 6, 1861, from Headquarters of the Army to Banks.

8 Hall, *Cayuga in the Field*, 80.

9 *Ibid.*, 81, letter dated November 4, 1861, from Banks to Clark.

10 *Ibid.*, 81.

handled in a way that would keep them in harness with opposites like Massachusetts and Ohio. Recognition of Democratic Party leaders, both politically and militarily, would take a long stride toward the kind of cooperation Banks had achieved with the Free Soil Party when it supported Henry Wilson, now the Republican chairman of the Senate Committee on Military Affairs. A man of expedient principles, he could and would adopt the views that would facilitate his advancement. As a major-general he would exemplify recognition and appeasement of Democrats, Know-Nothings, and abolitionists. He would be palatable to Radical Republicans.

When Banks was commissioned, wild rumors circulated about his assignment: he would be quartermaster general because of his strong administrative ability; he would command a department on the Atlantic where he would cooperate with Butler at Fortress Monroe. Although Banks had the support of Adjutant-General Colonel Lorenzo Thomas and Lieutenant Colonel Ebenezer Sprout Sibley, the secretary of war and others wanted Captain Montgomery C. Meigs and had worked the political halls of appointment effectively on his behalf.[11] Nor was Meigs's appointment strictly a contest between different candidates. Banks had his opponents. "What does it mean," wrote Edward L. Pierce from Boston to a Cabinet officer, "that Banks is to command at Fort Monroe? Has the Administration turned mad? What earthly qualifications does he have? He is without military experience or even theoretic education. Above all he lacks the essential quality of a military chief. The disposition to observe and collate carefully and compare all facts large and minute bearing on the main result. He jumps at conclusions. He always attempts show and display."[12] One of Chase's correspondents urged that Banks be sent to command the northwest because Governor Yates was "drunk all the time and utterly unfit for his Post and particularly at such a critical moment." Instead, Scott preferred that Banks relieve the ineffective George Cadwalader as commander of the Department of Annapolis.

The most difficult task in his assignment was control of the headquarters city of Baltimore. Butler had handled the department by the unauthorized use of troops, for which he had been reprimanded and removed. Cadwalader had done nothing.

Banks assumed command of the Department of Annapolis on June 11, 1861. Applying the skills so well honed in his political career, he began with an essentially conciliatory approach to the civilian population in the Baltimore area. Toward the end of his tenure he used a firmer hand, bringing eighteen hundred troops into the heart of Baltimore in the middle of the night to arrest Marshall George P. Kane, a

11 Nicolay MSS (L.C.) Meigs MS diary, entry dated June 10, 1861; Gurowski, *Diary*, 1, 43, entry for May; Harrington, *Banks*, 56.

12 Chase MSS (U.P.I.) letter dated June, 1861, from Edward L. Pierce in Boston to Chase.

disloyal secessionist. When ninety percent of the Baltimore police force quit in response, he designated a new police force at once and Colonel John R. Kenley of the First Maryland Union Volunteers gave the oath. A short time later Banks arrested the police commissioners. Working with the United States marshals, he began, among a series of strong steps, to conduct successful searches for hidden arms.[13]

During this time Banks's friends continued to advocate him as a logical candidate for a Cabinet post. He had the backing of moderate Republicans; worked well with Seward, who was a moderate in the Republican Party; and opposed the Radical policies of Salmon P. Chase, the secretary of the treasury. Having used the slavery issue for his political betterment in a state that was particularly sensitive to it, Banks knew it would be an issue every bit as volatile for an officer as it had been for a politician. As always, he was careful not to choose an extreme position with an uncertain future. Fremont attempted to free the slaves in Missouri; and Butler called for abolition, all of which caused the Lincoln administration, still having taken no firm position, considerable embarrassment. Banks successfully avoided offending either side. Fugitive slaves coming into his camps would be given rations and work when possible. At the same time he would tell those who came to find them that he did not have time to meet with them or to return their slaves, and he would not allow outsiders to search his camps.[14]

At the camp of the Nineteenth Massachusetts, fugitive slaves from the countryside were anxious to find work serving the officers. Nearly every day a local citizen would arrive at camp hunting for a runaway slave. When a man went to Colonel Edward W. Hinks,[15] the regimental commander, to say he was certain one of

13 Chase MSS (U.P.I.) letters dated May 8, 1861, from Soloman Sturgis to Chase; letter dated June, 1861 from Edward L. Pierce to Chase; Nevins, *Strong Diary*, 3, 163, entry dated July 1, 1861; Gurowski, *Diary*, 1, 43, entry dated May, 1861; *OR*, 2, 172; Harrington, *Banks*, 56.

14 Harrington, *Banks*, 61.

15 According to Warner, *Generals in Blue*, 229, the colonel's name was "Edward Winslow Hincks." Relying on letters from the Boston Public Library (1957) and the Mount Auburn Cemetery (1961), Warner concluded that the colonel dropped the "c" when he entered the army. He has no explanation for the middle name "Winslow," which Hinks used during the war (*ibid.*, 630, n. 229). In Heitman, *Historical Register*, 532; *Official Army Register*, 1, 175; and Historical Committee, *History of the Nineteenth Regiment Massachusetts Volunteer Infantry 1861-1865* (Salem, 1906), caption of picture facing 9 (Committee, *Nineteenth Massachusetts*) his last name is noted as "Hincks." Heitman and the history of the Nineteenth Massachusetts have his middle name as Ward, not "Winslow." The several members of the Historical Committee who served with him for more than a year can be presumed to have the best knowledge. Under the photograph, which gives his name as "Edward Ward Hincks," the Committee gives a terse explanation for the confusion. After stating his name as "Edward W. Hinks" the caption continues, "Since changed by authority of the Massachusetts Legislature to 'Edward Winslow Hincks.'"

his blacks was in the camp, Hinks sent for Sergeant McGinnis of Company K and ordered him to assist the man in a search. Hinks gave McGinnis a look that said the slave was not to be found. McGinnis went into the woods with the man. As soon as they were out of sight in the woods, he halted and cut a switch.

"Look here" said McGinnis reinforcing his argument by touching the old man with the switch. "Do you suppose we left Massachusetts to come out here to hunt Negros?"

The man was indignant. He would report McGinnis, he said.

"Go ahead, and I will go with you."

They both went to the colonel. The citizen told the story with tears in his eyes.

Hinks turned to McGinnis saying, "Sergeant McGinnis, is this true!"

"Colonel, Do you think I would *be seen* doing such a thing?"

"No," replied Hinks. To the citizen he said, "Sergeant McGinnis is a man of truth and I must take his word. You have deceived me, sir. Leave this camp and never enter it again."[16]

Banks's principal characteristics were more political than military, skills that had served him extremely well as a politician and helped him keep peace in a troubled civilian area like Baltimore. Would they serve him as a significant military leader with a large, independent command? Not unlike McClellan, Banks did not communicate with his subordinates, even his brigade commanders, about his intended movements. Though always pleasant and courteous, again like McClellan, he was not the kind of "companionable person" that McClellan was. Excellent judgment and good sense he had but no familiarity with military concepts or routine. The novelty of the untried position he held seemed to oppress him, and the large new responsibilities, so different from those of his past, seemed to make him ill at ease. The weakness of his adjutant, the representative of any commanding officer, his obvious political influence in Washington, and the Regular Army officers who seemed to believe that no man could qualify for general officer without fifteen years "as a clerk in an army bureau," all worked against his standing in his new military community.[17]

Banks's adjutant-general, R. Morris Copeland, knew even less than he did about military life and etiquette. To his provost marshal, Charles F. Morse, he gave a great deal of discretionary power to shut down hotels, stores, and other places whenever he had trouble with liquor. The discipline of the army improved quickly.

16 Adams, *Reminiscences of the 19th Massachusetts*, 14.

17 Quaife, *Williams' Letters*, 40, December 7, 1861, from Williams to his daughter.

The soldiers and officers stayed in their camps except for special occasions. A board of officers was created to dispose of inefficient officers.[18]

The camps of the Second and Twelfth Massachusetts overlooked each other and were separated by a shallow gully. Looking into the camp of the Second one morning, the officers and men of the Twelfth Massachusetts saw a private tied to a tree near the guardhouse. The private had been sentenced to this punishment by a court-martial. He was to be tied to the tree for three days in succession, an hour each day. When the Twelfth saw him, they gave loud shouts of disapproval.

"Cut him down! Cut him down!" they cried.

They advanced threateningly toward the Second's camp. In vain their officers tried to control them. The Second's guard appeared under arms. Its officers and soldiers calmly awaited the issue. At length expostulations prevailed where orders had been useless. The officers of the Twelfth urged their men to desist, and during the remainder of the hour they were quiet.

In the afternoon Colonel Webster told Gordon that, if the man were tied again in full view of his regiment, he would not be responsible for the consequences.

Gordon snidely asked if Webster could control his men.

"Yes, I can control my men," he replied.

The man would be tied in the same place, Gordon assured him.

"Then I shall take my men out to drill at that hour."

This assurance by Colonel Webster was serious. Was a rush into the Second's lines possible? As Gordon saw it, he was looking at a mutiny in the division. The time had come for Banks to interfere. Gordon laid the matter before him in time for action before the next punishment.

"It is quite evident," Gordon said, "that Colonel Webster cannot control his men; and it is equally clear these men must be controlled. The punishment I am inflicting is by sentence of a court. It is not cruel."

"You are quite right, sir," replied Banks.

"Then, sir, will you order to report to me to-morrow at my encampment, a squadron of cavalry and a battery, with authority to use their arms in the suppression of any mutiny that my take place near my camp?"

"I will order them," replied Banks.

Gordon thanked him. As he left, he saw Colonel Webster approaching General Banks's headquarters.

18 Charles F. Morse, *Letters Written During the Civil War, 1861-1865* (n.p., 1898), letter dated August 11, 1861, from Morse (Morse, *Letters*.)

Next morning, a few minutes before the appointed hour for the execution of the sentence, an orderly delivered a note from Banks. He had not left the politician behind in Massachusetts:

> SIR,—Since publicity is no part of the sentence of the court-martial in the case of a man to be tied up, I would suggest that the remainder of the sentence be executed in a less conspicuous place.

Instantly, Gordon ordered Major Dwight to tell Banks the harmful result of yielding to a mutinous demand and to protest any change in the punishment. The major returned in a few minutes to say that as soon as he had despatched the note, Banks had ridden away rapidly, leaving no word at his headquarters about his destination. Only a few moments remained before the hour—not enough time to pursue Banks.

The general was "a most sagacious trimmer," Gordon wrote years later. If bloodshed occurred, he had suggested a prevention; if nothing happened, he had not ordered a concession. Neither battery nor cavalry reported, and the hour for the execution of the sentence had arrived. Gordon sent for the officer of the day and ordered him to make no change in the execution of the sentence.

At the appointed hour, while the sentence was being carried into effect in the same place, the colonel of the Twelfth Massachusetts Regiment hastily marched his men far beyond sight and sound of the Second's camp. They returned long after the hour had expired overcome with fatigue but without a trace of mental laceration. On the third and last morning, Webster adopted the same expedient while the remainder of the sentence was executed.

Even before Banks published the order announcing his assumption of command of the Department of the Shenandoah, he and Scott had resumed the inconclusive Harpers Ferry correspondence suspended at the end of Patterson's tenure. Scott deemed it useful, "perhaps highly important," he wrote, to hold the Ferry. "It will probably soon be attacked."[19]

Banks agreed that he was facing "a probable attack" and believed twenty thousand men would be needed to hold the Ferry. This report, enhanced by rumors circulated by those below the "need to know" line, swept through Banks's troops, keeping them in a "state of expectancy."[20] Like Patterson and Porter before him, he concluded that, to occupy the town itself, he needed to hold Loudon Heights, Bolivar

19 *OR*, 2, 174.

20 Edwin Bryant, *History of the Third Regiment of Wisconsin Volunteer Infantry, 1861-1865* (Madison, 1891), 21 (Bryant, *Third Wisconsin*).

Heights, and Maryland Heights but to deny the town to the Rebels, he need occupy only one height. If attacked, he would withdraw across the Potomac to Maryland Heights. Orders had already been sent to Hagerstown to ready the stores for removal if necessary.[21]

At once, Scott began to equivocate about occupation and evacuation, an indecisiveness that pre-dated Banks and one that would continue into 1863. Shades of his correspondence with Patterson, he said he did not intend Banks to hold the Ferry at great hazard even if he had been significantly reinforced. With a force of fifteen thousand men and a prospect of attack by twenty thousand, a defensive battle Banks should expect to win easily, he should nevertheless cross the Potomac to positions on Maryland Heights and opposite Leesburg.[22] But as his numbers grew, his force became too large for a quick, orderly retreat across the Potomac. And a crossing by his army in retreat might well be prevented altogether if the rains that were threatening raised the level of the river.[23]

When McClellan arrived in Washington, he found Banks's command "distant, . . . unorganized, demoralized, and unfit to march or fight."[24] On the second of August he received a letter from Colonel Fitz-John Porter. "That the government should not suffer by my withdrawal from this command, on the arrival of Genl. Banks I consented to remain, and had myself assigned to the position of acting inspector-general in order to accomplish what no-one else here can—a re-organization of this demoralized force. I think within a week I shall have placed it in excellent order for brigade commanders to perfect."[25] For now, the Army of the Shenandoah remained too weak to defend against a determined attack.

Banks received a steady stream of reports that the Confederates were advancing against him. Continuing the Patterson image, Banks consulted his officers, including Fitz-John Porter. They unanimously recommended that he withdraw the majority of his force to the Maryland side of the river. He agreed, reported his intentions to Washington, and began the movement. To make communication across the river easier, he would construct a temporary bridge.[26]

By the next day, July 29, he had established his headquarters on the eastern side of the river at the Miller house on the bluff above Sandy Hook, a tiny village

21 *OR*, 2, 764.

22 *OR*, 2, 765.

23 *OR*, 2, 767.

24 *M.O.S.*, 73.

25 McClellan MSS (L.C.) letter dated August 1, 1861, from Porter to McClellan. Part of this letter is quoted in *M.O.S.*, 74.

26 *OR*, 2, 767.

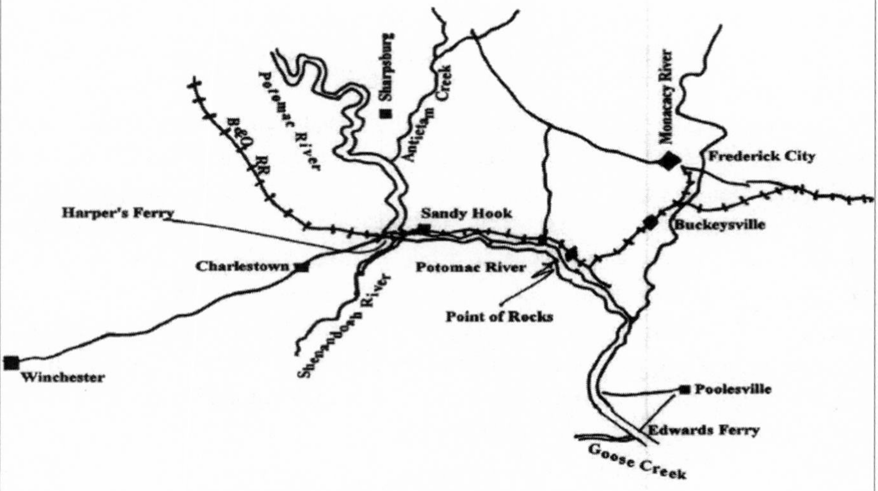

Upper Potomac in the Vicinity of Harpers Ferry

crammed into the narrow lane between the river and the canal on one side and the sharply rising Catoctin Mountains on the other. The road along the north bank of the Potomac toward Harpers Ferry was a narrow route cut into the mountainside just wide enough for a team of horses and a wagon but not for two wagons to meet and pass each other. Infantry, artillery, and trains passed along it slowly; and very little was required to block it.

Banks ordered three companies of the Second Massachusetts Infantry and the twenty cavalrymen to stay in Harpers Ferry as a garrison. Lieutenant Colonel Andrews remained behind with the three infantry companies. The remaining companies of the Second with three guns of Battery A, First Rhode Island Artillery, took position on the rocky face of Maryland Heights. From there, the troops would be able to see the Rebels in positions west of the Ferry beyond Boliver Heights.[27]

The army left behind by Patterson had been rapidly disintegrating as the three-month troops reached the end of their tour of duty and started for home. Arriving at

27 Strother, "Personal Recollections," *Harpers New Monthly Magazine*, vol. 33, no. 196, 411; Gordon, *Brook Farm*, 30-31. The artillery was undoubtedly Battery A, First Rhode Island Artillery. Quaife, *Williams' Letters*, 18-19, letter dated October 12, 1861, from Williams to his daughter; James E. Taylor, *With Sheridan up the Shenandoah Valley in 1864: Leaves From a Special Artist's Sketch Book and Diary* (Cleveland, 1989), 25-26, and sketch of Point of Rocks, 26 (Taylor, *With Sheridan*); Malles, *Brainerd's Memoir*, 87.

Harpers Ferry at 3:00 in the afternoon on July 29, Colonel John White Geary, commanding the Twenty-eighth Pennsylvania, "found the whole army retiring from Virginia to the Maryland side. Helter skelter men, horses, cannons, wagons, etc., etc., 'ad infinitum.' I never saw more confusion. I thought the army was again defeated, but was soon informed that that was the way the three months men done the thing up. They are leaving for home—the service will not lose much . . ."[28]

Unlike Patterson, Banks received a steady flow of three-year men. By July 29, he had five or six thousand long-term men, some totally unreliable "short-timers" as they would be known a century later, and three hundred wagons.[29] All Patterson's personal aides were gone; but the bureau heads were still in place, giving Banks an experienced transition group although some like Fitz-John Porter and John Newton were known candidates for brigadier general.[30]

Starting from scratch, he created a new division from his new regiments and new officers. His premier regiment continued to be the Second Massachusetts Infantry, commanded by Colonel George H. Gordon, West Point class of 1846; Lieutenant Colonel George L. Andrews, first in the West Point class of 1851; and Major Wilder Dwight, Harvard class of 1853.[31] By early August he had twelve thousand men progressing in discipline and drill.[32]

Banks had entered the army as a major general, thus making his proper command a division, a corps if they were ever formed, or even an army.[33] He had responsibility for the Department of the Shenandoah, which included a long stretch of the Potomac and Harpers Ferry, a command which demanded more than the four thousand men of an infantry brigade. The command structure of the Army of the Shenandoah, created under Patterson in May and inherited by Banks in July, had undergone a complete transformation. Like his army, Banks's officer corps had to be rebuilt from the ground.

One of Patterson's division commanders, Major General George Cadwalader of the Pennsylvania militia, had come to the end of his commission at the same time

28 Blair, *Geary's Letters*, 2-3, letter dated July 30, 1861, from Geary to "My Beloved Mary" (his wife) (Blair, *Geary Letters*). The date of the event described is not stated but seems clear from the text of related *OR* dispatches.

29 *OR*, 2, 767.

30 Strother, "Personal Recollections," *Harpers' New Monthly Magazine*, 33, no. 197, 412.

31 Dwight, *Letters*, 110, letter dated October 4, 1861, from Dwight to his family; Quaife, *Williams Letters*, 20, letter dated October 12, 1861, from Williams to his daughter, 2, *Cullum* nos. 1314 and 1494.

32 *OR*, 2, 554.

33 By the end of the war Banks would have completed a truly mediocre career in which he had commanded them all.

that Patterson's tenure ended on July 19. A prominent Democrat of Philadelphia, Cadwalader had supporters who continued to write in favor of high rank for him. Lincoln endorsed the recommendations, "I am willing to make General Cadwalader a Brigadier, or a Major General, any moment when Gen. Cameron says so."[34] Secretary Cameron sent these letters to McClellan endorsing them, "I will be very glad to act in this matter as General McClellan will advise."

No doubt recalling Cadwalader unfavorably from Mexico, where he had been a *voluntarios* brigade commander, McClellan responded on September 16:

> I cannot recommend the appointment of General Cadwalader. I do not think it would promote the interests of the country. If he be appointed from any political considerations—which I do not think are proper to be considered in the present exigency—I would respectfully request that he may not be assigned to duty with the Army under my command.[35]

Some of Banks's best officers were lost to promotion or transfer.[36] Promoted to brigadier-general, George H. Thomas was transferred to Kentucky in August.[37] To McClellan's forces around the capital went Surgeon Charles S. Tripler, chief medical officer; Major Fitz-John Porter, chief of staff to both Patterson and Banks; John Newton, chief engineer, and brigade commander Charles P. Stone, the last three being West Point graduates, Regular Army officers, and Mexican War veterans.[38]

From the capital came Brigadier General Alpheus Starkey Williams, who had hoped to command a brigade of Michigan regiments in the nascent Army of the Potomac. Instead, he went to Banks with the promise that Banks would have a responsible position for him.[39] Born in Connecticut in 1810 the son of a wealthy manufacturer, Williams managed to overcome an 1841 degree from Yale. He spent his vacations in travel to all states in the Union and to Texas while it was part of

34 Basler, *Lincoln's Works*, 4, 525, endorsement dated September 19, 1861, and 525, n. 1.

35 Sears, *McClellan's Correspondence*, 102, letter of September 16, 1861, from McClellan to Cameron, and 102, n. 1; Jack K. Bauer, *The Mexican War, 1846-1848* (Norwalk, 1990), 295-296, 309-310 (Bauer, *Mexican War*).

36 Dwight, *Dwight Letters*, 103, letter dated September 15, 1861, Dwight to his family; *OR*, 5, 592.

37 *D.A.B.*, 9, pt. 2, 433; *Cullum*, 1, no. 1028; Warner, *Generals in Blue*, 500; Hall, *Cayuga in the Field*, 76.

38 NA RG 393, General-in-Chief's Ledger of Documents Sent, 220, dispatch dated August 6, 1861, from Headquarters of the Army to Stone. Warner, *Generals in Blue*, 345, 379; *Cullum*, 2, nos. 1112, 1238.

39 Quaife, *Williams' Letters*, 18, letter dated October 12, 1861, from Williams to his daughter.

Mexico. After three years at Yale Law School, he traveled in Europe from 1834 to 1836, where he dissipated much of the $75,000 fortune[40] he had inherited when his father died. His reduced circumstances forced him to develop a career. For no reason now apparent, he chose to establish a law practice in Detroit, Michigan.

After a few years he married a young widow and began a lifetime of procreation, which produced five children in the next decade.[41] He was elected to the Probate Court, became a minister, became president of the St. Clair Bank, owner of a Detroit daily newspaper, and recorder of the Board of Education.

While this kaleidoscopic career was proceeding, its creator was active in the peacetime military of Michigan, beginning with service in the Brady Guards, a newly organized infantry company. Sporting one month of active service on Canada's border, he was elected first lieutenant of the company in 1839, then captain in 1843 and 1846. Michigan sent to the Mexican War a regiment of infantry in which Williams was the lieutenant colonel. Although his regiment reached Mexico before the peace, he took part in no battle. In his year of service Williams won no glory, acquired no combat experience, and was involved only in guerilla warfare; but he did learn the duties of military life and the responsibilities of managing a military unit.

After the war he served as postmaster of Detroit from 1849 to 1853, then as president of the Michigan Oil Company, as a member of the city council, as president of the Detroit Board of Education, and as president of the state military board. He continued his place in the Brady Guards, then the Grayson Guards, and finally the Detroit Light Guard, in which he was the captain. In 1859 the company was expanded to a battalion of two infantry companies, Williams in command as a major. By 1861 his varied career had made him a prominent citizen in Detroit.

A brigadier-general's star in the Michigan militia appeared when the South fired on Fort Sumter. In May he went to Washington on military business for the State of Michigan. With him he carried a letter of introduction addressed to Simon Cameron. It said,

> This letter is no mere formal introduction. The Bearer thereof is General Alpheus Williams of the First Brigade of Michigan Volunteers, appointed by Governor Blair and truly prophesying the confidence and general respect and affection of *our* people. He is a military man by education and experience.

40 In 1861 the income from $100,000, carefully invested, would have provided an upper middle class style of life for the recipient. Interview, John S. Gordon, financial historian for *American Heritage*.

41 After the war and a decade as a widower, Williams remarried and produced several more children. *D.A.B.*, 10, pt. 2, 248.

> Courteous and courageous, honorable and high minded, intimately acquainted with the theory and details of military science from a captain to colonel, and from company drill, to the government of a Brigade, to him, more than any one else among us . . .

With this endorsement, which wandered from Cameron to the Radical Republican senator from Michigan, Zachariah Chandler, Lincoln found it easy on August 9 to appoint Williams a brigadier general of volunteers to rank from May 17.

Fifty-one when he was commissioned, he was much older than the "Scott Rule" officers who were also being commissioned as general officers by Lincoln. He had been a widower for more than ten years, two of his children had died in childhood, and his full beard and ferocious mustache made him look his age. To his men he would be known as "Old Pap" and, could be easily recognized astride his favorite horse, a large white mare he called "Snowball."[42]

On Monday, October 7, he and his staff with their tents and other equipment in three wagons left Washington for Banks's division. That evening a torrential downpour forced them into a small inn at Rockville. Next morning, they started in a drizzle and, about noon, reached Banks's headquarters, which were on top of a hill. At the bottom of Banks's headquarters hill was a small rapid stream, and below it spread a valley bounded on the opposite side by higher hills. There he dined with Banks and received orders to assume command of a brigade.

After completing the usual initial pleasantries, he selected a campground for the eight or ten tents of his headquarters. Like Banks, Williams and his staff pitched the tents themselves. They were sheltered by woods in their rear. Just within the woods were servants' tents and, farther back, picket stakes for the horses.[43]

As brigade commander, Williams spent a great deal of time on horseback visiting his regiments. His staff did the administrative work while his adjutant

> kept employed with a clerk and one or two other assistants and a mounted orderly in answering applications, making the daily details for guard, pickets, duty officers, recording orders, and generally providing for our large military family of 5,000 men, to say nothing of the hundreds of teams and horses . . . Our daily routine is: up at reveille (sunrise); William gives us a cup of strong coffee soon after and breakfast in an hour. By eight o'clock the reports begin to arrive

42 Chandler MSS (L.C.) letter of May 29, 1861, from Ross Wilkins to Cameron; Alpheus S. Williams MSS (Detroit Public Library) letter of September 17, 1865, from Williams to "My dear Lew"; Quaife, *William's Letters*, Intro., 3-8; *D.A.B.*, 10, pt. 2, 247-248; Heitman, *Historical Register*, 1, 1030; Warner, *Generals in Blue*, 559-600; Clowes, *Detroit Light Guard*, 490-494.

43 Quaife, *Williams' Letters*, 18-20, letter dated October 12, 1861, from Williams to his daughter.

> from the several regiments, and then sergeant-majors [begin] to copy orders and the general applications for leave furloughs, for quartermaster's or commissory's stores, for all kinds of wants. Orders from division headquarters follow, all to be copied, repeated in a new order and distributed to the several regiments. We have improvised a few desks out of packing boxes, and on these we do most of our writing.

Included in his brigade were the Second Massachusetts under Colonel Gordon, the Fifth Connecticut under Colonel Ferry, the Twentieth New York under Colonel Donnelly, the Forty-sixth Pennsylvania under Colonel Knipe, the Nineteenth New York under Major Ledlie, and Battery A of the First Rhode Island Artillery. Williams considered the Second Massachusetts a splendid regiment. The commander of the Fifth Connecticut, Colonel Ferry, was a member of Congress from Connecticut, "a man of great energy and industry," Williams wrote in a letter, "but I think not much of a soldier."

Alpheus Williams, an early attempt to begin rebuilding the officer corps of the Army of the Shenandoah, was joined by other brigade commanders, Brigadier Generals Charles S. Hamilton and John J. Abercrombie. Later taken to McClellan's forces at Washington, they would be succeeded by senior regimental colonels, George H. Gordon of the Second Massachusetts Infantry, a former Regular Army officer and McClellan's classmate at West Point in the Class of 46; and John White Geary, another veteran of the Mexican war and a man with political aspirations past and future.[44] For artillery, Banks had only fourteen field guns and Major Abner Doubleday's heavy artillery, the heavy guns too cumbersome for use in the field. He needed additional mobile artillery before he could put his force on the march against the enemy.[45]

For his main force, which lay east of the Potomac in Maryland, Banks needed to establish a supply depot and hospital. Hagerstown, too far north, would not serve his purposes. At Sandy Hook the strip of land along the edge of the river could not accommodate new structures because the canal, the railroad, and the highway took too much of the narrow space and because it lay exposed to artillery fire from heights on the Virginia side.[46] Needing a place removed from the river and with railroad facilities in every direction, he chose the village of Buckeystown.

44 Quaife, *Williams' Letters*, 10-20, letter dated October 12, 1861, from Williams to his daughter; Warner, *Generals in Blue*, 3, 199; *Cullum*, 1, no. 322; *Cullum*, 2, nos. 1192, 1314.

45 *OR*, 5, 560, 565.

46 *OR*, 2, 770.

Banks had responsibility northwest along the Potomac past Harpers Ferry through Shepherdstown to Williamsport. His main force was on the march for Pleasant Valley between Frederick and the river.[47]

While Banks was building his command, McClellan tried to protect the Potomac River between the capital and the area around Harpers Ferry and Point of Rocks. For Brigadier-General Charles P. Stone, his West Point classmate, he created a small brigade from the First Minnesota, Thirty-fourth New York, and one company of Regular cavalry. Familiar with this area from his march to join Patterson before Bull Run, Stone took command of the troops on August 5. As quickly as he could, McClellan gave him more regiments.

On August 11, McClellan ordered Stone and his force to the vicinity of Poolesville. He was to guard the Potomac River from Seneca Mills to Point of Rocks, keep his main force in the central position at Poolesville, picket the dangerous fords strongly, and reinforce the pickets wherever the Rebels tried to cross. McClellan also wanted his flank units to maintain contact on the north with Banks's pickets near Point of Rocks and to the south with McCall near Langley. Stone should also arrange for McCall to support him in any strong position which could be held with his available forces. Forbidding all activity that might bring on a general engagement, McClellan had great confidence and trust in Stone. "Should you see the opportunity of capturing or dispersing any small party by crossing the river, you are at liberty to do so, though great discretion is recommended in making such a movement."

Observation was Stone's general mission. Any Confederate attempt to cross the river was to be disputed in order to allow reserves from the main army to concentrate. "I leave your operations much to your own discretion, in which I have the fullest confidence," McClellan said to him.[48]

Connecting with Stone's right flank was the Twenty-eighth Pennsylvania under Colonel John White Geary at Point of Rocks, the left regiment of Banks's division. Like Banks, Geary was an officer with much political and limited military experience. In Stone's opinion Geary and his troops showed too much nervousness and their conduct disrupted his men.[49] He was right. Geary himself found his position unsettling. "I have been very busy here for several days," he wrote his wife, "and indeed I sometimes begin to think that we are in a pretty tight place. My Regiment is extended as guard from Harpers Ferry to Monocacy, distance 18 miles.

47 *OR*, 5, 560, 565.

48 *OR*, 5, 557-560, especially 557-558.

49 *OR*, 5, 568, 578-579.

General Banks is a c – – – – d or something worse, (but this is for your own eyes), else he would sustain my precarious condition better. If the enemy attacks my lines, we will make it a Thermopilae, for we have no support, and unless I am ordered to do so I will not retreat."[50]

More officers than Geary had doubts about Banks's military abilities. "Tomorrow morning our Brigade is to be reviewed by Genl Banks," wrote one of the general's intelligent, Harvard-educated field-grade officers. "Napoleon, as the newspapers are fond of saying, used to precede his great battles and important movements by grand reviews. Genl Banks is not Napoleon."[51]

Guarding a stretch of the Potomac twenty-two miles in length, Stone, like Banks, needed more than the usual brigade of infantry. By the middle of August, he had six regiments of infantry, a battery of artillery, and a company of cavalry, a total approaching on division strength.[52] Willis A. Gorman, to whose command the Eighty-second New York and the Fifteenth Massachusetts had been added in the meantime, was appointed Brigadier General of Volunteers on September 7, 1861, and assigned a brigade in Stone's division.[53]

50 Blair, *Geary's Letters*, 11, letter dated August 22, 1861, from Geary to his wife.

51 Dwight, *Dwight Letters*, 172, letter dated December 16, 1861, from Wilder Dwight to his mother.

52 *OR*, 5, 560, 565, 592-593.

53 N.A. Off's MS Rpts (Gorman); *OR*, 5, 560, 565, 592-593; *M.O.S.*, 79-81.

Chapter 27

"The vital importance of rendering Washington perfectly secure, and its *imminent danger*, impel me to urge these requests with the utmost earnestness and that not an hour be lost in carrying them into execution."

– *McClellan to Scott*

Growing Friction with Scott

Banks, meanwhile, collected additional intelligence that the Confederates at Winchester were advancing on Harpers Ferry, that a large force under Johnston would soon reoccupy Leesburg, and that a thrust across the Potomac River would be made north of the capital. Thinking that the Confederates, emboldened by their victory at Bull Run, still intended to press their advantage in the form of a classic pursuit, McClellan accepted Banks's intelligence. He concluded that the Confederates would cross the Potomac in the vicinity of Poolesville where Stone's headquarters were located, march to Baltimore, sever all land communication between Washington and the loyal states to the north, then advance on the unfortified rear of the capital. Pinning attacks would hold the troops on the Alexandria–Aqueduct line to prevent them from assisting the sparse defensive forces of Banks, Stone, and McCall north of the capital.[1] With the forces available to

1 *OR*, 5, 80; McClellan in *B&L*, 2, 161.

the Rebels, as McClellan and his headquarters staff evaluated them, the threat had reality.

"Be sure Beauregard has one hundred thousand ready to attack us," said Lieutenant-Colonel A. V. Colburn to Lieutenant-Colonel William Dwight, "and why he don't do it I can't imagine."[2]

Whether or not this force existed, Stone was a wiser, shrewder, and more experienced observer than Banks. Carefully, he examined the Confederate positions across the river from Poolesville. They were constructing entrenchments about three and a half miles to the rear of Edward's Ferry on the Leesburg Road. Excellent for defense but, in Stone's opinion, "good for nothing for offensive operations." Stone could see no preparation of rafts or boats for crossing a Potomac that was now unfordable by wagons or artillery. He concluded that very few troops were across the river from him.

Banks's concerns about the length of the Potomac River between Washington and Harpers Ferry were not fanciful, at least not in the minds of officers in the danger zone.[3] Several colonels, expecting severe cavalry attacks most probably in the form of Napoleonic cavalry pursuit, discussed the best method of forming squares against them.[4] Even in the middle of August they still expected to need this formation. Early in the month McClellan warned Banks to have his men ready to defend against a crossing. The same alert he sent to his brigade commanders,[5] and he renewed it two days later.[6] During the nights of the fifth, sixth, and seventh of August, he was so distraught at the prospect of a Confederate attack and the unprepared state of his army that he hardly slept a wink,[7] a fear that stayed with him and many others through the month.[8]

Scott seemed as unconcerned about this possibility as he had been about a brigade of elephants on the Long Bridge. Although he had feared this very stroke

2 Dwight Family MSS (M.H.S.) letter dated August 17, 1861, from William Dwight to his father; Howe, *Sherman Howe Letters*, 215, letter dated August 17, 1861.

3 Blair, *Geary's Letters*, 10, letter dated August 17, 1861, from Geary to his wife.

4 Dwight Family MSS (M.H.S.) letter dated August 19, 1861, from William Dwight to his father.

5 Sears, *McClellan's Correspondence*, 79, telegram dated August 4, 1861, from McClellan to Banks, and 79, n. 1.

6 *OR*, 5, 553.

7 Sears, *McClellan's Correspondence*, 81, letter dated August 8, 1861, from McClellan to his wife.

8 Dwight Family MSS (M.H.S.) letters dated August 19, 22, 28, and 30, 1861, from William Dwight to his father; Sears, *For Country Cause and Leader (Haydon Diary)*, 74-75, entry dated August 20, 1861.

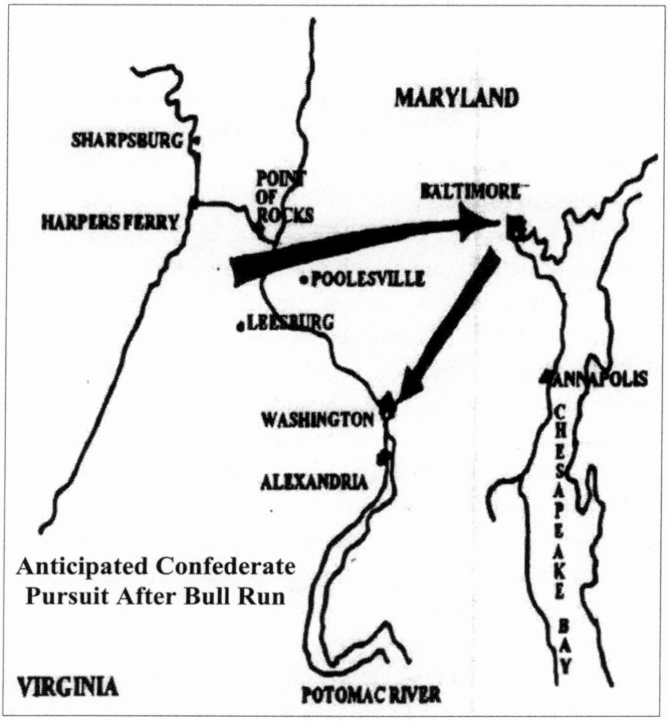

after the fall of Fort Sumter, his experience and judgment now told him the Rebels would not do it. After the surrender of Sumter they had not. While McDowell gathered his army for its advance, they had not. During the confusion immediately after their victory at Bull Run, they had not. When Stone was guarding the upriver area with a tiny force after Bull Run, they had not. Why should he anticipate an attack now? The Confederate army, victorious though it had been, "was badly hurt," according to his adjutant general, who was probably speaking Scott's views, "and will not be ready to advance to the attack of our forces, I imagine, at any rate for some days."[9] As the old general put it, "I have not the slightest apprehension whatsoever for the safety of the government."[10]

This difference, along with many others, escalated the troubles between McClellan and Scott. McClellan wrote his wife on August 8, "I do not know whether he is a dotard or a traitor. I can't tell which . . . that confounded old Genl always

9 Porter MSS (L.C.) letter dated July 27, 1861, from Townsend to Porter.

10 *OR*, 11, pt. 3, 3.

comes in the way—he is a perfect imbecile. He understands nothing, appreciates nothing & is ever in my way."[11]

On August 10 at 1:00 a.m. he continued his tirade: "Genl Scott is the great obstacle—he will not comprehend the danger & is either a traitor, or an incompetent. I have to fight my way against him."[12]

Others had recognized the problem as early as the end of July. The scrivener in the State Department wrote in his diary, "McClellan ought to be altogether independent of Scott; be untrammeled in his activity; have direct action; and not refer to Scott . . . Scott, as [if] by concession, cuts for McClellan a military department of six square miles. Oh, human stupidity, how difficult thou art to lift!"[13]

McClellan decided to address the problem with a straightforward violation of the rules of military etiquette, something already unintentionally encouraged by the president. The disagreement with Scott, at least the major-general's side of it, he formally recorded for the first time in a letter. The letter, addressed to Scott, was delivered to him by hand "in the usual course of official correspondence," as McClellan endorsed his personal copy. But in the unusual course, McClellan's aide Thomas M. Key delivered a copy directly to the president. Many personal characteristics that would loom larger as McClellan's military career progressed were plainly foretold in this letter and the surrounding incidents.

He believed, he said, that the Confederates would concentrate all their efforts and resources to defeat his army. Large Rebel reinforcements known to be passing through Knoxville would, he was certain, go to Richmond to reinforce Beauregard and Johnston on the Potomac. Beauregard already had at least one hundred thousand men and would attack. The federal army, believed McClellan, was wholly insufficient to meet this attack. All garrisons in the rear should be stripped and their forces sent to him. Every new regiment and every piece of Regular artillery should be sent to him. The core of the West Virginia army, his first command, should be ordered east to him. The Departments of Northeastern Virginia, Washington, Pennsylvania, the Shenandoah, Baltimore, and Fort Monroe should be merged into one department "under the immediate control of the Commander of the main army of operations."

He appealed to the fear most easily evoked in Lincoln and his Cabinet: the safety of the capital. They had survived the long, emotionally draining period of

11 Sears, *McClellan's Correspondence*, 81, letter of August 8, 1861, from McClellan to his wife.

12 Sears, *McClellan's Correspondence*, 81-82, letter of August 9, 1861, 1:00 a.m., redated August 10 by the editor, from McClellan to his wife.

13 Gurowski, *Diary*, 1, 75, entry dated July 1861.

March, April, and May when the capital seemed available for the taking. He must have touched a tender spot when he said, "The vital importance of rendering Washington perfectly secure, and its *imminent danger*, impel me to urge these requests with the utmost earnestness and that not an hour be lost in carrying them into execution."[14]

This was a simple effort to free the dispute about the danger to the capital from the confines of his military relationship with Scott. It should include Scott's civilian superiors, McClellan believed. His plan, and it could have been nothing less than a carefully devised plan to have his own way and to compromise the aged general, was to frighten the civilians, concentrate the country's military assets in his hands, replace Scott as general in chief, and end the war in a single huge battle.

The day after he sent this letter he worked long and hard. Setting out for the south side of the river on horseback at 7:00 a.m., he rode the advanced positions, was caught in a heavy rain, and returned soundly drenched. At last reaching his headquarters, where he would do his daily paperwork, he concluded that everything was improving. Three new regiments had arrived that day. Two new batteries of artillery had arrived in the last two days, two more were to arrive tomorrow, and no less than five the day after. McDowell had gone to battle with forty-five guns, one battalion of cavalry, and fewer than forty-five regiments. McClellan now had twenty-one batteries of approximately one hundred twenty-four guns, almost two regiments of cavalry, and seventy regiments of infantry. On his problem with Scott, he believed "the question will probably be solved by giving me absolute control independently of him."[15]

When Scott received McClellan's letter, it was more than he could bear. He had no long, growing line of fortifications he could review with pride while his damaged feelings mended. Unable to ride a horse or walk more than a few steps, immobile except for a carriage, he was a prisoner in his quarters. He went to his only place of refuge, his desk, and raised the only weapon he could, his pen. In the letter that followed, he exploded.

He disagreed, he wrote, with almost every statement in McClellan's letter; but although he was the principal military officer of his country, he could not refute any of it with military facts. McClellan's opinions had never been expressed during any of their few meetings. Scott had freely given his views and opinions but McClellan had never responded. The old general had tried to draw him out; but "[h]e has stood

14 Sears, *McClellan's Correspondence*, 79-80, letter dated August 8, 1861, from McClellan to Scott.

15 Sears, *McClellan's Correspondence*, 81, letter of August 9, 1861, redated August 10 by the editor, from McClellan to his wife; Gurowski, *Diary*, 1, 77, entry dated July, 1861.

on his guard, now places himself on record. Let him make the most of his unenvied advantages . . . [B]eing broken down by many particular hurts, besides the general infirmities of age—I feel that I have become an encumbrance to the Army as well as to myself, that I ought, giving way to a younger commander—to seek the palliatives of physical pain and exhaustion. Accordingly I must beg the president at the earliest moment, to allow me to be placed on the *officers' retired list* then quietly to lay myself up—probably forever—somewhere in or about New York."[16]

Disturbed by this dispute,[17] Lincoln went to work promptly to resolve it. For all Scott's faults, the old general had an uninterrupted chain of military successes McClellan had not had time to match. The president was simply not prepared to continue without Scott's advice. And he did not want to multiply McClellan's responsibilities by making him general in chief as well as head of what was soon to become the Army of the Potomac. He would meet with McClellan and use his great personnel skills to persuade his fractious young major-general to withdraw the offending letter. Then, he would convince Scott to withdraw the resignation.

McClellan responded to his president's request with a prompt, sanctimonious letter which exalted form over substance, the proper appearances he had been taught over his real feelings. Naively or disingenuously, he described his August 8 bomb as a "plain and respectful" statement of his opinions and a part of his duty. "The command with which I am entrusted was not sought by me and has only been accepted from an earnest and humble desire to serve my country in the moment of extreme peril . . . above all I would abstain from any word or act that could give offense to General Scott . . . as you requested my authority to withdraw the letter, that authority is hereby given, with the most profound assurances of respect for General Scott and yourself."[18] He sent the withdrawal to Lincoln the same day the president requested it. From McClellan's point of view, retraction was meaningless because he had accomplished his purpose: he had released the "danger-to-the-capital" genie from the bottle. Nothing, certainly not retraction of the letter, could put it back.

Armed with McClellan's letter, the president went to Scott's quarters to persuade the old general in chief to make the second retraction.[19] Lincoln produced

16 Lincoln MSS (L.C.) letter dated August 9, 1861, from Scott to Cameron. This letter appears in *OR*, 11, pt. 3, 4.

17 *N&H*, 4, 463.

18 Lincoln MSS (L.C.) letter of August 10, 1861, from McClellan to Lincoln. It also appears in *OR*, 11, pt. 3, 4-5; and in Sears, *McClellan's Correspondence*, 82-83.

19 No sources expressly discuss the visit or establish the place of the meeting. McClellan, unfortunately, did not write the usual newsy letters to his wife between August 9-13, 1861. Nevertheless, the context of all correspondence suggests this chronology and this location.

McClellan's letter. While they were talking one of the general in chief's servants brought him an unaddressed envelope. It contained an unsigned copy of McClellan's retraction. Scott had addressed his letter of resignation to the secretary of war, his superior. McClellan, of course, had not sent his retraction to Scott, his superior, but to the president. An unsigned copy in an unaddressed envelope to his commanding officer? "This slight," wrote Scott later, "was not without its influence on my mind."

The president pleaded his case, but Scott did not succumb. When the president left, the lieutenant-general remained undecided. He knew Lincoln had come to him for the "patriotic purpose of healing differences," a high purpose which weighed heavily on him. But it was not enough to tip the balance. The original offense, the letter of August 8, had been committed by McClellan intentionally and, worse yet, with the complicity of Cabinet members. Of course, Scott had no way to relieve himself from the indignities, no way to discipline McClellan, and no way to cure his crippling physical infirmities. He lacked the troops to review with pride and had no growing line of fortifications to ride. Although he had a comfortable, European, Balzacian marriage, he had no soulmate to whom he could unburden himself, pour out his own soul. His former conversational companions had vanished: Keyes was a brigade commander about to become a division commander; the old southern officers with whom he had surrounded himself had chosen their parochial loyalties over their national loyalties and "gone south."

On August 12, 1861, two days after the meeting, Scott prepared his answer and addressed it pointedly to the secretary of war, the proper recipient. Quickly, it found its way to the president. The general in chief refused to withdraw his resignation.[20] But Lincoln was too shrewd. Relying on a tactic he would use more than once, Lincoln kept the resignation but did not act on it.

With his resignation in the hands of the president, no acceptance of it forthcoming, and no retirement being suggested, Scott remained in an equivocal position. He decided to do the only thing a man of his stature and dignity could do: he would keep at his job until the president did something. Seeing this, McClellan doubled his efforts to make the sensitive old man's life intolerable.

Outright, face-to-face rudeness? The thought would never have crossed McClellan's mind. He would have been governed by the old rule that a gentleman never gives personal affront unintentionally. But innumerable slights, breaches of military courtesy, withholding of basic military information? These had been early transgressions encouraged by the president, who knew less about military protocol

20 Lincoln MSS (L.C.) letter dated August 12, 1861, from Scott to Lincoln. This letter is reprinted in *OR*, 11, pt. 3, 5.

than a housewife. McClellan continued them. In the immediate future, he would raise their level.

Studiously he ignored his superior officer,[21] gave him no reports about troop arrivals, and withheld information about troop locations.[22] The steady stream of direct communication with the president and members of the cabinet, begun while he was in Ohio and encouraged by both, he continued.[23] This course of conduct, aided if not strengthened by the president and his Cabinet officers, continued in an unmistakable way. On September 7, Cameron wrote directly to McClellan, to buttress inferentially by conduct and expressly by words the major-general's view of the situation. McClellan sent a prompt, long, self-serving response supporting his contentions that he had inadequate forces under his command; that he differentiated between a field army and overall troop strength, including a garrison for the capital; that he needed more men for his field army; and that all available forces should be brought to him from all sources. He sent no copy to Scott.[24]

By the middle of August the men guarding the river had concluded that the Confederates would attempt to cross at the place presenting the fewest obstacles. From a reliable, loyal citizen Stone learned that a force of Rebels had occupied one of the Potomac islands and had under construction an immense raft for a crossing. Stone went to the island himself but found no trace of human occupation except for a large accumulation of driftwood probably mistaken for the raft in construction. A quiet cigar in the tent would cure the anxieties.[25]

Small units and parts of units were shifted nervously about the Harpers Ferry area. The Second Massachusetts ended this mobile suffering when it finally occupied a position on the eastern slope of Maryland Heights where it could cover the river from Harpers Ferry to Sandy Hook.

By August 19, signs of Confederate presence were increasing. A force of Confederate cavalry appeared in Harpers Ferry and exchanged fire with Union pickets. Late that night, the officer of the guard roused Colonel Gordon from his sleep to read a message by the lantern's light:

21 *N&H* 4, 463.

22 Morse, *Welles' Diary*, 1, 242-243, entry dated February 25, 1862.

23 *N&H*, 4, 464.

24 Sears, *McClellan's Correspondence*, 95-97, letter dated September 8, 1861, from McClellan to Cameron.

25 Strother, "Personal Recollections" in *Harpers' New Monthly Magazine*, vol. 33, no. 196, 415.

Colonel Gordon:

I am directed by Colonel Donnelly to send a messenger to you with information that the rebels are marching on Harpers Ferry six thousand in numbers strong.

Yours very respectfully,

E. F. Brown Lieut.-Col.
Twenty-eighth Reg. N.Y.V.

Berlin, Md., August 19, 1861.

Gordon hastily questioned the messenger, who said he had to hurry back to his regiment. The colonel recalled the recent signs of Confederate movements. These confirmed that the dispatch was well-founded. Remaining alone a moment, Gordon surveyed the area about him from the small height on which his tent was pitched. He was partially surrounded by trees. He looked down on the thousand men of his regiment. In the near distance he could hear the rushing sound of the Potomac. The faint light of the moon revealed the heights on all sides.

Any attempt by the Confederates to cross the river would be in his front; and if it were made, it was, he thought, likely to succeed. He had no artillery, the three Rhode Island guns having gone to Banks's main force. Having neither the guns nor the numbers to meet an attack successfully, he saddled his horse, mounted, and rode rapidly into Sandy Hook to the hotel where the telegraph office was located. After a lengthy struggle, he managed to awaken the operator, who established a connection with another station. At least the wires were not cut even though they paralleled the Potomac River for twelve miles to Point of Rocks before they turned eastward to Frederick. Gordon gave silent thanks to God.

"Where shall I telegraph?" asked the operator.

Gordon responded, "To headquarters."

The instrument began to sound. No response.

"What's the matter?" Gordon asked.

"I am afraid there's no night operator," replied the telegraph operator.

"Continue your call. Don't cease."

Gordon was impatient. The instrument continued to clatter in the dimly lit room. Gordon waited anxiously. Minutes passed. No response. A quarter of an hour passed. Still no answer. Finally Gordon became impatient.

"Try some other place."

"Where, sir?"

"Where? Someplace where we have troops and artillery. Try Frederick."

The operator worked the key again, but again he could not provoke a response.

"Keep on," urged Gordon.

Again there was no answer.

"What can you do?"

"I might try Baltimore. Perhaps someone is awake there," the operator suggested.

Gordon was ready to try anything.

"Well, try Baltimore then." Again the telegraph clicked monotonously. Yet again, no response.

"Is this a failure, too? Try some other station in Baltimore, then."

Again the machine began to clatter. For moments Gordon strained his eyes as if he were expecting to see a response. At long last, Baltimore, ninety miles distant, responded from a railroad station. The telegraph key clattered, "What do you want?"

"Is there a night operator within twenty miles of me?" Gordon asked.

The operator at Baltimore responded, "Yes, at Frederick."

Gordon then asked, "Who is there at Frederick?"

The telegraph key responded, "Troops and General Fitz John Porter."

Once again, the telegraph operator transmitted to Frederick. After a long effort, the machine finally responded, "What do you want?"

Gordon dictated to the machine. "Who there is of our army at Frederick, is what I want."

The machine clattered back, "General Porter."

With a few more transmissions, Gordon learned that Porter was sleeping at a hotel. He ordered the dispatcher at the far end to record the following dispatch, give it to Porter, and tell Porter that he would await a response:

"The enemy, numbering six thousand, is marching upon Harpers Ferry. I am here with my regiment, but no artillery. If the enemy has artillery, I cannot hold the place. What shall be done. Answer quickly."

The operator in Frederick telegraphed back, "I will carry him this dispatch and answer in twenty minutes."

By this time it was one o'clock in the morning, August 20. Very little time remained, certainly not enough to make preparations to meet an advancing force. Gordon was nervous. As patiently as he could, he counted off ten minutes. Then twenty, and then thirty. The telegraph key lay silent. At last he could stand it no longer.

"Ask for an answer."

But the key spoke no response. Some time passed. Finally, came a reply.

"I have important dispatches to Baltimore and cannot leave to carry your message."

Gordon was furious. "Tell him he *must* go."

But Gordon's operator was helpless.

"I cannot," he responded. "He has cut off all communication with this place and will not get my dispatch." Gordon was desperate. "Can you jump him to a place beyond?"

"Yes, I can reach Baltimore again."

"Do so, and tell the operator there to tell the operator at Frederick that he *must* deliver my message immediately."

The telegraph operator at Baltimore received the message and obviously applied some secret magic to the anonymous operator in Frederick. In a moment, the Frederick operator telegraphed, "Now I will go."

In a short while the telegraph machine began to record Porter's response.

"Colonel Gordon has his orders."

"Tell him to come down to the telegraph office and talk with me."

In a few moments the key began to respond again.

"Here he comes."

Over the telegraph wire, Gordon told Porter about the three hundred cavalry and infantry and the scouts who had been seen in the vicinity of Harpers Ferry. Then he summarized the dispatch about the advance of six thousand men. He concluded that in his view he would probably be attacked at daylight.

"Well, General Banks' instructions are to dispute the passage of fords," Porter responded, "and if too strongly pressed, to retire slowly towards Buckeystown. Colonel Donnelly has two pieces of artillery, which he is directed to send to you if required. Call on Colonel Geary to send you two by express train. Can the enemy ford the river? I suggest you send your baggage to the rear. Daylight will show the enemy not so strong as represented. Send a messenger to Colonel Leonard to withdraw toward Boonesboro and Buckeystown and send your baggage there; but don't retire entirely without making your enemy feel you. He will not follow or attack a determined front."

It was two o'clock when Gordon said a telegraphic good night to Porter, mounted his horse, and returned to camp. He roused his field officers and told them the news. The men were awakened, tents struck, horses harnessed, wagons packed, fires lighted, and rations cooked.

Gordon sent dispatches to the regiments on his right and left and prepared to receive the Rhode Island battery that would be sent to him. Having done all he could to be ready, he fell exhausted on a bundle of straw and slept. He awakened to a faint daylight creeping over the surrounding mountains, pointing into the trees, and slowly driving the shadows from the gorge bottomed by the Potomac River.

During the day, he received conflicting orders from Banks and Fitz-John Porter and in the afternoon re-entered Harpers Ferry to complete the destruction of the flour mill and its contents. When this was done, he destroyed the remaining supplies in Harpers Ferry.[26]

That day, the structure of command in the east changed in a way that served McClellan well and must have pleased him. He had originally been assigned to command the Division of the Potomac, which had in it the Department of Northeast Virginia under McDowell and the Department of Washington under Mansfield. He had wanted to abolish the departments and divisions but been frustrated, as always, by General Scott. Now, Banks's Department of the Shenandoah was merged with McClellan's departments. At once, McClellan formed the Army of the Potomac, which was composed of all military forces in the former Departments of Northeastern Virginia, Washington, Baltimore, and the Shenandoah. Banks's troops became an infantry division in the Army of the Potomac.[27] This did not end his disagreement with Scott about departments and armies, but it did give him his way locally. What would happen in the future if he took his army into another department remained to be seen. Problems of that sort, a distant thought if in his mind at all, could be addressed later.

Now that Banks was under his command, McClellan ordered him to cross to the eastern bank of the Monocacy River, a tributary of the Potomac between Poolesville and Point of Rocks. Banks's position at Sandy Hook and Buckeystown was too far from the capital and the forces protecting its north flank. He was to leave one regiment to cover the river above Harpers Ferry and another from the Ferry to the mouth of the Monocacy, the main body of his division to be in the vicinity of Hyattstown and Darnestown. There he would hold the ground between Stone and McCall. His supply base he changed from Frederick to Baltimore or Washington. This would allow him to cover the Potomac above Harpers Ferry but be able to join the Washington forces if the Confederates crossed below the Monocacy. His mission was to oppose any crossing, avoid being severed from the capital forces, and protect the Baltimore & Ohio Railroad without weakening himself by detachments. The uncertain condition of Maryland made exclusion of all Rebel forces, even small ones, important.[28]

The following morning, August 21, Gordon was ready to withdraw to Buckeystown. He had barely completed the withdrawal of his new artillery from the hill and his pickets from the front when Rebels swarmed into Harpers Ferry.[29]

26 Gordon, *Brook Farm to Cedar Mountain*, 29-31, 36-38.

27 *M.O.S.*, 67, 81, 94.

28 *M.O.S.*, 93-95.

29 Gordon, *Brook Farm to Cedar Mountain*, 36-38; and Strother, "Personal Recollections," in *Harpers' New Monthly Magazine*, vol. 30, no. 196, 415.

Still unstable, Maryland presented more complex problems than a simple invasion by victorious Confederate infantry. The military peace established by Butler and precariously maintained by Banks was neither perfect nor complete. It did not mean political peace even if McClellan's weak measures with Banks and Stone were mistakenly thought by the Confederates to be strong. The threat of an ordinance of secession by the Maryland legislature continued to be real. The legislature had twenty-two senators, twelve of whom were needed to pass a law. Fourteen were not loyal.[30]

The Maryland secessionists, Lincoln and Seward believed, had not abandoned their hope of dragging Maryland into the Confederacy by a vote for secession, by a military thrust from across the Potomac, or by both. The Maryland legislature was to meet at Frederick on September 17, where a majority favoring secession were expected to take seats. An ordinance of secession was expected to be tendered and passed. This would be regarded as a call to active revolt by many Maryland residents who opposed federal rule. The Union members of the Legislature were thought to be divided about their course: go to Frederick to oppose secession or stay away to prevent a quorum.

The administration in Washington decided to take a bold step to prevent secession. From the beginning of Lincoln's Administration, Secretary of State Seward and the Department of State had responsibility for disloyal persons.[31] Seward would naturally be involved in any program to control the Maryland dissidents. On Saturday, September 7, Lincoln, Seward, and his son, Assistant Secretary of State Frederick Seward, arrived in a carriage at the headquarters of the Army of the Potomac.[32]

A few moments later McClellan emerged and took the vacant seat in the carriage, which then rolled rapidly toward Georgetown Heights. It seemed to be headed for an inspection of the camps and fortifications now covering the hills in the direction of Tennallytown on the northwest corner of the capital. But as the carriage reached the heights, it did not stop. No more than cursory glances were cast at the troops in the camps as the occupants of the carriage passed silently through them. The September day was bright. Once outside the military lines, they began to converse.

30 *OR*, Series 2, 1, 679.

31 Banks MSS (L.C.) letter dated September 16, 1861, from McClellan to Banks; Van Deusen, *Seward*, 288-289.

32 Seward, *Personal Recollections*, 174-175. Neither Secretary Seward nor anyone else dates this meeting except that Seward states that it occurred on a Saturday. From the known dates of other events, Saturday, September 7 is the only logical date. Regrettably, it is not in Miers, *Lincoln Day by Day*.

"General Banks will be expecting us, I reckon," observed Lincoln.

"Yes sir," replied McClellan. "I have telegraphed him. He will meet us at his headquarters at Rockville and will provide a quiet place for conference."

McClellan then asked in turn, "I suppose that General Dix has his instructions also."

"Yes," answered the president. "Governor Seward went over to Baltimore a day or two ago and spent some hours with him at Fort McHenry. So he is fully informed."

Seward smiled. "General Dix's views on the subject of hauling down the American flag are pretty well known. He can be depended upon."

The carriage traveled as fast as the rutted, broken road would permit. Some hours later it drew to a halt at the door of a tavern in the little village of Rockville, where Banks awaited them. Banks's aides and one or two squads of soldiers were with him. After greeting the visitors, the general led them to a small nearby grove which had shaded seats and no obstructing bushes. Here they could talk freely without being overheard, and they could see anyone who could see them. The participants had thought it wise not to trust the subject of the discussion to paper or to subordinates.

Forcibly preventing a legislative body from exercising its functions would be an act of despotism, they all agreed; but they also believed the legislature would be departing from its legitimate functions by inviting a public enemy to plunge the state into anarchy. Dissolution of the legislature, therefore, became commendable, proper, and necessary.

The fewest possible persons were informed beforehand. Generals Dix and Banks, commanding the eastern and western portions of the state (Banks along the Potomac and Dix in Baltimore), were to watch the members of the legislature carefully, particularly those expected to respond to the summons to Frederick. Banks, Dix, and McClellan agreed that loyal members could come and go as they pleased, perform their legislative duties, or stay away. Secessionists should be quietly turned back and not allowed to reach Frederick at all. Those favoring disunion had proclaimed their views loudly and were well known. The federal troops would have little difficulty, Lincoln remarked, "separating the sheep from the goats."

Late in the evening, and with agreement on the program, the carriage party returned to Washington. Sentries had taken their posts for the night, but McClellan had the countersign, and all reached their homes without incident.[33] McClellan sent

33 Seward, *Personal Recollections*, 174-178.

word to his subordinates along the Potomac River to be especially watchful because he had positive information that a concerted action was intended by the Confederates.[34]

On September 11, McClellan asked Secretary Cameron for a letter of instructions to Major General Dix to arrest six civilian residents of Maryland, three of whom were members of the Maryland legislature. Once in custody the men were to be taken by ship to Fort Monroe, then to New York City for incarceration. Allan Pinkerton would deliver the instructions, take charge of the prisoners, and review their documents.[35] While issuing the requested instructions to Dix, Cameron ordered Banks to prevent the passage of an ordinance of secession by arresting the secessionist members.[36]

At 10:30 in the evening Pinkerton arrived at Dix's headquarters, where he delivered the secretary's letter to Dix. Pinkerton believed it was too late to find all the men to be arrested. He and Dix agreed to delay the work until the next evening. The steamer, ready in the Baltimore harbor for a rapid trip to Fort Monroe, was held over. The delay would not be harmful because the legislature was not to meet until Tuesday, September 17.[37]

Before the secessionists could attend, the two generals, both Democrats, carried out their instructions faithfully, with tact and with discretion. By September 14, fourteen men were imprisoned in Fort Monroe; and pursuant to orders from McClellan,[38] Banks had readied Lieutenant Colonel Thomas B. Ruger of the Third Wisconsin to arrest the remainder of the legislature, including the heads of both houses, secretaries, clerks, and subordinate officials.[39] This left the Union members of the legislature in control. No ordinance was adopted, Baltimore remained peaceful, and Maryland continued quietly in the Union.[40]

The events in the Departments of Baltimore and the Shenandoah involving Dix, Banks, and the civilian Maryland legislature could not have occurred without effect on the struggle for power at the head of the Union armies. McClellan's dismissive conduct toward Scott had again been validated, this time by his involvement with

34 McClellan MSS (L.C.) letter dated September 6, 1864, from Burns to McClellan.

35 *OR*, Series 2, 1, 678; *M.O.S.*, 146.

36 *OR*, Series 2, 1, 678-679; in *M.O.S.*, McClellan confused the date as September 10, rather than September 11.

37 *OR*, Series 2, 1, 679.

38 Sears, *McClellan's Correspondence*, 99, letter of September 12, 1861, by the editor from McClellan to Banks.

39 *OR*, Series 2, 1, 680-681.

40 Seward, *Personal Recollections*, 174-178.

Lincoln and Seward in important political events with military overtones.[41] Physically and intellectually Scott could have participated. Decades earlier he had dealt deftly with the North Carolina nullifiers, who were early versions of the secessionists. But he seems not to have been invited. If these circumstances had any effect on George McClellan, he concluded that his campaign of silence against General Scott had the tacit approval of the president and his primary cabinet advisors.

The strong steps in Maryland had stopped any attempt to secede but did not end secessionist sentiment or a desire to assist the Rebels. The Potomac River, unguardable over its length, was a porous wall through which information was passed by disloyal citizens. And while generals and Cabinet officers dealt with legislatures and legislation, the company grade officers responsible for the river still had delicate, unsolvable problems presented by the mixed population of Maryland.

Picket duty along the river did not have a huge army immediately available as it did between Alexandria and the Chain Bridge. Henry Ropes, one of the many highly educated Harvard graduates serving as company grade officers in the Twentieth Massachusetts, found picketing duty fascinating enough to send home a lengthy letter to his mother detailing his experience.[42]

On Saturday night, September 13, the weather was dark and rainy. Captain Casper Crowninshield, a wealthy, twenty-three year old graduate of Harvard University, class of 1860,[43] finished posting extra pickets before he took tea at the house of a secessionist name Chiswell. Two other men, Chiswell's brother, a dirty, Indian-looking boy of nineteen years, and Joe White, a man with light hair and complexion, were present. They were talkative. After tea, the younger Chiswell and White rode away on horseback. About 9:00 p.m. one of Crowninshield's sentinels reported seeing signal lights in the Chiswell house. Crowninshield went to a hill, saw the lights, and concluded without doubt that they were signals.

He posted men around the house with orders to arrest every man who could not give the countersign, then sent a lieutenant to report to Colonel William Raymond Lee and request further orders. The lieutenant returned with orders to arrest both White and the younger Chiswell. Crowninshield arrested Chiswell, who denied any knowledge about the lights. Crowninshield searched the house but found nothing.

41 Sears, *McClellan's Correspondence*, 99, 102, 565; *M.O.S.*; Ser. 2, *OR*, 1, 670-690.

42 Henry Ropes MSS (B.P.L.) letter dated February 10, 1862. Though this letter was written after Ball's Bluff, it evidences no reason to believe picket duty changed over that period.

43 Roger D. Hunt, and Jack R. Brown, *Brevet Brigadier Generals in Blue*, 138; *Report of the Class of 1860, Harvard College 1895-1900* (Cambridge, 1900). After the war Crowninshield would be described as a "gentleman of leisure."

Although he found the elder Chiswell to be "a plausible man," they had long been suspects. He was almost certain of their guilt or at least of their knowledge of the signals but did not think he could prove anything against them. Their slaves said White was a captain in the Confederate army. More to the immediate point, they said "Massa White be drefful smart. He cross river and come back no one know how."

Crowninshield ate his meals with the prisoners at Chiswell's house. They did not appear guilty, but Crowninshield knew they were. Many sources reported that both men had drilled a Rebel company in that area a month earlier.

On Sunday, September 21, 1861, Crowninshield released the younger Chiswell on parole; but early that evening the sentinels again saw signals from the house and answers from the other side. During the rest of the night everything was quiet. On Monday, September 22, 1861, Colonel Lee arrived, collected the prisoners, and took them to General Lander.

During the night of September 22-23, Crowninshield saw signals from the woods on his side of the river and was told by sentinels that they were answered from the other side. The men were taken to Stone on the afternoon of Monday, September 23. Stone asked them if they would take the Oath of Allegiance. They refused. He then made them take an oath that they would not give any signals or assist the Confederates in any way. They said the oath would hold good only so long as Maryland remained in the Union. If Maryland seceded, they would "secede."[44]

Around this time Stone decided to test his artillery on Confederate camps and earthworks around the mouth of Goose Creek. He took two batteries to the high bluffs at Edward's Ferry where he could see the redoubts north and south of the Creek. The guns could not reach the upper work, which was crowded with men. Still under construction, the lower work was well within range. A section of 10-pounder Parrotts took position in the hollow of the road while the others went to a position for a crossfire. Couples from the area came to watch.

The topographer who had drawn Stone his map of the area, offered his binoculars to the prettiest of the female guests.

"And can we really see the Southern soldiers?" she asked.

She could tell the color of their eyes, he told her, adjusting the glasses.

"How charming," she replied. "How romantic it seems. And are you really going to throw shells at them?"

The topographer confirmed their purpose.

"What! Without giving them notice beforehand? Ah, that will be cruel."

44 Casper Crowninshield MS diary (M.H.S.) entries dated September 13-24, 1861.

Not so cruel, he explained, as it might appear because the first shell would probably miss and they could hide.

"Ah, the gallant fellows! But it would be a shame," she said, proving the usual intelligence level for women on military issues, "if you should happen to hurt any of them."

"From the interest you express, Miss," giving her the benefit of the doubt, "I suppose you are from the South."

"No," she replied. "I have never been in Virginia." She sighed. Then she sparkled. "I had a cousin who once lived in Virginia for several years, and I do so love and admire Virginians."

The guns roared. The conversation halted. The Union gunners, true to form, covered the near earthwork with their first salvo. The Rebel construction crews scattered into the woods. The guns went for the distant work, but their fire fell short, and the Confederate occupants applauded their futility with gesticulations "disrespectful and contemptuous in the highest degree."[45]

45 Strother, "Personal Recollections," in *Harpers' New Monthly Magazine*, vol. 30, no. 196, 417-418.

Chapter 28

"I *must* ride every day for my army covers much space, and unfortunately I have no one on staff to whom I can entrust the safety of affairs—it is necessary for me to see as much as I can every day, and more than that to let the men see and gain confidence in me."

–McClellan to his wife

The Men of Headquarters

Shortly after arriving in the capital McClellan established his residence and headquarters in Captain Charles Wilkes's house, an elegant structure on the northwest corner of Jackson Square. There, he began to build the staff he would need for the large army he foresaw. And there, as one of his brigadier-generals later wrote, he "received the homage which always bows before power, there he welcomed the officers who flocked around him to ask from favor what their merit did not deserve." Headquarters were, he told Ellen in a letter, near the house occupied by her father's cousin while he was secretary of state to President Franklin Pierce. The general took the front three rooms on the second floor, Van Vliet the room behind them; then Key, A. V. Colburn, an aide, had the third floor.

Breakfast was at Wormley's, a restaurant on I Street around the corner. Occasionally, McClellan had it sent to headquarters. Each morning around 10:00 and each evening at 9:00 he received reports from his staff. Meetings and staff reports took place upstairs in the living quarters, where McClellan was always attended by Captains Edward McK. Hudson, N. B. Schweitzer, and A. V. Colburn, members of his personal staff. A growing group it was, composed of outstanding officers, and one of which he was justly proud. "A fine looking set," he reported home.[1]

On the ground floor the telegraph key rattled continuously, with everyone hard at work at his desk. The outside doors were always open. People came and went or sat and waited as their circumstances required. Headquarters had an air of democracy, an attitude of equality, like the English. No junior officer would think of rising to salute when a general entered.

The selection of the city as the location for his headquarters was natural but, like everything else he did, at least mildly controversial. In Washington, he could have constant, prompt, personal communication with the general in chief, the president, and Cabinet officers. That would be more effective, he no doubt believed, than the vulnerable technology of communication over distance. He does not seem to have considered that he might have been better served if he had been immune from presidential "drop-in" visits that became customary in the evening[2] or that were routine for many others who wished to see the country's principal military leader. At once he found that the crush of work required him to decline invitations for dinner from prominent officials and for other social events.[3] Quickly, he began to refuse to meet civilians not directly concerned with his army.[4] Even his military subordinates found it difficult to see him;[5] and in a short while he would decide that he really needed to be free of the president's visits.[6]

In early October, Lincoln went to see McClellan at his headquarters. Brigadier General Van Vliet, McClellan's quartermaster general, was at work in the offices.

"Well," said Lincoln, "is George in?"

1 Comte de Paris MS diary (large diary) (A.N. de la M. de F.) entry dated September 28, 1861; Sears, *McClellan's Correspondence*, 84, letter dated August 13, 1861, from McClellan to his wife and, 89, letter dated August 23, 1861, from McClellan to his wife; De Trobriand, *Four Years*, 139.

2 Comte de Paris, in *B&L*, 2, 112-114; Burlingham, *Hay Diary*, 24-32, entries for the months of October and November.

3 Sears, *McClellan's Correspondence*, 70, letter dated, July 27, 1861, from McClellan to his wife.

4 Milroy MSS (Indiana Historical Society) letter dated September 6, 1861, from Colfax to Milroy. Ordinarily, he refused his presence to civilians, including members of congress, unless they were accompanied by the president.

5 Heintzelman MS diary (large diary) (L.C.) entry dated November 29, 1861, and generally, entries for November; DePeyster, John Watts, *Personal and Military History of Philip Kearny Major-General United States Volunteers* (New York, 1869), 225, 226, letter dated February 19, 1862, from Kearney to n.a. (DePeyster, *Kearny*).

6 Sears, *McClellan's Correspondence*, 113, letter dated October 31, 1861, by the editor, from McClellan to his wife.

"Yes, sir, he's come back but is lying down, very much fatigued. I'll send up, sir, and inform him you wish to see him."

"Oh, no. I can wait. I think I'll take supper with him. Well, and what are you now—I forget your name—are you a major, a colonel, or a general?"

"Whatever you like to make me."

The next time the president visited a precisely instructed orderly rebuffed him directly. McClellan had gone to bed, the orderly told him, and could not be disturbed even for the president.

Ten minutes later "Bull Run" Russell, the correspondent for the London *Times*, appeared wishing to see the general. The orderly gave him the same response.

"The general's gone to bed tired and can see no-one. He sent the same message to the president who came inquiring after him ten minutes ago."[7]

At least a few men believed he would have been better served if he had established his headquarters and residence across the river with his army.[8]

But his growing army was not deprived of his presence or his inspiration. Almost daily, he spent long hours in the saddle visiting his various commands and making himself familiar to all. Frequently, he stayed overnight with one of his units.[9] As he wrote his wife, "I *must* ride every day for my army covers much space, and unfortunately I have no one on staff to whom I can entrust the safety of affairs—it is necessary for me to see as much as I can every day, and more than that to let the men see and gain confidence in me."[10]

On a tour of inspection near Bailey's Cross Roads he and Israel B. Richardson arrived at the Second Michigan with their escort. Was the regiment "ready for a brush," McClellan asked.

The men replied, "Yes."

He then said he would "risk the night with us," recorded a junior company grade officer in his diary that evening, noting indirectly that this showed, among other things, confidence in the troops. The officer continued, "I do not like to see them exposing themselves so much. I know that if I knew of Beauregard coming out in

7 Comte de Paris MS Diary (large diary) (A.N. de la M. de F.) entry dated September 28, 1861; Russell, *My Diary*, 256-257, entry dated October 8, 1861.

8 Sherman, *Memoirs*, 1, 191-192; Rusling, *Men and Things*, 24-25.

9 Comte de Paris MS diary (large diary) (A.N. de la M. de F.), entries dated October 9, 10, 11, and 12, 1861; Sears, *McClellan's Correspondence*, 75, 81, 89, 90-91, 92, letters dated August 2, 1861; August 8, 1861; August 10, 1861, by the editor, and August 23, 1861, August 25, 1861; August 31, 1861, from McClellan to his wife; Rusling, *Men and Things*, 25; *M.O.S.*, 69.

10 Sears, *McClellan's Correspondence*, 95, letter dated September 6, 1861, by the editor, from McClellan to his wife.

that way toward our camp I would try to shoot him. They go out in sight of the enemy every day. They went out again today just after dinner."[11]

The end of these long days was unpredictable and irregular. "Dinner . . . takes its chances," McClellan wrote home, "& generally gets no chance at all, as it is after ten o'clock when I get back from my ride & I have nothing to eat all day."[12]

What kind of man was McClellan? What personality traits did he bring to the command? Consistent with his upbringing as a patrician and his affinity for aristocratic Southerners, he was dignified, reserved, friendly, quiet, and magnetic. He had splendid talents as an organizer, administrator, and drillmaster. His distaste for, even disgust at, the volunteer soldiers and officers of the Mexican War he had, to some extent, put aside; but he had doubts about their willingness and ability to fight. His personal intercourse with the men about him was marked by kindness, modesty, and courtesy, even toward his enemies, military and civilian. In fact, one of his close friends thought he treated his enemies better than his friends. His manners were simple and unaffected. Nor was his personal conduct subject to criticism. No drinker, no gambler, no womanizer, he was known for the highest truthfulness and integrity.[13]

A connoisseur of the arts, he read Latin and Greek, spoke French and Spanish fluently in a good voice without being very musical, and rode his huge horse, Dan Webster, like a professional horseman. His work, especially the mountains of organizational and administrative work necessary to create an army where none had existed, he did with tireless patience, energy, and good humor, which earned him the loyalty and support of all who dealt with him.[14]

11 Sears, *For Country, Cause and Leader (Haydon diary)*, 79, entry of August 28, 1861; John S. Applegate, *Reminiscences and Letters of George Arrowsmith of New Jersey, Late Lieutenant-Colonel of the 157th Regiment, New York State Volunteers* (Red Bank, 1893); letters dated August 4, 1861, and September 19, 1861, from Arrowsmith, to n.a.

12 Sears, *McClellan's Correspondence*, 89, letter dated August 20, 1861, by the editor, from McClellan to his wife.

13 Porter MSS (L.C.) letters dated November 6, 1889, from Smith to Porter; and June 1, 1896, from Wright to Porter; McLaughlin, *Olmstead Letters*, 4, letter dated September 12, 1861, from Olmstead to his father; Cox, *Reminiscences*, 1, 9, 57; Howard, *Autobiography*, 1, 167; Rusling, *Men and Things*, 36; Herman Haupt, *Reminiscences of Herman Haupt . . . giving Hitherto Unpublished Orders. Personal Narratives of Important Military Operations* (Milwaukee, 1901), 305 (Haupt, *Reminiscences*), 305; Schurz, *Reminiscences*, 1, 334; De Trobriand, *Four Years*, 350. The characteristics that appear repeatedly in the descriptions of McClellan are his quiet, reserved manner and his great dignity.

14 Porter MSS (L.C.) letter of June 1, 1896, from Wright to Porter; Rusling, *Men and Things*, 36; Averell, *Recollections*, 315-316; Ford, Worthington Chauncey, ed., *A Cycle of Adams Letters*, 2 vols. (Boston and New York, 1920), 1, 38, letter dated September 3, 1861, from Charles Francis Adams, Jr., to his father; Stephen Minot Weld, *War Diary and Letters of Stephen Minot Weld 1861-1865* (Boston, 1979, 2nd ed.), 76 (Weld, *Diary and Letters*).

In camp, he was genial, charming, and friendly to the men around him, a sociable, modest man "with a taste for jokes and good cigars." Always in uniform, he could nevertheless be approached by a junior officer or an enlisted man at any time. The hard-nosed confrontation born of a disagreement on an important subject was beyond him. Cursing, the emotional outburst, damning those who were wrong, vilifying his enemies, relief of a defaulting subordinate from command were not part of his personality.

In disagreement he showed a stubbornness exceeded by no man; but with his natural reserve, he always avoided antagonism. His resistance, according to a subordinate who saw him during the early days of the war and intermittently until the end of his military career, was unshakable but was of "the feminine sort." He would discuss, re-discuss, raise, and reraise a question.[15] Because many of the disagreements he had with his superiors involved time and McClellan usually wanted more, further talking gave him his way.

Great personal courage of the natural, relaxed sort would allow him to maintain his intellectual powers, presence of mind, and coolness of judgment in the heat of battle.[16] Officers of all ranks were expected to be fearless, set an example for their men by their indifference to danger, expose themselves to enemy fire even when their men were under cover, and walk or ride among their men during the fighting.

Many variations of courage would be shown during the war, and they would not produce the same conduct or the same results. Under fire some, like Robert H. Milroy, would be excitable, even lose all control. Run from the enemy? The thought did not exist for Milroy to consider it. But deranged by the excitement of battle, he would be disruptive on the battlefield. Some would be excitable and lose all sense of dignity like Winfield Hancock, even all sense of decency like Philip Sheridan. But unlike Milroy, neither Hancock nor Sheridan would lose the animal faculties that told them how to defeat the enemy.

Many would be cool as ice, relaxed and calm to sight, but only so because they used most of their mental energies to maintain their apparent composure. The negative consequence of this was the disruption caused, for example, by wounds like those suffered by Hooker at Antietam and later at Chancellorsville.

Leaders like McClellan, Andrew Atkinson Humphreys, and Darius N. Couch were simply not conscious of danger. They kept their intellects sharply focused on the events and forces confronting them, and suffered no disruption or diminution of their mental abilities by the mayhem about them or by their effort to keep calm.

15 Cox, *Reminiscences*, 1, 367.

16 Niven, *Chase Papers*, 1, 581, diary, entry dated June 28, 1865. Cox, *Reminiscences*, 1, 368; McClure, *Lincoln and Men*, 208, 210.

In his headquarters in 1861, as one of his young staff officers described him, "McClellan was surrounded for the most part by young officers. He was himself the most youthful of them all not only because of physical vigor, the vivacity of his impressions and the noble candor of his character and his growing patriotism but also by his 'inexperience of men.' His military bearing breathed a spirit of frankness, benevolence, and firmness. His look was piercing, his force gentle, the word of command clear and definite, his temper equitable. His encouragement was most affectionate, his reprimand couched in terms of perfect politeness. Discreet, as military or political chiefs should be, he was slow in distilling his confidence; but, once given, it was never withdrawn. Himself perfectly loyal to his friends, he knew how to inspire others with an absolute devotion."[17]

When McClellan first arrived in Washington, he contemplated a "main Army of Operations" numbering two hundred seventy-three thousand infantry, cavalry, artillery, and engineers, a "main Army" that was, of course, to be his.[18] By the end of October he had compromised on these grandiose plans and described to the secretary of war a more realistic "column of active operations" numbering one hundred fifty thousand men.[19]

Whatever the size of the army he would finally put in the field, no man could command it without a large, skilled, and efficient staff. More was necessary than a hill from which he could see the flanks of his forces in battle, sharp eyes, a pair of binoculars, and aides with fast horses. He needed men who could stand in his place on those inevitable parts of the battlefield that were beyond his field of vision and who could represent him fully, even to giving orders in his name but in his absence, men who knew his plan, who understood his inattentions, and who could accomplish them. These would be his personal aides.[20] And the bureau chiefs? They must assure him that the army would have a continuous supply of weapons, ammunition, clothing, and equipment; depots filled with food for the troops and forage for the animals; medical supplies, as crude as they were by comparison with today's medical armamentarium; accurate records; and communication of his orders to his far flung units in camp, on the march, and in battle.

17 Comte de Paris in *B&L*, 2, 112-113.

18 Sears, *McClellan's Correspondence*, 71-75, memorandum dated August 2, 1861, by the editor, from McClellan to Lincoln.

19 Sears, *McClellan's Correspondence*, 114-119, letter dated October 31, 1861, by the editor, from McClellan to Cameron.

20 Webb, *Peninsula*, 3-6, and select entries. For an anecdotal account of his aides at work on the battlefield, see Steven R. Jones, *The Right Hand of Command: the Use and Disuse of Personal Staffs in the American Civil War*, chap. 2, 12-31 (Mechanicsburg, 2000).

McDowell had begun with a handful of officers, not nearly enough even for the tiny army he took into battle on July 21. In spite of the many mishaps he suffered, he might have carried the day had he not been failed by his staff. Its small size hampered him. Its inexperience complicated his preparation for the advance. Its incapabilities crippled his attack. And its failure of judgment cost him the turning point in the battle on Henry House Hill. McClellan had recognized at least part of the problem and obtained legislation authorizing an essentially unlimited number of aides. These men, his aides, his personal staff, would do his bidding, carry his messages, and see that his orders were executed. They would not and could not act independently on his behalf.

The officer corps came from two independent authorities, the federal government and the state governments. Neither had authority over the other. Each governor was his own authority and controlled the appointment of officers in his regiments. Officers in the Regular Army and all general officers were appointed by the federal government. A true pool of officers for assignment where they were needed did not exist. All officers appointed by the governors, like officers commissioned upon graduation from the Military Academy, had specific places in their regiments. Unassigned company and field grade officers, men who did not have a specific position in a specific regiment, did not exist. Staff officers were taken from the regiments but continued to hold their regimental assignment even while they did not serve with the regiment. Their unoccupied slots could not be filled by another appointment or a promotion.

A member of the prestigious Schuyler family of New York thought staff service, particularly at army headquarters, guaranteed an officer recognition throughout the army, even if it did not increase his rank. That alone was a good thing. Living at headquarters rather than with the "crunchies," staff officers had the greatest comfort possible under the circumstances; and when taking his staff appointment, the officer left his regiment but retained his rank and position in the regiment even though he did not continue to serve in it.

"[I]f I go," wrote Schuyler to his father, "I become more generally acquainted and known to those men—who hereafter will no doubt be of service to me—and when I return to my Regiment: in a year or even less—I come back to my same position i.e. Captain: but with an increased knowledge of persons and things—in a much greater circle of acquaintances both personal and official—than five years of line duty could give me . . ."[21]

21 Philip Schuyler MSS (New York Historical Society) letter dated November 15, 1863, from Schuyler to his father.

Unit commanders disliked losing their subordinates to staff positions. Asked to approve a staff appointment for one of his company grade officers, one senior commander, responded ferociously:

> This application for the transfer of Lieutenant Crossman 10th U.S. Infantry is most respectfully *disapproved*. Scarcely a day passes without an appointment from other Corps or Divisions for the removal of some officer of my Command, to other spheres of duty. My best officers are taken from me and my Regiments are so weakened that in some of them but a *single captain* remains for duty.
>
> I have already furnished the Third Corps with Major Hayden who should command the 10th U.S. Infantry and the Second Division same Corps with Captain Poland Second U.S. Infantry who, were he present, would be in command of his Regiment. Every one expects something of the Regular Infantry, and nobody cares to recollect, that its officers are the main element of its strength and, in that forgetfulness are willing to lose sight of its own reputation altogether. It is not probable that Lieutenant Crossman will receive promotion even were he assigned to the staff of General Birney. I judge though from the fact that I have steadily advocated the promotion of two of my own Staff and the War Department has steadily refused it unless they would give up their rank in the regular service . . . I have uniformly opposed the transfer of my officers, and I beg that my wishes on the subject may be regarded.[22]

As Brigadier General Christopher C. Auger wrote to a fellow officer about his opposition to a staff appointment for one of his line officers, "It's a feeling I have a good deal of sympathy for. At the same time I must have my staff."[23]

Rather than raid a regiment with an existing officer structure, a general creating his staff could use regiments forming or with openings, especially in the early part of the war. If he had identified the person he wished to appoint to his staff, he could arrange to have that man commissioned in a new regiment with the understanding that the officer would come immediately to his staff. James S. Wadsworth, to become a general soon, would select as one of his personal aides, James H. Kress, a West Point cadet who preferred to serve rather than finish school. "Some difficulties

22 N.A. RG 94, reel 6, no. 322, DB 1863, endorsement dated May 28, 1863, by George Sykes; previous correspondence including letter dated June 9, 1863 from Birney to Thomas; letter dated May 17, 1863 from Birney to Seth Williams; endorsement dated May 28, 1863, by Sickles; and endorsement dated May 29, 1863, by Sykes; endorsement dated June 1, 1863, by Meade; and endorsement, dated June 2, 1863, by Joseph Hooker; Howard MSS (Bowdoin College) letters dated October 19, 1861, and November 4, 1861, from Charles Howard to Oliver Howard; Hyndman, *History of a Cavalry Company*, 30.

23 Collection (American Wars, Civil War Union Generals) (P.H.S.) letter of January 4, 1862, from Auger to Patrick; Joinville, *Army of the Potomac*, 52; Hyndman, *History of a Cavalry Company*, 29-30.

have arisen as to the acceptance of the Resignation of Cadet Kress," Wadsworth wrote to Governor Morgan of New York, "and if you have not forwarded him a commission, as I requested in Col. Lords Regiment, please withhold it until further advised. I should be gratified by a commission as Second Lieutenant for my son Craig W. Wadsworth in any of my Regiments where a vacancy may exist."[24]

When the higher ranking line officers made "raids" for their staff officers, nothing could compete with the huge promotions available to junior officers in the line commands. A cure that would preserve skill and experience in the staffs arrived at headquarters upon the appointment of a chief of topographical engineers for the Army of the Potomac.

The day he received command of the topographical engineers, Major Andrew Atkinson Humphreys proposed to McClellan that his topographical officers should at least be given temporary increases in rank and pay. McClellan expressed approval and requested a statement in writing. Prompt, proper, and punctilious, as he always was, Humphreys wrote a concise page-and-a-half letter explaining the problem, giving examples, and suggesting the solution.

"I beg to propose to the Commanding General," he wrote, "that he should[,] so far as it lies in his power, carry out the views approved by him of confirming additional temporary rank upon Officers of the Corps of Topog. Engineers on duty with Armies in the field . . . Lieut. Abbott has been offered the command of a regiment of volunteers more than once, but permission to accept it has been refused on the ground that his services were more valuable in the duties of his Corps. Lieut. Poe now commands a regiment, but if the additional rank proposed were confirmed he would doubtless consider it no hardship to return to Corps duties. I do not find a single Officer of Topog. Engineers in my command below the rank of Major, the officers of lower-grade preferring to serve with increased rank in the volunteer service. Conferring this additional rank would induce them to seek to return to the duties of their own Corps." McClellan in turn recast the letter for his signature seeking the appropriate legislation from Senator Henry Wilson and his Committee on Military Affairs.[25]

24 Edwin D. Morgan MSS (New York State Library) letters dated July 15, September 10, and September 19, 1861, and March 26, 1862, from Wadsworth to Morgan; Heitman, *Historical Register*, 1, 609. The quoted letter is dated September 19, 1861. During the war Wadsworth resigned which probably forced Kress to switch from the volunteers to the Regular Army, from infantry to ordnance, and from lieutenant colonel to second lieutenant. Kress retired after 1900 as a Regular Army lieutenant colonel in the ordnance. *Heitman, op. cit. supra*. Both became his aides.

25 Andrew Atkinson Humphreys MSS (Pennsylvania Historical Society) draft letter dated March 5, 1862, from Humphreys to Marcy and March, 1862, from McClellan to Senator Wilson.

The staff of a general officer had two parts: his personal aides and the bureau heads. McClellan's personal aides, selected by him, reflected his personality, his beliefs, his likes and dislikes, and his circumstances. On the recommendation of the Prussian minister to the United States, McClellan took two Germans as aides on his personal staff, both of whom were typical of McClellan's mentality. Baron Paul von Radowitz, a member of a noble German family, was handsome and carried himself with a very distinguished air.[26] The other was from an old military family, his father having been a general and his brothers and cousins lower ranking officers in the Austrian army.[27] Others saw this as a rejection of things Americans, a loss of "our previous simplicity" and an undesirable adoption of a large European staff composed of high titles and foreign princes.[28]

More traditional Americans on McClellan's staff were Captain N. B. Schweitzer, First United States Cavalry; Captain Edward McK. Hudson, Fourteenth Infantry; Captain Lawrence A. Williams, Tenth Infantry;[29] Captain William F. Biddle, who had held a civilian staff position with McClellan the railroad man in Chicago and Cincinnati before the war; and Arthur McClellan, the general's younger brother.[30] As time passed, McClellan collected a number of bright, recent graduates of the Military Academy: Wesley Merritt, Alexander Stewart Webb, John Wilson, George Armstrong Custer, and James Harrison Wilson, a hard-working, hard-riding group.[31] His staff would produce, among other things, two of the best cavalry officers in American history. An early member of this most personal part of his military family was Judge Thomas M. Key, who had been involved in the scrape with Simon Buckner in Cincinnati.

In September, McCellen met the Prince de Joinville, a member of the French royal family, and his two nephews, Robert D'Orleans, Duc de Chartres, and his brother Phillipe d'Orleans, Comte de Paris and distant heir to the throne of France. The two brothers were sons of the direct heir to the throne. The prince was traveling in the United States at the outbreak of the war in order to place his sixteen-year-old son in the naval school at Newport, Rhode Island.[32]

26 Cecil D. Eby, Jr., ed. *A Virginia Yankee in the Civil War: the Diaries of David Hunter Strother* (Chapel Hill, 1961), 4, entry dated February 27, 1862, (Eby, *Strother Diary*).

27 *M.O.S.*, 144.

28 Kearny MSS (L.C.) letter dated December 3, 1861, from Kearny to Parker.

29 Sears, *McClellan's Correspondence*, 87-88, General Orders, No. 1, dated August 20, 1861.

30 Military Historical Society of Massachusetts MSS (John C. Ropes letters) (B.U.) letter of March 27, 1985, from Biddle to Ropes.

31 Wilson, *Under the Old Flag*, 1, 103.

32 *M.O.S.*, 144.

The two nephews believed the Great American Conflict presented an opportunity. If the North won, Phillipe confided to his diary, "[W]e will have undertaken a great campaign. Our name will be linked to the restoration of a great liberal government, an ally of France with a great destiny for which we will have earned strong feelings in the country. We will have worn a Republican uniform into victory which, in the eyes of those we rely on in France, is wrong."[33]

They decided to take a chance. In Washington in September of 1861 they offered through Seward their services to the United States Army.[34] A European serving in the Department of State

> warned the government against admitting the Count of Paris, saying that it would be a *deliberate* breach of good comity towards Louis Napoleon, and towards the Bonapartes, who prove to be our friends; I told them that no European government would commit itself in such a manner, not even if connected by ties of blood with the Orleans. At the start, Mr. Seward heeded a little my advice, but finally he could not resist the vanity to display untimely spread-eagleism, and the Orleans are in our service. Brave boys. It is a noble, generous, high-minded, if not altogether wise, action.[35]

Lincoln welcomed them personally, and they reported for duty on McClellan's staff on September 20.[36] A few days later their commissions arrived from Seward.[37]

Robert, the duc de Chartre, had received a military education at the military school at Turin. Reflecting his fair complexion and fine appearance, he was happy, active, and lively with a frank, easy conversational manner. A lower-class joke told by a trooper was as welcome to him as a well-told anecdote.

Phillipe, the Comte de Paris, had been given military instruction by his tutors. He was tall, lean, awkward, youthful-looking, spoke with a high-pitched voice, had a friendly face, and rode less than gracefully. In conversation, both formal and informal, he avoided the subject of his role as pretender to the throne of France. Freely and sensibly he spoke on general subjects, and he judged the characteristics of the American military forces well.

33 Comte de Paris MS Diary (large diary) (A.N. de la M. de F.) entry dated October 22, 1861.

34 *M.O.S.*, 144-145.

35 Gurowski, *Diary*, 1, 101, entry dated September, 1861.

36 *M.O.S.*, 144-145.

37 Comte de Paris MSS (A.N. de la M. de F.) letter dated September 25, 1861, from Seward to Comte de Paris; Lonn, *Foreigners in the Union Army*, 277-279.

Although they were officially guests at headquarters, they acted as aides to McClellan, bearing dispatches, making reconnaissances, sharing the dangers of an aide's life like the other aides, making friends with their peers, and blending into the general's staff as if they were young Americans.[38] As Lincoln's secretary described them, ". . . the Royal blood in their veins does not prevent their being very intelligent, amiable, and courteous gentlemen who impress very favorably everyone that meets them."[39]

Because of their unusual family status, they extended their relationships beyond an ordinary circle of friends, as they knew they must; and they did not belong to any clique. They came and went freely, associating comfortably with McClellan's general officers.[40]

While the army remained in Washington, they lived in a house on I Street and were frequent visitors at the Seward house. At lunch one day, the secretary of state asked about their situation in the army.

"I should think your names and titles might occasion some embarrassment. What do your brother officers call you?"

The Duc de Chartre laughed.

"Oh!" he said. "That is all arranged. My brother is Captain Paris, and I am Captain Charters. And we are excellent friends with all our comrades."[41]

With the Prince de Joinville and the d'Orleans brothers were two men, a physician and a *chasseur-á-pied*, the latter a man of great size who would not mount a horse. The faithful *chasseur* followed his royal charges on foot like an ordinary infantryman. Being men of wealth and station the princes had their own little establishment, which McClellan found to be "the jolliest in camp." Severely burdened by the size of his command and its unreadiness, McClellan would seek relief from the stress of the day by visiting them to hear "the laughter and gaiety that resounded from their tents."[42]

Because any role the members of the House of Orleans might play on his staff had potential international implications, McClellan had sought approval from Seward and the State Department. On September 21, 1861, he was sent a letter

38 Eby, *Strother Diary*, 4, entry dated February 27, 1862; Burlingame, *Hay Diary*, 25, entry dated October 10, 1861; *M.O.S.*, 144-145; Evan R. Jones, *Four Years in the Army of the Potomac: A Soldier's Recollections* (London, n.d.), 64 (Jones, *Four Years*); de Trobriand, *Four Years*, 139-140.

39 Nicolay MSS (L.C.) letter dated September 20, 1861, from Nicolay to Therena.

40 Seward, *Reminiscences*, 186.

41 Nicolay MSS (L.C.) letter of September 20, 1861, from Nicolay to Therena; Seward, *Reminiscences*, 184.

42 *M.O.S.*, 144-145.

saying the department had no objection to the use of the military services of the French princes.[43] McClellan was right to foresee a problem. The appointments angered the Emperor Louis Napoleon, the current French ruler, who did not favor any enhancement of Bourbon prestige; and they required the efforts of August Belmont to smooth relations at a time when uncertainty prevailed in America's foreign affairs.[44]

A few days later Seward mailed the Comte de Paris his commission as a captain in the United States Army. The president, he said, had agreed to the three conditions: no oath that would modify his allegiance to France would be required, he could resign at any time he wished in order "to obey the cause of duty in France, or in Europe, and he would be allowed—gratefully—to serve without compensation."[45]

The Prince de Joinville was the son of King Louis Phillipe of France. Tall, slender, but bent in his figure, the prince was somewhat deaf and in colder weather wore an unattractive fur hat. He appeared to be undistinguished, but his appearance was deceiving.[46] About him McClellan wrote many years later, he "sketched admirably and possessed a most keen sense of the ridiculous so that his sketchbook was an inexhaustible sense of amusement, because everything ludicrous that struck his fancy on the march was sure to find a place there. He was a man of far more than ordinary ability and of excellent judgment. His deafness was, of course, a disadvantage to him, but his admirable qualities were so marked that I became warmly attached to him as, in fact, I did to all three . . ."[47]

Although the prince held no official position, he frequently rendered "important service."[48] In the balance, the deaf, older uncle played a more important role than the two young princes. The "American government," most probably Secretary of State Seward, wanted de Joinville to command a naval expedition. To do that he would have required superior rank, an appointment with political and emotional overtones that would have engendered "jealousy and mistrust." It could not be done. "Therefore, he dedicates himself to an amateur's role . . . but he can do a lot and be more useful to the Americans than in an official position . . ." He went everywhere

43 McClellan MSS (L.C.) letter dated September 21, 1861, from Seward to McClellan.

44 Seward MSS (University of Rochester) letters dated September 25, 1861, and October 21, 1861, from Belmont to Seward; Katz, Irving, *August Belmont: A Political Biography*, 104 (New York & London, 1968).

45 Comte de Paris MSS (A.N. de la M. de F.) letter of September 25, 1861, from Seward to Comte de Paris.

46 Nicolay MSS (L.C.) letter of September 20, 1861, from Nicolay to Therena; Eby, *Strother Diary*, 4, entry dated February 27, 1862; Seward, *Reminiscences*, 184.

47 *M.O.S.*, 144-145.

48 Lonn, *Foreigners in the Union Army*, 277-279.

with McClellan and discussed everything with him. Having McClellan's trust de Joinville gave him a great deal of advice. "As a consequence, my uncle may be the person who knows the most about everything here . . .," wrote Phillippe in his diary.[49]

Long before accumulating the "column of active operations," whatever its size, McClellan had begun to collect the bureau heads who would help him manage it throughout his career as commander of the Army of the Potomac. McClellan made his first significant report to Scott after his appointment by Governor Dennison less than ten days after the surrender of Fort Sumter. In it he asked assignment of his friend Major Fitz-John Porter as his adjutant-general and his father-in-law Major Randolph B. Marcy as his paymaster, among others.[50]

The next day he had witten to Allan Pinkerton, a private detective who had served him well while he was a railroad executive. A practice that would continue throughout McClellan's service in the war he established in this letter. "If you telegraph me, better use your first name alone. Let no one know that you come to see me, and keep as quiet as possible." Allan Pinkerton would become E. J. Allen.[51] A short time later, Fitz-John Porter being busy with Pennsylvania and Patterson, he asked successfully for Captain Seth Williams to be his adjutant general.

When he came east, McClellan brought Marcy, Williams, George Stoneman, and Pinkerton with him.[52]

49 Comte de Paris MS diary (large diary) (A.N. de la M. de F.) entry dated October 22, 1861.

50 Sears, *McClellan's Correspondence*, 7-9, esp 8, letter dated April 23, 1861, from McClellan to Scott.

51 Sears, *McClellan's Correspondence*, 11, letter dated April 24, 1861, from McClellan to Pinkerton; Allan Pinkerton, *The Spy of the Rebellion* (New York, 1883), 140-141 (Pinkerton, *Spy*); Edwin C. Fishel, *The Secret War for the Union: The Untold Story of Military Intelligence in the Civil War* (Boston, 1996), 53-54 (Fishel, *Secret War*); *D.A.B.*, 9, pt. 2, 92.

52 Sears, *McClellan's Correspondence*, 16-18, letter dated May 9, 1861, from McClellan to Scott; *M.O.S.*, 45, 122, 140-141.

Chapter 29

"The duties of the chief of artillery and the chief of cavalry are exclusively administrative and these officers will be attached to the headquarters of the Army of the Potomac."

–McClellan in general orders

The Bureau Heads and Command

The bureau chiefs, the chief of artillery, chief of cavalry, chief engineer, medical officer, provost marshall, and adjutant general, among the most prominent, were altogether different staff officers than the personal aides. Before the war friction had existed in the army over the independence of the staff bureaus, particularly the engineers, who had a peculiar peacetime alliance with civilian society.[1] Because of their high academic standing upon graduation, the

1 Skelton, *American Profession of Arms*, 232-233. The problems of independent status for staff organizations like the engineer units and engineer officers did not end in the nineteenth century. Both the air and armored forces served in the early twentieth century as subordinate parts of the infantry. The armored forces, a metallic replacement for cavalry, were not generally massed in their own organizations until World War II. Those who early advocated theoretical or practical creation of an independent armored arm, B. H. Liddel Hart, J. F. C. Fuller, Heinz Guderian, Charles de Gaulle, and George Patton, labored "long in the vineyards" to produce the

engineers received the best assignments, which made them objects of jealousy, criticism, and animosity among both Regular and volunteer officers in the less exalted branches. Their favored position annoyed those risking their lives in the infantry and cavalry.[2] McClellan had given no sophisticated thought to the household part of his army. Changes from the prewar, peacetime structure would occur; but experience in the field, rather than European example or analytical thought, would dictate them. To confuse matters more, some of the bureau chiefs had responsibility for combat troops; but, allowed no more than administrative authority,[3] they lacked the power to perform combat duties. Instead of leading field

extraordinarily successful armored forces of World War II and the Israeli army. Brian Bond, *Liddell Hart: A Study of his Military Thought* (New Brunswick, 1977), 4, 28-30; Kenneth Macksay, *Guderian: Creator of the Blitzkrieg* (New York, 1975), 40-52; Jean Lacouture, *DeGaulle: The Rebel 1890-1944*, 2 vols. (New York and London, 1990, Patrick O'Brian, tr.) *The Rebel 1890-1944*, 1, 129-178. An excellent example of the difficulties faced by innovators in unyielding, tradition-bound military organizations appears in the brief opening of Guderian's memoirs. After the First World War the Inspectorate of Cavalry projected heavy cavalry for battle and light cavalry for reconnaissance, all horsemen. Following early concessions to the infant armored forces, the Inspectorate yielded little or no role for tanks. They opposed, or never even considered, the organization of tank battalions, tank regiments, the great panzer divisions, corps, and armies. The Chief of the General Staff, a highly respected officer of the von Moltke school, opposed tank units and wanted the tanks divided among the infantry units. Heinz Guderian, *Panzer Leader* (London, 1952), 26-39, especially 32 and 36 for problems with Beck. In his memoirs Guderian describes the tribulations of the infant German armor between the two wars. First, the horse cavalry failed to recognize tanks as the successor to cavalry and mechanized infantry as the successor to dragoons. The Chief of the General Staff, General Beck, refused to allow the creation of armored units, treating tanks as a support weapon organic to an infantry unit like a machine gun. Only with the greatest difficulty was he convinced to allow the creation of a tank regiment. Nothing could have been farther from Beck's mind than a panzer division of tank and mechanized infantry punching a hole in an infantry line, racing tens of miles into its rear area, and causing chaos in deep sanctuaries as Rommel's Seventh Panzer Division did in 1940. Panzer corps, the huge tank armies of the Russians in 1944 and 1945 stood beyond the conception of all but the few thinkers. Capt. B. H. Liddell-Hart, ed., *The Rommel Papers* (New York, 1953), especially the map on page 23. Like armor, the air force did not end domination by the army until the middle of the twentieth century. These developments, obvious today, did not come any more easily than the recognition of artillery and engineers as independent combat arms in the nineteenth century.

2 Dwight Family MSS (M.H.S.) letter dated August 30, 1861, from William Dwight to his father; T. C. H. Smith MSS (O.H.S.) MS acct of 2nd Bull Run, 48-49; Skelton, *American Profession at Arms*, 101, 104-105, 225, 228-230; W. A. Ketcham MS Rem. (Indiana Historical Society), 70; de Peyster, *Kearny*, 226, letter dated February 19, 1862, from Kearny to n.a. Citing Jomini as authority for the proposition, Smith wrote "the mental quality & training of the engineer entirely unfits him for the part of a general in the field. The professional methods of mind are such as unfit one for the active requirements of war. War is not a science, as such, but an art, not a game of chess, but rather like those games which are half skill & half chance. We have only to look at the history of this great war to see the truth of Jomini's observation." Smith, MS *Bull Run* 2, 48; Gurowski, *Diary*, 1, 127, entry dated November, 1861.

3 *C.C.W.*, 2, 91 (Hunt).

artillery battalions, engineer brigades, infantry regiments, or cavalry divisions,[4] they were part of army headquarters. As John P. Hatch wrote to his father when he became chief of cavalry for McDowell, he would have office duty but hoped he would have an opportunity to distinguish himself and be mentioned favorably in dispatches.[5]

Nor could they, as staff officers, command troops of other arms even if they were the senior officer. Essentially thought to be subordinate to infantry commanding officers, all arms were treated as if they were part of the infantry, batteries being assigned to brigades and being denominated artillery "companies," an infantry term, and troops of cavalry being assigned as companies, not "troops," to the headquarters of brigades, divisions, and corps. Applying a significantly different science and coming from their unique, separate peacetime existence, the engineers had some chance for independence that would provide line authority for the chief engineer.[6]

The size, sources, and composition of the staffs for McClellan's army and its divisions and brigades remained a matter of controversy for some time. On January 29, 1862, Senator Henry Wilson rose on the floor of the Senate to describe a bill providing for the organization of division staffs. It authorized as staff bureau heads for each division commander one assistant adjutant general, one quartermaster, one commissary of subsistence, and one assistant inspector general. All would be majors and were to be appointed by the president. In addition, the division commander was to have three personal aides, one major and two captains, to be appointed by the president on the recommendation of the division commander. When an officer took a staff position, he automatically took the rank fixed for it by law, which was usually higher than the rank he carried in his line unit. But at the end of an officer's staff duty, he resumed his prior position in his regiment and reverted to his pre-staff rank.

4 By the end of the twentieth century, the combat arms were infantry, armor (cavalry), artillery, engineer, and communication. At the beginning of the Civil War the combat arm was the infantry, the "Queen of Battles." Others with combat characteristics, artillery, cavalry, and engineers, were service organizations subordinate to infantry.

5 John P. Hatch MSS (L.C.) letter dated March 17, 1862, from Hatch to his father. By this time McDowell had been given a corps; and according to Hatch, each division had one or two regiments of cavalry for which he would have some responsibility.

6 McClellan MSS (L.C.) letter of December 16, 1861, from Hunt to McClellan; *M.O.S.*, 114; Hunt, Henry Jackson, "Artillery," in *P.M.H.S.M.*, 13, 98; L. Van Loan Naisawald, *Grape and Cannister: The Story of the Field Artillery of the Army of the Potomac, 1861-1865* (New York and Oxford, 1960), 24-25 (Naisawald, *Grape and Cannister*). As an example Hunt noted that an infantry company under a second lieutenant, a line officer, and an engineer company under a first lieutenant, a staff officer, would be commanded by the infantry second lieutenant "because the engineer, as a 'staff officer,' is ineligible to command troops other than his own arm." Hunt in *P.M.H.S.M.*

Of course, the commanding officer could terminate the staff officer's assignment, which would end automatically when the commanding officer left the unit or was killed. The senior officer of artillery in each division was to act as chief of artillery and ordnance for the division with the grade and pay of a major. The four division staff officers, one major and the rest captains, were intended to outrank the comparable brigade officers. The bill also detailed officers from the army; but if they could not be detailed from the army, they were to be appointed by the president. Wilson acknowledged that this proposal would cause some additional expense.

In a long speech, Maine Senator William Pitt Fessenden opposed the bill and argued that all provisions for new officers should be stricken. "I think it is not only our right, but our duty," claimed Fessenden, "to keep the control of that matter with regard to an increase of the number of officers, and especially of these ranks, within our own power; and, therefore, I suggest to the honorable chairman of the Military Committee that it would be better to strike out all the provisions of this bill which provide for an increase of the number of officers at the discretion of the president for so it is substantially, and leave it in all cases a matter to be settled by congress."

He also opposed the automatic increase in rank for an officer who was junior to the staff rank when he received a staff appointment. This kind of promotion improperly satisfied the injurious tendency of officers "to have an increase of rank." And he saw no reason for the office of division quartermaster or division commissary. Every regiment had one, and every brigade had one. The only reason for one at the division level was symmetry, and the cost was too great.

Sounding like a spokesman for von Seeckt's hundred-thousand-man army, he argued that increases in the number of officers were not necessary. The men to serve as staff officers could be detailed from already existing units. They were available because the adjutant general had, with the concurrence of the secretary of war, "refused to detail officers in the Regular Army to duty in the volunteer service when called upon to do so by regiments in the field or by the Governors of States."

Wilson thought it would have been best if the Regular Army officers had been scattered through the volunteer regiments to give the volunteers training and experience. Many of the old privates and sergeants could have been good company grade officers in the volunteer regiments and would thus have given immediate experience to the army in the field. An act had been passed earlier authorizing the secretary of war to detail officers from the Regular Army "when he saw fit to do so, and it has been done to some extent, but has generally met the resistance of those who were so careful to preserve intact the little Army we had on hand . . ."[7] Some

7 *Cong. Globe*, 37th Cong. 2d Sess., January 29, 1862, 537-538.

comments reflected continuing hostility to a standing army. Other statements were hypothetically sound but actually absurd: like the Radicals, many senators thought volunteer officers were better than Regular Army officers because they were more zealous and more devoted to the cause.[8]

No different than his companions in arms, McClellan thought of a military staff far differently than his European counterparts.[9] No similarity did his ideas have to the German general staff,[10] whose members were easily recognized by the claret colored stripe down the outer seam of their trousers. The German staff officers had the skill, training, and authority to speak on behalf of their commander; and through the general staff network they had almost direct access to their commander's superior officers. Many reasons, therefore, existed for paying attention to them. In battle they could and would give orders in their superior's name, orders that seemed right to them under the circumstances but had never been discussed with their superior. They could rally a defeated army, give advice to their superior, and speak to the king.[11]

The interaction of line and staff in the nineteenth-century European army was intended to merge the tactical skills and personal courage of a line officer with the intellect, education, and judgment of a staff officer. Von Bulow, with the supremely effective assistance of his brilliant chief of staff, von Gneisenau, had crushed Napoleon's right wing at Waterloo; and when he later received an honorary degree at Oxford, he commented, "If I am to become a doctor, you must at least make Gneisenau an apothecary, for we two belong always together."[12] Throughout his time with the Army of the Potomac, McClellan had few officers he would trust with independent command and no men who could perform as his eyes, ears, and local decision-maker like a Prussian staff officer.

A comparison of the German general staff of the 1860s with the staff of the United States Army or the Army of the Potomac would leave a pair of unresolved questions for the Americans. First, could staff officers exercise the authority of line officers and command troops in battle? For the cavalry, answers to this question would appear in the sharp contrast between Alfred Pleasonton in 1863 and a short,

8 *Cong. Globe*, 37th Cong. 2d Sess., 1133-1136; 38th Cong. 1st Sess. 3196-3197; Tap, *Over Lincoln's Shoulder*, 18, 26, 46-47.

9 de Joinville, *Army of the Potomac*, 18.

10 *M.O.S.*, 111, 120.

11 Walter Goerlitz, Brian Battershaw, trans., *History of the German General Staff 1857-1945* (New York, 1953), 20, 21, 46; Archer Jones, *The Art of War in the Western World* (New York and Oxford, 1983), 392 (Jones, *Art of War*).

12 Craig, *Politics of the Prussian Army*, 62-63.

nasty-tempered man whose uncanny leadership ability and combat skill would rise to the fore in 1864 and 1865. For the artillery, a vigorous dispute between the commander of the Army of the Potomac and Henry Hunt at a little Pennsylvania town in 1863, and a lifetime quarrel between Hunt and Winfield Hancock, would highlight a lasting difference of opinion. Before McClellan marched his army against the enemy, he gave his answer to the question: "The duties of the chief of artillery and the chief of cavalry are exclusively administrative and these officers will be attached to the headquarters of the Army of the Potomac."[13]

Second, were the bureau chiefs administrative clerks or were they analytical contributors to, and planners for, events of the future? The war would end with no watershed event to answer the question.

Unlike McClellan's personal aides, the bureau heads were, by law, selected by the president. Of course, McClellan had much say in many of these appointments but not in all of them. Three he surely selected were Seth Williams, his father-in-law Randolph B. Marcy, and his classmate at West Point George Stoneman. Allan Pinkerton, whose status as a staff officer was never clear, served, in effect, as McClellan's G-2, his intelligence officer, throughout McClellan's time with the Army of the Potomac.

The United States Army did not have a chief of staff. In foreign armies the chief of staff controlled and accounted for the staff of the command. He also originated and issued orders in the name of the commanding officer and was, for practical purposes, his *alter ego*. In the fighting at Quare Bras, Marshal Grouchy was to keep the Prussians separated from Wellington's Allied forces at Waterloo. Von Blucher, commanding the Prussian forces and personally involved in the battle, fell to the ground trapped under his dead horse with French cavalry swirling past him. Battered by the French and leaderless, the Prussians at nightfall had two choices: withdraw east to a position of safety or risk further fighting with Grouchy's French troops by regrouping toward Wellington's left wing. Von Gneisenau, Blucher's chief of staff, took command and chose the dangerous course when he ordered a regrouping nearer Wellington. This made possible the arrival of the Prussian army on the French right and sealed Napoleon's defeat on June 18.[14]

13 *OR*, 11, pt. 3, 40. General Orders No. 110, March 26, 1862. The order is quoted in Edward G. Longacre, *The Man behind the Guns: A Biography of General Henry J. Hunt, Commander of Artillery, Army of the Potomac*, (New York, 1977), 99 (Longacre, *Hunt*). Today, the command of artillery units extends, as Hunt wished more than a century earlier, well beyond division level. By combining complex procedures and indirect fire, the fire of the guns of three divisions in line, for example, can be concentrated in front of one division if that becomes necessary.

14 Peter Hofschröer, *1815, the Waterloo Campaign*, 2 vols. (London, 1998), *Wellington, his German Allies, and the Battles of Ligne and Quartre Bros*, 1, 126, 321-322.

In the American armies, the adjutant generally served as a chief of staff but had no real power. He issued, "in the name of the commander, all orders relating to the discipline, instruction, movements, and supply of the troops, whether directly to the fighting organization or to the other staff corps; and through it pass to the commander all written reports on such subjects."[15]

Adjutant-General Major Seth Williams, wrote one officer, was:

> simple in manner, courteous in intercourse, constant in friendship, honest in his convictions, and tolerant of adverse opinion. His personal magnetism, inextinguishable cheerfulness, genial nature, and almost feminine gentleness endeared him to all who came within the sunshine of his presence. He never forgot the amenities of life: his politeness was proverbial, his patience was inexhaustible, and it was his highest gratification to devote himself to the pleasure of others. Hence it was that his unselfishness, modesty, sincere sympathy, and steadfast affection made him the loved companion of young and old of both sexes.
>
> Yet with all his light-hearted nature and avoidance of the asperities of life, Williams was a manly man, a firm patriot, and a brave soldier, who never neglected his fealty to a friend nor a duty to his country.

A simple, modest, devoted gentleman he was, but not the stuff of an alter ego for an army commander in battle. Over many years of service as a staff officer, Williams had mastered the paperwork of an army. Line command he had never held, and no exercise of line command would occur during the war. McClellan found him to be honest, careful, laborious, and conscientious but lacking self-reliance, drive, and initiative. "He was, if anything, too modest," McClellan wrote after the war.[16]

Frederick T. Locke, adjutant for the Fifth Corps, with tongue firmly planted in cheek, described the duties of an adjutant-general after the war. He "should be able to ride a horse without falling off, and to handle his sabre and revolver without wounding himself or killing his horse. He should know how to write the name of the commanding general and his own; and the larger the letters, the better. He should be adept in military correspondence, and be able with Chesterfieldian courtesy to apply the cold steel of official rebuke to subordinate commanders."[17]

15 Nathaniel P. Banks MSS (L.C.) copy of a letter dated September 16, 1861, from McClellan to Banks (the original is in the Seward MSS at the University of Rochester); *M.O.S.*, 110.

16 *M.O.S.*, 141; de Trobriand, *Four Years*, 139; Lieutenant Colonel William H. Powell, ed., *Officers in the Army and Navy (Volunteer) who Served in the Civil War* (Philadelphia, 1893), 407 (Powell, *Officers*).

17 Frederick T. Locke, "Recollections of an Adjutant General," in *Broadfoot MOLLUS New York*, 20, 42-43.

The army McClellan commanded was simply too large and too far-flung to be viewed at all moments or even at one moment by one man. But McClellan could not trust Williams with the kind of discretionary authority an alter-ego needed. Nor could he make his father-in-law, to whom he would be willing to entrust the discretion on occasion, adjutant-general. He solved his problem with a little sleight of hand: *de facto* his father-in-law, who served as his inspector-general, became his chief-of-staff.[18] Although Marcy would always attempt to execute McClellan's plans literally, he came in time to exercise discretionary power to issue orders in McClellan's name when the major general was not readily accessible. William F. Biddle, who had worked several years with McClellan the railroad man, who then served as an aide, and who remained devoted to the general long after he died, described this appointment: ". . . [A] worldly wise man, thoroughly convinced that his father-in-law was the very best possible chief of staff to be found, would have quietly appointed the *next best* man, simply because the other was his *father-in-law*. Not so McClellan, who simply wanted the very best, no matter who it was,—and was sure he had got it."[19]

A European with a pretense to knowledge about military structures confided to his diary, "McClellan makes his father-in-law, a man of *very* secondary capacity, the chief of staff of the army. It seems McClellan ignores what a highly responsible position it is, and what a special transcendent capacity must be that of a chief of staff—the more so when of an army of several hundreds of thousands. I do not look for a Berthier, a Gneisenau, a Diebitsch, or a Gortschakoff, but a Marcy will not do."[20]

Born in Greenwich, Massachusetts, on April 9, 1812, of a family that had come to America in 1685, Marcy graduated from the Military Academy in 1832, twenty-eighth in a class of forty-five, and was commissioned in the infantry. For more than a decade he served on the frontier in Michigan and Wisconsin, then for another ten years in Texas and New Mexico. This long period of arduous frontier duty was broken only by occasional stints of recruiting duty and service with Taylor's army on the Rio Grande in the War with Mexico, including battles at Palo Alto and Resaca de la Palma. Short campaigns against Indians in Florida, then against the Mormons in Utah included some fascinating and rugged frontier adventures. By the outbreak of the war his report of explorations in the southwest had been published by the Senate; and *The Prairie Traveler*, a practical guide

18 Burlingame, *Hay Diary*, 80, entry dated September 9, 1863; *M.O.S.*, 120.

19 Biddle, "Recollections of McClellan" in vol. xi, *The United Service* (1894), 467.

20 Gurowski, *Diary*, 1, 94, entry dated September, 1861.

covering no less than thirty-four frontier trails and giving the frontier traveler many helpful suggestions, was published by authority of the War Department. In 1859 he was promoted to major.

Married in 1833, he had three children: a son who died in infancy; Mary Ellen, the wife and soulmate of George McClellan; and a second daughter. From his many years on various frontiers, he was an outdoorsman and big-game hunter with a tall, broad shouldered physique and a military bearing. Unlike his son-in-law, who was always in uniform, he almost always wore casual civilian attire about headquarters. In August of 1861, he was promoted to colonel in the Regular Army.[21]

Knowing well the organization of European armies, McClellan felt that a major-general commanding an army should have a brigadier-general to do the administrative paperwork as adjutant and a second brigadier to assure the fighting condition of his troops as inspector general.[22] During the fall of 1861, Seth Williams, Randolph Marcy, John G. Barnard, William F. Barry, Andrew Porter, and George Stoneman were promoted to brigadier-general, probably at McClellan's request.[23] In spite of their stars they held anomalous positions in an army that could not define a modern staff;[24] and the Senate, which did not consider staff positions as important as line commands, resisted promoting staff officers to the rank of general. Senator Henry Wilson, chairman of the Committee on Military Affairs, wrote to Marcy that no one opposed their confirmation as brigadier-generals on personal grounds. "The opposition to you and Williams is that you are doing staff duties. But I think Senators are coming to understand that your duties are as important as field duties."[25]

George Stoneman, McClellan's chief of cavalry, a classmate in the outstanding Class of 1846 and one of the men on McClellan's July 29 list of recommendations for promotion to brigadier general, was undoubtedly McClellan's choice. Some members of McClellan's staff, including John G. Barnard, who had been McDowell's chief engineer, and William F. Barry, McDowell's chief of artillery, McClellan inherited. He kept Andrew Porter in his assignment as provost marshal for the capital until he appointed him provost marshal of the Army of the Potomac when it took the field.[26]

21 Comte de Paris MS diary (large diary) (A.N. de la M. de F.) entry of September 28, 1861; *D.A.B.*, 6, pt. 2, 273-274; *Cullum*, 1, no. 690; Warner, *Generals in Blue*, 310-311.

22 *M.O.S.*, 112.

23 *M.O.S.*, 108-110, 113-117, 124.

24 Skelton, *An American Profession of Arms*, 221-232.

25 McClellan MSS (L.C.) letter dated June 22, 1862, from Wilson to Marcy.

26 *M.O.S.*, 130-131. Only Barnard was not listed on McClellan's July 29 memorandum to Lincoln.

In 1836, young Andrew Porter, then only sixteen, had entered the military academy as a plebe; but a year later he resigned. When war broke out with Mexico, he obtained a commission as a first lieutenant in the Mounted Rifles, winning promotion to captain and a brevet to lieutenant-colonel, recognition of exceptional achievement by an army that did not have enough slots to reward by full promotion. A captain in the Mounted Rifles with fourteen years of service in Texas and the southwest at the fall of Fort Sumter, he was another beneficiary of the Scott Rule and was promoted to colonel on May 14, 1861.[27]

Handsome, stout, and well-proportioned, Porter had clear, strong eyes "beaming with intelligence" and luxuriant hair atop a fine head. By the outbreak of the Civil War, he had begun to put on weight. His family could not have hurt his standing for promotion. His grandfather had risen to colonel during the Revolutionary War, and to major-general of militia thereafter. His father served as territorial governor of Michigan, and his mother was a cousin of Mary Todd Lincoln. A charming mixture of good humor and formality with courtly manners, Andrew Porter was just the kind of man who would appeal to McClellan, a good friend, a brave man, and a true gentleman.[28]

Heading the equivalent of the modern, uniquely unpopular military police, the provost marshal, as McClellan defined his duties and Andrew Porter superbly executed them, had responsibility for all points of contact between the military and the civilian worlds. This was a delicate task under any circumstances but far more delicate in a civil war with loyal and disloyal citizens mingled and often indistinguishable. His duties included suppression of marauding, depredation, and disturbances by the army; prevention of straggling; suppression of gambling houses, drinking houses, bar rooms, and brothels; regulation of hotels, taverns, markets, and places of public amusement; searches, seizures and arrests; execution of sentences of general courts martial, including firing squads; handling of deserters from the enemy; handling of prisoners of war; managing countersigns; handling passes for citizens within the lines for purposes of trade; and handling complaints of citizens about the conduct of soldiers.[29]

Even though he could not join his good friend at the beginning of the war, Fitz-John Porter tried to help by suggesting men for his staff. Knowing that

27 Warner, *Generals in Blue*, 377-378; James Wilson, and John Fiske, eds., *Appleton's Cyclopedia of American Biography*, 6 vols. and 6 supplements (New York, 1887-1891), 5, 72 (*C.A.B.*).

28 Comte de Paris MS Diary (large diary) (A.N. de la M. de F.) entry of November 27, 1861; Averell, *Recollections*, 98; Warner, *Generals in Blue*, 377-378; *D.A.B.*, 8, pt. 1, 82; Heitman, *Historical Register*, 1, 798.

29 *M.O.S.*, 132-133; *OR*, 5, 30.

McClellan would be building a large organization requiring a broad range of skills, Porter recommended Surgeon Charles Stewart Tripler, who was serving as medical director of Patterson's Valley army and who wished to join McClellan. "A more able and willing assistant in his branch you cannot get," Porter wrote.[30]

Apparently accepting Porter's recommendation, McClellan arranged for the appointment of Major Tripler as medical director of the Army of the Potomac.[31] Born in New York City in 1806 and educated at the College of Physicians and Surgeons from which he graduated in 1830, Charles Tripler was an "energetic, spasmodic, crotchety, genial old man," according to George Templeton Strong. Tripler's first army assignment was a post on the Michigan frontier. As medical director to General Twiggs, he served at several western outposts in the Mexican War. After the outbreak of the Civil War, he became medical director for General Patterson in the Shenandoah Valley.[32]

When Tripler assumed his duties with McClellan's army on August 12, 1861, he found a large organization of completely inexperienced regimental surgeons who stood at zero on the learning curve for military medicine.[33] At the heart of the problems Tripler faced in his early tenure were the simple, routine changes from civilian to soldier. Describing a life now lost to most men through the ravages of "progress," he noted, "The individual man at home finds his meals well cooked and punctually served, his bed made, his quarters policed and ventilated, his clothing washed and kept in order without any agency of his own, and without his ever having bestowed a thought upon the matter. The officer in ninety-nine cases in a hundred has given no more reflection than the private to these important subjects. When the necessity for looking after these things is forced upon his attention, he is at a loss how to proceed. Too frequently he lacks the moral courage and the energy to make his men do what neither he nor they stipulated for or understood when they entered the service. To bad cooking, bad police, bad ventilation of tents, inattention to personal cleanliness, and unnecessarily irregular habits we are to attribute the greater proportion of the diseases . . ."[34]

30 McClellan MSS (L.C.) letter dated August 1, 1861, from Porter to McClellan.

31 Sears, *McClellan's Correspondence*, 75-76, letter dated August 2, 1861, McClellan to his wife; Heitman, *Historical Register*, 1, 970-971.

32 Nevins, *Strong Diary*, 3, 181, entry dated September 16, 1861; Maxwell, William Quentin, *Lincoln's Fifth Wheel: The Political History of the United States Sanitary Commission* (New York and London, 1956), 348 (Maxwell, *Fifth Wheel*).

33 *M.O.S.*, 126.

34 *OR*, 5, 83.

Unfamiliar with the deleterious effects caused by the lack of routine hygienic procedures, the regimental and brigade surgeons and their commanding officers had to learn them before they knew to make their men do them. Numerous other problems arose as both immediate and future concerns. They covered a broad range: the use of quinine and whiskey to treat "malarial disease," creation of regimental hospital funds, the best form of ambulance, organization of an ambulance corps, vaccination to prevent spread of smallpox, a regular system of inspections by officers from army headquarters, and for the Napoleonic battles to be fought, preparation to treat the Napoleonic numbers of wounded.[35]

Knowing the army would not go into winter quarters because McClellan intended to advance before winter, the medical director delayed winterizing the men's tents and other sleeping quarters. Finally, circumstances made it necessary whether or not the army advanced. In December, Tripler learned that some of the men were using fire pits in the ground inside their tents, an unhealthy heating method. Healthy alternatives were suggested to the troops and at last in January he recommended housing the troops for winter.[36]

Tripler found a bed capacity of two thousand seven hundred in hospitals above the brigade level. The Sanitary Commission believed the capacity should be five thousand, but foreseeing huge battles Tripler attempted to convince the Commission he would need twenty thousand beds in cities like Alexandria, Washington, Georgetown, Baltimore, Philadelphia, and New York. Others had begun to see the need for hospitals with large capacity in cities north of Washington even before McDowell's battle at Bull Run. Compromising with the Commission, he wrote McClellan on September 9, 1861, to request permission to contract for buildings capable of housing fifteen thousand men.[37]

Confronting the complexities of officer appointment by both state and federal authorities, the medical service, like the combat arms, fell victim to "federalism." This resulted in dispersion of effort and absence of overall direction. Surgeons were appointed to the regiments by the governors. Brigade and division surgeons did not exist at all. As long as the army was in position about Washington, the system was adequate. The real test was to come when the army took the field, and the result then no one could predict.[38] Nor did they foresee the magnitude of the test.

35 *OR*, 5, 83-85, 87-88, 89, 99, 102-103.

36 *OR*, 5, 84.

37 Union Defense Committee MSS (N.Y.H.S.) letter dated April 25, 1861, from Turner to Wood; *OR*, 5, 90, 100-101.

38 *OR*, 5, 77-78; George Worthington Adams, *Doctors in Blue: the Medical History of the Union Army in the Civil War* (Baton Rouge and London, 1952), 10-11, 25, 63, 71 (Adams,

Tripler found many men who were not truly disabled on the sick lists. Because the only hospital above the regimental level was the army hospital, the sick who did not remain with the regiment were carried as "absent-sick" and lowered the paper strength of the army. To reduce the number of absent men, Tripler initiated a policy of keeping them with their regiments when they were not severely ill. The army hospitals were cleared of many patients. The number and percentage of men "absent-sick" declined. But these indications of improved army-wide health lacked reality. The regimental facilities acquired full complements of men disabled by serious diseases like typhoid, malaria, and dysentery.[39]

Compounding the administrative problems, essential elements of medical care fell outside the control of the medical officers. Medical supplies and transportation were the responsibility of the quartermaster's department. Ambulances were supplied by the quartermaster. And the ambulance drivers were civilian contractors. Overall direction by the medical department could not exist. Once again, these conditions presented no severe problem as long as the army lay around the capital. But would that continue when the army took the field and everything inevitably changed?[40]

Legislation approved August 3, 1861, authorized the use of female nurses. The choice was generally between Protestant women and the Catholic Sisters of Charity. Writing to McClellan later in the fall of 1861, Tripler articulated the continuing prejudice against Catholics in an essentially Protestant country: "It is a very damaging position for any one to take and avow," he forthrightly explained to the general, "but in the honest discharge of my duties, though a Protestant myself, I do not hesitate to declare that in my opinion the [Sisters of Charity] are far preferable to the [Protestant women], being better disciplined, more discreet and judicious, and more reliable."[41]

While Tripler worked to create a medical service for the army, another organization grappled with the issues confronting him. It had powerful supporters, independence, imagination, creativity, and a very strong mind of its own. The

Doctors in Blue); Maxwell, *Fifth Wheel*, 19. McDowell's chief medical officer Surgeon W. S. King and his assistant lacked the power to compel a surgeon commissioned by one state to treat a casualty from a different state. Maxwell, *op. cit.*, 19. For an army of thirty-five thousand McDowell provided no care for his men above the regimental level; and during the battle had only one hospital, a spontaneous facility at the Sudley Church and a few outbuildings. Captain Louis C. Duncan, *The Medical Department of the United States Army in the Civil War* (Gaithersburg n.d. reprint; orig 1900).

39 *OR*, 5, 79, 94-95; Adams, *Doctors in Blue*, 71-72.

40 *OR*, 5, 102; Adams, *Doctors in Blue*, 6, 72, 75.

41 *OR*, 5, 102-103.

leaders of the United States Sanitary Commission, strong-willed, productive men, stood outside the lines of military authority. In June, Secretary of War Cameron had issued an order establishing "a Commission of inquiry and advice in respect to the sanitary interests of the United States forces." The Commission would have mixed leadership of five civilians and three army officers. On June 13, Lincoln approved Cameron's order. But he was uncertain that the Commission would be helpful and, in fact, feared it would not.

The volunteer infantry, thought to be from a higher social class than the infantry of the Regular Army, were believed to present different problems than the Regulars and might benefit from something different than Regular Army medical care. This was "an important factor in inducing the government to accept the offer of advice from a voluntary body." Surgeon General Clement A. Finley agreed to the formation of the Commission only after extracting the commitment that it would confine its efforts to the volunteers.

The civilian members of the Commission represented the professions, rather than business. They came from the eastern seaboard, primarily New York City, not from the West. The Commissioners of 1861 included the assistant surgeon general, the head of a government scientific bureau, two clergymen, a pair of lawyers, and a half-dozen physicians or physician-scientists. Alexander Dallas Bache, superintendent of the United States Coast Survey, regent of the Smithsonian Institution, and a great grandson of Benjamin Franklin, served with New Yorkers Henry W. Bellows, George Templeton Strong, Dr. W. H. Van Buren, Wolcott Gibbs, and Cornelius Agnew.[42]

In a very early meeting, the Commissioners appointed Frederick Law Olmsted general secretary or executive officer. Not yet forty at the time of his appointment, Olmsted was, in his own words, a "growler." According to a later historian of the Commission, Olmsted was "restless, anxious, irritable, and fault-finding." Though irregular and unpredictable in personal habits, he was the personification of order and efficiency in his professional commitments. Olmsted had already published tracts widely read across the United States that condemned the institution of slavery—not only because it was inhumane but also because he found it wasteful and inefficient.

The members of the Commission knew that the recent Crimean War had set a new low for the medical care of fighting troops. The death toll from disease had been four, seven, even ten times as large as it was from wounds in battle. In addition, for

42 Allan Nevins described the Commission as a "combination of specialized skill, sturdy common sense, and concentrated devotion to a great aim." In his opinion, nothing like it "had previously been known in American annals." Nevins, *War for the Union*, 1, 416.

every man who died from disease, scores suffered illnesses that adversely affected the strength and efficiency of the army.[43]

By the end of 1861, the Commission had recruited and hired fourteen physicians to inspect military camps and posts. The members created a schedule of inspections, and the inspectors trooped from one place to another to determine whether or not the installations complied with the requirements for good health. Wisely, the Commission saw that the medical officers provided care for the men while the Commission inspected to assure that it was done properly. Nevertheless, the Commission and its inspectors became involved in the delivery of health care. For example, they sometimes attempted to solve critical shortages of supplies and hospitals. In August, 1861, Bellows complained that short-term work giving cures for illness and comfort for soldiers impaired the Commission's handling of its real responsibility: prevention.[44] Tripler could look forward to dealing with the Commission as his equal because both the medical director and the Commission dealt with the same vital part of the army's life and neither had authority over the other.

On September 12, Olmsted, the Commission's secretary, and Henry W. Bellows, its founder and president, visited McClellan to discuss medical affairs. After an hour McClellan, Bellows, and Olmsted went to meet the secretary of war. McClellan sat casually on the sofa smoking a cigar, playing with a dog, and occasionally spitting on the rug. To Olmsted, he seemed "direct, frank and familiar as if he never saw a politician or heard of rank. The degree of his independence of political considerations, of red tape and circumlocution, was magnificent."

Henry Bellows saw the same man. "He spoke to the point with earnestness, honesty, and intelligence. His humanity and sympathy fitted him for earnest love of women and common soldiers," he wrote home.

"We are working for the same ends," McClellan said. "I have entire confidence in you. You know more of medical and sanitary matters than I do. Tell me what ought to be done and it shall be done. I do not care who is in the way nor what. He and it shall be overridden."

43 A parliamentary investigation and critical newspaper reports followed the Crimean War. Care of the health of the troops had reached an all time low for the troops of a civilized nation. In April 1856 the British army had 111,000 men. Of the 20,899 deaths, only 2,755, approximately ten percent, were killed in action, 2,019 died of wounds, 5,705 were discharged with disabilities. Losses from disease were more than 16,000. Maxwell, *Fifth Wheel*, 5.

44 Robert Bremner, *The Public Good: Philanthropy and Welfare in the Civil War Era* (New York, 1980), 39-44 (Bremner, *Public Good*); Maxwell, *Fifth Wheel*, 5-7; Charles J. Stille, *History of the United States Sanitary Commission Being the General Report of its Work During the War of the Rebellion* (Philadelphia, 1866), 109-138 (Stille, *History of the U.S.S.C.*).

The concurring remarks of Secretary Cameron promised "the most wonderful revolution in medical affairs."

"Find me a Larrey,[45] and he shall be at the head of everything and have everything he can ask for tomorrow."

The general turned to Olmsted. "I will do anything you will ask for your Commission, anything that you say will increase your usefulness in this Department."

Olmsted, a vigorous activist, was also careful. He must reflect before replying, he said.

McClellan responded that Olmsted should come to see him whenever he had anything to ask. The general would see him whenever he had time.

Cameron echoed these sentiments, then turned to Bellows. "You have never asked anything of me yet that you have not got it—and you never will."

They all took a drink of Pennsylvania whiskey, and the Commission members left. The clock showed midnight.[46]

The United States Sanitary Commission operated at the seat of power. By background, upbringing, and preference, bright, hard working, successful, and socially prominent professional men attracted McClellan. The board of the Commission with its powerful, prominent patricians included some of the best representatives of this class. A young patrician himself, McClellan found them kindred spirits.

The Commission already waged open warfare with Surgeon General Clement A. Finley and most of the time-honored policies of the Medical Bureau in Washington. Could Tripler perform his duties amid this turmoil? Could the Commission and the Bureau look forward to coordination and cooperation? Or would they produce conflict between different methods intended to achieve the same goals?[47]

45 Dominique Jean Larrey, the outstanding medical officer of Napoleon's army, served as surgeon-in-chief to the Imperial Guard. A baron, Commandant of the Legion of Honor, and Knight of the Order of the Iron Cross, an organizer, teacher, and inventor, Larrey was thought by the emperor to be the most virtuous man he had ever known and was a proponent of the principle that the most seriously wounded should be treated first (the line colonels wanted the slightly wounded treated first and returned to the line). Elting, *Swords Around a Throne*: *Napoleon's Grande Army* (New York and London, 1988), 229, 283, 291; McLaughlin, *Olmstead Letters*, 4, 198, n. 10, and 191, n. 31.

46 Bellows MSS (M.H.S.) letter dated September 12, 1861, from Bellows to his wife, quoted in Maxwell, *Lincoln's Fifth Wheel*, 27; McLaughlin, *Olmstead Letters*, 4, 196-197, letter dated September 12, 1861, from Olmstead to his father.

47 McLaughlin, *Olmstead Letters*, 4, 1, 3-12, 16-18, 243-244 (n. 1), 367 (n. 19); Bremner, *Public Good*, 49-50; Stille, *History of the U.S.S.C.*, 111-112; Adams, *Doctors in Blue*, 27-29.

The Army of the Potomac, McClellan believed, would confront and defeat the main Confederate army in the style of Napoleon, Jomini, and Mahan: one campaign by a huge army, ending with one great battle, a single Armageddon in which the enemy would not be defeated—he would be destroyed.[48] As McClellan saw it, this would be a difficult task. The Rebel army was flush with victory, infused with high morale, well-drilled, and ready for battle.[49]

McClellan's plans for his army would test the outer limits of the abilities of all his bureau chiefs. Tripler would find his test far beyond the greatest any medical officer had faced in the history of the American army, and the personal strain even greater.

48 The idea of a Napoleonic-style campaign ending in a single, monstrous, decisive battle, not unlike the Franco-Austrian War that ended with the Battle of Wagram, the Napoleonic campaign he had studied under the watchful eye of Professor Mahan at West Point after his return from Mexico, runs repeatedly through his personal and official correspondence, e.g., Sears, *McClellan's Correspondence*, 74, memorandum dated August 2, 1861, by the editor, from McClellan to the president; 75, letter dated August 2, 1861, from McClellan to his wife.

49 Sears, *McClellan's Correspondence*, 95-97, letter of September 8, 1861, from McClellan to Cameron.

Chapter 30

"For all present for duty of cavalry on the Upper Potomac, volunteers will suffice as they will have nothing to do but carry messages & act as videttes."

–McClellan to Banks

The Cavalry: Learning It All

Alexander the Great created—and often led personally—his Companion Cavalry, a powerful mass of Macedonian horsemen.[1] The Greeks and Macedonians made good use of cavalry on the battlefield. Their defeats had proven to them that a mass of cavalry mattered at critical times.[2] Centuries later, the young Napoleon Bonaparte found the cavalry assigned to his infantry divisions in small, ineffective units, less than a regiment. First, he concentrated them as full strength regiments. Then, he concentrated the regiments as a "Cavalry Reserve" under Marshall Joachim Murat, who would lead it to success, glory, and the huge ten-thousand-man charge at Eylau.[3]

1 Green, *Alexander*, 74-76, 177-179, 228-233, 396-397.

2 Spence, I. G., *The Cavalry of Classical Greece: A Social and Military History With Particular Reference to Athens*, (Oxford, 1993), 97-99 (Spence, *Cavalry of Greece*). Dixon, Karen R., and Southern, Pat, *The Roman Cavalry From the First to the Third Century AD*, (London and New York, 1992), 141-143, 144-146 (Dixon and Southern, *Roman Cavalry*).

3 Elting, *Swords Around a Throne*, 229; Chandler, David G., ed., *Napoleon's Marshals*, Pickles, Tim, "Prince Joachim-Murat," 341, 347 (New York, 1987).

McClellan, however, did not know his Napoleon as well as he thought. He splintered his cavalry into small units, none larger than a brigade but most no larger than a troop. He gave it no overall commander for battlefield leadership and no overall mission. "As to the Regular cavalry," he wrote Banks on the Upper Potomac, "I have directed all of it to be concentrated in one mass [the Reserve Brigade, a very small concentration] that the numbers in each company may be increased & that I may have a reliable & efficient body on which to depend in a battle. For all present for duty of cavalry on the Upper Potomac, volunteers will suffice as they will have nothing to do but carry messages & act as videttes." Were larger units necessary in the rugged terrain of Virginia?[4] Could they be effective if they were assembled? Was massed cavalry still useful in 1861?[5]

McClellan's plan for organizing the cavalry of the Army of the Potomac showed how little he understood the role it would play in the next four years even though he had been commissioned a captain in a cavalry regiment and had studied the cavalry forces of several nations in the Crimean War. Initially, he would assign one regiment to each division. When corps were formed, he would reassign the regiments to corps headquarters in the form of a "strong brigade." A small force would be detailed from the brigade to each division in the corps, merely enough for "the necessary duty." At army headquarters he would create a "cavalry reserve" of no predetermined strength. He perceived no large force of cavalry capable of independent operations to be necessary.

Nor did his division commanders have any constructive ideas about the use of cavalry. Testifying before a congressional committee intent on maligning General McClellan's army and his administration of it, most of them claimed they had too much cavalry. Half of it, they testified, should be disbanded.[6] No division needed an entire regiment of horse. The Virginia countryside made it useless except as messengers, orderlies, and guards for the division commander. No one mentioned a cavalry force organized into a corps. In fact, none of them recommended even a division of cavalry. Perhaps they thought about a Reserve Brigade to be kept at army headquarters.

The combat characteristics of modern armor, the direct descendant of horse cavalry, are firepower, maneuverability, and shock action.[7] These characteristics

4 Banks MSS (L.C.) letter dated September 16, 1861, from McClellan to Banks; Harris in *Wisconsin MOLLUS Broadfoot*, 46, 348-349; *M.O.S.*, 118-119.

5 *M.O.S.*, 118, 119.

6 *C.C.W.*, 1, 114 (Richardson), 119 (Heintzelman), 124 (Franklin).

7 They are known with somewhat derisive affection to infantry (the "crunchies") and artillery (the "cannon konkers") as firewater, manureability, and shack action.

were no different in the cavalry of ancient Greece, Macedonia, and Rome.[8] The mission of cavalry remained the same over two millenia: reconnoiter, screen the main army, raid behind enemy lines, disrupt the enemy's rear areas, provide mobile defense, protect the flanks, fight along side the great infantry force in battle, and make the crushing pursuit after a victory.[9]

On the advance to Bull Run, McDowell had proven how little he knew about cavalry by inching forward blindly while he kept his scant horsemen in the rear of an infantry column. In the Shenandoah Valley, Patterson demonstrated that this was an army-wide deficiency, not just the shortcomings of a single officer. The column marching up the Pike from Martinsburg in July had Thomas's brigade of infantry tramping in front, followed by Patterson and his staff, Cadwalader and his staff, a battery of horse artillery, then two companies of Regular cavalry and the remainder of the column. As one non-commissioned officer, soon to be an officer in another regiment, put it in a letter home the next day, "We moved with a great deal of caution, halting often to examine the woods as the enemy had their pickets posted along the road."[10] Nor was the cavalry as a screen, scouting force, and light advance combat element new art. Napoleon's fighting cavalry, primarily his gaudy hussars, performed well-known services of this sort, which earned them renown and desirable female attention.[11]

Before the war the cavalry of the Regular Army included two regiments of dragoons, the equivalent of mounted light infantry; one regiment of mounted rifles; and two of cavalry. In May the entire force had been redesignated as cavalry, the regiments renumbered consecutively, and a new Sixth United States Cavalry Regiment authorized. For years before the war cavalry had been non-existent or a stepchild with no apparent reason for its existence. The sparse mounted forces were scattered far and wide, one regiment "stationed" from Kansas to Oregon. Nevertheless, the small units were in excellent condition, boasted a high morale, and were hardened to the rigors of service in the field. From them came the core of

8 Dixon and Southern, *Roman Cavalry*, 141-147; Spence, *Cavalry of Greece*, 36-33, 49-51, 103-105. On the issue of shock action, which he calls "hitting power" in the chapter on "Combat Potential," Spence adopts the position of John Keegan in his classic *Face of Battle* (156-159), that cavalry could not successfully charge well-formed, steady infantry. This does not affect the shock action characteristic of cavalry. Even the Israeli tankers, the best cavalrymen of the twentieth century, found the well-armed, motivated Arab infantryman to be its most dangerous enemy—especially at close quarters. Moshe Dayan, *Moshe Dayan: Story of my Life*, 246, 507-508, 510, 616 (New York, 1976).

9 Spence, *Cavalry of Greece*, 127-162; Dixon and Southern, *Roman Cavalry*, 141-147.

10 Thomas, *Thomas Letters*, 21, letter dated July 16, 1861, from Thomas to his father.

11 Chandler, *Napoleon*, 1, 354-355.

Rebel military leadership in the early part of the war, Robert E. Lee, Joseph E. Johnston, Albert Sidney Johnston, and William J. Hardee.[12]

At least some believed volunteer cavalry would be needed, but the road to acceptance would be long, difficult, and frustrating. The creation of the First New York Cavalry, the first volunteer cavalry regiment, would exemplify the trials that confronted the early cavalry regiments. Two days after Sumter surrendered, recruiting for a regiment of New York cavalry began with an advertisement in the *Tribune* of April 16 calling for a captain of cavalry, offering to equip the first fifty volunteers free, and suggesting that interested men contact G. W. Richardson at 21 Maiden Lane. According to the summons, "The Cavalry department of the Northern army is, without a doubt, the one most lacking in efficiency."

The response was so great that Richardson and his compatriots advertised for a meeting on April 19 at 765 Broadway, a large meeting hall reached by a long, dimly-lit, narrow corridor. Richardson, who would chair the meeting, selected Ezra H. Bailey, a bright young friend, to serve as secretary. More than one hundred fifty men appeared at the meeting. Recruits were induced to enroll; and candidates for commissions presented themselves on the stage, where they declaimed their qualifications, extolled their experience, and demonstrated their skill with the sabre. Those present decided to raise a company and offer it to the government. Colonel O. Forest offered the use of the Palace Garden for a recruiting office, which was opened the next day. The response was again so strong that the organizers decided to raise a regiment. Favorable press coverage of the first session[13] produced a large increase in numbers; but some of those who had addressed the group in their own favor as candidates for commissions, including a former member of Her Majesty's cavalry, failed to reappear. Capable men like Ezra Bailey, Daniel Harkins, Joseph Stearns, Henry Hidden, and a large "politician" bobbed to the surface. In the game of "Can-You-Top-This" storytelling no man could match the "politician," whose "topping" stories always featured himself as the hero. Growing quickly, the group began to drill.[14]

12 Captain Moses Harris, "The Union Cavalry," 3 vols. (Milwaukee, 1891) (*Wisconsin MOLLUS Broadfoot*), 46, 341-351; Stephen Z. Starr, *The Union Cavalry in the Civil War*, 3 vols., *From Fort Sumter to Gettysburg 1861-1863* (Baton Rouge, 1979), 1, 47-53 (Starr, *Union Cavalry*); J. Roemer, *Cavalry: its History, Management, and Uses in War* (New York, 1863), 359-360.

13 James Stevenson, *Boots and Saddles: A History of the First Volunteer Cavalry of the War, known as the First New York (Lincoln) Cavalry and also as the Sabre Regiment. Its Organization, Campaigns and Battles* (Harrisburg, 1879), 5-7 (Stevenson, *Boots and Saddles*).

14 F. Colburn Adams,, *The Story of a Trooper: With Much of Interest Concerning the Campaign on the Peninsula, Not Before Written* (New York, 1865), 14-19 (Adams, *Story of a Trooper*). The identity of the "politician" mentioned in this work remains a small mystery.

Lincoln had not specified any cavalry in the call for seventy-five thousand militia. In his subsequent call for three-year volunteers and more Regulars, he had said the men should be "mustered into service as Infantry and Cavalry. The proportions of each arm, and details of enrollment and organization will be made known through the Department of War."[15] Of these volunteers only one regiment was to be cavalry.[16]

To overcome the government's equivocal, if not negative, attitude toward cavalry, the organizers, led by the seller of jewelry from Maiden Lane, sent Bayard Clarke, a "polished gentleman," a former officer who in the Second Dragoons had served with Harney in the Florida War, and later a member of congress, to offer his services and persuade the government to accept the regiment aborning. Clarke met with Lincoln, who received him cordially and who conceded that cavalry would be needed. When Clarke told him the need would reach twelve to fourteen regiments, Lincoln did not deny it. But the president did not think the country would stand the expense. Without skill on military matters but duty bound, he said, to satisfy the expectations of the people, who would hold him accountable for adopting the best means of suppressing the rebellion, he had entrusted the organization of the army to General Scott and Secretary Cameron. Clarke should see them.

Across he went to the War Office Building, a manful struggle he had with the screening mechanisms, and finally a meeting with the secretary. Cameron was neither indecisive nor vague. Clarke could not have authority to raise a cavalry regiment. Cameron could see no clear need for cavalry, nor did he disagree with Scott's antipathy for volunteer cavalry. Other negative reasons abounded, all common, all hypothetical, none verifiable, but none refutable—expense, geography, topography, time, strategy, and on and on. Bizarrely, Cameron urged Clarke to maintain the regiment but would not say whether it would ever be accepted. The secretary left the impression, verified by his well-known affinity with local Pennsylvania corruption, that any cavalry would come from his home state as political spoils.

Clarke, despondent, returned to New York City. The three cheers that greeted him did not enliven his spirits. The government would not take the regiment and had no need of his services, he reported. He would retire to private life. Top to bottom the men were depressed by the news. Many thought of abandoning the project. But

15 Basler, *Lincoln's Works*, 4, 331-332, Proclamation Calling Militia and Convening Congress, dated April 15, 1861, and 353-354, Proclamation Calling for 42,034 Volunteers, dated May 3, 1861.

16 Beach, William H., *The First New York (Lincoln) Cavalry from April 19, 1861, to July 7, 1865* (New York, 1892), 11-12 (Beach, *First New York Cavalry*).

others knew that "young hearts, full of fire and spirit" beat in men like Hidden and Bailey and that they needed nothing more than a leader they could respect, a man of experience, energy, and will. Under the cloud of the bad news, the drill masters put the men through a series of evolutions.

A few friends quietly escorted Clarke to a nearby saloon, "where good cheer was to be had"; and the politician took him under his wing. He was a man of fortune, he said, had held positions of high trust, had filled them with honor, and was making sacrifices to serve. He would see justice done, would spend half his fortune to accomplish it, and would take any amount of time to do it. Influence in the capital he had, and he knew how to use it. Any senator would be delighted to serve him, and a word from him was enough. He would see Clarke made a colonel, a general even. He could do it.

Silently, Clarke listened. The politician, though he meant well, was adrift "in his cups," Clarke must have decided.[17] But in spite of this early setback, the core of New Yorkers intent on serving as cavalry continued their efforts to complete a regiment of horse.[18]

Carl Schurz, a prominent German-American who had fled his homeland after the unsuccessful revolutions of 1848 and a personal acquaintance of the president, had been appointed ambassador to Spain; but when the war erupted a few days later, he preferred to participate in the fighting. Schurz approached Lincoln to suggest that the army would need an efficient cavalry force in the war. To shorten the long time needed to create skilled cavalrymen from raw material, Schurz suggested that the government recruit able-bodied German immigrants who resided in New York and had served in German cavalry regiments. He thought they need only be armed and mounted to make good cavalrymen immediately. They would include experienced cavalry officers trained in the Prussian or other German armies. Known to and respected by the German-born citizens of the United States, he would be a good person, he thought, to organize that kind of regiment.[19] Lincoln said he would authorize him to recruit one cavalry regiment and to serve as its colonel, but he should go to the secretary of war to discuss the necessary arrangements.

Cameron appeared to favor the idea; and wrote a letter to the governors of all the states asking them to support the regiment by contributing mounts and equipment

17 Adams, *Story of a Trooper*, 8-24; Heitman, *Historical Register*, 1, 306.

18 Beach, *First New York Cavalry*, 12, memorandum dated May 1, 1862, Cameron to "the Governors of the Several States and all whom it may concern," and 9-13; Adams, *Story of a Trooper*, 6.

19 Carl Schurz, *The Reminiscences of Carl Schurz*, 3 vols. (New York, 1907-1908), vol. 2, 228-230 (Schurz, *Reminiscences*); Beach, *First New York Cavalry*, 12-13.

because the government could supply no more than weapons.[20] Although Cameron favored Schurz's idea, he thought General Scott should consider it.

Schurz had never seen Scott. But having heard the general in chief was a pompous old man who did not tolerate contrary opinions on military matters, he anticipated the forthcoming meeting with some misgivings. Schurz asked Secretary Cameron for a letter of introduction describing his proposal and recommending it to Scott as strongly as possible. He hoped that Scott would not disregard him as a mere intruder.

The general read Cameron's letter and invited Schurz to sit down. When Schurz, slender, bespeckled, and ascetic, explained his project for a cavalry regiment, Scott's face became stern and impatient. He asked if Schurz had any practical experience in organizing and drilling mounted troops.

Taking this as an ill omen, Schurz confessed that he had none.

Scott had concluded that much from the proposition, he replied. He believed the war would end long before any volunteer cavalry would be fit for service. He also thought the theater of war would be Virginia, whose hilly and wooded surface was so marked with fences and other obstructions that large bodies of cavalry would be impracticable. He could see no other use for it. Once again proving that his art had outstripped him, the lieutenant-general said the Regular cavalry would be sufficient for all needs.

Seeing that he could not persuade the disagreeable old general in chief, Schurz returned to the president and the secretary of war, who said that Scott took too narrow a view. They gave him the desired authority to raise a regiment of cavalry in New York, and to that city he started.[21] He would command the one volunteer cavalry regiment to serve against the Confederacy.

On his way from Washington to New York with Lincoln's permission to raise a cavalry regiment of Germans and a commission as its colonel in his pocket, Schurz stopped in Philadelphia. He had learned that a few men there were raising a regiment of cavalry. He met with them to see if they wished to become part of his regiment, the only volunteer cavalry regiment to be authorized in the war, he assured them.

20 Beach, *First New York Cavalry*, 12, letter of May 1, 1861, from Cameron to the Governors of the Several States and Others.

21 Joseph Schafer, ed., *Publications of the State Historical Society of Wisconsin, Collections,* (Madison, 1928); *Intimate Letters of Carl Schurz 1841-1869*, 30, 252, letter dated March 28, 1861, from Schurz to his wife (Schafer, *Schurz Letters*); Harris in *Wisconsin MOLLUS Broadfoot*, 47, 350-351; Schurz, *Reminiscences*, 2, 229-231; *D.A.B.* 8, pt. 2, 466-467; Adams, *Story of a Trooper*, 21-22, 23, 25-27; Averell, *Recollections*, 333; Historical Committee, *Henry Wilson's Regiment: the Twenty-second Infantry, Second Sharpshooters, Third Light Battery, Massachusetts Volunteers* (Boston, 1887), 2 (Committee, *Henry Wilson's Regiment*); DeTrobriand, *Four Years*, 90.

Among his listeners only Lieutenant William H. Boyd accepted his offer of a captaincy in exchange for a company. When he reached New York, he learned about the troops being raised by Ezra Bailey, Joseph Stearns, and Alonzo Adams. In addition, parts of several companies of Germans who had served in Europe were tendered by Frederick von Schickfuss, a New Jersey resident with "an honorable record as a cavalry officer in the German army." Schurz invited them to join his group.

No doubt expressing the common anti-foreigner sentiment embodied in the Know-Nothing Party, many men in the Bailey group opposed acceptance of the Germans. But good men with distinguished careers ahead of them were going to other units that had a more certain military future. Reluctantly, they agreed to work with Schurz and the von Schickfuss group because it seemed the only way to find a place in the war. At the same time yet another problem arose: Lincoln had decided that Schurz should proceed to his post as minister to Spain. They must find a replacement for him.

By the middle of May the government had not changed its general attitude toward cavalry. The "regiment," if it could be called that, continued without a replacement for Clarke or Schurz; and "the question of how to get a colonel to act with us either temporarily or permanently," wrote one officer later in the war, "was now troubling us more than any other."[22] A regimental commander had to be found. Ezra Bailey was sent to interview George D. Bayard, an instructor at West Point. He was willing, but could not obtain his release to accept a volunteer commission. Bayard recommended a fellow instructor named Owen, who would accept if he could obtain relief from duty in the Regular Army.[23]

Owen and Bailey traveled to New York City to meet with Schurz. To accept the colonelcy, for which he was found acceptable, Owen needed a leave of absence from his regiment in the Regular Army. An application for this would require paperwork through "regular channels." Those who have enjoyed this exercise know the frustration and delay "regular channels" can present, today and then—and the application, after wandering slowly through "red tape" and "channels," might then be denied. Bailey had to go to Washington.[24]

22 Adams, *Story of a Trooper*, 45.

23 Beach, *First New York Cavalry*, 13-15.

24 Stevenson, *Boots and Saddles*, 20-21. In 1961, the author was serving in Korea as a first lieutenant and executive officer of a rifle company (M-1's from the days of the great "bow and arrow" wars). After a hair-raising flight in an L-19 from the DMZ to Seoul, he presented himself to the personnel actions warrant officer at Eighth Army headquarters to request that he be given orders for a transfer to Vietnam in order to "see the elephant." Scheduled for an early release to enter law school, he was willing to "go voluntary indefinite" if orders to Vietnam would be

Cool, nonchalant, genial, active, indefatigable, Bailey went to Washington to obtain Owen's release. He carried with him a letter from Schurz to Montgomery Blair. When Bailey and Blair saw Cameron, he said he needed approval from Scott or Adjutant General Lorenzo Thomas for any order involving Owen. Both were too busy to meet with them. After business hours Bailey, resourceful and persistent, went to Scott's residence. While the sentinel was busily turning Bailey away, Scott saw them through the window and gestured to the sentinel to let him pass. Bailey explained his purpose. Scott responded with his diatribe on volunteer cavalry. He did not believe in allowing young Regular Army officers to command volunteer regiments, did not believe in volunteer cavalry at all, opposed spending the half million or more dollars necessary to mount and fully equip a cavalry regiment, and thought the war would end before the mounted regiment would be fit for active service.

Depressed, Bailey left Scott's headquarters and began to walk aimlessly along Washington's streets. With no particular purpose in mind he eventually found himself headed toward the White House, then in a gathering crowd in front of it. It was a reception day. Am I not one of the people? Bailey asked himself. He would visit the president.

"What can I do for you, General?" asked the president who seemed to grant extra rank to every officer he met.

"Not general yet, Mr. President, but hope to be if the war lasts long enough."

"I hope the war will not last long enough to make generals of *all* who aspire to that position."

Bailey explained his mission involving Owen. Unless it were absolutely necessary, the president said, he did not like to interfere in army matters. Bailey should see Scott or Cameron.

That had been done, Bailey said, but Scott would give no encouragement, and Cameron would not see him at all. "Oh, it's the old story. You tried all other sources first and then came to me as a last resort."

Bailey laughed. "Just so, Mr. President; and I hope I shall not have come in vain."

assured. The warrant officer had a direct radio contact with the personnel office in the Pentagon and could have sought the orders on the spot; instead, he said, "Well, lieutenant, you sign for voluntary indefinite and we will see what we can do." He opened his desk drawer, removed some papers, and tendered them. Prior experience suggested this was a bad idea without the guaranteed result. The papers were not signed. Satisfaction came too late. A few years later, then at the beginning of a career with a large law firm on Wall Street, the author felt compelled to decline an unsolicited offer of increased rank and choice of assignments if he would return to the service.

Lincoln smiled. "I can't see why you should have so much difficulty about getting a colonel. Why, I could supply you with a hundred from Illinois alone in a week. Go back and tell Colonel Schurz to hurray up this regiment as soon as possible, and I will see that it is accepted." Bailey returned to New York, where he and the other organizers renewed their search for a regimental commander.[25] They had failed with Bayard.[26] They could not pry Owen loose.

Willing to leave a successful law practice on Wall Street, Hamilton Merrill, a West Point graduate in the class of 1838, a former Regular Army cavalry officer with a good reputation, and a man with battle experience and a brevet for gallantry at Molino del Rey, wanted to return to the service. Representatives visited him to tender command of the regiment. Anything within his power he would do, he said; but he had already tendered his services and been summarily rebuffed by Cameron. He could join them, give advice, preside over their deliberations, and help them create a temporary organization, but no more.[27]

Even without a colonel, they needed a temporary structure. One evening during drill the "candidates" for positions in the structure caused "a great stir at headquarters . . . soliciting influence and votes." The politician sought the quartermastership, an opportunity to make a fortune with a little unscrupulous bookkeeping; but only the colonel, if they ever found one, could fill the quartermaster position. The politician would compromise. He was willing to take Company A, usually the right flank company in the regimental line and the holder of the position of honor.

When drill ended, the men who were to be the rank and file went home. The "candidates" remained in the gallery at a long table with Merrill seated at the head. After his short but sound speech—followed by three cheers—Merrill supervised the voting. Harkins, Stearns, and the politician received temporary captaincies. The rest became first lieutenants. The temporary structure complete, they adjourned to the omnipresent saloon for what Merrill referred to as "a social glass."

The days now became June with no increase in certainty, no authorization, and no commanding officer. Another delegation, Lieutenant Alonzo Adams and another man, went to the capital to see if the secretary would accept the regiment with

25 Stevenson, *Boots and Saddles*, 21-22; Beach, *First New York Cavalry*, 13-15, Adams, *Story of a Trooper*, 43.

26 Samuel J. Bayard, *The Life of George Dashiell Bayard: late Captain, U.S.A., and Brigadier-General of Volunteers, Killed in the Battle of Fredericksburg, Dec. 1862* (New York, 1874), 261, letter dated November 22, 1862, from Bayard to his father (Bayard, *Bayard*).

27 Beach, *First New York Cavalry*, 13-15.

Merrill as its colonel.[28] Once again, Cameron gave no encouragement except to urge maintenance of the regiment for needs that might arise in the future.[29]

Unsatisfactory candidates for colonel were interviewed and rejected. Now the officers turned to Philip Kearny, a native New Yorker, a graduate of Columbia College, and an experienced cavalry officer. Too late. The governor of New Jersey had offered Kearny a brigade of infantry; but Kearny, like Bayard, suggested another candidate, Andrew T. McReynolds, a fellow cavalry officer of the Mexican War.

Alonzo Adams had a copy of *Gardiner's Military Dictionary*, which gave McReynolds's biographical data and address. A telegram to Grand Rapids, Michigan, and a train ride produced in New York the next day a fifty-five year old Irishman of medium height, solid build, broad face, and hair to the collar. McReynolds had participated in Kearny's famous charge on the Bel¾n causeway to the gates of Mexico City. There Kearny lost his arm and McReynolds suffered a disabling wound to his bridle arm. McReynolds's mother, a cousin to Andrew Jackson, provided a helpful family connection. In addition, he had become interested in politics and was a member of the Michigan state legislature. Less impressive than Kearny and a sharp contrast to the nervous, fast talking Schurz, McReynolds met the officers and men with Schurz presiding. They were satisfied. But they still needed approval from the War Department and had internal problems to resolve.

Meetings of Schurz, McReynolds, and others addressed the internal problems of command and composition. Once laid on the table, they resolved themselves in a few points of agreement: Schurz would assign his commission and the authority to raise a regiment of cavalry over to McReynolds. In addition, the New York contingent from the Palace Garden would form part of the regiment, the companies of Germans would become part of the regiment, the Germans could elect their officers from their countrymen, and a German would be lieutenant colonel of the regiment.

On June 5, 1861, Schurz endorsed his commission to McReynolds with a request that McReynolds replace him at the head of the regiment. "I would invite

28 Adams, *Story of a Trooper*, 46-52; Heitman, *Historical Register*, 1, 705; *Cullum*, 1, 965. *Story of a Trooper* was written, according to the title page, by F. Colburn Adams, a company grade officer in the regiment. However, rosters in Beach, *supra*, 45, 545-579, and Stevenson, *supra*, 363-388, show no Adams named F. Colburn. From the narratives in all three sources, the author appears to have been Alonso Adams, who later rose to command the regiment.

29 Adams, *Story of a Trooper*, 46-52, 63-65.

you to see the authorities at Washington," he wrote, "for the purpose of inducing them to ratify this transfer of authority."[30]

A group of officers, McReynolds, Adams, Boyd, and Stearns, again took the road to the capital, where Lincoln again referred them to Cameron. They handed Cameron the authorization for the regiment and Schurz's colonelcy. Authority to raise the regiment, the secretary said, had been personal to Schurz and had been given as a political favor, not as an indication of a need for cavalry. When Schurz committed to the post in Spain, no need for the regiment—or any volunteer cavalry—existed; and the authorization for it lapsed. He was "glad to have that *document* in [his] possession once more." He had regretted it ever since it had been granted. He placed it in a drawer. He would keep it.

The members of the Committee were demoralized by this development. The quick-witted Adams said he had a personal interest in the document. Schurz had endorsed it with some commendations of him, and he would not like to lose them. Could he have the paper back? Cameron hesitated long, then consented. A wily politician with decades of practice and years of demonstrated skill, Cameron did not stand alone in the higher tricks of politics. Adams and the other officers took the commission back to the president—fortuitously collecting, because Adams knew him, ex-governor Newell of New Jersey on the way. Newell agreed to help.

When Lincoln heard their "statement of affairs," he endorsed their papers:[31]

> Hon. Secretary of War:
>
> Please say to Col. A. T. McReynolds that when he will present the cavalry regiment according to the within authority, they will be received under him as they would have been under Col. Schurz.
>
> A. Lincoln
> June 13.[32]

30 Adams, *Story of a Trooper*, 72; Beach, *First New York Cavalry*, 20, endorsement dated June 5, 1861, from Schurz to McReynolds, and 13-20. Adams's account of the creation of the regiment is informative and amusing but often inaccurate. Preferring the sensational to the factual, he infers without corroboration and exaggerates with freedom. One of the most glaring examples of inaccuracy is his treatment of Schurz. Without saying it in so many words, he leaves the impression that Schurz was a coward who preferred the European drawing room to the American battlefield, *op. cit.*, 68-72. Schurz would end the war a barely tolerable, if mildly incompetent, military leader. But no one could question his courage on the field of battle or his willingness to risk personal danger to serve his adopted country.

31 Stevenson, *Boats and Saddles*, 24-25.

32 *Ibid.*, 20-21, Basler, *Lincoln's Works*, 4, 406, endorsed June 13, 1861, from Lincoln to Cameron.

The officers returned to Cameron with their undeniable authority. When they showed it to him, Cameron saw he had been outplayed at his own game. He reacted "like a wounded tiger."

"This is what you wanted the papers for, is it?" he stormed at the committee. "I wish the president would remember there is a War Department."

Unable to ignore Lincoln, Cameron could still make life miserable for the regiment. He would do nothing without approval from Scott. The infantry forces having recently crossed to Virginia and being involved with plans for the Bull Run campaign, Scott was unavailable; but Adams knew Lieutenant-Colonel Schuyler Hamilton, a New Yorker on Scott's staff. Through him, he obtained just enough time to extract a hurried note from Scott approving acceptance of the regiment. Not recovered from his fury and embarrassment, Cameron grudgingly accepted the regiment "on condition" that the entire regiment be at Washington or "wherever ordered" by August 1 and that portions be presented before July 15.[33] They had one month.

While in the War Office Building, the committee began to discuss a name for the regiment that, even though it had struggled so hard for its life, still had no way to refer to itself. McReynolds proposed "The Lincoln Cavalry," a suggestion promptly accepted by all because the president had called for the regiment despite severe opposition.[34]

Company C, Boyd's Philadelphia company, received enough additional Philadelphia recruits to achieve full strength. Von Schickfuss's German companies became a battalion and would later become favorites of a short, sharp-tempered man with a peculiar shape to his head. Company F rose from the street trash and reprobates of Syracuse and Company K from McReynolds's hometown of Grand Rapids, Michigan.

As McDowell was preparing for his advance on Manassas, he reportedly said he did not have one cavalry officer on whom he could rely to reconnoiter an enemy position. In the middle of July the War Department began to urge the regiment to fill its companies quickly and come forward. After Bull Run the army decided "with some reluctance and hesitation" to create a small mounted force. The number first mustered, however, was too small to be of much value. For more than eighteen months the cavalry regiments would be divided and subdivided and assigned in

33 Stevenson, *Boats and Saddles*, 25-26, endorsement dated June 15, 1861, by Cameron.

34 Letter dated November 14, 1864, from Lieutenant Colonel Alonso Adams to Lorenzo Thomas, in Records of the Adjutant-General's Office, First New York Cavalry Regiment: Letters, Endorsements, Orders and Roster Book (several volumes, only two surviving), Record Group 94, National Archives; Stevenson, *Boots and Saddles*, 27.

detachments to different corps and division headquarters. When they arrived at Washington, they were armed, equipped, mounted, and sent immediately across the river to different division headquarters. The regimental organizations were often delayed until late in the fall. No one should have expected that effective cavalry would be available in time for the spring campaign.[35]

When he received the message from the War Department, McReynolds sent Cameron a memorandum reporting the condition of the regiment. The Philadelphia company was equipped and mounted. It would be ready to be mustered in a week. In New York City the others needed horses and equipment. The usually helpful Union Defense Committee would do nothing because, carefully guarding its limited resources, it would not expend them when it saw the federal government spending its money on other regiments "not so essential to the public service."[36] And no company could be mustered until it had a minimum number of men, at least seventy-nine.[37] Quartermaster General Montgomery Meigs was at last ordered to supply horses to cavalry, particularly to McReynolds's regiment. This would, in Meigs's view, "relieve the regiment from the only important difficulty attending its organization and delaying its entrance upon field service."[38] He also took the last step, ordering the mustering officers to requisition clothing and equipment for camp and garrison.[39]

Recruiting became urgent, and permanent officers had to be chosen to replace the earlier temporary choices. At headquarters, Adams, Stearns, Harkins, Bailey, Hidden, and Ogle sat quietly smoking their pipes, until a man arrived with news that the politician had been seen downtown wearing a uniform with a yellow stripe down the outer seam of his trousers. That was the color for cavalry. Hidden turned to Bailey and shook his head.

"If there is any manhood left in the fellow, he won't make another attempt to get into this regiment."

35 Miller, William E., Captain, *War History: Operations of the Union Cavalry on the Peninsula, in which some Cumberland County Soldiers Took Part*, (pamphlet, Carlisle, 1908). This was a speech read before the Hamilton Library Association of Carlisle, Pennsylvania, on October 23, 1908 and reprinted.

36 Memorandum from McReynolds to Cameron dated July 8, 1861, in Record Group 94, File R&S 462632, National Archives.

37 Adams, *Story of a Trooper*, 87-88; Beach, *First New York Cavalry*, 22-28; and Stevenson, *Boots and Saddles*, 14.

38 Letter from Meigs to Seward dated July 9, 1861, endorsed "approved" on the same day by Lincoln, Records of the Adjutant General's Office, Correspondence of the Record and Pension Office, File R&P 462629, in RG 94, NA.

39 Letter from Meigs to Thomas dated July 10, 1861, File R&P 462631, RG 94, NA.

"He will," said the man with the news. "He is doing it now. He has got authority from the colonel to raise a company of Germans for this regiment; and as he won't understand a word they say, much happiness may he have with them. And I can tell you this, too. He is raising money from citizens to pay his recruiting expenses."

"Money!" interjected one of the officers. "Why, where is the fortune he has been boasting about. Like his common sense, we have not seen the color of it yet."

The politician and a man who had failed to receive a captaincy in the preliminary organization joined forces to recruit a fourth German troop for the regiment. When it was raised, the defeated former candidate was elected captain. The politician wanted to be the first lieutenant, but he met highly qualified competition in the form of a German with experience and credentials.

At the final session, the men gave three cheers for the German candidate, a bleak development for the politician. He sought the help of the new company commander as a translator.

"Say to them, sir, that I am their particular friend. I don't lack courage, I don't. I will show them I don't when we meet the enemy!"

He pushed his fingers through his bushy hair. His speech became ponderous.

"Tell them I am ready to give any man satisfaction who says I'm a coward. Don't forget to put that in."

He tapped the captain on the shoulder.

"You see, I cannot understand a word they say; yet it seems to me, the more I tell them I am their friend, the more they take me for their enemy. If it is more lager they want, they shall have five kegs. And if that is not enough, ten! In addition to this, each man shall have a dollar as soon as I have proof that he has given me his vote."

The captain smiled, then translated for the politician. He was asking for a position that involved life and death for them. His condescending speech incensed the men so badly that they showed signs of assaulting him. McReynolds saved the day. He asked the men to listen.

"Ja, ja, ja," they responded through the ranks.

Once again the captain interpreted.

The candidate was worthy of their favor in every way, the colonel said. The politician wanted the post as a platform for advancement and would, the colonel pledged, resign in less than three weeks, thus leaving the space for a man of their choice.

Some cheered.

Others shook their heads.

The remainder could not understand "what they were required to do in this strange and irregular" proceeding.

The vote that followed vindicated McReynold's leadership by electing the politician. McReynolds thanked them. The politician could not resist a gush of gratitude. They would not be sorry, he said. Although he would not be with them long, he would not forget their kindness. Unable to understand his speech the men nevertheless accepted him with hearty laughter. The German battalion was full.

Proving once again that the personal characteristics preferred by civilized society could not predict the men who would be chosen to lead, the officers of the regiment were a polyglot group: McReynolds, stolid and pedestrian; von Schickfuss, genial, quick-witted, self-possessed; Bailey, cool, generous to his last dollar, and a man of few but to-the-point words; Harkins, active, impulsive, with an inspiring laugh and an endless collection of amusing stories; the politician, who spoke often of his political influence, which he would, he said, use for himself and be willing to use for his fellow officers and who also talked about his great wealth and bragged about his future deeds in battle; and Hidden, handsome, impeccable in attire, piercing black eyes "armed with intelligence," restless, impatient for the field, and with a contemptuous curl of his lip for the despondent ready to quit. By his demeanor Hidden, a young man in his early twenties, made those around him believe that in his former lives he had served in every war, fought beside every soldier, and enjoyed a survivor's drink with each.

The completion of the regiment produced some strange coincidences. About the time Captain Boyd's Company A saved its reputation and dispersed the Confederate cavalry force in its first charge, the German battalion defended its honor against a hated enemy. The regiment had adopted the name Lincoln Cavalry because of the president's many intercessions on its behalf. But a nearby regiment composed primarily of Austrians called itself the "Lincoln Greens," an offensive attempt, it seemed, to pirate the name. The Prussians in McReynolds's regiment disliked the Austrians because they were inferior, arrogant blowers. The Poles had long hated Austrians because old national scores remained unsettled. Deep down, the Hungarians simply despised them. The "Greens" responded full well in kind. The men had already enjoyed numerous "little fights." At two o'clock on Sunday, August 4, the animosity exploded. Several pistol shots cracked in rapid succession near the local hotel, where most of the trouble usually occurred. Loud calls for help were followed by the clang of sabres, the thud of clubs, and noises made by other handy weapons. The German officers and men in camp seized their weapons. More pistol shots. Reports of casualties. The fighting covered the top of a nearby hill. McReynolds's Germans were slowly driven off the crest by the superior numbers of the Austrians. The American officers, typical anti-foreigners, held their men in check. The Europeans could do unto each other as they wished. Colonel McReynolds shouted numerous orders to the Germans, who understood nothing he said and did not care. The frail bugler intensified the situation by blowing a confused series of unidentifiable calls. The regiment's second bugler, a fat Dutchman, added blasts with such a great effort that his face turned purple. To the rescue went the

Germans from camp, some of them armed with the few old sabres supplied by the Union Defense Committee. One after another, wounded men were carried off the hill to safety.

Now the "Greens" lost ground. Fighting without their officers, who had initiated the fight then adjourned to the kitchen of a nearby hotel, the Greens soon suffered a general rout. The Germans pursued them mercilessly. McReynolds ordered the buglers to sound "Recall." The little bugler jumped from one stone wall to another, blowing to no avail. The fat Dutchman had no more success. But less than thirty minutes after the beginning the hill stood clear. Having completed their pursuit, the enlisted men slowly, victoriously reappeared in camp.

McReynolds's officers cursed the men and sent them to their tents, both groups knowing the officers secretly approved and were proud of the result. Once the men were peacefully in place, some of the officers searched out the officers of the Greens to berate them for cowardice. McReynolds's chaplain forestalled a renewal of the battle by interceding with a plea for God's day and offering to hold a service for both sides. He was supported by the tearful pleas of two sweethearts of Green officers.[40]

On August 25, McReynolds's regiment prepared to leave for Washington and the war. Overcoming the usual mishaps and with good dispatch, they boarded ships at Canal Street and set sail. On September 10, the last company joined the regiment from New York; and it began to draw horses, equipment, and weapons. The last field and staff positions were finally filled, von Schickfuss as lieutenant-colonel and Bailey, over the politician, as the quartermaster. The standard cavalry regiment, intended at this time to serve more often by troop (one company), squadron (two troops or companies), and battalion (four troops or two squadrons) than an infantry regiment, had twelve troops in three battalions. It had, therefore, three majors. The regiment needed a real designation, the "Lincoln Cavalry" being historically accurate but not sufficient for the adjutant general's office. In November it was ordered to accept the designation First New York Cavalry.[41]

40 Adams, *Story of a Trooper*, 111-114.

41 Records of Adjutant General's Office, First New York Cavalry Regiment Regimental Letter Book, Endorsements, Orders, and Roster Book, letter dated November 14, 1864, from Alonzo Adams to Thomas, NA, RG 94. The men were proud that they were the first regiment of cavalry raised in the war. In fact, they rose to protect their status in 1864 when the Seventh New York Cavalry called itself the First New York Mounted Rifles, the Seventeenth New York Cavalry called itself the First New York Veteran Cavalry, and the Nineteenth New York Cavalry called itself the First New York Dragoons. Adams, commanding the regiment, asked that this confusion be eliminated because mail went to the wrong place, orders were wrongly directed, and great feats were sometimes not properly attributed, to the disappointment of the public and the "friends of this regiment at home." *Ibid.*

The candidacy of the politician for the majority, a rank made vacant by von Schickfuss's promotion was opposed by a vicious protest signed by the other officers in the regiment. He was "a detriment . . . and . . . unfit to associate with officers and gentlemen," it said.

Above conniving, Captain Ogle would not send the protest to McReynolds without first showing it to the politician. The officers gathered in Ogle's tent and were joined by the smiling politician, who was happy to be among friends, he thought, and fellow officers.

"Lieutenant," said Ogle, "we have sent for you on business not of the most agreeable kind . . ."

The politician interrupted. "It doesn't matter. I am accustomed to kicks and never take them as unkind when I know a man's a particular friend."

"You have resolved to honor this regiment with your presence. And believing that you are neither fit for a soldier nor an honest man . . . that you do the service much harm and no good . . . that this regiment would be better without you, we have subscribed to this protest."

In a loud, clear voice he read the document. The politician listened. He shook his head.

"I'd have you know that is no compliment to a man to set him down for a fool. And no one said I was not an honest man when I had the honor of holding a position in the New York Custom House . . ."

"A night watchman, I suppose," interrupted Ogle.

The politician frowned deeply. "Nothing less than a full inspector, if you please," he retorted with an injured air. "You must know that I have come to the war not so much to fight as to make peace between the contending parties. As for your opposition to me, this I can tell you. I do not mean to stay but a week or two in the regiment. As to the position, it will only serve me until I am made a General, which I will soon show you I have friends enough to do. Why, I have great respect for my enemies and never speak ill of them."

Again he bowed, then withdrew in a spirit of victory to circulate his petition for the majority. After a brief discussion with the regimental chaplain about seeking satisfaction, he decided that he had already prevailed and that further proceedings were unnecessary. Although his successful pursuit of the promotion to major provoked a protest to General McClellan and an order directing McReynolds to investigate, the inquiry "was never made, and General McClellan's order . . . found a quiet sleeping place in the Colonel's pocket."[42] The politician, one of his regimental

42 Adams, *Story of a Trooper*, 111-114, 135-139, 152-153.

colleagues wrote later in the war, was "like a man of vulcanized rubber, of such elasticity that the hardest blows were followed by an instant rebound, leaving no visible or permanent impression." And his self assurance did not fail him in battle.[43]

As negative as Scott was, he could not suppress the desire of many to serve in the cavalry rather than the infantry or the artillery. It had the romance of legendary officers of the Revolution like "Light Horse Harry" Lee and Francis Marion, the "Swamp Fox." It offered a means of transportation other than the feet. It had an aura of the upper class, an appearance of eliteness.[44]

By October 15, McClellan had one regiment and two companies of Regular cavalry and eleven regiments of volunteer cavalry, a force he considered woefully inadequate. As he described it later, "The newly arriving regiments reported to General Stoneman, the chief of cavalry . . . There was a total lack of equipment for the cavalry, and it was very long before this difficulty was removed . . . Many of the officers and men were quite ignorant of the management of horses, and could not ride well. Moreover, there was too little appreciation on the part of the government of the necessities and advantages of that arm of service."[45]

Into the thankless assignment as chief of cavalry for the Army of the Potomac stepped George Stoneman without complaint. Somewhat younger and slightly more pedestrian in his background than other staff officers, McClellan's chief of cavalry had been born in upstate New York in 1822, the first of ten children. He received his primary schooling at an academy in a nearby town. In 1846, he graduated from the Military Academy, where he and McClellan would have known each other well. As a second lieutenant in the First Dragoons and a captain in the Second Cavalry, he served as quartermaster of the Mormon Battalion in the California part of the Mexican War. During the 1850s he developed hemorrhoids while serving in Texas

43 Adams, *Story of a Trooper*, 140-145, 148, 151, 177.

44 Beach, *First New York Cavalry*; Tobie, *First Maine Cavalry*, 3-4; Benjamin W. Crowninshield, *A History of the First Regiment of Massachusetts Cavalry Volunteers* (Boston, 1891), 9-11 (Crowninshield, *First Massachusetts Cavalry*); Christopher Ward; John Richard Alden, ed., *The War of the Revolution*, 2 vols., (New York, 1952), 2, 604, 661.

45 In fact, a debate over the massing of cavalry in the form of armor carried well into the Twentieth Century. In 1940, the Wehrmacht took 2,500 tanks into battle. The French had approximately 4,000. But the Germans fought with a sound tactical doctrine, i.e., they concentrated their tanks with mechanized infantry in ten armored divisions. This made units like Rommel's Seventh Panzer Division a terror to the French rear areas. The French used tanks as infantry support weapons like mortars and recoilless rifles, and scattered them throughout their infantry units. Liddell Hart, *The Rommel Papers*; Tom Schactman, *The Phony War, 1939-1940*, 186 (New York, 1982); Thomas Parrish , ed., *The Simon and Shuster Encyclopedia of World War II* (New York, 1978), 221, 223. The Americans, featuring Yankee ingenuity, George S. Patton, and the United States Third Army, took massed cavalry and deep lightning thrusts to the next level. See generally, Victor Davis Hanson, *The Soul of Battle*.

and underwent an unsuccessful operation. Stationed at Fort Brown, Texas, in 1861, he refused to join his superior General David Twiggs in a treasonous surrender and escaped with part of his regiment. After temporary duty at the cavalry school at Carlisle Barracks, he and a small cavalry force led the bridge columns advancing into Virginia on May 24. He then served on McClellan's staff in West Virginia and came east with McClellan to the Army of the Potomac as chief of cavalry.[46]

In appearance, he was tall, thin, and full bearded with large eyes. In performance and demeanor, he was an experienced, reliable cavalry officer who understood more about cavalry than his two superiors and who, like his immediate superior, was a reserved gentleman. Not the kind of blustery person many would expect as a cavalry officer, his look of habitual gravity approaching sadness or sleepiness was most likely a product of the health problems that plagued him.[47]

Other men, driven by personal preferences, undertook to convince the government to accept three-year volunteer cavalry. In Maine, a state of lumbermen and sailors, a cavalry regiment came together early and quickly, once again under uncertain authority from the War Department. All horses were on hand by the first of November, and by November 5 the last company had been mustered, but the regiment was not called to Washington. Both mounted and dismounted drill began at once. While the regiment was being reviewed by Governor Israel Washburn, one of the companies, composed primarily of sailors and led by a captain more familiar with the quarterdeck than the saddle, had difficulty maintaining its position in formation.

"Come up there!" he shouted, anxious to perform well for the governor but not fully separated from his seafaring background, "What in hell are you falling astern for?"

"Why, Captain, I can't get the damn thing in stays."

"Well, give her more headway, then!"[48]

But the hostility to cavalry continued. Cameron, who had become generous in authorizing cavalry regiments, would be replaced as secretary of war by Edwin Stanton. Honest, unyielding, grudge bearing, motivated by personal animosities, and a man of absolute rigidity on debatable wartime issues, Stanton had entered

46 *Cullum*, 2, no. 1304; Warner, *Generals in Blue*, 481; *D.A.B.*, 9, pt. 2, 92; Jack D. Welsh, M.D., *Medical Histories of Union Generals* (Kent and London, 1996), 323 (Welsh, *Medical Histories*).

47 Robertson, *McAllister Letters*, 253, letter of January 7, 1863; Cox, *Reminiscences*, 2, 139; de Trobriand, *Four Years*, 337; Gould, *Berry*, 211, letter dated November 12, 1862; *D.A.B.*, 9, pt. 2, 92; Warner, *Generals in Blue*, 481; *Cullum*, 2, no. 1304; Heitman, *Historical Register*, 1, 930.

48 Tobie, *First Maine Cavalry*, 15-16.

office with enough negative predispositions to stop the development of cavalry. A general order directed that all volunteer cavalry regiments be disbanded, including the First Maine.[49]

Writing from the Headquarters of the Department of New England, Benjamin Butler sent two letters suggesting that the men of the First Maine be distributed to infantry and artillery units, that the officers be mustered out, and that the valuable horses be given to him for artillery and transportation.[50]

Governor Washburn went to James G. Blaine, who knew Stanton personally, to obtain assistance that would preserve his regiment. Like his predecessors working to preserve the First New York Cavalry, Blaine went to Washington. He would argue hyperbolically: even if all other cavalry regiments were disbanded, the Union could not be saved without the First Maine Cavalry. During several conversations, Stanton, a man of mindless stubbornness, was intractable. Even Vice President Hannibal Hamlin, Senator William Pitt Fessenden, and Senator Justin Morrill could not budge the secretary. Fortuitously, a Regular Army officer who happened to be at the War Department on other business became an inadvertent participant in the campaign, saying the First Maine had no equal in American cavalry history and the United States could not afford to disband it. Confronted by this speech and a "good, round, square cavalry oath," Stanton yielded at last.[51]

After a long hard winter in its quarters in Maine, the regiment traveled to Washington. The few ancient muskets issued for guard duty and the wooden sabers made from lathes were replaced in March by real sabres and pistols. Training with real weapons was about to begin.

At the beginning of the war cavalrymen received various mixtures of rifles, carbines, lances, pistols, and sabers. Pistols and sabers were perfect weapons for the close fighting of a great cavalry charge. Scouting, screening, reconnaissance, fighting on foot, and other activities requiring longer range weapons? McClellan would not give these assignments to his cavalry in the early period of his command. The future of cavalry was so uncertain and its duties so poorly defined that no one knew how to arm it. In any event longer range weapons did not exist for all who needed them.[52] The pistols and sabres had the great convenience of availability.

But even these available weapons were not always functional. In December of 1861, the Eighth Illinois cavalry, commanded by Colonel John F. Farnsworth, was

49 Blaine in Tobie, *First Maine Cavalry*, 11, Speech at 1876 Regimental reunion.

50 Rebellion Record, letters dated February 12 and 14, 1862, from Butler to Stanton.

51 Blaine, 1878 regimental reunion speech, reprinted in Tobie, *First Maine Cavalry*, 11.

52 *M.O.S.*, 109-110, 118-119; Reverend S. L. Gracey, *The Annals of the Sixth Pennsylvania Cavalry* (Philadelphia, 1868), 34-35 (Gracey, *Sixth Pennsylvania Cavalry*).

armed with pistols. When put to the test, many misfired several times before discharging; and some could not be made to fire at all. Colonel Farnsworth and his quartermaster made several unsuccessful attempts to exchange them. Finally, Elon J. Farnsworth, John's younger brother, who was known for his shrewdness and wit, said he could arrange to have them exchanged.

He selected a number of the worst pistols, took a few men, went to General Edwin V. Sumner, and told him the problem.

"The men should be satisfied with the arms furnished them and not be finding fault," responded Sumner.

"But, General, let me show you," said Farnsworth. The men began loading the pistols. Talking rapidly to the general in his quick, nervous way, Farnsworth explained the problem.

Sumner must have seen what was coming. "But stop," he said, "You are not going to shoot here?"

Farnsworth had already decided on his next step.

"Well, well. Just let me show you."

By this time the men had loaded the pistols. They pointed at the fireplace and prepared to pull the triggers.

"Hold! Hold!" commanded Sumner. "You must not shoot here."

"No danger. Not the least danger," said Farnsworth still pulling away in vain at the trigger. "I assure you they are perfectly harmless."

When Farnsworth concluded that he had demonstrated the worthlessness of the pistols, he handed one to Sumner. The white-haired old general threw it aside and wrote an order to have them exchanged, remarking, "They are not fit to go to war with."[53]

53 Abner Hard, *History of the Eighth Cavalry Regiment Illinois Volunteers* (Aurora, 1868), 56-57 (Hard, *Eighth Illinois Cavalry*).

Chapter 31

"When I found you had gone a thousand yards in front, I cannot tell you my feelings."

–Andrew Porter to Charles Griffin

The Artillery: The Middle Class Dominates

The chief of artillery, Major William F. Barry, began the war as a staff officer of great promise. In 1838, he graduated seventeenth in his West Point class. He served in Mexico, then in Florida. Before the firing on Fort Sumter, Barry was one of the numerous officers giving substance to Colonel Browne's geography rule. Assigned to Washington, he participated in the hospitality normally enjoyed by the military. Receptions and balls were accompanied by many parties. The light artillery returned these compliments by show drills. "My Captain Barry was full of dash and show," wrote Tidball after the war, "and made his exercises fascinating to the onlookers, to most of whom a light battery was a novel sight."

Barry was tall, slender, forty-three years old, dignified in his bearing, and very reserved, but with a happy disposition. He was a hard worker, systematic, and "just the person needed to organize new artillery." In a long inspection of various artillery units on a cold day in December, Barry sat his horse impervious to the elements while his subordinates' teeth chattered. He conducted a thorough inspection, examining every strap of harness, every key of the carriages, and every implement in the boxes.

Barry sailed from New York as part of the successful expedition to reinforce Fort Pickens. On May 14, he was promoted to major; and on July 5, he re-embarked with his battery from Fort Pickens for New York. When he arrived in New York ten days later he received orders to take the battery to Washington at once and report to General McDowell. Arriving in Washington the next day, he drew ammunition, collected additional horses, marched after McDowell, and joined the army on July 16 at Fairfax Court House. Three days later and only two days before the battle he yielded command of his battery in order to assume his duties as a major of artillery and chief of artillery of the army.[1]

Napoleon, an artilleryman by training, believed that huge concentrations of artillery were essential for a good infantry attack, sometimes creating a gun line of as many as one hundred pieces,[2] the lower the quality of the infantry, the more guns needed.[3] Concentration of artillery fire, a problem of artillery tactics and theory for decades to come, presented itself at Bull Run. Any solution, no matter how rudimentary, owed little to Barry. After the eleven guns bounced up the steep northern slope to the Henry house yard, Barry seemed to watch the effect of their shells on the tree line to his front. Their supports, improperly placed, had found positions themselves; and Griffin was forced to order one of the two regiments away from his immediate rear where all the counter battery "overs" would land in it.[4]

But the most culpable act of all was Barry's order not to fire on the Confederate regiment which eventually shot the two batteries to pieces.[5] Before that critical volley, the position was relatively secure, the guns safe, and the unknown steadiness of the infantry supports immaterial. The crushing Confederate volley was the first sound of federal defeat. Whatever the circumstances may have been, Barry was at fault. The fact that the Confederate regiment broke and ran after it fired showed that

1 Tidball MS Rem (L.C.), 112-113; NA Off's MS Rpts (Barry) letter of March 2, 1864; Nevins, *Wainwright Diary*, viii; *D.A.B.*, 1, pt. 1, 22-23; Warner, *Generals in Blue*, 22-23.

2 Chandler, *Napoleon*, 1, 363.

3 Chandler, *Napoleon*, 1, 340.

4 *C.C.W.*, 1, 168 ff (Griffin).

5 An unavoidable mistake? Today as always, the army has two rules for evaluating the conduct of its officers: "You can't argue with success" (if an officer fails to follow procedures but produces the right result, without being insubordinate, his conduct is approved, perhaps even lauded); and "You are responsible for everything that happens under your command" (even if you follow the rules, you are at fault for everything that goes wrong without regard for extenuating circumstances).

it would not have withstood the blast of canister Griffin wanted to give it at two hundred yards.

On July 23, Scott ordered Barry to return to Washington in order to reorganize the field artillery forces of the entire United States Army. A few days later, he was appointed by McClellan chief of artillery of what would become the Army of the Potomac. On August 20, McClellan asked that he be appointed brigadier general of volunteers by the president, and Lincoln endorsed the request favorably.[6] Unlike Barnard, Barry liked and respected McClellan; his favorable attitude would continue uninterrupted beyond McClellan's tenure with the Potomac army.[7] But he was naive and susceptible to being misled.

Forty-five guns of all caliber went into battle on Sunday, July 21. Two of them were the boat howitzers organic to the Seventy-First New York.[8] Disregarding these two guns, which were part of an infantry regiment and were served by infantrymen, General McDowell's army had eleven batteries of four or six guns each, all served by Regulars except for two: the six-gun Rhode Island battery under Reynolds and the six-gun battery belonging to the Eighth New York Infantry. The officers of the Regular batteries were West Point graduates ranging back to the Class of 1851,[9] all of whom had been continuously on active duty since graduation. Most had seen active service. All knew well the use of their arm. Because no Regular Army battery had undergone a wholesale change of command as a result of the promotions on May 14, 1861, the artillery officers occupied positions they had previously held for some time and were often leading the units they had trained in peacetime. Of the two volunteer batteries, the men of Varian's Independent Battery, attached to the Eighth New York, claimed their discharge on the morning of July 21. Their guns were served by volunteers who had previous experience as artillerymen in European armies.

Although the overall organization of the artillery was deficient in the eyes of sophisticated and thoughtful critics,[10] command of the artillery for a battle as small

6 Basler, *Lincoln's Works*, 4, 494, letter dated August 20, 1861, from Lincoln to Cameron and endorsement.

7 Comte de Paris MSS (A.N. de la M. de F.) letter dated September 20, 1864, from Barry to the Comte de Paris.

8 In his report, *OR*, 2, 345-46, Barry disqualifies the six guns attached to the Eighth New York Militia, Varian's Independent Battery, but they were served during the day by volunteers after their crews demanded discharge. The total should not be Barry's forty-nine, but rather fifty-five.

9 See generally the *Cullum* and *Heitman* sketches of these men. Lieutenant John Edwards was the youngest Regular artillery officer in command of a battery.

10 Henry Jackson Hunt MSS (L.C.) draft letter dated December 16, 1861, from Hunt to McClellan (the final version, bearing the same date is in the McClellan MSS); Misc. Civ. War

as Bull Run was stable; and individual batteries were well led. Field artillery, resting on principles of chemistry, physics, geometry, and mathematics, would thrive in a middle-class bourgeois society of shopkeepers, bookkeepers, surveyors, and artisans.[11] An agrarian, aristocratic planter society like the South could certainly create skilled artillerymen; but they would be creations, not natural products. And they would not be numerous.[12] Although it was not clear at Bull Run, the Union officers in this branch were far superior to their Confederate counterparts. Quality, quantity, and superiority characterized the early artillery officers of the Union army. The finest artilleryman to serve on either side during the war, Henry Jackson Hunt, made his debut at Blackburn's Ford.

In the battle at Bull Run Creek the artillery introduced one of the problems that would baffle both artillery and infantry throughout the war, ammunition resupply on the battlefield. Both the Regular and volunteer batteries were equipped helter skelter with guns of varying calibers, light twelves, 10-pounder rifles, 13-pounder James rifles, 6-pounders, 12-pounder howitzers, 10-pounder Parrott rifles, and boat howitzers. Worst of all, the guns were not necessarily uniform within a battery.[13] Many of the old Regular Army batteries had mixed equipment, a supply officer's worst nightmare. Once on the field of battle, each gun in a battery armed with a variety of pieces was limited to the ammunition in its chest and its limber. When that had been expended, it was useless. Worse, it then became a battlefield liability because it could not defend itself; and its men were not equipped with firearms. To be certain that a gun without ammunition was safe, it would be sent off the field.

The unavailability of ammunition resupply probably encouraged an uncontrolled rate of fire. Once the ammunition was gone, the gunners could expect to be sent to the rear—and safety. On July 21, the firing of the Rhode Island battery "was exceedingly rapid, every one appearing to feel that the great object was to make as much noise as possible, and get an immense quantity of iron into the enemy's line in the shortest possible space of time, without regards to whether it hit anything or not . . . very little attention was paid to the effect of the shot for some

Letters (N.Y.H.S.) endsmnt by W. T. Sherman on the rpt of William F. Barry, dated March 31, 1865, and letter dated April 1, 1864, from John Bigelow to "Judge"; McClellan MSS (L.C.) letter dated December 13, 1867, from Hunt to McClellan; *C.C.W.*, 2, 91 (Hunt).

11 Elting, *Swords Around a Throne*, 250; Goerlitz, *History of the German General Staff*, 8; Rothenberg, in Paret, *Makers of Modern Strategy*, 66; Chandler, *Napoleon*, 1, 69. As far back as the reign of Louis XIV the commissaire general d'artillerie was "a man of the middle class." Rothenberg, *supra*.

12 Byrne, *Haskell Letters*, 114-115, letter of July 16, 1863, from Haskell to his family.

13 *OR*, 2, 345-346.

time," commented one officer after the war.[14] Good artillery officers, many of whom received their baptism in this battle, would come to be appalled at this.[15]

Drilling in the artillery, like that of other combat arms, involved individual training and unit training—drilling with a single gun; drilling of a two gun "section" commanded by a lieutenant; and drilling by battery under the battery commander. As this work progressed, it identified proficient and deficient officers. Battery L of the Second New York Artillery Regiment had been assigned to the Artillery Reserve in Camp Barry in the vicinity of Franklin's division on the Seminary grounds near Alexandria, the camp for the twenty-three batteries in Barry's Reserve Brigade. The battery had achieved a high level of proficiency at section drill, and its officers had been tested by the artillery board. The unit, however, had performed no battery exercises because the battery commander, Captain Thomas L. Robinson, never appeared for drill. First Lieutenant Jacob L. Roemer, a naturalized German who had funded many of the battery's original financial obligations, reported to the battery commander that the unit had made good progress. He inquired whether Captain Robinson would join it for section drills.

Robinson said he would appear that day, but would do battery drill. Roemer remonstrated that the unit was not yet ready for battery drill. Robinson did not care.

But General Barry, Roemer protested, always watched the drills of his batteries. This, too, had no effect. On the drill ground, the battery halted in a single column of guns. Robinson guided his mount over to Roemer. He wanted to change the formation from a column to a line.

"Lieutenant Roemer, the first movement will be 'Battery Front into Line.'"

"All right, captain."

Robinson rode to a position by the middle of the column.

"Forward into line, march," ordered the captain.

Defective, the command could not be executed. Roemer raised his saber.

"Halt!" he commanded.

Robinson rode back to him. "Lieutenant Roemer, what is the matter?"

"Captain, you did not give the right command for the execution of the maneuver you wish to have performed."[16]

14 Monroe in *Broadfoot MOLLUS Rhode Island*, 32, 36.

15 *OR*, 21, 49, 827-828; Longacre, *The Man Behind the Guns*, 126-127

16 William French, William F. Barry, and Henry J. Hunt, *Instructions for Field Artillery* (Philadelphia, 1861), 94, paras. 53 and 54, depending on whether the battery was marching left in front or right in front but it had to be marching before the preparatory command and the command of execution could be given.

"Well, I will give it again."

He gave exactly the same command. Roemer again raised his saber and called for a halt. Robinson turned his horse and rode toward camp. The two junior lieutenants commanding sections rode to Roemer.

"What shall we do now?"

"Lieutenants, we are all right. General Barry and Colonel Bailey have not as yet noticed the blunder. Take your respective stations and we will see if we cannot perform the maneuver 'Battery Front into line;'" but be careful to give the right commands to your sergeants."

Roemer rode to the left, raised his saber, and gave the commands.

"Column, forward march." The guns began to move.

"Column forward into line, left oblique, march!" The guns veered into line "like veterans."

"Halt."

"Right dress."

"Front."

To the front of the line of guns, now in position to fire, Roemer guided his horse. "Officers and men, that was well done."

The lieutenants asked about the next maneuver.

"Recollect, this is now 'Battery Front.' The next command will be 'Battery Forward.'"

"Attention. Battery forward, march. Right section, right wheel. Left section, left wheel. Center section, forward, march." Having sent each two gun section in its own direction, Roemer now commanded, "Each lieutenant will take command of his own section and drill it in section drill."

After excellent additional drilling, the battery prepared to leave the drill ground for camp. Colonel Guilford D. Bailey, chief of artillery of Camp Barry, appeared. He congratulated the men on a splendid drill and asked for the battery commander.

Roemer responded loyally that the captain had come out with them but had returned to camp earlier.

"Well, lieutenants, you have had a very fine drill. General Barry was very much pleased with it and wished me to present you with his compliments and congratulate you on your efficiency."

When the battery reached camp, Roemer reported the good news to Captain Robinson. The battery commander had not recovered from the slight unintentionally administered by his subordinate.

"Lieutenant Roemer," he said, "I want you to understand that I command this battery and not you."

The conversation marked the end of all cordiality between the two men. Roemer and one other lieutenant agreed that the captain was inadequate. Although all battery officers had taken their examinations before the artillery board, nothing had been heard. Everyone believed nothing would happen as a result. Roemer, a forty-three-year-old lieutenant, found all this and other indignities intolerable. He decided to resign and return home with his wife and son, who were visiting. The other lieutenant intended to join him. They sent resignations to Colonel Bailey. The next day Bailey came to visit them.

"Gentlemen," he began, "General Barry and I have had a talk about the papers. We know who are the workers in this battery. I came to return these papers, but now I will hold them until there are some developments relating to the affairs of your battery, and they will most likely occur soon."

Meanwhile, Roemer and his fellows learned, to their unpleasant surprise, that Robinson had not reported the battery ready for the field. As a result they were to be cannibalized to bring a battery trained for the field to its full complement of animals. They were ordered to deliver sixty of their best horses. The men who had trained the fine horses they were about to lose stole them from the stable and took them for an all day ride out the Bladensburg Road. Others drowned their feelings in "the flowing bowl" and cursed the captain.

Meanwhile, Roemer's wife was preparing to leave. She wanted to know if Roemer and the other lieutenant had tendered their resignations. Roemer said the resignations were awaiting acceptance by General Barry.

"I don't want you to resign. What would the people of Flushing say if you should depart the battery here? No! I would rather have your dead body brought to me from the battlefield than have this happen just now. It was a struggle for me in the first place to give my consent for your going into the army, but now that you have undertaken this work and have promised the wives of most of the men to stand by their husbands, I will make all sacrifices for your honor and will gladly care for our children if you shall fall in so just a cause."

"I will heed your words, my dear wife," said Roemer, inspired by her staunch speech. "And as Heaven is my witness, I will stand by the battery amid shot and shell. You are a woman who has taught a soldier his duty to his country."

Several unpleasant months, marked by severe vilification of the captain, passed. Finally, the cloud dispersed. All others learned they had passed the Board. Captain Robinson, however, had failed and was discharged from the service. Governor Morgan promoted Roemer to battery commander, another junior officer to first lieutenant, and others to fill other gaps.

"Gentlemen," said Colonel Bailey, "this is the reason why I asked the two of you to withhold your resignations. After the examination of February twenty-fifth, I knew what must happen in the battery; but I was not permitted to explain matters until we had heard from Governor Morgan. The papers just received and presented to Captain Robinson have been under way three months. Now, gentlemen, work together and see how soon the battery can be made ready for active service in the field."[17]

After Bull Run the field artillery entered a new era governed by new attitudes. Both McDowell and McClellan considered their artillery important. In fact, McClellan believed the war "had become a duel of artillery" and refused "to move until he [had] . . . 600 guns."[18] An artillery contingent of this size demanded many changes in the ancient system, even though that had been as effective as it had in Mexico. Barry proposed a number of improvements for the artillery McClellan eventually inherited. With its losses the artillery had only parts of nine batteries amounting to thirty pieces of various calibers, most of the batteries having mixed calibers and insufficient other equipment. He suggested that the artillery initially have two and a half guns per thousand men, later to be increased to three pieces per thousand. With all artillery used only for direct fire, in which the men at the guns could see their targets, the exceptional range and greater accuracy of rifled artillery was generally useless in the uneven, wooded Virginia–Maryland countryside.[19] The proportion of rifled guns was to be restricted. Parrots and smoothbores were to be exclusively the 12-pounder model of 1857, the Napoleon, with the exception of a few howitzers for special service. Ordinarily, each battery would have six guns but no less than four in any case, and all guns in a battery should be the same caliber. Each gun should carry four hundred rounds of ammunition into battle.

To facilitate training and concentration of fire (the latter a signal failing at Bull Run), each division would have a battalion of four batteries, no batteries to brigades or regiments, one battery of Regulars and the remainder volunteers. The captain of the Regular battery would command the artillery of the division. Instruction in the theory and practice of gunnery, tactics of artillery, and other basics would be given to officers and non-commissioned officers of the volunteer batteries through suitable textbooks and by recitations in each division. The Regular officer commanding division artillery would direct this course of instruction. He would perform frequent personal inspections and report the improvement of officers and enlisted men and their fitness for field service.

"In the event of several divisions constituting an army corps," Barry wrote in his plan, "at least one-half of the divisional artillery was to constitute the reserve artillery of the corps." The artillery reserve for the army would consist of one

17 Jacob Roemer, ed. by L. A. Furney, *Reminiscences of the War of the Rebellion 1861-1865*, 17, 19-24, 28-29 (New York, 1897); Heitman, *Historical Register*, 1, 181.

18 Gurowski, *Diary*, 1, 99, 107, entries dated September and October, 1861.

19 In the case of the artillery, unlike the cavalry, this analysis of the effect of Virginia's topography was correct.

hundred guns, composed of light mounted batteries, guns of position, and all horse artillery "until the cavalry was massed." A siege train of fifty pieces would accompany the army. To command the Reserve Artillery, McClellan on September 12, 1861, selected Major Henry Jackson Hunt, who had served at Bull Run, and arranged for him to be promoted to colonel. This was probably the largest artillery line command in the history of the United States Army to that date.[20]

The immediate and obvious problems of the artillery were well considered in Barry's report to McClellan, but more subtle problems were recognized by more subtle thinkers. Barry was not one of them, and McClellan realized it. On December 13 he received an apparently unsolicited letter from Major Hunt. In it, Hunt described a system of training and drill he thought equally applicable to infantry, artillery, and cavalry.[21] McClellan was intrigued; and Hunt, he must have known, was a well-regarded, thoughtful artillery officer. He asked Hunt to propose revisions for the artillery structure. On December 16, Hunt drafted a long response and with slight tinkering prepared a final version the same day. Although he did not say it in so many words, he addressed the anomalous staff-line position of the chief of artillery, gave a short lecture on artillery history, and suggested remedies for several problems. The letter was prophetic.

Within the last two years before the war, Hunt wrote, the artillery had been employed at extreme frontier stations on duties unrelated to artillery service. "This arrangement, the prominent feature of what is now called the *treasonable* dispersion of the army by the late Secretary of War, was instigated and brought about by an army officer, his confidential advisor, against the earnest and repeated remonstrances of the General in Chief and other officers." The wretched condition of the Regular Army field artillery, as Hunt saw it, was "the legitimate result of this act . . . Great evils might probably have been spared the country had its artillery been under the direction of a proper chief, and thus secured against the interference of vagrant advisors ignorant of its duties and wants." Involved in a full-scale war, the army could no longer afford to treat its artillery like an illegitimate child surviving on hand outs from its infantry and cavalry parents. "At present the batteries scramble for what they can get, and the supplies depend more upon the whims and caprices of officers of other arms rather than upon the knowledge and experience of their own. This leads to great waste without securing efficiency."

20 *OR*, 5, 67; *M.O.S.*, 114, 117; Longacre, *Man Behind the Guns*, 98-99.

21 Hunt MSS (L.C.) letter of December 13, 1861, from Hunt to McClellan. The treatment of Hunt's system would rankle him lifelong because it was taken without attribution or credit by the French for their infantry, and by Upton for his tactics. Longacre, *Man Behind the Guns*, 66-67.

To begin, Hunt would put the artillery under a chief to ensure unity of administration. "All supplies and stores relating to the batteries should be taken up and accounted for on returns rendered to the chief of artillery . . ." The regimental organization would be abandoned, and the batteries consolidated into one corps. "Artillery acts by batteries as units not by battalions," he wrote. The batteries would also be more independent and flexible than the typical relationships among the infantry companies of a regiment. But when a number of batteries fell under a common commander, a staff was necessary for their management and supplies. Commissioned and non-commissioned officers equal to those of a regiment would be retained in a pool for distribution to the commands needing them.

The troops would be organized for artillery duties, and the officers and men given the same advantages offered to other branches of the service. A "platoon from the ranks" would be created for the non-commissioned staff and clerks.[22] This was necessary in the artillery to avoid losing talented men to staff functions outside their batteries. Ordnance sergeants were necessary. Prior to 1832 the artillery, like the artillery in other countries, performed all ordnance duties, which included care of the guns and equipment, and development of new artillery and techniques.[23]

Between 1832 and 1838, a separate ordnance department had existed but without officers below the rank of captain. The duties of lower grades were performed by lieutenants of artillery. In 1838, the grade of lieutenant was given to the ordnance, which then began to receive its officers directly from the Military Academy. Hunt wished to revert to the system of 1832 and pass all artillery lieutenants through a course of practical instruction at the arsenals, filling vacancies occurring in the captaincies of ordnance by selection from the first lieutenants of artillery. This would leave all artillery officers free to serve only in the artillery, and the promotion of artillery officers in the subsistence and quartermaster departments could then be prohibited. If it were not done, Hunt wanted a second captain to be created for the artillery, the second captain to be available for non-line responsibilities.

Hunt considered the term "light artillery" to be very vague and indefinite. "Field artillery" was the proper name, he wrote. He wanted to drop the term "company,"

22 Probably a forerunner of today's gunless headquarters battery in a battalion.

23 The artillery had already won itself a position of high regard for its performance in the Mexican War. Around the corner was indirect fire and the forward observer, which would replace the "battery commander" system for adjustment of artillery fire. These two developments would make American artillery the best in the world and the most feared of all American battlefield weapons.

which more properly referred to infantry or cavalry. The term "battery" would be used in its place.[24]

Although Hunt and Barry may have disagreed about some aspects of organization, administration, and equipment, they managed to work together with William H. French, an artilleryman gone to the infantry, and were probably friends. In the late 1850s the three men were appointed a Light Artillery Board to prepare a revised system of Light Artillery Tactics. In January of 1859, they made their submission: *Instruction for Field Artillery*, which was approved by the president. In March of the following year the secretary of war adopted their recommendation and prohibited any maneuver inconsistent with their system.[25]

For both the artillery and the cavalry the line and staff disagreement continued; and the problem of overall management remained without a solution in spite of the creation of division artillery organizations. Wisely, Barry wanted full tactical or line authority over all artillery in the army. Administrative supervision was not enough. McClellan convened a board of officers to report on the artillery command structures in foreign armies. The board reported wide variations and made no firm recommendations. McClellan made his own decision, based surely on his thoughtful consideration and logic. He knew that no one man could exercise direct command over six hundred guns in more than one hundred batteries deployed from flank to flank, especially along a battle line of several miles. McClellan had already announced in orders that the duties of the chief of artillery—would be "exclusively administrative." He would serve at headquarters of the Army of the Potomac.[26]

Henry Hunt did not overtly pursue Barry's job as chief of artillery for the Army of the Potomac, but he was certainly a competitor. He had all the natural instincts of an artilleryman. He understood its science, organization, and administration. Barry was a fine artilleryman and a good officer but had the "black spot" for his failure at

24 Hunt MSS (L.C.) draft letter of December 16, 1861, from Hunt to McClellan; the original final copy, bearing the same date is in the McClellan MSS (L.C.) letter dated December 16, 1861, from Hunt to McClellan. "Field artillery" and "battery" remain terms of art in the artillery today. Overall command of artillery units above the battery level would remain an important question of coordination throughout the twentieth century.

25 French, Barry and Hunt, *Instructions for Artillery*, preface, letter dated January 15, 1859, from French, Barry, and Hunt to Cooper; letter dated March 6, 1860, from John B. Floyd.

26 William E. Birkhimer, *Historical Sketch of Artillery* (Washington, 1884), 213; Henry J. Hunt, "Artillery Administration," in *Journal of the Military Institute of the United States*, 12, 217-218 (1891), discussed in Longacre, *Man Behind the Guns*, 99. At the time the issue amounted to an academic discussion. Later, Hunt, the most respected artillery officer in the Union forces, would have a severe and lifetime disagreement with one of the most respected Union corps commanders. Today, the United States Army has complicated procedures for coordinating and concentrating artillery fire across regimental and division lines through division artillery and corps artillery commanders.

Bull Run. Although his error might have been forgotten, it was not. Stephen Minot Weld, an aide on Fitz-John Porter's staff, wrote that Griffin's battery had been lost at Bull Run "through the want of military knowledge of other parties, who ordered him within musket range of the enemy without supporting him by sufficient infantry." Weld thought the federal army had lost the battle in great measure because Barry ordered Griffin not to fire on regiments marching in front of him, saying that they were Union troops.[27] Others agreed.

The events on Henry House Hill among Barry, Griffin, and Ricketts remained unknown to many. Charles Griffin, described after the war as "bellicose" and "disposed to be cynical," was a sharp-tongued, sarcastic, excellent young officer with a bright future.[28] Ricketts, a wounded prisoner in Confederate captivity, could not become involved in any controversy. Griffin did not suffer this or any other disability on the subject, nor was he timid about expressing his opinions. In the late fall or early winter Andrew Porter queried Griffin "very severely," as Griffin recalled it, about his vulnerable position near Judith Henry's house.

"Sir, I want to know how you got into such a situation."

"I went in accordance with the order of General Barry from General McDowell."

Porter responded that he relied on Griffin's battery because it was his only one. "When I found you had gone a thousand yards in advance, I cannot tell you my feelings. I was afraid I had allowed you to go there upon my order."

Had the captain used his own discretion to go on the hill? Porter believed this Griffin decided.[29] Even worse, few people knew that Griffin's battery had been ready to blow the Confederate regiment to pieces when Barry stopped him. Unwilling to allow this misinformation to continue, Griffin denounced Barry. Naive, Barry for some time did not realize he was being criticized both inside and outside the army.

On February 7, 1862, Barry sent a letter by Major Alexander S. Webb to Griffin. He had just learned "with surprise," he said, that Griffin was criticizing his conduct at Bull Run. Barry wanted to know what Griffin was saying in order to determine whether or not he should request a court of inquiry.[30] Barry could not wait, and the next day sent a request to McClellan for a court of inquiry because of "statements of

27 Weld, *Diary and Letters*, 59-60, letter dated February 18, 1862, from Weld to Hannah. Military Historical Society of Massachusetts MSS (John C. Ropes Letters) (B.U.), letter dated August 8, 1861, from Bache to Ropes.

28 Warner, *Generals in Blue*, 190-191; *D.A.B.*, 4, pt. 1, 617-618; Powell, *Officers*, 327.

29 *C.C.W.*, 2, 172 (Griffin).

30 Webb MSS (Y.U.) letter dated February 18, 1862, from Griffin to Webb.

a nature derogatory to [Barry's] official character which are rumored to have been made by him." He enclosed a copy of his letter to Griffin.

McClellan found the letter from Barry to Griffin "personal rather than official in tone and expression" and was indisposed to take official action on it. "As to the rest there are obviously grave objections to the summoning [of] a Court of Inquiry at the present time and the commanding general would be glad if the subject were not pressed." Nevertheless, Barry could ask for the court if "the necessity is found by you to be imperative."[31]

Because he had made no secret of his opinions since the battle, Griffin was surprised that Barry had been so long hearing them. He scrutinized the letter. It appeared to be official; but it also appeared not to have been sent through proper channels. He returned it to Webb.[32]

"It is just the thing I wished. General Barry must send it through the proper official channels."[33]

A short time later Griffin asked Webb if, in fact, Barry had sent the letter in the proper manner. Webb responded that it had been sent through General McClellan's headquarters. This would have satisfied Griffin because it would give widespread publicity to his criticism, but Barry withdrew the letter.[34]

Barry's personal problems did not change the diverse responsibilities of the chief of artillery or the developing artillery forces. Apart from the field artillery units necessary for the army on the battlefield, artillery had to be prepared for the fortifications around Washington when McClellan departed. As early as September, the major general had begun to accumulate heavy artillery regiments that would be left behind to man the guns in the forts.[35] Larger than the standard one thousand men and thirty-six officers of an ordinary infantry regiment, they would number almost two thousand men each.[36] And the duty would not inflict the difficult living

31 Letters Sent, 16, RG 108, NA, letter dated February 14, 1862, from McClellan to Barry.

32 Webb MSS (Y.U.) letter dated February 18, 1862, from Griffin to Webb.

33 Webb MSS (Y.U.) letter dated February 19, 1862, from Webb to Griffin. The language in the letter is in quotation marks but is phrased in indirect discourse. Here, it is kept in quotation marks and converted to direct discourse.

34 Webb MSS (Y.U.) letters dated February 18, 1862, from Griffin to Webb and February 19, 1862, from Webb to Griffin. The dates of the events described in the letters cannot be determined from the letters' content, but they were earlier.

35 Union Defense Committee MSS (N.Y.H.S.) dispatch of September 25, 1861, from Draper to McClellan (in response to a letter of request from McClellan dated September 23, 1861-not found); de Joinville, *Army of the Potomac*, 26-27.

36 Hyland Kirk, *Heavy Guns and Light: A History of the 4th New York Heavy Artillery* (New York, 1890), 9-10; Henry Hall, *Cayuga in the Field: A Record of the 19th N.Y. Volunteers, and Third New York Artillery Comprising an Account of Their Organization, Camp Life, Marches,*

conditions of ordinary infantrymen and artillerymen. Billets would be in the capital. As one recruiting poster said, "The regiment being quartered in the forts around Washington, never to leave them, affords to persons wishing to enter the military service the inappreciable advantage of being exempted from all the hardships and privations of camp life."[37] This appealed to many, even some already in the army, who tried to arrange the transfer of their regiments to this life.[38] The Nineteenth New York Infantry was a perfect candidate for the Washington defenses.

Disgruntled over ragged uniforms, inadequate food, mistreatment by Patterson, and apparent sleight of hand in its conversion to two-year service, the Nineteenth became mutinous and was subdued only when army headquarters threatened a trip to the Dry Tortugas. Its lieutenant-colonel, James H. Ledlie, a young man of Irish descent, medium stature, good proportions, dark eyes, active mind, and exceptional talents as an engineer and politician, met McClellan and Governor Morgan of New York while at lunch at Seward's house. Ledlie had great popularity in the army and powerful influence in Washington. When the conversation centered on the needs of the army and the heavy fortifications being built around the capital, Ledlie used his "remarkable affability and dignity" to tout his regiment.

"Colonel," said McClellan to Ledlie, "how would you like to have your regiment converted to engineers?"

"If you want to do anything for me, general, I can tell you something I would like better than that."

"What is it?"

"Give me authority to raise an artillery regiment."

Morgan and Seward supported the suggestion. McClellan invited Ledlie to see him the next day.

Seward accompanied Ledlie to the meeting, where McClellan and Ledlie agreed that Ledlie would use the Nineteenth New York as a base from which to recruit an artillery regiment of one thousand nine hundred men. McClellan sent instructions to the adjutant-general for the necessary papers.

Regimental commander Colonel Charles H. Stewart reported the news to Brigadier General Alpheus Williams, his brigade commander. The unwelcome

Battles, Losses, Toils and Triumphs in the War for the Union, With Complete Rolls of their Numbers (Auburn, 1873), 57, 85 (Hall, *Cayuga in the Field*); George W. Ward, *History of the Second Pennsylvania Veteran Heavy Artillery from 1861 to 1865 (112th Regiment Pennsylvania Volunteers) from 1861 to 1865 including the Provisional Second Penn. Heavy Artillery*, 2 (Philadelphia, 1904).

37 Comte de Paris MS diary (large diary) (A.N. de la M. de F.) entry of January 8, 1862.

38 Sears, *For Country Cause & Leader (Haydon Diary)*, 155-158, December 23, 1861.

thought of losing an experienced regiment prompted Williams to say he did not believe the Nineteenth would ever wear the red stripe of an artilleryman.[39]

"You will never see anything larger than calibre .69," he added.

"Yes, I will."

Stubbornly, Williams said, "No, you won't."

But on December 11, McClellan issued Special Orders No. 326 from Headquarters of the Army converting the Nineteenth to a regiment of heavy artillery.[40]

39 Each combat arm has its own color, now and then, infantry light blue, cavalry yellow, and artillery red.

40 Banks MSS (L.C.) letter of September 12, 1861, from Marcy to Banks; Hall, *Cayuga in the Field*, 27, 57, 58-59, 85. Originally a three-month regiment, the regiment was reorganized as the Nineteenth New York Volunteers, a two-year regiment, and then changed to the Third New York Light Artillery on January 31, 1862. *Official Army Register*, 2, 392.

Chapter 32

"Why, President Lincoln can make a brigadier-general in five minutes; but it has taken five years to make you an engineer soldier."

– Captain J. C. Duane to an enlisted engineer who wanted to seek a commission

Barnard's Engineers Make a Fortress

To undertake his plans, McClellan knew he must have freedom to leave the capital, freedom to maneuver with his field force, freedom to defend Washington with a garrison. He simply could not accomplish his task of defeating and destroying the Rebel army if Lincoln compromised his maneuverability by requiring that he keep his army between the capital and the Confederates. Especially if he decided to leave the capital area by water, he had to make Washington a stand-alone, fortified area safe against attack by a large force. Safe it must be without the presence of his army. He needed a system of fortification that would allow a small garrison to repulse persistent attacks by a major Confederate army until friendly fighting forces could come to the rescue. He, Barnard, and Barry must design, build, equip, and garrison the capital's fortifications.

The safety of Washington had been a matter of grave concern from the outbreak of hostilities. On July 8, 1861, after the federal forces occupied the west bank of the Potomac River, the House of Representatives passed a resolution requesting information about defensive works to be constructed around the capital on both sides of the river "to reduce to the minimum the number of troops required for the defense of the capital." The resolution was addressed to the secretary of war, but by its terms it was to be answered by the engineers. Toward the middle of the month McClellan referred the resolution to John G. Barnard, McDowell's chief of engineers.

Barnard had already begun to make secure the means of access to the west bank, the Aqueduct, the Long Bridge, and Alexandria. In the seven weeks between May 24 and July 16, he and his junior engineer officers supervised the construction of forts, infantry parapets, and block houses in those locations. "When the army first crossed the Potomac . . . ," he wrote later to Secretary Chase, "no extended system of fortifications for Wash'n was contemplated" and in that short time, he reported in December, the "general reconnaissances and studies necessary for locating a line of defensive works around the city and preparing plans and estimates of the same" were not possible. But he believed the basic work had been "nearly completed" when he marched with McDowell on July 16. When McDowell's defeated army and George McClellan reached Washington after July 21, they found works "far from constituting a defensive system which would enable an inferior force to hold the long line from Alexandria to Georgetown."[1]

"An engineer of distinction, McClellan himself devised in all its details the system of defensive works from Alexandria to Georgetown,"[2] wrote the Comte de Paris after the war. Additional works to complete the encirclement of Washington were planned on the Baltimore or "back" side. Asked when he would drill his

1 Chase MSS (U.P.I.) letter dated [February ?] 25, 1862, from Barnard to Chase; *M.O.S.*, 68; *OR*, 5, 678-679.

2 Comte de Paris, "McClellan Organizes the Army," in *B&L*, 2, 113; Comte de Paris MSS (A.N. de la M. de F.) galley proof of B&L article with notations; Prince de Joinville, trans. William Henry Hurlbert, *The Army of the Potomac: Its Organization, Its Commander, and Its Campaign* (New York, 1862), 26 (de Joinville, *Army of the Potomac*); McClellan in *B&L*, 2, 161; Ferdinand LeComte, *Campagne de Virginie et de la Maryland en 1862: Documents Officials Sounies au Congress traduits de L'Anglais avec Introduction et Annotations* (Paris, 1863); *M.O.S.*, 72-73, 93, 141; John G. Barnard, *The Peninsular Campaign and its Antecedents as Developed by the Report of Maj.-Gen. George B. McClellan and other published Documents* (New York, 1864), 14-16 (Barnard, *Peninsular Campaign*). In his mean-spirited, hyper-critical account of the Peninsular Campaign, *supra*, Barnard used his nineteenth century pamphleteering skills to attack his former chief mercilessly—and without a great deal of integrity. In it he claims, *ibid.*, n. 3, 62-63, that he selected the location for every fortification but one; and that the one was selected by General Richardson; and he implies that this was done before McClellan arrived. At best, his chief "examined" some of the sites and "in general . . . approved" all of them; but the creative work, he tells us, was his own. McClellan's claim, confirmed by the Comte de Paris and by Barnard's correspondence with Congress and Secretary Chase, has been accepted. Barnard's accounts, especially when they involve McClellan, are always suspect.

regiment, one colonel replied, "We can't drill! Our men are building forts back of the city."[3]

After McClellan finished the fortifications, he invited the president and the cabinet to inspect them. The tour began at Arlington, moved south toward Alexandria, crossed the river, traversed the southern edge, rounded the eastern end, and moved along the works facing north until they reached the most formidable of them all. Lincoln asked McClellan to explain the need for such a strong fortification north of the capital.

"Why, Mr. President, according to military science, it is our duty to guard against every possible contingency that may arise. For example, if under any circumstances, however fortuitous, the enemy, by any chance or freak, should in a last resort get in behind Washington, in his efforts to capture the city, why there the fort is to defend it."

"Yes, that's so, general. The precaution is doubtless a wise one, and I'm glad to get so clear an explanation, for it reminds me of an interesting question once discussed for several weeks in our Lyceam or moot court in Springfield, Illinois, soon after I began reading law."

"Ah, Mr. President, what question was that?"

"The question was, 'Why does man have breasts?' After many evenings' debate the question was submitted to the presiding judge, who wisely decided that under any circumstances however fortuitous or by any chance or freak, no matter of what nature or by what cause a man should have a baby, there would be the breasts to nurse it."[4]

Whether Lincoln meant to be serious, sarcastic, or humorous, he would find himself in three years in debt once again to McClellan's professional skill and good judgment.

McClellan based his design, a massive extension of the work begun on the morning of May 24, on the great Torres Vedras lines built by the Duke of Wellington to make the base for his Peninsular Campaign a place of refuge, if necessary.[5] The Torres Vedras fortifications were the best modern example of unconnected field works designed to defend extended lines.[6] Less than every yard of perimeter was to

3 Dwight Family MSS (M.H.S.), letter dated August 19, 1861, from William Dwight to his father; Nevins, *Strong Diary*, 178, entry dated September 16, 1861.

4 *New York Tribune*, October 21, 1885, p. 7, col. 4, quoting a speech by John G. Barnard. The operative paragraph, somewhat altered, is quoted in Ferenbacher, Don E., and Ferenbacher, Elizabeth, *Recollected Words of Abraham Lincoln*, 22 (Stanford, 1996).

5 Barnard and Barry, *Reports*, 13-14.

6 *M.O.S.*, 73. Sir Charles Oman, in his monumental *A History of the Peninsula War*, 7 vols. (Mechanicsburg, 1995), vol. 1, introduction ix-x (Oman, *Peninsular War*) described the origin

be guarded by an infantryman and a trench. Carefully designed fortifications would cover open areas with interlocking infantry and artillery fire. According to Napoleon, as Barnard and McClellan well knew, fifty thousand men with three thousand artillerymen protected by field fortifications could successfully defend a national capital against an assaulting army of three hundred thousand.[7]

Assisted by a growing engineer battalion, a group of bright young West Point subalterns,[8] the miraculous willingness and ability of the American infantryman with the axe and the shovel,[9] and the hard work of civilian engineers and contract labor,[10] Barnard built the engineering and Barry the artillery fortifications for the capital. The work went forward rapidly even though Company A, the old West Point Engineer Company, would not return from Fort Pickens until early October.[11]

At McClellan's request, Barnard supervised the complex construction work. He found it "an immense task." Each day the major would work at his office duties in the morning, then take to the saddle to oversee construction by the green troops. Long after dark he would return to headquarters too fatigued to think about other subjects. To him his work on the defensive fortifications around the capital was incidental to his real duties, which were to create, equip, and properly train engineer

and construction of the Torres Vedras works at some length. Wanting an absolutely safe place of refuge for his army, the Duke of Wellington, recently appointed to command the Allied forces in Spain and Portugal, selected the Lisbon peninsula in Portugal. Two lines of fortifications were constructed across the peninsula, but the word "line" is misleading. No continuous rampart ran from water to water. Separated, independent fortifications, each for approximately two to three hundred infantry and three field guns, were located on carefully chosen heights in two irregular lines that made maximum use of land and water to enhance their natural defensive strength. Between the forts the ground was made completely open. Buildings were torn down, ditches filled, mounds leveled, and excess dirt carted away. No cover existed for great distances; and any attacking force would suffer a long, unendurable fire before it reached its objective. Wherever possible, the fortifications were placed on heights behind rivers; and the rivers were dammed creating impassable swamps sometimes more than a mile wide. Infantry advancing across the swampy area would be under constant artillery fire, but their own field guns could not be brought close enough to support them. Where the ascents to the forts were steep and rugged, cover would always be available for slow approaches and sharpshooters. In these places blasting converted steep slopes to unscalable vertical escarpments. Of course, the usual man-made obstructions, trees, *chevaux de frise*, abatis, and others, added the final degree of impossibility to any assault. Oman, *Peninsular War*, 3, 191-192 (the original idea), 395-410 (first use against the French), 419-429, 433-436 (construction).

7 Barnard and Barry, *Reports*, 12, 13. The Rebels would never have, even in the deranged eyes of the Union intelligence service, a field army of 300,000. In fact, neither side would field an army of that size in the entire war.

8 Barnard and Barry, *Reports*, 13-14; *M.O.S.*, 72-73; *OR*, 5, 684.

9 Comte de Paris MSS, MS diary (large diary) (A.N. de la M. de F.) entry of September 28, 1861, account of September 22, 1861, and entry dated September 29, 1861; *M.O.S.*, 72.

10 *OR*, 5, 684-685.

11 Thompson, *Engineer Battalion*, 2.

units for a large field army; but the demands of the fortifications made him unable to train the engineer troops, collect bridging and other equipment, and create the engineer trains.

Finally deciding that he must be relieved of the fortification burdens, Barnard broached the subject with McClellan, suggesting that he assign the task to his subordinates, Colonels Benjamin S. Alexander and Daniel P. Woodbury, both of whom he praised highly. McClellan approved the idea, but Alexander and Woodbury were also severely burdened. The fortification work clung to Barnard like a leech.

In response to Barnard's complaints about the lack of trained engineer troops and his own recognition of the woeful inadequacy of McDowell's staff, McClellan tried to remedy both problems. He drafted and presented to the Senate in person legislation allowing him to appoint as many staff officers as he wanted along with legislation creating three additional companies of Regular Army engineers and an entirely new company of topographical engineers. The staff and the creation of new engineer companies passed on August 3 and authorization for the topographical engineer company on August 6.[12]

Built from the old Company A in which McClellan had served during the Mexican War, the new engineer battalion collected an extraordinary number of young officers whose exploits, for good or ill, would become well known during and after the war: Captain James C. Duane in command of the battalion, with First Lieutenants Cyrus B. Comstock, Godfrey Weitzel, C.B. Reese, and Charles B. Cross and Second Lieutenant Orville E. Babcock commanding the companies. The Regular battalion, by its expansion really a battalion of newly recruited civilian volunteers,[13] was augmented by two volunteer infantry regiments, the Fifteenth New York and the Fiftieth New York, which were designated as engineer regiments.[14]

Recruited as engineers, the Fifteenth and Fiftieth New York Regiments had been serving as infantry but had a large percentage of sailors and mechanics in their ranks. They were combined to serve as an engineer brigade under the command of Colonel Alexander, then under Colonel Woodbury, "a mild, unassuming Christian gentleman, a fine Engineer [and] a talented officer but too retiring in his disposition to attain an exalted position."[15] The brigade camp was established near the navy yard

12 Sears, *McClellan's Correspondence*, 71, letter dated July 30, 1861, from McClellan to his wife; Thompson, *Engineer Battalion*, 2; *OR*, 5, 684.

13 Thompson, *Engineer Battalion*, 4.

14 John D. Billings, *Hard Tack and Coffee or the Unwritten Story of Army Life* (Boston, 1887), 378 (Billings, *Hard Tack and Coffee*).

15 *M.O.S.*, 119; Malles, *Brainerd's Memoirs*, 58.

on the Anacostia River, the east branch of the Potomac River. Once in this position the regiments built shops to manufacture bridging equipment and made it a depot for storage of engineering materiel.

Once again, change met the resistence posed by an old, entrenched system. The Regular Army engineer officers opposed the creation of volunteer engineers. Not until mid-winter and after much lobbying did Congress finally pass legislation recognizing the two volunteer regiments as engineer troops and conferring on their officers and men the same rank and pay as those in the Regular engineer battalion. "For nearly a year after the act was passed," wrote an officer of the Fiftieth after the war, "those high in Authority would not consent to allow us to wear the Engineer button though the privilege of wearing the castle on our hats could not be denied us."[16]

Then and now, engineer troops received basic infantry training and carried infantry weapons; but their most important work, a task that would be done by them rather than infantry labor, was the laying of bridges, a subject McClellan had studied while in the Crimea.[17] Bridge building for armies had a long history with tortured beginnings. In 450 B.C. Xerxes arrived at the Hellespont with an army of almost two hundred thousand men intending to cross for a campaign against the Greeks. His engineers built two bridges, each one more than a mile in length. No sooner had they finished than a mighty storm smashed both bridges to floating timber.

Not a patient or tolerant man, Xerxes ordered three hundred lashes and branding with red-hot irons for the unruly Hellespont. Somewhat more realistically he decapitated the engineers and commissioned replacements. When the work reached completion, the Great King went to the bridge site, poured wine from a golden goblet into the sea, prayed against failure, hurled the goblet into the water, and began an uneventful crossing.[18]

Preferring the French and English system of engineering, McClellan had recommended the Birago Trestle system for bridging. He particularly disliked the India rubber pontoon and apparently had no desire to use the canvas pontoon. If Virginia were to be, as everyone expected, the battleground for the war, the army needed the ability to cross its many rivers rapidly and perhaps in the face of opposition. As Barnard saw it, preparation for this was his real responsibility.

16 Malles, *Brainerd's Memoirs*, 44, 45-46.

17 Billings, *Hard Tack and Coffee*, 378; McClellan, *Armies of Europe*, 36-56 (and especially 55-56).

18 *Herodotus*, 7, chp. 35; Peter Green, *The Greco-Persian Wars* (Berkeley, 1996), 75-76; Donald Featherstone, *Bridges of Battle: Famous Battlefield Actions at Bridges and River Crossings*, 35-36 (London, 1998).

Born in 1815 and older than most of his fellow officers in McClellan's army, Barnard had graduated from the Military Academy before most of them. He stood second in the class of 1833. A relative had been secretary of war to President John Quincy Adams. Commissioned an engineer, the usual branch for high-ranking graduates, he was given the standard engineering assignments of the time: construction of coast defenses, improvement of rivers and harbors, and supervision of the Military Academy. He served on coastal fortification projects in the east, the south, and the west.[19] On the subject of secession he convinced himself that, because of his fifteen years of duty in the South and the personal attachments he had made there, he had the ultimate detachment and objectivity—even when he delivered a tirade.[20] A man with intellectual and literary attainments, he had investigated scientific and mathematical questions, published several scholarly works on engineering subjects, and participated in the original incorporation of the National Academy of Science before the war.

In April 1861, Barnard, by then a major, was serving in New York in charge of engineers working on the harbor defenses. On April 19, he received orders to go to Washington where he was assigned to duty as an engineer with Brigadier General Mansfield, the commanding officer of the Department of Washington. He continued under Mansfield until the advance of McDowell's army when he was assigned to duty with McDowell as chief of engineers and served in that capacity at the Battle of Bull Run.

Barnard performed the reconnaissance on July 19 and recommended that still another be made, neither of which produced information McDowell did not have. Although the waste of July 20 must in the end be McDowell's responsibility, the ineffectual reconnaissances for the Sudley Ford roads were Barnard's fault. Because Heintzelman's guide, one of Barnard's engineers, failed to identify the turn to the middle ford where Heintzelman's division was to cross, the army lost the middle prong of the turning movement; Heintzelman's division marched twelve sweltering miles rather than five; and Heintzelman and Hunter had to fight their way to Henry House Hill. Barnard's poor reconnaissance and his ignorant guides ruined any chance of recouping the time lost by Tyler. Meanwhile, the Confederates were given time to react, march north, deploy, and delay the advance of the turning column after it had crossed the Run at Sudley's Ford.

19 *D.A.B.*, 1, pt. 1, 626; Warner, *Generals in Blue*, 19-20; Heitman, *Official Register*, 1, 191; *Cullum*, 1, no. 708.

20 Barnard, *CSA and Bull Run*, preface, 3-4.

After he was assigned to duty as chief engineer under McClellan, he was appointed brigadier general on September 23, 1861. As chief engineer, though a staff officer, he was responsible for the engineer forces of McClellan's army.[21]

Thoughtful, self-contained, humorous, and earnest, he was not as aloof as he appeared to be; and he took great interest in the progress of the young officers serving under him. His cold demeanor resulted from inherited deafness, which made his social dealings difficult. To peril, he was indifferent, ignoring enemy fire and any suggestions for safety by his pickets. In the reconnaissances that led to the plan of battle for Bull Run, he was restrained by fear that he might disclose McDowell's plan if the Rebels discovered his reconnaissance, not by any fear for his personal safety. Different from his military courage and scientific skills was his love of music. A *Te Deum* from his pen long survived him.[22]

Next to his long list of admirable talents and characteristics must be added some less attractive qualities. He did not take criticism well and did not willingly assume responsibility for his mistakes.[23] Nor was he particularly scrupulous about the facts when disputes arose about his own conduct, and he was willing to lie when it suited him. These characteristics made him unusually adept at the snippy pamphleteering of the late eighteenth and early nineteenth centuries.

William Howard Russell, the fleet-footed, cowardly military correspondent of the *London Times*, had published an account of the retreat from Bull Run Creek that angered many people in the North.[24] Dated July 22, 1861, the day after the battle, and published in the London *Times* of August 6, 1861, Russell's narrative was republished as a small pamphlet in the United States later in the year. The first twenty lines of his account characterized the Union forces and their performance as "disgraceful conduct," "a cowardly rout," "a miserable, causeless panic," and "scandalous behavior." He could not resist the temptation to mention the "superior fighting powers" of the enemy.[25] His depiction of terror stricken federal troops, unfair to most of McDowell's army, roused Barnard's anger and loosed the chief engineer's sharp pen. To be certain, a few units had run; and a few individuals had carried their flight as far north as New York City. But even in retreat the majority of

21 NA Off's MS Rpts (Barnard).

22 *D.A.B.*, 1, pt. 1, 627.

23 For criticism of his written accounts of his own activities, in which he would praise himself for conduct performed by others and ignore his own faults in a military failure, see McClellan MSS (L.C.) letter dated April 3, 1863, from Fitz-John Porter to Barnard and February 8, 1864, from Humphreys to Barnard. The letter from Porter is unusually caustic.

24 Russell, *My Diary*, entries dated August 22, 1861, 245-246, and September 1, 1861, 249-250.

25 William Howard Russell, *The Battle of Bull Run* (New York, 1861), 5-7.

the men, though inexperienced and individualistic, kept their weapons and stayed with their colors. Barnard drew his retaliatory pen from its scabbard to write his own account of the battle and the federal army in retreat. In it he found space for the conduct of Mr. Russell.

As the literary ombudsman for McDowell's Army of Northeastern Virginia, Barnard adopted the form of an open letter to a British friend and produced a slim volume entitled *The CSA and the Battle of Bull Run*. It was completed and published in early 1862. Not a journalist with the usual self-created license, he relied on lengthy quotations from the reports of higher ranking officers like McDowell, Heintzelman, Sherman, and Porter, as well as the available reports of comparable Confederate officers. The result was a disjointed but reasonably accurate and thorough account of the campaign and the battle. The officers who led the Union army that fought at Bull Run, he showed, were not at fault for the defeat. The ungentlemanly member of the British press he featured in "retreat." Aside from depicting Russell as a coward, he demonstrated that Russell had no way to know anything about the battle because he had been too much afraid to go anywhere near it. "Bull Run" Russell had never crossed the Run, never heard the whine of a rifle bullet, and fled in terror.[26] An uninvolved spectator, McClellan could sit quietly on the sidelines, from which he could watch the rapier thrusts and saber slashes of Barnard's pen with equanimity.

Shortly after McClellan arrived in the capital Barnard presented him with the deficiencies of the Engineer Corps, insisting that McClellan go to Senator Wilson to demand rank for the engineer officers and the addition of sappers and miners. "Without some such decided and active step on your part," he wrote, "I fear it will not be carried out."[27] For the advance to Bull Run, he complained, he had been

26 John G. Barnard, *The CSA and the Battle of Bull Run: (A Letter to an English Friend)* (New York, 1862), 119-121 (Barnard, *CSA and Bull Run*).

27 McClellan MSS (L.C.) letter dated November 2, 1861, from Barnard to McClellan and undated mem (arbitrarily included in the November correspondence by the curator) from J. G. B. to no addressee. The value of the trained troops in the Regular Army engineer units was recognized by everyone at the outset. As the history of the engineer battalion described one of the "old hands" from the "Old Army," "The recruits looked up to him with a reverential feeling; he had been 'in Mexico' and 'on the plains,' and was a real 'old soldier.' He was expert in all the mysteries of camp life and military routine, was quartermaster and drillmaster, butcher and blacksmith, rigger and boatman. Practical and punctilious in all his duties, he considered that to be the ranking non-commissioned officer was a greater honor than to hold a commission. He received a medal of honor from Congress . . ." Thompson, *Engineer Battalion*, fn., 4. And when the enlisted men were pursued with offers of commissions in the explosive growth of the volunteer forces, one of them asked Captain J. C. Duane, commanding the Regular battalion, for advice about taking a commission. Irritated at the prospect of losing one of his experienced men, Duane spoke his mind quickly, "Why, President Lincoln can make a brigadier-general in five minutes; but it has taken five years to make you an engineer soldier." *Ibid.*

forced to create four engineer companies, which were nothing compared to trained engineer soldiers.

In McClellan's view the engineers were responsible for the conduct of reconnaissances; the selection of positions, particularly those of defense; siege operations; and construction of field works, temporary defenses, bridges, and roads. They could not do their duties without "accurate judgment of ground, and great intelligence."[28]

Barnard wanted Colonel Alexander to begin work on the canvas boats, pontoon bridges, Birago trestles, and Russian canvas boats for the army's bridging train. "In accordance with long formed intentions," he wrote to McClellan, "I . . . addressed your active recommendations as to organizing Engineer troops and getting up Engineer trains." He had given Alexander preliminary instructions. Then "to my utter astonishment I found the whole thing taken from my hands. The command of troops both Regular and Volunteer is taken from the Commanding Officer of Engineers." He did not know what it meant and could no longer define his duties as chief engineer. If it meant distrust in him, his course should be short and simple. If it did not mean distrust, "it is a blow to that unity of action and integrity of command, which it has been—in all else—one of the main labors of *your* administration here to establish."[29]

Ingenious as he was, McClellan did not know that Barnard, a defeated suitor for the hand of Mary Ellen and probably jealous of the young McClellan's rise to stardom, lay in wait with the pen he had used on "Bull Run" Russell. When the problem erupted, McClellan's duties had just multiplied, and he had many too many things on his hands to deal with personnel squabbles. His friend and former professor Dennis Hart Mahan had recently arrived from West Point to visit his former students now growing to maturity.

To Mahan, McClellan unburdened himself about his problem with Barnard. Mahan believed he could help. Unable to catch the galloping Barnard, Mahan sent him a note as he was leaving the army to return to West Point. He told the chief engineer, he reported to McClellan, "how kindly you had spoken of him and your high appreciation of his abilities and of your not desiring to trench upon his functions." If Barnard went through channels, Mahan had written to Barnard, time would be lost. He suggested that Barnard expedite his business by making a personal visit to McClellan with memoranda in hand because McClellan was too busy to

28 *M.O.S.*, 111.

29 McClellan MSS (L.C.) letter of n.d., from Barnard to McClellan; undated mem (arbitrarily included in November correspondence by the curator) from J. G. B. to no addressee.

answer letters himself. "This, with some good advice, growing out of what he said to me, I hope may do good, though I doubt it."[30]

During the fall the work done by Barry and Barnard on the fortifications reached a point at which McClellan could believe they would hold any force of onrushing Rebels at bay and they could be entrusted to junior, less experienced men. The major-general asked Barnard and Barry to evaluate the condition of the capital and determine the minimum infantry and artillery "to satisfy the conditions of a good defense."[31] Headquarters received two responses, one four and one six days later. The substance of both reports was the same.[32]

Barnard and Barry estimated that slightly more than eleven thousand infantry would suffice to garrison all forts, an additional twelve thousand would be enough reserves west of the Potomac from Fort Lyon to Fort Corcoran, and seven hundred fifty could defend the Chain Bridge. Last, ten thousand would suffice as reserves in the capital. In his August 2 report to the president, McClellan had estimated twenty thousand for the defense of Washington. Barnard and Barry, the primary experts on the question, had carefully and in detail determined that the grand total should be 33,795.[33]

In early December, Barnard wrote his report in response to the long outstanding House resolution of July 8. Comparing the fortifications with Wellington's Torres Vedras model, Barnard believed that a garrison of 22,674 men, plus 7,200 men to man the guns in the forts, would suffice. In number of guns Barnard's nine miles of fortifications were at parity with those of Torres Vedras but in weight of metal more than double because he had many guns of heavier caliber. Only refinements that could be completed in the spring remained to be done.[34] With thirty thousand men remaining behind, the army would presumably be free to leave the capital area and need not remain between the capital and the main Rebel force.

As long as Barry and Barnard adhered to their numbers and their opinions, satisfaction of these conditions for the Armageddon campaign ought to be easy. The careful thought and expert knowledge embodied in the two memoranda and the report to Congress left McClellan free to execute a new plan he was considering, and

30 McClellan MSS (L.C.) letter dated, November 6, 1861, from Dennis Hart Mahan to McClellan.

31 *OR*, 5, 622, order dated October 18, 1861.

32 *OR*, 5, 624, 626-627.

33 *OR*, 5, 683-684.

34 *OR*, 5, 624, 626-627. According to Barnard, the line of Washington defenses was two-thirds as long as those at Torres Vedras; but the garrisons and gunners were the same, Wellington having used only 34,124 mem. *OR*, 5, 683.

he went forward with radical ideas for the use of his army. But one of his bad habits guided his thoughts: once he had carefully considered an issue, decided that he knew enough to resolve it, and reached a conclusion, he treated his conclusion as if no right-thinking men could think differently. In the alternative he decided that he was the general in chief, the smartest and most knowledgeable person, and the sole arbiter of important military questions. In either case he gave no consideration to contrary opinions or to the people who might hold them, no matter who they were.

Two large question marks remained. First, although Barry was a man of honest consistency, Barnard was not. He could change his mind for no reason or would lie for undetectable personal reasons, and he could not predictably be entered in the ledger as a man irrevocably committed to anything. And the seeds for disagreement with McClellan lay well planted. They could burst forth in bloom at any time. In his naivete McClellan would not recognize the problem in its inchoate form.

Second, the horror Lincoln had survived and the psychological scars it had left when the capital could have been taken by a reinforced brigade might have receded. But they had not died. The monster of the capital uncovered by the main Union army and confronted by the Confederate's main army remained alive and needed only the right trumpet call to emerge from its lair.

McClellan went forward in his private way without thinking about either problem. After all, he was right. That was enough. Would either one arise to confound his plans for the future? Only time and the reality of the event would tell.

Appendix One

Officers and Battlefield Maneuvers

For the last time in any major war,[1] battlefield maneuvers in the American Civil War were executed with parade ground evolutions. Organized and trained armies usually entered battle in one of four general formations, closed order (column), open order (line), *orde mixte* (a combination of column and line), and skirmish order, all of which were generally based on the French techniques developed, refined, and used during the eighteenth century and the Napoleonic Wars. By the advent of Napoleon the French usually approached the enemy with clouds of skirmishers followed by the main force in column, deployed rapidly into line, and closed with the enemy line of battle.[2]

1 Save possibly the European wars of unification, e.g., the Franco-Prussian War.

2 See, generally, Robert S. Quimby, *The Background of Napoleonic Warfare: The Theory of Military Tactics in Nineteenth Century France* (New York, 1957), esp. 330-337 (Quimby, *Background of Napoleonic Warfare*).

In closed order the men were in mass, i.e. three or more ranks deep. Of course, only the first two ranks and the men on the flanks could fire. Although a few eighteenth-century theoreticians advocated the column as a formation with firepower, most found it weak as a firing formation.[3] Because the main battle weapon of the infantryman, a smoothbore flintlock or musket, was remarkably inaccurate beyond fifty yards, shock from human mass, not firepower, was the virtue of this formation in spite of Frederick the Great's devotion to infantry firepower in the eighteenth century,[4] and Napoleon's sophisticated appreciation of it.[5] The column remained an important formation well into the nineteenth century. Having lasted in various forms for centuries the deep, heavy striking force had been proven by the Thebans under Epaminondas at Leuctra and Mantinea and by Alexander's heavy infantry with their huge sarissas at Gaugamela and many other battles well before the birth of Christ.[6]

The open order, essentially two parallel lines two paces apart, maximized the firepower of the infantryman and dominated infantry tactics in the latter half of the nineteenth century. Although Napoleon, like Alexander and all other great generals, used every conceivable formation depending on the circumstances, he did not resolve the great debate among eighteenth-century theoreticians by making the open order his most often used formation and still argued at the end of the eighteenth century that he preferred the column.[7]

Skirmish order, the formation of virtually all tactical assaults in twentieth-century warfare, left four men, "comrades in battle," the equivalent of the modern fire team, to their own devices[8] and was a product of the nation in arms discussed by Machiavelli[9] and made famous, if not uniform for all major wars, by the French

3 Quimby, *Background of Napoleonic Warfare*, 31-33.

4 Gunther E. Rothenberg, *The Art of Warfare in the Age of Napoleon* (1995, Norwalk, Easton Press ed.), 17-18 (Rothenberg, *Art of Warfare*).

5 Quimby, *The Background of Napoleonic Warfare*, 334-336.

6 Archer Jones, *The Art of War in the Western World* (New York and Oxford, 1987), 20-21, 22; Victor Davis Hanson, *The Soul of Battle: From Ancient Times to the Present Day, How Three Great Liberators Vanquished Tyranny* (New York, 1999),46-53; Peter Green, *Alexander of Macedon 356-323 B.C. A Historical Biography* (Los Angeles, 1991), 177-179, 293-294; Rob Fox, in Lane, *Alexander the Great* (London, 1973), 76-77.

7 Quimby, *The Background of Napoleonic Warfare*, 333-334.

8 Brig. Gen. Silas Casey, *Infantry Tactics for the Instruction, Exercise, and Maneuvers of the Soldier, A Company, Line of Skirmishers, Battalion, Brigade, or Corps de Armée*, 3 vols. (New York, 1862), 1, 183, para. 12; 184, para. 17; 187, para. 27; diagram, pl. 26, facing 185; (Casey, *Infantry Tactics*).

9 Felix Gilbert, "The Renaissance of the Art of War," 18-21, 26-27, in Peter, Paret, ed., *Makers of Modern Strategy* (Princeton, 1986).

Revolution.[10] Skirmishers did not move in cadence or formation. They fought individually and dispersed. The individual was to stay several paces from the nearest men in his unit, and he was generally permitted to fire at will. His main battle weapon transformed over time from muzzleloader, to breechloader, to repeater, to semi-automatic weapon, to fully automatic weapon. Until the advent of real firepower, particularly automatic weapons, the skirmish order had no use as a tactical battle line. Inheriting this "formation" from the untrained, undisciplined, democratic armies of the French Revolution, Napoleon used it to disrupt the tactical formations of his adversaries.[11]

The *orde mixte*, a combination of column and line, combined firepower (line), shock (column), and flexibility (skirmishers). Generally, the column part was a formation for battlefield maneuver, not a formation designed for assault.[12] In the American army, the use of columns had fallen into disuse by the middle of the nineteenth century.

In the closed order, open order, and *orde mixte* formations, the arrangement of the infantrymen, shoulder to shoulder, marching in cadence, and maneuvering according to command, was important for preserving the ability of the regiment to execute its assignment in battle. For example, Thomas L. Livermore, entering the war as a second lieutenant in the First New Hampshire Infantry in 1861 and leaving it as colonel of the Eighteenth New Hampshire Volunteers in 1865 at Appomattox, was a civilian who became a shrewd participant in the war, a highly intelligent critic, and an excellent historian. Under the command of Colonel Edward Cross, Livermore's regiment, the superb Fifth New Hampshire Infantry executed a parade-ground evolution, under severe infantry and artillery fire at Antietam in 1862. When Cross gave the command, "By the right of companies to the front! By the right flank! March!" the regiment maneuvered from a standard two-line formation into a series of short parallel columns in order to pass through a regiment it was relieving under fire.[13]

To complete a maneuver of this sort or almost any tactical evolution on the battlefield, an officer had to command; and the unit had to respond. These parade ground evolutions were not performed willy-nilly at the personal option of the infantryman. They were "on command," and the orders had to be given at the proper moment. To perform the evolution "squad right about," for example, the preparatory

10 Quimby, *The Background of Napoleonic Warfare*, 327-328.

11 Chandler, *Napoleon*, 1, 67.

12 Quimby, *The Background of Napoleonic Warfare*, 334-355.

13 Thomas L. Livermore, *Days and Events, 1860-1866* (Boston, 1920), 134-135 (Livermore, *Days and Events*).

command ("squad right about") and the command of execution ("march,")[14] had to be given as the proper foot struck the ground or as any foot struck the ground.[15] Marching and maneuvering infantry lost their order, as well as respect for their officers, when commands were improperly given; and these losses are suffered as much today as they were in 1861. This aspect of command came easily with a little practice and a little experience. The novice from civilian life could learn it quickly. The militia officer from his Saturday and Sunday parades presumably already knew it. Much else was necessary to define a good officer, but failure of this test was an easy, early way to identify a man who was not qualified.

14 Brig. Gen. Philip St. George Cooke, *Cavalry Tactics: Or, Regulations for the Instructions, Formations, and Movements of the Cavalry of the Army and Volunteers of the United States, prepared under the direction of the War Department and authorized and adopted by the Secretary of War* (Philadelphia, 1862), vol 1, 43 (Cooke, *Cavalry*), *U.S. Infantry Tactics, for the Instruction, Exercise, and Maneuvers of the United States Infantry including Infantry of the Line, Light Infantry, and Riflemen prepared under the Direction of the War Department and authorized and adopted by the Secretary of War, May 1, 1861, containing the School of the Soldier; the School of the Company; Instruction for Skirmishers; the general calls, the calls for skirmishers, and the School of the Battalion; including the Articles of War and a Dictionary of Military Terms* (Philadelphia, 1861), 15, paras. 63, 64 (Casey, *U.S. Infantry Tactics*) .

15 Casey, *Infantry Tactics*, 1, 21, paras. 70-71, 82; para. 355; Cooke, *Cavalry*, 56, parag. 20; Casey, *U.S. Infantry Tactics*, 61, paras. 336, 338; 108, paras. 112, 114; 119, para. 174.

Bibliography

A handful of core publications and another handful of manuscript collections supply the vast bulk of research material for the military aspects of the American Civil War. They include, among other things, the *Official Records*, the *Report of the Joint Committee on the Conduct of the War*, and Tom Broadfoot's massive republication of the many collections of articles by the Military Order of the Loyal Legion of the United States. Of the manuscript sources, the *Officers Manuscript Accounts of Military Services* in the National Archives, the McClellan manuscripts, the Meade manuscripts, Ledgers of Orders and Correspondence sent from Headquarters of the Army of the Potomac in the National Archives, and files of Orders and Correspondence Received by Headquarters of the Army of the Potomac in the National Archives, the Heintzelman manuscripts, and the Kearny manuscripts are the best, most encyclopedic, and most informative. This bibliography applies to both volume one and volume two.

The great frustration for research in an area rich and deep in personal primary sources is the man who left nothing behind, e.g., Sumner, Pope, McDowell, Burnside (personal), Butterfield, etc., and the man who left it behind to be lost, e.g., Griffin, Candler, Townsend, etc. In many instances the gaps can be reliably filled by inference, but that always has its risks and certainly leaves the way open to healthy debate. For all these uncertain areas and others I am the last line of defense and share responsibility with no man. Mistakes are, like everything else here, attributable to me.

Manuscripts

William W. Averell MSS (New York State Library and the Gilder Lehrman Collection in the Morgan Library). Averell's letters are in Albany and his pocket diaries, excellent for confirming dates, are in the Morgan.

John B. Bachelder MSS (New Hampshire Historical Society). These voluminous papers are indispensable to any study of the battle of Gettysburg. They include correspondence between Bachelder and participants of all ranks on both sides commencing in August and December of 1863 and continuing until 1894. They particularly include detailed accounts of the activities of General Meade on July 3 and of General Hunt during the artillery bombardment on July 3. The letters have been edited and recently published by Morningside.

Bancroft-Bliss Family MSS (Library of Congress). The mass of Civil War material relates almost entirely to family business and personal matters, but interesting materials on sidelights exist in it.

Nathaniel Banks MSS (Library of Congress). Primarily official papers, the collection has some affectionate letters to Banks's wife.

Francis Channing Barlow MSS (Massachusetts Historical Society). The content of this collection is superb for the command structure of the Second Corps and the Eleventh Corps during the critical spring and summer months of 1863.

S. L. M. Barlow MSS (Huntington Library). Barlow was a prominent lawyer and Democratic politician with correspondents and business interests scattered nationwide as well as in Europe. His correspondence with McClellan and others contains a wealth of factual information about McClellan's difficulties with McDowell, his relations with the cabinet, his struggles with the abolitionists, and general attitudes of government officials.

James G. Bennett MSS (New York Public Library). The letters to Bennett from reporters with the Army of the Potomac contain excellent, revealing material on McClellan.

James C. Biddle MSS (Pennsylvania Historical Society). Serving first as a company grade line officer, Biddle became an aide to Ricketts, then to Meade. His letters contain excellent factual material and commentary.

Simon Cameron MSS (Library of Congress). Unlike his successor, Cameron did not involve himself in strategy, grand tactics, or army movements but left them to Scott, McDowell, Fremont, and McClellan. The absence of material of this sort from his papers supports the point.

Ezra Carmen MSS (New York Public Library). Less well known than the Bachelder papers, Carmen used a far-flung correspondence to prepare the Antietam Battlefield Board Maps, the Antietam counterparts to the Bachelder Gettysburg maps. Among other things the collection has interesting details about the discovery of the lost order, the death of Generals

Reno and Mansfield, and Alpheus Williams's personal campaign to establish the cowardice of General Crawford. The collection is huge.

Zachariah Chandler MSS (L.C.). A regrettably small collection for the vituperative senator from Michigan.

Chapman, George H., MS Diary (Indianapolis Historical Society). These two small pocket diaries for the years 1862 and 1863 contain sometimes continuous and sometimes sporadic entries during the period that Chapman worked his way from major of the Third Indiana Cavalry to continuous command of the cavalry brigade previously commanded by Colonel Gamble of the Eighth Illinois. When Chapman was not content, he faithfully recorded his views on a daily basis. When he was apparently content, his pen fell silent.

Salmon P. Chase MSS (University Productions, Inc.). Chase, a voluminous correspondent in his own hand, has large collections of letters, comments, etc., scattered all over the United States, particularly in the Library of Congress and the Pennsylvania Historical Society. Gathering letters to and from Chase wherever they could be found, this encyclopedic collection on microfilm is an excellent contribution to historians of the nineteenth century. A copy is available in the Bobst Library of New York University.

Miscellaneous Civil War Collection (Huntington Library). This collection of approximately five hundred sixty miscellaneous pieces contains a number of useful pieces for individual officers, including the only extant collection of letters from Israel B. Richardson. In addition to Richardson, it contains useful letters from McDowell and McClellan.

Miscellaneous Civil War Letters (New York Historical Society). Difficult to use in any systematic way, this polyglot collection, like the similar groups in the New Hampshire Historical Society, the Gratz Autograph Collection in the Pennsylvania Historical Society, the Palmer Autograph Collection in the Western Reserve Historical Society, and the century Collection in the New York Public Library will reward the plodding effort.

Edward Payson Clar MSS (Missouri Historical Society). This collection of approximately fifty letters written by a corporal of the Twelfth Vermont Infantry has interesting anecdotes about Generals Stoughton and Stannard.

Schuyler Colfax MSS (Indiana Historical Society). A small collection of letters most of them from Colfax to a generally unidentifiable group of recipients. A few letters to Colfax.

Casper Crowninshield MS Diary (Boston Public Library). This is a 93-page typewritten transcript of a diary kept, at least in part, by Casper Crowninshield during the early part of the war. Although Crowninshield served throughout the war, first in the Twentieth Massachusetts Infantry, then as a troop commander in the First Massachusetts Cavalry, and finally as the colonel in command of the Second Massachusetts Cavalry, the diary covers only the years 1861-62 while Crowninshield served in the Twentieth. The part for the early months appears to have been a daily diary with some later additions. The latter part, particularly from the withdrawal from the Peninsula by McClellan when Crowninshield's regiment rejoined the Army of the Potomac, is a chronological narrative more than a day-by-day diary. The manuscript contains a large number of interesting anecdotes and descriptions of senior officers.

John A. Dahlgren MSS (Library of Congress). For a naval officer unusually informative about the army because of Dahlgren's correspondents.

Phillippe D'Orleans, Comte de Paris, MSS primarily MS diaries (Archieve Nationale de la Maison de France, Paris). After three-and-one-half years of correspondence, the author finally obtained access from the royal family in Amboise and from the staff in Paris. The correspondence, which must have been large at one time, is now sparse—but the diaries are extraordinary.

Dwight Family MSS, particularly the letters of William and Wilder (Massachusetts Historical Society). A relatively recent acquisition of the Society, the letters of the two brothers, who served under Banks (Wilder) and Hooker (William) in the early period, supply excellent commentary from the viewpoint of two perceptive field grade officers. The published letters of Wilder were edited by the family in the frustrating, restrained style of the nineteenth century. The originals will reward the extra effort.

William B. Franklin MSS (Library of Congress). A distressingly small collection for an active correspondent who knew many important persons, this collection frustrates even more because Franklin had classic, legible nineteenth-century handwriting and because he was probably the most honest commentator of all corps commanders.

John Charles Fremont MSS including MS Reminiscences (University of California, Berkeley). Except for the official military papers, the papers, at least in information, are equally valuable from both John and Jessie.

William Frothingham MSS (New York Public Library). For the brief period Frothingham served as surgeon for the Forty-fourth New York, a literate record of daily life for officers.

John Gibbon MSS (Maryland Historical Society). This is a small collection of letters, many of which are quoted in the autobiography written by Gibbon after the war. One letter which is not quoted by Gibbon or even mentioned, notes that he was ordered at the end of the first day of fighting at the Wilderness to attack on the second day, the time when he and Hancock, according to the later controversy, did not understand each other.

John Gibbon MSS (Pennsylvania Historical Society). A much larger and more informative collection. Unfortunately, Gibbon's correspondence during the Second Civil War, in which he was a willing, active participant, appears to remain in the hands of a descendant and unavailable.

Horace Greeley MSS (New York Public Library). In spite of his long list of interesting and distinguished correspondents, Greeley unfortunately did not seem to save correspondence.

Francis Vinton Greene MSS (New York Public Library). A few letters from George Sears Greene to his family written during the war and particularly during the period 1861-63.

Halpine MSS (Huntington Library). A small but literate collection of personal letters by a writer who served as a staff officer.

John P. Hatch MSS (Library of Congress). This relatively small collection contains a number of interesting comments on general officers who served in the Shenandoah Valley and in the Army of Virginia, including Pope.

Louis M. Haupt MSS (Library of Congress). This is a typewritten transcript of letters written by Haupt to members of his family during the period 1862-1863 with texts from various unidentified sources included between the letters. Not all the letters are printed in full, and some are only summarized. Haupt was a great supporter and proponent of McDowell and gave information supporting McDowell and criticizing Pope and McClellan to the Committee on the Conduct of the War.

Samuel P. Heintzelman MSS (Library of Congress). A large collection of outspoken diaries and even handed letters, no work on the period is complete without contributions from this collection.

Edward W. Hinks MSS (Boston University). A small but interesting polyglot collection of personal letters and career correspondence.

Ethan Allen Hitchcock MSS (Library of Congress). This small, interesting, and frustrating collection has many useful—or probably useful—nuggets in it; but many of the draft outgoing letters cannot be said with certainty to have been sent.

Joseph Hooker MSS (Huntington Library). No useful personal papers from Hooker appear to survive, leaving us still with the official military papers which Hooker took with him whenever he left a command whether or not they belonged to the United States government.

Oliver Otis Howard MSS (Bowdoin College). A huge collection of personal and official correspondence. Howard was a vigorous and informative correspondent even after he was forced to switch hands and learn to write a second time.

Andrew Atkinson Humphreys MSS (Pennsylvania Historical Society). Engineer, staff officer, corps commander, and chief of staff to Meade, Humphreys was one of the few universally respected and admired men in the Army of the Potomac and his pronouncements on controversial issues can usually be taken as gospel limited only by human capacity to observe.

Henry Jackson Hunt MSS (Library of Congress). A potpourri of letters, drafts, memoranda, jottings, and notations with much indispensable information from a talented officer at the center of events throughout the war.

Reverdy Johnson MSS (Maryland Historical Society). This collection contains a number of letters from Fitz-John Porter, Johnson's client in the court-martial proceeding and his client in some of Porter's subsequent efforts to reargue or retry the case. It also contains an interesting letter from Meade after Meade was attacked in Congress for his "intention" to withdraw from Gettysburg and Johnson's defense of Meade on the floor of the Senate.

Phillip W. Kearny MSS (Library of Congress). These manuscripts include two collections of typewritten transcripts of letters, one to Phillip Courtlandt, a friend and supporter and a man who assisted him in his promotions, and another to his wife. The letters to

Courtlandt begin approximately July of 1861, and continue through early August 1862. The letters to Kearny's wife begin in March of 1862, and end two days before his death.

William A. Ketcham, MS Reminiscences (Indiana Historical Society). This typewritten transcript of approximately 100 pages records the reminiscences of an enlisted man and later a captain commanding a company in the Thirteenth Indiana Infantry from February 1864 through the end of the war. It is not organized chronologically except on a haphazard basis but it contains very interesting insights into general subject matters as well as certain incidents in the war and, although short, ought to be published.

Frederick W. Lander MSS (Library of Congress). Although only one or two letters from Lander to his wife survive, the collection contains virtually every other piece of paper that crossed Lander's desk, including drafts of official correspondence. It is invaluable for the early handling of the troops on the upper Potomac.

Robert Todd Lincoln MSS (Library of Congress). The correspondence and other materials received by Abraham Lincoln, especially during his presidency. Available on microfilm.

Theodore Lyman MSS (Massachusetts Historical Society). Edited and published as *Meade's Headquarters* by Edward Meade Agassiz, Lyman's complete letters in this collection including the postwar correspondence along with one or two other sources are indispensable for the Army of the Potomac from late 1863 to 1865.

J. K. F. Mansfield MSS (United States Military Academy). A small collection of letters primarily to his daughter Mary.

Manton Marble MSS (Library of Congress). Invaluable for the long, frank letters from Fitz-John Porter to Marble.

George B. McClellan MSS (Library of Congress). In spite of requests from the War Department and from Grant when the latter was general in chief McClellan refused to deliver his papers to the government or allow access to them. Several of the documents noted in "not found" *OR* can be found here, and no good work on the Army of the Potomac or McClellan can proceed without them.

George B. Meade MSS (Pennsylvania Historical Society). A huge collection, much of which has been published, it is nevertheless valuable for the unpublished letters and the incoming correspondence.

T. A. Meysenburg MSS (Missouri Historical Society). This collection consists in its entirety of three medium-size diaries for the period 1862-1864. They appear to have been diaries kept for the Eleventh Corps by Meysenburg, who was a staff officer for the corps commander. They contain one or two references to individual events by Meysenburg but the remainder include, without descriptive comment, changes of command and movements, sometimes by the hour, and sometimes by the minute.

Military Historical Society of Massachusetts MSS, John Codman Ropes letters (Boston University, Mugar Library). A collection that rewards every minute of study and requires little sifting, the Ropes collection, with one or two exceptions including an extraordinary letter on First Bull Run, contains letters responding to inquiries by Ropes about incidents covered in his history of the war and are invaluable at the corps and division level.

Robert H. Milroy MSS (Indiana Historical Society). Much interesting correspondence about political string-pulling for a commission and Second Bull Run.

William Robey Moore MSS. These manuscripts include letters, which are not particularly informative, and disjointed typewritten reminiscences of approximately one hundred twenty-five pages. The reminiscences contain some interesting anecdotal material but the overall accuracy of the accounts is poor.

Edwin D. Morgan MSS (New York State Library). Like all available governor's papers, a massive collection with particularly numerous incoming letters from persons whose letters are hard to find, e.g., the largest and most informative collection of Wadsworth letters.

MS Court of Inquiry in the case of Dixon S. Miles (National Archives).

James Nesmith MSS (Oregon Historical Society). Senator from Oregon, Nesmith left a small but valuable collection of correspondence with Union officers, particularly Joseph Hooker.

John G. Nicolay MSS (Library of Congress). In addition to Nicolay's personal letters and random memoranda, recently edited in his excellent style by Professor Burlingame, the collection contains the transcript of Montgomery C. Meigs MS diary.

Officers MS Reports of Services (National Archives). Intending to identify ineffective officers lost in the assignment mill but holding slots that could be given to more qualified junior officers awaiting promotion, Congress passed a law requiring all general officers to submit reports of their activities during the war, etc. For historical reasons Congress continued the requirement after the war. The result is an invaluable source for both narratival and personal information. The Archives have put them on microfilm, and the complete set is available at a very reasonable price.

Alfred Pleasanton MSS (Library of Congress). A small collection of letters from Pleasanton to Brigadier-General John F. Farnsworth, who was on duty in the Capitol. The collection includes a letter to Farnsworth from his nephew Elon J. Farnsworth, a staff officer for Pleasanton. With one exception, the letters are all in the month of June, 1863, prior to the promotion of Farnsworth, Merritt, and Custer, and the consequent reorganization of the cavalry. All are extremely useful.

Fitz-John Porter MSS (Library of Congress). Although devoted to every detail of the court-martial and the re-trial, this collection is indispensable for the first two years of the war in the east, especially the correspondence after 1865.

William Warren Potter MS Reminiscences (Buffalo Historical Society). *Three Years With the Army of the Potomac: A Personal Military History*. Typewritten unpublished manuscript of approximately 100 pages by an infantryman who enlisted from Buffalo.

Henry J. Raymond MSS (New York Public Library). Approximately 300 letters which include a wide variety of correspondence over a very lengthy period of time. It also includes various letters relating to McClellan, his attempt to suppress the *New York Times*, and the attitude of certain officers toward him.

John A. Roebling MSS (Rutgers University). A young civil engineer who became an accomplished military engineer, Roebling had the knack of being in the right place to see (and report) important events. The collection also contains an engineer "diary" that appears to have been kept for the Fifth Corps from the Wilderness to the end.

Henry Ropes MSS (Boston Public Library). The best published or unpublished letters of a junior company grade officer, who served in an active Massachusetts regiment, and the surviving record of one of the many literate graduates of Harvard University.

Schoff Collection (Clement Library, Univ. Mich.). Like the Palmer and Gratz Collections, a random, but excellent, gathering of miscellaneous collections and items.

Phillip Schuyler MSS (New York Historical Society). Approximately 140 pages of typewritten transcripts of letters for the period October 1863, through December 1864, during most of which time Schuyler served as a staff officer to Brigadier General M. R. Patrick, the provost marshall for the Army of the Potomac. The letters contain comments on Meade, Grant, their relations, and other officers.

Winfield Scott MSS (Library of Congress). A useful collection for the early period, particularly pre-Bull Run, the collection has little of a personal nature; but Scott's personality is so-well portrayed in the published accounts of others that the disappointing gap is nevertheless well filled.

John Sherman MSS (Library of Congress). Serving as an aide to Patterson, Sherman's letters are valuable for his participation in the Valley.

Daniel E. Sickles MSS (New York Historical Society). A collection of approximately 200 letters, a few of which have to do with the Civil War. Some, however, are extremely interesting and supply good details not found in other places. Another interesting collection of letters, primarily about the Second Battle of Gettysburg, can be found in the National Archives.

T. C. H. Smith MSS (Ohio Historical Society). Primarily a MS account from Pope's viewpoint of Second Bull Run, the best defense of Pope, an indefensible man, by anyone, then or now. Smith's narrative, however biased, deserves publication.

William F. ("Baldy") Smith MSS (Vermont Historical Society). Both MS Memoirs by Smith, one in the form of a letter to his daughter and recently published, are in this collection; but it has much more, primarily organized by and devoted to the many controversial incidents in which he participated.

Edwin McM. Stanton MSS (Library of Congress). Although they have very little personal correspondence, Stanton's papers contain valuable memoranda of important meetings and reports from his staff of diligent assistant secretaries about the Army of the Potomac.

Stevens Family MSS, primarily Isaac Ingalls and Hazard (University of Washington). This collection, cut short in part by Isaac's death at Chantilly, is very useful.

Charles Sumner MSS (Harvard University Library). Like the Chase manuscripts, Sumner's massive papers are available on a University Publications microfilm, a copy of which is in the Low Library of Columbia University.

Charles C. Suydam MS diary (New York Historical Society). The diary is one of the better records of the affairs of the short-lived Fourth Corps. Suydam served as an aide to Keyes.

Union Defense Committee (New York Historical Society). Active in critical ways at the beginning of the war, the Committee filled many important needs when the federal government could not and touched many important people.

John Caldwell Tidball MS Reminiscences (Library of Congress and United States Military Academy). There are parts of manuscript reminiscences. These segments cover the period from early 1861 and the arrival of Lincoln in Washington until the loss of the First Battle of Bull Run. It has interesting sketches of several individuals including McDowell, Barry, and French.

Wadsworth Family MSS (Library of Congress). Regrettably, only a small volume of material from James survives; and in spite of the statement by Pearson in his biography, no letters exist in the Charles Sumner Papers.

James S. Wadsworth MSS (University of Rochester). Another small collection.

Governor Kemble Warren MSS (New York State Library). Although, like the Porter manuscripts, Warren's collection has much of its shelf space devoted to a hearing on his removal from command of the Fifth Corps by Sheridan at Five Forks, it is still invaluable for the Army of the Potomac.

Alexander Stuart Webb MSS (Yale University, Sterling Library). Staff officer to Barry, brigade commander at the Bloody Angle at Gettysburg, and staff officer to Meade, Andy Webb's letters to his naggy wife are cited by all but read by few, until recently, especially the postwar correspondence.

Willey MS Reminiscences (Vermont Historical Society). These two short typewritten manuscripts of reminiscences written by Willey contain strong criticism of General Stoughton and some exaltation at his capture by Mosby. The Sixteenth Vermont, in which Willey served, was recruited in 1862 and mustered out at the end of its term shortly after the battle of Gettysburg in 1863.

William S. Tilton MSS (Boston Public Library). This is a collection of four letters with enclosures written by Tilton to the wife of Colonel Jesse A. Gove, the colonel who commanded the Twenty-second Massachusetts until his death at Gaines Mill in June 1862. The letters have a number of enclosures giving accounts of various enlisted men who were near the Colonel when he was killed. The letters themselves express sympathy at the death of Colonel Gove and later letters describe the fortunes of the regiment after Tilton succeeded to command of it.

John E. Wool MSS (New York State Library). A massive collection covering many years of both personal and professional affairs of the second highest ranking officer in the

United States Army at the outbreak. They give marvelous insight into the problems Wool inflicted on McClellan and the methods used to do it.

Officers' Biographies, Autobiographies, Diaries, Letters, and Reminiscences

Adams, F. Colburn, *The Story of a Trooper* (New York, 1865). This book, written at least as early as December of 1863 and finally published in 1865, gives a detailed account of the formation of the First New York Cavalry at the outset of the war. The author with part of the cavalry regiment was attached to Franklin's headquarters and remained with General Franklin through the end of the Seven Days Battles on the Peninsula in 1862. The latter portion of the book deals in some detail with General Franklin's activities and gives an account without benefit of Confederate sources of the campaigns of the Army of the Potomac through July 1, 1862. It is interesting for its discussions of Franklin and the effect of various conditions on the troops. It has the reliability of a contemporaneous diary because it was published so early. According to the regimental roster, no F. Colburn Adams ever served in the regiment, but the writer was probably Alonso Adams, who rose to be the regimental commander.

Alberts, Done E., *Brandy Station to Manilla Bay: A Biography of General Wesley Merritt* (Austin, 1980).

(Anonymous, ed.) *War Letters of William Thompson Lusk, Captain, Assistant Adjutant General, United States Volunteers 1861-1863 M.D. LL. D.* (New York, 1911). Lusk served in the Seventy-Ninth New York Highlanders under Stevens, then served as one of Stevens's aides until Stevens was killed at the battle of Chantilly. His letters have interesting anecdotal material about Stevens, Benham, and others.

Applegate, John S., *Reminiscences and Letters of George Arrowsmith of New Jersey, Late Lieutenant-Colonel of the 157th Regiment, New York State Volunteers* (Red Bank, 1893).

Arnold, T. J., *Early Life and Letters of General Thomas J. "Stonewall" Jackson* (New York, 1916).

Athearn, Robert G., *Thomas F. Meagher: An Irish Revolutionary in America* (Boulder, 1949).

Bayard, Samuel J., *The Life of George Dashiell Bayard: late Captain, U.S.A., and Brigadier-General of Volunteers, Killed in the Battle of Fredericksburg, Dec. 1862* (New York, 1874). Letters and text prepared lovingly by a family member for Bayard, who was about to become chief of cavalry of the Army of the Potomac when he was killed at Fredericksburg by a random artillery shell.

Benedict, George Grenville, *Army Life In Virginia: Letters From The Twelfth Vermont Regiment And Personal Experiences Of Volunteer Service In the War For The Union 1862-63* (Burlington, 1895). This small volume contains an excellent account of the life of an enlisted man during 1862 and 1863. Toward the end of the period, Benedict served as a staff officer for General Stannard of the Vermont brigade and was present when both Stannard and Hancock were wounded at Gettysburg.

Blair, William Alan, ed., *A Politician Goes to War: the Civil War Letters of John White Geary* (University Park, 1995).

Blake, Henry N., *Three Years in the Army of the Potomac* (Boston, 1865). As one of the most extreme critics of virtually every general he saw and all officers as a class (with the exceptions of Hooker, Kearny, and Grant), Blake ranks with the anonymous author of *Red Tape and Pigeon Hole Generals* and Wilkeson (*Personal Recollections of the Civil War*). It contains a large amount of interesting and valuable factual material, including a large number of very useful anecdotes devoted primarily to the Third Corps. However, its distortions are best summarized by the handwritten note in pencil at the end of the author's copy, "To understand this curious mixture of assertion, criticism, invective and abuse, one should know the peculiarities of the author, Capt. Blake. He was brave and faithful; but carried his independence to the very limit of military subordination. Some of his positive statements may be true as isolated facts, as he boldly asserts; but are no basis for the calmer and broader conclusions of the historian."

Bloodgood, Rev. J. D., *Personal Reminiscences Of The War* (New York and Cincinnati, 1893). These personal reminiscences at the company level in the One Hundred Forty-first Pennsylvania contain a number of interesting anecdotes about brigade commanders in the Second and Third Corps and about the attitude of the troops and the company officers toward a number of general officers.

Burr, Frank A., *Life and Achievements of James Addams Beaver* (Philadelphia, 1882). Burr's work is well-researched and sound. It includes much useful information obtained by correspondence and interview with many of the people who participated in the war with Beaver. It also gives interesting insights into Hancock.

Butler, Benjamin Franklin, *Butler's Book, A Review of his Legal, Political, and Military Career* (Boston, 1892). This huge book must be read to be appreciated and with a critical eye to be useful.

Butterfield, J. L., ed., *A Biographical Memorial of General Daniel Butterfield including many Addresses and Military Writings* (New York, 1904). This book is an interesting collection of contemporary documents and letters, postwar writings, and text, which draws together Butterfield's life, primarily his military life. It contains a number relating to the period when Butterfield served as chief of staff of the Army of the Potomac.

Byrne, Frank L., and Weaver, Andrew T., eds., *Haskell of Gettysburg: His Life and Civil War Papers* (Madison, 1970). Although this book has a considerable amount of biographical information about Haskell, its principal content are Haskell's war time letters to his family, including the famous letter on the Gettysburg campaign. In 1862, Haskell adopted the practice of writing lengthy accounts of each campaign and battle after the campaign had ended. His position as a staff officer for various members of the Second Corps gave him a good vantage point for many of the things done by the Second Corps and in some cases for decisions made at the army level.

Campbell, James Havelock, *McClellan: A Vindication of the Military Career of General George B. McClellan, A Lawyers Brief* (New York, 1916).

Cannon, LeGrand B., *Personal Reminiscences of the Rebellion: 1861-1866* (New York, 1895). Cannon served as a volunteer aide on the staff of General Wool during the first two years of the war. His memoirs contain a number of interesting anecdotes about Wool's conduct in command of Fort Monroe in 1861 and the relations between Wool and McClellan during the Peninsula campaign.

Casdorph, Paul D., *Prince John Magruder: his Life and Campaigns*, 108-109 (New York, 1996).

Chamberlain, Joshua Lawrence, *The Passing of the Armies* (Dayton, 1974). This is a series of articles prepared by Chamberlain during a period of approximately twelve years in the latter part of his life after his initial undertaking to write a history of the Fifth Corps of the Army of the Potomac was snatched from him by William H. Powell in 1896. The articles are a combination of a personal account by Chamberlain of his activity in the final movements of the war, and an overall account of the Fifth Corps and the cavalry with special emphasis on Warren, Griffin, and Sheridan. Chamberlain lauds Warren in a measured way and is critical of Sheridan in an extreme way.

Coco, Gregory A., ed., *Through Blood and Fire: The Civil War Letters of Major Charles J. Mills, 1862-65* (Gettysburg, 1982). This is a collection of superb letters by an officer who served first in the Second Massachusetts and then in various staff positions in the Ninth and Second Corps.

Cox, Jacob Dolson, *Military Reminiscences of the Civil War*, 2 vols. (New York, 1900). This is one of the standard, excellent, military reminiscences of the Civil War, which also discusses the overall military picture in addition to the personal involvement of the individual. The narrative itself is entertaining and appears quite reliable; but the judgments should be used with care. For example, Cox is one of the few strong supporters of Pope and one of the few who argues that Pope's competence was proven by his command of the Army of Virginia. In two separate footnotes, he discloses that one of his children married one of Pope's children and that the two families became close friends after the war.

Crary, Catherine S., ed., *Dear Belle—Letters from a Cadet & Officer to his Sweetheart, 1858-1865* (Middletown, 1965). This book includes substantial excerpts from letters written by a member of the class of 1862 at West Point to his sweetheart during his time as a cadet and his service in the Army of the Potomac from his graduation in 1862 through the end of the Battle of Gettysburg. The letters are valuable; the text could better have been relegated to footnotes as Robertson did in the editing of the letters of Colonel Robert McAllister. Most disappointing is the absence of the lengthy letter (16 pages) written by Custer to Macrae immediately after the first battle of Bull Run and a variety of other Custer letters which are mentioned in Macrae's letters.

Croffut, W. A., ed., *Fifty Years in Camp and Field—Diary of Major-General Ethan Allen Hitchcock* U.S.A. (New York, 1909). This book is a rambling collection of partial diary entries, letters, vignettes from newspapers and a variety of other unidentified sources, and personal commentary. It covers the lengthy military life of Ethan Allen Hitchcock. The brief segment treating the Civil War is useful only in its demonstration of the confusion of the civilian authorities in Washington at various times, particularly 1862.

Curtis, Newton Martin, *Bull Run to Chancellorsville* (New York, 1906). Martin, who rose to brevet major general covered his period in the Sixteenth New York in this volume.

deForest, B. S., *Random Sketches and Wandering Thoughts* (Albany, 1866). The Eighty-first New York, in which the author served, spent most of its time on the Atlantic Coast. The volume has a few useful descriptions.

deForest, John William, *A Volunteer's Adventures, a Union Captain's Record of the Civil War* (New Haven, 1946). DeForest served for the majority of the war as a company commander in the Twelfth Connecticut Volunteers. During the last months of his service, while in the Shenandoah Valley in the Nineteenth Corps, DeForest served as a staff officer to General William H. Emory. His reminiscences, written a short while after the war and in some parts during the war, have a delightful style and sufficient overview. Their primary interest is their accounts of the major battles in the Shenandoah Valley in 1864.

De Trobriand, Regis, trans. George J. *Four Years with the Army of the Potomac* (Boston, 1888). This is an excellent war memoir written by a general officer who served in the Army of the Potomac from late 1861 to the surrender. De Trobriand is highly partisan, for the Third Corps, against McClellan, etc., thus giving some interesting insights into a number of issues.

De Peyster, John Watts, *Personal and Military History of Phillip Kearny, Major General United States Volunteers* (New York, 1869). Cumbersomely written, excessively laudatory, and often irrelevant, this biography is nevertheless the best printed collection of original source material on Kearny. Although it was written by a worshipful relative, it nevertheless also points out many of Kearny's disabilities and the restraints they imposed on his Civil War career.

Dix, Morgan, *Memoirs of John A. Dix*, 2 vols. (New York, 1883). The war consumes only a small part of this work, another laudatory "family member" piece. It best shows the frustrations of early would-be leaders.

Donaghy, John, *Army Experience of Captain John Donaghy, 103d Penn'a Vols. 1861-1864* (Deland, 1926). Donaghy's regiment was part of Wessells's brigade, Casey's division, Fourth Corps. The book has a number of interesting anecdotes about the division before it was left behind on the Peninsula when McClellan withdrew. It also frankly recognizes that Casey's division fought poorly at Seven Pines and broke under Confederate pressure.

Doster, William E., *Lincoln and Episodes of the Civil War* (New York and London, 1915). Doster was ultimately the commanding officer of the Fourth Pennsylvania Cavalry, which served for a large part of the time in the defenses in Washington and with the cavalry corps during the Chancellorsville and Gettysburg campaigns. The book has a number of interesting anecdotes about various officers in both battles during crucial moments.

Dowdy, Clifford, *The Wartime Papers of R. E. Lee* (Boston, 1961). The best easy access to Lee's correspondence.

Draper, William F., *Recollections of a Varied Career* (Boston, 1908). Draper served as a second lieutenant in the Twenty-fifth Massachusetts Infantry and ultimately as a captain and later lieutenant colonel of the Thirty-Sixth Massachusetts Infantry.

Dwight, ed., *Life and Letters of Wilder Dwight* (Boston, 1867). This work discloses no author on the title page or at any other specific place, but it was obviously edited and written by a close relative of Dwight, most probably his mother or his father. It gives an interesting firsthand account of the formation and operations of the Second Massachusetts Infantry and an interesting insight into certain of the higher ranking officers in command of the Union forces in the Shenandoah Valley in 1862. Its content stops at the battle of Antietam where Dwight was mortally wounded. The Dwight family papers, including letters from William and Wilder, have recently been deposited in the Massachusetts Historical Society, which allows the compulsive author to fill the annoying nineteenth century editing gaps.

Eby, Cecil D. Jr., ed. *A Virginia Yankee in the Civil War—the Diary of David Hunter Strother* (Chapel Hill, 1961). A staff officer born and raised in the Shenandoah Valley in the area of Martinsburg, Virginia, and well-known because of publications showing his familiarity with the Valley. Strother served almost entirely in the Shenandoah Valley during his military career. The diary was apparently not prepared on a day-to-day basis and entries on many days were obviously made at later times. More interesting although requiring care and verification are the articles in *Harpers*.

Eckenrode, H. J., and Conrad, Bryan, *George B. McClellan: the Man who Saved the Union* (Chapel Hill, 1941).

Eckert, Edward K., and Amato, Nicholas J., Eds., *Ten Years in the Saddle—The Memoir of William Woods Averell* (San Raphael, 1978). Unfortunately, Averell's memoirs end in early 1862 while McClellan was still in command of the Army of the Potomac and before the Peninsula Campaign. They are extraordinarily well-written and very entertaining; but because they were unfinished, the most important parts of Averell's career, as a general officer in the battles in the east, are not covered.

Elliott, Charles Winslow, *Winfield Scott, the Soldier and the Man* (New York, 1937). The best biography of Scott by far and not likely to be replaced without the discovery of some huge cache of Scott correspondence.

Emerson, Edward W., ed., *Life and Letters Of Charles Russel Lowell* (Boston and New York, 1907). Lowell was one of the many members of the Harvard graduating classes of the 1850s who served with extraordinary distinction in the Union armies during the war. His letters to his family and friends are thoughtful and more valuable for their insights than they are for their anecdotes. The text about his life is valuable, as are the many footnotes which appear at the end of the book, for information about other officers.

Favill, Josiah Marshall, *The Diary of a Young Officer—Serving with the Armies of the United States During the War of the Rebellion* (Chicago, 1909). Although not actually a contemporary diary, this book was obviously written from a diary with post-war additions and, in the main, follows the format of a diary. Favill served as a company-grade officer in the Fifty-Seventh New York Infantry, then as a staff officer in various capacities in the Second Corps. His comments on brigade, division, and corps commanders are superb and enlightening.

Ford, Worthington Chauncey, ed., *A Cycle of Adams Letters*, 2 vols. (Boston and New York, 1920). A polyglot collection of Adams family letters describing political, diplomatic, and military events that concerned all generations during the war.

Ford, Worthington Chauncey, ed., *War Letters 1862-1865 of John Chipman Gray and John Codman Ropes* (Boston and New York, 1927). Ropes was in Boston throughout the war and spoke only of the home front and on the basis of comments he received from the many Bostonians who served in the Union forces. Gray served in part with the Army of the Potomac and in part on the eastern seaboard in the Carolinas. Letters from Gray that are particularly interesting are those about Generals George H. Gordon and Quincy A. Gillmore.

Forsyth, George A., *Thrilling Days in Army Life* (New York and London, 1900). This book contains four chapters, two on Indian fights in the west after the Civil War, one on Sheridan's ride from Winchester to Cedar Creek on October 19, 1864, and one on the closing scene at Appomattox Courthouse on April 9, 1865. Well and interestingly written, it makes one wish that Forsyth had seen fit to write about all his experiences as a staff officer with Sheridan.

Freeman, Douglas Southall, *Lee's Lieutenants: A Study in Command*, 3 vols. (New York, 1942). An original work with no equal for any war.

Freeman, Douglas Southall, *R. E. Lee*, 4 vols. (New York, 1934). Replaced in tone by many, it has never lost its, "Best biography by or about an American."

Gardner, Augustine V., ed., *Recollections Of A Civil War Quartermaster, An Autobiography of William G. Le Duc* (St. Paul, 1963). This is an extraordinary but regrettably short autobiography of a staff officer who served as a brigade quartermaster and corps quartermaster in the Second Corps and then as corps quartermaster in the Eleventh Corps. When the Eleventh Corps was transferred west, he went with it and became the quartermaster for the Twentieth Corps under Hooker. Biased and unusual as some of the views in it are, the only regret anyone can have about it is its brevity.

Gibbon, John, *Personal Recollections of the Civil War* (New York and London, 1928) reprint by Morningside Bookshop. This is one of the best reminiscences written by any officer who served in any American war. It is also one of the most well-conceived, well-designed, well-written, and well-constructed personal accounts published after the war. For the events in this account which became the subject of controversy after the war, the subtleties of Gibbon's treatment of relevant circumstances at other places in the book, e.g., the credibility of Hancock's aide Mitchell, are extraordinary. The touch is light but convincing and the style of writing is, like most of Gibbon's letters, far above average.

Gordon, George H., *Brook Farm to Cedar Mountain in the War of the Great Rebellion 1861-62* (Boston, 1883). This is one of the many personal narratives with fuller history based on published reports. Quick to criticize, particularly his superiors, Gordon should be read with care. He claims to have written most of the work from contemporaneous diaries he made while serving in the field. Although subject to careful use like all Gordon's works, this work is indispensable for the Valley through the end of 1862.

Gordon, George H., *A War Diary of Events in the War of the Great Rebellion, 1863-1865* (Boston, 1882). This is a continuation of Gordon's three volume work on the Civil War, which includes *Brook Farm to Cedar Mountain*, and *The Army of Virginia*. It contains some interesting anecdotes although the bulk of the time was spent in service on the Atlantic Coast.

Gould, Edward K., *Major General Hiram G. Berry, His Career As A Contractor, Bank President, Politician and Major General of Volunteers in the Civil War Together with His War Correspondence Embracing the Period from Bull Run to Chancellorsville* (Rockland, 1899). The bulk of the anecdotes about Berry in this work are based on private correspondence with officers who knew him and his letters home during the war. This is the only work of any substance on Berry.

Gregg, Reverend J. Chandler, *Life in the Army, In the Departments of Virginia, and the Gulf, including Observations in New Orleans, with an Account of the Author's Life and Experience in the Ministry* (Philadelphia, 1866). This is the typical chaplain's account of his service, heartfelt and plausible when written but sounding absurd today. Officers who did not drink and who worshiped regularly at church were the best leaders, others were ineffective—as it was seen by the chaplain.

Gunn, Moses, *Memorial Sketches of Doctor Moses Gunn With Extracts From his Letters and Eulogistic Tributes from His Colleagues and Friends* (Chicago, 1889). Although this book covers Gunn's entire life with a small section devoted to the Civil War, the letters quoted are interesting and useful. Gunn served in a regiment in the Third Corps through the end of the Peninsula Campaign.

Hagemann, E. R., ed., *Fighting Rebels and Redskins: Experiences in Army Life of Colonel George B. Sanford, 1861-1892* (Norman, 1969). This book is a combination of personal reminiscences of George B. Sanford for the period 1861-1865, then a historical work about the remainder of his military experiences between 1865 and 1892, and the later years of his life after his retirement from the army. Sanford began as a Regular Army officer and served in the Cavalry Reserve. In the latter years of the war he served on the staff of various high-ranking cavalry officers including Torbert and Sheridan. His accounts are invaluable for these cavalry operations, particularly the operations in the Shenandoah Valley in 1864, the period preceding Sheridan's remarkable campaign, and the period after the destruction of the Confederate forces at the Battle of Cedar Creek.

Hancock, Mrs. Almira, *Reminiscences of Winfield Scott Hancock* (New York, 1887). The portions of this work devoted to the Civil War are slight, it being based primarily on incidents in which Mrs. Hancock participated personally. The most valuable contribution is the reprinting of the narrative by Morgan, chief of staff in the Second Corps, of Hancock's activities from the time he assumed command of the corps until the conclusion of the battle of Gettysburg on July 3.

Harrington, Fred Harvey, *Fighting Politician: Major General N. P. Banks* (Philadelphia, 1948). This is a well-researched and well-documented current biography of Banks, which covers his political career prior to the Civil War in some detail, his Civil War services as a major general, and his brief career after the war. It is both sympathetic and critical.

Harris, Samuel, *Personal Reminiscences of Samuel Harris* (Chicago, 1897). This autobiography places its primary emphasis on Harris's service as a company grade officer in the Fifth Michigan Cavalry during the Civil War. It contains a number of interesting anecdotes about Custer, Alger, the cavalry fight on July 3 at Gettysburg, and the Dahlgren column of the Kilpatrick Raid in February and March of 1864. Inserted at the end is a small pamphlet of letters received by Harris from people familiar with the events described in the book.

Haupt, Herman, *Reminiscences of General Herman Haupt* (Milwaukee, 1901). These reminiscences are particularly valuable for the period when McDowell held the First Corps at Fredericksburg and for later operations leading to Second Bull Run. Haupt met McDowell frequently, being on his staff, and Pope. In the period after the battle of Gettysburg, Haupt resigned and returned to civilian life.

Hollandsworth, James G., Jr., *Pretense of Glory: the Life of General Nathaniel P. Banks* (Baton Rouge, 1998). The most recent biography of Banks.

Howard, O. O., *Autobiography of Oliver Otis Howard Major General United States Army* (2 volumes) (New York, 1907). Howard's autobiography is well-written and entertaining. It combines in a sound manner the general with the personal narrative and presents Howard's views of the controversial events in the latter half of the first day at Gettysburg.

Howe, Henry Warren, *Passages From the Life of Henry Warren Howe, Consisting of Diary and Letters Written During the Civil War, 1861-1865* (Lowell, 1899). Howe served as an enlisted man and a company grade officer in the Thirtieth Massachusetts Infantry, which was part of the Nineteenth Corps. His diary and letters describe incidents in the campaign in the Shenandoah Valley in 1864.

Howe, Mark DeWolfe, ed., *Home Letters of General Sherman* (New York, 1909).

——, ed., *Touched With Fire—Civil War Letters and Diary of Oliver Wendell Holmes, Jr. 1861-1864* (Cambridge, 1946). Holmes served first as a company grade officer in the Twentieth Massachusetts Infantry, then as a staff officer of General Sedgwick (and later General Horatio Wright) when he commanded the Sixth Corps.

Humphreys, Charles A., *Field, Camp, Hospital and Prison in the Civil War 1863-1865* (Boston, 1918). One of the many graduates of Harvard College who served in the Civil War, Humphreys was chaplain to the Second Massachusetts Cavalry commanded first by Charles

Russell Lowell and later by Casper Crowninshield. The book contains his reminiscences, some tributes at the end, his diary, and a few of his letters. It has interesting descriptions of Lowell and Crowninshield and some interesting anecdotes about the federal cavalry in the last two years of the war.

Hunter, David, *Report of the Military Services of General David Hunter, U.S.A., during the War of the Rebellion made to the United States War Department* (New York, 1873).

Hyde, Thomas W., *Following The Greek Cross or, Memories of the Sixth Army Corps* (Boston and New York, 1894) 2nd ed. Reminiscences of an officer from Maine who served through the war in the Sixth Corps. For a considerable period of time Hyde served on the staff of General John Sedgwick, and his accounts of Sedgwick and the Sixth Corps headquarters are invaluable. At the close of the war, particularly at the battles of Fort Steadman, the capture of Petersburg, and the Pursuit to Appomattox, Hyde commanded a brigade in the Sixth Corps.

Hyndman, Capt. William, *History of a Cavalry Company. A Complete Record of Company "A2" 4th Penn'a Cavalry* (Philadelphia, 1870). This is a laconic straightforward account of marches, bivouacs, etc.

Johnston, Joseph E., *Narrative of Military Operations during the late War between the States* (New York, 1872).

Jones, Evan R., *Four Years In The Army Of The Potomac: A Soldier's Recollections* (London, n.d.). The author served in the Fifth Wisconsin, one of the regiments in Hancock's original brigade. The memoirs contain a number of interesting anecdotes about Hancock.

Jordan, William B., Jr., ed., *The Civil War Journals of John Mead Gould, 1861-1866* (Baltimore, 1997). For its length and detail this is the most disappointing recent discovery and publication, especially for such an active participant in the Second Civil War.

Kennedy, Elijah R., *John B., Woodward, a Biographical Memoir* (New York, 1897).

Keyes, E. D., *Fifty Years' Observation of Men and Events Civil and Military* (New York, 1884). Although written in 1884, almost twenty years after the war ended, this book begins with Keyes's reminiscences from the 1830s when he served as military secretary to General Scott and ends with the withdrawal of the Union Army from Harrison's Landing in August of 1862. It is disjointed, sometimes confusing but withal an interesting and literate account of a controversial officer's participation in the early phases of the Civil War. It is the only significant known memoir of the Fourth Corps, which terminated its useful life after the Army of the Potomac withdrew from Harrison's Landing. Neither Couch nor Casey left any memoir or manuscript collection.

Keyes, E. D., *From West Point to California* (Oakland, 1950). This short piece was apparently written by Keyes some years after his service in California between the years 1849 and 1858 when he was stationed at the Presidio of San Francisco.

Kidd, James Harvey, *Personal Recollections of a Cavalryman with Custer's Michigan Brigade in the Civil War* (Ionia, 1908). This is undoubtedly one of the very best narratives written by any participant in the Civil War and clearly one of the best cavalry accounts. Its personal vignettes of Custer, Merritt, and other officers serving in the Cavalry Corps during the war rank at the top.

Kiefer, Joseph Warren, *Slavery and Four Years of War, a political history of slavery of the United States together with a narrative of the campaigns and battles of the Civil War in which the author took part: 1861-1865*, two volumes (New York and London, 1900). Both a history of the comprehensive type and a personal narrative, these two volumes cover a wide range of areas of the Civil War. Kiefer served in the West, in the Shenandoah Valley, and in the Sixth Corps of the Army of the Potomac. During most of his service in the Valley and in the Army of the Potomac he commanded a brigade or a division. His insights into various members of Milroy's command and the Sixth Corps are invaluable. Writing as late as he did, he had the benefit of the official records, the memoirs of other officers, and in some measure "the last word."

Lavery, Dennis S., and Jordan, Mark H., *Iron Brigade General: John Gibbon, A Rebel in Blue* (Westport and London 1993). Well researched in the primary sources this short biography does not fill the need for a full length biography of a devoted McClellanite, who survived the witch hunts to end the war in command of a corps.

Lewis, Lloyd, *Sherman: Fighting Prophet*, 2 vols. (Norwalk, 1991, Easton Press ed.). A longstanding biography that has stood the test of time but frustrates with sparse citations of original authorities.

Longacre, Edward G., *General John Buford* (Conshohocken, 1995). The standard, long-overdue biography of the keeper of the cavalry of the Army of the Potomac.

Longacre, Edward G., *The Man behind the Guns: A Biography of General Henry J. Hunt, Commander of Artillery, Army of the Potomac* (New York, 1977). Still the best of Longacre's many works on the Army of the Potomac.

Malles, Ed., ed., *Bridge Building in Wartime: Colonel Wesley Brainerd's Memoir of the 50th New York Volunteer Engineers* (Knoxville, 1997). One of the best recent contributions and one could only wish for more newly discovered works like this and the Willcox letters and diaries.

Marshall, Jessie Ames, ed., *Private and Official Correspondence of Gen. Benjamin F. Butler During The Period of the Civil War*, 5 vols. (Norwood, 1917). The widely varied contents compare in an interesting manner with Butler's memoirs.

Marvel, William, *Burnside* (Chapel Hill and London, 1991). At last a well researched biography of Burnside, but Marvel undertakes the impossible: unlike Pope, Burnside was a decent person with integrity; like Pope, however, he was indefensibly incompetent.

Maull, D. W., *The Life and Military Services of the Late Brigadier General Thomas A. Smyth* (Wilmington, 1870). This slim volume contains valuable quotes from Smyth's diary, which has apparently not been preserved and useful descriptions of Smyth's advancement in the Second Corps.

McClellan, George B., *McClellan's Own Story*, 67-69 (Norwalk, 1995) (Easton Press ed.). The most rewarding, frustrating, taxing, informative, confusing, and baffling of all postwar memoirs. From its terse style one wonders if the earlier draft, destroyed by fire, did not make the historian's task easier. Its real value appears only when used with the MSS.

McKinney, Francis F., *Education in Violence: the Life of George H. Thomas and the History of the Army of the Cumberland* (reprint Chicago, 1991).

Meade, George Gordon, ed., *The Life and Letters of George Gordon Meade Major-General United States Army*, 2 vols. (New York, 1913). Indispensable to the history of the army and its officers corps but like McClellan's memoirs should be used with the MSS.

Merington, Marguerite, *The Custer Story: The Life and Intimate Letters of General George A. Custer and His Wife Elisabeth* (New York, 1950). Because Custer will never want for biographers, this book will never want for readers until the unlikely "Complete works of . . ." It is composed primarily of lengthy quotations from letters written by Custer and his wife to various members of the family. It also includes a considerable amount of other original material written by persons who served with or knew Custer. Quotes from newspaper articles have been added. A small amount of connecting text has been written to give the book a narrative flow. The letters are excellent and an invaluable source on Custer.

Meyer, Henry C., *Civil War Experiences Under Bayard, Gregg, Kilpatrick, Custer, Raulston, and Newberry 1862, 1863, 1864* (New York, 1911). Meyer served as an enlisted man in the Second New York Cavalry (the Ira Harris Cavalry), then as a captain in the Twenty-fourth New York Cavalry. In both capacities he had close contact with numerous high-ranking officers, particularly while he was an enlisted man when he served as a clerk and de facto staff officer to David M. Gregg and others. The books contains many interesting anecdotes about cavalry operations during the war.

Michie, Peter S., *The Life and Letters of Emory Upton, Colonel of the Fourth Regiment of Artillery and Brevet Major General U.S. Army* (New York, 1885).

Miller, C. G., *Donn Piatt: his Work and his Ways* (Cincinnati, 1893). A biography of a junior but well-connected officer who spent much of his time defending the indefensible persons of the war, e.g., Schenk, Stanton, etc.

Miller, Edward A., Jr., *Lincoln's Abolitionist General: The Biography of David Hunter* (Columbia, 1997). One of the recent new biographies whose careful research has made a task of many lifetimes more or less possible in one, at least one hopes it is.

Mitchell, Donald G., ed., *Daniel Tyler: A Memorial Volume* (New Haven, 1883). An attempt at a defense that better produces an indictment.

Monaghan, Jay, *Custer: the Life of General George Armstrong Custer* (Boston, 1959).

Moore, James, M.D., *Kilpatrick and Our Cavalry* (New York, 1865). This is a highly laudatory and somewhat suspect biography of Kilpatrick. The evaluations are not reliable, some of the factual assertions are inaccurate, and the continuous descriptions of "routes" of the Rebel cavalry must be taken with a grain of salt. Still, the book does offer a considerable amount of useful factual information on Kilpatrick himself.

Morse, C. F., *Letters Written During the Civil War—1861-1865* (Boston, 1898). Morse served in the Second Massachusetts Infantry and later on the staff of General H. W. Slocum.

The letters are informative, thoughtful, and in some cases lengthy accounts of marches and battles of the regiment and the Twelfth Corps.

Myers, William Starr, *General George Brinton McClellan: A Study in Personality* (New York, 1934). The only fair and even-handed book about McClellan, the man.

Myers, William Starr, ed., *The Mexican War Diary of General George B. McClellan: A Campaign Journal Written in Camp and Field, in 1846-47 and Now for the First Time Published* (Princeton, 1917).

Nagle, Theodore M., *Reminiscences of the Civil War* (Erie, 1923). A slim volume of reminiscences written long after the war and, by the numerous factual mistakes in it, after some of the memory had faded. It contains a few useful anecdotes relating to the Twenty-first New York Infantry and General M. R. Patrick, who commanded the brigade.

Nash, Howard P., Jr., *Stormy Petrel: The Life and Times of General Benjamin F. Butler, 1818-1893* (Cranbury, 1969). A superficial biography of a controversial subject who deserves more but will probably never receive it.

Nevins, Alan, *Fremont: Pathmarker of the West* (New York, 1955).

A staff officer [Newhall, Frederick C.], *With General Sheridan in Lee's Last Campaign* (Philadelphia, 1866). This volume, written by Colonel Frederick C. Newhall, of Sheridan's staff, is a superb and invaluable, although disputatious, account of Sheridan's cavalry from the battle of Dirwiddie Court House to the surrender of Lee's army at Appomattox Court House.

Nolan, Dick, *Benjamin Franklin Butler: the Damnedest Yankee* (Novato, 1991). Another short biography of a complicated man.

Noyes, George F., *The Bivouac and the Battlefield; or Campaign Sketches in Virginia and Maryland* (New York, 1863). Obviously written from a diary kept by a member of the staff of General Abner Doubleday, it is dedicated to Doubleday, contains a number of interesting anecdotes based on contemporaneous observations, and was published when the war had not yet ended and some of the great debates had not yet commenced. Hence, while it may be subject to inaccuracies from incorrect observations, it is not generally vulnerable to the kind of revisionism that makes many of the memoirs and other publications written long after the war suspect.

Palfrey, Francis Winthrop, *Memoir of William Francis Bartlett* (Boston, 1878). This is one of the many works produced by Palfrey about men from Harvard in the Civil War. It quotes extensively from Bartlett's personal letters and his diary and is both a valuable work on an unusual individual and a good collection of information about men who served with Bartlett.

Pearson, Henry Greenleaf, *James S. Wadsworth of Geneseo, Brevet Major General of United States Volunteers* (New York, 1913). This biography of General James Samuel Wadsworth is well written, relatively detached, and extremely well researched. Its detail about Wadsworth is the more remarkable because Wadsworth himself left behind virtually no manuscripts. Much of the material used by Pearson in the biography would be useful today if it could be located because it included manuscript reminiscences of a number of officers whose papers have not found their way into public repositories and have not been published. Pearson has also successfully shown the circumstances in which Wadsworth functioned as well as the day to day performance of those functions by Wadsworth.

Perry, Martha Derby, *Letters From A Surgeon Of The Civil War* (Boston, 1906). These letters were written to the editor by her husband, one of the numerous young Harvard graduates who served in the Twentieth Massachusetts Infantry.

Piatt, Don, *Memories of the Men who Saved the Union* (New York and Chicago, 1887). This book contains a large number of interesting and illuminating anecdotes, many of which are based on personal observation and personal participation. It also contains some very interesting insights into the character of Lincoln, Stanton, Seward, Chase, and McClellan. Its military analyses show the kind of mindless bias against West Point of many midwesterners, who believed the United States Military Academy created an aristocratic military elite. His views on military issues are generally absurd.

Pinchon, Edgcumb, *Dan Sickles, Hero of Gettysburg and Yankee King of Spain* (New York, 1945).

Pisani, Lieutenant-Colonel Camille Ferri, *Prince Napoleon in America 1861, Letters from his Aide-de-Camp* (Bloomington, 1959).

Poore, Ben: Perley, *The Life and Public Services of Ambrose E. Burnside, Soldier-Citizen-Statesman* (Providence, 1882). This is a laudatory and in the main uncritical biography of Burnside, which surprisingly has more to it on a second reading than meets the eye on the first.

Porter, Admiral David D., *Incidents and Anecdotes of the Civil War* (New York, 1885). A man with a hyperactive, indefatigable pen, Porter left behind much valuable material; but he has never attracted a definitive biographer.

Quaife, Milo M., ed., *From the Cannon's Mouth, the Civil War Letters of General Alphius S. Williams* (Detroit, 1959). This exceptional collection of letters written by General Williams to his daughters covers his tenure with the Army of the Potomac from 1861 through the fall of 1863, and continues after the transfer of the Eleventh and Twelfth Corps to the west. While they contain less information about specific individuals than one might expect, they contain an extraordinary amount of information about life in the army, the activities of the Twelfth Corps, and particularly the First Division of that corps.

Randall, Ruth Painter, *Colonel Elmer E. Ellsworth, a Biography of Lincoln's Friend and first Hero of the Civil War* (Boston and Toronto, 1960).

Revere, Joseph W., *Keel and Saddle: A Retrospect of Forty Years of Military and Naval Service* (Boston, 1872).

Robertson, James I., Jr., ed., *The Civil War Letters of General Robert McAllister* (New Brunswick, 1965). This volume contains more than 900 letters written by McAllister to his family during the course of the war. They cover him day to day from the time he entered the war until the surrender of Lee's army and reflect his advancement from lieutenant colonel of the First New Jersey Volunteers to brigadier general commanding a brigade in the Third Division, Second Army Corps. They are an invaluable reference tool for the day to day happenings of the army, in some measure the officers who commanded it, and McAllister himself.

Robertson, James I., Jr., *Stonewall Jackson: the Man, the Soldier, the Legend* (New York, 1997).

Rockwell, A. D., *Rambling Recollections and Autobiography* (New York, 1920). The author served as a surgeon in the Sixth Ohio Cavalry, Davies brigade, which was later commanded by C. H. Smith. The book contains a number of interesting anecdotes about Davies, Smith, Sheridan, and Gregg.

Roemer, Jacob, ed. by L. A. Furney, *Reminiscences of the War of the Rebellion 1861-1865*, (New York, 1897). Useful autobiographical account of a battery commander during the war.

Rusling, James F., *Men And Things I Saw In Civil War Days* (New York, 1899). A number of excellent first-hand accounts of major officers in the Army of the Potomac. It also includes letters sent by Rusling during the war while he was a quartermaster in the Third Corps and for some time on the staff of the Army of the Potomac.

Schafer, Joseph, ed. and trans., *Intimate Letters Of Charles Schurz 1841-1869 (Publications the State Historical Society of Wisconsin, Collections, Vol. 1130)* (Madison, 1929). A small part of this volume contains letters relating to Schurz's service as an officer in the Union army.

Schmitt, Martin F., ed., *General George Crook, His Autobiography* (Norman, 1946). Written between 1885 and 1890 but undiscovered until the Second World War and not published until after that, Crook's autobiography is rough, filled with minor errors, but a valuable piece of work. Burdened with the view that his successful efforts almost invariably redounded to the credit of others, Crook has little complimentary to say about any of his fellow officers of any rank.

Schurz, Carl, *The Reminiscences of Carl Schurz*, 3 vols. (New York, 1907-1908). Schurz appears never to have acquired an objective view of his part in the war or his performance.

Scott, Robert Garth, ed., *Forgotten Valor: the Memoirs, Journals, & Civil War Letters of Orlando B. Willcox* (Kent, 1999). One of the major recent publications of firsthand material about the Army of the Potomac.

Scrymser, James A., *Personal Reminiscences of James A. Scrymser in Times of Peace and War* (1915, n.p.). This slim volume was written by a man who first served as a non-commissioned officer in Butterfield's Twelfth New York Infantry, then as an officer of the Forty-first New York, during which time he was a staff officer for Baldy Smith. The book contains fascinating anecdotes about various incidents during the first three years of the war. One wishes that Scrymser had written a full-fledged memoir if these are only a sampling of the things he saw.

Sears, Stephen W., ed., *For Country, Cause & Leader: The Civil War Journal of Charles B. Haydon* (New York, 1993). This is a superb journal of a junior company grade officer who rose to the rank of lieutenant colonel by 1864 in the Second Michigan. It gives an excellent picture of the duties and responsibilities of a junior company grade officer, the hazards of picket duty, and a variety of other responsibilities that all tend to be lost in the usual Civil War narrative.

Sears, Stephen W., *George B. McClellan: The Young Napoleon* (New York, 1988). The most current major work on the war's most controversial leader.

Sears, Stephen W., ed., *The Civil War Papers of George B. McClellan, Selected Correspondence 1860-1865* (New York, 1989). If this work, extremely valuable, had been published twenty-five years ago, it would have saved the author a great deal of work.

Sedgwick, Henry D., *Correspondence of John Sedgwick, Major General* (2 volumes) (privately printed, 1902). These two slim volumes contain correspondence from Sedgwick to his family, primarily to his sister, the bulk of which was written during the Mexican War and the Civil War. In addition, the volumes contain a number of official dispatches and some official correspondence which does not appear in the *Official Records* and which is very interesting on the issues of officer promotion and the means by which various candidacies were advanced.

Small, Abner, *Road to Richmond the Civil War Memoirs of Major Abner R. Small of the Sixteenth Maine Volunteers, together with the diary which he kept when he was a Prisoner of War* (California, 1939). A very good personal reminiscence by an officer.

Stevens, Hazard, *The Life of Isaac Ingalls Stevens*, two volumes, (Boston and New York, 1900). This work is written by Stevens's son Hazard and was based in part on unpublished family papers. Much of the Civil War material is based on Stevens's personal knowledge, having served as an aide to his father in many of the battles and during most of his time in the service. Although perhaps excessively laudatory, the biography is well written and does not have the same level of adulation contained in many post Civil War biographies.

Swanberg, W. A., *Sickles the Incredible* (New York, 1956). The best reasonably current biography of a highly visible, always controversial officer.

Taylor, James E., *With Sheridan up the Shenandoah Valley in 1864: Leaves from a Special Artist's Sketch Book and Diary* (Cleveland, 1989).

Thompson, Jerry, ed., *Fifty Miles and a Fight: Major Samuel Peter Heintzelman's Journal of Texas and the Cortina War* (Austin, 1998).

Tilney, Robert, *My Life In The Army: Three Years and a Half with the Fifth Army Corps, Army of the Potomac, 1862-1865* (Philadelphia, 1912). This is part narrative and part letters. To the end of 1863 it is narrative, and from the Wilderness Campaign through the end it is letters. It contains some interesting information about Warren and the Fifth Corps headquarters.

Townsend, Brevet Major-General Edward D., *Anecdotes of the Civil War in the United States* (New York, 1881). This small volume contains a variety of disjointed and unconnected anecdotes by the adjutant general of the United States Army throughout the Civil War. It is interesting for the light it throws on a variety of top-ranking government officials and officers. Its primary use is confined to the early part of the war, particularly the year 1861, but it contains some useful incidents from later periods. Townsend had an opportunity to write one of the major military reminiscences of the War but passed it with a short, superficial, uncontroversial book.

Tremain, Henry Edwin, *Last Hours of Sheridan's Cavalry* (New York, 1904). During this campaign Tremain, who later formed a law partnership with Mason Tyler Whiting, served as an aide to General George Crook, commander of the Second Cavalry Division of the Army of the Potomac, formerly Gregg's division. The account includes details of Crook's maneuvers as well as a critique, highly favorable to Sheridan, of the cavalry activities from the initial advance on the White Oak Road by the Fifth Corps and the cavalry battle at Dinwiddie Court House through the grand review in Washington after the surrender of the Army of Northern Virginia. Tremain's partialities, very strong, are the Third Corps, Sheridan, his cavalry, and Crook.

Tremain, Henry Edwin, *Two Days of War: A Gettysburg Narrative and Other Excursions* (New York, 1905). A superb series of articles about the experiences of a staff officer who served on the staffs of Sickles and Hooker at the Battle of Chancellorsville and the Battle of Gettysburg. The clarity, precision, and beauty of the prose, although perhaps not its objectivity, are superior; and the first-hand accounts of important events involving the transmission of orders at both battles is exceptionally interesting. Tremain's home letters, regrettably, do not appear to have survived.

Trumbull, H. Clay, *War Memories of an Army Chaplain* (New York, 1898). A few interesting anecdotes.

Wainwright, Charles S., Nevins, Allan, ed., *A Diary of Battle: The Personal Journals of Colonel Charles S. Wainwright, 1861-1865* (New York, 1962). One of the best diaries maintained by anyone during the entire Civil War, it has extraordinary insight into the officers with whom Wainwright served, including many army, corps, and division commanders, and gives the personal views of a conservative democrat serving the length of the war in the eastern United States. The editing by Nevins is, of course, superior.

Walker, Charles N. and Rosemary, *Diary of the War by Robert S. Robertson, 93d Reg't. N.Y. Vols. & A.D.C. to Gen. N. A. Miles, Commanding 1st Brigade, 1st Division, 2d Army Corp, 1861-2-3-4* (Indiana, 1965). This diary, kept from November of 1861 until early June of 1864, is an excellent daily account of activities in the Fourth Corps, the Second Corps, and Miles's Brigade. It also contains useful information about various other individuals.

Wallace, Lewis, *Lew Wallace: an Autobiography*, 2 vols. (New York, 1905).

Weigley, Russell F., *Quartermaster General of the Union Army: a Biography of M. C. Meigs* (New York, 1956).

Weld, Stephen Minot, *War Diary and Letters of Stephen Minot Weld, 1861-1865* (Boston, 1979, 2nd ed.). Originally prepared by Weld and published in 1912 in fifty copies for his family, this is one of the most invaluable works written by any of the participants in the war. Weld's service as a small unit commander, staff officer, and regimental commander gave him contact with numerous important and controversial officers in the army including Burnside, Ledlie, Porter, and Reynolds, among others. The diary and letters are interspersed with text written 50 years after the events, and the style is everything that would be expected of the usual Harvard graduate.

Whittaker, Frederick, *A Complete Life of Gen. George A. Custer, Major-General of Volunteers, Brevet Major-General, U.S. Army, and Lieutenant-Colonel, Seventh U.S. Cavalry* (New York, 1876). Custer's incomplete reminiscences of the war appear without attribution verbatim in the text.

Williams, Frederick D., ed., *The Wild Life Of The Army: Civil War Letters of James A. Garfield* (Michigan, 1964). This volume contains a collection of Garfield's letters to his wife, his family, and certain friends. The letters are collected from a variety of sources. They are most valuable for the period August 1862 through February 1863, during part of which time Garfield served as a biased member of the board of officers who presided over the court-martial of Fitz-John Porter.

Wilson, Calvin Dill, ed., *Sword and Gown by John R. Paxton D. D. Soldier And Preacher, A Memorial Volume* (New York, 1926). A compilation of speeches, lectures, sermons, and letters. Paxton served in the One Hundred Fortieth Pennsylvania Infantry and relates a number of interesting anecdotes about Hancock.

Wilson, James Harrison, *Under the Old Flag—Recollections of Military Operations in the War for the Union, the Spanish War, the Boxer Rebellion, etc.*, 2 vols. (New York and London, 1912). This is one of the outstanding military reminiscences written by any general officer. However, it is marred from time to time by "if only they had . . . I would have . . ." and a variety of other statements about better courses of action which would have produced better results although, in fact, many of the courses suggested by Wilson completely ignore the real purpose of the activity he criticizes, e.g., his criticism of Sheridan's march for Trevillian as having departed too soon when one of the purposes of the march was to draw the Confederate cavalry away in order to permit an undiscovered march by the Army of the Potomac to the James River and the crossing to Petersburg.

[Wister, Sara B.] *Walter S. Newhall, A Memoir* (Philadelphia, 1864). This slim volume, printed during the war after Newhall's death, contains parts of a number of interesting letters written by Newhall during the war. Newhall himself served, after a brief tour of duty in Missouri at the outset of the war, in a distinguished regiment, the Third Pennsylvania Cavalry.

Youker, J. Clayton, ed., *The Military Memoirs Of Captain Henry Cribben of the 140th New York Volunteers* (n.p., 1911). Cribben served as an officer in the One Hundred Fortieth New York, the first regiment to occupy Little Round Top on July 2. His memoirs contain an interesting account of the conversation between Colonel O'Rourke and Warren prior to seizing the hill.

Pamphlets and Articles

Allen, Lewis F., "Memorial of the late Gen. James S. Wadsworth delivered before the New York State Agricultural Society at the close of its annual exhibition at Rochester, September 23rd, 1864, by the Hon. Lewis F. Allen, of Buffalo, (ex-President of the Society). (Buffalo, 1864).

Banes, Charles H., *An Address Delivered at Gettysburg, August 27, 1883, by Alexander S. Webb, at the dedication of the 72nd PA. Vols Monument. Also, a historical sketch of the 72nd regiment* (Philadelphia, 1883). Webb delivered the address; Banes wrote the sketch of the regiment.

Biddle, "Reminiscences of McClellan," vol. xi, *The United Service* (May, 1894).

Cullum, George W., *Biographical Sketch of Major-General Henry W. Halleck of the United States Army* (New York, 1880). This brief sketch of Halleck by his chief of staff and most ardent supporter is frustratingly short about his service as general in chief.

Gould, John Mead, *Joseph K. Mansfield, Brigadier General of the U.S. Army. A narrative of events connected with his mortal wounding at Antietam, Sharpsburg, Maryland, September 17, 1862* (Portland, 1895). Gould maintained a spirited correspondence on this subject with anyone who would respond to him, e.g., the Carmen MSS in N.Y.P.L.

Griess, Thomas Everett, *Dennis Hart Mahan: West Point Professor and Advocate of Military Professionalism 1830-1871* (MS, Ph.D. dissertation, Duke University, 1969).

Hicks, John D., "The Organization of the Volunteer Army in 1861 with special Reference to Minnesota," *Minnesota Historical Bulletin*, no. 5, Feb. 1918.

Hunt, Henry J., "Artillery Administration" in *Journal of the Military Institute of the United States*, vol. 12 (1891).

LeComte, Ferdinand, *Campagne de Virginie et de la Maryland en 1862: Documents Officials Sounies au Congress traduits de L'Anglais avec Introduction et Annotations* (Paris, 1863). A reprint in French, with valuable footnotes by one of McClellan's European aides, of the first report of the Joint Committee about the Army of the Potomac. Although somewhat critical of McClellan and misleadingly used by Barnard, LeComte had no use for the Joint Committee, which received in his notes the treatment it deserved.

Olmsted, Frederick Law, Secretary, United States Sanitary Commission, "Report of the Secretary with Regard to the Probable Origin of the Recent Demoralization of the Volunteer Army at Washington and the duty of the Sanitary Commission with Reference to Certain Deficiencies in the Existing Army Arrangements as Suggested Thereby"(Washington, 1861) reprinted in McLaughlin, Charles Capen, ed., *The Papers of Frederick Law Olmsted*, 5 vols. (incomplete) (Baltimore and London 1977-).

Parker, Daingerfield, "The Regular Battalion in the First Battle of Bull Run," in *The United Service: A Monthly Review of Military and Naval Affairs*, xiii, no. 5 (November, 1885).

Porter, Fitz-John, "In Memory of Gen. Chas. P. Stone (n.p., n.d.).

Prince de Joinville, trans. William Henry Hurlbert, *The Army of the Potomac: its Organization, its Commander, and its Campaign* (New York, 1862).

Robinson, John C., and John Watts de Peyster, "Obituaries of Major General Samuel P. Heintzelman, first Commander of the Third Army Corps, and Major General Joseph Hooker" (New York, 1881).

Scheips, Paul J., *Albert J. Meyer, Founder of the Army Signal Corps: A Biographical Study*, 2 parts (MS Ph.D. dissertation) (U.M.I. Dissertation Services).

Schenck, R. C., "Major-General David Hunter," *Magazine of American History*, vol. 15, no. 2, February, 1887.

Weik, Jesse W., "Side Lights on Lincoln, How Lincoln Was Convinced of Scott's Loyalty," *Century Magazine* (1911).

Wilson, William B., *A Leaf from the History of the Rebellion: Sketches of Events and Persons* (Philadelphia, 1888).

Enlisted Men's Letters, Diaries, and Reminiscences

Adams, John G. V., *Reminiscences of the 19th Massachusetts Regiment* (Boston, 1899). This slim volume has a number of interesting anecdotes about Colonel Hinks and also about the campaigns in which the regiment took part, particularly the pontoon crossing at Fredericksburg.

Allen, Stanton G., *Down in Dixie: Life in a Cavalry Regiment in the War Days from the Wilderness to Appomattox* (Boston, 1893). The author enlisted in one of four new companies to be added to First Massachusetts Cavalry and took part in the campaigns from the Wilderness through the end of the war. During part of that time, he served in Davies's brigade, Gregg's division, Sheridan's Cavalry Corps. During the remainder of the time, including the period until the surrender at Appomattox, he was part of the First Massachusetts Cavalry, which was detailed to army headquarters as the escort for General Meade.

(Anonymous) A Citizen-Soldier, *Red Tape and Pigeon-Hole Generals: As Seen From the Ranks During a Campaign in the Army of the Potomac* (New York, Carleton, 1864). This extraordinary book was written by a member of Tyler's brigade of Humphrey's division, Fifth Corps after the battle of Antietam. The division was composed primarily of short-term enlisted men and was disbanded almost immediately after the battle of Chancellorsville. It should be compared with Wilkeson for its vituperative criticism of virtually every senior officer in the army.

Armstrong, Dr. Nelson, V. S., *Nuggets of Experience—Narratives of the Sixties and Other Days, with Graphic Descriptions of Thrilling Personal Adventures* (San Bernadino, 1904, Times—Mirror, P. and B. House). A few anecdotes.

Bennett, Edwin C., *Musket and Sword or the Camp, March, and Firing Line in the Army of the Potomac* (Boston, 1900).

Benton, Charles E., *As Seen From The Ranks—A Boy in the Civil War* (New York, 1902). Memoir of an enlisted man who served in the One Hundred Fiftieth New York, part of Lockwood's brigade at Gettysburg and later part of the Twelfth Corps, which was ultimately sent to the west in the fall of 1863. It has a few interesting anecdotes, particularly about Lockwood.

Billings, John D., *Hard Tack and Coffee or the Unwritten Story of Army Life* (Boston, 1887).

Borton, Benjamin, *On the Parallels or Chapters of Inner History: A Story of the Rappahannock* (Woods Town, 1903). The author served in the Twenty-fourth New Jersey, a nine-month regiment. The narrative covers only the battles of Fredericksburg and Chancellorsville and has a few useful anecdotes in it.

Bristol, Frank Milton, *The Life of Chaplain McCabe, Bishop of the Methodist Episcopal Church* (Cincinnati and New York, 1908).

Calvert, Henry Murray, *Reminiscences of a Boy in Blue 1862-1865* (New York, 1920). These informal reminiscences by a member of the Eleventh New York Cavalry, a regiment which served for some period of time with the Army of the Potomac, then in the Louisiana campaign, contain a few interesting anecdotes about its officers and its original organization.

Cole, Jacob H., *Under Five Commanders or a Boy's Experience with the Army of the Potomac* (Patterson, 1906). This is a superb narrative by an infantryman who served in the Fifty-seventh New York. It contains a great number of useful anecdotes and information about French and Zook, among others.

Crotty, D. G., *Four Years' Campaigning in the Army of the Potomac* (Grand Rapids, 1974). This slim book of personal reminiscences by a non-commissioned officer in the Third Michigan Infantry contains a number of minor errors on dates and descriptions of events not in Crotty's immediate view. It contains interesting anecdotes about various brigade and division commanders and describes the feeling of the troops toward various changes in command. It remains one of the better reminiscences written by any soldier in the Union army.

Crowell, Joseph E., *The Young Volunteer: the everyday Experiences of a Soldier Boy in the Civil War* (Patterson, 1906). This book is an excellent first-hand account of an infantryman in the Twelfth Corps of the Army of the Potomac and has a number of useful anecdotes about various officers, including particularly the conversation between Pleasanton and Major Harman of the Eighth Pennsylvania Cavalry before the fatal charge at Chancellorsville.

Deane, Frank Putnam, 2nd, ed., *"My Dear Wife . . ." the Civil War Letters of David Brett Ninth Massachusetts Battery, Union Cannonier* (n.p., 1964). This collection of letters contains a few interesting anecdotes about the change in command in the winter of 1863 and the battle of Gettysburg.

Don Pedro Quaerendo Reminisco, *Life in the Union Army by a Two Years Volunteer: a History in Verse of the Fifteenth Regiment N.Y.V. Engineers, Col. John McLeod Murphy . . .* (New York, 1864).

Foster, Alonzo, *Reminiscences and Records of the Sixth New York Veteran Volunteer Cavalry* (1892). This small volume, based on a diary maintained during the war, recites a number of interesting incidents, particularly relating to Brigadier General Thomas C. Devin. It contains the usual number of mistakes when it discusses matters not within direct sight of the author.

Foster, Alonzo, *Reminiscences and Records of the Sixth New York Veteran Volunteer Cavalry* (n.p., 1892). This small book contains a series of articles about the Sixth New York Cavalry, including extensive text "from Foster's own diary and a few anecdotes from his personal participation in the war." It contains a number of interesting anecdotes about various general officers.

Galwey, Thomas Francis Colonel W. S. Nye, ed., *The Valiant Hours* (Harrisburg, 1961). These memoirs are extremely valuable for the period from the beginning of the war to the end of the fighting on the North Anna River. The Eighth Ohio served throughout the war in Sprigg Carroll's brigade.

Gause, Isaac, *Four Years With Five Armies, Army of the Frontier, Army of the Potomac, Army of the Missouri, Army of the Ohio, Army of the Shenandoah* (New York and Washington, 1908). This is an excellent personal reminiscence of service in the Second Ohio Cavalry, which joined the Army of the Potomac in 1864 as part of the Ninth Corps and was then reassigned to the Cavalry Corps. It casts interesting light on Wilson's reputation in his division but is sometimes difficult to follow because the author makes no effort to describe events beyond his personal participation.

Goss, Warren Lee, *Recollections of a Private. A story of the Army of the Potomac* (New York, 1890). This is one of the best accounts by a private serving in the infantry during the war. Although it undertakes some of the history of the army as a whole, the accounts of the troops are excellent. Parts of it were printed in Battles and Leaders.

Greenleaf, Margorie, ed., *Letters to Eliza From a Union Soldier, 1862-1865* (New York, 1970). George Fowle, the writer of the letters, served in the Thirty-ninth Massachusetts in the Fifth Corps. The letters were written to his sweetheart, whom he married after the war. They were edited with some comments by his granddaughter.

Hamilton, William Douglas, *Recollections of a Cavalryman of the Civil War after Fifty Years 1861—1865* (Columbus, 1915). The author served in the Thirty-Second Ohio Infantry and Ninth Ohio Cavalry.

Hill, A. F., *Our Boys. The personal experiences of a soldier in the Army of the Potomac* (Philadelphia, 1864). The author served in the Eighth Pennsylvania Reserves until he was wounded at Antietam. The book contains a number of useful anecdotes about various general officers in the reserves including McCall, Meade, and Reynolds.

Jackson, Harry F. and O'Donnell, Thomas F., eds., *Back Home in Oneida: Hermon Clarke and His Letters* (Syracuse, 1965). These letters contain a few anecdotes and some reflections of views of the enlisted men of the 117th New York Infantry, a regiment recruited in western New York.

Jones, Evan R., *Four Years in the Army of the Potomac: A Soldier's Recollections* (London, n.d.).

Kennedy, Elijah R., *John B. Woodward A Biographical Memoir* (New York, 1897). This small work is part biographical and part a publication of Woodward's letters. Woodward served for some time in the Baltimore area, then in the Peninsula, and finally with the militia at Gettysburg.

Kieffer, Harry M., *The Recollections of a Drummer Boy* (Boston and New York, 1881) revised ed. 1888. A few interesting anecdotes. The author was the drummer for the One Hundred Fiftieth Pennsylvania, a regiment that served in the First Corps.

Locke, E. W., *Three years in Camp and Hospital* (Boston, 1870). This book contains many interesting anecdotes and opinions about various officers to 1864.

Lockwood, James D., *Life and Adventures of a Drummer-Boy; or Seven Years a Soldier* (Albany, 1893). Lockwood served as a drummer boy in the Fourth New York Heavy Artillery. The book contains a few interesting anecdotes about General Wadsworth and General Kitching.

Loving, Jerome M., ed., *Civil War Letters of George Washington Whitman* (Durham, 1975). Whitman served in the Fifty-first New York Infantry, part of Burnside's coast expedition, then part of Reno's division, Ninth Corps throughout the war. The letters are interesting from a number of points of view, including the relationship between the Ninth Corps and the Army of the Potomac.

Lyle, Rev. W. W., *Lights and Shadows of Army Life: Or, Pen Pictures from the Battlefield, the Camp, and the Hospital*. (Cincinnati, 1865) 2d Ed. A few anecdotes about Cox in the fighting at Second Bull Run and Antietam.

Lynch, Charles H., *The Civil War Diary, 1862-1865, of Charles H. Lynch, 18th Conn. Vol's.* (Hartford, 1915). This diary, perhaps originally contemporary, was obviously substantially modified after the war. It contains information about the Eighteenth Connecticut Volunteers, which served in the Shenandoah Valley.

McKinney, E. P., *Life In Tent And Field: 1861—1865* (Boston, 1922). A few interesting anecdotes about the Sixth New York Cavalry, Devin, and Sheridan, but little else of real value, it is a cross between a campaign history and a personal narrative but in fact neither one.

Miller, Delavan S., *Drum Taps in Dixie—Memories of a Drummer Boy 1861-1865* (Watertown, 1905). The author served as drummer boy throughout the war in the Second New York Heavy Artillery. The book has a number of useful anecdotes.

Norton, Oliver Willcox, *Army Letters* 1861-1865. *Being Extracts from private letters to relatives and friends from a soldier in the field with an appendix containing copies of some official documents, papers, and addresses* (Chicago, 1903). Norton served as an unlisted man in the Eighty-third Pennsylvania Infantry, part of Butterfield's brigade and later commanded by Vincent in the fighting at Little Round Top at Gettysburg. The letters contain interesting comments on Butterfield, Rice, Vincent, and Chamberlain as well as speeches and papers written by Norton after the war on the same subjects.

Noyes, George F., *The Bivouac and the Battlefield or Campaign Sketches in Virginia and Maryland* (New York, 1863).

Opie, John N., *A Rebel Cavalryman With Lee, Stuart, and Jackson* (Chicago, 1899).

Parker, David D., *A Chatauqua Boy in '61 and Afterward* (Boston, 1912). Parker served for a short time as a member of an infantry regiment, the Seventy-second New York, and then as Superintendent of the Mails.

Rauscher, Frank, *Music on the March, 1862-65, with the Army of the Potomac. 114th Regt. P.V., Collis' Zouaves* (Philadelphia, 1892). Rauscher's band served initially with the One Hundred Fourteenth Regiment, Pennsylvania Volunteers, but in spite of its small numbers was soon recognized as one of the better bands in the army. During the last year of the war it served a considerable amount of time at army headquarters. The book contains a number of interesting anecdotes relating to Meade and Grant, as well as anecdotes about Third Corps officers before the band was taken to army headquarters.

Ryder, John J., *Reminiscences of Three Year Service in the Civil War* (New Bedford, 1928). The author wrote these memoirs many years after the war, and it shows.

Spangler, Edward W., *My Little War Experience with Historical Sketches and Memorabilia* (York, 1904).

Stone, James Madison, *Personal Recollections Of The Civil War, By One Who Took Part In It As A Private Soldier In The Twenty-first Volunteer Regiment Of Infantry From Massachusetts* (Boston, 1918). The book contains an interesting account of Kearny's conduct immediately prior to the time he was killed at Chantilly.

Truxall, Qida Craig, ed., *"Respects to All" Letters of Two Pennsylvania Boys in the War of the Rebellion* (Pittsburgh, 1962). Although these letters contain few significant battle descriptions, they do contain a great deal of valuable information about the attitudes of the fighting men toward various generals.

Tyler, William S., ed., *Recollections of the Civil War by Mason Whiting Tyler* (New York, 1912). This volume is composed in part of a personal narrative unfinished at Tyler's death and a collection of his diary entries and letters after the end of the draft in existence at his death. The narrative is a combination of an overall history of the Army of the Potomac, an account of the Thirty-Seventh Massachusetts Regiment, and the personal experiences of Tyler, with interesting anecdotal information about the Sixth Corps.

Urban, John W., *In Defense of the Union; or, Through Shot and Shell and Prison Pen* (Chicago, 1887). The author served in the First Pennsylvania Reserves from the beginning of the war until he was captured in the fighting at Spotsylvania in 1864. His narrative is more valuable for its discussions of events seen personally and far less for its discussion of the Army of the Potomac. It contains a number of interesting anecdotes about the Reserves. Urban was one of the prisoners freed by Custer's cavalry at Beaver Dam Station during the Yellow Tavern Raid in 1864 and remained with the cavalry column on the remainder of the raid.

Vanderslice, Catherine H., ed. *The Civil War Letters of George Washington Beidelman* (New York, 1978). These letters were written by an infantryman who served in the Seventy-first Pennsylvania, the "California Regiment" originally recruited by Edward D. Baker, who was killed at Ball's Bluff. For all practical purposes, they end after the Battle of Fredericksburg.

Wilkeson, Frank, *Recollections of a Private Soldier in the Army of the Potomac* (New York, 1887). Wilkeson makes three points in this small book, which deals with fighting beginning with the Wilderness and ends with the early stages of the siege of Petersburg: generalship on the Union side ranged from poor to cowardly, the volunteers from earlier years were excellent troops, the draftees and bounty troops were abysmal. Like all "exposees," this book vastly overstates everything.

Williams, G. F., *Bullet and Shell. War as the Soldier saw It: Camp, March, and Picket; Battlefield and Bivouac; Prison and Hospital* (New York, 1882). Williams first served as an enlisted man in the Fifth New York Volunteers and apparently at some point became a company-grade officer. This command was part of Warren's brigade, Fifth Corps. He later served as an officer in the One Hundred Forty-Sixth New York Volunteers, again in the Fifth Corps, this time in Weed's brigade. Many of the incidents seem to be apocryphal; but, upon examination, the surrounding circumstances for virtually every one of them can be verified. No doubt, the colloquy is not verbatim; but like all colloquy in any narrative written with the intent of being historically accurate, the narrator intended to be accurate in the substance of the discussions, stood in a position to observe the event or participate in it, and had the motivation to record it as accurately as possible.

Wing, Samuel B., *The Soldier's Story: A Personal Narrative of the Life, Army Experiences and Marvelous Sufferings Since the War of Samuel B. Wing* (n.p., 1898). For reasons totally unrelated to the present work this is a fascinating little piece, which also has in it some interesting anecdotes.

Young, Jesse Bowman, *What A Boy Saw in the Army, A Story of Sight-Seeing and Adventure in the War for the Union* (New York, 1894). Young served for some time in the western armies, then moved east for service in the Eighty-fourth Pennsylvania in time for the Battle of Fredericksburg. He then served on the staff of various division commanders in the

Third Corps including Humphreys and Prince. The book contains a number of interesting anecdotes about various officers in the Third Corps.

Unit Histories

Albert, Allen D., ed., *History of the Forty-fifth Regiment Pennsylvania Veteran Volunteer Infantry 1861-1865* (Williamsport, 1912).

Banes, Charles H., *History of the Philadelphia Brigade Sixty-ninth, Seventy-first, Seventy-second, and One Hundred and Sixth Pennsylvania Volunteers* (Philadelphia, 1876).

Bates, Samuel P., *History of the Pennsylvania Volunteers 1861-1865*, originally published as 5 vols. (Harrisburg, 1869, 1871). This series is far more accurate and useful than one would think at first glance.

Bates, Samuel P., *Martial Deeds of Pennsylvania* (Philadelphia, 1875).

Beach, William H., *The First New York (Lincoln) Cavalry from April 19, 1861, to July 7, 1865* (New York, 1892).

Boyce, C. W., *A Brief History of the Twenty-Eighth New York State Volunteers, First Brigade, First Division, Twelfth Corps, Army of the Potomac* (Buffalo, 1896).

Bryant, Edwin E., *History of the Third Regiment of Wisconsin Volunteer Infantry 1861-1865* (Madison, 1891). Much more than a "we went here, we went there" regimental history.

Clowes, Walter F., *The Detroit Light Guard* (Detroit, 1900).

Cooke, S. G. and Benton, Charles E., EDS., *The Dutchess County Regiment, (One Hundred Fiftieth Regiment of New York State Volunteer Infantry, in the Civil War)* (Danbury, 1907). This is a typical regimental history. It has very little information about individuals and almost nothing about general officers. The regiment did not join the Army of the Potomac until June 29, 1863 and was part of the Twelfth Corps when it was sent west in the fall of 1863.

Crowninshield, Benjamin W., *A History of the First Regiment of Massachusetts Cavalry Volunteers* (Boston, 1891).

Cudworth, Warren H., *History of the First Regiment* (Boston, 1866).

Davis, W. W. H., *History of the 104th Pennsylvania Regiment, From August 22, 1861, to September 30, 1864* (Philadelphia, 1866). This book, dedicated to Henry M. Naglee, is an interesting description and defense of Naglee's service during the Peninsula Campaign and the period that preceded it. The account is both a regimental history and a personal narrative. Davis organized the One-Hundred-Fourth Pennsylvania and was its only commander throughout the war. Hence, the narrative describes both his own activities and those of the regiment in considerable detail.

Denison, Rev. Frederick, *Sabres and Spurs: The First Regiment Rhode Island Cavalry in the Civil War, 1861-1865* (Central Falls, 1876). This is a standard regimental history with little comment about individuals either in the regiment or higher but generally gives the history of the regiment in diary form. It is most valuable for the early part of the war.

Fairchild, C. B., *History of the 27th Regiment N.Y. Vols. being a record of its more than two years of Service in the War for the Union from May 21st, 1861, to May 31st, 1863* (Binghamton, 1888).

Freemont, Jessie Benton, *The Story of the Guard: A Chronicle of the War* (Boston, 1863). This is a brief account of the Zagonyi Guard, a unit composed of four companies of cavalry, and a variety of events relating to General Fremont. The two subjects, the life of the Guard and the incidents and anecdotes of Fremont's headquarters in 1861, are important. The book also shows the importance of Fremont's wife in the management of his headquarters.

Fry, Frinkle, "Wooden Nutmegs" at *Bull Run: a Humorous Account of some of the Exploits and Experiences of the Three Months Connecticut Brigade, and the Part they Bore in the National Stampede* (Hartford, 1872).

Gates, Theodore B., *The Ulsterguard and the War of the Rebellion* (New York, 1879). Although this volume apparently covers the entire war, it really ends, with the exception of the discussion of the first day at the battle of Gettysburg, with the battle of Antietam. The regiment was not engaged at Fredericksburg and after January of 1863 it served as a detached regiment in the provost marshall brigade under General Patrick. Aside from being relatively good on the overall efforts of the army (see the long footnote in Starr, *The Union Cavalry*, about the inaccuracy of regimental histories on matters concerning the army as a whole and not the regiment), the book contains a number of very useful incidents and anecdotes. This book strongly favors McDowell, the Ulsterguard having served in the First Corps from its earliest enlistment, and criticizes McClellan. Almost by default it supports Pope in his disputes with McClellan, a herculean task wtih no possibility of success.

Goff, Alan D., ed., *The Second Wisconsin Infantry* (Dayton, 1994).

Gracey, Rev. S. L., *Annals of the Sixth Pennsylvania Cavalry* (Pennsylvania, 1868). This book covers the Sixth Pennsylvania Cavalry day by day, in some cases almost in diary form, throughout its active service during the war in the east. It has little about the officers who led it or any of the other officers, but some valuable information and some interesting anecdotes.

Hall, Henry, *Cayuga in the Field: A Record of the 19th N.Y. Volunteers, and Third New York Artillery Comprising an Account of Their Organization, Camp Life, Marches, Battles, Losses, Tails and Triumphs in the War for the Union, with Complete Rolls of their Numbers* (Auburn, 1873). With hard work and attention to detail this unit history can be made useful.

Hard, Abner, *History of the 8th Cavalry Regiment Illinois Volunteers, During the Great Rebellion* (Aurora, 1868). An excellent account of an outstanding cavalry regiment, which produced three brigadier generals, John F. Farnsworth, Elon J. Farnsworth, and William Gamble. It contains interesting anecdotes about all three men.

Haynes, Martin H., *A History of the Second New Hampshire Volunteer Infantry in the War of the Rebellion* (Lakeport, 1896).

Historical Committee, *Henry Wilson's Regiment: the Twenty-second Infantry, Second Sharpshooters, Third Light Battery, Massachusetts Volunteers* (Boston, 1887).

Historical Committee, *History of the Nineteenth Regiment Massachusetts Volunteer Infantry 1861-1865* (Salem, 1906).

Holcombe, R. I., *History of the First Regiment Minnesota Volunteer Infantry* (Stillwater, 1916). Supplemented if not replaced (but still useful) by later, more detailed works.

Hutchinson, Nelson V., *History of the Seventh Massachusetts Volunteer Infantry in the War of the Rebellion of the Southern States Against Constitutional Authority, 1861-1865, with description of battles, army movements, hospital life, and incidents of the camp, by officers and privates* (Taunton, 1890). This is the standard history of a regiment which produced a number of superior infantry commanders during the war including Darius N. Couch, David A. Russell, and others.

Isham, Asa B., *An Historical Sketch Of The 7th Regiment Michigan Volunteer Cavalry From Its Organization, in 1862, to its Muster out, in 1865* (New York, n.d.). This is a short, typical regimental history with interesting descriptions of the activities of the Michigan brigade and anecdotes about Custer.

James, Henry B., *Memories of the Civil War* (New Bedford, 1898). This small slim volume contains a few interesting anecdotes about Griffin, in whose brigade and division the Thirty-Second Massachusetts Infantry served. It also has the usual general opinions about different events.

Kirk, Hyland C., *Heavy Guns and Light: A History of the 4th New York Heavy Artillery* (New York, 1890).

MacNamara, Daniel George, *The History of the Ninth Regiment Massachusetts Volunteer Infantry, Second Brigade, First Division, Fifth Army Corps, Army of the Potomac June 1861 to June 1864* (Boston, 1899).

Mills, J. Harrison, *Chronicles of the Twenty-first Regiment New York State Volunteers, embracing a full History of the Regiment, from the enrolling of the first Volunteer in Buffalo April 15, 1861 to the final mustering out May 18, 1863* (Buffalo, 1887).

Newell, Captain Joseph Keith, *"Ours." Annals of the 10th Regiment, Massachusetts Volunteers, in the Rebellion* (Springfield, 1875). Presented in general in the form of a diary with extensive biographical information at the end, much of it contains narrative material. The core of this volume was used for the later history of the regiment published shortly after the turn of the century as a result of funding by the Massachusetts Legislature.

Norton, Chauncey S., *The Redneck Ties, or History of the Fifteenth New York Volunteer Cavalry* (Ithaca, 1891). This brief volume describes the recruitment and service of the

Fifteenth New York Cavalry, which spent most of its time in the mountains in West Virginia until the latter part of the campaign in the Shenandoah and the Appomattox campaign. It contains a few interesting anecdotes about April 8 and 9, 1865.

Osborn, Captain, and others, *Trials and Triumphs the Record of the Fifth-Fifth Ohio Volunteer Infantry* (Chicago, 1904). This regimental history includes a number of chapters which are, in effect, personal reminiscences about limited aspects of the war. It contains a considerable amount of information about various officers who served in the Eleventh Corps.

Powell, William H., *The Fifth Army Corps (Army of the Potomac) A Record of Operations during the Civil War in the United States of America 1861-1865* (New York, 1895). An excellent labor of love that managed to consider the many controversial incidents and persons with some, if not entire, dispassion.

Publication Committee, *History of the Eighteenth Regiment of Cavalry, Pennsylvania Volunteers (163d regiment of the line) 1862-1865* (New York, 1909). This regimental history is composed of a brief overview of its term of service, a detailed diary of events, and various anecdotal contributions by members of the regiment. It does not follow the more normal format of a continuous narrative from recruitment to discharge.

Quint, Alonzo H., *Record of the Second Massachusetts* (Boston, 1867).

Reichardt, Theodore, *Diary of Battery A, First Regiment Rhode Island Light Artillery* (Providence, 1865).

Roe, Alfred S., *The Tenth Regiment Massachusetts Volunteer Infantry 1861-1864, a Western Massachusetts Regiment* (Springfield, 1909). This regiment served from the early stages of the war until the siege of Petersburg in 1864 when its three year enlistment expired. The history is in part a daily diary of the activities of the regiment but includes excerpts from various personal reminiscences, letters, and diaries.

Smith, James E., *A Famous Battery and its Campaigns, 1861-1864* (Washington, 1892). As an old artilleryman denied a real opportunity to "see the elephant," the author found this the best narrative on service in the artillery.

Stevenson, James H., *"Boots and Saddles," a History of the First Volunteer Cavalry of the War, known as the First New York (Lincoln) Cavalry and also as the Sabre Regiment, its Organization, Campaigns and Battles* (Harrisburg, 1879).

Swinton, *History of the Seventh New York State Militia*, 2 vols. (New York, 1902).

Thompson, Gilbert, *The Engineer Battalion in the Civil War: a Contribution to the History of the United States Engineers* (Washington, 1910).

Todd, William, *The Seventy-Ninth Highlanders New York Volunteers in the War of the Rebellion 1861-1865* (Albany, 1886).

Walcott, Charles F., *History of the Twenty-first Regiment Massachusetts Volunteers in the War for the Preservation of the Union 1861-65* (Boston, 1882). This excellent, often opinionated, history of the Twenty-first Massachusetts makes a number of judgments about commanding officers, particularly brigade and division commanders, that are not often found in regimental histories. It is particularly laudatory of Reno, who commanded the brigade to which the Twenty-first Massachusetts was assigned, and by absence of reference and one or two specific statements somewhat critical of Ferraro, the later brigade commander.

Walker, Francis A., *History of the Second Corps in the Army of the Potomac* (New York, 1891, 2d ed.). An excellent work, as one would expect from a man like Walker.

Ward, George W., *History of the Second Pennsylvania Veteran Heavy Artillery from 1861 to 1865 (112th Regiment Pennsylvania Volunteers) from 1861 to 1865 including the Provisional Second Penn'a Heavy Artillery* (Philadelphia, 1904).

Waring, George E., Jr., *The Garibaldi Guard* (New York, 1893). A good history of a horrible regiment of European scavengers.

Williams, K. P., *Lincoln Finds a General*, 5 vols. (New York, 1952). Alan Nolan, whose opinions are not to be taken lightly, and the author will never agree on the value of this work, left incomplete by Professor Williams's untimely demise.

Willson, Arabella M., *Disaster, Struggle, Triumph: the Adventures of 1000 Boys in Blue from August, 1862, to June, 1865* (Albany, 1870).

Battles

Barnard, John G., *The C.S.A. and the Battle of Bull Run: a Letter to an English Friend* (New York, 1862).

Barnard, Brig-Gen. J. G., and Barry, Brig. Gen. W. F., *Report of the Engineer and Artillery Operations of the Army of the Potomac from its Organization to the Close of the Peninsula Campaign* (New York, 1863).

Barnard, John G., *The Peninsular Campaign and its Antecedents as Developed by the Report of Maj.-Gen. George B. McClellan and other published Documents* (New York, 1864).

Beatie, Russel H., Jr., *Road to Manassas: The Growth of Union Command in the Eastern Theatre from the Fall of Fort Sumter to the First Battle of Bull Run* (New York, 1961).

Davis, William C., *Battle at Bull Run: A History of the First Major Campaign of the Civil War* (Garden City, 1977).

Fry, James B., *McDowell and Tyler in the Campaign of Bull Run* (New York, 1884).

Heller, Charles E., and William A. Stafft, eds., *America's First Battles 1776-1965*; esp. W. Glenn Robertson, "First Bull Run 19 July 1861," Chap. 4, 81-108 (Lawrence, 1986).

Hennessy, John, *The First Battle of Manassas: An End to Innocence July 18-21, 1861*, 2d ed. (Lynchburg, 1989). A worthy effort, although it does not rank with Hennessy's irreplaceable tour de force on Second Bull Run.

Huey, Pennock, *A True History Of The Charge Of the 8th PA Cavalry At Chancellorsville* (Pennsylvania, 1885).

Johnston, R. M., *Bull Run: Its Strategy and Tactics* (Boston and New York, 1913). Still the best bilateral account of the first major encounter of the War.

Newell, Clayton R., *Lee vs. McClellan: the First Campaign*, esp. 116-132 (Washington, 1996).

Patterson, Robert P., *A Narrative of the Campaign in the Valley of the Shenandoah in 1861* (Philadelphia, 1865).

Pond, George E., *The Shenandoah Valley in 1864* (New York, 1883).

Webb, Alexander S., LLD., *The Peninsula: McClellan's Campaign of 1862* (New York, 1881). Written by a McClellanite with a critical but fair eye.

Wert, Jeffrey D., *From Winchester to Cedar Creek: the Shenandoah Campaign of 1864* (Carlysle, 1987).

Collected Articles

Dwight, Theodore F., ed., *Papers of the Military Historical Society of Massachusetts*, 13 vols. (Boston, 1881) (Broadfoot Reprint). Freeman was right: "Sound and in the main detached."

Everett, Edward G., "Pennsylvania Raises an Army, 1861," *Western Pennsylvania Historical Magazine* (Summer, 1956).

Johnson, Robert Underwood, and Buell, Clarence Clough, eds., *Battles and Leaders of the Civil War, being for the most part contributions by Union and Confederate Officers. Based upon* "*Century War Series*," 4 vols. (New York, 1956, Yoseloff-Reprint).

McClure, A. K., ed., *The Annals of the War written by Leading Participants North and South originally published in the Philadelphia Weekly Times* (Philadelphia, 1879).

Military Essays and Recollections: Papers Read before the Commandery of the State of Illinois, Military Order of the Loyal Legion of the United States, 4 vols. (Chicago, 1894) (Broadfoot edition, 1992, vol. 11).

Military Order of the Loyal Legion of the United States, 66 vols. (Wilmington, 1991-1997). This reprint by the indefatigable Tom Broadfoot saves the researcher great expense and years of frustration.

Collected Letters

Basler, Roy P., ed., *The Collected Works of Abraham Lincoln*, 9 vols. and 2 supps. (New Brunswick, 1953). Indispensable to all students of the period.

Burnett, Edmund C., ed., *Letters of Members of the Continental Congress*, 7 vols. (Washington, 1923).

Crist, Lynda C., ed., *The Papers of Jefferson Davis*, 9 vols. (incomplete) (Baton Rouge, 1971-1995).

McLaughlin, Charles Capen, ed.-in-ch., *The Papers of Frederick Law Olmsted*, 5 vols. (incomplete) (Baltimore and London 1972).

Moore, John Bassett, *The Works of James Buchanan, Comprising His Speeches, State Papers, and Private Correspondence*, 11 vols. (New York, 1960).

Pennsylvania Archives: Papers of the Governors, 9 Series (Harrisburg, 1902).

Showman, Richard K., ed., *The Papers of General Nathaniel Greene*, 3 vols. (Chapel Hill, 1980).

Multi-Biography

Bartlett, John Russell, *Memoirs of Rhode Island Officers who were engaged in the Service of their Country during the Great Rebellion of the South* (Providence, 1867).

Brown, Russel K., *Fallen in Battle: American General Officer Combat Fatalities from 1775* (Westport, 1988).

Fiske, John, eds., *Appleton's Cyclopedia of American Biography*, 6 vols. and 6 supplements (New York, 1887-1891).

Hassler, Warren W., Jr., *Commanders of the Army of the Potomac* (Baton Rouge, 1962).

Hunt, Roger D., and Brown, Jack R., *Brevet Brigadier Generals in Blue* (Gaithersburg, 1990).

Hunt, Roger D., *Colonels in Blue: Union Army Colonels of the Civil War, The New England States Connecticut, Maine, Massachusetts, New Hampshire, Rhode Island, Vermont* (Utglen, 2001).

Kirshner, Ralph, *The Class of 1861: Custer, Ames, and their Classmates after West Point* (Carbondale, 1999).

Lewry, Thomas P., M.D., *Tarnished Eagles: The Courts-Martial of Fifty Union Colonels and Lieutenant Colonels* (Mechanicsburg, 1997).

Lonn, Ella, *Foreigners in Union Army and Navy* (Baton Rouge, 1951). Until someone is able to computerize for statistical analysis figures relating to foreigners who served at all levels in the Union Army and Navy, this book will not be replaced. It is an extraordinary piece of research, well-organized and well-presented. From time to time the subject matter itself makes the presentation a bit tedious but the overall result is outstanding.

Malone, Dumas, ed., *Dictionary of American Biography*, 10 vols. (New York, 1964).

Piatt, Donn, *Memoirs of the Men Who Saved the Union* (New York, 1887).

Powell, Lieutenant Colonel William H., ed., *Officers in the Army and Navy (Volunteer) who Served in the Civil War* (Philadelphia, 1893).

Report of the Class of 1860, Harvard College 1895-1900 (Cambridge, 1900).

Spencer, John, *Civil War Generals: Categorical Listings and a Biographical Directory* (New York, 1997).

Warner, Ezra J., *Generals in Blue: Lives of the Union Commanders* (Baton Rouge, 1964).

Waugh, John C., *The Class of 1846: from West Point to Appomattox: Stonewall Jackson, George McClellan and their Brothers* (New York, 1994).

Welsh, Jack D., M.D., *Medical Histories of Union Generals* (Kent, 1996).

Official and Semi-Official Publications

Adjutant General's Office, *Official Army Register of the Volunteer Force of the United States Army for the Years 1861, '62, '63, '64, '65*, 10 vols. (n.p., n.d. reprint Gaithersburg, 1987).

Annual Report of the Adjutant General of the Commonwealth of Massachusetts 1861 (Boston, 1861).

Annual Report of the Adjutant General to the Legislature of Minnesota 1861 (Boston, 1861).

Annual Report of the Adjutant General of New York 1861 (Albany, 1862).

Annual Report for the Adjutant General of the State of Connecticut for the Year 1861 (Hartford, 1861).

Annual Report of the Adjutant General of the State of New Jersey for the Year 1861 (Trenton, 1861).

Congressional Globe, 36th to 41st Congress (Washington, 1860-1865).

Everly, Elaine, et al. (National Archives), *Preliminary Inventory of the Records of United States Army Continental Commands, 1821-1920, Record Group 393*, 4 vols. (Washington, 1973).

Heitman, *Historical Register and Dictionary of the United States Army, 1789-1903*, [no.] vols. (Washington, 1903).

Hewitt, Janet B., ed., *Supplement to the Official Records and Confederate Armies*, 100 vols. (Wilmington, 1990-2001).

The Massachusetts Register of 1862 Containing a Record of the Government and Institutions of the State together with a very Complete Account of the Massachusetts Volunteers (Boston, 1862).

Report of the Joint Committee on the Conduct of the War, 9 vols. (Wilmington, 1998, Broadfoot ed.).

Miscellaneous

Adams, George Worthington, *Doctors in Blue: the Medical History of the Union Army in the Civil War* (Baton Rouge and London, 1952).

Allen, Oliver E., *New York, New York: a History of the World's most exhilarating and challenging City* (New York, 1990).

Anbinder, Tyler, *Nativism and Slavery: The Northern-Know-Nothings and the Politics of the 1850's* (New York, 1992).

Andrews, J. Cutler, *The North Reports the Civil War* (Pittsburgh, 1955). Based on an exceptional collection of contemporary newspaper accounts, privately held and publicly available manuscript collections, books, articles, and other sources published after the war, and information of a secondary nature, this scholarly work is clearly the best of the several studies of the corps of newspaper reporters who gave the public their knowledge of the Civil War while it was occurring.

Bassford, Christopher, *Clausewitz in English: the Reception of Clausewitz in Britain and America* (New York, 1994).

Bates, David Homer, *Lincoln in the Telegraph Office: Recollections of the United States Military Telegraph Corps During the Civil War* (New York, 1907). Although limited almost entirely to matters relating to the Telegraph Corps and the four men who were the primary operators of the telegraph office in the War Department during the war, this book contains a number of interesting and important anecdotes, particularly about relations between McClellan and the government.

Bauer, K. Jack, *The Mexican War, 1846-1848* (Norwalk, 1990, Easton Press ed.). Now and probably for a long time, the standard work.

Beale, Howard K., ed., *The Diary of Edward Bates 1859-1866* (Washington, 1933), Volume 4, *Annual Report of the American Historical Association for the year 1930*. Edward Bates served as attorney general under Lincoln. The diary describes those matters presented to the cabinet for consideration, discussion, and decision; the business of the attorney general including arguments presented to the Supreme Court of the United States; and Bates advice to the President as attorney general.

Bickers, Richard Townsend, *Friendly Fire: Accidents in Battle from Ancient Greece to the Gulf War* (London, 1994).

Birkhimer, William E., *Historical Sketch of Artillery* (Washington, 1884).

Block, Eugene B., *Above the Civil War—The Story of Thaddeus Lowe, Balloonist, Inventor, Railway Builder* (Barclay, 1966). A few useful anecdotes.

Bond, Brian, *Liddell Hart: a Study of his Military Thought* (New Brunswick, 1977).

Bradley, Omar N., *A Soldier's Story* (New York, 1951).

Bremner, Robert H., *The Public Good: Philanthropy and Welfare in the Civil War Era* (New York, 1980). This book is a well written, well researched study of, in the main, the United States Sanitary Commission during the American Civil War although its more generally intended purpose was to study philanthropy during the latter half of the nineteenth century.

Brockett, L. P., M.D., *Battle-Field and Hospital; or Lights and Shadows of the Great Rebellion including Thrilling Adventures, Daring Deeds, Heroic Exploits, and Wonderful Escapes of Spies and Scouts, Together with the Songs, Ballads, Anecdotes, and Humorous Incidents of the War* (n.d., n.p.) The title is given as it appears on the title page. The printed title on the front of the book is *Camp, Battle-field, and Hospital*. This is a collection of anecdotes taken from a variety of sources including letters, newspapers, and word of mouth. A few of the incidents are interesting. Because of the unreliability of many of the sources, only those consistent with other information have been used.

Buchanan, James, *Mr. Buchanan's Administration on the Eve of the Rebellion* (New York, 1866).

Burke, Thomas, *Abstract of Debates of the New York Provisional Congress, February 12 to 19, 1777* (1838).

Burlingame, Michael, and Ettinger, John R. Turner, eds., *Inside Lincoln's White House: the complete Civil War Diary of John Hay* (Carbondale and Edwardsville, 1997).

Chandler, David, *The Campaigns of Napoleon*, 2 vols. (Norwalk, 1991, Easton Press Ed.). We should all emulate the grasp and presentation of this truly extraordinary work.

Churchill, Winston S., *Marlborough: His Life and Times*, 4 volumes in two (London 1933, reprint 1966).

Coffman, Edward M., *The Old Army: A Portrait of the American Army in Peacetime, 1784-1898* (New York, 1986).

Comte de Paris, *History Of The Civil War In America*, 3 vols. (Philadelphia, 1875).

Craig, Gordon A., *The Politics of the Prussian Army 1640-1945* (Oxford, 1955).

Craig, Gordon, and Loewenheim, Francis L., eds., *The Diplomats 1939-1979* (Princeton, 1994).

Dana, Charles A., *Recollections of the Civil War: With the Leaders at Washington and in the Field in the Sixties* (New York, 1898). These recollections, confined to the period of the Civil War, were written by Dana very late in his life, were completed only a few months before his death on October 17, 1897, and were published after his death. A large part of the narrative was published serially in *McClure's Magazine*. The recollections attempt some overall views about the war but more particularly follow Dana in a variety of ad hoc assignments throughout the war and provide interesting insights into a number of different important persons.

Dayan, Moshe, *Moshe Dayan: Story of my Life* (New York, 1976).

Dixon, Karen R., and Southern, Pat, *The Roman Cavalry from the First to the Third Century AD* (London and New York, 1992).

Donald, David, ed., *Inside Lincoln's Cabinet, the Civil War Diaries of Salmon P. Chase* (New York, 1954). The diary of Chase, kept intermittently throughout the war, records in considerable detail the development of the Union army from late 1861 through the end of 1862. This was the time when the cabinet was most heavily involved in the command structure of the Army of the Potomac. Chase describes in what appears to be a relatively dispassionate way the activities of those people with whom he dealt and his own activities in advancing or compromising the aspirations of various officers.

Duncan, Captain Louis C., *The Medical Department of the United States Army in the Civil War*, (Gaithersburg n.d. reprint; orig 1900).

Eltinge, John R., *Swords Around a Throne, Napoleon's Grande Armee* (New York and London, 1988).

Epstein, Robert M., *Napoleon's Last Victory and the Emergence of Modern War* (Lawrence, 1994).

Featherstone, Donald, *Bridges of Battle: Famous Battlefield Actions at Bridges and River Crossings* (Loudon, 1998).

Fishel, Edwin C., *The Secret War for the Union: The Untold Story of Military Intelligence in the Civil War* (Boston, 1996). The only work on this subject worth reading.

Ford, Worthington Chauncey, ed., *A Cycle of Adams' Letters 1861-1865* (Boston, 1920). This is a collection of letters written during the Civil War by the principal members of the Adams family, Charles Francis Adams, who was ambassador to England during the majority of the War; Henry Adams; and Charles Francis Adams, Jr., who served as an officer in the First Massachusetts Cavalry. The letters of Charles Francis Adams, Jr. are particularly relevant to the Army of the Potomac after the First Massachusetts joined the Army prior to Antietam. Many of the judgments about persons in the army were not necessarily shared by the vast majority of his brother officers, and some of them showed the prejudices of a well-born Bostonian.

Franklin, John Hope, *The Militant South 1800-1861* (Cambridge, 1956).

Fraser, Antonia, *Cromwell: the Lord Protector* (New York, 1973).

French, William H., William F. Barry, and Henry J. Hunt, *Instructions for Field Artillery* (Philadelphia, 1861).

Fry, James B., *The History and Legal Effect of Brevets in the Armies of Great Britain and the United States from their Origin in 1692 to the Present Time* (New York, 1877).

Fuller, Major-General J. F. C., *The Generalship of Alexander the Great* (Norwalk, 1990) (Easton Press ed.).

Gienapp, William E., *The Origins of the Republican Party, 1852-1856* (New York, 1987). This work apparently vaulted Professor Gienapp from the hustings to Harvard University, and deservedly so.

Goerlitz, Walter, trans. Brian Battershaw, *History of the German General Staff 1857-1945* (New York, 1953).

Gordon, Harold J., Jr., *The Reichswehr and the German Republic 1919-1926* (Princeton, 1957).

Green, Peter, *The Greco-Persian Wars* (Berkeley, 1996, rev. ed.).

Greene, Peter, *Alexander of Macedon: 356-323 B.C. A Historical Biography* (Berkeley, Los Angeles and London, rep. 1991).

Guderian, Heinz; trans., Constantine Filzejibbon, *Panzer Leader* (Norwalk, 1990, Easton Press ed.).

Hagerman, Edward, *The American Civil War and the Origins of Modern Warfare: Ideas, Organization, and Field Command* (Indianapolis, 1988).

Hart, B. H. Liddell, *The Rommel Papers* (New York, 1953, Easton Press ed.). The best of the many works about the Desert Fox.

Herrmann, David G., *The Arming of Europe and the Making of the First World War* (Princeton, 1996).

Hofschröer, Peter, *1815, the Waterloo Campaign*, 2 vols. (London, 1998).

Hungerford, Edward, *The Story of the Baltimore & Ohio Railroad 1827-1927*, 2 vols. (New York and London, 1928).

Jones, Archer, *The Art of War in the Western World* (New York and Oxford, 1983).

Katz, Irving, *August Belmont: A Political Biography* (New York & London, 1968).

Keegan, John, ed., *Churchill's Generals* (New York, 1991).

Lacouture, Jean, *DeGaulle: the Rebel 1890-1944*, 2 vols. (New York and London, 1990, Patrick O'Brian, tr.) *The Rebel 1890-1944*.

Leech, Margaret, *Reveille in Washington 1860-1865* (New York, 1941).

Lowenfells, Walter, ed., *Walt Whitman's Civil War* (New York, 1960). Except for one or two quotes, this book is basically useless. About the only commentary of any substance in the entire book is Whitman's various descriptions of hospitals and the wounded. The rest are essentially non-substantive discussions of matters about which he knew nothing.

Macksay, Kenneth, *Guderian: Creator of the Blitzkrieg* (New York, 1975).

Maxwell, William Quentin, *Lincoln's Fifth Wheel: The Political History of the United States Sanitary Commission* (New York, London, and Thrato, 1956). A fine work that reads well, perhaps too well because the author appears to take literary license with the sources, which are not rigorously cited in footnotes.

McClellan, George B., *The Armies of Europe: comprising Descriptions in Detail of the military Systems of England, France, Russia, Prussia, Austria, and Sardinia adopting their Advantages to all Arms of the United States Service; and Embodying the Report of Observations in Europe during the Crimean War, as Military Commissioner from the United States Government in 1855-1856* (Philadelphia, 1861).

McClure, A. K., *Abraham Lincoln and Men of War Times: Some Personal Recollections of War and Politics during the Lincoln Administration* (Lincoln and London, 1996, 4th ed.).

McKay, Ernest A., *The Civil War and New York City* (Syracuse, 1990).

McLaughlin, Charles Capen, ed., *The Papers of Frederick Law Olmsted*, 5 vols. (incomplete) (Baltimore and London 1977-).

Montgomery, Sir Bernard, *The Memoirs of Field Marshal the Viscount Montgomery of Alamain, K. G.* (New York, 1958).

Morse, John T., ed., *Diary of Gideon Welles: Secretary of the Navy Under Lincoln and Johnson*, 3 vols. (Boston and New York, 1911).

Naisawald, L. Van Loan, *Grape and Cannister: the Story of the Field Artillery of the Army of the Potomac, 1861-1865* (New York and Oxford, 1960).

Nevins, Allan, *The Emergence of Lincoln, Prologue to Civil War 1859-1861*, 2 vols., (New York, 1950).

Nevins, Allan, and Thomas, Milton Halsey, eds., *The Diary of George Templeton Strong*, 4 vols. (New York, 1952).

New York Monuments Commission for the Battlefields of Gettysburg and Chattanooga, *Final Report on the Battlefield of Gettysburg*, 3 vols. (Albany, 1900).

Nicolay, John G., *Outbreak Of The Rebellion* (New York, 1882).

Nicolay, John G., and Hay, John, *Abraham Lincoln, a History*, 10 vols. (New York, 1914). Not unbiased, not fair to McClellan, not replaced by Sandburg or Randall; we must wait and see how the work in progress by Professor Richard Burlingame sizes up.

Niven, John, ed., *The Salmon P. Chase Papers*, 4 vols. (incomplete), (Kent and London, 1993).

Otto, Eisenschiml, *Why Lincoln Was Murdered* (Boston, 1937).

Paret, Peter, ed., *Makers of Modern Strategy from Machievelli to the Nuclear Age* (Princeton, 1986).

Parrish, Thomas, ed., *The Simon and Shuster Encyclopedia of World War II* (New York, 1978).

Pflanze, Otto, *Bismarck and the Development of Germany*, 3 vols., (Princeton, 1990).

Pinkerton, Allan, *The Spy of the Rebellion* (New York, 1883). Until the recent work by Fishel, no one, participant or historian, has come close to an accurate account of intelligence activities in the War; but we wait impatiently for the "Complete Works of Civil War Intelligence" in progress in the expert hands of my old friend Tom Broadfoot, who promises to return my microfilm of the McClellan MSS when he publishes at last.

Poore, Ben: Perley, *Perley's Reminiscences of Sixty Years in the National Metropolis*, 2 vols. (Boston, 1986).

Rhodes, James Ford, *History of the United States from the Compromise of 1850 to the McKinley-Bryan Campaign of 1896*, 8 vols. (New York, 1920).

Riddle, Albert Gallatin, *Recollections of War Times: Reminiscences of Men and Events in Washington 1860-1865* (New York, 1895).

Robertson, John, *Michigan in the War* (Lansing, 1882).

Roemer, J., *Cavalry: its History, Management, and Uses in War* (New York, 1863).

Schactman, Tom, *The Phony War 1939-1940* (New York, 1982).

Schouler, William, *Massachusetts in the War*, 2 vols. (Boston, 1868).

Searcher, Victor, *Lincoln's Journey to Greatness: a Factual Account of the Twelve Day Inaugural Trip* (Philadelphia, 1960).

Sellers, Charles, *James K. Polk*, 2 vols. (Princeton, 1966).

Seward, Desmond, *Henry V, Scourge of God* (New York, 1987).

Seward, Frederick H., *Seward at Washington*, 2 vols. (New York, 1891).

Seward, Frederick W., *Reminiscences of a War-Time Statesman and Diplomat, 1830-1915* (New York, 1916).

Shannon, Fred Albert, *The Organization and Administration of the Union Army 1861-1865*, 2 vols. (Cleveland, 1928).

Skelton, William B., *American Profession of Arms, the Army Officer Corps, 1784-1862* (Lawrence, 1992).

Spence, I. G., *The Cavalry of Classical Greece: a Social and Military History with Particular Reference to Athens* (Oxford, 1993).

Starr, Stephen Z., *The Union Cavalry in the Civil War*, 3 vols. (Baton Rouge, 1979).

Stewart, Edgar I., *Custer's Luck* (Norman, 1955).

Stille, Charles J., *History of the United States Sanitary Commission Being the General Report of its Work During the War of the Rebellion* (Philadelphia, 1866). This semi-official document was written by a member of the Commission contemporaneously with the war. In fact the history of the Commission during the war was prepared as a result of a resolution adopted at a session of the Commission in July of 1865. Stille was assigned the task of preparing the general history and it was published by the Commission as "the official Report of its operations during the war."

Summers, Festus P., *The Baltimore and Ohio in the Civil War* (Gettysburg, 1939).

Triumph in the West: A History of the War Years Based on the Diaries of Field Marshall Lord Alanbrooke, Chief of the Imperial General Staff (New York, 1959).

Turner, George Edgar, *Victory Road the Rails: The Strategic Place of the Railroads in the Civil War* (New York, 1952).

Van Dusen, Glynder G., *William Henry Seward* (New York, 1967). After all these years, not replaced or superceded.

Ward, Christopher, *The War of the Revolution*, 2 vols. (New York, 1952).

Whitman, William E., and True, C. H., *Maine in the War for the Union* (Lewiston, 1865).

Williams, T. Harry, *Lincoln and his Generals* (New York, 1952).

Worby, Leslie J., *Hippies: the Cavalry of Ancient Greece* (San Francisco, 1994).

The Detroit Post & Tribune, *Zacharia Chandler: An Outline Sketch of His Life in Public Services* (Detroit, 1879).

INDEX